PREACHING THE WORD

Edited by R. Kent Hughes

JEREMIAH AND LAMENTATIONS

JEREMIAH AND LAMENTATIONS

From Sorrow to Hope

PHILIP GRAHAM RYKEN

R. Kent Hughes
Series Editor

:: CROSSWAY®
WHEATON, ILLINOIS

Cover design: Jon McGrath, Simplicated Studio

Cover image: Adam Greene, illustrator

First printing 2001

Reprinted with new cover 2012

ESV edition 2016

Printed in the United States of America

Unless otherwise indicated, Scripture quotations are from the ESV® Bible (The Holy Bible, English Standard Version®), copyright © 2001 by Crossway, a publishing ministry of Good News Publishers. Used by permission. All rights reserved.

Scripture references marked JB are from The Jerusalem Bible. Copyright © 1966, 1967, 1968 by Darton, Longman & Todd Ltd. and Doubleday & Co., Inc.

Scripture quotations marked KJV are from the King James Version of the Bible.

Scripture quotations marked NASB are from The New American Standard Bible®. Copyright © The Lockman Foundation 1960, 1962, 1963, 1968, 1971, 1972, 1973, 1975, 1977, 1995. Used by permission.

Scripture references marked NIV are taken from The Holy Bible, New International Version®, NIV®. Copyright © 1973, 1978, 1984, 2011 by Biblica, Inc.™ Used by permission. All rights reserved worldwide.

Scripture references marked NKJV are from The New King James Version. Copyright © 1982, Thomas Nelson, Inc. Used by permission.

All emphases in Scripture quotations have been added by the author.

Hardcover ISBN: 978-1-4335-4880-2
ePub ISBN: 978-1-4335-4883-3
PDF ISBN: 978-1-4335-4881-9
Mobipocket ISBN: 978-1-4335-4882-6

Library of Congress Cataloging-in-Publication Data

Ryken, Philip Graham, 1966–
   Jeremiah and Lamentations : from sorrow to hope / Philip Graham Ryken.
      p.   cm.—(Preaching the Word)
   Includes bibliographical references and index.
   ISBN 13: 978-1-58134-167-6 (alk. paper)
   ISBN 10: 1-58134-167-9
   1. Bible. O.T. Jeremiah Commentaries. 2. Bible O.T. Lamentations—Commentaries. I. Title. II. Series.
BS1525.3.R94   2001
224'.2077—dc21   00–010769

*This expositional commentary is dedicated to
the Lord Our Righteousness
in memory of James Montgomery Boice,
who inspired a generation of preachers to teach the Bible.*

Let him who has my word speak my word faithfully.

JEREMIAH 23:28

My joy is gone; grief is upon me; my heart is sick within me.

JEREMIAH 8:18

*For I know the plans I have for you,
declares the Lord,
plans for welfare and not for evil,
to give you a future and a hope.*

JEREMIAH 29:11

Contents

LAMENTATIONS

Acknowledgments

The publication of the present volume is an occasion for thanksgiving. I thank the Reverend R. Kent Hughes for the opportunity to contribute to Crossway's valuable Preaching the Word commentary series. I thank the Session of Tenth Church for granting the study leave necessary to edit this manuscript for publication. I also thank Tenth's wonderful congregation for their extraordinary enthusiasm for expository preaching. You are always on my mind and in my heart as I prepare to teach God's Word. I especially want to thank the Tenth members and others who helped prepare the indices: Rick and Jenny Brown, Wilma and Lydia Brownback, Leland and Mary Ryken. Above all, I thank God for the life and teachings of Jeremiah, a remarkable man who has become one of my mentors in ministry.

A Word to Those Who Preach the Word

There are times when I am preaching that I have especially sensed the pleasure of God. I usually become aware of it through the unnatural silence. The ever-present coughing ceases and the pews stop creaking, bringing an almost physical quiet to the sanctuary—through which my words sail like arrows. I experience a heightened eloquence, so that the cadence and volume of my voice intensify the truth I am preaching.

There is nothing quite like it—the Holy Spirit filling one's sails, the sense of his pleasure, and the awareness that something is happening among one's hearers. This experience is, of course, not unique, for thousands of preachers have similar experiences, even greater ones.

What has happened when this takes place? How do we account for this sense of his smile? The answer for me has come from the ancient rhetorical categories of *logos*, *ethos*, and *pathos*.

The first reason for his smile is the *logos*—in terms of preaching, God's Word. This means that as we stand before God's people to proclaim his Word, we have done our homework. We have exegeted the passage, mined the significance of its words in their context, and applied sound hermeneutical principles in interpreting the text so that we understand what its words meant to its hearers. And it means that we have labored long until we can express in a sentence what the theme of the text is—so that our outline springs from the text. Then our preparation will be such that as we preach, we will not be preaching our own thoughts about God's Word, but God's actual Word, his *logos*. This is fundamental to pleasing him in preaching.

The second element in knowing God's smile in preaching is *ethos*—what you are as a person. There is a danger endemic to preaching, which is having your hands and heart cauterized by holy things. Phillips Brooks illustrated it by the analogy of a train conductor who comes to believe that he has been to the places he announces because of his long and loud heralding of them. And that is why Brooks insisted that preaching must be "The bringing of truth through personality." Though we can never *perfectly* embody the truth we preach, we must be subject to it, long for it, and make it as much a part of our ethos as possible. As the Puritan William Ames said, "Next to the Scriptures, nothing makes a sermon more to pierce, than when it comes out of the inward affection of the heart without any affectation." When a preacher's *ethos* backs up his *logos*, there will be the pleasure of God.

Last, there is *pathos*—personal passion and conviction. David Hume, the Scottish philosopher and skeptic, was once challenged as he was seen going to hear George Whitefield preach: "I thought you do not believe in the gospel." Hume replied, "I don't, but he *does*." Just so! When a preacher believes what he preaches, there will be passion. And this belief and requisite passion will know the smile of God.

The pleasure of God is a matter of *logos* (the Word), *ethos* (what you are), and *pathos* (your passion). As you *preach the Word* may you experience his smile—the Holy Spirit in your sails!

R. Kent Hughes
Wheaton, Illinois

Preface

What can be gained from reading and studying Jeremiah? After spending several weeks listening to daily readings from this Old Testament prophet, the writer Kathleen Norris concluded that the point of listening to him is "coming unglued":

> The prophet, after all, is witness to a time in which his world, the society surrounding the temple in Jerusalem, meets a violent end, and Israel is taken captive to Babylon. Hearing Jeremiah's words every morning, I soon felt challenged to reflect on the upheavals in our own society, and in my life. A prophet's task is to reveal the fault lines hidden beneath the comfortable surface of the worlds we invent for ourselves, the national myths as well as the little lies and delusions of control and security that get us through the day. And Jeremiah does this better than anyone.[1]

Norris is right: Better than anyone else, Jeremiah reveals the spiritual fractures beneath the comfortable surface of daily life. This was true in the prophet's own time, as he watched his society suffer the devastating consequences of life without God. It was true in the 1960s as well, when Francis Schaeffer boldly identified Jeremiah as a prophet for post-Christian times. "Jeremiah," he wrote, "provides us with an extended study of an era like our own, where men have turned away from God and society has become post-Christian."[2] It is still true today as Western civilization accelerates towards the godless abyss.

This commentary began as a long series of sermons straight through Jeremiah. During the year and a half we studied the book at the Tenth Presbyterian Church in center-city Philadelphia, we were often amazed at its relevance for life in these postmodern times. The barbaric relativism Jeremiah witnessed in ancient Israel has come to America. As one parishioner said, "Sometimes I feel like Jeremiah has a job where I work."

Because of his ongoing relevance for spiritual life, Jeremiah is a wonderful prophet to study. This commentary was written to help Christians read, understand, and teach the books of Jeremiah and Lamentations. It has several distinctives. First, it shows some of the connections between the ministry of Jeremiah and the saving work of Jesus Christ. Some commentaries give too little attention to the presence of Christ in the Old Testament; this one tries to present the gospel according to Jeremiah.

Second, the present volume explains the implications of Jeremiah and Lamentations for practical Christianity. It is an expositional commentary, which means (among other things) that it applies biblical truth to daily life. I have tried not only to explain what Jeremiah meant but also to illustrate what he means for the contemporary Christian. Strictly speaking, the commentary is not exegetical, and pastors looking for in-depth grammatical analysis of Jeremiah and Lamentations will undoubtedly wish to consult more technical works.

A third distinctive of this commentary is that it views Jeremiah and Lamentations as literary unities. Some contemporary scholars approach Jeremiah's books as hopeless jumbles of prophecy that they must cut and paste back into the proper order. Such cutting and pasting is unnecessary because the organization of Jeremiah and Lamentations is not merely chronological, it is also topical. It is important to understand from the outset that this is by design rather than by accident. Although there are enough historical clues to provide dates for most of Jeremiah's material, the prophet's own concerns were more theological than historical.

Finally, it should be noted that some of the material in this volume has appeared in print before, in a much shorter book called *Courage to Stand: Jeremiah's Battle Plan for Pagan Times*.[3]

JEREMIAH

1

A Prophet to the Nations

JEREMIAH 1:1–10

THE RABBIS CALLED HIM "The Weeping Prophet." They said he began wailing the moment he was born. When Michelangelo painted him on the ceiling of the Sistine Chapel, he presented him in a posture of despair. He looks like a man who has wept so long he has no tears left to shed. His face is turned to one side, like a man who has been battered by many blows. His shoulders are hunched forward, weighed down by the sins of Judah. His eyes also are cast down, as if he can no longer bear to see God's people suffer. His hand covers his mouth. Perhaps he has nothing left to say.

His name was Jeremiah. His story begins like this:

> The words of Jeremiah, the son of Hilkiah, one of the priests who were in Anathoth in the land of Benjamin, to whom the word of the LORD came in the days of Josiah the son of Amon, king of Judah, in the thirteenth year of his reign. It came also in the days of Jehoiakim the son of Josiah, king of Judah, and until the end of the eleventh year of Zedekiah, the son of Josiah, king of Judah, until the captivity of Jerusalem in the fifth month. (1:1–3)

This introduction tells us a great deal about Jeremiah. He was a preacher's son, for his father Hilkiah was a priest. He was born in the village of Anathoth, close enough to Jerusalem to see the city walls, but at the edge of the wilderness, where the land slopes down to the Dead Sea. He labored as God's prophet for forty years or more, from 627 BC to some time after 586 BC. Four decades is a long time to be a weeping prophet.

Jeremiah lived when little Israel was tossed around by three great superpowers: Assyria to the north, Egypt to the south, and Babylon to the east. He served—and suffered—through the administrations of three kings: Josiah the reformer, Jehoiakim the despot, and Zedekiah the puppet. He was a prophet during the cold November winds of Judah's life as a nation, right up to the time God's people were deported to Babylon. Jeremiah himself was exiled to Egypt, where he died.

A Divine Call

Jeremiah's sufferings began with a divine call:

> Now the word of the LORD came to me, saying,

> "Before I formed you in the womb I knew you,
> and before you were born I consecrated you;
> I appointed you a prophet to the nations." (vv. 4, 5)

God did wonderful things for Jeremiah before he was even born. He knew him. He formed him. He set him apart and appointed him as a prophet to the nations. He did all this long before Jeremiah drew his first breath or shed his first tear.

The call of Jeremiah is rich in its doctrinal and practical content. Among its important teachings are the following:

1. *God is the Lord of life.* God formed Jeremiah in the womb. Jeremiah had biological parents, of course, but God himself fashioned him and knit him together in his mother's womb. Telling children who ask where babies come from that they come from God is good theology. And it is not bad science either. The Lord of life uses the natural processes he designed to plant human life in the womb.

2. *A fetus is a person.* A person is a human being, created in the image of God, living in relationship to God. This verse testifies that the personal relationship between God and his child takes place in the womb, or even earlier.

Birth is not our beginning. Not even conception is our real beginning. In some ineffable way, God has a personal knowledge of the individual that *precedes* conception. "Before I formed you in the womb I knew you." This is the strong, intimate, Hebrew word for "know" that is also used to describe sexual intimacy between husband and wife.

"I knew you." What a beautiful thing for God to say to his children! "I loved you and cared for you in eternity past. I made a personal commitment to you even before you were born." And what a beautiful thing for parents to say to their children: "God knows you, God loves you, and God has entered into a personal relationship with you." This verse holds special comfort for mothers who have had miscarriages. It gives hope to parents who have lost children in infancy, and even for women who aborted their own babies. God knew your child, and he knows your child.

3. *We do not choose God before God chooses us.* If you want to know *who* you are, you have to know *whose* you are. For the Christian, the answer to that question is that you belong to Jesus Christ.

When did Jeremiah start belonging to God? When did God choose him? The prophet was set apart before he was born. While Jeremiah was being carried around in his mother's womb, God was making preparations for his salvation and his ministry. To set something apart is to sanctify it or to dedicate it to holy service. Long before Jeremiah was born, God chose him and consecrated him for ministry.

Given the intimacy of God's knowledge of Jeremiah, it is appropriate for Jeremiah to address him with the title "Lord GOD" (v. 6). God is sovereign. He not only forms his people in the womb, he sets them apart for salvation from all eternity.

God's choice is not unique to Jeremiah; it is true for every believer. This is known as the doctrine of divine election. "You did not choose me," Jesus said to his disciples, "but I chose you and appointed you that you should go and bear fruit" (John 15:16a). "Blessed be the God and Father of our Lord Jesus Christ . . . he chose us in him before the foundation of the world, that we should be holy and blameless before him" (Ephesians 1:3–4). This promise is for the whole church. Therefore, it is for the comfort of every Christian. God not only knows you, he chose you, and he did so long before you were ever conceived.

Eugene Peterson offers these practical conclusions about God's choice of Jeremiah:

> My identity does not begin when I begin to understand myself. There is something previous to what I think about myself, and it is what God thinks of me. That means that everything I think and feel is by nature a response, and the one to whom I respond is God. I never speak the first word. I never make the first move.
>
> Jeremiah's life didn't start with Jeremiah. Jeremiah's salvation didn't start with Jeremiah. Jeremiah's truth didn't start with Jeremiah. He entered the world in which the essential parts of his existence were already ancient history. So do we.[1]

4. *Every Christian has a calling.* There is a general call, of course, to believe in Jesus Christ. But everyone who believes in Christ also has a special calling to a particular sphere of obedience and ministry. Jeremiah was not just

set apart for salvation, he was set apart for vocation. God had work for him to do. The prophet had a mission to accomplish and a message to deliver to his generation.

Jeremiah's unique appointment was to be a prophet to the nations. God intended his ministry to be international in scope. Part of Jeremiah's job was to promise God's grace to the nations, proclaiming, "All nations shall gather to . . . the presence of the LORD in Jerusalem" (3:17).

But to be a prophet to the nations also includes announcing God's *judgment*. By the time he reached the end of his ministry, Jeremiah had pronounced a divine sentence of judgment upon every nation from Ammon to Babylon. Just as all nations receive God's sovereign grace, all nations are subject to God's severe justice.

Jeremiah's calling is not for everyone. The first chapter of Jeremiah is mainly about his call for his times, not your call for your times. But you do have a call. God not only knows you and chose you, he has a plan for your life. As F. B. Meyer so eloquently puts it, "From the foot of the cross, where we are cradled in our second birth, to the brink of the river, where we lay down our armor, there is a path which he has prepared for us to walk in."[2]

Perhaps you are still trying to figure out what God's plan is for you. Many Christians long to know what God is calling them to do. If you are not sure, there are at least two things you ought to do.

The first is to do everything you already know God wants you to do. You cannot expect to be ready for God's call, or even to recognize God's call, unless you are obeying what God has already revealed to you. This includes the obvious things, such as spending time in prayer and Bible study, serving the people with whom you live, remaining active in the worship of the church, and being God's witness in the world.

Second, ask God to reveal his will for your life. If you ask, he has promised to answer. "If any of you lacks wisdom, let him ask God, who gives generously to all without reproach, and it will be given him" (James 1:5).

A Dubious Candidate

Jeremiah knew what God wanted him to do. Yet even after he received his divine call, he was still a dubious candidate: "Ah, Lord GOD," he said, "I do not know how to speak, for I am only a youth" (v. 6).

Jeremiah had two main objections to becoming a prophet: his lack of eloquence and his lack of experience. To paraphrase: "Ahhh, wait a second, Lord, about this whole prophet-to-the-nations thing . . . It doesn't sound like that great an idea. Prophecy is not one of my spiritual gifts. As you know, I am getting a C in rhetoric at the synagogue. Besides, I am just a teenager."

Was Jeremiah being modest or faithless? Was it right for him to object to God's call or not?

A good way to answer those questions is to compare Jeremiah with some other prophets. Later the Lord reaches out his hand and touches Jeremiah's mouth (v. 9). This reminds us of Isaiah's experience when he saw "The Lord sitting upon a throne, high and lifted up; and the train of his robe filled the temple" (Isaiah 6:1).

Isaiah had one or two doubts about his calling too, but his doubts were different. Isaiah's main problem was that he had a guilty conscience: "And I said: 'Woe is me! For I am lost; for I am a man of unclean lips, and I dwell in the midst of a people of unclean lips; for my eyes have seen the King, the LORD of hosts!'" (v. 5). Isaiah did not doubt his ability, he doubted his integrity. When the seraph flew from the altar to touch Isaiah's lips with a live coal, he said: "Behold, this has touched your lips; your guilt is taken away, and your sin atoned for" (v. 7).

Isaiah's experience was somewhat different from Jeremiah's. When God touched Jeremiah's lips, it was not to take away his sins, it was to give him God's words.

What about the call of Moses? Was Jeremiah's call like the call of Moses? Jeremiah's objection sounds very much like the objection Moses made when God called him: "Oh, my Lord, I am not eloquent, either in the past or since you have spoken to your servant, but I am slow of speech and of tongue" (Exodus 4:10). Unlike Isaiah, Moses doubted his competence rather than his righteousness.

This was precisely Jeremiah's objection. He was not sure what to say or how to say it. He may have even been concerned about his foreign language skills, since God was calling him to an international ministry. Perhaps his grasp of Akkadian and Ugaritic was deficient. In any case, Jeremiah had his doubts about whether he could do the job.

Jeremiah's doubts find an echo in J. R. R. Tolkien's novel *The Fellowship of the Ring*. A hobbit named Frodo has been chosen to make a long and dangerous quest to destroy the one ring of power, a quest he himself would not wish to choose. "I am not made for perilous quests," cried Frodo. "I wish I had never seen the Ring! Why did it come to me? Why was I chosen?"

The answer Frodo is given is similar to the one God's prophets often receive: "Such questions cannot be answered. . . . You may be sure that it was not for any merit that others do not possess; not for power or wisdom, at any rate. But you have been chosen and you must therefore use such strength and heart and wits as you have."[3]

When God gives his servants a clear calling, he does not accept any excuses. "Then the LORD said to him [Moses], 'Who has made man's mouth? Who makes him mute, or deaf, or seeing, or blind? Is it not I, the LORD? Now therefore go, and I will be with your mouth and teach you what you shall speak'" (Exodus 4:11, 12).

God said much the same thing to Jeremiah. To put it plainly, he said, "Don't give me that stuff!" "Do not say, 'I am only a child.' You must go to everyone I send you to and say whatever I command you'" (1:7). "Then the LORD put out his hand and touched my mouth. And the LORD said to me, 'Behold, I have put my words in your mouth'" (v. 9).

God did not disqualify Jeremiah on the basis of his youth and inexperience. In fact, he treated him the same way he treated Moses. He did not deny the basis for the prophet's objection. He did not argue with Jeremiah about his speaking credentials or quibble with him about his age. Jeremiah may have had reasonable doubts. But God exposed his false humility for what it really was: a lack of faith.

Jeremiah had forgotten that God is not limited by human weakness. God himself possesses everything Jeremiah needs to answer his call. In fact, enabling weak tools to do strong jobs is God's standard operating procedure. His entire work force is comprised of dubious candidates. When God calls someone to do a job, he gives him or her all the gifts needed to get the job done. With God's calling comes God's gifting.

This does not mean that your gifts and abilities do not matter when you are trying to figure out what God wants you to do with your life. They do matter. If you do not know what God is calling you to do, take an honest look at the gifts he has given you. If necessary, ask others to help you figure out what your gifts are.

But once you know what God has called you to do, trust him to equip you to do it. God equipped Jeremiah to be an international prophet in some amazing ways. He was a polymath, a great scholar, a man of prodigious learning. He was able to converse in the fields of politics, economics, comparative religion, geography, theology, botany, zoology, anthropology, military strategy, architecture, industry, agriculture, fine arts, and poetry.[4]

If God has actually called you to do a particular job, then he will do for you what he did for Jeremiah: He will give you everything you need to do that job. If you think you know what the Lord wants you to do with your life, get busy, trusting him to give you the grace to answer his call.

A Dangerous Commission

Once God had issued his divine call and dealt with his dubious candidate, he gave him a dangerous commission: "For to all to whom I send you, you shall go, and whatever I command you, you shall speak. Do not be afraid of them, for I am with you to deliver you" (vv. 7, 8).

Frankly, that sounds a little ominous! God does not spell things out, but it is easy to tell that Jeremiah's job will be dangerous. Telling someone "Do not be afraid" is the kind of advice that tends to have the opposite effect than the one intended. The more people tell you not to be afraid, the more you start to wonder what you ought to be afraid of! It is like the king who sent one of his knights off to rescue his fair princess. Just as the knight rode away from the castle, and just as the drawbridge was closing behind him, the king yelled down from the ramparts, "Don't be afraid of the dragon!" "Dragon? What dragon? You didn't say anything about dragons!"

God's promise to rescue Jeremiah is also a bit worrisome. Rescued from what? The promise suggests that the prophet will fall into grave danger. God does not promise that Jeremiah has nothing to fear or that he will not need to be rescued. But he does command him not to be afraid, and he does promise to rescue him.

The reason Jeremiah did not need to be afraid was that he had the promise of God's presence. The Lord gave him the same promise he made to Moses, to Joshua, and to all his children: "I am with you."

Once there was a man who understood the danger of the prophet's commission and the comfort of God's presence. He was an evangelist God used to bring renewal to the Colombian church during the 1980s and 1990s. Since he was an enemy of the drug cartels, his life was in constant danger, until he was finally gunned down by assassins. Yet shortly before he died, he said, "I know that I am absolutely immortal until I have finished the work that God intends for me to do." God's servants are indeed immortal until they have completed their service.

Not only did Jeremiah have God's presence at his side, he also had God's words on his lips: "Then the LORD put out his hand and touched my mouth. And the LORD said to me, 'Behold, I have put my words in your mouth'" (v. 9). This is another connection between Jeremiah and Moses. God promised that he would raise up a prophet for his people like Moses: "I will put my words in his mouth, and he shall speak to them all that I command him" (Deuteronomy 18:18).

Whenever Jeremiah spoke in God's name, God was the one doing the talking. Who wrote the book of Jeremiah? From one point of view, it contains the words of Jeremiah, as the Scripture says: "The words of Jeremiah, the son of Hilkiah" (1:1). From another point of view, however, these are the words of God himself: "To [him] the word of the LORD came" (v. 2).

The Bible is never embarrassed to speak this way. There is a meaningful sense in which the words of Jeremiah are recorded in the pages of the Old Testament. The book of Jeremiah gives us a glimpse of the personality and experiences of the man, Jeremiah. But at the same time the Holy Spirit is the One who breathed out the words of the book of Jeremiah. "For no prophecy was ever produced by the will of man, but men spoke from God as they were carried along by the Holy Spirit" (2 Peter 1:21). The book of Jeremiah is God's words and Jeremiah's words. When we read them, we do not just see God through Jeremiah's lens; God speaks to us directly.

The reason Jeremiah has authority "over nations and over kingdoms" (1:10) is that he is not speaking on his own behalf. God is sovereign over the nations, and he rules them by his Word. When prophets speak in his name they are mightier than kings. When preachers preach according to God's Word they are mightier than presidents.

Once when I was interviewed by a pastoral search committee, I was asked if I was easily intimidated. (The church was frequented by scholars and other learned individuals.) "Would you feel comfortable preaching to so-and-so?" I was asked. Before taking time to think about my answer, I blurted out, "Yes, I'd preach to the Queen of England."

I think it was a good answer. God rules the nations of this world by his Word. Those who have been appointed to preach that Word have a spiritual authority over the nations. The Lord instructed Jeremiah to be a bold prophet, not because of his preaching ability or because of his age and experience, but because he was called to speak God's own words.

A Depressing Conclusion

It was not always easy for Jeremiah to speak God's words. His commission was not only dangerous, it was often depressing. We have already been given a clue that the book of Jeremiah does not have a happy ending. It ends with the people of Jerusalem being sent into exile. Thus the book of Jeremiah is a tragedy rather than a comedy. It is about the unraveling of a nation. It is the sad story of the decline of God's people from faith to idolatry to exile.

It is this decline that makes Jeremiah a prophet for post-Christian times. He lived in a time very much like our own, when people no longer think God matters for daily life. Public life is increasingly dominated by pagan ideas and rituals. Some people still meet their religious obligations, but they do so out of duty rather than devotion.

The spiritual problems we face at the dawn of the twenty-first century were the same problems that Jeremiah found depressing twenty-five hundred years ago. The discouragement of his ministry is evident from the verbs God uses to describe it: "See, I have set you this day over nations and over kingdoms, to pluck up and to break down, to destroy and to overthrow, to build and to plant" (v. 10). The prophet's job description includes six tasks, and four of them are negative. Two to one, his words to the nations will be words of judgment.

"To pluck up" is to dig up nations by the roots and turn them under. It is a word that Jeremiah uses more than all the other Biblical writers combined, often to describe the uprooting of idols (e.g. 12:14–17). "To break down" is to tear down a standing structure, like knocking down a city wall or toppling a tower. "To destroy" is another word for knocking things down. "To overthrow" is to demolish, to bring to complete ruin.

Once the Lord plucks up, breaks down, destroys, and overthrows a nation, there is not much left. There is a great deal of that kind of judgment in the rest of Jeremiah's book. This verse is not only Jeremiah's job description, it is also a helpful plot-summary of his book. He lives in such evil days that judgment will outnumber grace two to one.

But grace will have the last word. When the cities of evil have been torn down and plowed under, God will start afresh. He will begin a new work. He will "build," and he will "plant." He will bring renewal out of demolition.

This is God's plan for the kingdoms of this world (cf. 18:7–10). He is the one who is in charge of the beginnings and endings of history. He is the one who uproots some nations and plants others. He is the one who tears down some kingdoms and rebuilds others.

This is also God's plan for salvation in Jesus Christ. Jesus said, "Destroy this temple, and in three days I will raise it up" (John 2:19). The temple of Jesus' body was uprooted and torn down from the cross. It was destroyed and overthrown to the grave. But God built and planted resurrection life into the body of Jesus Christ.

Now God builds and plants that same resurrection power into the life of every believer. First the Holy Spirit uproots and tears down sin in your heart, and then he plants faith and builds obedience into your life. Like Jeremiah, you were a dubious candidate at the beginning. Yet God has known you from all eternity, and he has set you apart for new life in Christ.

If God has done all that for you, will you go wherever he tells you to go and say whatever he wants you to say, even if it turns out to be a dangerous commission?

2

When the Almond Tree Blossoms

JEREMIAH 1:11–19

GOD FINISHED HIS CALL TO JEREMIAH with a flourish. It was an audiovisual presentation, a spiritual show-and-tell.

The second half of Jeremiah 1 consists of three object lessons. First God shows the prophet an almond tree (vv. 11, 12), a boiling pot (vv. 13–16), and an iron pillar (vv. 17–19). Then God tells Jeremiah what the tree, the pot, and the pillar mean: his word will blossom forth, his judgment will be poured out, and his prophet will stand firm.

The Almond Tree

What is the sign that winter is over and spring is on the way? In the northern United States, the first harbinger of spring is the robin. In my Midwestern childhood, a better indicator of spring was the forsythia bush on the side of the house. When tiny yellow blossoms started to appear on the forsythia, spring was definitely on its way, and the urge to get out a baseball glove was irresistible. In Washington, D.C., cherry blossoms mean spring. In Oxford, England, it is daffodils.

In Anathoth, where Jeremiah was born, it was almond blossoms. If they had wanted to, they could have held an almond-blossom festival there every spring. Even to this day that region of Judea is a center for almond-growing. The almond tree is always the first to blossom. Already in January the almond trees in Jeremiah's hometown were covered with white blossoms.

"And the word of the LORD came to me, saying, 'Jeremiah, what do you see?'" The prophet's answer was predictable: "I see an almond branch" (v. 11). Very likely the branch was covered with white blossoms. Or perhaps it had not yet blossomed, but its tiny buds were just beginning to appear. In any case Jeremiah understood what the branch meant. It was the first sign of spring. When the almond tree blossoms, the promise of spring is about to be fulfilled, and warm weather is on the way.

The almond blossom was the show. Next comes the tell: "Then the LORD said to me, 'You have seen well, for I am watching over my word to perform it'" (v. 12). God used a play on words to teach Jeremiah the spiritual significance of the almond branch. This is how he stoops to the level of human understanding. He speaks—indeed, he puns—so that we might comprehend.

The word for "watching" is the Hebrew *shoqed*. It sounds very much like the Hebrew for "almond": *shaqed*. In fact, those two words—*shoqed* and *shaqed*—are different forms of the same word, the word for waking or watching. The almond tree was the waking tree. It was the first tree to wake up after a long winter's nap. It was also the watching tree, the tree one watched for in the spring.

God showed Jeremiah the almond tree to teach him that he is wide awake. He is not asleep. He does not slumber. He never goes into hibernation. God is still on his watch. He is wide awake, watching and waiting.

What God is watching for is to make sure that everything God has promised comes to pass. He is watching to see that his Word is fulfilled. This is one of the main themes of the book of Jeremiah, what Douglas Rawlinson Jones calls "The power and inescapability of the divine word moving inexorably towards fulfilment (sic)."[1] God is going to do everything he has promised to do. He is bringing his plans to fruition. Even when it seems dormant, God's Word is waiting to burst into flower. It is not dead, it is alive. Like the almond tree, it is starting to blossom. One can no more prevent God's promise from being fulfilled than one can keep the almond tree from blossoming in springtime.

God made a similar promise to Isaiah:

> For as the rain and the snow come down from heaven
>   and do not return there but water the earth,
> making it bring forth and sprout,
>   giving seed to the sower and bread to the eater,
> so shall my word be that goes out from my mouth;
>   it shall not return to me empty,
> but it shall accomplish that which I purpose,
>   and shall succeed in the thing for which I sent it. (Isaiah 55:10, 11)

The almond branch gives solid hope and lasting joy to every Christian. It assures us that everything God has promised will come to pass. Every last one of his very great and precious promises will be fulfilled.

It is good to recount the promises of God. There is the promise of "redemption" in Jesus Christ (Colossians 1:14). There is the promise of forgiveness of sins (1 John 1:9). There is the promise of "The water of life without price" (Revelation 22:17). There is the promise of the gift of the Holy Spirit, for this generation and the next (Acts 2:39). There is the promise that you will be comforted when you mourn, shown mercy when you are merciful, and filled with righteousness when you hunger and thirst after it (Matthew 5:4–7). There is the promise that God will give you wisdom (James 1:5, 6). There is the promise that God will never leave you nor forsake you (Joshua 1:5).

These promises are only the beginning. There is the promise that "The pure in heart . . . shall see God" (Matthew 5:8). There is the promise that God's people will be with him (Revelation 22:3). There is the promise that Jesus has gone to prepare a place in his Father's house, and that he will come back soon to take you there (John 14:2, 3). There is the promise that the Lord Jesus Christ will transform your body to be like his glorious resurrection body (Philippians 3:21).

All those promises are true. Every last one of them will be fulfilled. Some have already begun to blossom, like almond blossoms in springtime. Soon all of them will burst into full flower in the everlasting springtime of paradise. The Apostle Paul wrapped up all these promises together (and many more besides) when he wrote: "For all the promises of God find their Yes in him. That is why it is through him that we utter our Amen to God for his glory" (2 Corinthians 1:20).

The Boiling Pot

What about words of judgment? Will they come to pass too? Does God fulfill his threats as well as his promises?

Here is the show: "The word of the LORD came to me a second time, saying, 'What do you see?' And I said, 'I see a boiling pot, facing away from the north'" (1:13). Once again God used something common to teach Jeremiah. First it was an almond branch. This time it is a plain, old, ordinary cooking pot, probably made of iron or copper.

The prophet must have seen this pot on an open fire. As anyone who has ever been camping knows, it does not take long for water to boil on an open flame. Imagine the pot resting on logs or coals and heating to a rolling boil. The Hebrew does not literally say "boiling"; actually it says "blown upon."

In other words, the fire is being stoked, the flames are being fanned, and the embers are bursting into flame. As the pot resettles in the fire, it tips to one side, the boiling water bubbles over the side of the pot, and steam goes hissing up from the flames.

That was the show. Here is the tell: "Then the LORD said to me, 'Out of the north disaster shall be let loose upon all the inhabitants of the land. For behold, I am calling all the tribes of the kingdoms of the north, declares the LORD" (vv. 14, 15a). Trouble is brewing, and it is not hard to tell which way the wind is blowing. The cauldron is tipping ominously away from the north.

The Bible does not yet identify the northern peoples who will come spilling down toward Jerusalem, but one can round up the usual suspects. Maybe it will be the Scythians from northern Asia, whom Herodotus mentions in his history. Perhaps it will be the Assyrians, although their power was on the wane in Jeremiah's day. Probably it will be the Babylonians, who were going from strength to strength.

But the real point is that God himself will do the judging. God is *summoning* the northern kingdoms. When the Babylonians come, they will be marching to God's orders. God is the one who will tip the "boiling pot" and pour it out over Judah. Judging sin is God's prerogative. He is the righteous judge who uproots and tears down nations, who destroys and overthrows kingdoms (v. 10). As he says in verse 16, "I will declare my judgments against them."

What will it be like for Jerusalem to be scalded by the boiling pot of divine judgment? The northern kings "shall come . . . against all its walls all around and against all the cities of Judah" (v. 15b). This is a hint that when judgment comes, Jerusalem will be a city under siege. Enemy armies will camp around her walls, waiting for the people of God to starve. While they are at it, these armies will have their way with the defenseless towns and villages in the surrounding countryside.

But here is the real kicker: "Every one shall set his throne at the entrance of the gates of Jerusalem" (v. 15b). What total humiliation! When an ancient king wanted to show his complete domination over vanquished foes, he would set up his throne in the gates of their capital city. There is an ancient mural, for example, that shows Sennacherib sitting in the gates of Lachish, ruling as a judge over that city.

Consider how degrading this would be for the city of Jerusalem. Jerusalem is the city where the son of David is supposed to sit on his throne. Indeed, it is intended to be the throne of God himself (cf. 3:17). But when the boiling pot spills over Jerusalem, the Babylonian generals will park their thrones right in the middle of the city gates. This prophecy was fulfilled, of course. Later

Jeremiah will recount how Nergal-sar-ezer of Samgar, Nebu-sar-sekim, and another Nergal-sar-ezer camped out in the Middle Gate of Jerusalem (39:3).

Why would God allow his own people to experience such a defeat? And not just allow it—God will actually bring this judgment to pass! But he will do it with good reason. His people have rejected him. They have decided to follow other gods. He holds a cauldron over them, he says, "for all their evil in forsaking me. They have made offerings to other gods and worshiped the works of their own hands" (1:16).

God's people will get no more than they deserve. They have burned incense to other gods, which was a blatant violation of the first commandment God ever gave them: "You shall have no other gods before me" (Exodus 20:3). The word God uses for burning incense can include offering sacrifices. So perhaps the Jews had even tried to get atonement from other gods. They also worshiped idols they had made with their own hands, which was a blatant violation of the second commandment: "You shall not make for yourself a carved image . . . You shall not bow down to them or serve them" (Exodus 20:4, 5). No wonder, then, that the tribes of Judah and Benjamin found themselves under the boiling pot!

This show-and-tell is a warning to anyone who does not have a personal relationship with Jesus Christ. If you are like the people of Jeremiah's day, you stand under the boiling pot of divine judgment. Do not repeat their mistake. They did not believe that God punishes sin. They decided that Jeremiah was just breathing idle threats and that Jerusalem would never be destroyed. Their dismissive attitude is summed up in this taunt: "Where is the word of the LORD?" (17:15). That is a dangerous attitude to take if God is the God of the almond tree. His threats of judgment are as certain as his promises of grace. He watches to see his Word fulfilled, as the people of Jerusalem eventually discovered.

If you do know Christ, think twice about bowing down to idols. The values of this world have a way of getting mixed up with the values of the kingdom of God. That is why the church always needs to be on its guard against worldliness. The gods of self, sex, power, luxury, popularity, and beauty are always clamoring for attention. Turn a deaf ear to them, for it is against such sins that the wrath of God is about to be revealed.

The Iron Pillar

There was more show-and-tell to come, but first God repeated Jeremiah's call: "But you, dress yourself for work; arise, and say to them everything that I command you. Do not be dismayed by them, lest I dismay you before them"

(1:17). Sometimes important things need to be repeated, especially for dubious candidates for Christian service.

Jeremiah had heard most of this before. God had already put words into his mouth and had already told him not to panic. What is new is the sense of urgency. By telling his prophet to get ready, God was telling him to brace himself. Literally he said, "Gird up your loins." Today Jeremiah would be told to roll up his sleeves or to put on some sweats and lace up his sneakers. Back then God told him to hike up his robe and tuck it into his belt so it would not get in his way.

The other thing that is new is the warning: "Do not be dismayed by them, lest I dismay you before them" (v. 17). If Jeremiah does panic, God will give him something to really panic about. The point is that if Jeremiah loses his nerve in front of mere human beings, God will unnerve him.

John Calvin's commentary on this verse is worth repeating:

> This passage contains a useful doctrine, from which we learn that strength shall never be wanting to God's servants, while they derive courage from the conviction that God himself is the author of their calling . . . for God will then supply them with strength and courage invincible, so as to render them formidable to the whole world: but if they be unhinged and timid, and turn here and there, and be influenced by the fear of men, God will render them base and contemptible, and make them to tremble at the least breath of air, and they shall be wholly broken down. . . . [2]

Jesus Christ repeats this warning for the benefit of his disciples: "For whoever is ashamed of me and of my words in this adulterous and sinful generation, of him will the Son of Man also be ashamed when he comes in the glory of his Father with the holy angels" (Mark 8:38). Anyone who speaks a word of testimony in behalf of Christ—even in the face of ridicule or persecution—needs to do it with spiritual courage.

If Jeremiah is going to be as bold as that, he will need supernatural strength, which is exactly what God promised to give him.

> And I, behold, I make you this day a fortified city, an iron pillar, and bronze walls, against the whole land, against the kings of Judah, its officials, its priests, and the people of the land. They will fight against you, but they shall not prevail against you, for I am with you, declares the LORD, to deliver you. (1:18, 19)

How strong will Jeremiah be? God has made him "a fortified city." He will be a metropolis of a man. He will be like a city on a hill, with high walls and strong towers, defended by a mighty army. He will be like Pharaoh Thutmose III, a man described as "a hero, excellent fortress of his army, a wall of iron."[3] Jeremiah was no military hero—he was a man of the cloth—but he was just as strong.

God also made him "an iron pillar," a steel beam of a man. The word for "pillar" is not the word for a free-standing column; it is the word for a prop or foundation post that supports a building. Jeremiah will be a tower of strength. He will be like a flying buttress holding up the wall of a cathedral. He will support and uphold the people of God.

God made Jeremiah a "bronze [wall]," a metal bulwark of a man. Actually there were no bronze walls in the ancient world. The British Museum in London houses bronze gates from Assyria. But they are only gates, and they are actually wooden gates with bronze overlay. They are strong gates, but imagine how much stronger they would be if they were bronze all the way through. That is how strong God made Jeremiah.

Jeremiah needed that kind of strength. He needed the triple protection of being "a fortified city, an iron pillar, and bronze walls." God commanded him to take his stand against the kings, the officials, the priests, and the people of Judah, which did not leave him with many allies. In fact, it did not leave him with any. The kings of Judah—Josiah, Jehoiakim, and Zedekiah—were against him. The courtiers, advisers, and civil servants of the kingdom were against him. So were the people of the land, meaning the regular folks, the rank-and-file working people. Even his own colleagues in ministry turned against him. With friends like these, who needs enemies?

God warned Jeremiah that he would not win many popularity contests. His warning was accompanied by strong words for confrontation. "They will fight against you," God said, using a word for military conflict. The people would declare war on Jeremiah, ambushing him at every turn and trying to destroy his ministry. When God told Jeremiah to gird up his loins, what he was really telling him to do was to put on his combat fatigues.

Jeremiah was appointed over nations and kingdoms, to tear them down and to build them up (v. 10). This included standing up to God's enemies, refusing to give in to political pressure. How could he do it? How can any believer, let alone a youngster who does not know how to speak, have the courage to stand against the enemies of God in a wicked world?

Courage and strength come from the Lord. Jeremiah did not construct himself into "a fortified city." He did not fashion himself into "an iron pillar." He did not raise himself into a "bronze [wall]." Instead God said, "I make you this day a fortified city, an iron pillar, and bronze walls" (v. 18). God himself is the foreman for this construction project. Right from the beginning of his calling, God equipped Jeremiah with the courage he needed to finish his calling.

The great Jewish scholar Moses Maimonides (1135–1204) had this to say about the prophetic calling:

> Thus, we find prophets that did not leave off speaking to the people until they were slain; it is this divine influence that moves them, that does not allow them to rest in any way, though they might bring upon themselves great evils by their action. Thus, when Jeremiah was despised, like other teachers and scholars of his age, he could not, though he desired it, withhold his prophecy or cease from reminding the people of the truths which they rejected.[4]

It was not just Jeremiah's call that made him indomitable, it was God's protection. God did not just make Jeremiah strong; he promised to stay at his side, to rescue him, to help him stand and not be overcome. God kept those promises, of course. He is the God of the almond tree, the God who watches to see that his Word is fulfilled.

Derek Kidner makes a striking point about the fulfillment of these promises. He observes that verse 18 sounds like a wild exaggeration. How can one man be "a fortified city" and "an iron pillar" and a "bronze [wall]"? But Kidner points out that when one looks at the whole career of Jeremiah, this verse turns out to be an understatement, because the prophet held out longer than the walls of his fortified city, Jerusalem.[5] Jerusalem cracked and crumbled before Jeremiah did.

Jeremiah was like the Puritan described in John Geree's *The Character of an Old English Puritane*: "a man foursquare, immoveable in all times, so that they who in the midst of many opinions have lost the view of true religion, may return to him and there find it."[6]

Are you a foursquare Christian? The command to stand firm in the day of spiritual battle is not just for Jeremiah; it is a command for every follower of God. Jeremiah is a picture of the Christian who stands and is not overcome. Like Jeremiah, you must "be strong in the Lord and in the strength of his might" (Ephesians 6:10). You must get ready for combat, putting on "The whole armor of God, that you may be able to stand against the schemes of the devil" (Ephesians 6:11). You must gird up your loins, standing firm, "having fastened on the belt of truth" (Ephesians 6:14). Is anything in this world stronger than a believer who stands firm in the promises of God?

The calling to be strong in the Lord is not just for prophets like Jeremiah. It is for every Christian because every Christian faces spiritual danger. In John

Bunyan's *Pilgrim's Progress* (1678), Christian answers the call of God and embarks upon a great journey to the Celestial City. On the way he overtakes Mr. By-ends, a man who differs from what he calls Christians "of the stricter sort." He is a fair-weather believer. He cannot be bothered with the demands of discipleship. He is not willing to hazard everything for God if that is going to include any suffering. "We never strive against wind and tide," says Mr. By-ends. "We are always most zealous when religion goes in his silver slippers; we love much to walk with him in the street, if the sun shines and the people applaud it."

Christian replies to Mr. By-ends with words that apply to Jeremiah and to everyone who stands with Jesus Christ for the gospel: "If you will go with us, you must go against wind and tide, the which, I perceive, is against your opinion. You must also own religion in his rags, as well as when in his silver slippers, and stand by him, too, when bound in irons, as well as when he walketh the streets with applause."[7]

3

God Files for Divorce

JEREMIAH 2:1–37

I WALKED PAST the notice board on the street, and I was shocked by my own sermon title, chosen some weeks before: "God Files for Divorce." I ran up to my office and pulled out a Bible to make sure I had it right. God files for *divorce*? Can it be true? Would the God of the eternal covenant end his marriage to his own people?

Yes, he would. "'Therefore I still contend with you, declares the LORD, and with your children's children I will contend'" (2:9). The honeymoon is over. God is taking his people to divorce court. Jeremiah 2 is his legal testimony.

The Honeymoon

God remembers what the honeymoon was like. He pages through the photos in his wedding album. As he looks back on the early days of his marriage, there is an ache in his heart. He can remember how his bride adored him when they were first married. "The word of the LORD came to me, saying, 'Go and proclaim in the hearing of Jerusalem, Thus says the LORD , "I remember the devotion of your youth, your love as a bride, how you followed me"'" (vv. 1, 2a).

God is on the witness stand in the agony of love, the kind of agony Sheldon Vanauken describes in his book *A Severe Mercy*:

> To hold her in my arms against the twilight and be her comrade for ever—
> this was all I wanted so long as my life should last. . . . And this, I told my-
> self with a kind of wonder, this was what love was: this consecration, this
> curious uplifting, this sudden inexplicable joy, and this intolerable pain.[1]

Once Israel loved God like a newlywed. Wives should take careful note of Jeremiah's picture of the devoted wife. Actually the word "devotion" is not strong enough! God remembers the covenant faithfulness of Israel. This is a word for unbroken promises, unshakable loyalty, unceasing devotion, and unfailing loving-kindness. It is the perfect word to describe marriage because marriage is a covenant relationship. It is more than a legal contract; it is a steadfast love commitment of fidelity and adoration.

Christians sometimes get the idea that being faithful to God's covenant is simply a matter of obeying God's Law. This is because we are legalists at heart. But God never intended our relationship with him to be mere obedience of the will. God wants our hearts as well as our wills. Redemption is a romance.

The children of Israel gave their hearts to God when they first got married. They reveled in the romance of redemption. Like a newly married bride, Israel loved her divine husband. She loved him the way Julian of Norwich (c. 1342–1413) did when she said, "I saw him and sought him, and I had him and I lacked him."

The proof of Israel's love was that she followed God wherever he led. "In the wilderness, in a land not sown" (v. 2b), this bride submitted to the guidance of her husband. Israel was young and in love, and all she wanted was to be close to her husband. Barren wilderness was not much of a bridal suite, but that didn't matter! Israel followed God out of Egypt, through the wilderness, and into the Promised Land (vv. 6, 7).

If Israel was a loving wife, God was a faithful husband. He did not fail to keep any of his wedding vows. Here husbands ought to take careful note of Jeremiah's picture of the perfect husband.

God had *passion* for his bride. "Israel was holy to the LORD, the firstfruits of his harvest" (v. 3a). He took her to love and cherish. He treated her with honor and respect, setting her apart as "holy." Israel was the firstfruits of God's harvest among the nations of the world. She was God's best and most valuable possession, the apple of his eye, dedicated to him alone.

So God *protected* his bride. He would not allow anyone else to taste his fruit. "All who ate of it incurred guilt; disaster came upon them" (v. 3b). If anyone threatened Israel or encroached on her territory, God treated it as an attack on his own person. Remember what happened to the Egyptians? Or the Philistines? God saved his wife and kept her safe.

Then God *provided* for his bride: "I brought you into a plentiful land to enjoy its fruits and its good things" (v. 7a). God gave Israel a beautiful home. There was plenty of food in the fridge—mostly milk and honey—and fine bone china on the table.

The Grounds for Divorce

That was then, but this is now. Time to wake up and smell the burnt toast. The honeymoon is over. My wife and I decided our honeymoon was over when the no-stick frying pan we bought when we first got married started to stick. Well, in Jeremiah 2 the frying pan is sticking like the floor of a movie theater.

How could this be happening? If you were there for the nuptials, when Jerusalem was espoused to God, you never would have believed it would all end in divorce. The wedding was so beautiful! The honeymoon was so wonderful! The bride was so devoted! The husband was so faithful! Where did it all go wrong?

God is on the witness stand in divorce court asking the same question.

> Hear the word of the Lord, O house of Jacob, and all the clans of the house of Israel. Thus says the LORD:
>
> "What wrong did your fathers find in me
>   that they went far from me,
> and went after worthlessness, and became worthless?
> They did not say, 'Where is the LORD
>   who brought us up from the land of Egypt,
> who led us in the wilderness,
>   in a land of deserts and pits,
> in a land of drought and deep darkness,
>   in a land that none passes through,
>   where no man dwells?'" (2:4–7; cf. 2:31)

God did not leave his people—they dumped him. God's people were the ones who walked out on the marriage. They used to love him, but it's all over now. This is worth remembering whenever God seems distant. "Have you not brought this upon yourself by forsaking the LORD your God, when he led you in the way?" (v. 17). As the saying goes, "If God does not seem as close as he used to, who moved?"

Why would anyone ever move away from God? It makes no sense! Why would a bride leave a perfect husband? Why would she abandon a spouse who fulfilled all his vows to her? There is no explanation, no excuse. God's bride separated from her husband without the slightest provocation.

God is the one who has been wronged. He is the plaintiff, and this is his accusation: "They went far from me, and went after worthlessness, and became worthless" (v. 5b). This is the only legitimate ground for divorce—adultery (cf. Matthew 5:32). In this case the adultery is spiritual. God's people have been having affairs with "worthless" idols. This is the same word used in Ecclesiastes for "vanity." It means "mist" or "vapor." Idolaters grasp at thin air. Actually, they worship nothing at all.

The marriage between God and his people is dying of neglect. God's people no longer seek after God. They no longer say, "Where is the LORD?" (2:6a). They no longer recount and recite the mighty acts of salvation. They forget the love that saved them. They suffer from self-induced spiritual amnesia.

This is a reminder for Christians to thank God daily for salvation in Jesus Christ. Recount and recite the saving acts of God in history. Remember what God has done in your life. The road to spiritual adultery begins when you stop reveling in the love of God. Few Christians plan to fall into grievous sin. It is only after falling that they realize they have drifted away from the God of love.

Jeremiah places the blame for Jerusalem's marital difficulties squarely on the shoulders of her spiritual leaders:

> The priests did not say, "Where is the LORD?"
>   Those who handle the law did not know me;
> the shepherds transgressed against me;
>   the prophets prophesied by Baal
> and went after things that do not profit. (2:8)

The prophets, priests, and kings were not part of the solution—they were part of the problem. "As a thief is shamed when caught, so the house of Israel shall be shamed: they, their kings, their officials, their priests, and their prophets" (v. 26). The leaders got caught with their hands in the cookie jar. They were committing secret sins. Like everyone else, they were sleeping around with idols.

The middle of verse 8 ought to keep ministers and other spiritual leaders awake at night: "Those who handle the law did not know me." A holy calling does not make a holy man. The priests of Jeremiah's day were handling the Scriptures, studying the Bible, and teaching God's Word, but they did not know God himself (cf. John 5:39, 40). Their ministry was a dead ritual rather than a living relationship.

The Evidence

Jeremiah 2 does not describe a situation of "irreconcilable differences." This is not a no-fault divorce. God has legitimate grounds for terminating the marriage.

The rest of the chapter gives evidence of the infidelity of God's people. It is like a judicial slide show. As part of his prosecution, God introduces into evidence image after image of spiritual adultery. He lays out his case with the logic of a lawyer and the longing of a lover, proving beyond a shadow of a doubt that his people have forsaken their first love.

What is it like when God's people leave their husband? It is unheard of! Exhibit A: It is like a nation changing its gods.

> For cross to the coasts of Cyprus [in the West] and see,
>> or send to Kedar [a tribe in the far East] and examine with care;
>> see if there has been such a thing.
> Has a nation changed its gods? (vv. 10, 11a)

Of course not! Travel the world from east to west, no nation has ever changed its gods. Shoes, maybe, or hairstyles, but not gods.

Even the pagans are loyal to their gods. They cart them around wherever they go. Did the Canaanites ever abandon Baal or Asherah? Never! Did the Babylonians ever forsake Bel or Merodach? Ridiculous!

> Has a nation changed its gods,
>> even though they are no gods?
> But my people have changed their glory
> for that which does not profit. (v. 11)

It is hard to believe, but God's people exchanged the glorious effulgence of the divine presence for idols made of wood or stone. "For as many as your cities are your gods, O Judah" (v. 28b).

The people of Judah were so confused that they were "cross-worshiping": "[They] say to a tree, 'You are my father,' and to a stone, 'You gave me birth'" (v. 27). That is, they call the feminine goddess (represented by the wood) "Father" and tell the masculine god (represented by the stone) that he gave them birth!

By partner-swapping, Israel bartered away the living God. This was a religious crime without precedent in the ancient world. The pagans never abandoned their dead gods, but God's people abandoned the living God. The members of the jury, namely, the "heavens," ought to be so appalled at what they hear that they are "shocked . . . [and] utterly desolate" (v. 12).

What is it like when God's people leave their husband? Exhibit B: It is like leaving a spring of living water:

> [for] my people have committed two evils:
> they have forsaken me,
>> the fountain of living waters,
> and hewed out cisterns for themselves,
>> broken cisterns that can hold no water. (v. 13)

Imagine living in the desert. It is always dry. The thing you always need and can never find is water. Then imagine finding a desert spring that continuously bubbles up fresh from the ground. Would you leave a never-ending supply of water behind? Never! Only a lunatic would abandon a desert spring.

Now imagine leaving the spring behind and digging a cistern to catch rainwater. If you went to such trouble, would you then leave cracks in the limestone seal? Yet God testifies, "My people have . . . hewed out cisterns for themselves, broken cisterns that can hold no water" (v. 13). If leaving a spring is dumb, building a cracked cistern is dumber. It would be like shutting off your water supply and then digging a trench to get water from the nearest industrial canal.

What Jerusalem did made even less sense. God's people were worried about getting squashed by world superpowers. They were afraid of being plundered. So just to be safe, they propositioned their neighbors. They substituted political alliances for their love covenant with God:

> And now what do you gain by going to Egypt
>   to drink the waters of the Nile?
> Or what do you gain by going to Assyria
>   to drink the waters of the Euphrates? (2:18; cf. v. 36)

But these nations are not friends, they are enemies. In the end the alliances will fail, and Israel will be disappointed by her former partners.

> Is Israel a slave? Is he a homeborn servant?
>   Why then has he become a prey?
> The lions have roared against him;
>   they have roared loudly.
> They have made his land a waste;
>   his cities are in ruins, without inhabitant.
> Moreover, the men of Memphis and Tahpanhes
>   have shaved the crown of your head. (2:14–16)

> How much you go about,
>   changing your way!
> You shall be put to shame by Egypt
>   as you were put to shame by Assyria.
> From it too you will come away
>   with your hands on your head,
> for the LORD has rejected those in whom you trust,
>   and you will not prosper by them. (2:36, 37)

These prophecies came true, as Israel was later to lament: "I called to my lovers, but they deceived me" (Lamentations 1:19a).

Defense treaties with Egypt and Assyria are like broken cisterns. They cannot hold water the way God can. Worse still, their water turns out to have a bitter aftertaste compared to the sweet living water from God's eternal wellspring.

> Your evil will chastise you,
>   and your apostasy will reprove you.
> Know and see that it is evil and bitter
>   for you to forsake the LORD your God;
>   the fear of me is not in you,
>   declares the Lord GOD of hosts. (2:19)

This is partly a lesson about the coming Messiah. No water can compare with the living water God pours out in Jesus Christ (John 4:10). When the Scottish theologian Thomas Boston (1676–1732) preached on this text, he said, "God in Christ is the fountain, all-sufficient in himself. All the creatures are but cisterns; if there is no water brought into them from heaven, or from the spring, they are dry."[2]

It is also a lesson about God and country. Politics is a broken cistern. When Christians trust in political solutions to save the nation, they bring judgment on themselves. One reason for the precipitous decline of the mainline church in America has been its engagement in liberal politics. And by aligning itself with the right-wing agenda, the conservative church has fallen into the same trap. The quest for political power destroys the spiritual influence of the church.

Next comes Exhibit C: God's people leaving their husband is like a beast breaking free from its yoke. "For long ago I broke your yoke and burst your bonds; but you said, 'I will not serve'" (2:20a). Jerusalem is like a wild ox with a broken yoke that runs off into the fields. On their way into the spiritual wilderness, God's people yell back over their shoulders, "We will not serve you!" As a result, God finds himself wondering:

> Have I been a wilderness to Israel,
>   or a land of thick darkness?
> Why then do my people say, "We are free,
>   we will come no more to you"? (2:31)

God's people were made to serve him. To reject servanthood is not freedom but bondage. Anyone who knows Christ has put his shoulder to the easy yoke (Matthew 11:30). Breaking that yoke to go off and sin is hard slavery.

What is it like when God's people leave their husband? Exhibit D: It is like a prostitute on the street corner waiting for some action. "Yes, on every

high hill and under every green tree you bowed down like a whore" (2:20b).
As Derek Kidner explains, Israel is here depicted as "a restless wife to whom
the bonds and burdens of true love were slavery, and the lure of the forbidden
irresistible."[3]

God's people were guilty of religious prostitution. They were shacking up
with gods they hardly knew. Very likely Jeremiah was referring to Baal worship, which included ritual prostitution at leafy hilltop shrines.

> Their worship digressed to highly charged eroticism. Somehow an of-
> fering was made to these fertility gods through illicit orgasm. But Baal
> and Ashteroth weren't real gods at all. Both were satanic counterfeits that
> snatched away the sexuality given by the Creator, reduced it to eroticism,
> and propped up that eroticism as an object of worship. Submission to these
> gods meant bowing the knee to the demonic principalities of sexual perver-
> sion. In effect, idealized, eroticized images of the creature were being wor-
> shiped, and worship degenerated into nothing more than orgies. The col-
> lision of body parts between faceless, nameless people marked the depths
> of Israel's idolatry.[4]

Once the people of Jerusalem had been seduced by the gods and goddesses of Canaan, they became adept at idol worship. "How well you direct
your course to seek love! So that even to wicked women you have taught your
ways" (v. 33). The Jews knew enough about worshiping idols to give lessons
to the most experienced pagans.

This was scandalous, as it always is when religious people turn away from
the Lord. A regular churchgoer who does not worship God from the heart is
more wicked than an unbeliever who has never heard the gospel.

Worshiping other gods was not only scandalous, it was also futile, as Israel would discover on the day of her judgment: "But where are your gods that
you made for yourself? Let them arise, if they can save you, in your time of
trouble" (v. 28a)

More Evidence

When God's people forsake him, it is also like a wild vine. This is Exhibit E:

> Yet I planted you a choice vine,
>   wholly of pure seed.
> How then have you turned degenerate
>   and become a wild vine? (v. 21)

Usually animals are the ones who turn on their masters; this time it is a
plant. Back in the springtime, when God planted his garden, he took some

cuttings and planted "a choice vine." He was expecting to get rich, red grapes from the vine and, as one writer describes it, squeeze them into a nice bottle of Sorek wine from the Wadi al-Sarar.[5] But the vine turned on him.

God's people are supposed to be fruitful branches of the true vine, Jesus Christ (John 15:1–8). But when they forsake their first love, they go back to their wild natural state and yield sour fruit.

What is it like when God's people leave their husband? Exhibit F: It is like an indelible stain.

> Though you wash yourself with lye
>   and use much soap,
>   the stain of your guilt is still before me,
>   declares the Lord GOD. (2:22)

Sin is not simply a cosmetic problem. Even after the detergent, the exotic cleansers, the turpentine, and the tomato juice, the stain of sin remains. What soap can wash away sin from the soul? There is no home remedy to take away guilt. Only the blood of Jesus Christ can purify us from all sin (1 John 1:7).

When God's people leave their husband, it is like a young camel running loose in the desert, which is Exhibit G:

> Look at your way in the valley;
>   know what you have done—
> a restless young camel running here and there. (2:23b)

Listen to this description of a young camel:

> Literally, this camel is criss-crossing her tracks. The young camel is the perfect illustration for all that is "skittery" and unreliable. It is ungainly in the extreme and runs off in any direction at the slightest provocation, much to the fury of the camel-driver. To sit in a village courtyard and watch such a young camel go scooting through, with some alarmed peasant dashing madly after it, is an unforgettable experience; such a young camel never takes more than about three steps in any direction. To this day the young camel provides a dramatic illustration for anything unreliable. Thus "inter-lacing her paths" is an accurate description of a young camel—it provides Jeremiah a perfect illustration for the fickleness of Israel.[6]

Jeremiah's point is that God's people run all over the place to sin. They are unable to decide which god they want to serve.

The reference to "The valley" is particularly ominous. It probably refers to the Valley of Ben Hinnom, where children were sacrificed to Molech (v. 23;

cf. 7:30–32). Then there is a further reference to murder. "Also on your skirts is found the lifeblood of the guiltless poor; you did not find them breaking in" (2:34a). The people of Jerusalem had blood on their hands and sleeves. They practiced both child sacrifice and the wanton abuse of the urban poor. When God is forbidden, everything is permissible, as abortion and the lack of concern for the poor in the pagan West now confirm.

For Exhibit H, God moves from dromedaries to donkeys. To forsake him is to behave like a donkey in heat, "a wild donkey used to the wilderness, in her heat sniffing the wind! Who can restrain her lust?" (v. 24a).

Sin is like the uncontrollable sexual urge of an animal.

> The habits of the female [donkey] in heat are dramatic and vulgar. She sniffs the path in front of her, trying to pick up her scent of a male (from his urine). When she finds it, she rubs her nose in the dust and then straightens her neck, and with head high, closes her nostrils and "sniffs the wind." What she is really doing is sniffing the dust which is soaked with the urine of a male [donkey]. With her neck stretched to the utmost, she slowly draws in a long, deep breath, then lets out an earthshaking bray and doubles her pace, racing down the road in search of the male.[7]

Idols do not need to chase the people of Jerusalem. "None who seek her need weary themselves; in her month they will find her" (v, 24b). Looking for some action, God's people found their own way to the temples of the pagan gods.

Their hankering after false worship shows the power of addictive sin. Even God's warnings are not enough to stop them:

> Keep your feet from going unshod
>   and your throat from thirst.
> But you said, "It is hopeless,
>   for I have loved foreigners,
>   and after them I will go." (v. 25)

Those who are compulsive gamblers or drug addicts or habitual sex offenders can hardly help themselves. They crave their addictions so much that they feel incapable of giving them up. "It's no use," they say. "I must have my sins." They run after them until they wear out their shoes.

God's testimony is almost finished, but he has one final piece of evidence, Exhibit I:

> Can a virgin forget her ornaments,
>   or a bride her attire?

Yet my people have forgotten me
days without number. (v. 32)

It would be unthinkable for a bride to forget her wedding dress. Ask any bride what she wore on her wedding day, what her wedding ring was like, and how her hair was done, and she will tell you. Yet God's bride has forgotten her husband. All comparisons fail. No wife has ever been this forgetful.

The Defense

All the evidence has been heard. What is the verdict? Is there enough evidence for a conviction?

Enough evidence! God can make this accusation stick like taffy on a two-year-old! He has every right to sue for divorce. Jerusalem has no defense. She has turned away from God to foreign idols and foreign alliances.

Like most guilty parties, however, Jerusalem tries to defend herself anyway. Throughout chapter 2, God's bride mounts a defense in her own behalf. She protests her innocence: "I am not unclean, I have not gone after the Baals" (v. 23). But her lie is exposed during cross-examination, when she is forced to admit that she loves foreign gods (v. 25). How fickle! Yet still another claim of innocence follows: "You say, 'I am innocent; surely his anger has turned from me.' Behold, I will bring you to judgment for saying, 'I have not sinned'" (v. 35).

God's people are in denial. "But in the time of their trouble they say, 'Arise and save us!'" (v. 27c), as if nothing is wrong. Worse still, they are starting to play the blame game, as often happens when marriages start to fall apart. Each spouse refuses to take responsibility for his or her own actions. In this case the accused has been doing all the cheating, but she has the audacity to bring charges against her husband: "Why do you contend with me? You have all transgressed against me, declares the Lord" (v. 29).

In the end, Judah's plea of innocence leads to her condemnation: "I will bring you to judgment for saying, 'I have not sinned'" (v. 35). God is not only the spurned husband and the prosecuting attorney—he is also the righteous judge. He weighs all the evidence and renders his verdict: guilty as charged.

The important question to ask is this: What verdict would God render about the contemporary church? The dominant sin of Jerusalem—forgetting God—has become a predominant sin in the American church.

Raymond Ortlund Jr., imagines what the evangelical church would look like without the gospel:

What might our evangelicalism, without the evangel, look like? We would have to replace the centrality of the gospel with something else, naturally. So what might take the place of the gospel in our sermons and books and cassette tapes and Sunday school classes and home Bible studies, and above all, in our hearts?[8]

Ortlund suggests a number of substitutes for the gospel: A "drive toward church growth." Or "sympathetic, empathetic, thickly-honeyed cultivation of interpersonal relationships." Or "a determination to take America back to its Christian roots through political power."[9] Or, one might add, any number of otherwise good things that now usurp the throne of a forgotten God.

To make the question personal, what verdict do you deserve? Do you love God like a newlywed, or have you been looking for love in all the wrong places? Whether forgetting God is compared to changing gods or getting water from a broken cistern or sleeping around with idols, the sin is the same. So is the verdict: guilty as charged.

The Reconciliation

So God went through with the divorce, right? He certainly had every right to. He had already tried to rescue the marriage, but even this had failed.

> In vain have I struck your children;
> > they took no correction;
> your own sword devoured your prophets
> > like a ravening lion. (2:30)

The marriage seemed to be beyond recovery. But it wasn't. Just half a chapter later Jeremiah writes, "Return, O faithless children, declares the LORD; for I am your master" (3:14). It is a breathtaking command. It is God's grace for the ungracious, his faithfulness to the unfaithful. Even when God's love goes unrequited, he does not cease to love. Although his marriage is violated, he does not break covenant.

If you have never entered into a love relationship with God, he is courting you at this moment. He invites you to enter into a love that will never let you go. He calls you to leave behind the sins that carry you here, there, and everywhere in the spiritual desert. He invites you to embrace Jesus Christ.

If you have already entered the romance of redemption, consider whether you love God the way you did when you first "got married." If not, do not try to dance around this betrayal. If you are not passionately in love with God, then you have been behaving like a floozy, spiritually speaking. But your divine husband still wants you back. More amazing still, he can restore the passion and purity of your love for him.

There is a hint of such restoration later in Jeremiah's book.

> The LORD appeared to him from far away.
> I have loved you with an everlasting love;
>   therefore I have continued my faithfulness to you.
> Again I will build you, and you shall be built,
>   O virgin Israel! (31:3–4; cf. 31:21)

It is amazing enough that God still considers Israel his bride. But there is more. His cleansing is so complete that he restores her to passion and purity.

How can he do that? What detergent can wash away the stain of sin? Nothing but the blood of Jesus. "Christ loved the church and gave himself up for her, that he might sanctify her, having cleansed her by the washing of water with the word, so that he might present the church to himself in splendor, without spot or wrinkle or any such thing, that she might be holy and without blemish" (Ephesians 5:25b–27; cf. Revelation 21:2, 9). Jesus Christ died on the cross to remove the promiscuity and restore the virginity of his spiritual bride.

4

The Way Back Home

JEREMIAH 3:1–18

THERE'S NO PLACE LIKE HOME, there's no place like home, there's no place like home." That is what Dorothy says at the end of *The Wizard of Oz*. The trouble with life in this world is that we are never at home, even when we get back to Kansas.

There is a passage from an unpublished novel by Walker Percy that captures the homelessness of humanity. Percy imgines this dialogue between two men in a tuberculosis sanitarium:

> "What's the matter, Willy?"
> "I don't know, Scanlon. I'm homesick."
> "How long have you been homesick?"
> "All my life."[1]

Percy's dialogue captures the restlessness of the soul that wanders through this world until it finds a home with God.

Jeremiah 3 is about the way back home. At the end of verse 1 God's people start to experience the first pangs of homesickness. They telephone God, long distance, from a pay phone in a brothel. God is overheard to say, "You have played the whore with many lovers; and would you return to me?" (v. 1).

Far from Home

The first thing for God's people to realize is how far away from home they really are. They have broken their marriage vows. They have been spiritually promiscuous. They have been looking for love in all the wrong places. When God's people cheat on him, it is like leaving a fresh mountain spring to drink from a sewer (2:13) or like a wild donkey in heat (2:24).

In chapter 3, the Lord is still thinking about divorcing his unfaithful spouse. In words reminiscent of the prophecies of Hosea, who married a prostitute, he asks,

> If a man divorces his wife
>   and she goes from him
> and becomes another man's wife,
>   will he return to her?
> Would not that land be greatly polluted? (v. 1a)

Think about it for a moment. If a man divorces his wife, and she goes off and gets married to someone else, should the man move back in with his ex?

The answer is no, as the Scripture plainly teaches (Deuteronomy 24:1–4). Derek Kidner explains:

> This law, which forbade a divorced couple to reunite, was aimed against what would amount to virtually lending one's partner to another—for if an authoritarian husband could dismiss his wife and have her back when the next man had finished with her, it would degrade not only her but marriage itself and the society that accepted such a practice.[2]

The Old Testament is often dismissed as patriarchal, but the Bible protects the dignity of women. God has always forbidden his people to treat women like chattel. He also forbids them to play fast and loose with their marriage vows. When people do that—as they do in postmodern society—the whole land is completely defiled.

If it would defile the land for a man to move in with his former wife and her new spouse, then how can God move back in with his people? That would seem to violate his own law, for what God's spouse has done is much, much worse. She has lived as a prostitute with many lovers!

The children of Israel have been sleeping with every god they can get their hands on. They have become equal-opportunity worshipers. They do not have just one or two idols—they have a whole closet full of them. "Lift up your eyes to the bare heights, and see," says God. "Where have you not been ravished?" (3:2a). This verse alludes to the worship of Baal and Asherah, which included sex with temple prostitutes at hilltop shrines. The word "ravished" is especially powerful. It is an obscene word for sexual violence. Although God's people have been looking for a good time, they have been getting raped. False gods are always abusive.

The middle of verse 2 shows how far away from home God's people have strayed: "By the waysides you have sat awaiting lovers like an Arab in the wilderness" (v. 2b). They have behaved like so many prostitutes sitting at a crossroads in the desert. They are like Bedouin salesmen, advertising their wares, waiting for a caravan to pass by. They are just sitting there, trafficking in the world's currency, waiting to make love to idols.

They have no shame. "You have the forehead of a whore," God says. "You refuse to be ashamed" (v. 3b). This verse reminds me of a painting by Henri Toulouse-Lautrec, who wasted much of his time exploring the red-light district of Paris. The painting depicts a young prostitute. Her gaze is fixed straight forward without fear or modesty. Her chin is lifted in defiance, challenging anyone to pass judgment on her sins.

Prostitution is a shameless sin. Homosexual prostitutes sometimes strut on the corners around Tenth Presbyterian Church in Philadelphia. This is such common knowledge that in 1996 *Philadelphia* magazine ran an article about the prostitutes entitled "The Vampires of Delancey Street." Some of the things in that article sounded like they came right out of Jeremiah. The prostitutes were described as "nomads." The article also talked about the way they call themselves "hustlers" to make it sound like they are the ones who are getting something. Sadly, of course, they are being used and abused. "The very name for it, *hustling*, seems like a defiant insistence that it's their customers, and not the boys themselves, who are getting played, getting used, eaten up by the street and by each other."[3]

I do not mention these things because I despise homosexual prostitutes, who are made in the image of God and can receive forgiveness for sin in Jesus Christ. I mention these things because they give us a picture of the shameful-ness of sin in the church. Jeremiah is a prophecy for people who know God in a personal way and yet have wandered away from him. It is a warning about apostasy, the sin of having a home with God and then running away.

Running away was especially reprehensible in Judah's case because God gave her ample warning that she would be punished for her sins. Already the spring rains have been shut up in the heavens, which was the proper punish-ment for idolatry (Deuteronomy 11:16, 17). "Therefore the showers have been withheld, and the spring rain has not come" (3:3a). God proceeds to remind Judah what happened to her sister:

> The LORD said to me in the days of King Josiah: "Have you seen what she did, that faithless one, Israel, how she went up on every high hill and under every green tree, and there played the whore? And I thought, 'After she has done all this she will return to me,' but she did not return, and her treacherous sister Judah saw it. She saw that for all the adulteries of that faithless one, Israel, I had sent her away with a decree of divorce. Yet

her treacherous sister Judah did not fear, but she too went and played the whore. Because she took her whoredom lightly, she polluted the land, committing adultery with stone and tree. Yet for all this her treacherous sister Judah did not return to me with her whole heart, but in pretense, declares the LORD." And the LORD said to me, "Faithless Israel has shown herself more righteous than treacherous Judah." (vv. 6–11)

Even after the people of God divided into two kingdoms—north and south, Israel and Judah—they were still sisters. God gave Judah the opportunity to learn from her sister's mistakes. In 722 BC the ten northern tribes of Israel were carried off by the Assyrians because they had been unfaithful to God. God refers to this event as giving Israel her "decree of divorce" and sending her away (v. 8). He hoped Israel would grow tired of her spiritual adultery, but she never did.

Now God pleads with Judah to learn from her sister's mistakes. But does she listen? Sadly, no; apostasy ran in the family. God saw that Judah, like Israel, continued shamelessly to commit spiritual adultery. Some people never learn.

Has the contemporary church learned the lessons of church history? Not very well. Evangelicals are prone to chastise the government, Hollywood, the media, or drugs for national problems. But Jeremiah indicts the church first of all. When he starts to talk about what is wrong with society, he hands God's people a mirror and invites them to take a long, hard look. The church is supposed to be married to Jesus Christ, but we have many mistresses. If we kept a little black book with the names of our lovers, it would read something like this: "For a good time, call material prosperity, idle entertainment, political power, sexual license, and self-indulgence."

Homeward Bound

How do we get back home? Jeremiah mentions four milestones along the way. First, the way back home begins with *a divine call*. You are sitting out in the desert by the side of the road, waiting for sin to come along. You have no idea how to get back home to God, and even if you did know how, you would not want to go.

The way back home starts with God's call: "Go, and proclaim these words toward the north, and say, 'Return, faithless Israel, declares the LORD. I will not look on you in anger, for I am merciful, declares the LORD; I will not be angry forever'" (v. 12). And again: "Return, O faithless children, declares the LORD; for I am your master" (v. 14a).

As he loves to do, Jeremiah is playing on words in these verses. Different forms of the word for "Turn" or "return" occur eighteen times in this chapter. What the prophet is really saying is, "Return, turnable children," or perhaps "Come back, backsliders." God is calling his kids back home.

Why does God do it? He does it for no reason at all except that he is a God of love. This is the inscrutable grace of God. He is gracious to the ungracious, faithful to the unfaithful, loving to the unloving. His call comes first. God issues the invitation to come back home before anything else happens, before we have made the slightest motion back toward him. This is the priority of the divine call in salvation.

Through the words of the Bible, God is calling you back home. He is saying, "Come back home, little child, come home. Daddy wants you to come on home." He makes the same call through Jesus Christ, who says, "Come to me, all who labor and are heavy laden, and I will give you rest" (Matthew 11:28).

Electing Grace

The second milestone on the way back home is *God's election*. God's grace is not for those who help themselves. It is sometimes suggested that although God calls you to repent, he leaves it up to you to decide whether you want to repent or not. God has his part in salvation, and you have yours. Max Lucado puts it like this: "If there are a thousand steps between us and God, he will take all but one. He will leave the final one for us. The choice is ours."[4]

According to this kind of teaching, Jesus Christ did not save you when he died on the cross. He only made salvation possible. Jesus offers you salvation and you can take it or leave it. It is up to you. This is the gospel according to Arminianism, named after the Dutch theologian Jacob Arminius (1560–1609).

Is this the teaching of Scripture? Certainly not in Jeremiah 3: "Return, O faithless children, declares the LORD; for I am your master" (v. 14a). That is the divine call, the free invitation of God to come to him for salvation. It is the free offer of the gospel that is offered to all men, women, and children in Jesus Christ. But notice what the Lord goes on to say: "I will take you, one from a city and two from a family, and I will bring you to Zion" (v. 14b). That is divine election, God's choice. God's choosing stands behind God's calling.

The call to salvation is not like a mother calling her child home for dinner. When God calls you to come home, he does not just say, "It's time to come home now." His call comes with much greater force than that. It comes with a stronger compulsion. The Westminster divines called it effectual calling. God calls all people everywhere to repent. But when it comes to salvation, God's calling has an effect; it gets the job done.

When my son Joshua learned to walk, I took him to the park every day.

We would walk down the sidewalk, over the bridge, through the woods, and into the meadow. It took a long time, but he could manage all that on his own. He had enough strength in his little legs to leave home and go out and play in the world. But he did not have enough strength to get back home.

It was not enough, therefore, for me to call him home. He was neither willing nor able to go home. In fact, if it had been up to him, we would probably still be out there! He needed his father to scoop him up, put him on his shoulders, and carry him home, sometimes kicking and screaming. When God calls you to salvation in Jesus Christ, he does not just yell down the block; he scoops you up, plants you on his shoulders, and marches you all the way home.

Someone might object, "But what about my rights? What about my free choice in the matter?" But the truth is that if God did not come and put you on his shoulders, you would never come home. You do not know the way home without his call, and you do not want to come home without his electing grace. You need God's sovereign grace to completely transform you and bring you back home. One by one and two by two, God brings each and every one of his children home.

Leaving the World Behind

The third milestone on the way back home is *repentance*. When God calls you to return to him, he calls you to turn away from sin. Returning to God's embrace means turning your back on all your other lovers.

It is easy to mistake false repentance for true repentance. There was much false repentance in Jeremiah's day. People returned to God but not wholeheartedly, only "in pretense" (v. 10). Judah's repentance was merely a charade. It is possible to fool yourself into thinking you have repented for your sins and that you have gone back home to God, when the truth is that you are still out wandering around in the desert. The most dangerous spiritual condition in the world is to think you have already done all the repenting you need to do.

Notice how true repentance differs from false repentance. It is *wholehearted*. The problem with Judah's repentance was that she did not return to God with her whole heart. The believer's relationship to God is a love-relationship. Redemption is a romance; true love requires an undivided heart.

True repentance is also *God-directed*. Here is the kind of repentance God is looking for:

> Only acknowledge your guilt,
>   that you rebelled against the Lord your God
> and scattered your favors among foreigners under every green tree,

and that you have not obeyed my voice
declares the LORD. (v. 13)

Repentance cannot be on a merely human level. First and foremost, repentance is telling God that you are sorry you have sinned against him. King David committed adultery and murder, which are crimes against humanity. Yet he repented to God with these words: "Against you, you only, have I sinned and done what is evil in your sight" (Psalm 51:4a).

True repentance is *grace responsive*. We do not work up repentance from somewhere inside us. Repentance is a response to the love of God. "I will not look on you in anger, for I am merciful, declares the LORD; I will not be angry forever" (3:12). The word used here for mercy (*hesed*) is a word for covenant mercy (cf. 2:2), for unbroken promises and vows of eternal love. God never went through with his divorce. When you are an unfaithful wife, God is still a faithful husband (3:14). He had every right to slam the door on you forever. But he is your loving, merciful, all-suffering husband. He keeps on welcoming you back home.

Finally, true repentance is also *obedience producing*. The problem with God's people in Jeremiah's day was that they were just giving lip service to repentance. They uttered prayers of repentance, but they did not change their ways. They talked the talk without walking the walk. Their conversations with God were casual. They did not have a proper sense of reverence and awe in his presence. So God says:

Have you not just now called to me,
    "My father, you are the friend of my youth—
will he be angry forever,
    will he be indignant to the end?"
Behold, you have spoken,
    but you have done all the evil that you could. (vv. 4, 5)

What is surprising about this flippant attitude is that the people of Jerusalem had experienced spiritual reformation. This part of Jeremiah's message was delivered during the reign of Josiah. It was during Josiah's reign that reformation came to Judah. The Book of the Law was found in the temple, and the worship of God's people was reformed (2 Kings 22). Now Jeremiah says that if you do not repent with a wholehearted, God-directed, love-prompted, obedience-producing repentance, you only have half a reformation, which is no reformation at all.

John Calvin understood that Jeremiah 3 is about reformation. The chapter reminded him of people he knew during the Protestant Reformation in Europe who "seemed at first to embrace the doctrines of the Gospel" but went on to lead sinful lives, even though "They boldly claim to be the advocates of reformation."[5]

Do you desire reformation in the church? The way back home for the evangelical church passes through fields of repentance. The Cambridge Declaration signed by the Alliance of Confessing Evangelicals in April 1996 speaks to this issue with real power: "Evangelical churches today are increasingly dominated by the spirit of this age rather than by the Spirit of Christ. As evangelicals, we call ourselves to repent of this sin and to recover the historic Christian faith."

The Declaration ends with this prayer:

> We repent of our worldliness. We have been influenced by the "gospels" of our secular culture, which are no gospels. We have weakened the church by our own lack of serious repentance, our blindness to the sins in ourselves which we see so clearly in others, and our inexcusable failure adequately to tell others about God's saving work in Jesus Christ.

Until the church learns to live out that prayer, it will experience no authentic reformation.

Shepherds after God's Own Heart

The final milestone on the way back to God is *the faithful preaching of God's Word*. God promises that when his people return to him, he will give them godly shepherds—"shepherds after my own heart" (v. 15).

The promise of good shepherds applies first of all to kings—for example, David, who was a shepherd after God's own heart (1 Samuel 13:14; cf. Psalm 78:70–72). But this verse also contains a promise pertaining to the New Testament, when God gave pastors to the church to preach and teach his Word. Like the Old Testament kings, pastors shepherd God's flock.

A good pastor is a pastor after God's own heart. He is a man of strong affection. Having received the love and compassion of God, he is filled with love for God's people and compassion for the lost. Then notice what he does: he shepherds God's people with knowledge and understanding.

The Dutch artist Anton Mauve created a beautiful painting called "The Return of the Flock" (c. 1886–1887). It depicts a flock of sheep, viewed from the rear, walking down a broad path through brown fields. But the focal point of the picture is the man the sheep are following down the road. The shepherd is leading his sheep back home.

This is the picture Jeremiah has in mind when he describes the shepherd who will lead God's sheep back home. The word he uses for "feed" (v. 15) is a shepherding word. A pastor after God's own heart is a teaching pastor. The Puritan pastor John Shaw put it like this:

> In a word, ministers according to God's heart preach Jesus Christ. Christ is the end, He is the scope, He is the design of their ministry. That design is to bring sinners to Christ, to build up believers in Christ. They preach Christ in His person, Christ in His natures, Christ in His offices, Christ with the free offers and tenders of His grace, Christ in His righteousness, Christ with His unsearchable riches. . . . [6]

A good minister is exactly what someone needs in order to figure out what Christianity is all about. If you want to find your way home to God, find a minister after God's own heart who will teach you the Bible.

That is also what the church needs today. There has never been an authentic revival or a true reformation in the church that did not begin with the sound preaching of God's Word. The Word of God is oxygen for the fire of revival. There can be no reformation without proclamation. This was true in Josiah's day, when the rediscovery of the Law reformed the temple (2 Kings 22). It was true in Ezra's day, when the Law was explained and the people of Jerusalem cried aloud for mercy (Nehemiah 8, 9). It was true in Peter's day, when Christ was preached and thousands were baptized unto salvation (Acts 2:14–41).

The same thing was true when the Reformation came to Scotland. The main thing John Knox (c. 1514–1572) did to bring reformation to Scotland was to preach the Word of God. Knox did not become a Reformer until he put down his sword and picked up his Bible, the sword of the Lord. If we desire reformation in our own churches, we must pray for our ministers, because reformation comes through proclamation.

The way back home begins with God's call, which is based on God's choice. Going back home means leaving the world behind and listening to God's voice. But will we ever make it all the way back home? Jeremiah promises that we will:

> And when you have multiplied and been fruitful in the land, in those days, declares the LORD, they shall no more say, "The ark of the covenant of the LORD." It shall not come to mind or be remembered or missed; it shall not be made again. At that time Jerusalem shall be called the throne of the LORD, and all nations shall gather to it, to the presence of the LORD in Jerusalem, and they shall no more stubbornly follow their own evil heart. In those days the house of Judah shall join the house of Israel, and together

they shall come from the land of the north to the land that I gave your fathers for a heritage. (3:16–18)

Jeremiah looks ahead to the day when God's people Israel will be brought back home to Jerusalem from their exile in Babylon. He prophesies that all the nations of the world will turn away from evil and gather in Jerusalem. He even prophesies that Judah and Israel will put aside their differences and come back home to the land God gave them. Instead of worshiping separately, they would worship together at the temple.

These promises began to be fulfilled by the end of the Old Testament, but they find their ultimate fulfillment in the church of Jesus Christ. It is in the church that all God's people, from every nation, gather together in God's presence. We no longer need the ark of the covenant because God himself is with us, by his Holy Spirit. We are no longer divided by pride or race; we all worship together, drawn by the attractive power of God's presence.

The poet John Oxenham expressed it like this:

From North and South, and East and West,
    They come!
The sorely tried, the much oppressed,
Their Faith and Love to manifest,
    They come!
They come to tell of work well done,
They come to tell of kingdoms won,
To worship at the Great White Throne,
    They come!
In a noble consecration,
With a sound of jubilation,
    They come! They come!

We gather at God's throne for one reason: to honor his name. This is the way it always is when you go home to God. When you get there you want to submit to his gracious rule. Worship is always the result of personal conversion. Once you have answered God's call to salvation and repented for all your sins, what you want to do more than anything else in the whole world is to worship God. That is also where reformation always leads. A reformed church is a worshiping church.

When you come home to God the only thing you can say is, "To God alone be the glory." Look back at the long and winding road that led you home to God. You were sitting in the desert acting like a spiritual whore. You had no idea how to get back home.

Who called you home? God did. Who chose you and brought you back from the wilderness? God did. You did the repenting, of course, but your repentance was a response to God's love. God also provided the faithful preachers who taught you God's Word. So from beginning to end, your salvation is the work of God.

All you can say is, "To God alone be the glory," and you will say it for all eternity:

> Lift your eyes, ye sons of light!
> Zion's city is in sight;
> There our endless home shall be,
> There our Lord we soon shall see.[7]

5

True Repentance

JEREMIAH 3:19—4:4

THINGS DO NOT ALWAYS TURN OUT the way you want them to. Disappointment is part of life. Like when you expect to be the first to use the peanut butter, only to discover that someone has already taken a bite out of it. Or when you take your beach ball to the park and a big dog comes bounding up to take a bite out of it.

Or like when you are newly married, and you do not have much money, and you cut out coupons from the back of the cereal box to get free ice cream treats, and you walk hand-in-hand to the ice cream parlor, pockets empty, clutching your coupons, and you get all the way up to the cash register . . . where the guy in the little white hat says, "Oh, we don't make that size anymore."

All those things have happened to me, but they are just the little disappointments. Add to them the real disappointments of life, like losing a loved one, or not landing the job you really want, or finding out that marriage is not quite what you expected, or having prodigal children, or having a handicap that robs you of your joy. It is little wonder that writer Philip Yancey sold so many copies of his book *Disappointment with God*.[1]

A Disappointed Father

But look at things from God's point of view for a moment. If God wanted to write a book about us, he might give it this title, *Disappointment with People*:

> I said,
>> How I would set you among my sons,

and give you a pleasant land,
    a heritage most beautiful of all nations.
And I thought you would call me, My Father,
    and would not turn from following me." (3:19)

That was the way God wanted things to be. He wanted to treat his people like sons and daughters. He wanted to love them with a father's love and delight in them with a father's delight. He wanted to give them every good thing. He wanted to plant them in a beautiful garden. He wanted to grant his children a legacy far beyond any inheritance any other father could imagine.

That was the way God wanted things to be from the very beginning. It was the way he intended things to be for our first parents. When he planted Adam and Eve in a beautiful garden, he wanted them to live in that garden as a loyal son and a loving daughter.

That was also the way God intended things to be for the children of Israel. He wanted to treat them like sons. In fact, he *did* treat them like sons. He gave them a desirable land, a beautiful heritage. All he wanted from them in return was their loyalty. He wanted them to stay at home, call him "Father," and really mean it.

That was the way God wanted it to be, but that is not how things turned out. He wanted a son like Beaver Cleaver, and he got Bart Simpson instead. Listen to his lament for his children: "Surely, as a treacherous wife leaves her husband, so have you been treacherous to me, O house of Israel, declares the LORD" (v. 20). This vocabulary is starting to become familiar. The last two chapters have been filled with the imagery of spiritual adultery. God's people were supposed to be devoted to him like a bride to a husband, but they have been fooling around, behaving like cheap prostitutes.

These verses show that the relationship between God and his people is too rich to be defined by any single human relationship. The Lord reminds his people that they are like unfaithful spouses. But he also compares them to wayward sons who are unworthy of their inheritance. Not only is God a spurned husband, but he is also a disappointed father.

God's disappointment should bring grief to the hearts of all his sons and daughters. If you had a good father, then you know that a father's disappointment brings greater shame than a father's anger. When a father says, "I am disappointed with you," that cuts to the heart in a way that the words "I am angry with you" never can. The same is true of our relationship with God. We want to be able to sing the second verse of "Be Thou My Vision" with full confidence:

Be thou my wisdom, and thou my true word;
I ever with thee and thou with me, Lord;
Thou my great Father, I thy true son;
Thou in me dwelling, and I with thee one.[2]

God is always our great Father, but we are not always his true sons and daughters.

The Bitterness of Sin

Sin makes life very bitter. It is a bitter thing for a child to turn away from his father, and it is a bitter thing to bring disappointment to God's heart. Jeremiah describes it like this:

A voice on the bare heights is heard,
    the weeping and pleading of Israel's sons
because they have perverted their way;
    they have forgotten the LORD their God. (v. 21)

It is hard to know what to make of this verse. Some commentators treat it as the beginning of Israel's repentance. They may be right. It is true that sorrow is often attached to repentance. "In the spiritual life lost power can only be regained when the sinner retraces his steps to the point where he sinned, and seeks forgiveness and restoration with God."[3] Perhaps the children of Israel have gone back to the high places to confess their sins.

But their cries may not be cries of repentance at all. The real prayer of repentance seems to begin at the end of verse 22, after God has promised to cure their backsliding. Furthermore, there is something suspicious about the fact that God's people are still standing up on the barren heights, which were places for idolatry. If they really want to repent for their sins, they need to come down from the place of sin and go back to the temple to meet with God.

The reason they are weeping and pleading is because they have perverted their ways and forgotten their God. This may mean that they have recognized their sin as sin and are sorry for it. But it may simply mean that their sin was making them bitter. Calvin's opinion was that these prayers did not arise from faith, "but simply that they were such lamentations as betokened misery and wretchedness,"[4] the kind of distress that always comes from not following God. In that case, they were not shedding sweet tears of repentance, but salty tears of sinful bitterness.

Parents quickly learn to recognize the difference between these two kinds of crying. It is one thing to shed tears because the consequences of sin make us miserable. It is a far different thing to weep over the disobedience itself.

One way to interpret "bare heights" is to take them as a reference to the time when the centers for idol worship were destroyed. This prophecy was given, remember, during the reign of Josiah the reformer. The Scripture says that when Josiah was only twelve, "he began to purge Judah and Jerusalem of the high places, the Asherim, and the carved and the metal images. And they chopped down the altars of the Baals in his presence" (2 Chronicles 34:3b, 4a). That may not have been very popular with some of his subjects. One can imagine the people of Israel going back to those idolatrous temples, now nothing more than barren hilltops, and pleading for the return of their false gods. Their tears may have been tears of protest rather than remorse.

No matter how verse 21 is interpreted, it shows the despair of a godless society. In lectures entitled *Death in the City*, Francis Schaeffer (1912–1984) concluded that "The 'Christian culture' of Jeremiah's day was disintegrating into a 'post-Christian culture.'"[5] That is what this verse is about—a culture that has forgotten God and is discovering the bitterness of life without him. And that is exactly why Jeremiah is so relevant for postmodern times.

Jeremiah is not just a book about what happened to Judah; it is a book about what happens to anyone who abandons God. Loud cries may be heard from the barren heights of our own culture. We hear the cries in modern art, as in Edvard Munch's painting *The Scream*, in which a wraithlike figure stands on a bridge, holds his ears, and howls in agony at the world. We hear the cries in modern literature, as at the end of T. S. Eliot's poem "The Hollow Men:"

This is the way the world ends
This is the way the world ends
This is the way the world ends
Not with a bang but a whimper.[6]

We hear cries from the barren heights of the families of our nation, like in Merton P. Stromann's books *Five Cries of Youth* and *Five Cries of Parents*.[7] We can even hear them from within the womb in ex-abortionist Bernard Nathanson's famous film, *The Silent Scream*.

Many people hear the same cry welling up from somewhere deep within the soul. It is a cry from the barren heights, the weeping and pleading of people who have perverted their ways and forgotten the Lord their God.

Come Back Home

Cries of despair and abandonment do not go unheard. God is not deaf to the weeping and pleading of his people. Nor is he silent.

Jeremiah 3 is full of divine speech. Four times he speaks in this passage to invite his people to come back home. These invitations need to be underscored. As we listen to everything Jeremiah has to say about sin and judgment, we may find ourselves asking, "Where is the grace?" When I preached a long series of sermons on Jeremiah, someone in the congregation confessed that Jeremiah sometimes made him feel like hiding under his pew. This is understandable. But when the grace of God does come in Jeremiah's book, it shines like a lighthouse on a stormy night.

God's grace is inviting. "Return, faithless Israel . . . for I am merciful" (v. 12). "Return, O faithless children . . . for I am your master" (v. 14). "Return, O faithless sons; I will heal your faithlessness" (v. 22). "If you return, O Israel . . . to me you should return" (4:1). The message is starting to get through. Even though you have been unfaithful to God, like a cheating wife or a prodigal son, God loves you and wants you to come back home.

If God gave gracious invitations in Jeremiah's day, he gives them all the more in our own day, because now he has given us Jesus Christ. The gospel is full of sweet invitations:

Follow me. (Matthew 4:19)

Come to me, all who labor and are heavy laden, and I will give you rest. (Matthew 11:28)

Come to the wedding feast. (Matthew 22:4)

Enter into the joy of your master. (Matthew 25:21)

And let the one who is thirsty come; let the one who desires take the water of life without price. (Revelation 22:17)

The grace of God is present in the divine call to salvation, the invitation to come back home. God is like the father in the story of the prodigal son. "But while he [the son] was still a long way off, his father saw him and felt compassion, and ran and embraced him and kissed him" (Luke 15:20).

A Prayer of Repentance

How will you respond to God's invitation? The best answer to give is the answer Israel gave: "Behold, we come to you, for you are the LORD our God" (3:22b).

That verse ought to have an exclamation mark at the end of it. The children of Israel answer God's proposal in the exclamatory affirmative. The answer is not "Maybe," or "Let me sleep on it," or "I need to talk this over with a few people." When God goes out and finds his people in the desert, selling themselves to false gods, and invites them to come back home, they say, "Yes!" Something of their joy and exuberance is captured in a song recorded by Jars of Clay, "Love Song for a Savior":

> Someday He'll call her and she will come running
> And fall in His arms and the
> Tears will fall down and she'll pray,
> "I want to fall in love with You."[8]

Falling back in love with God includes repenting for sin. Repentance is not something we do so that God will let us come back home, it is what going back home is all about.

The prayer Israel offers is a model of true repentance:

> Behold, we come to you,
>   for you are the LORD our God.
> Truly the hills are a delusion,
>   the orgies on the mountains.
> Truly in the LORD our God
>   is the salvation of Israel.
>
> But from our youth the shameful thing has devoured
>   all for which our fathers labored,
> their flocks and their herds,
>   their sons and their daughters.
> Let us lie down in our shame,
>   and let our dishonor cover us.
> For we have sinned against the LORD our God,
>   we and our fathers,
> from our youth even to this day,
>   and we have not obeyed the voice of the LORD our God. (3:22b–25)

First, *the prayer recognizes who God is*. True repentance begins with the confession that God is God. As we noted in the previous chapter, repentance is God directed.

Admitting that God is God may seem rather obvious, but it was Israel's whole problem. It is the same basic problem that every unbeliever has: worshiping everything else except God. Notice that the phrase "The LORD our God" is repeated four times in this prayer of confession. The entire prayer is uttered with a proper sense of the majesty, holiness, and righteousness of

God. It is offered to the Lord God Almighty, Jehovah, the great "I AM." True repentance testifies that the Lord is God.

At the same time, recognizing who God is means speaking to him in personal terms. It is "The Lord *our* God," the God with whom we have a personal relationship. God's people speak to God as their own God. They have made a personal appropriation of the living God. They belong to him, and he belongs to them. Confession restores the intimacy of a love relationship.

Another part of recognizing who God is involves recognizing that he is the Lord of salvation. God's people confess that he is the salvation of Israel. True repentance looks for salvation from God alone. It requires true faith in the true God. The only God it makes sense to repent to is the God who can really save.

The New Testament reveals that salvation comes through God's Son Jesus Christ. Jesus says, "I am the way, and the truth, and the life. No one comes to the Father except through me" (John 14:6). True repentance testifies that salvation is found in Jesus Christ and in no other.

The second thing true repentance recognizes is *how sinful sin is*. Once we are squared away on who God is, we need to come clean about what we have done to offend him.

Israel's prayer of confession offers full disclosure of sin. God's people admit that all their worship has been false. All their worship on the high places—the hubbub in the hills, it might be called—has been nothing more than a lot of noise. True repentance renounces every attempt to save itself. When we come to God we must renounce anything and everything else we have ever trusted to bring us joy and meaning in life.

Next God's people confess how costly their sin has been. False gods are harsh taskmasters. They always damage the people who worship them. In this case they have consumed the "flocks and . . . herds" of Israel (3:24). Worse still, they have even consumed "Their sons and their daughters." This is not pleasant to talk about, but the evidence is mounting that God's people were guilty of child sacrifice. Some of the gods they worshiped demanded the lives of their children, and they were willing to offer them. We will learn the sad details when we get to Jeremiah's sermon at the Valley of Slaughter (chapter 7).

Little wonder that the people of Israel were utterly humiliated by their sins. "Let us lie down in our shame," they said, "and let our dishonor cover us" (3:25a). They made their beds, and now they have to lie in them.

Confessing the sinfulness of sin also means confessing that we have lived our whole lives in disobedience to God. "From our youth even to this day," the Scripture says, "we have not obeyed the voice of the Lord our God" (v. 25c). True repentance includes repenting for past sins as well as present sins. On occasion the Scottish divine Thomas Boston spent an entire day repenting of his sins and covenanting to follow God in new obedience. When he did so, he confessed not only his sins of recent days and weeks, but also the many sins of his youth.

True repentance is thorough. It even extends to corporate sins. Notice how the children of Israel repent not only for their own sins, but for the sins of their fathers: "We have sinned against the Lord our God, we and our fathers" (v. 25b). We are reminded by these words that sin is an offense against God, first of all. But we also see that confessing the sinfulness of sin extends to the sins of our nation, our race, our denomination, our church, and our family, not only in the present, but also in the past.

We learn from all this that the healing of our backslidden condition demands radical repentance. Repentance must go right down to the historical root of our sins. True repentance exposes the heart of sin's darkness. To return to God is to bring the blackest sins right out into the light of his glorious presence and to freely admit that you have done and thought evil things.

Repentance is not easy, but the words of this confession give comfort because they teach us that God is willing to forgive even the vilest sins. His invitation to return to him is given to everyone . . . even those who have murdered their own children.

More Than Just Words

As comprehensive as Israel's confession was, it was inadequate. It recognized both the holiness of God and the sinfulness of sin. And yet, shockingly, it was not true repentance!

True repentance requires more than just a prayer of repentance. True confession must give something more than lip service to our rebellion against God. It must be repentance in deed as well as in word. God has heard Israel's prayer of confession, but he has heard it all before (cf. 3:10), and sometimes it has been a sham. This time he warns his people to follow through.

God's warning includes some advice about spiritual agriculture. "For thus says the LORD to the men of Judah and Jerusalem: 'Break up your fallow ground, and sow not among thorns'" (4:3). Most Christians are content with the size of their present obedience to God. That obedience is about the size of a hanging basket, or maybe a window box, or perhaps even a small garden plot in the city. But God wants his people to break new ground in their obedience.

In other words, God wants you to do more than just tend the little garden you keep planting year after year. He wants you to do some real farming. It is time to put away your hoe and your shovel. Get the John Deere out of the barn, hitch up the plow, go out into the fields, and break up the rocky soil of your heart.

And take care of those weeds while you are at it! Even a hanging basket can be beautiful, as long as it is tidy. I once had a neighbor who tended a beautiful hanging basket bursting with peach-colored begonias. My flowerpots never compared to hers. Usually they contain as many weeds as flowers. They need to be plowed under before the pots are planted, or I will be throwing good seed after bad.

God says that the same thing is true in the spiritual realm. Do not sow obedience to Christ among the thorns of Satan. The reason we are weak and ineffective in the Christian life is that we want to plant the flowers of Heaven in the same pot with the weeds of the world. It is not so much that we are against Christ as it is that we want to follow Christ and the world at the same time.

The Lord is asking for a deep repentance, a much deeper repentance than we are used to giving, a *true* repentance that gets to the very root of sin and digs it out. He wants more than just prayers of repentance—he wants deeds of repentance. He wants more than just circumcised Israelites—he wants circumcised hearts. And he wants more than just baptized Christians—he wants baptized lives.

God describes the kind of repentance he wants with three conditional sentences. They all begin with "If." "If you return, O Israel, declares the LORD, to me you should return" (v. 1a). God's people have said that they want to return, but God says, "Okay, if you really do return." And he adds, "If you remove your detestable things from my presence, and do not waver" (v. 1b). They said their idol worship was a deception, but now God says, "Okay, if you really do get your idols out of my sight."

And finally, "If you swear, 'As the LORD lives,' in truth, in justice, and in righteousness" (v. 2a). This verse has to do with worship. Anyone who comes to praise God's name must speak truly (so that your heart echoes your lips), justly (so that your dealings with others please God), and righteously (so that your own holiness pleases God). God's people have been saying "The LORD our God" over and over again, so now God says, "Okay, if you really do confess my name."

Then what? What will happen if God's people meet all the conditions of true repentance? "Then nations shall bless themselves in him, and in him shall they glory" (v. 2). This shows the vital importance of true repentance. Nothing less than the evangelization of the world depends on it. The church's effectiveness in evangelism and world missions is directly tied to the sincerity of its repentance.

Christians usually blame social and national problems on the sinful ideas of secular people. But this passage teaches that if the people of God would truly confess their own sins, the nations of the world would be blessed. If born-again Christians in the evangelical church would return to God with all their hearts and get their idols out of God's sight, then the world would give glory to God.

But what if we do not repent for our sins? Children who test the boundaries of authority sometimes want to know what will happen if they disobey. "What if I don't turn in my homework?" "What if I don't clean my room?" "What if I don't repent for my sins?"

God's answer to that question shows his respect for the choices we make:

> Circumcise yourselves to the LORD;
>   remove the foreskin of your hearts,
>   O men of Judah and inhabitants of Jerusalem;
> lest my wrath go forth like fire,
>   and burn with none to quench it,
>   because of the evil of your deeds. (v. 4)

This portion of Jeremiah's prophecy thus ends with a solemn warning. You have heard the invitation to come back home to God. You have heard the free offers of Jesus Christ in the gospel. But do not think that God's grace allows him to ignore your sin. "For if we go on sinning deliberately after receiving the knowledge of the truth, there no longer remains a sacrifice for sins, but a fearful expectation of judgment, and a fury of fire that will consume the adversaries. . . . It is a fearful thing to fall into the hands of the living God" (Hebrews 10:26, 27, 31)

6

Lament for a City

JEREMIAH 4:5–31

IT IS TIME FOR A BRIEF REVIEW. Chapter 1 was Jeremiah's calling. God called him to be a prophet to the nations and warned him that he would have to preach judgment before he would get to preach grace.

Chapter 2 was the trial. Even though he never went through with it, God filed for divorce. He presented enough evidence to prove that although he was always a faithful husband, his people dumped him after the honeymoon and prostituted themselves to other gods.

Chapter 3 was the invitation to come back home. Time and again God pleaded with his people to turn away from idols, confess their sins in true repentance, and come back to their husband. He even gave them a solemn warning about the dangers of refusing to come back home.

What a Nightmare!

Sadly, Judah never heeded those warnings. God's people rejected God's invitation to come back home. That is why Jeremiah 4 is a living nightmare of divine judgment.

The terrible things that befall Judah for refusing to turn back to God are jumbled all together. Like most nightmares, you are not always sure where you are. Events sometimes seem out of sequence; thoughts and images appear without any logical order. You are not always sure what is happening, but whatever it is, it is absolutely frightening.

First, there is a battle cry in the countryside:

Declare in Judah, and proclaim in Jerusalem, and say,

> "Blow the trumpet through the land;
> cry aloud and say,

> 'Assemble, and let us go
> into the fortified cities!'" (v. 5)

The rams' horns are sounding all over Judah, like so many civil defense sirens, warning the people to run for the walled cities. This is the first sign that something is amiss.

Then a signal flag is raised in Jerusalem, or perhaps a fire beacon is lit, warning the Judeans to gather within the walls of Zion. "Raise a standard toward Zion, flee for safety, stay not" (v. 6a). There is not a moment to lose!

Why all the commotion? "For I bring disaster from the north, and great destruction" (v. 6b; cf. Deuteronomy 28:49). An enemy army is approaching from the north.

> A lion has gone up from his thicket,
>   a destroyer of nations has set out;
>   he has gone out from his place
> to make your land a waste;
>   your cities will be ruins
>   without inhabitant. (v. 7)

An army has left its den and is on the prowl.

"Lion" may be a reference to Assyria, or perhaps Babylon. R. K. Harrison reports that the "lion was depicted elegantly in sixth-century BC Assyrian reliefs, at a time when Assyria was at its height, while beautiful representations of lions in enamel have been recovered from the Processional Street of ancient Babylon."[1]

Whoever this lion is, his pursuit is a nightmare. He will bring terrible destruction.

> For this put on sackcloth,
>   lament and wail,
> for the fierce anger of the LORD
>   has not turned back from us. (v. 8)

Jeremiah instructs the people to get out their handkerchiefs, possibly to repent. Their situation will be desperate:

In that day, declares the LORD, courage shall fail both king and officials. The priests shall be appalled and the prophets astounded. (v. 9)

Jeremiah prophesies a complete collapse of leadership in Judah. The three pillars of Judean society—the "king," "The priests," and "The prophets"—

will be completely demoralized. Politicians are not much help in the face of divine judgment. The coming disaster will totally overwhelm their capacity to govern.

Everything Jeremiah has described so far will happen while the disaster is still on its way, before it even strikes. Even the rumors of impending disaster are a disaster. "At that time it will be said to this people and to Jerusalem, 'A hot wind from the bare heights in the desert toward the daughter of my people, not to winnow or cleanse, a wind too full for this comes for me. Now it is I who speak in judgment upon them'" (vv. 11, 12).

The kind of wind Jeremiah describes is called a *sirocco*. It is an oppressive desert wind, too dry to bring refreshment, too strong to separate the wheat from the chaff. Over a century ago Sir George Adam Smith described the approach of a sirocco in his diary: "Atmosphere thickening. At 1.45 (p.m.) wind rises, 93°; 2.30 gale blowing, air filled with fine sand, horizon shortened to a mile, sun not visible, grey sky, but a slight shadow cast by the tents. View from tent-door of light grey limestone land under dark grey sky. . . ."[2]

The wind will lift up the sand and turn the whole world gray. Then it will get stronger still. The winds whip up to gale force, and storm clouds appear on the horizon.

Behold, he comes up like clouds;
  his chariots like the whirlwind;
his horses are swifter than eagles—
  woe to us, for we are ruined! (v. 13)

God's judgment is coming like a cyclone. But the disaster has yet to strike. A watchman in Dan—in the northern part of Israel, beyond Galilee, at the headwaters of the River Jordan—can see the enemy mobilizing. "For a voice declares from Dan" (v. 15a) that invasion is impending. Then all of a sudden the messenger "proclaims trouble from Mount Ephraim" (v. 15b), just ten miles north of Jerusalem. The prophet gives us a vivid description of an unidentified flying army gathering like a storm in the north and then sweeping down toward Jerusalem.

"Warn the nations," Jeremiah says, "announce to Jerusalem, 'Besiegers come from a distant land; they shout against the cities of Judah'" (v. 16). Get the word out! The whole nation is surrounded. Spread the news so people will hear how much trouble Judah is in. Maybe someone will send help!

Then the disaster comes right to the walls of the city. The juggernaut has been coming closer and closer, until finally it advances on Jerusalem. Jeremiah himself is in the capital city. He says, "I hear the sound of the trumpet, the alarm of war" (v. 19b). The enemy soldiers are so close, the prophet can hear their voices. All the while he is cowering in his flimsy tent.

> Crash follows hard on crash;
>   the whole land is laid waste.
> Suddenly my tents are laid waste,
>   my curtains in a moment. (v. 20)

Having seen the destruction in the countryside, Jeremiah is waiting for the storm troopers to show up in his bedroom. He peeps out of his tent, peers over the city wall at the surrounding army, and longs for the battle to end: "How long must I see the standard and hear the sound of the trumpet?" (v. 21). Jeremiah is weak from fear, weary from the sights and sounds of battle. As bad as things are, they are about to get worse:

> I looked on the earth, and behold, it was without form and void;
>   and to the heavens, and they had no light.
> I looked on the mountains, and behold, they were quaking,
>   and all the hills moved to and fro.
> I looked, and behold, there was no man,
>   and all the birds of the air had fled.
> I looked, and behold, the fruitful land was a desert,
>   and all its cities were laid in ruins
>   before the LORD, before his fierce anger. (vv. 23–26)

If these verses sound familiar, it is because Jeremiah deliberately repeats the vocabulary of Genesis 1. The destruction of Judah will be so catastrophic that it will be like the un-creation of creation.[3] When God created the world he brought order out of chaos, light out of darkness, and fullness out of emptiness. Now the judgment of God is bringing chaos out of order, darkness out of light, and emptiness out of fullness.

The acts of creation are reversed by the judgment of God. In verse 23 the earth is formless and void, and light has been snuffed out of the heavens (cf. Genesis 1:2–5). In verse 24 the mountains and the hills are starting to crack and crumble (cf. Genesis 1:9, 10; Psalm 46:2, 3). In verse 25 the people have vanished, and the birds have flown the coop (cf. Genesis 1:20–23, 26–28). In verse 26 the fruitful land has been turned into desert (cf. Genesis 1:11–13). God has gone day by day through the creation of the world. His judgment has unglued, dismantled, and un-created his creation. It is as if Jeremiah takes the documentary film of the creation of the world and runs it backward.[4]

The Judgment to Come

When did the judgments Jeremiah prophesied take place? Scholars of an earlier era suggested that he was describing an invasion by the Scythians. Herodotus gives the historical evidence for an invasion of Scythians who came down from Russia into Palestine.[5] Others say Jeremiah was afraid of an Assyrian invasion. Ultimately, of course, it was the Babylonians who swept down from the north and carried Judah into captivity, but Jeremiah 4 does not give the time and date of the invasion.

That is often the way it is with nightmares. Usually the details are forgotten, and all that remains are confused images of horror and a feeling of fear in the pit of one's stomach. Most likely, this nightmare of divine judgment came early in Jeremiah's ministry. The prophet described the invasion so vividly because he was given a divine vision. But the prophecies themselves were not fulfilled until much later, when the Babylonians attacked Jerusalem. If so, then chapter 4 serves as a warning to God's people to turn away from their sins and back to God.

It serves as a warning for us as well. It is a reminder that God says what he means and means what he says. "For this the earth shall mourn, and the heavens above be dark; for I have spoken; I have purposed; I have not relented, nor will I turn back" (v. 28). All the judgments described in Jeremiah come from God. His prophecies are not about politics; they are about religion. Even when some earthly army carries out the attack, it is really God himself who marches against his people.

When God judged Jerusalem, he was well within his rights. Every sin deserves the wrath and curse of God. There can be no doubt that when these punishments finally came, they were well deserved. The opening chapters of Jeremiah prove that God's people were desperately wicked. They did everything from sleeping with the enemy to sacrificing their children to idols. The reason for judgment is not hard to find:

Like keepers of a field are they against her all around,
    because she [Judah] has rebelled against me,
    declares the LORD.
Your ways and your deeds
    have brought this upon you. (vv. 17, 18a)

Anyone who is honest will admit to deserving the same punishment. Jeremiah's prophecies have a way of touching the conscience and exposing sins that usually go unnoticed. Do you not worship success, beauty, wealth, happiness, comfort, or control over others? Is it not true that you fail to put the Lord first in your life, that the glory of God is not your only motivation?

We deserve no more than judgment. The same was true of Jeremiah's people, and yet their judgment was only partial. "For thus says the LORD, 'The whole land shall be a desolation; yet I will not make a full end'" (v. 27). The Lord did not completely destroy his people. God preserved the people of Judah through captivity. Eventually he brought them back to their land. As terrible as their judgment was, it was not final.

However, there will come a day when the earth and the heavens will be destroyed. The language Jeremiah uses—particularly when he foretells the destruction of the cosmos—is a reminder that a day is coming when God will un-create the heavens and the earth. Do you believe this? Do you believe that Jeremiah's nightmare will come true?

It is tempting to say, "God will not *really* judge me for my sins." But the Bible warns against that temptation:

> [Know] this first of all, that scoffers will come in the last days with scoffing, following their own sinful desires. They will say, "Where is the promise of his coming? For ever since the fathers fell asleep, all things are continuing as they were from the beginning of creation." For they deliberately over-look this fact, that the heavens existed long ago, and the earth was formed out of water and through water by the word of God. . . . But by the same word the heavens and earth that now exist are stored up for fire, being kept until the day of judgment and destruction of the ungodly. . . . But the day of the Lord will come like a thief, and then the heavens will pass away with a roar, and the heavenly bodies will be burned up and dissolved, and the earth and the works that are done on it will be exposed . . . the heavens will be set on fire and dissolved, and the heavenly bodies will melt as they burn! (2 Peter 3:3–5, 7, 10, 12b)

Fatal Attraction

The threat of judgment raises an important question: When the Bible speaks about divine judgment, how should we respond? How should one think, act, or even feel about the news of judgment by God?

One way to respond to the wrath of God is to ignore it. That seems to be what the people of Judah did, and Jeremiah could hardly believe it. "And you, O desolate one, what do you mean that you dress in scarlet, that you adorn yourself with ornaments of gold, that you enlarge your eyes with paint?" (4:30a). Jeremiah understood the fickleness of the human heart, but even he was amazed. Disaster was coming. An enemy army was on the march. Yet God's people dressed up like prostitutes, putting on fancy red dresses with spangles and sequins. They took out all their gaudy jewelry and cosmetics.

What incredible naiveté! This was no way to prepare for an invasion! God's people ought to be repenting in sackcloth and ashes, or at least skipping town, as Jeremiah describes:

> At the noise of horseman and archer
>   every city takes to flight;
> they enter thickets; they climb among rocks;
>   all the cities are forsaken,
>   and no man dwells in them. (v. 29)

Instead they are dabbing on eyeliner and eye shadow so they can go out and seduce some soldiers.

This may be a reference to Judah's last-ditch attempt at diplomacy, to the way she tried to make herself attractive to Egypt and Assyria so she would not be destroyed. In any case, it is a completely inappropriate way to prepare for battle. Soldiers are not to be seduced—they are to be feared. And it is a completely inappropriate way to prepare for divine judgment. Salvation requires more than a good cosmetologist.

Even after all her primping, Judah will be destroyed. "In vain you beautify yourself. Your lovers despise you; they seek your life" (v. 30b). To put it another way, Judah had a fatal attraction. Jeremiah warned God's people again and again that false gods abuse their worshipers. This northern army has not come for love, but for violence. Judah's fancy dress and shiny beads cannot save her. She will die, it seems, in childbirth:

> For I heard a cry as of a woman in labor,
>   anguish as of one giving birth to her first child,
> the cry of the daughter of Zion gasping for breath,
>   stretching out her hands,
> "Woe is me! I am fainting before murderers." (v. 31)

That is what happens to anyone who tries to ignore God's wrath against sin. You can dress up for a night on the town, seeking satisfaction and salvation from someone else, but you will not be saved.

Lamentations

Jeremiah responded to God's judgment in a different way. First he responded with *accusation*. He was so confused by what God was doing that he blamed God for Judah's troubles. "Then I said, 'Ah, Lord GOD, surely you have utterly deceived this people and Jerusalem, saying, "It shall be well with you," whereas the sword has reached their very life'" (v. 10). In effect, Jeremiah accused God of a cover-up, of misleading Judah by promising peace.

Perhaps Jeremiah was speaking ironically. Yet he does not seem to have his facts straight. Is the Lord the one who promised peace to Judah? Far from it! He warned Judah again and again about the inevitability of judgment if they refused to repent. The only people who said, "'Peace, peace,' when there is no peace" were the false prophets (6:14). Jeremiah should know better than to listen to them.

Later Jeremiah seems to respond with *frustration*.

> For my people are foolish;
>   they know me not;
> they are stupid children;
>   they have no understanding.
> They are "wise"—in doing evil!
>   But how to do good they know not. (4:22)

Calvin and others have thought that these words could only be spoken by God.[6] I am not so certain. Since this speech falls in the middle of Jeremiah's lament, it could well express his frustration about his preaching ministry.

Jeremiah was so gripped by the message of divine judgment that he was completely exasperated when God's people ignored him. His sermons could hardly have been clearer or more forceful. Yet most of his parishioners continued to go about their business without heeding his warnings. Jeremiah himself had such a palpable sense of impending judgment that he could believe God's people would not listen to him.

One senses the prophet's inner turmoil. Although he responded to divine judgment with accusation and frustration, his primary response was *lamentation*:

> ". . . It is bitter;
>   it has reached your very heart."
> My anguish, my anguish! I writhe in pain!
>   Oh the walls of my heart!
> My heart is beating wildly. (vv. 18b, 19a)

The word translated "anguish" (*meah*) is a word for intestinal discomfort. Literally, Jeremiah was "sick to his stomach" about what was going to happen to Judah. Not only did God's judgment make his stomach churn, it gave him heart palpitations. When God's people suffered, his prophet suffered with them. Somewhere the Dutch theologian Geerhardus Vos (1881–1949) has given this apt characterization: "Though he surrendered to God for the sake of God, there always seems to have remained in his mind a scar of the tragic conflict between the stern things without and the tender things within. His soul sometimes found it difficult to enter self-forgetfully into the message."

Jeremiah was not smug about God's wrath; he took no satisfaction in the death of the wicked. Instead, he practiced what he preached (v. 8), putting on sackcloth to wail a lament when the Babylonians finally conquered Jerusalem. He was the "Weeping Prophet" who offered God the tears shed at the beginning of the book of Lamentations:

> How lonely sits the city
>   that was full of people! . . .
> She weeps bitterly in the night,
>   with tears on her cheeks;
> among all her lovers
>   she has none to comfort her;
> all her friends have dealt treacherously with her;
>   they have become her enemies. . . .
> "For these things I weep;
>   my eyes flow with tears;
> for a comforter is far from me,
>   one to revive my spirit." (Lamentations 1:1a, 2, 16a)

However bold and stern Jeremiah may have seemed when he preached in public, he had his doubts, anxieties, fears, and sorrows in private.

Where are the Jeremiahs of the evangelical church in these postmodern times? Where are the men and women who have such awe for the justice of God, such love for the church of Jesus Christ, and such pity for the lost souls of the world that they weep over the sins of the nation? Christians spend a great deal of time wringing hands about the state of the church, bemoaning the ills of pagan society, and looking back with nostalgia for a "Christian America" that probably never existed. But that is not lamentation; it is just feeling sorry for ourselves.

Genuine lamentation arises out of a solemn sense of the dishonor that is done to God by sin, and out of a godly fear of the consequences of divine judgment. Where are the men and women who have tender hearts like Jeremiah, who "was filled with the utmost sorrow at the heavy tidings he was called to announce"?[7] Where are the men and women who weep to the glory of God?

Such lamentation would bring glory to God by properly acknowledging the church's need of reformation. It would also enable Christians to do effective evangelism. In his commentary on this passage, F. B. Meyer writes that

> when thoughts have saturated our hearts of the dishonor done to God, the loss sustained by Christ, the anguish wrought into the texture of one disobedient life—we shall be able to speak to men of the judgment to come, with streaming tears, tremulous voice, and breaking heart. Such [evangelism] will always be a convincing and irresistible argument to turn sinners from the error of their ways.[8]

Wash Yourselves

We have mentioned two ways to respond to news of divine judgment. One is to ignore it, which is the way of death. Another is to lament it, which is the way of tears. A third way is to escape it, which is the way of life.

How can anyone escape the wrath to come? There is nowhere to hide. But even in Jeremiah 4, in the heat of battle and the destruction of the cosmos, God offers salvation. The invitation is so short it is easy to overlook: "O Jerusalem, wash your heart from evil, that you may be saved. How long shall your wicked thoughts lodge within you?" (v. 14).

It is not certain how Jeremiah would have understood this invitation. How could Jerusalem have washed the evil from her heart? Could she have performed some repentance to turn away the wrath of God? Could she have sacrificed some perfect lamb to drive the enemy away from the walls of Jerusalem? Jeremiah does not say.

But know this: God's purpose for the salvation of the world is to offer cleansing from sin through the blood of Jesus Christ. There is nothing in the whole world that can wash away the stain of sin except the blood of Jesus Christ, shed on the cross to take away sin. His blood can cleanse us from all sin. "How much more will the blood of Christ, who through the eternal Spirit offered himself without blemish to God, purify our conscience from dead works to serve the living God" (Hebrews 9:14). In Christ God says to us, as he said to the people of Judah, "Wash your heart from evil, that you may be saved."

God can offer that kind of cleansing because Jesus Christ has taken the wrath of God upon himself. There is a faint reminder of this in Jeremiah. "Woe is me! I am fainting before murderers" (v. 31). These words were spoken by the people of Judah to describe the agony of their devastation. They seem to be without hope.

Christians can draw comfort from them, however. Consider how appropriate they would sound in the mouth of Jesus Christ, who knelt in the garden of Gethsemane and declared that he was fainting. "My soul is very sorrowful, even to death," he told his disciples (Matthew 26:38). Then Jesus died on the cross, for his life was given over to murderers. In his great sermon on the history of redemption, Stephen accused the Sanhedrin of homicide: ". . . the Righteous One, whom you have now betrayed and murdered" (Acts 7:52). Thus the fainting Christ was given over to murderers.

Christians may say that Jesus suffered the judgment of Jeremiah 4 in their place. There is great comfort in knowing that Jesus Christ has already suffered all of the wrath of God against your sin. On the day of judgment, when human history is rewound, creation is un-created, and the heavens and the earth are consumed by fire, you will have nothing to fear. You will be safe in Jesus Christ.

7

A Good Man Is Hard to Find

JEREMIAH 5:1–19

GOD GAVE JEREMIAH A CHANCE to save his civilization. All he needed to find was one righteous man. Just one. Not one hundred, or fifty, or ten, or even two. Jeremiah was not looking for a few good men; he was looking for only one.

This is the offer God made to his prophet:

> Search her squares to see
> if you can find a man,
> one who does justice
> and seeks truth,
> that I may pardon her. (5:1b)

The challenge was to find a plain dealer, just one citizen who could be trusted. For the sake of one person of real integrity, God would forgive the sins of the entire city.

Jerusalem, A to Z

According to the bargain, Jeremiah could take as long as he wanted to look. And he had the whole city of Jerusalem to choose from.

> Run to and fro through the streets of Jerusalem,
> look and take note!
> Search her squares . . . (v. 1a)

So Jeremiah scoured the streets of the capital to find one righteous man. He started with the common people, the regular folks, "The poor," as he called them (v. 4). He seemed to be cruising the right neighborhood, because he overheard plenty of religious jargon. "As the LORD lives," they said (v. 2). Among

87

people giving lip service to God, a prophet might expect to find at least one good person.

Sadly, although the common people had God's name on their lips, they did not have his glory on their minds. They had little respect for the Almighty:

> For the house of Israel and the house of Judah
> > have been utterly treacherous to me,
> > declares the LORD.
> They have spoken falsely of the LORD
> > and have said, "He will do nothing;
> no disaster will come upon us,
> > nor shall we see sword or famine." (vv. 11, 12)

These poor people were in spiritual denial. They doubted that God judges sin or rules in history. For all their religious talk, they refused to follow God. Their worship was false because they did not give glory to God in their hearts. By "swear[ing] falsely" (v. 2), they actually committed perjury when they worshiped.[1] This is a strong warning for anyone who claims to worship God. Whenever hymns are mumbled or prayers are mindlessly repeated, perjury is committed in God's house.

As Jeremiah walked the streets of Jerusalem, he found many people who had endured suffering. They had been struck down and crushed by the hardships of life. Among people who had endured such adversity, he might have expected to find someone who feared God. Or someone who had learned obedience through suffering. Surely Jeremiah could find at least one!

Sadly, suffering had not produced character among the common folk.

> O LORD, do not your eyes look for truth?
> You have struck them down,
> > but they felt no anguish;
> you have consumed them,
> > but they refused to take correction.
> They have made their faces harder than rock;
> > they have refused to repent. (v. 3)

They were callous, stubborn, and obstinate. They were men and women of steel. Their suffering did not produce godliness because they were immune to pain. They would not receive correction. Even after all of Jeremiah's warnings, they refused to repent.

Jeremiah began to realize he was not getting anywhere in his search, so he changed his strategy. Perhaps he had been looking in all the wrong places. Instead of looking low, perhaps he should look high:

Then I said, "These are only the poor;
    they have no sense;
for they do not know the way of the LORD,
    the justice of their God.
I will go to the great
    and will speak to them." (vv. 4, 5a)

"What can you expect from the poor?" Jeremiah said to himself. "They cannot read the Bible. They have not studied theology. They are sinning out of sheer ignorance."

So Jeremiah went to the high-rent district, where the priests and politicians lived. After all, the religious leaders had been to seminary. They could read the Torah. "For they know the way of the LORD, the justice of their God" (v. 5b).

Not so. "But they all alike had broken the yoke; they had burst the bonds" (v. 5c). Jeremiah compares the cultural elite to dumb oxen who have shattered their yokes. This image captures their willful disobedience. They sinned, not out of ignorance like regular folks, but in defiance of the Word of God. Since they broke free from divine authority, they were doubly culpable.

Jeremiah still needed to find one good man to save his city. Where else could he look? Not among the children. They, too, had forsaken the living God. "How can I pardon you? Your children have forsaken me and have sworn by those who are no gods" (v. 7a). They were worshiping the gods of the lower case, not God with a capital G. But lower-case gods are no gods at all. As Os Guinness shows in one of his best books, there is *No God but God.*[2]

Jeremiah could not find even one righteous child. Nor could he find a righteous adult, for they were too busy committing religious adultery. "When I fed them to the full, they committed adultery and trooped to the houses of whores" (v. 7b). Like most good preachers, Jeremiah often repeated himself. Here he gives another reminder that although his people were married to the living God, they had been lavishing their affection on dead idols. As noted in the first chapter, this adultery may have been literal as well as figurative, since many of the ancient religions—for example, Baal worship—included temple prostitution.

In this case, the people of Jerusalem "Trooped to the houses of whores" (v. 7b). The word for trooping here is a word for organizing an army into ranks and files. God's people lined up to worship idols. Anyone who worshiped at the temples of the false gods had to take a number.

As Jeremiah had mentioned before (2:23–25), the people were behaving like wild animals in heat. In their desperation to commit spiritual adultery, they were like "well-fed, lusty stallions, each neighing for his neighbor's wife" (v. 8). Judah was a sex-crazed society, saturated with sexual immorality.

Not that they were deprived. God had given them everything they needed. They were well supplied (v. 7) and "well-fed" (v. 8). But instead of praising God for their affluence, they turned to sexual sin. Jeremiah's Jerusalem was much like the post-Christian West, a culture Professor A. J. David Richards of New York University has termed a "pornotopia." All Jeremiah needed was one righteous man, but he could not find him among the wild broncos of Judah.

What about the preachers? Jeremiah offers a glimpse of the spiritual condition of his colleagues in ministry:

> The prophets will become wind;
>   the word is not in them.
> Thus shall it be done to them! (v. 13)

Prophets ought to speak God's Word, but the only thing coming from these men was hot air. The irony is that the Hebrew word for *wind* is the same as the word for *spirit*. Whereas the prophets were supposed to be filled with the Spirit, they were just windbags.

Not Even One

All Jeremiah needed was one good man, but he could not find so much as one righteous person among the poor, the leaders, the children, the adults, or the prophets.

The futility of Jeremiah's quest echoes Abraham's argument with God over the fate of Sodom (Genesis 18:16–33). Sodom was such a wicked city that God planned to destroy it. But Abraham was unwilling to write the city off, so he bartered with God for its salvation. He started by getting God to agree to spare Sodom for the sake of fifty righteous people. The more he thought about it, however, the more impossible finding fifty honest pagans seemed. Gradually he worked God down to forty, down to twenty, and finally down to just ten righteous souls. God said, "For the sake of ten I will not destroy it" (Genesis 18:32).

The sins of Sodom are well known and often condemned, especially its homosexual ones. What Jeremiah discovered, however, was that Jerusalem had become New Sodom. Salemites were no more righteous than Sodomites. Like Abraham before him, Jeremiah was unable to answer God's challenge to find the righteous among the wicked.

Jeremiah's search would have been equally futile if he had walked up and down the streets of my adopted city, Philadelphia. He would have had as much trouble finding one good man in the luxury apartments on Rittenhouse Square or among the tourists at Independence Mall. He would have found hatred and intolerance in Bridesburg and Gray's Ferry. He would have found drugs and violence in the Badlands of North Philly. Up on Society Hill he would have found selfishness and greed.

The search would be every bit as disappointing if Jeremiah walked all the towns and cities of the United States. He would have as much trouble finding a righteous man in Washington or Peoria or Kalamazoo as anywhere else. Could he have found truth among our journalists, honesty among our politicians, generosity among our businessmen, integrity among our clergy, or love within our families?

Indeed, Jeremiah's quest would have been equally hopeless if he had walked all the pages of human history. Where and when could he have found one man to be righteous for the people? If Jeremiah had lived for three thousand years he would have had ample time to pace the streets of humanity, searching for "one who does justice and seeks truth" (5:1).

He could have investigated the Vandals who sacked Rome. He could have taken a survey among the serfs of the Middle Ages. He could have searched through the tribes of Africa and lived among the emperors of China. He could have hunted buffalo with the Plains Indians and sipped tea with the Victorians. He could have observed the moral habits of the Eskimo, or even examined the members of your local church. But he would still be looking for one good person, righteous to the very core of his being, without any dissemblance or falsehood.

Would he have found anything different if he had knocked at your door?

Anyone who has ever looked for a perfectly good man has reached the same verdict. The philosophy major who wrote Ecclesiastes searched high and low and concluded that "There is not a righteous man on earth who does good and never sins" (Ecclesiastes 7:20). The Apostle Paul put it like this, loosely quoting King David:

What then? Are we Jews any better off? No, not at all. . . . as it is written:

> "None is righteous, no, not one;
>   no one understands;
>   no one seeks for God.
> All have turned aside; together they have become worthless;
>   no one does good,
>   not even one." (Romans 3:9–12; cf. Psalm 14:1–3)

This is one aspect of the doctrine of total depravity. The Bible does not teach that every human being is as bad as he or she can be. But it does teach that every aspect of every person has been corrupted by sin. Bodies perform sinful acts, and minds think sinful thoughts. The understanding, the heart, the will, and the imagination are all corrupted by sin. To paraphrase the title of an autobiography by basketball player Dennis Rodman, we are as "Bad as We Wanna Be."

Depravity is total because it affects the whole person. It is also total because it affects the whole of humanity. Total depravity is the one Biblical doctrine that has been proven by every era of human history. Even the pagan philosophers recognized the sinfulness of the human race, although they could not fully explain it. Diogenes the Cynic (c. 350 BC) carried a lantern by daylight, looking for one honest person. He failed in his quest.

Like Diogenes, Jeremiah received a lesson in total depravity. The longer he walked the streets of Jerusalem, the clearer the lesson became: "None is righteous, no, not one."

The Wages of Sin Is Death

If no one "is righteous, no, not one," then what will become of the human race? Paul answered that question well: "The wages of sin is death" (Romans 6:23). *The Catechism for Young Children* puts the same truth slightly differently: Every sin deserves "The wrath and curse of God" (Q & A 31). Total depravity leads to total destruction.

Even someone who does not believe in God must admit that sin deserves to be punished. God's moral law is imprinted on the conscience. *Time* magazine once ran a story about the vile things mass murderer Richard Speck did while he was in prison. Among other things, he managed to star in his own pornographic video. A caption for the story read, "The Wages of Sin Is . . ." Underneath the caption was this quotation from Speck's video: "If they only knew how much fun I was having in here, they would turn me loose."[3] The caption was intended to provoke outrage. The reason it had such an effect is because every human being has an inherent sense of justice. Whatever the wages of sin may be, they *cannot* include goofing off in jail.

Jeremiah 5 teaches that the proper wages of sin is divine judgment. Having watched the leaders of Judah break free from their yokes, Jeremiah explained what happens to domesticated oxen when they leave the farm and roam free:

Therefore a lion from the forest shall strike them down;
  a wolf from the desert shall devastate them.

A leopard is watching their cities;
    everyone who goes out of them shall be torn in pieces,
because their transgressions are many,
    their apostasies are great." (v. 6)

Like a wounded cow, Judah would be stalked by one predator after another. A lion would attack from the forest, a wolf would ravage from the desert, and leopards would lie in wait in suburbia.

The message of judgment continues with another image. Israel was planted to be a *choice vine* bearing good grapes for God (cf. 2:21), but now the vine is to be plucked.

Go up through her vine rows and destroy,
    but make not a full end;
strip away her branches,
    for they are not the LORD's. (v. 10)

Then God's people are compared to kindling:

Because you have spoken this word,
behold, I am making my words in your mouth a fire,
    and this people wood, and the fire shall consume them. (v. 14b)

Jeremiah's words of judgment were like a consuming fire.

This language about wild animals, vines, and fire is metaphorical. What God really threatened was an attack from some unidentified foreign army.

Behold, I am bringing against you
    a nation from afar, O house of Israel,
    declares the LORD.
It is an enduring nation;
    it is an ancient nation,
a nation whose language you do not know,
    nor can you understand what they say. (v. 15)

This prophecy referred to the Scythians, the Assyrians, or perhaps the Babylonians. In any case, the enemy was to speak a foreign language, adding to the terror of being defeated.

There is a horrifying scene in the movie *Platoon* in which an American military outpost is attacked by the Viet Cong at night. The outpost screams for help and maintains radio contact with headquarters. But when the Viet Cong win the skirmish, all the operator hears through his headset back at command is soldiers chattering in Vietnamese. The battle has been lost, and the alien tongue adds to the horror of conquest.

Jeremiah speaks of an army so strong that even its wimps are bullies: "Their quiver is like an open tomb; they are all mighty warriors" (v. 16). A three-year-old football fan once asked me about the New York Giants. He said, "But, Dad, if they're *giants*, then nobody could tackle them because they'd be too big!" Judah would face that kind of enemy—every last man a giant, much too big to tackle.

By the time these voracious warriors are finished, they will have swallowed Judah whole:

> They shall eat up your harvest and your food;
>   they shall eat up your sons and your daughters;
> they shall eat up your flocks and your herds;
>   they shall eat up your vines and your fig trees. (v. 17a)

The next sentence is especially foreboding. "Your fortified cities in which you trust they shall beat down with the sword" (v. 17b). The truth of this verse has been confirmed by archaeology. As William Foxwell Albright concluded concerning Israel's eventual destruction, "Many towns were destroyed at the beginning of the sixth century BC and never again occupied. . . . Others were destroyed and reoccupied after a long period of abandonment."[4] "The wages of sin is death."

By the grace of God, some of the people of Judah would be granted a stay of execution. "But even in those days, declares the LORD, I will not make a full end of you" (v. 18). A few grapes would be left on the vine (v. 10). But even their future looked bleak. Once they were carried off into exile, they would wonder why all these terrible things had happened to them. Their children, especially, would wonder what they had done to deserve such misfortune. God has a good answer:

> And when your people say, "Why has the Lord our God done all these things to us?" you shall say to them, "As you have forsaken me and served foreign gods in your land, so you shall serve foreigners in a land that is not yours." (v. 19)

God could hardly be any more fair! The people of Jerusalem had worshiped foreign gods all along. What could be more appropriate than sending them to a place where they could serve those gods to their hearts' content?

Be careful what you desire: God might grant it!

The Righteous One

This is a good place to summarize the condition of Jerusalem as presented in the fifth chapter of Jeremiah. God promised to forgive the sins of the city if his prophet could find one honest, righteous, and truthful person left in it. But Jeremiah could not find a single one. As a result, the people of Jerusalem were about to receive the wages of sin through divine judgment.

This was not just the condition of Jerusalem. It is the condition of the entire human race. "None is righteous, no, not one." "The wages of sin is death." If you belong to the human race, it is your condition as well.

If only the good man Jeremiah was looking for could be found! If only one man could be found who is honest in all his dealings and who seeks the truth. If only one man could be found to be righteous for the people's sake. If only that one man could be found, a man of such perfect integrity that he could turn away the wrath of God.

There is that man—Jesus Christ. What about him? Can he meet Jeremiah's conditions?

Jeremiah was told to look for a man "who deals honestly" (NIV). Jesus Christ was straightforward in all his dealings. He gave an honest presentation of his deity, performing miracles to prove his divine power over creation. Jesus Christ dealt honestly with his disciples, not hiding from them the necessity of his own sufferings and death. Jesus Christ also dealt honestly with sinners, like the woman at the well (John 4), exposing their secrets and inviting them to trust in him. And Jesus Christ dealt honestly with his enemies, like the Pharisees, confronting the enmity in their hearts. There was nothing false or deceptive in anything Jesus said or did.

Jeremiah was told to look for one man "who . . . seeks truth." Jesus Christ not only sought the truth—he *is* the Truth! At the beginning of his Gospel, John says Jesus Christ came into the world "full of grace and truth" (John 1:14). That is truth with a capital *T*, the Truth of God himself. Thus when the disciples wanted to know the way to eternal life, Jesus said, "I am the way, and the truth, and the life" (14:6).

The challenge God gave to Jeremiah was answered in Jesus Christ. He is the one man, the plain dealer, the truth-seeker, the righteous man for whose sake God can forgive his people.

However, in order to achieve this forgiveness, it was necessary for Jesus Christ to die on the cross. Atonement had to be offered for the sins of God's people. In Jeremiah's prophecy, this need is recognized: "Shall I not punish them for these things? declares the Lord; and shall I not avenge myself on a nation such as this?" (5:9). "How *can* I pardon you?" (v. 7). This is the basic problem of salvation: How can God be just *and* justify the ungodly?

Only if one perfect man, the God-and-man, would offer himself as a perfect sacrifice for sin. Such a man would be righteous, not only for himself, but also for others. Then God the Father would be able to forgive his people for their sins.

This is why the New Testament writers took such pains to prove that Jesus Christ is the one man who could and who did atone for all the sins of God's people. In Mark's Gospel it is a demon who recognizes Jesus Christ, crying out, "I know who you are—the Holy One of God" (Mark 1:24b). In the book of Acts, Peter calls Jesus "The Holy and Righteous One" (Acts 3:14), while Stephen calls him "The Righteous One" (Acts 7:52; cf. 22:14). John said the same thing in his first epistle: "We have an advocate with the Father, Jesus Christ the righteous. He is the propitiation for our sins" (1 John 2:1b, 2a).

In John's Gospel it is Caiaphas who testifies that Jesus is the answer to Jeremiah's quest. Caiaphas, who served as high priest in Jerusalem, was no friend of Jesus. Yet this is what he said, by the Holy Spirit: "It is better for you that one man should die for the people, not that the whole nation should perish" (John 11:50). Exactly what Jeremiah was looking for: *one man* to save the nation from perishing! That one man was Jesus Christ, who died for the sins of his people so they might not perish, but have everlasting life (John 3:16).

The Apostle Paul said the same thing. He "concluded this: that one has died for all" (2 Corinthians 5:14). He compared the death that came through Adam with the life that comes through Christ:

> For if many died through one man's [Adam's] trespass, much more have the grace of God and the free gift by the grace of that one man Jesus Christ abounded for many . . . [how] much more will those who receive the abundance of grace and the free gift of righteousness reign in life through the one man Jesus Christ . . . one act of righteousness leads to justification and life for all men. For as by the one man's [Adam's] disobedience the many were made sinners, so by the one man's [Christ's] obedience the many will be made righteous. (Romans 5:15b, 17b, 18b, 19)

Through the grace, the life, the righteous act, and the obedience of the one man, justifying grace comes to many.

Look as long as you like, there is no other answer to Jeremiah's quest. God sent his own Son, Jesus Christ, the Righteous One, to save the city. A good man is hard to find, but not impossible.

8

What Will You Do in the End?

JEREMIAH 5:20—6:15

NOBODY PAYS ANY ATTENTION TO CAR ALARMS. They go off day and night, sometimes for no reason at all, but nobody ever seems to do anything about them. People have become so used to the pattern of whistles, buzzers, sirens, and beepers that they hardly even notice them anymore.

This often happens with warnings that are repeated over and over, like fire alarms, Surgeon General's Warnings, and boys who cry "Wolf!" The more you hear them, the less you heed them.

Under Siege

Jeremiah was up against the same problem in the early years of his ministry. Chapter after chapter, day after day, he warned the people of God to flee from the wrath to come. He could tell that his alarms were falling on deaf ears.

> To whom shall I speak and give warning,
>   that they may hear?
> Behold, their ears are uncircumcised,
>   they cannot listen;
> behold, the word of the LORD is to them an object of scorn;
>   they take no pleasure in it. (6:10)

Jeremiah's modern readers face the same temptation. Already by this point in the book we feel like we have heard it all before. We *have* heard it all before. Jeremiah continues to preach against the sins of God's people and to tell them that God will punish them as a result.

Chapter 6 begins with another warning to flee, another order to sound the trumpet, and another command to light the signal fires:

> Flee for safety, O people of Benjamin,
>   from the midst of Jerusalem!
> Blow the trumpet in Tekoa,
>   and raise a signal on Beth-haccherem,
> for disaster looms out of the north,
>   and great destruction. (6:1)

Once again disaster is threatened by Israel's ancient enemies to the north (cf. 4:5, 6), and the people are warned to flee to the south.

Once again Jeremiah uses feminine vocabulary to show how vulnerable his people are. Previously he suggested that Jerusalem was preparing for battle by putting on makeup (4:30). Now he says Jerusalem is more like a maiden than a warrior: "The lovely and delicately bred I will destroy, the daughter of Zion" (6:2).

Once again Jeremiah prophesies that Jerusalem will be a city under siege (cf. 4:16): "Shepherds with their flocks shall come against her; they shall pitch their tents around her; they shall pasture, each in his place" (6:3). Foreign rulers will surround the city with their armies to wage unholy war. "Prepare war against her," they say (v. 4). The word translated "prepare" suggests they will offer pagan sacrifices to determine when they should attack. "Arise, and let us attack at noon!" the commander says. "Woe to us, for the day declines, for the shadows of evening lengthen! Arise, and let us attack by night and destroy her palaces!" (vv. 4, 5). This change of plans is frightening because to fight by night violates ancient Near Eastern rules of engagement.

Once again Jeremiah makes it clear that Jerusalem will get no more than she deserves.

> For thus says the LORD of hosts: . . .
>
> > "This is the city that must be punished;
> >   there is nothing but oppression within her.
> > As a well keeps its water fresh,
> >   so she keeps fresh her evil." (vv. 6, 7a)

Jerusalem is Sin City. There is always a fresh supply of evil welling up like poison within her and overflowing into her streets.

> Violence and destruction are heard within her;
>   sickness and wounds are ever before me. (v. 7b)

Her streets are noisy with violence. Sin covers the city like an open sore.

For all these reasons God must punish Jerusalem. His holiness and his justice require him to judge sin. His character does not allow him to allow us to sin with impunity. It is against God's very nature to overlook sin. So once again the Lord himself will punish his people. It is the Lord himself who orders the soldiers to cut down trees, build siege ramps, and batter down the gates of Jerusalem (v. 6).

> Be warned, O Jerusalem,
> lest I turn from you in disgust,
> lest I make you a desolation,
> an uninhabited land." (v. 8)

It is the Lord himself who rejects Jerusalem. The foreign soldiers who besiege her are mercenaries in his army.

Once again Israel is compared to a vine to be gleaned.

> Thus says the LORD of hosts:
> "They shall glean thoroughly as a vine
> the remnant of Israel;
> like a grape gatherer pass your hand again
> over its branches." (v. 9; cf. 5:10)

In the famous words of "Battle Hymn of the Republic," God is "Tramping out the vintage where the grapes of wrath are stored."

Once again judgment will fall on the whole city, from the greatest to the least. Jeremiah is filled with the wrath of God, a wrath that will cut across age and gender distinctions. It will be poured out on everyone in Judah, from the toddlers to the senior citizens.

> Therefore I am full of the wrath of the LORD;
> I am weary of holding it in.
> "Pour it out upon the children in the street,
> and upon the gatherings of young men, also;
> both husband and wife shall be taken,
> the elderly and the very aged.
> Their houses shall be turned over to others,
> their fields and wives together,
> for I will stretch out my hand
> against the inhabitants of the land,"
> declares the LORD. (vv. 11, 12)

Their property will be turned over to their conquerors. One spring the *Philadelphia Inquirer* ran a series of interviews with Serbs who were living in Croatian homes, using Croatian china and paging through Croatian photo albums. This is what happens in war; to the victors go the spoils.

As we have listened to Jeremiah, we have heard all of this before. We have heard before, too, that the judgment God poured out on Jerusalem was a foretaste of the wrath to come. A day is still coming when "The heavens will pass away with a roar, and the heavenly bodies will be burned up and dissolved, and the earth and the works that are done on it will be exposed" (2 Peter 3:10). A day is still coming when the earth will crack, the heavens will melt, and the whole universe will be destroyed by fire (2 Peter 3:12). A day is still coming when ungodly men will be judged and destroyed (2 Peter 3:7), when God will render to men, women, and children according to their deeds (Matthew 25:31–46).

What will you do then? To put it the way Jeremiah put it, when all is said and done, "What will you do when the end comes?" (5:31).

Blind Fools

Jeremiah's question is multiple choice. He preaches to three different groups of people in this passage, and they each give a different answer to the threat of divine judgment.

The first group is the "blind fools" (5:20–25). John Guest points out that there were several things these blind fools were without.[1] First, they were *without understanding*. Not that there was anything wrong with their natural capacities. They had eyes, ears, and brains. But they were closed minded:

> Declare this in the house of Jacob;
>   proclaim it in Judah:
> "Hear this, O foolish and senseless people,
>   who have eyes, but see not,
>   who have ears, but hear not." (vv. 20, 21)

Their problem was not intellectual but spiritual. Their eyes and ears and minds were shut to the Word of God. They were in denial, denying that the living God had a claim upon their lives and would judge them for their sins.

The ignorance of these blind fools made Jeremiah's preaching ministry extremely frustrating. He complained:

> To whom shall I speak and give warning,
>   that they may hear?
> Behold, their ears are uncircumcised,
>   they cannot listen;
> behold, the word of the LORD is to them an object of scorn;
>   they take no pleasure in it. (6:10)

Jeremiah was not the only prophet who experienced this struggle. He was in good company. The prophet Isaiah had some blind fools in his congregation too. The Lord said to him:

Go, and say to this people:

> "Keep on hearing, but do not understand;
> keep on seeing, but do not perceive."
> Make the heart of this people dull,
>   and their ears heavy,
>   and blind their eyes;
> lest they see with their eyes,
>   and hear with their ears,
> and understand with their hearts,
>   and turn and be healed. (Isaiah 6:9, 10)

These prophets learned that it is only by the grace of God that anyone ever understands the message of salvation. The mind and heart of the natural man is closed to God's Word until he is regenerated by the Holy Spirit.

Though discouraging, this reality is an encouragement for Christian evangelism. It is easy to become frustrated when people fail to understand the gospel. The good news about Jesus Christ is offered more often than it is accepted. Often people do not seem to "get it." They remain unconvinced of their sin, unmoved by Christ's sacrifice, and unconcerned about the final judgment.

An elder once met with a woman who wanted to join the church. As they talked, he could sense that she was not really trusting in Christ for her salvation; she was still trusting in her own good deeds to appease God. So he confronted her, reminding her that her good deeds could not atone for her sins and that only the merits of Jesus Christ could save her. The woman listened to the elder very carefully, nodding her head and saying, "Yes, yes, I understand." When he was finished, she said, "Okay, *now* am I good enough to get in?" Then the elder realized he was right back where he'd started.

Jeremiah's experience is a reminder that such encounters are not surprising. Faith in Jesus Christ is a spiritual dynamic, and spiritual results can only be accomplished by the Holy Spirit.

Consider the preaching ministry of Jesus Christ himself. Jesus knew a thing or two about how to preach. There were no deficiencies in his homiletical method. Yet not everyone who heard his sermons trusted him for salvation. In fact, many listeners rejected him. Why was this? Because receiving the message of salvation is a work of the Holy Spirit. As Jesus himself said, "To you it has been given to know the secrets of the kingdom of heaven, but to them it has not been given. . . . This is why I speak to them in parables, because seeing they do not see, and hearing they do not hear, nor do they understand" (Matthew 13:11, 13). Then he proceeded to quote from Isaiah 6: "You will indeed hear but never understand," and so forth. The spiritual insight to understand the message of salvation is a gift from God. The blind fools of Jeremiah's day were without this understanding.

What else did they lack? They were *without reverence* for the power of God. "Do you not fear me? declares the LORD. Do you not tremble before me?" (5:22a). Yes, every human being ought to fear God and tremble in his presence. Why? For many reasons, one of which is his mighty power over the sea:

> I placed the sand as the boundary for the sea,
>   a perpetual barrier that it cannot pass;
> though the waves toss, they cannot prevail;
>   though they roar, they cannot pass over it. (5:22b)

How mighty God must be to rule the sea! He rules over the rolling waves, and the stormy seas obey him. He has set the oceans in their places and bounded them with the dry land. If God can rule over the chaos of the sea, he deserves our reverence and awe.

Yet our culture refuses to give God glory for his work of creation. The secular mind recognizes some beauty in the created order, but refuses to praise the God who made all things beautiful. In the words of Carl Sagan, "Design? Absolutely—without question. Designer? Not a hint." The secular mind thinks in merely natural terms, viewing the whole universe as nothing more than molecules in motion. It never acknowledges that the principles that govern the universe come from a Mind, the mind of God.

Only a stubborn heart would refuse to revere the God of creation. "But this people has a stubborn and rebellious heart; they have turned aside and gone away" (v. 23). If even the seas obey him, then he ought to be praised and obeyed.

The other thing these blind fools lacked was gratitude. They were *without gratitude* for God's grace:

> They do not say in their hearts,
>   "Let us fear the LORD our God,
> who gives the rain in its season,
>   the autumn rain and the spring rain,
> and keeps for us
>   the weeks appointed for the harvest." (v. 24)

Jeremiah has already mentioned God's work of creation, the way he made the sea and the dry land in the first place. Now he addresses God's work of providence, the way he continues to sustain and uphold everything he has made. God did not make the world, then walk away. He did not wind the world up to let it wind down on its own. Instead in summer and winter, in springtime and harvest, the Lord is great in his faithfulness.

But these blind fools had forgotten all that, and now they are beginning to reap the consequences of their ingratitude. There is a drought in Israel. The autumn and spring rains have not watered the land. "Your iniquities have turned these away, and your sins have kept good from you" (v. 25). This makes sense, because Deuteronomy 11:16, 17 teaches that the proper punishment for idolatry is drought.

This principle is worth pondering whenever there is news of drought or some other natural disaster. Are hurricanes, earthquakes, floods, and droughts a sign of God's judgment against idolatry? Perhaps they are. If so, God would be perfectly within his rights, because we live in a nation that worships many false gods.

Fat Cats

One response to the news of divine judgment is to ignore it like a blind fool, living without understanding, reverence, or gratitude to God. Another response is the response of the fat cats (5:26–31).

The word "cats" does not actually appear in these verses, but the wicked men Jeremiah describes are "fat and sleek" (5:28). Furthermore, they liked to catch birds, which is one of the things cats like to do.

> For wicked men are found among my people;
>   they lurk like fowlers lying in wait.
> They set a trap;
>   they catch men.
> Like a cage full of birds,
>   their houses are full of deceit;
> therefore they have become great and rich. (vv. 26, 27)

These poachers were skilled at what they did, for their houses were full of birds.

The problem with these fat cats was not just that they were rich and powerful. The Bible does not condemn the rich for being rich (although it does explain how hard it is for the rich to trust God for their salvation). Nor does the Bible condemn the powerful for being powerful (although it does warn against the abuse of power). No, the problem with these fat cats was that they had gained their wealth and power by defrauding the poor.

There are many bird catchers in our own society. I think of the officers convicted in a Philadelphia police corruption scandal, or a lawyer who used insurance fraud to bilk the State of New Jersey out of millions of dollars. The "haves" use the system to take advantage of the "have-nots."

What Jeremiah says about spiritual responsibility for the have-nots is very challenging. It is easy to think that as long as you do not take advantage of the poor, you are not guilty of social injustice. But the Lord maintains a much higher standard:

> They know no bounds in deeds of evil;
>   they judge not with justice
> the cause of the fatherless, to make it prosper,
>   and they do not defend the rights of the needy.
> Shall I not punish them for these things?
>   declares the Lord,
>   and shall I not avenge myself
> on a nation such as this? (vv. 28, 29)

It is not enough to not exploit the poor, although the Bible does command us, "Do not oppress the widow, the fatherless, the sojourner, or the poor" (Zechariah 7:10). But God cares as much about sins of omission as he does about sins of commission. He commands his people to be *advocates* for the poor. It is not even enough to fight on behalf of the needy—we must fight to *win*.

The reason for this is that God himself is a Father to the fatherless and a defender of the poor: "For the Lord your God is God of gods and Lord of lords . . . He executes justice for the fatherless and the widow, and loves the sojourner, giving him food and clothing" (Deuteronomy 10:17, 18). All true sons and true daughters of God show their love for their heavenly Father by being champions for the cause of the poor.

Jeremiah's preaching about fat cats condemns us all. Political liberals and political conservatives alike have a false compassion for the poor. Most liberals give the poor money to care for their immediate needs, but lack the compassion to get to the spiritual causes at the root of poverty. Most conservatives recognize that some kinds of so-called aid do more harm than good, but what they really want is for the poor to go away and solve their own problems.

The living God, who is neither a Republican nor a Democrat, has a higher standard. He asks, "What are you doing to plead the case of the fatherless to win it, or to defend the rights of the poor?" If you are not doing anything for orphans or for the destitute, then you are just one of the fat cats. Unless you are doing something already, it is time to do something about the poor in your neighborhood.

Lying Prophets

Ministers do not get very good press in the book of Jeremiah. In almost every chapter so far, Jeremiah has been clergy bashing. I doubt he was very popular at denominational meetings. Yet he was not speaking on his own behalf; he was bringing the Lord's condemnation against a wayward clergy.

The great evangelist George Whitefield (1714–1770) began his sermon on this passage by observing, "As God can send a nation of people no greater blessing than to give them faithful, sincere, upright ministers, so the greatest curse that God can possibly send upon a people in this world is to give them over to blind, unregenerate, carnal, lukewarm, unskillful guides."[2]

Whitefield's words describe exactly what was happening in Jeremiah's day. "The prophets prophesy falsely, and the priests rule at their direction; my people love to have it so" (5:31a). The other prophets were liars. They say "'Peace, peace,' when there is no peace" (6:14b). "Shalom, shalom," they say, but there is no shalom.

This is the "Big Lie" of liberal theology—that God does not punish sin. Liberal theology tries to reassure people that everything is okay, even if everything isn't okay. It does what Neville Chamberlain did in 1940 when he was Prime Minister of Great Britain. After his negotiations with the Nazis, he announced, "We have achieved peace in our time." He said, "Peace, peace," but there was no peace, and shortly afterwards the world was plunged into war.

In the same way, pastors who fail to preach the judgment to come are saying "peace, peace" when there is no peace. The Bible teaches that God is holy and righteous and will judge every person according to what he or she has done. Only those who trust in Jesus Christ will be saved, while everyone else will be cast into an eternal "lake of fire" (Revelation 20:14, 15). To preach anything less is to be a lying prophet.

Prophets ought to be surgeons of the soul, correctly diagnosing the spiritual condition of God's people. In Jeremiah's day surgery was needed, but the prophets turned out to be quack-doctors; they did no more than apply a tourniquet. "They have healed the wound of my people lightly" (6:14a). "There, there," they said, "let me give you a Band-Aid." But what the people really needed was a heart transplant.

The prophets were shameless. They conducted their spiritual malpractice without blushing.

> Were they ashamed when they committed abomination?
>> No, they were not at all ashamed;
>> they did not know how to blush.
> Therefore they shall fall among those who fall;
>> at the time that I punish them, they shall be overthrown,"
> says the LORD. (v. 15)

Not only were the prophets shameless liars, but the priests were abusing their authority. They were in cahoots with the prophets, preaching their own messages rather than the Word of God. When my son was very small he composed his own impromptu hymns. Once he sang about "royal pastors leading us astray." My wife was alarmed about this, but I said, "The royal pastors are the ones you have to watch out for, the pastors who think they are kings." That is what the priests of Jeremiah's day were like. They were not bringing themselves under God's authority but were ruling by their own authority.

The priests were partly motivated by greed, which was a problem for the whole culture.

> For from the least to the greatest of them,
>> everyone is greedy for unjust gain;
> and from prophet to priest,
>> everyone deals falsely. (v. 13)

Although Jeremiah had failed to find a righteous man, he knew plenty of wicked ones. He lived in the same kind of "greed is good" culture that we live in, and ministers are not immune from its influence.

A minister who ceases to believe in the authority of Scripture, who denies the certainty of the Last Judgment, or who sees the pastorate as a prosperous career rather than a sacrificial calling ought to drop out of the ministry. One can sense Jeremiah's outrage about what the lying prophets were doing: "An appalling and horrible thing has happened in the land" (5:30). But here is another shock: "My people love to have it so" (5:31b). Despite the false teaching and deplorable behavior of the clergy, the people of Jerusalem were delighted with their ministry.

In the summer of 1995 an Anglican minister was removed from his parish for heresy. He had written a book entitled *God in Us*, in which he argued that God is not personal, but a force whose "mercy and grace are mediated through human beings." The headline of the article in the London Times read, "Sacked priest compares his fate to Jeremiah's."[3] The minister was right that the book of Jeremiah was relevant to his situation, but he was missing the point. He was like the lying prophets whom Jeremiah opposed, not like the true prophet Jeremiah.

But the real shocker was the way the minister's congregation responded. One parishioner called his dismissal "an appalling situation." "The Church of England has always prided itself on being very liberal," he said. "There ought to be room for experiment in this sort of fashion."

The Apostle Paul warned that there would be days like this. He wrote to Timothy:

> Preach the word . . . For the time is coming when people will not endure sound teaching, but having itching ears they will accumulate for them-selves teachers to suit their own passions. (2 Timothy 4:2, 3)

Unless I am very much mistaken, this is exactly what is happening in the contemporary church. Preaching that entertains more than it instructs, soothes more than it convicts, and appeases more than it confronts has become the rule rather than the exception in the evangelical church. What H. Richard Niebuhr (1894–1963) said about the liberals a generation ago can now be applied to the preaching of the evangelical church: "A God without wrath brings men without sin into a kingdom without judgment through the ministrations of a Christ without a cross."

What Will You Do?

Well, what are you going to do about it? That is the question Jeremiah asks at the end of chapter 5: "What will you do when the end comes?" We live in the kind of post-Reformation church and post-Christian nation Jeremiah lived in. There are blind fools, fat cats, and lying prophets all around us. In truth, there is more blind fool or fat cat or lying prophet in each one of us than there ought to be. But what will we do in the end? Or to translate Jeremiah's question another way, "What will happen to you when it is over?"

Jeremiah's question is multiple choice, so there is one more option: none of the above. The answer, if we obey God, is that we will *not* do what the people of Jerusalem were doing.

We will not be blind fools. We will understand and believe the message of salvation in Jesus Christ. We will fear God, giving all honor and reverence to him for his sovereignty over sea and sand. We will thank God, giving all praise and gratitude to him for rain and harvest.

We will not be fat cats. We will not use social structures to take advantage of the disadvantaged. We will be advocates for the orphans and the unborn. We will defend the rights of the poor and the needy.

And we will not be lying prophets. We will not hide the wrath of God from people. We will warn them that God judges sinners, and that the only protection from his curse is the righteousness of Jesus Christ, received by faith.

9

At the Crossroads

JEREMIAH 6:16–30

IN HIS FIRST INAUGURAL ADDRESS President Franklin Delano Roosevelt (1882–1945) admitted that the United States of America had lost its way. "We don't know where we are going," he said, "but we are on our way."[1]

Roosevelt was right. We didn't know where we were going. At least that is the conclusion Harvard scholar Oscar Handlin reached in a remarkable 1996 article called "The Unmarked Way."

> At some point, midway into the twentieth century, Europeans and Americans discovered that they had lost all sense of direction. Formerly, familiar markers along the way had guided their personal and social lives from birth to maturity to death. Now, disoriented, they no longer trusted the guideposts and groped in bewilderment toward an unimagined destination. Wandering in the dark, men and women in all Western societies, stumbling blindly along, strained unavailingly for glimpses of recognizable landmarks.[2]

Jeremiah could have said the same thing about his times. People had lost all sense of direction. They were disoriented. They groped in bewilderment and wandered in the dark. They needed a landmark. So Jeremiah gave them one:

> Stand by the roads, and look,
>   and ask for the ancient paths,
> where the good way is; and walk in it,
>   and find rest for your souls. (6:16)

This is a verse for people who have come to the crossroads and do not know which way to turn.

A Fork in the Road

The first thing to do is recognize the crossroads for what it is. Look around; get your bearings. You have come to a fork in the road.

The people of God often find themselves at the crossroads. The children of Israel were at a crossroads when they gathered at Shechem. Joshua, their general, was about to die, so he said:

> Now therefore fear the Lord and serve him in sincerity and in faithfulness. Put away the gods that your fathers served beyond the River and in Egypt, and serve the LORD. And if it is evil in your eyes to serve the LORD, choose this day whom you will serve, whether the gods your fathers served in the region beyond the River, or the gods of the Amorites in whose land you dwell. But as for me and my house, we will serve the LORD. (Joshua 24:14, 15)

The people of God were at a crossroads when Elijah confronted the prophets of Baal on Mount Carmel. It was the same crossroads, offering the same two choices—God's way or the highway. Elijah said, "How long will you go limping between two different opinions? If the LORD is God, follow him; but if Baal, then follow him" (1 Kings 18:21).

Western civilization now stands at the crossroads. We have started down the road to destruction, perhaps, but the way of life still stretches out before us. The ethical dilemmas we face show that we are at the crossroads. Will we cherish the lives of the innocent, or will we permit abortion on demand? Will we protect the lives of the defenseless, or will we allow involuntary euthanasia? Will we preserve the sanctity of marriage, or will we tolerate no-fault divorce and homosexual unions? Will we love the true and the beautiful, or will we gaze upon images of sex and violence? These are the questions a culture faces at the crossroads.

The evangelical church is also standing at the crossroads. Will we glorify God in our worship, or will we entertain ourselves? Will we bear witness to the Law of God and the grace of the gospel, or will we tone down our message so as not to offend anyone? Will we expound the eternal Word of God, or will we seek some new revelation? Will we defend the doctrine of justification by faith alone, or will we add works to grace? These are the questions a church faces when it stands at the crossroads.

Perhaps you are at a personal crossroads. Some Christians wonder what God wants them to do with their lives. Others contemplate a change of career, the pursuit of a new educational opportunity, the possibility of marriage, or a change of ministry within the church. Still others wrestle with deep spiritual questions, wondering who Jesus Christ is or if the Bible is really true.

The thing to do at such times is to recognize that you are standing at the crossroads. Two roads stretch before you. You can go in only one of two directions. Either you can keep going the way you have been going, or you can go down a different road altogether. Your destiny depends upon which road you take.

On the Beaten Track

The second step is to ask for directions. When a nation, a church, or an individual comes to a crossroads, it helps to have good road signs, good directions, or a good map. Jeremiah knew what kind of directions to get: "Ask for the ancient paths," he said. Ask "where the good way is" (6:16).

In a paved society it is hard to understand what Jeremiah means. For automobiles, newly paved roads are best, not old roads full of potholes. But in Jeremiah's day people liked to travel on ancient pathways. Pedestrians wanted to follow a well-established route. According to the old Latin maxim, *via trita via tuta*: "The worn way is the safe way." In the wilderness it is best to walk on a well-beaten path that has been trampled by many feet.

When Jeremiah asked for the ancient paths, he did not mean to suggest living in the past. He was not nostalgic. He did not propose "That old-time religion."

There is too much talk these days about the alleged Christian faith of the Founding Fathers of America. There is also overmuch talk about the glories of the Reformation. Some Christians pine away for some golden age of the historical church. But the Bible counsels against longing for the good old days. The philosopher warns, "Say not, 'Why were the former days better than these?'" (Ecclesiastes 7:10).

Jeremiah would have agreed with the philosopher. He did not tell God's people to live in the past. Instead he tells us to walk, here and now, according to the Word of God. The ancient path is the Biblical path. The good way is the way marked out in the Scriptures. According to God himself, the problem with the people of Jerusalem was that "They have not paid attention to my words; and as for my law, they have rejected it" (6:19). In other words, they had made a bad choice back at the crossroads. And the reason they made a bad choice was that they rejected God's Word.

The people of God did exactly the opposite of what Psalm 119 recommends. Psalm 119, the longest chapter in the Bible, is all about walking in the ancient way of God's Word. It starts out like this: "Blessed are those whose way is blameless, who walk in the law of the LORD!" (Psalm 119:1).

Staying on track in life means going down the Biblical path. The psalmist loved, read, meditated on, and prayed through God's Word. As he did all those things, he discovered that the Bible is like a smooth pathway for a difficult journey.

The psalmist often compares the Word of God to a pathway: "I will run in the way of your commandments when you enlarge my heart!" (v. 32). "Lead me in the path of your commandments, for I delight in it" (v. 35). "When I think on my ways, I turn my feet to your testimonies" (v. 59). "Through your precepts I get understanding; therefore I hate every false way" (v. 104). "Your word is a lamp to my feet and a light to my path" (v. 105). "Keep steady my steps according to your promise" (v. 133). Even in the very last verse of the psalm (v. 176), when the psalmist confesses that he has strayed like a lost sheep, the only reason he knows he has gone down the wrong road is that he has not forgotten God's commands.

The ancient path, the good way, is the Bible. Jeremiah's advice for people at the crossroads was to walk in the ancient path of Biblical faith.

There is another way to interpret the ancient path and the good way. Jeremiah may have been speaking not only about the Bible, but also about sound theology in the history of the church. Other Christians have walked down the ancient path of the Bible before us, and they can show us the way.

Christians can learn from the past without living in the past. The evangelical church of the twenty-first century will live in post-Christian times. It cannot repeat the experiences of the Early Church Fathers, the Reformers, the Puritans, or anyone else in church history. But wherever Christians have followed in the footsteps of Christ, their footsteps should be followed. This is one good reason to recite the ancient creeds of the church. They represent what all Christians everywhere have always believed about God the Father, God the Son, and God the Holy Spirit.

It is possible to trace a straight pathway from the prophets and apostles to Augustine of Hippo, to Martin Luther, to John Calvin, to the Puritans, to the defenders of evangelical faith in modern times. These are the theologians of the church who brought themselves under the authority of God's Word and testified to the sovereignty of God's grace in salvation. They maintained the glory of God as their chief end, the Scriptures of the Old and New Testaments as their only authority, and the righteousness of Christ received by faith as their only hope. Anyone who follows them as they follow Scripture has found the good way.

When the great evangelical theologian Charles Hodge (1797–1878) was named a full professor at Princeton Seminary in 1872, he testified that he was "not afraid to say that a new idea never originated in this Seminary."[3] Hodge did not mean that he could not think for himself; he was one of the leading intellects of his day. What he meant was that he wanted to be sound in his theology. He knew that sound theology does not go off in new directions. Hodge was not interested in being an innovator. He wanted to follow the ancient path, the good way.

Theological orthodoxy sounds old-fashioned. It seems out-of-date or even obsolete to some. But sound theology is like fine wine—it gets better with age. Jesus said, "No one after drinking old wine desires new, for he says, 'The old is good'" (Luke 5:39). For novelty, go to the church that follows the latest fad. But novelty is the enemy of orthodoxy. It is much better to go where the eternal Word of God is faithfully preached and freshly applied to contemporary culture and the living church.

He Is the Way

The ancient path, the good way, is the teaching of Scripture. It is orthodox theology. And it is also Jesus Christ. Those who seek the ancient path and the good way are seeking for Jesus Christ.

Jesus told his disciples he was going to his Father's house to prepare a place for them (John 14:1, 2). He promised he would come back to take them there (vv. 3, 4). He also told them they knew the pathway to the place where he was going (v. 4). But the disciples were confused. They were not quite sure what Jesus was talking about. Frankly, they *didn't* know the way.

They could sense they were standing at a crossroads, however, and they knew they needed better directions. "Thomas said to him, 'Lord, we do not know where you are going. How can we know the way?' Jesus said to him, 'I am the way, and the truth, and the life. No one comes to the Father except through me'" (vv. 5, 6).

Jesus Christ *is* the way. He is the ancient way and the good way. And he is the only way. Jesus is the only way to God, the only way to salvation, and the only way to eternal life.

Jesus Christ is also the peaceful way. There is one place in the New Testament where Jesus seems to quote from Jeremiah 6:16. Jeremiah promised rest for the soul. Jesus said: "Come to me, all who labor and are heavy laden, and I will give you rest. Take my yoke upon you, and learn from me, for I am gentle and lowly in heart, and you will find rest for your souls" (Matthew 11:28, 29). Those who walk in the ancient path and the good way find rest for their souls, which is exactly what people find when they come to Jesus Christ. He is the ancient, good, restful, and peaceful way. In Christ there is rest for the soul.

If you are standing at a crossroads—culturally, ecclesiastically, or personally—what you need is Biblical teaching, sound theology, and a personal relationship with Jesus Christ.

The Obstacle Course

What happens to those who go down the other road? In the rest of chapter 6 Jeremiah looks a little way down the other road. It seemed broad and easy, but it was a foolish route to take.

The state of Israel seemed to be at a crossroads in the spring of 1996 when a new Prime Minister was elected. Israelis were asked to choose between Shimon Peres, who offered peace, and Benjamin Netanyahu, who promised security. *Time* magazine had this to say about the importance of their choice: "Sometimes statesmen stumble blindly over an epochal crossroads they do not know is there. Others are given the chance to see the fork in the road ahead and decide deliberately which way to go. Folly, wrote historian Barbara Tuchman, is when leaders knowingly choose the wrong path."[4]

True, isn't it? Folly is when people knowingly choose the wrong path. Here is a historical example:

> Stand by the roads, and look,
>   and ask for the ancient paths,
> where the good way is; and walk in it,
>   and find rest for your souls.
> But they said, "We will not walk in it." (6:16)

This is one of those Biblical passages that causes one to scratch one's head and ask, "What were these people thinking?" The good and peaceful way was set before them, but they wanted nothing to do with it.

God placed Jerusalem at the crossroads. He put up road signs to show them which way to go. They were marked with a directional arrow and they read, "HERE, GO THIS WAY." God even handed them a road map in case they got lost, but they still insisted on taking the road not to be taken.

So God offered them even more help:

> I set watchmen over you, saying,
>   "Pay attention to the sound of the trumpet!"
> But they said, "We will not pay attention." (v. 17)

The watchmen were the prophets—like Isaiah and Jeremiah—who warned the people of Israel to leave their idols and return to God. But God's people did not listen, even when trumpets of prophecy were blaring in their ears.

So God summoned the nations and the earth itself into his cosmic jury box to be witnesses to their folly:

Therefore hear, O nations,
    and know, O congregation, what will happen to them.
Hear, O earth; behold, I am bringing disaster upon this people,
    the fruit of their devices,
because they have not paid attention to my words;
    and as for my law, they have rejected it.
        (vv. 18, 19; cf. Deuteronomy 30:19, 20)

God filed for divorce back in chapter 2. Here in chapter 6 he seems to render his final verdict. Disaster would befall God's people for refusing to walk in the good path.

Why did God's people go the wrong way? The next verse seems to give some insight into the nature of their sin:

What use to me is frankincense that comes from Sheba,
    or sweet cane from a distant land?
Your burnt offerings are not acceptable,
    nor your sacrifices pleasing to me. (v. 20)

Some commentators conclude that Jeremiah was opposed to the Old Testament system of temple sacrifices.[5] They see contradictions between the Torah's regulations for sacrifices and later criticisms of temple worship from the prophets. But Jeremiah was not speaking against the sacrifices themselves; he was only opposed to offering them with a wrong spirit.

The people of Jerusalem were very religious. They were becoming sophisticated, fashionable, up-to-date, and contemporary in their worship. Their services were lavish and ornate. No expense was spared. They imported exotic perfumes by camel—frankincense from Saudi Arabia and calamus from India—in order to spice up their worship. They were on an insatiable quest for the "latest thing." But their hearts had wandered far from God.

The ancient path is the simplicity of Word and Sacrament. The good way is simply the people of God meeting in the presence of God to pray, sing, break bread, and listen to the Word of God (see Acts 2:42–47). Whenever buildings, instruments, sermons, or fellowship are used to entertain or fascinate rather than to glorify God, worship becomes unacceptable. The people of Jerusalem thought Biblical worship was old-fashioned. They wanted to try something newfangled. Yet John Guest writes this epitaph on their religious experiment: "Ritual performance perfumed with imported incense will never hide the stench of moral disobedience."[6]

So the Lord threatened to turn their new road into an obstacle course:

Behold, I will lay before this people
    stumbling blocks against which they shall stumble;
fathers and sons together,
    neighbor and friend shall perish. (6:21)

It seemed like a good road at the beginning. It was wide and smooth. But the further they went, the narrower it became. The highway became a street. The street became a gravel road. The gravel road became a muddy track. Eventually, what started out as a Sunday drive turned into a steeplechase.

Some years ago I made a pilgrimage to Thomas Boston's church in the Scottish village of Ettrick. The longer I drove, the more difficult the road became, until I was dodging sheep on single-lane roads through the hills. This often happens when people get off the beaten track; there are obstacles in the road.

The obstacles Judah faced were formidable. Soldiers were on the march, renowned for their cruelty and armed to the teeth. Approaching like thunder, they would take no prisoners and show no mercy.

Thus says the LORD:

"Behold, a people is coming from the north country,
    a great nation is stirring from the farthest parts of the earth.
They lay hold on bow and javelin;
    they are cruel and have no mercy;
    the sound of them is like the roaring sea;
they ride on horses,
    set in array as a man for battle,
    against you, O daughter of Zion!" (vv. 22, 23)

Judah was no more than a girl—the "daughter of Zion." She was hardly a match for hardened military veterans. Even the scouting reports of the northern army were enough to paralyze her with fear.

We have heard the report of it;
    our hands fall helpless;
anguish has taken hold of us,
    pain as of a woman in labor.
Go not out into the field,
    nor walk on the road,

for the enemy has a sword;
  terror is on every side.
O daughter of my people, put on sackcloth,
  and roll in ashes;
make mourning as for an only son,
  most bitter lamentation,
for suddenly the destroyer
  will come upon us. (vv. 24–26)

Going down the wrong road brings the kind of grief usually reserved for the loss of "an only son."

It is much safer to stay at home. For those who refuse to go down the ancient path of the Bible and the good way of sound theology, even Jesus Christ becomes a stumbling block. The Apostle Paul called Jesus Christ a "stumbling stone" (Romans 9:32), "a stone of stumbling, and a rock of offense" (v. 33). If you refuse to walk in God's way, eventually the crucified and risen Christ will be your Judge, not your Savior.

If you have already gone down the wrong road, it is time to head back home. Somewhere the English apologist Gilbert Keith Chesterton (1874–1936) offered this sound advice for people who are off-track: "When you have lost your way quite hopelessly, the quickest thing is to go back along the road you know to the place from which you started. You may call it reaction, you may call it repetition, you may call it tiresome theory, but it is the quickest way out of the wood."

The prophet Jeremiah expressed the same idea in a single command: "Return" (3:12, 14). As you repent and obey, God will help you find your way to the ancient path and the good way.

From Crossroads to Crucibles

At the end of chapter 6, Jeremiah's theme shifts from crossroads to crucibles. It is not easy to see the connection, but verses 27–30 seem to show what happens when one tries to go down two roads at the same time.

These verses start with God adding "metallurgist" to Jeremiah's job description:

I have made you a tester of metals among my people,
  that you may know and test their ways. (v. 27)

Jeremiah had become an assayer, a tester of metals. The prophet seems to have known something about metallurgy, because these verses give an accurate description of ancient Near Eastern smelting practices.

God's people were like silver ore. There seemed to be some real silver in the rock, but it was mixed up with various impurities and alloys.

> They are all stubbornly rebellious,
>   going about with slanders;
> they are bronze and iron;
>   all of them act corruptly. (v. 28)

Bronze and iron were clinging to the silver.

Following God's instructions, Jeremiah took the ore and placed it in a crucible. He added lead to the compound to serve as a flux and then heated it all up in the fire. First the bellows stoked the fire, and then they sent a blast of air onto the compound. The blast was supposed to oxidize the lead so that all the impurities and alloys would bond with it. The rock, the bronze, and the iron would then be stripped away with the lead, leaving nothing behind but pure silver.

What actually happened in Jeremiah's test?

> The bellows blow fiercely;
>   the lead is consumed by the fire;
> in vain the refining goes on,
>   for the wicked are not removed. (v. 29)

The fire burned in the crucible, but the bronze of wickedness and the iron of godlessness were not refined. The silver thus proved to be spurious, and it was time to throw the ore on the scrap heap.

Jeremiah's talk of silver and iron had a spiritual point: "Rejected silver they are called, for the LORD has rejected them" (v. 30). God's people were supposed to be righteous, like pure silver. But even after they passed through the crucible of divine testing and felt the heat of divine judgment in the prophetic message, they proved to be nothing but dross, the slag of metallic waste.

Many Christians assume they can have Christ and the world at the same time. They want to mix the bronze of the devil and the iron of the world in with the pure silver of Christ. They think they can walk down the ancient path and the new highway at the same time. They end up mixing a little greed, pride, immorality, gluttony, idleness, worry, bitterness, and selfishness in with faith, hope, and love.

But all those little impurities add up. Derek Kidner gives this final lab report on Jeremiah's testing of metals: "It emerges that the people of Judah are not, so to speak, precious metal marred by some impurities, but base metal from which nothing of worth can be extracted."[7]

This is a solemn warning for everyone who stands at the crossroads and wonders which road to choose. The only safe thing to do is walk in the way of Christ alone. For someday Christ himself will come and cause everyone to pass through his crucible. "But who can endure the day of his coming, and who can stand when he appears? For he is like a refiner's fire. . . . He will sit as a refiner and purifier of silver" (Malachi 3:2, 3a).

10

What the Church Needs Now Is Reformation!

JEREMIAH 7:1–15

IN JANUARY 1519 something shocking happened at the Great Minster in Zurich. Everyone in the city was talking about it. One man said he was so excited he felt as if someone had grabbed him by his hair and lifted him out of his pew.

What was the cause of all this commotion? Simply this: Ulrich Zwingli (1484–1531), the new pastor of the church, was preaching the Word of God. At the first service in January he opened his Bible to Matthew 1 and began to preach from the Scriptures. At the next service he picked up where he left off in the Gospel of Matthew and kept preaching. He did the same thing at the third service and thereafter, verse by verse, chapter by chapter, book by book, right through the New Testament.

Then Zwingli started preaching through the Old Testament. Amazing! Unheard of! Soon men, women, and children came from all over Zurich to hear the minister explain the Bible in words they could understand.

Zwingli's systematic Bible exposition was the beginning of the Reformation in Switzerland. To this day there is an inscription over the portal of that church that reads, "The Reformation of Huldrych Zwingli began here on January 1, 1519." Reformation begins with preaching God's Word!

The Temple Sermon

Long before Ulrich Zwingli, Martin Luther, or John Calvin, there was a reformer named Jeremiah. If that great prophet were alive in these post-Christian times, he would do what the Protestant Reformers did: He would preach God's

Word. He would tell the evangelical church to mend its ways. He would teach that religious observance without moral obedience cannot save. He would say that what the church needs now is reformation.

Jeremiah 7 contains one of the great reformation sermons in the history of God's people. It is often called Jeremiah's Temple Sermon because God commanded him to preach it at the temple. "The word that came to Jeremiah from the LORD: 'Stand in the gate of the LORD's house, and proclaim there this word, and say, Hear the word of the LORD, all you men of Judah who enter these gates to worship the LORD'" (vv. 1, 2).

One can imagine Jeremiah standing at one of the temple gates, watching the people of Israel come thronging up the temple steps to worship. Since his message was delivered to all the people, it was most likely preached during one of the great religious festivals, such as Passover or the Feast of Tabernacles, when the whole nation came to Jerusalem to worship. The Lord wanted the Temple Sermon to get the widest possible hearing.

One thing that made the Temple Sermon great was that it was preached at a moment of historical destiny. The sermon is reprinted in chapter 26, with this additional detail: "In the beginning of the reign of Jehoiakim the son of Josiah, king of Judah, this word came from the LORD" (26:1).

Jeremiah preached his courageous sermon, therefore, at a time of national crisis. The people of Judah had lost hope in the power of political solutions to solve their problems. "In his [Josiah's] days Pharaoh Neco king of Egypt went up to the king of Assyria to the river Euphrates. King Josiah went to meet him, and Pharaoh Neco killed him at Megiddo, as soon as he saw him" (2 Kings 23:29). Josiah, the great reforming king of Judah, was dead.

After the light of Josiah's reformation, Judah slipped back into spiritual darkness. Josiah's son Jehoahaz only reigned in Jerusalem for three months before Pharaoh Neco carried him off to Egypt, where he died (2 Kings 23:31–34). Jehoiakim took the throne, but how long would he last? Judah was at another crossroads—politically and spiritually—when Jeremiah mounted the temple steps to preach.

His message was very simple. "Thus says the LORD of hosts, the God of Israel: Amend your ways and your deeds, and I will let you dwell in this place" (7:3). However simple Jeremiah's message may have been, popular it was not!

> And when Jeremiah had finished speaking all that the LORD had commanded him to speak to all the people, then the priests and the prophets and all the people laid hold of him, saying, "You shall die! Why have

you prophesied in the name of the LORD, saying, 'This house shall be like Shiloh, and this city shall be desolate, without inhabitant'?" . . . Then the priests and the prophets said to the officials and to all the people, "This man deserves the sentence of death, because he has prophesied against this city, as you have heard with your own ears." (26:8, 9, 11)

The religious establishment wanted to wring Jeremiah's neck. This often happens to reformers. The same thing happened to Martin Luther (1483–1546) when he started to preach his reformation sermons. The Pope attacked Luther's preaching and called him a wild boar, a serpent, and a "pestiferous virus."[1]

A False Hope

What was so pestiferous about Jeremiah's message?

The content of his Temple Sermon can be summarized in this way: Religious observance without moral obedience cannot save. John Calvin put it like this: "Sacrifices are of no importance or value before God, unless those who offer them wholly devote themselves to God with a sincere heart."[2] It can be stated even more briefly: Those who seek justification without sanctification need reformation.

The first thing to understand about Jeremiah's message is that it was delivered to a religiously observant people. Jeremiah was preaching to people who were on their way to the temple to offer sacrifices to God. The people he told to mend their ways were devout. They were "churchgoers." They wore their Passover best and had their scrolls tucked under their arms.

Reformation always begins with the people of God. Reformation is something that starts in the church. It begins when God's own people are convicted of their sins and turn to God with new repentance, trust in God with new faith, and walk with God in new obedience. That kind of spiritual reformation always has an influence on the city, the society, or the civilization. But it always starts in the hearts of God's people.

The people of Judah were in desperate need of reformation because they had put their trust in the outward trappings of religion. Their approach to theology—which could be called their "Temple Theology"—can be summarized as follows: "This is the temple of the LORD, the temple of the LORD, the temple of the LORD" (7:4b). Obviously, it was not the most complicated theology in the world. The people had taken their faith in the living God and reduced it to faith in a building. They knew enough not to put their trust in kings. After all, they had watched Josiah die in battle at Megiddo, and they had seen Jehoahaz dragged down to Egypt. But they still believed that the temple in Jerusalem would keep them safe. They were putting their confidence in outward religion.

They were half right, which is the way false theology usually works. Most heresies are half made up of truth. It is the other half one has to worry about. In this case the people knew God had chosen Jerusalem to be his holy city. They knew God promised he would never abandon his dwelling place. They knew he would defend and save his city (Isaiah 37:35). Each year when they went up to worship at the temple in Jerusalem, they sang:

> For the LORD has chosen Zion;
> he has desired it for his dwelling place:
> "This is my resting place forever;
> here I will dwell, for I have desired it." (Psalm 132:13, 14)

The problem was that God's people thought God's promise about the temple gave them the freedom to be immoral. The temple had become a superstition. They assumed that as long they fulfilled their religious obligations, they could do whatever they wanted with the rest of their lives.

Their Temple Theology had nothing to say about holy living. They assumed God would never judge them for their sins, which is why Jeremiah tried to reason with them: "Behold, you trust in deceptive words to no avail" (v. 8). They wanted faith without practice. They wanted covenant blessing without covenant obedience. They wanted to be justified without being sanctified.

What they were really doing was presuming upon divine election. They were assuming that because they were God's chosen people, living in God's chosen city, worshiping in God's chosen temple, no harm could ever come to them. But they were living in sin, which means they had never truly understood the marvel of God's grace.

That is a strong warning for anyone who has experienced God's sovereign grace, yet continues to live in sin. God has saved you *from* sin, not *for* sin. If you are unrepentant about lust, bitterness, greed, anxiety, or any sin whatsoever, you are presuming upon God's grace. Know this: You cannot separate justification (God's *declaring* you righteous) from sanctification (God's *making* you righteous). If you have done so, what you need is reformation.

Jeremiah's message is also a strong warning to everyone who seeks to be justified before God by religious observance. Some put their trust in church attendance and say, "I go to church, I go to church, I go to church." Some put their trust in religious experience and say, "I'm born again, born again, born again." Some put their trust in a sacrament and say, "I've been baptized, baptized, baptized." Some put their trust in church affiliation and say, "I belong to an evangelical church, evangelical church, evangelical church." Others put their trust in religious duties and say, "I have daily devotions, daily devotions, daily devotions." Still others put their trust in some theological principle separated from a personal relationship with Jesus Christ. They say, "I believe in the doctrines of grace, doctrines of grace, doctrines of grace."

All these things are good in themselves. That is what is so dangerous about the temptation to put confidence in outward religion. There was absolutely nothing wrong with the temple in Jerusalem. The people of God were *supposed* to go there to worship. Nor is there anything wrong with going to church, being born again, being baptized, becoming a member of a particular church, having daily devotions, or believing the doctrines of grace. Not only is there nothing wrong with these things, all of them are positively necessary for growing in the Christian faith.

But do not put your trust in these things. Do not trust church attendance, a conversion experience, a sacrament, church membership, or spiritual exercises for salvation. Instead, like the Apostle Paul, "worship by the Spirit of God and glory in Christ Jesus and put no confidence in the flesh" (Philippians 3:3). Trust in the righteousness that comes from God and is by faith in Jesus Christ (Philippians 3:9). Trust in Christ *alone* for salvation. He is all our hope and trust.

A Life of Sin

That was half the problem. God's people were trusting in superficial religiosity to save them. What about the other half?

Remember the message of Jeremiah's Temple Sermon: Religious observance without moral obedience cannot save. The other half of the problem was that God's people were not obedient. They were living sinful lives. They did not realize that moral integrity was more important to God than showing up at a house of worship on the Sabbath.

They said to God, "The temple, the temple, the temple." But God said to them "if, if, if": "If you truly amend your ways and your deeds, if you truly execute justice one with another, if you do not oppress the sojourner, the fatherless, or the widow, or shed innocent blood in this place, and if you do not go after other gods to your own harm, then I will let you dwell in this place, in the land that I gave of old to your fathers forever" (7:5–7).

This is a catalog of the sins of God's people. A close look shows that they violated virtually every one of the Ten Commandments (Exodus 20:1–17). The first commandment says to have no other gods before God. Well, they followed other gods (7:9). The second commandment says not to make idols, but the people of Judah burned incense to Baal (also v. 9). The third commandment says not to take the name of the Lord in vain, but they profaned the house that bore God's name (v. 10). The fourth commandment says to honor the Sabbath, but they gave false worship on the day of worship. They violated all the commandments that deal with one's relationship to God.

What about the commandments that govern human relationships? The fifth commandment gives honor to parents, but the people neglected their social responsibilities to the fatherless and the widow (v. 6). Commandments six through nine say, "You shall not murder . . . commit adultery . . . steal . . . bear false witness." All these sins are mentioned in verse 9: "Will you steal, murder, commit adultery, swear falsely, make offerings to Baal, and go after other gods that you have not known?" Run a finger down the list: Judah rejected every basic principle of God's Law.

Although the people broke all the commandments, Jeremiah had a special concern for social justice. God wanted his nation to be a caring society, but his people did not deal justly with one another. They did not take care of the disadvantaged. To learn how compassionate a society is, and how just, find out what happens to the underclass. How orphans, immigrants, and single-parent families are treated indicates how godly a society is.

A church can be tested using the same standard. How active is its concern for the homeless, the elderly, and the disabled, or for broken families? What Jeremiah saw when he walked around Jerusalem was that people were not very concerned.

It would be bad enough to commit all those sins, but what God's people did was even worse. They violated all God's commandments, and then they went to worship in God's house as if they had done nothing wrong. They thought reformation had to do with Sabbath worship. They did not understand that reformation has to do with all of life. They thought they could spend six days breaking all God's commandments as long as they spent one day singing Scripture songs and taking sermon notes. They thought they could divorce worship from daily life.

Here is what God wants to know: How could they do all these things and "Then come and stand before me in this house, which is called by my name, and say, 'We are delivered!'—only to go on doing all these abominations?" (v. 10). God's people used God's temple as a safe house. They went out on crime sprees and then went back and used the temple for their hideout. They were wolves in sheep's clothing.

That is why the Lord says, "Has this house, which is called by my name, become a den of robbers in your eyes?" (v. 11a). Jesus said the same thing when he went to the temple. In his day the people of Jerusalem used the temple courts as a place to do shady business. So Jesus threw over the tables of the money changers. "He said to them, 'It is written, "My house shall be called a house of prayer," but you make it a den of robbers'" (Matthew 21:13).

The people of Judah operated on the assumption that God neither saw nor cared what they did during the week. They thought they could fool God by showing up for worship on the Sabbath and on the major holy days, and then go out and do whatever they wanted the rest of the time. They wanted to be justified without being sanctified.

Well, they say you can fool some of the people some of the time, but God is no fool. Ever. His people could run back to their den of thieves, but they could not hide, because God had them under constant surveillance: "Behold, I myself have seen it, declares the LORD" (7:11b). God is omniscient. He knows all things, which includes knowing when people come into his house with dirty shoes.

A History Lesson

Jeremiah's reformation message was that religious observance without moral obedience cannot save. But what happens if a church or a nation refuses to mend its ways?

Jeremiah often answered such questions. He explained what happens to those who refuse to follow God. In this case he offered to take God's people on a historical field trip: "[The LORD said] Go now to my place that was in Shiloh, where I made my name dwell at first, and see what I did to it because of the evil of my people Israel" (v. 12).

What was there to see at Shiloh? Not much. Hardly enough even to constitute a tourist trap. Shiloh was where the temple used to be, where God first made his dwelling in Israel. Many years before, "The whole congregation of the people of Israel assembled at Shiloh and set up the tent of meeting there" (Joshua 18:1). The Tent of Meeting was where the ark of the covenant was located, the ark that contained the earthly presence of Almighty God. The ark of God's presence stayed at Shiloh for many years. When Samuel went to serve Eli at the temple, for example, he did not go to Jerusalem, but to Shiloh (1 Samuel 1:3).

The ark of the covenant did not remain in Shiloh, however, because the people did not obey God. They carted the ark off to the battlefield to use it as a lucky charm against the Philistines. It was captured in battle, only to be returned when the Philistines discovered how dangerous it is to live in God's presence, as embodied in the ark (1 Samuel 4—6). The ark was taken first to Beth Shemesh and then to Kiriath Jearim, where David later found it and brought it up to Jerusalem (2 Samuel 6:2).

If God's people went to Shiloh in Jeremiah's day, they would not find God or God's living presence, but only a pile of rubble. The archaeological evidence shows that Shiloh was destroyed twice over—once by the Philistines and once when the Assyrians carried the northern tribes into captivity.[3]

When Jeremiah told the people to go to Shiloh, he was telling them to go to the place where God is not. Shiloh is the place where God once was and is no longer. As Asaph wrote:

> For they provoked him to anger with their high places;
>   they moved him to jealousy with their idols.
> When God heard, he was full of wrath,
>   and he utterly rejected Israel.
> He forsook his dwelling at Shiloh,
>   the tent where he dwelt among mankind. (Psalm 78:58–60)

Shiloh thus represents the absence and abandonment of God along with the end of his worship.

The people of Jerusalem thought such a disaster would never happen to them. "We have the temple of the LORD, the temple of the LORD, the temple of the LORD," they said. They knew what had happened to Shiloh, but they did not realize it could happen to them as well. They knew it had happened to the liberals, but they did not think it could ever happen to conservatives. They remembered all the time and energy they'd invested in repairing the temple—all the fund-raising they did, all the stone they cut, all the timber they bought (2 Kings 22:3–7)—and they could not imagine the temple ever being destroyed.

But they were wrong, for they had put their confidence in the outward trappings of religion rather than in a living relationship with God himself. "And now, because you have done all these things, declares the LORD, and when I spoke to you persistently you did not listen, and when I called you, you did not answer, therefore I will do to the house that is called by my name, and in which you trust, and to the place that I gave to you and to your fathers, as I did to Shiloh. And I will cast you out of my sight, as I cast out all your kinsmen, all the offspring of Ephraim" (7:13–15). Religious observance without moral obedience cannot save.

The ruins of Shiloh stood as a warning in Jeremiah's day, and also in ours. There are Shilohs all around the post-Christian West.

There is a Shiloh in Cape May, New Jersey. The Admiral, an immense Christian conference center, used to dominate the Cape May skyline. But the Admiral has been destroyed, with the property subdivided into housing lots.

There are dozens of Shilohs in Philadelphia. There is a Shiloh at 15th and Locust, where the old First Presbyterian Church used to stand. Now it is a parking garage. Another Presbyterian church building still stands at 34th and Chestnut. It is not a church anymore—it has been turned into a Creative Motions Dance Studio.

There is a Shiloh at 22nd and Walnut, where an Episcopal church has been torn down and replaced by a minimart. The steeple of the old church is visible only in the mural on the wall next to the store. The church has become a shadow in the city, nothing more than a reflection in a painted window on an urban wall.

There are Shilohs all around, like so many skeletons on the pilgrim road. They are places where God used to be worshiped in Spirit and in truth. They are places where praise was given to God in the name of Jesus Christ. They are places where the counsel of God was preached. But they are all places where God is worshiped no longer.

The Shilohs on the post-Christian landscape stand as warnings. They are reminders that the living God does not dwell in buildings made by human hands (Acts 17:24). No building, no church, no congregation has a permanent hold on his presence. The perseverance of God's people in any place depends upon God's grace. There is nothing sacred about buildings. Church structures provide no protection on the day of judgment.

One place where the church shows little danger of becoming a Shiloh is in the Chinese city of Wenzhou. Christians there know the security of God's presence, with or without a church building. The Chinese government, of course, takes a dim view of religious devotion. So in the mid–1990s they commandeered a church building in Wenzhou and appointed one of their own officials to "pastor" the church. Talk about letting a wolf into the sheepfold!

The church had a large congregation, more than one thousand members in all. They had also built their church building with their own hands. Yet the government told them either to accept the new "pastor" or to leave the premises. The pastoral council decided to leave the church building with as many members as were willing to go. Within two days they divided the congregation into dozens of house churches. They needed dozens because nearly one thousand members were willing to leave their building behind.

What they wanted, more than anything else, was the living presence of God in their worship. They did not say "Wenzhou Church, Wenzhou Church, Wenzhou Church." They had placed their confidence not in the outward trappings of Christianity, but in Jesus Christ himself. They were unwilling to settle for anything less than the pure worship of God and the unhindered presentation of the gospel. As long as they remain faithful to God, they will never become a Shiloh.

This is an example for the Western church, which has fallen on post-Christian times. What the church needs now is not more building programs or new methods of church growth. What the church needs now is reformation.

11

The Family That
Worships Together

JEREMIAH 7:16–29

JEREMIAH'S TEMPLE SERMON was a reformation classic. But nobody listened. "So you shall speak all these words to them, but they will not listen to you. You shall call to them, but they will not answer you. And you shall say to them, 'This is the nation that did not obey the voice of the LORD their God, and did not accept discipline'" (7:27, 28a).

To quote baseball great Yogi Berra, it was like "déja vu all over again." Israel was having another hearing problem. God's people had a long history of not listening. They never listened.

> But they did not obey or incline their ear, but walked in their own counsels and the stubbornness of their evil hearts, and went backward and not forward. From the day that your fathers came out of the land of Egypt to this day, I have persistently sent all my servants the prophets to them, day after day. Yet they did not listen to me or incline their ear, but stiffened their neck. They did worse than their fathers. (vv. 24–26)

Sometimes a man of God preaches and nobody listens. It happened to the prophet Isaiah. The Lord made the heart of his people callous; he made their ears dull and closed their eyes (Isaiah 6:9, 10). It even happened to Jesus Christ. He spoke to the people in parables. Though seeing, they did not see; though hearing, they did not hear or understand (Matthew 13:11–15).

And it happened to Jeremiah. Jeremiah preached, but nobody listened. He gave Israel his best shot. He preached repentance as well as he knew how to preach it, but the people did not listen. They were so busy with their little rituals that their hearts were far from God. What should Jeremiah do next?

Intercession Prohibited

Surely Jeremiah should pray. That is what Moses did. When Moses came down from Mount Sinai with the Ten Commandments he found the people of God worshiping a golden calf. He told them:

> You have sinned a great sin. And now I will go up to the LORD; perhaps I can make atonement for your sin." So Moses returned to the LORD and said, "Alas, this people has sinned a great sin. They have made for themselves gods of gold. But now, if you will forgive their sin—but if not, please blot me out of your book that you have written. (Exodus 32:30–32)

David prayed too. When the judgment of God was about to fall upon Israel because he had numbered the fighting men, David said to God, "It is I who have sinned and done great evil. But these sheep, what have they done? Please let your hand, O LORD my God, be against me and against my father's house. But do not let the plague be on your people" (1 Chronicles 21:17).

Ezra the priest did the same thing. When he heard that the people of God had intermarried with pagans, he tore his tunic and cloak, pulled out his hair, and went into mourning. After his self-abasement he fell on his knees, spread his hands out to God, and prayed, "O my God, I am ashamed and blush to lift my face to you, my God, for our iniquities have risen higher than our heads, and our guilt has mounted up to the heavens" (Ezra 9:6).

The first job of a spiritual leader is to pray for the people of God. When the people sinned, the prophets, priests, and kings were to intercede for their salvation. Surely Jeremiah should pray!

But God did not tell Jeremiah to pray. In fact, he specifically told him *not* to pray. "As for you, do not pray for this people, or lift up a cry or prayer for them, and do not intercede with me, for I will not hear you" (7:16). The command could hardly be clearer. God spelled it out for Jeremiah five different ways: "Do not pray for this people. Do not offer a plea for them. Do not make a petition for them. Do not plead with me. I will not listen to you."

Nor is this the only time God gave Jeremiah this instruction. "Therefore do not pray for this people, or lift up a cry or prayer on their behalf, for I will not listen when they call to me in the time of their trouble" (11:14). "Do not pray for the welfare of this people" (14:11). There can be no mistake. God told Jeremiah not to pray. But why?

God's prohibition of intercession is hard to understand. In order to make sense of it, several things need to be kept in mind. First, God knew one or two things that Jeremiah did not know. He knew that the people of Israel would neither listen to the prophet's message nor repent. Furthermore, he knew he would certainly send unquenchable judgment upon Israel (7:20).

Once God's intention was to do all that had been revealed to Jeremiah, it would have been wrong for the prophet to pray for deliverance. To do so would have been to pray against the purposes of God. God is glorified by his justice. Whenever he judges sin, it is wrong to pray against his judgment. Praying for the glory of God to come includes accepting his justice.

Remember also that there will be grace beyond judgment for the people of God. Jeremiah was called to build as well as to tear down. Eventually he would even proclaim a new covenant. God had promised the ultimate deliverance of his people. But they must pass through the crucible of judgment before they can shine like silver. There is no other way for them to be refined and purified but to pass through punishment. Jeremiah was not allowed to pray for a temporary deliverance that would fall short of full salvation.

The same principle applies to some of our own prayers. We are often aware of friends and family members who are in bondage to sin. But we cannot rescue them. Only God can do that, and sometimes he allows people to hit rock bottom in their sin so that they have nowhere else to turn but back to him for salvation.

Some of these considerations help explain God's hard instruction for Jeremiah. But the most important thing to remember is that God's command to Jeremiah for Jeremiah's times is not his command to us for our times. Often we are impressed with the similarities between the way God's grace works in the Old and New Testaments. But other times we are confronted with the difference between the old covenant and the new, between before Christ and after. This is one of those times.

We live in gospel times. We live in the age of the risen Christ. One of the biggest differences between living then and living now is that we have a Priest who prays incessantly for our salvation. Jesus "holds his priesthood permanently, because he continues forever. Consequently, he is able to save to the uttermost those who draw near to God through him, since he always lives to make intercession for them" (Hebrews 7:24, 25). The writer to the Hebrews is emphatic: Jesus Christ always prays, and he *completely* saves his people.

Because Jesus always prays, we can always pray. No sinner is beyond the reach of God's grace, and thus no sinner is beyond the need for our prayers. When the Apostle Paul wrote to young Timothy, he gave him these instructions for prayer:

> First of all, then, I urge that supplications, prayers, intercessions, and thanksgivings be made for all people. . . . This is good, and it is pleasing in the sight of God our Savior, who desires all people to be saved and to come to the knowledge of the truth. For there is one God, and there is one mediator between God and men, the man Christ Jesus, who gave himself as a ransom for all. (1 Timothy 2:1, 3–6a)

God desires all kinds of men and women to be saved. So he instructs us to pray for the salvation of all kinds of men and women. No boundary is set to limit our prayers for the salvation of the lost.

The Hidden Life of the Home

Why were Jeremiah's people beyond prayer? Why were they so far gone? Why were they beyond the hope of redemption? It was because of a collapse of family values. The people of God were not worshiping God in their homes.

In the middle of the nineteenth century, a Swedish visitor came to visit the homes of the United States. Her name was Frederika Bremer (1801–1865), and she traveled widely, visiting such notables as Ralph Waldo Emerson, Henry Wadsworth Longfellow, and Washington Irving. Bremer explained her purpose, saying, "I came hither . . . in particular, to study the women and the homes of the New World, and from the threshold of the home to obtain a view of the future of humanity, because, as the river is born from the springs of heaven, so is the life and fate of a people born from the hidden life of the home."[1]

Bremer was right. The life and fate of a people is born from "The hidden life of the home." That is why God took Jeremiah by the hand and led him to the threshold of the homes of Jerusalem. "Do you not see what they are doing in the cities of Judah and in the streets of Jerusalem?" (v. 17). In other words, "Just look what they are doing!" What Jeremiah saw was this: "The children gather wood, the fathers kindle fire, and the women knead dough, to make cakes for the queen of heaven. And they pour out drink offerings to other gods, to provoke me to anger" (v. 18).

It seemed to be a model of family harmony. It almost sounds like the Cleavers having a Labor Day cookout. The kids run around to gather kindling. Dad builds the fire just the way he always builds it. And Mom, of course, is doing the cooking. She mixes the batter and is about to get out some pans to bake her cakes. Later Jeremiah provides their secret recipe: "When we made offerings to the queen of heaven and poured out drink offerings to her, was it without our husbands' approval that we made cakes for her bearing her image and poured out drink offerings to her?" (44:19). These cakes would be imprinted with or shaped into the form of a woman. Every holiday weekend the people of Jerusalem spent quality family time together.

But notice what is wrong with this picture. While these families were drawing closer together, they were moving farther away from God. The women were turning pagan religion into a cottage industry.

Scholars are not completely agreed about the identity of this "queen of heaven." Perhaps she was the Assyrian goddess Anat. Perhaps she was the Canaanite goddess Asherah (cf. 2 Kings 21:1–7; 23:4–16), called Ishtar by the Persians, from whom we get the word *Easter*. Both of these pagan goddesses were associated with the planet Venus. In any case, in the hidden life of the home the people of Israel were trying to match the Lord God up with a spiritual mistress.

Such idol worship made God angry. "Behold, my anger and my wrath will be poured out on this place, upon man and beast, upon the trees of the field and the fruit of the ground; it will burn and not be quenched" (7:20).

God's main point is not that he will punish you when you worship idols, but that you are punishing *yourself* when you worship them. "Is it I whom they provoke? declares the Lord. Is it not themselves, to their own shame?" (v. 19). Remember, false gods always abuse their worshipers. Satan wants a piece of your soul, or your body, or both. He lusts after you and has an infernal plan for your life.

When it came to worship in Jerusalem, there was trouble at home. But that is not where the trouble ended. The families left their homes and went to worship in God's house, where burnt offerings were usually offered by households.[2] "Thus says the Lord of hosts, the God of Israel: 'Add your burnt offerings to your sacrifices, and eat the flesh" (v. 21). That was a shocking thing for God to say. The burnt offering was a crucial sacrifice. Derek Kidner points out that it was the Israelite's "highest bid" for atonement, his best bet for salvation from sin.[3] The burnt offering was not to be eaten at all. Like the bull Elijah offered on Mount Carmel (1 Kings 18:38), it was supposed to be wholly devoted to the Lord.

Yet God told them that their burnt offerings meant nothing to him. He was saying something like this: "Look, if you're going to worship like this, save yourself the trouble. If you're going to treat me this badly, you might as well just save the meat and make yourself some barbecue." It would be like God telling us to keep our tithes and offerings so we can get a burger after the service.

Why was God so upset? It is not hard to understand: "For in the day that I brought them out of the land of Egypt, I did not speak to your fathers or command them concerning burnt offerings and sacrifices. But this command I gave them: 'Obey my voice, and I will be your God, and you shall be my people. And walk in all the way that I command you, that it may be well with you'" (7:22, 23).

Some scholars conclude from this passage that Jeremiah was calling for an end to Old Testament sacrifices. Far from it. Rather, like many other prophets (cf. Isaiah 1:10–17; Amos 5:21–25; Micah 6:1–8), he was reminding God's people that God wants their obedience as well as their worship. It was not wrong for them to sacrifice, but their sacrifices were in vain because they were not pursuing holiness. "I desire steadfast love and not sacrifice," the Lord said through the prophet Hosea (6:6). But it was never an either/or proposition. God wants obedience *and* sacrifice.

To make his point, Jeremiah used a historical example. When God saved his people out of Egypt, he did not just give them rules and regulations for sacrifices. The first thing he gave them—once he had saved them—was the Ten Commandments. Obedience to command was at the heart of the covenant, the relationship in which God belonged to his people and his people belonged to him.

Apparently the people of Jerusalem were making little or no attempt to be God's people. They did not do justice or love mercy or walk humbly with their God (cf. Micah 6:8). If one wanted to take all the sins of Israel and reduce them to one spiritual failing, it was the loss of truth: "Truth has perished; it is cut off from their lips" (7:28b). There was no truth in family worship, for the people worshiped false goddesses rather than the one true God. Nor was there truth in public worship. The people were just giving him lip service, which is what people do when they call Jesus Savior but do not live for him as Lord.

Back to Basics

Jeremiah's indictment was meant to fill his people with sadness. It was followed by a strange set of instructions: "Cut off your hair and cast it away; raise a lamentation on the bare heights, for the LORD has rejected and forsaken the generation of his wrath" (v. 29). In Biblical times, shaving one's head was a sign of sorrow and repentance. It was the only suitable response to the loss of truth.

"Truth has perished; it is cut off from their lips." Jeremiah's indictment would make a suitable epitaph for our own post-Christian culture. Truth has vanished from our homes and from the lips of our preachers. One writer who has taken up the lament is Os Guinness:

Contemporary evangelicals are no longer people of truth. . . . A solid sense of truth is foundering in America at large. Vaporized by critical theories, obscured by clouds of euphemism and jargon, outpaced by humor and hype, overlooked for style and image, and eroded by advertising, truth in America is anything but marching on.

With magnificent exceptions, evangelicals reflect this truth decay and reinforce it for their own variety of reasons for discounting theology. Repelled by "seminary theology" that is specialized, professionalized, and dry, evangelicals are attracted by movements that have replaced theology with emphases that are relational, therapeutic, charismatic, and managerial (as in church growth). Whatever their virtues, none of these emphases gives truth and theology the place they require in the life and thought of a true disciple.[4]

Guinness is right. We are not people of the truth, and we do not live among people of the truth (cf. Isaiah 6:5). We have truth decay in the same places Jeremiah could detect it.

Start with goddess worship. Goddess worship is all around us. It can be seen in the veneration of Mother Earth and the rise of witchcraft. It can be seen in the fascination of the New Age movement with ancient goddesses. It can be seen wherever liberal Protestants pray to Sophia. It can even be seen at Toys-R-Us®, where Barbie doll serves as the goddess of the plastic age. Barbie exemplifies an unrealistic ideal of feminine beauty and an immoral attachment to material possessions. Goddess worship can be seen wherever supermodels are found—on television and billboards, in newspapers and magazines.

There is goddess worship in the Roman Catholic religion, where Mary is sometimes given the title "The Queen of Heaven." This title sets off alarm bells for anyone who knows the book of Jeremiah. There is no queen in Heaven, only a King. But the Catholic Church persists in its devotion to Mary. During his 1996 visit to Guatemala, Pope John Paul II said, "All those who have at some time prayed to the Most Holy Virgin, even though they may have strayed from the Catholic church, conserve in their hearts an ember of faith which can be revived. The Virgin awaits them with maternal arms open wide."[5]

The official Catholic dogma that makes Mary effectively a mediatrix of salvation remains unchanged. The veneration of the Virgin Mary in Roman Catholicism and Eastern Orthodoxy is not a harmless, quirky addition to the gospel. Rather, it is a denial of the sufficiency of Jesus Christ. Mary, the mother of Jesus, played a role in the history of redemption. She gave birth to the incarnate Son of God. But she has no role to play in personal salvation. To pray to her is to treat her like a goddess. It is merely a baptized paganism.

We see goddess worship at work in feminism, both inside and outside the church. It is one thing to recover the truth that women are made in the image of God. It is another thing to make a goddess in the image of woman. Katherine Kersten has written a compelling critique of feminism called "How the Feminist Establishment Hurts Women." She writes:

> The metamorphosis of feminism from a campaign for equal rights to an existential crusade has had a curious result. Too often, contemporary feminism holds itself out as a source of ultimate meaning for women. It claims to answer the fundamental theological question: "Why do we suffer?" For many, it has become a religion.[6]

The religious nature of feminism is freely acknowledged by its leaders. Betty Friedan describes the feminist movement as a "religion." Vivian Gornick speaks of her "conversion" to feminism. Susan Faludi describes it as "bringing salvation in the promised land." According to Naomi Goldenberg, author of *Changing of the Gods*, "The feminist movement in Western culture is engaged in the slow execution of Christ and Yahweh. . . . It is likely that as we watch Christ and Yahweh tumble to the ground, we will completely outgrow the need for an external God."[7]

The frightening thing about all of this is that false goddesses always abuse their worshipers. Our nation is paying the price for its various forms of goddess worship. It is paying the price in broken relationships between men and women, in the decline of marriage and the rise of divorce, in schisms in the church over the role of women, in eating disorders, in violence against women, and in a pervasive warping of normal male-female relations.

Then add the evils of abortion. Where feminism becomes a religion, child sacrifice is its rite of atonement. The belief that lies behind the so-called right to choose is that someone else may have to die in order to keep me happy. It is not surprising that Jeremiah's Temple Sermon ends with a cry against infanticide (7:30—8:3). There is a straight path from the adoration of the Queen of Heaven to the abomination of the Valley of Slaughter.

Where else has truth perished? It has vanished from the hidden life of our homes. The summer 1996 issue of *The American Scholar* featured a lament over the loss of direction in Western culture. The article, entitled "The Unmarked Way," lamented the way the "profound transformation of family" in the twentieth century has slackened our religious ties:

> *The family that prays together stays together* had been the old-time slogan. But now families neither stayed together nor prayed together, as the soaring number of single-parent households testified. Drastic changes in the

role of women and in birth control effaced the image of the home as citadel of faith and replaced it with the image of home as the location of the VCR.[8]

Families are made to worship together. They must worship. They cannot help but worship. A family may worship the living God. If not, they may worship their VCR, or television sitcoms, or Harley-Davidson motorcycles, or the Washington Redskins, or junk food, or music and art, or anger, or violence, or deception. A family may worship a thousand gods and goddesses. But it must worship.

That is why it is so absolutely necessary for us to worship God in our homes. Do you want to see reformation come to America and revival to the church? It starts in the hidden life of the home. It starts in your apartment, where you consecrate your living space to God by beginning every day with prayer and Bible reading. It starts in your dorm room, where you make a commitment to spend an hour in prayer with your roommate every week.

If you live with a family, it starts wherever you live. There are so many different ways to foster the spiritual life of your family that I hesitate to suggest any one way in particular. My own family has adopted different practices at different times. In the morning before school we read and discuss a few verses from the Proverbs. We keep the children's memory verses and catechism questions looped together on a ring. We often work on them during meals. After dinner we read a Bible story and sing a hymn together. Often my wife and I have our own short devotional reading and prayer together at bedtime.

Figure out what works in your own home. Establish good habits of home worship. Do not burden your children with unrealistic demands, but draw them into a worship of God that you and they enjoy. If you do not worship Christ at home, then you must be pagans, because families are made to worship. If you are not worshiping the one true God in the name of Jesus Christ, then you must be worshiping some other gods and goddesses.

My edition of the Westminster Standards begins with a letter written sometime after the signing of the Westminster Confession of Faith. The letter is signed by some of the greatest Puritans of the seventeenth century, men such as Thomas Goodwin, William Whitaker, Matthew Pool, and Thomas Manton. It is addressed "To the Christian Reader, Especially Heads of Families." It begins with words that are as relevant today as they were on the day they were written:

> As we cannot but with grief of soul lament those multitudes of errors, blasphemies, and all kinds of profaneness, which have in this last age, like a mighty deluge, overflown this nation; so, among several other sins which

have helped to open the flood-gates of all these impieties, we cannot but esteem the disuse of family instruction one of the greatest.[9]

The letter goes on to give Biblical examples of the instruction of children, to exhort fathers to take heed to themselves first of all, and to commend the use of the catechisms of the church for family devotions. The letter closes like this:

If, therefore, there be any spark in you of love to God, be not content that any of yours should be ignorant of him whom you so much admire, or any haters of him whom you so much love. If there be any compassion to the souls of them who are under your care, if any regard of your being found faithful in the day of Christ, if any respect to future generations, labour to sow these seeds of knowledge, which may grow up in after-times.[10]

12

The Valley of Slaughter

JEREMIAH 7:30—8:3

PLACING YOURSELF IN THE HANDS OF the prophet Jeremiah is something like getting a ride from a friend who turns out to be a more reckless driver than you expected. Once you are in the car, the only thing you can do is grab on to the dashboard and pray for God's mercy. Nowhere is this more true than in Jeremiah's sermon on the Valley of Slaughter.

Temples of Doom

The end of chapter 7 through the beginning of chapter 8 is a horrible passage of Scripture, in the sense that it describes horrible actions and contains horrible images. It is one of the low points of Jeremiah's book.

The way the passage begins is bad enough. "For the sons of Judah have done evil in my sight, declares the LORD. They have set their detestable things in the house that is called by my name, to defile it" (7:30). They had taken idols made of stone and wood and placed them in the temple of the Lord God. "If one God is good," they said to themselves, "Two would be better, and three would be better yet." They were hedging their bets. They were putting their trust in the Lord God of Israel, but at the same time they were trusting in Baal, the Queen of Heaven, and anyone else they could think of.

Of course, trusting in God plus any other god is not trusting in the one true God at all. The gospel is Christ plus nothing. To start adding to the gospel is not to improve it, but to destroy it. You cannot walk down two or three roads at the same time. It is either God's way or the highway. As Jesus said, "No one can serve two masters" (Matthew 6:24).

When the people of Judah brought their idols into the temple, they were defiling it, profaning it, and making it completely unsuitable for the worship of the one true God. What they did was detestable; it was an abomination in God's sight. It would be like setting up a Shinto shrine or opening an adult book shop in your church fellowship hall. Even if everything else in the church remained the same—pews, Bibles, songbooks—the place of worship would still be defiled. What the people of Judah were bringing into the temple was such an affront to everything God stands for that it made the temple uninhabitable. Worshiping extra gods does not enhance worship—it makes true worship impossible.

All of that was bad enough, but the other thing the people of Judah did was even worse: "And they have built the high places of Topheth, which is in the Valley of the Son of Hinnom, to burn their sons and their daughters in the fire" (7:31).

The "high places" of Biblical times were not always very high. These particular high places, for example, were down in a valley. It was an inaccessible rocky ravine south and west of the city of Jerusalem. But a "high place" is a shrine, a raised platform built out of stones for the purpose of worship.

In Jeremiah 7 the high places are called by the name "Topheth." Topheth is not the name of a god, but means something like "fireplace" or "oven." It is not hard to see why that name was appropriate for this place. Topheth was the place where the people of Judah took their sons and their daughters and cast them into the flames.

Child sacrifice was practiced in ancient Near Eastern places such as Cyprus, Sardinia, Sicily, and Tyre.[1] The remains of hundreds of children have been discovered at Carthage, apparently sacrificed to Baal.[2] But child sacrifice also had a long history in Israel. Already in the book of Leviticus the children of Israel had been warned not to sacrifice their children to Molech (18:21), an offense punishable by death (Leviticus 20:1–5). Molech, the god of the Ammonites, had a way of turning up in Israel. Ahaz, King of Israel, sacrificed his own son in the fire (2 Kings 16:3). The same thing happened in Manasseh's day, when children were sacrificed to the gods of Canaan (2 Kings 21:6).

People conducted child sacrifices when Isaiah was prophet too, for he said, "[You] slaughter your children in the valleys, under the clefts of the rocks" (Isaiah 57:5b). When Josiah reformed temple worship in Jerusalem, one of the things he had to do was to tear down the high places of Topheth (2 Kings 23:10). But even that does not seem to have solved the problem, because the theme of child sacrifice comes up several times in the book of Jeremiah. Later Jeremiah explains that these sacrifices were offered to both Baal and Molech: "They built the high places of Baal in the Valley of the Son of Hinnom, to offer up their sons and daughters to Molech" (32:35).

There is little need to press home the horror of the imagery in this passage. Understand that it describes a real fire, a literal holocaust. Down in this valley, almost within sight of the temple of the Lord, the people of God were committing their infants to the flames.

What possible justification could they have had for these unholy flames and unspeakable sacrifices? Calvin writes, "It was a horrible and prodigious madness for parents not to spare their own children, but to cast them into the fire; for they must have been seized with a diabolic fury as to divest themselves of all human feelings."[3] I am not sure Calvin is right. I do not think that we can attribute the sins of the Valley of the Son of Hinnom to either insanity or demonic possession.

To understand this passage is to recognize that these people thought they were doing what God wanted them to do. Very likely these mothers and fathers loved their children. They had the natural feelings of care and protection that made them recoil at the very thought of harming their kids. They did not commit atrocities for the sake of committing atrocities. Instead, they carried out child sacrifice as an act of misguided piety and devotion to God. The sacrifice of the child was a religious act. They were killing their children out of the very best of intentions. They thought this was what God wanted them to do to atone for their sins.

This is a theme that recurs throughout Jeremiah: False gods are always harsh taskmasters. God is the only God who actually loves his people. Other gods may promise to save your soul, but they will tear your heart out in the process.

This is also a reminder that not everything done in God's name is pleasing to him. Not everything done out of zeal for God is acceptable to God. The people of Judah loved themselves more than they loved their kids. They were trying to buy their own salvation at the expense of their children. This is an extreme example, but it shows what happens when people try to worship God in ways that Scripture does not teach that he wants to be worshiped.

That is why God takes great pains in this passage to make it clear that what the people of Judah were doing was *not* pleasing to him, that in fact they were doing the very *opposite* of what he intended them to do. It is something, God says, "I did not command, nor did it come into my mind" (7:31).

The way this is phrased suggests that some of the religious leaders in Judah were claiming that child sacrifice had entered the mind of God, that he *did* command it. Some scholars point out that the priests of Topheth may have used the Torah to justify child sacrifice: "The firstborn of your sons you shall give to me . . . on the eighth day" (Exodus 22:29, 30). They were taking that verse out of context; it had nothing to do with child sacrifice. This is why we need to be careful not to tear Bible verses out of their Biblical contexts, especially when we are talking about the way of salvation. What the verse actually meant was that God wanted his people to circumcise their sons on the eighth day, not that he wanted them to kill their sons.

Topheth in America

That way of misreading the Bible sounds utterly foolish. But be careful not to write Jeremiah off. The practices he describes in this passage are so primitive and barbaric, and the reasoning behind them is so unconscionable, that it is tempting to think that they have nothing to do with life in these postmodern times. Where can the Valley of the Son of Hinnom be found in America? Where are the high places of Topheth? Where do parents burn their sons and daughters in the fire?

One might go to the Planned Parenthood office at Market East, on the corner of 11th and Filbert in Center City Philadelphia. Some years ago I saw a couple of young girls walk in the door of Planned Parenthood, wearing bobby socks and plaid school uniforms, carrying their books and their lunches. In my mind's eye, I could see them going down into the Valley of the Son of Hinnom.

Jeremiah's sermon on the Valley of Slaughter suggests important parallels between child sacrifice and abortion on demand. The more barbaric Jeremiah's culture seems, the more obvious the barbarities of our own culture become. Scholars such as MIT psychologist Steven Pinker have gone beyond abortion to argue in favor of infanticide. Writing in *The New York Times Magazine*, Pinker accepts that "The right to life must come . . . from morally significant traits that we humans happen to possess." However, he goes on to say that babies "don't possess these traits any more than mice do."[4] This is the postmodern barbarism of America.

One does not have to be a Christian to see that abortion is immoral. Anyone who has ever prepared to welcome an infant home knows how a fetus becomes a member of the household as soon as his existence is known, affecting virtually every family decision. Anyone who has ever carried a child in her womb knows how intimate a relationship forms between mother and child, how a fetus responds to the moods and schedules of her mother. Anyone who has ever seen pictures, videotapes, or ultrasounds of children in the womb knows how early the human heart forms, and how the fetus can respond to pleasure and pain. To know those things is to know instantly and instinctively that abortion is the murder of an unborn child. There is no substantive moral difference between the child sacrifices offered in the Valley of the Son of Hinnom and abortion as practiced in America.

It is easy to think of the people involved in the abortion industry as barbarians, as cruel and malicious murderers. But thinking about things in this way will not win anyone to Jesus Christ. Jeremiah teaches that abortion is a spiritual problem. The act of abortion is a religious ritual, a form of idol worship. The high priests of the abortion industry tell women that their physical comfort, their economic status, and their career plans are all more important than the life of their unborn child. Every abortion is a sacrifice to those ungodly gods.

Realizing that abortion is an essentially religious activity makes sense of the pro-choice movement. The pro-choice movement believes that pro-lifers are immoral, even wicked. Why is that? It is because the pro-choice position is a religious belief, and people always have a sense of moral outrage when you attack their religious beliefs. For abortion advocates, an abortion is an act of piety, an act of religious devotion. It is a ritual sacrifice to the gods of materialism and pleasure.

That kind of thinking is completely immoral, but the only way to combat it is to recognize that it is a spiritual problem. It is the kind of spiritual problem Paul describes in his letter to the Romans: "Since they did not see fit to acknowledge God, God gave them up to a debased mind to do what ought not to be done" (1:28).

The evil of abortion must be attacked on spiritual terms. It would be good and right if the Supreme Court overturned *Roe v. Wade*, or if the President agreed to ban partial-birth abortions, or if the states adopted a constitutional amendment banning abortion. But the issues at the heart of the abortion debate cannot be solved judicially or legislatively. The battle is a spiritual battle, and our weapons are spiritual weapons: prayer, the Word of God, the peace of the gospel, and the love of Christ.

Norma McCorvey, who was the plaintiff in *Roe v. Wade*, has become a born-again Christian. How was she won for Christ? Not by pro-life advertisements or by pickets and protests (although those things may have their place), but simply by the love and friendship of a pro-life family.

There is one more place to see a connection between the Valley of the Son of Hinnom and contemporary American culture, and that is in your own home. Christian parents should consider whether there are any ways in which they are guilty of the sins of the Valley of the Son of Hinnom.

Abortion is not the only form of child sacrifice in our culture. Many parents are guilty of lesser forms of child sacrifice. What Jeremiah teaches is that it is a wicked thing for parents to put their own needs and desires ahead of the needs and desires of their children. Obviously the Valley of the Son of Hinnom is an extreme example. But every time a career is put ahead of a family, every time anger prevents the exercise of loving discipline, and every time children must adjust to their parents' interests rather than the other way around, parents display the same heart attitude that the people of Judah displayed when they went down to the Valley of the Son of Hinnom.

Parents who love themselves more than they love their children are not parenting the way God intends. How you spend your money, how you discipline your children, and how you use your time all reveal whether you make sacrifices for your children, or whether you offer them up as sacrifices for yourself.

The Wages of Sin Is Death

What are the consequences of child sacrifice? The wages of sin is always death (Romans 6:23), but especially so in a case where the sin in question is infanticide. The whole rest of this passage reeks of death. The Valley of the Son of Hinnom will become the Valley of Slaughter.

The people of Judah will be slaughtered in the very place where they once slaughtered their children. R. K. Harrison observes that what was once "Their sanctuary would become their cemetery."[5] They have chosen death over life, and God will give them what they have chosen. "Therefore, behold, the days are coming, declares the LORD, when it will no more be called Topheth, or the Valley of the Son of Hinnom, but the Valley of Slaughter; for they will bury in Topheth, because there is no room elsewhere" (7:32). Jeremiah prophesies some great battle or some great catastrophe that will fill the valley with the dead.

What will happen when there is no more room to bury the dead in Topheth? "And the dead bodies of this people will be food for the birds of the air, and for the beasts of the earth, and none will frighten them away" (v. 33). Jeremiah prophesies death without dignity. There will be no room left to perform a decent burial, which will be a sign of God's curse, even after death. The corpses jumbled around the valley will become scavenger bait, since no one will be left to chase away the vultures or the hyenas from their grisly feast.

Even the leaders of Israel will meet this awful fate. "At that time, declares the LORD, the bones of the kings of Judah, the bones of its officials, the bones of the priests, the bones of the prophets, and the bones of the inhabitants of Jerusalem shall be brought out of their tombs" (8:1). God shows no favoritism. Royal bones, ecclesiastical bones, and the bones of the general public will all be treated alike.[6] The remains will all be disturbed, disinterred by grave robbers. Then they will be desecrated. "And they shall be spread before the sun and the moon and all the host of heaven, which they have loved and served, which they have gone after, and which they have sought and worshiped. And they shall not be gathered or buried. They shall be as dung on the surface of the ground" (v. 2).

The punishment fits the crime. These leaders did not cherish the bodies of their children, so their own bodies deserve to be treated like fertilizer. They have worshiped the celestial bodies, so they deserve to have their bodies exposed to the sun, moon, and stars. Then it will be clearer than ever that those gods cannot save, that the wages of sin is death. Worst of all, those who are left alive will long for death. "Death shall be preferred to life by all the remnant that remains of this evil family in all the places where I have driven them, declares the LORD of hosts" (8:3). God's people will endure a living death.

There is one more form of death described in this passage: the death of marriage. What happens in a society when parents violate their sacred trust to nurture their children? "And I will silence in the cities of Judah and in the streets of Jerusalem the voice of mirth and the voice of gladness, the voice of the bridegroom and the voice of the bride, for the land shall become a waste" (7:34).

This is one of the saddest verses in the book of Jeremiah. It is a prophecy of God's judgment on the family. Joyful families produce joyful weddings. But in a society in which parents sacrifice their children for their own comfort, the family is doomed. Infanticide, abortion, bad parenting, and divorce all undermine a society's confidence in the institution of marriage.

If this is true, then the postmodern West is in desperate trouble. On television sitcoms, characters use their words to tear down their family members. At the zoo, parents treat their children badly, and vice versa. These are harbingers of the death of the family in our culture. Given what is happening to families in our society, it is little wonder that marriages are on the decline, or that young people, especially, are afraid to get married.

Where Is the Grace?

One of the troubling things about this passage is that it does not contain any grace. In the words of one commentator, the sermon "ends without relief."[7] This is surprising because Jeremiah usually gives at least a little taste of the grace of God, even if it only amounts to half a verse. But Jeremiah's sermon about the Valley of Slaughter seems to be graceless.

The reason there is no grace in this passage is very simple: The Valley of Slaughter is the Valley of Hell. The common New Testament term for Hell is *Gehenna*. It occurs in places like Luke 12, where Jesus tells his disciples to fear the one who "has authority to cast into hell" (v. 5), or Matthew 23, where Jesus warns the Pharisees that they are in danger of "being sentenced to hell [Gehenna]" (v. 33).

What or where is Gehenna? In Jesus' day it was the ravine south of Jerusalem where the refuse of the city was burnt, and so Jesus used it as a picture of the fires of eternal judgment. But *Gehenna* is the same word as *Son of Hinnom*. So when the New Testament speaks about Hell, it is speaking about the very place that Jeremiah described in his sermon on the Valley of Slaughter. The Valley of the Son of Hinnom is the Valley of Hell. It is a place of abomination, wickedness, burning, and cruelty. It is a place of living death.

The reason Hell is such a terrible place is that God is not there. It is the absence of God that makes Hell to be Hell, just as it is the presence of God that makes Heaven to be Heaven. There is no grace in the Valley of Slaughter because there is no grace in Hell. There is no atonement in Hell, no preaching of the gospel, no sacraments. Hell is the place of endless torment where God banishes those who have decided to have nothing to do with him.

If you have not yet made friends with Christ, there is not a moment to lose. Jeremiah pulls back the curtains of Hell far enough to reveal what it might be like to remain an enemy of Christ for all eternity. If you will not have Christ, be assured that Christ will not have you. Now is the time to repent of your sins and believe in Jesus Christ and so be saved.

If you do know Jesus Christ in a personal way, the reality of eternal Hell should produce a sober lamentation for the sins of the lost. There seem to be plenty of angry Christians these days, condemning sinners for society's ills. There seem to be plenty of self-righteous Christians around these days too, chastising the nation for leaving the faith of its fathers. There is a place for righteous anger about the sins of America, and there is some truth to the idea that our nation is in spiritual decline. But our primary response to the lostness of the lost ought to be lamentation over the dishonor done to God and over the prospect of eternal judgment.

It is that kind of lamentation with which this passage actually begins: "Cut off your hair and cast it away; raise a lamentation on the bare heights, for the Lord has rejected and forsaken the generation of his wrath" (7:29). One of the chief marks of godliness in the days of Jeremiah was baldness. The Lord commanded the children of Israel to wear their hair long and to let their sideburns grow—but not in times of sin and judgment. Then they were to cut off their hair as a sign of despair and anguish. When children are being sacrificed down in the valley, the appropriate thing to do is to shave your head, climb to the top of a high mountain, and wail over the sins of your neighbors.

Most Christians do not leave enough tearstains on their prayer lists. This is because we do not have a due sense of the weightiness of God's holiness or the fearsomeness of God's justice. One of the chief marks of godliness in a sinful generation is lamentation over the sins of the times.

As we lament the sins of our times, we also testify that Jesus Christ has made the only sacrifice that is necessary for sin. There is no need to sacrifice our children to save our souls. God taught this lesson to his people once and for all on Mount Moriah, where Abraham went to sacrifice his son. Abraham was about to carry out the kind of sacrifice they performed in the Valley of the Son of Hinnom. But God said, "Do not lay your hand on the boy or do anything to him" (Genesis 22:12). God himself had provided a lamb. Yes, God had commanded Abraham to offer up his son, but as a test of the patriarch's faith, not because God really meant for Isaac to be sacrificed.

God never commanded child sacrifice in Israel, nor did it ever enter his mind. The prophet Micah asked, "Shall I give my firstborn for my transgression, the fruit of my body for the sin of my soul?" (Micah 6:7b). The answer has always been "No!" But here is something that *did* enter God's mind—providing a sacrificial lamb for us, as he provided for Abraham. His own Son would sacrifice himself for our sins.

One of the things that made that sacrifice acceptable was that Jesus Christ offered *himself* as an atonement for sin. He was not bound and gagged by his Father and dragged to Calvary against his will. If that had happened, then God the Father would have been just as cruel as the parents of Ben Hinnom. But Jesus Christ willingly gave himself up for us all. Because of his voluntary sacrifice, there is no need to go to Hell.

Although there is no grace in the Valley of Slaughter, there is a gracious promise about the valley later in Jeremiah's book. It appears among the promises of the new covenant at the end of chapter 31: "Behold, the days are coming, declares the LORD, when the city shall be rebuilt for the LORD from the Tower of Hananel to the Corner Gate. . . . The whole valley of the dead bodies and the ashes . . . shall be sacred to the LORD. It shall not be plucked up or overthrown anymore forever" (31:38, 40). The valley mentioned in this promise is the Valley of the Son of Hinnom, formerly filled with the bodies and ashes of child sacrifice.

In the new Jerusalem, where God's people live with God forever and ever, even that valley will become holy to the Lord: "Death shall be no more, neither shall there be mourning, nor crying, nor pain anymore, for the former things have passed away" (Revelation 21:4). There is a Hell, but there is no Hell in the eternal city of God.

13

Wrongly Dividing
the Word of Truth

JEREMIAH 8:4–17

ONCE HE HAD CONCLUDED HIS SERMON on the Valley of Slaughter, Jeremiah confronted the people with three more sins—willful disobedience, deliberate ignorance, and criminal negligence.

Bucking Broncos

The passage begins with two questions that are so easy to answer that the Lord does not wait around for a response:

> You shall say to them, Thus says the LORD:
> When men fall, do they not rise again?
>   If one turns away, does he not return? (8:4)

These are no-brainers. Of course people get up when they fall down; of course they return when they have turned away. That is just common sense.

This phenomenon is commonly observed among toddlers. Little kids are always falling down. Their parents spend a good deal of time saying, "You're okay, you're all right, just get back up." And toddlers always do; they get back up as many times as they fall down.

Gymnasts do the same thing. Watch a young gymnast perform a floor exercise. She does a spectacular tumbling run, but gets too much height on her last flip and ends up falling on her seat, right off the edge of the mat. But she does not sit there and mope; she hops right back up and finishes her routine. That is what people do when they fall down. They dust themselves off and get back on their feet, one way or another.

That is why Jeremiah was so amazed by what the people of Judah were doing. They had fallen down in their sins, and they were not getting back up again. The problem was not that they *couldn't* get up, because they could. The problem was that they *wouldn't* get up. This amazed Jeremiah because it was unnatural, foolish, and inexplicable. When people fall down, they always get back up. So why were the people of Jerusalem still lying in the dust?

To put the same question another way, why haven't they come back home? Here is another no-brainer: "If one turns away, does he not return?" Of course he does. When a mother goes out to the store to buy bread and milk, she always comes back home. If she does not come back home, something is badly wrong. It is time to call the police. She must be lost or had an accident or met with foul play.

Hence Jeremiah's consternation:

Why then has this people turned away
   in perpetual backsliding?
They hold fast to deceit;
   they refuse to return. (v. 5)

Jeremiah uses variations of the word "Turn" or its equivalent six times in these verses. The people of Jerusalem had wandered far away from God and would not come back home. They had turned, but they would not return. They were perpetual backsliders. They had not learned from their spiritual mistakes.

One way to describe their situation is to say that they were still stuck back in the third chapter of the story of the prodigal son (Luke 15:11–32). Actually, the story is more appropriately called "The Prodigal Father," since it is about a man who squanders his love on his rebellious sons.

In the first chapter of the story, the younger of two sons is sick of home. He has just about had it with life at home with his father. He wishes the old man would go ahead and die so he could have his inheritance. He wants to run away from home. Reluctantly, his father sends him off with his full share of his inheritance, so that the son can set up housekeeping on his own.

The second chapter of the story tells how the son takes the money and runs off to see the big city lights. He rents his own place and squanders his money on wine, women, and song.

As the third chapter opens, he hits rock bottom. He finds himself in the middle of a recession, homeless and unemployed. He hires himself out to clean pig sties for less than the minimum wage. He has fallen all the way down, he is wallowing in swine manure, and he refuses to get back up. "And he was longing to be fed with the pods that the pigs ate, and no one gave him anything" (Luke 15:16).

That is just where the people of Jerusalem were, stuck in the third chapter of the story of the prodigal son. To use the words that Jesus used to describe the wayward son, they had not yet "come to [their] senses" (cf. Luke 15:17 NIV). They were still far away from home, wallowing in the mire. They had fallen, and they would not get up.

The prophet Jeremiah, speaking for God, offers this assessment of their problem:

I have paid attention and listened,
    but they have not spoken rightly;
no man relents of his evil,
    saying, "What have I done?" (8:6a)

This is a failure of repentance. The people ought to get up. They ought to come back home to God. They ought to say, "What have we done?"

In other words, they ought to be doing what the prodigal son did in the fourth chapter of his life story. Once he was sick of home, but now he is homesick, and it is time for him to go home:

But when he came to himself, he said, "How many of my father's hired servants have more than enough bread, but I perish here with hunger! I will arise and go to my father, and I will say to him, 'Father, I have sinned against heaven and before you. I am no longer worthy to be called your son. Treat me as one of your hired servants.'" And he arose and came to his father. (Luke 15:17–20a)

If the people of Jerusalem would do all that, if they would repent for their sins and go back home, they would receive a Father's welcome. Every prodigal sinner can receive the same thing. If you have wandered away from God, all you need to do is go back home and tell your Father that you are sorry for your sins. Then you will receive the Father's welcome that the prodigal son received:

But while he was still a long way off, his father saw him and felt compassion, and ran and embraced him and kissed him. . . . "Bring quickly the best robe, and put it on him, and put a ring on his hand, and shoes on his feet. And bring the fattened calf and kill it, and let us eat and celebrate. For this my son was dead, and is alive again; he was lost, and is found." (Luke 15:20b, 22–24)

Sadly, the people of Jerusalem had yet to do that. They were still stuck in chapter 3 of that story, still wallowing in the muck of their sins. So Jeremiah compared them to wild stallions: "Everyone turns to his own course, like a horse plunging headlong into battle" (8:6b). Warhorses usually wear blinders so they will not be frightened by the horrible sights of battle. They just put their heads down and charge. Each pursues his own course, paying no attention to where he is going, simply rushing headlong into the fray. The warhorse, so like a bucking bronco, is a picture of wild disobedience, of mindless attraction to sin. Like the people of Jerusalem, we are incorrigible sinners. We do not just wander into sin—we gallop into it.

That is why Christians need to be regular in repentance. We must be as penitent as we are sinful. We must engage in serious, soul-searching, conscience-probing repentance. If one of the marks of the ungodly is refusing to repent for sin, one of the marks of the Christian is regular repentance.

The main difference between believers and unbelievers is not that believers do not sin, while unbelievers do. There ought to be some difference between Christians and non-Christians in their outward behavior, of course. "They will know we are Christians by our love," as the song says. But Christians are sinners too. "None is righteous, no, not one" (Romans 3:10). Thus the primary difference between Christians and non-Christians is not whether or not they sin.

The difference lies in how people deal with their sin. The Christian lives a life of repentance. A Christian man may fall down into sin, but he does not stay down. A Christian woman may wander away from God, but she does not stay away. Christians return after they have turned. They carry their sin back to God and ask him to forgive their sins for the sake of Jesus Christ.

Hence the need to be regular in repentance. As the Puritan William Bradshaw observed, "The Lord looks upon my sins, they are now before Him; and we should never rest till we have by repentance moved Him to blot them out. Yea, to this end we should ourselves call them to remembrance. For the more we remember them, the more God forgets them; the more we forget them, the more God remembers them."[1]

Birdbrains

Willful disobedience without repentance is bad enough, but now add deliberate ignorance:

> Even the stork in the heavens
> knows her times,
> and the turtledove, swallow, and crane
> keep the time of their coming,

but my people know not
  the rules of the LORD. (8:7)

To put it bluntly, the people of God were acting like birdbrains. Compare them to birds in their ability to obey their Creator's instructions, and they come out way behind. If any animal knows its way back home, it is a migratory bird. Geese are not the cleverest creatures, but they do not need to be told to head south in November. They just know. Jeremiah mentions a number of birds that passed through Israel on their annual migrations. Like swallows going back to Capistrano, the stork, the turtledove, the swallow, and the crane all know their appointed seasons. They know when it is time to go back home.

That is more than could be said for the people of God. Not only did they refuse to repent for their sins, they did not even know the way back home. They did not know God's requirements. One might say they were birdbrains, but according to this passage, that would be an insult to the birds! There is something unnatural about deliberate ignorance among the people of God.

Jeremiah attacked the widespread Biblical illiteracy of his day. His people did not know God's requirements. They did not go to hear the scribes read the Torah. They did not recite the Ten Commandments or teach them to their children. They were deliberately ignorant about spiritual things.

It is not hard to make the same indictment about the American church. This ought to be the golden age of Biblical knowledge. We have all kinds of advantages that the people of Jeremiah's day did not have. We have the New Testament as well as the Old. We live under the new covenant, so the full plan of redemption in Jesus Christ has been laid out before us. We have the printing press, so we can get our own copies of the Bible and read them for ourselves. After more than two millennia of additional Biblical scholarship, we have more tools to help us understand the Bible than ever before—commentaries and concordances, cross-references and study notes right in the margins of our Bibles. We can listen to tapes and radio broadcasts.

Yet what Jeremiah said about the people of God in his day is equally true of the contemporary church. The birds know God's requirements for them, but we do not know his requirements for us. Only one in five evangelicals reads the Bible every day.[2]

The practical remedy for our ignorance is not hard to find. If you are not in a weekly Bible study, find one and start attending. If you are not reading your Bible every day, get one and start reading. If you are reading your Bible, but not very carefully, get a pencil and start underlining.

Whatever you do, do not just read the Bible, but put it into practice. When

Jeremiah said that the people of Jerusalem did not *know* the requirements of the Lord, he was not talking about Bible trivia. The kind of knowledge he meant is a warm embrace of the teaching of Scripture in the mind, the heart, and the will. It is the kind of knowledge that becomes such a part of us that Biblical teaching governs everything we think and do.

An old preacher, whose name is now forgotten, had this to say about the Bible:

> This book contains the mind of God, the state of man, the way of salvation, the doom of sinners, the happiness of believers. Its doctrines are holy, its precepts are binding, it histories are true, and its decisions are immutable. Read it to be wise, believe it to be safe, and practice it to be holy. It contains light to direct you, food to support you, and comfort to cheer you. It is the traveler's map, the pilgrim's staff, the pilot's compass, the soldier's sword, and the Christian's character. Christ is its grand subject, our good its design, and the glory of God its end. It should fill the memory, rule the heart, and guide the feet.[3]

That kind of beautiful, practical, complete knowledge is available in the Bible. Anyone who refuses to study it is living in deliberate ignorance.

Wise Guys

When the people of God do not know the Law of God, professional theologians usually deserve part of the blame. True, the people of Jerusalem were willful in their disobedience and deliberate in their ignorance. Yet this was mainly because their spiritual leaders were guilty of criminal negligence.

> How can you say, "We are wise,
>   and the law of the Lord is with us"?
> But behold, the lying pen of the scribes
>   has made it into a lie." (v. 8)

The Apostle Paul told Timothy to handle the Bible carefully, to be an "approved . . . worker who . . . rightly handl[es] the word of truth" (2 Timothy 2:15). The scribes of Jerusalem did just the opposite. They mishandled the Bible. They were wrongly dividing the word of truth. They distorted the Scriptures to their own destruction.

It is not entirely clear what the job description of a scribe was in the days of Jeremiah. The scribes seem to have been priests, since the Chronicler reports that "some of the Levites were scribes and officials and gatekeepers" (2 Chronicles 34:13). That verse comes from Jeremiah's time period, when

King Josiah reformed the temple. Some of the Levites were scribes. They were scholars, experts in the Law. They copied and taught the Scriptures in Israel.

But something had gone badly wrong. This is apparent from what the scribes were saying: "We are wise." Whenever someone boasts how wise he is, it is a sure sign that he is a fool. Someone who is truly wise does not trust his own wisdom. True wisdom exercises the humility of the Christian mind. So rather than being wise men, these scribes must have been a bunch of wise guys.

They wrote with lying pens. They were tampering with the Word of God. They were involved in a cover-up of Biblical truth. The problem was not with the Scripture itself. Some commentators are a little careless on this point. They make it sound like the Bible is a dead letter that gets in the way of listening to God's Spirit. For example, R. E. O. White argues that "a religious movement dependent upon a book" can "become a substitute for the living voice of God speaking in contemporary circumstances."[4] That is not what Jeremiah was saying.

Jeremiah understood that God speaks in his Word rather than through contemporary circumstances. His point was that the scribes were handling that Word falsely. The problem was not the Bible—it was how the scribes were using the Bible. To use the proper term for this, the problem was with their Biblical interpretation, or hermeneutics.

There is so much strange teaching these days that it is easy to forget there is nothing wrong with the Bible. The meaning of the Bible is plain, particularly when it comes to salvation in Jesus Christ alone. If the church is not hearing that plain message, the problem is not with the Holy Bible; the problem is with unholy ministers.

How, exactly, were Jeremiah's scribes mishandling Scripture? There was a problem both with their motivation and with their content. The problem with their motivation was closely related to one of the "Seven Deadly Sins"—avarice.

> . . . from the least to the greatest
>   everyone is greedy for unjust gain;
> from prophet to priest,
>   everyone deals falsely. (v. 10b)

These scribes were the original naughty televangelists. They were in the ministry for the money and the glory. This is a reminder to anyone who is involved in full-time Christian ministry that a high calling is not protection from the lowest of temptations. Be on guard against discontent with your material circumstances. Resist the temptation to seek the flattery of men rather than the approval of God. You are not in the Lord's service for money or for praise. If you are, find another line of work.

The wrong motivation of the scribes started to influence their teaching:

> They have healed the wound of my people lightly,
>   saying, "Peace, peace,"
>   when there is no peace. (v. 11)

That verse sounds familiar because it appeared verbatim in Jeremiah 6:14. The scribes of Jerusalem denied that God would judge their sin. Their people needed an emergency heart transplant, but these quack-pastors came around with their Band-Aids and their lollipops. "There, there," they said, "you're okay. God will not judge your sin." "Peace, peace," they said. "Shalom, shalom." One reason they wrongly divided the word of truth was because they did not take God seriously.

More than anything else, failing to take God seriously is the problem with the contemporary church. We trivialize the holiness of God, so we end up with a trivial view of sin. We trivialize the majesty of God, so we end up with trivial worship. We trivialize the truth of God, so we end up with a trivial grasp of his Word. We trivialize the judgment of God, so we end up with a trivial appreciation for the atonement of Jesus Christ. Our God is too trivial!

Liberal theologians used to be the ones who trivialized God. Saying "peace, peace" was the big lie of liberal theology (God will not judge sin—not our sins anyway). But now the evangelical church has also been taken over by a lesser deity. Too many ministers offer a kinder, gentler God. He is everything anyone ever wanted in a God, only less.

In his book *God in the Wasteland* David Wells writes wistfully about the "weightlessness" of God in the contemporary church:

> It is one of the defining marks of Our Time that God is now weightless . . . he has become unimportant. He rests upon the world so inconsequentially as not to be noticeable. . . . Those who assure the pollsters of their belief in God's existence may nonetheless consider him less interesting than television, his commands less authoritative than their appetites for affluence and influence, his judgment no more awe-inspiring than the evening news, and his truth less compelling than the advertisers' sweet fog of flattery and lies. That is weightlessness.[5]

Wells concludes, "The fundamental problem in the evangelical world today is that God rests too inconsequentially upon the church. His truth is too distant, his grace is too ordinary, his judgment is too benign, his gospel is too easy, and his Christ is too common."[6]

Ministers who do not have some sense of the weightiness of God ought to be ashamed of themselves, but these scribes were as shameless as they were deceptive. "Were they ashamed when they committed abomination? No, they were not at all ashamed; they did not know how to blush" (8:12a). An example of such shameless clergy appeared in the Philadelphia newspapers in the summer of 1996. A group of ministers announced their support of the mayor's initiative to provide health benefits to the partners of gay and lesbian employees. "Not all of Christianity condemns it as sinful," they said. Some churches "have not changed with the times." "As people of faith we find no difference in the basic morality of committed, loving relationships and different-sex couples." "Peace, peace," they were saying to the homosexual lifestyle, even though Scripture roundly condemns it. They were saying it without shame, holding a press conference and getting their names and pictures into the news.[7]

The sad reality is that there is no peace for those who rebel against God. The rest of the passage describes what happens to those who turn but do not return:

> The wise men shall be put to shame;
>   they shall be dismayed and taken;
> behold, they have rejected the word of the LORD,
>   so what wisdom is in them?
> Therefore I will give their wives to others
>   and their fields to conquerors. (vv. 9, 10a)

> Therefore they shall fall among the fallen;
>   when I punish them, they shall be overthrown,
> says the LORD. (v. 12b)

> When I would gather them, declares the LORD,
>   there are no grapes on the vine,
>   nor figs on the fig tree;
> even the leaves are withered,
>   and what I gave them has passed away from them. (v. 13)

Those who wrongly divide the word of truth will be punished for their sins. Appropriately enough, they will fall down and stay there. Their crops will fail. Their wives and their fields will be given to others. As they sense disaster coming, they will huddle together in the fortified cities.

Why do we sit still?
Gather together; let us go into the fortified cities
   and perish there,
for the LORD our God has doomed us to perish
   and has given us poisoned water to drink,
   because we have sinned against the LORD. (v. 14)

All their attempts to save themselves will fail.

The passage ends on an ominous note. The people of Jerusalem put all their hopes in the message of peace, but when the army swoops down from the north and destroys them, they will say,

We looked for peace, but no good came;
   for a time of healing, but behold, terror. (v. 15)

The whole land will tremble as the invasion approaches from the north.

The snorting of their horses is heard from Dan;
   at the sound of the neighing of their stallions
   the whole land quakes.
They come and devour the land and all that fills it,
   the city and those who dwell in it. (v. 16)

The invaders will scorch the earth, devouring everything in their path.

It is easy to imagine that many people will say the same thing on the day of judgment, when Jesus Christ will judge every man, woman, and child according to his or her deeds. "We hoped for peace," some will say. "My pastor told me there wouldn't be any hell." Or "My spiritual advisor said God would accept me as long as I did my best."

They said, "peace, peace," but there will be no peace. Judgment cannot be escaped. "'For behold, I am sending among you serpents, adders that cannot be charmed, and they shall bite you,' declares the LORD" (v. 17).

The picture of poisonous snakes slithering all over Jerusalem is frightening. Whenever I take my children to the Reptile House to see the snakes, I hear the word "ugh" a lot. People have a natural dread of snakes. That dread goes back to Genesis 3, when Satan used a serpent to tempt humanity, and when God cursed the serpent to crawl on his belly all the days of his life. Satan is always biting at the heels of humanity, and God sometimes permits Satan's minions to carry out his divine judgment against sin. Such snakes cannot be charmed.

But there is an antidote for spiritual snakebite. Jesus Christ can take away the sting of death. In the days of Moses, God sent snakes to punish the people of Israel for their sins. "Then the L ord sent fiery serpents among the people, and they bit the people, so that many people of Israel died" (Numbers 21:6). But the Lord himself provided the antidote for snakebite. He took away the sting of death. He said to Moses, "Make a fiery serpent and set it on a pole, and everyone who is bitten, when he sees it, shall live" (Numbers 21:8).

Jesus came to reveal God's antidote for spiritual snakebite:

> And as Moses lifted up the serpent in the wilderness, so must the Son of Man be lifted up, that whoever believes in him may have eternal life. For God so loved the world, that he gave his only Son, that whoever believes in him should not perish but have eternal life. For God did not send his Son into the world to condemn the world, but in order that the world might be saved through him. (John 3:14–17)

Jesus Christ is the antidote for the venom of sin. God's judgment cannot be charmed, but anyone who looks to Christ can live.

14

There Is a Balm in Gilead

JEREMIAH 8:18—9:11

IT IS TIME TO HAND JEREMIAH another handkerchief:

Oh that my head were waters,
and my eyes a fountain of tears,
that I might weep day and night
for the slain of the daughter of my people! (9:1)

The Weeping Prophet proposes a perpetual lamentation, an endless flow of tears for the people of God. And with his lamentation comes confusion. Jeremiah is a jumble of conflicting emotions and contradictory ideas.

Consider what the prophet says about his relationship with God. He had the strongest possible sense of God's presence. He spoke to him directly, as a friend to a friend: "My joy is gone; grief is upon me; my heart is sick within me" (8:18). But by the time he gets to the middle of the next verse he is starting to doubt whether God is really there for his people at all: "Is the LORD not in Zion? Is her King not in her?" (8:19b). God is supposed to be in Zion because he has chosen Zion for his dwelling place (Psalm 132:13). But where is he? God does not seem to be at home. In his grief, Jeremiah is at once close to God and far away from him. He senses both the presence and the absence of God.

C. S. Lewis (1898–1963) wrote about the way sorrow confuses one's relationship with God in his book *A Grief Observed*, written after the death of his wife, Joy:

Meanwhile, where is God? This is one of the most disquieting symptoms. When you are happy, so happy that you have no sense of needing Him, so happy that you are tempted to feel His claims upon you as an interruption, if you remember yourself and turn to Him with gratitude and praise, you will be—or so it feels—welcomed with open arms. But go to Him when your need is desperate, when all other help is vain, and what do you find? A door slammed in your face, and a sound of bolting and double bolting on the inside. After that, silence. You may as well turn away. The longer you wait, the more emphatic the silence will become. There are no lights in the windows. It might be an empty house. Was it ever inhabited? It seemed so once. And that seeming was as strong as this. What can this mean? Why is He so present a commander in our time of prosperity and so very absent a help in time of trouble?[1]

Jeremiah's confusion about his own relationship to God was mirrored by his paradoxical relationship to God's people. He announced his absolute solidarity with them: "For the wound of the daughter of my people is my heart wounded; I mourn, and dismay has taken hold on me" (8:21). The prophet identified so strongly with the people of God that their sufferings became his sufferings.

Yet just a few verses later Jeremiah decides to abandon them completely:

Oh that I had in the desert
    a travelers' lodging place,
that I might leave my people
    and go away from them!
For they are all adulterers,
    a company of treacherous men. (9:2; cf. Psalm 55:6–8)

The prophet seems not to want to stay with the people of God after all. He wants to purchase his own private Heartbreak Hotel, a resort property in the desert far away from his people and their problems.

Did Jeremiah love God's people, or did he hate them? Is God present, or absent? It is all very confusing. But it is not surprising. These confusions and contradictions remind us that Jeremiah wrote from the very depths of despair. Despair troubles the soul and confuses the mind. In his grief, Jeremiah was not always sure what he thought or how he felt.

Truth Decay

What plunged Jeremiah into such perplexities of despair? There were two reasons for his sorrow. The first was that the people of God were no longer people of the truth. Lying and deceit are mentioned repeatedly in these verses. Jeremiah's people were not true in their personal relationships. They were "a company of treacherous men" (v. 2). "With his mouth each speaks peace to his neighbor, but in his heart he plans an ambush for him" (v. 8b).

This last verse reminds me of the time I was speaking with a well-known

English writer at a tea party in one of the Oxford colleges. She had just asked me about the subject of my doctoral work, but before I had a chance to give an answer we were all invited to go into another room. "Well," I said, "I guess I will have to tell you about my dissertation some other time." "Oh, do tell me about it," she purred, "I am so interested." The conventions of polite society would not permit her to abandon our conversation. She was speaking cordially, but it seemed to me she was lying through her smile. That is the way it was in Jeremiah's Jerusalem. People were polite, but they were not truthful.

Nor did they speak the truth to God. Their relationship with him was false. "Why have they provoked me to anger with their carved images and with their foreign idols?" God asked (8:19c). They worshiped many false gods rather than the one true God. "They proceed from evil to evil, and they do not know me," God lamented (9:3). He told Jeremiah, "Heaping oppression upon oppression, and deceit upon deceit, they refuse to know me" (v. 6).

This is the biggest lie of all, the lie that God does not exist. The people of Jerusalem did not praise God for his majesty, thank him for his mercy, or ask him for his forgiveness. Their silence was a denial of God's existence, which is the mother of all lies.

Their family relationships were equally false. Husbands and wives were cheating on one another (v. 2). Brothers and sisters were betraying one another:

> Let everyone beware of his neighbor,
>   and put no trust in any brother,
> for every brother is a deceiver,
>   and every neighbor goes about as a slanderer.
> Everyone deceives his neighbor,
>   and no one speaks the truth. (vv. 4, 5a)

God placed a "Beware of Thy Neighbor" sign over Jeremiah's relationships. With friends like these, who needs enemies?

When the Lord says that every brother is a "deceiver," literally he is saying that every brother is a "Jacob." The pun calls to mind the story of Jacob and Esau, where Jacob deceives his father and tricks his brother out of his blessing (Genesis 27). The point is that the people of Jerusalem treated their friends as falsely as they treated their families, and vice versa.

Trust is the basis of any society. But in this city, every personal relationship, every spiritual relationship, and every family relationship was corrupted by untruth. Thus Jeremiah repeatedly described the tongue as a weapon:

They bend their tongue like a bow;
    falsehood and not truth has grown strong in the land. (9:3a)

Their tongue is a deadly arrow;
    it speaks deceitfully. (v. 8a)

The words that came from their mouths were like so many poison darts. They even took their tongues to boot camp, training them for verbal combat: "They have taught their tongue to speak lies" (v. 5).

No wonder Jeremiah was overcome with grief! When a society loses its love for truth, it is in a lamentable condition. If Jeremiah could have, he would have run away and managed a quiet bed-and-breakfast in the Negev, just to get away from all the deceit. But he was bound to the people of God by his divine calling, by flesh and blood, and by God's love. He could not leave them—he could only grieve for them.

Truth . . . or Consequences

There is another reason Jeremiah grieved for the people of God. He grieved because he knew God would judge them for their sins. Judgment was inevitable. Because they did not speak the truth, they would have to bear the consequences.

God laid out his case against his people:

Behold, I will refine them and test them,
    for what else can I do, because of my people? (9:7)

Shall I not punish them for these things? declares the LORD,
    and shall I not avenge myself
    on a nation such as this? (v. 9; cf. 5:9, 29)

It is impossible to argue with God's logic. He had no choice. His people were unfaithful to him and unfaithful to one another. What else did they deserve except to be punished for their unfaithfulness? The problem was not that God was absent from Zion, but that he was angry with Zion.

Throughout this passage we get glimpses of the kind of judgment God will send. It will include exile, for Jeremiah begs God, "Behold, the cry of the daughter of my people from the length and breadth of the land" (8:19a). As the prophet of God, he could see things that had not yet happened as if they were happening before his very eyes. He could see the people of Judah already captured and carted off to Babylon.

Judgment will mean death as well as exile, for Jeremiah mourns the slain of his people (9:1). It will include great natural disasters. The prophet takes up a bitter lament for the land and its creatures:

> I will take up weeping and wailing for the mountains,
>   and a lamentation for the pastures of the wilderness,
> because they are laid waste so that no one passes through,
>   and the lowing of cattle is not heard;
> both the birds of the air and the beasts
>   have fled and are gone. (v. 10)

The mountains and the deserts are desolate. Jeremiah listens, but he cannot hear any mooing or chirping. All the animals are gone. The prophet groans along with the creation, which itself is groaning under the weight of Judah's sin (cf. Romans 8:22).

It sounds as if Jeremiah is describing "The day after" a nuclear holocaust. Or perhaps one should say "The day of the jackal," for the Lord says,

> I will make Jerusalem a heap of ruins,
>   a lair of jackals,
> and I will make the cities of Judah a desolation,
>   without inhabitant. (9:11; cf. 10:22)

Jackals were the wild scavengers of ancient Israel. They prowled in the remote places, living off leftovers, scraps, and carcasses. "A lair of jackals" is an uninhabitable place of darkness, death, and destruction, fit only for beasts, not for humans.

Is there any hope for the people of Judah? Is there any chance that they will escape divine judgment? The futility of their situation is summarized in one of the saddest verses in the Old Testament: "The harvest is past, the summer is ended, and we are not saved" (8:20).

There were two harvests in the ancient Near East—a spring harvest and a summer harvest. If the spring harvest failed, one could always hope for a bumper crop in the summer. But not this time. Both harvests failed. No hope was left. Even the backup plan failed. Thanksgiving is past, Christmas has ended, and there will be no turkey dinner.

True Lies

"The harvest is past, the summer is ended, and we are not saved." The same might well be said of our own culture. Everything Jeremiah says about his culture is true in these post-Christian times.

Jeremiah lived in a culture of deception. So do we. The title of a 1994 film captures the attitude of postmodern society toward truth and falsehood: *True Lies*. Is a "True lie" true or false? If it is a lie, then it must be false and not true. But if it is false, then it is truly a lie. We have lost the wisdom to know where truth ends and falsehood begins.

Family relationships are false. Many people live together as if they were married, but without the sanction of marriage vows. Others have taken marriage vows but have made themselves liars by breaking the marriage covenant.

There is falsehood in advertising. Television ads, magazines, and billboards manipulate us with false promises, misleading conclusions, and vain hopes. I was once informed, "WE NOW HAVE PROOF: PHILIP G. RYKEN IS THE NEW $1,666,675.00 WINNER!" After I had calmed down a little bit I noticed the fine print: "If you have and return the Grand Prize winning number . . ." That is deceptive, misleading, and manipulative.

There is falsehood in politics, where campaign season is the season for lies, deceptions, and half-truths. There is falsehood in business, where corporations hide their intentions from their own employees and investors.

There is falsehood at the university. Already in the 1960s Francis Schaeffer was warning that "Truth is worn down in the philosophy of our generation."[2] If truth was worn down in the 1960s, it is worn-out in the twenty-first century. The presupposition upon which the postmodern academy operates is that there is no such thing as an absolute truth, only a host of conflicting interpretations of reality, each as valid as the next.

There is even falsehood in the church. Os Guinness's telling indictment of American evangelicalism is worth quoting again:

> Contemporary evangelicals are no longer people of truth. . . . A solid sense of truth is foundering in America at large. Vaporized by critical theories, obscured by clouds of euphemism and jargon, outpaced by humor and hype, overlooked for style and image, and eroded by advertising, truth in America is anything but marching on. With magnificent exceptions, evangelicals reflect this truth decay and reinforce it for their own variety of reasons for discounting theology. Repelled by "seminary theology" that is specialized, professionalized, and dry, evangelicals are attracted by movements that have replaced theology with emphases that are relational, therapeutic, charismatic, and managerial (as in church growth). Whatever their virtues, none of these emphases gives truth and theology the place they require in the life and thought of a true disciple.[3]

We live in the midst of deception. What should we do? First, we need to repent for our own untruthfulness. That is what the prophet Isaiah did. Like Jeremiah, he lived in the midst of deception. As a prophet of God, speaking the

Word of God, it would have been easy for him to be smug about his own truthfulness. But when Isaiah "saw the Lord sitting upon a throne, high and lifted up," he cried, "Woe is me! For I am lost; for I am a man of unclean lips, and I dwell in the midst of a people of unclean lips; for my eyes have seen the King, the LORD of hosts!" (Isaiah 6:1, 5). We are no better than Isaiah. Our lips are no cleaner, our words are no more truthful—and we should be no less penitent.

Second, we need to be people of the truth. One of the memorable characters in John Bunyan's *Pilgrim's Progress* is called "Valiant-for-truth." His name is taken from the Authorized Version of this passage: "They are not valiant for the truth upon the earth" (9:3).[4]

We need to be Valiant-for-truth. We need to speak the truth in all our words and do the truth in all our actions. We must be faithful in our personal relationships, keeping our word even in trivial matters. We must be faithful in our family relationships. We must keep our marriage vows, honor our parents, and be forthright with our children.

We must also be faithful in our relationship with God. We must love him in our hearts so that the praise on our lips when we worship is true and not false. We must be devoted to the truth of Scripture because God's Word is truth (John 17:17). We must be devoted to reading, meditating, memorizing, and teaching the Bible.

Third, we must lament all kinds of untruth. Jeremiah's example teaches that one of the chief duties of the Christian in declining times is lamentation. Jeremiah is a prophet for post-Christian times, and post-Christian times call for lamentation from God's people.

Lamentation does not mean going around wringing one's hands or living in the nostalgic past. We are not gloomy but joyful, because we know that "Those who trust in the LORD are like Mount Zion, which cannot be moved, but abides forever" (Psalm 125:1). We are full of hope because we know that our salvation is sure in Jesus Christ, who will bring all things in Heaven and on earth under his authority. But at the same time we lament the untruthfulness of our generation. We are moved to tears by the deceptions of our age and the judgment of the age to come. Even as we lament, we ask the Lord to impress us with a still greater sense of the sadness of sin.

Our Comforter in Sorrow

Lamentation is hard service. The life of Jeremiah teaches how costly it can be to have both a passion for God's righteousness and a love for God's people. If Jeremiah had not had a passion for God's righteousness, he would not have been troubled by human sin. If he had not had a love for God's people, he would not have been troubled by divine judgment. But because he had both a passion for righteousness and a love for the people of God, he suffered greatly in his soul. He speaks of his sorrow, his faintness of heart, his mourning, his horror, his tears, his weeping, his wailing, and his lamentation. So great was his love for God's people that when they were crushed, he was crushed.

Some may think that these verses are very bitter. They are not bitter; they are bittersweet. They may be bitter because of sin and judgment, but they are sweet because of the consolation of the Holy Spirit.

In the midst of his great sorrow Jeremiah had a Comforter. True, there were times when he felt comfortless. On at least one occasion he lamented, "A comforter is far from me, one to revive my spirit" (Lamentations 1:16b). Yet what the prophet says in Jeremiah 8 is amazing. There is no other claim like it in the Old Testament: "You who are my Comforter in sorrow," he sighs (v. 18 NIV).

The word for "Comforter" here is a tricky one. The New International Version margin notes that its meaning is uncertain. Most other translations remove the concept of comfort from the verse altogether. Although there are some uncertainties about the text, the translation "Comforter" is a valid possibility. Literally the word means "one who brightens" or "one who restores a smile." Very likely the reason that most Jewish scribes and some Protestant commentators have tried to do something else with this verse is that they do not understand the ministry of the Holy Spirit in the Old Testament.

Jeremiah did not suffer alone. He had a companion in grief, a friend in sorrow. He spoke to him directly, as a friend to a friend. We are bound to conclude from the title he uses that his friend was none other than the Holy Spirit of God, the third person of the Trinity.

It is no surprise to discover the Holy Spirit in the Old Testament. At the creation the Spirit of God hovered over the waters (Genesis 1:2). The Spirit of God descended upon the seventy elders of Moses (Numbers 11:25). He came in power upon the judges of Israel, like Gideon (Judges 6:34), Jephthah (Judges 11:29), and Samson (Judges 13:25). David pleaded with God not to remove his Holy Spirit from him (Psalm 51:11). The Spirit of the Sovereign Lord also anointed Isaiah "To bring good news to the poor" (Isaiah 61:1).

Nor is it a surprise to see the Holy Spirit offering comfort. Within the three persons of the Godhead, it is the special function of the Holy Spirit to comfort. Not that the Spirit is the only one who gives succor. God is "The Father of mercies and God of all comfort, who comforts us in all our affliction . . . through Christ we share abundantly in comfort too" (2 Corinthians 1:3, 4a, 5). Nevertheless, it is the particular ministry of the Holy Spirit to comfort us in our sorrow.

Whether Jeremiah knew this Comforter or not, the Christian certainly knows him. The *King James Version* of the Bible captured an important dimension of the person and work of the Holy Spirit when it called the Holy Spirit "The Comforter." Jesus promised his disciples that he would send his Spirit to be with them forever (John 14:16). The word he used for the Spirit is the Greek word *paraclete*, which can be translated several ways. The Holy Spirit is a "Counselor" who teaches us all things. The Spirit is an "Advocate" who pleads our case before the Father. But the Holy Spirit is also a "Comforter."

The Holy Spirit ministers in the midst of earthly sorrow. "The whole creation has been groaning together in the pains of childbirth until now. And not only the creation, but we ourselves, who have the firstfruits of the Spirit, groan inwardly as we wait eagerly for adoption as sons, the redemption of our bodies" (Romans 8:22, 23). These verses teach that lamentation is an inescapable dimension of our present spiritual experience. We groan inwardly as we await the sanctification of our souls, the resurrection of our bodies, and the glorification of our whole beings.

Who can minister to us in the midst of such lamentable groaning? The Holy Spirit, our Comforter, can. As Paul goes on to write, "The Spirit helps us in our weakness. For we do not know what to pray for as we ought, but the Spirit himself intercedes for us with groanings too deep for words" (v. 26).

This is the comfort Jeremiah discovered. In his bitterness he had sweet consolation. As he wept over the sins of his people, he discovered that someone was weeping beside him. As he wailed over the judgment to come, he found that someone was wailing beside him. In his mourning, he received the blessing of comfort, and thus his lamentations were made bittersweet.

This is a beautiful picture of the personal friendship between God and his child. In this life we experience depths of grief and despair that far exceed our capacity to express them. But do not imagine that the secret sorrows and hidden wounds of the heart exceed the Spirit's capacity to understand and to heal. We may lament the sins of the church and the sins of the nation in private, but we do not weep alone. We have a Comforter in sorrow.

Our Balm in Gilead

We also have a balm in Gilead, which Jeremiah did not have but desperately wanted. The prophet needed medical supplies. He went to the pharmacy and discovered that the pharmacist was completely out of balm of Gilead. He asked if there was a doctor in the house, but there was no answer. Without doctor or medicine, the illness would be terminal. "Is there no balm in Gilead?" Jeremiah laments. "Is there no physician there? Why then has the health of the daughter of my people not been restored?" (8:22).

Gilead was the land just east of the Jordan River. It was known for its healing balsams. When Joseph was sold into slavery by his brothers, he was sold to a caravan taking balm from Gilead down to Egypt (Genesis 37:25). Scholars have been unable to determine how the balm of Gilead was made, but it seems to have been a soothing, aromatic resin made from a tree or plant. It might be compared to aloe vera. The balm of Gilead was useful in keeping wounds from putrefying.

But Jeremiah could find no balm in Gilead. Not for these wounds. As he examined the vital signs of his people, he realized he could do nothing to bring them back to spiritual health. There was no medicine to cure them and no doctor to heal their wounds. The people of God were in need of salvation from sin, but Jeremiah did not know where to find a Savior.

What the people of Judah needed was someone who could heal all their diseases. They needed a Great Physician. What they needed, of course, was Jesus Christ. They needed the Christ who, like Jeremiah, wept over the sins of Jerusalem (Luke 19:41). But Jesus did more than weep for his people. The Scripture says that he went around "proclaiming the gospel of the kingdom and healing every disease and every affliction among the people" (Matthew 4:23). More than that, he died to heal them from the wounds of sin. Jesus Christ is the balm in Gilead. He is the physician who heals the wounds of God's people.

The double comfort of Jesus Christ and the Holy Spirit is perhaps best expressed in the words of the old African-American spiritual:

> There is a balm in Gilead,
> to make the wounded whole;
> There is a balm in Gilead,
> to heal the sin-sick soul.
> Sometimes I feel discouraged,
> and think my work's in vain;
> But then the Holy Spirit,
> revives my soul again.

The balm of Gilead is not for this life only. In Heaven there is either the balm of Gilead or some better balsam. A river flows in the eternal city of God. On each side of the river stands the tree of life, the leaves of which are "for the healing of the nations" (Revelation 22:2). There at the tree of life, in the city of God where Christ rules, Jeremiah will find soothing balm for God's people. He will put away his handkerchief once and for all, for God will wipe every tear from his eyes (Revelation 21:4).

15

Something to Boast About

JEREMIAH 9:12–24

WHEN I BECAME A MEMBER OF Tenth Presbyterian Church in Philadelphia, I received a booklet explaining my responsibilities as a church member. The first page featured a Bible verse written out and signed by the senior pastor, Dr. James Montgomery Boice.

I later learned that Dr. Boice often chose verses appropriate for the new member's name, occupation, or spiritual condition. Here is the verse he chose for me:

> Let him who boasts boast about this:
>   that he understands and knows me,
> that I am the LORD, who exercises kindness,
>   justice and righteousness on earth,
>   for in these I delight." (Jeremiah 9:24 NIV)

On the occasion of my ordination to the pastoral ministry, my sister-in-law wrote to give me the same verses in a different translation:

> Let not the wise man glory in his wisdom,
> Let not the mighty man glory in his might,
> Nor let the rich man glory in his riches;
> But let him who glories glory in this,
> That he understands and knows Me,
> That I am the Lord, exercising lovingkindness,
> judgment, and righteousness in the earth.
> For in these I delight," says the LORD. (Jeremiah 9:23, 24 NKJV)

I never had the courage to ask either Dr. Boice or my sister-in-law why these verses seem so appropriate for me! Perhaps it is because I am boastful by nature. If so, then I receive these verses gladly, for they remind me not to boast about things that are nothing to boast about. Or perhaps this passage is suitable for me because it is my job to boast. I am a professional boaster, for to preach is to boast. And Jeremiah 9:23–24 gives a preacher—or any other Christian, for that matter—plenty to boast about.

The Grim Reaper

Because they are often sung or memorized, these verses are familiar to many Christians. Yet the place they occupy in Jeremiah's teaching is rarely considered. Calvin commented, "This is a remarkable passage, and often found in the mouth of men, as other notable sentences, which are known as proverbial sayings: but yet few rightly consider how these words are connected with the previous context."[1]

As Calvin well knew, the context of these verses is divine judgment. Jeremiah's invitation to boast comes in the middle of a recitation of punishment for sin. Chapter after chapter, verse by verse, over and over again the book of Jeremiah teaches the same lesson: God is a holy God who does not overlook sin but brings sinners to judgment.

Jeremiah 9 contains many righteous judgments. The God who once gave his people manna in the wilderness and water from the rock would offer them wormwood and gall: "Therefore thus says the LORD of hosts, the God of Israel: Behold, I will feed this people with bitter food, and give them poisonous water to drink" (v. 15). This prophecy is about a national calamity in the food and water supplies.

It is followed by a prophecy of exile: "'I will scatter them among the nations whom neither they nor their fathers have known, and I will send the sword after them, until I have consumed them'" (v. 16). Prophecies of exile became more frequent as the Babylonians marched closer and closer to Jerusalem. When judgment finally came, the land would be destroyed.

> For a sound of wailing is heard from Zion:
> "How we are ruined!
> We are utterly shamed,
> because we have left the land,
> because they have cast down our dwellings." (v. 19)

The Babylonians would ravage Jerusalem's infrastructure.

They would also decrease Jerusalem's population. The prophet provided lyrics for a dirge. His song for the dead sends shivers up and down the spine, like a chilling passage from a Stephen King novel: "For death has come up into our windows; it has entered our palaces" (v. 21a). This is death personified. According to Jeremiah, Death is the prowler who comes by night, the stalker who peeks in the window, the intruder who climbs into the house to commit murder. Death is the stealthy assassin who penetrates the defenses and slips into the fortified castle. Or Death is a body snatcher: "It has . . . [cut] off the children from the streets and the young men from the squares" (v. 21b). Death even grabs kids off the city playground. There is nowhere to run and nowhere to hide.

Worse still, Death treats the dead like so much garbage, denying them a proper burial:

> Speak: "Thus declares the LORD,
> 'The dead bodies of men shall fall
>   like dung upon the open field,
> like sheaves after the reaper,
>   and none shall gather them.'" (v. 22)

This macabre massacre is well-illustrated in a painting by Winslow Homer called "Veteran in a New Field." The painting shows a wide field of wheat against a blue horizon. In the foreground a man swings a scythe; dark cut grain is strewn all around him. The painting is not about farming; it is about war and death. It is evident from the farmer's garments that he has recently returned from fighting for the Union in the Civil War. The wheat he mows down before the blue horizon represents the destruction of the South.

Death is the Grim Reaper who leaves the dead bodies of men like cut grain in an open field. Longfellow described him like this:

> There is a Reaper, whose name is Death,
> And, with his sickle keen,
> He reaps the bearded grain at a breath,
> And the flowers that grow between.[2]

The School of Sadness

Jeremiah must have been disturbed by these images of death. He asked, "Who is the man so wise that he can understand this? To whom has the mouth of the LORD spoken, that he may declare it? Why is the land ruined and laid waste like a wilderness, so that no one passes through?" (v. 12). The answer was not hard to find. Death is the inevitable consequence of sin. "And the LORD says: 'Because they have forsaken my law that I set before them, and have not obeyed my voice or walked in accord with it, but have stubbornly followed their own hearts and have gone after the Baals, as their fathers taught them'" (vv. 13, 14).

God's people received judgment the old-fashioned way—they earned it. The question is not, "What have these people done to deserve this?" The question is, "What *haven't* they done?" You name it, they had done it: idol worship, adultery, lying, child sacrifice, not praising God, prostitution, unfaithfulness, treachery, shady dealings, false preaching, not fearing God, covenant-breaking, violence, greed, not walking in God's way, hypocrisy, racism, murder, goddess worship, slander, and rejecting the Word of God. In a word, they were stubborn (v. 14), which means to exhibit "a defiant attitude toward the Lord, a rejection of his law, a preference for other gods, and a refusal to repent."[3]

If these sins sound familiar, it is because they are the sins of post-Christian times—adultery, dishonesty, godlessness, racism, goddess worship, and so on. Such sins call for lamentation, which is one of the chief duties of the Christian in declining times. Christians are to weep over the sins of the church, the transgressions of the nation, and the fearfulness of the judgment to come.

Jeremiah beckoned the skillful wailing women to come in haste.

Thus says the Lord of hosts:

> "Consider, and call for the mourning women to come;
>   send for the skillful women to come;
> let them make haste and raise a wailing over us,
>   that our eyes may run down with tears
>   and our eyelids flow with water." (vv. 17, 18)

These women were mourners by occupation. They were real pros. "In the Middle East even today, on the occasion of deaths or calamities, mourning is carried out by professional women who follow the funeral bier uttering a high-pitched shriek."[4] Jeremiah invited the wailing women to let their tears flow into the eyes of their friends and neighbors so the whole nation could weep together.

Jerusalem would need as many mourners as she could get. Lamentation would become a growth industry:

> Hear, O women, the word of the Lord,
>   and let your ear receive the word of his mouth;
> teach to your daughters a lament,
>   and each to her neighbor a dirge. (v. 20)

There were to be plenty of job opportunities for professional wailing women. Perhaps God spoke to women here because they are more given to tears, but these verses are not just for women. Every Christian is called to weep with those who weep (Romans 12:15).

In these post-Christian times, Christians will need to rediscover the lost art of lamentation. In addition to teaching sons and daughters how to hate sin and fear its consequences, we must impress upon them the sadness of sin. As we pass a playground on the way to worship on the Lord's Day, my son might say, "Why aren't those guys going to church?" "Oh," I say, "it's a very sad thing, but some people do not love the Lord. They do not know that Sunday morning is a time for worship and not for basketball." Or we see parents fighting with children at the shopping mall. Dysfunctional families are distressing to watch. The primary emotion they ought to evoke is sadness for sin.

If Jeremiah 9 is any indication, the Lord calls some Christians to a ministry of lamentation. He "gave the apostles, the prophets, the evangelists, the shepherds and teachers" (Ephesians 4:11). Others exercise the gifts of helps or intercession. But where are the wailing women and mourning men of the evangelical church? Francis Schaeffer reminds us that

> with love we must face squarely the fact that our culture really is under the judgment of God. . . . We must proclaim the message with tears and give it with love. . . . It will not do to say these things coldly. Jeremiah cried, and we must cry for the poor lost world, for we are all of one kind. . . . I *must* have tears for my kind.[5]

Who will lament the sins of the church, the transgressions of the nation, and the fearfulness of the judgment to come?

Nothing to Boast About

It is just at this point—right in the context of sin, judgment, and lamentation—that we are warned about improper boasting.

> Thus says the LORD: "Let not the wise man boast in his wisdom, let not the mighty man boast in his might, let not the rich man boast in his riches." (9:23)

Wisdom, strength, and riches are nothing to boast about.

Wise men do love to boast about their wisdom. It starts early in elementary school: "I got a sticker on my paper; what did you get?" By the time some people get to university, their boasting is out of control. During my first term at Oxford I had the misfortune to walk behind two first-year students in the High Street. "So," said one Fresher to the other, "how's your arrogance coming along?"

Such boasting is not new. Back in the nineteenth century a scholar from

Padua paid a visit to Oxford. He did not find any members of the university who knew everything, but he did find plenty of know-it-alls:

> Elsewhere I have asked a professor of astronomy some questions regarding anatomy, or botany, and he had the courage and honesty at once frankly to answer, 'I do not know'. But at Oxford it really seemed as if everybody considered himself equally bound to be universal, to know everything, and to be able to give some sort of affirmative answer to every question, however foreign it might be to his ordinary and proper pursuits. There is so much wisdom in answering seasonably, 'I do not know', that in a university which has been celebrated, and accounted most wise for nine or ten centuries, I thought for the credit of the place, I ought to get it once, at least, before I went away; so I tried hard, but I could never attain it. Why was this?[6]

The Apostle Paul had a simple answer for the mystified academic from Padua: "'Knowledge' puffs up" (1 Corinthians 8:1). Intellectual accomplishments feed the ego.

The wise person may boast of his wisdom, but a high IQ is nothing to boast about. Only God knows all things, and all wisdom comes from him. Whatever is good, true, wise, or beautiful is known already by God. Therefore the best intellectual accomplishment is to think God's thoughts after him.

> Where is the one who is wise? Where is the scribe? Where is the debater of this age? Has not God made foolish the wisdom of the world? ... we preach Christ crucified, a stumbling block to Jews and folly to Gentiles, but to those who are called, both Jews and Greeks, Christ the power of God and the wisdom of God. For the foolishness of God is wiser than men. (1 Corinthians 1:20, 23–25a)

To be truly wise, begin with the fear of the Lord (Proverbs 1:7), then seek the knowledge of God in the face of Jesus Christ (2 Corinthians 4:6).

So much for the wise. What about the strong? Strong men, too, like to boast about their strength. Athletes are no longer content to score touchdowns, tackle quarterbacks, or make three-pointers. They want to strut, dance, taunt, jump into the crowd, and humiliate their opponents. Boxers and wrestlers seem to spend as much time jawing as they spend working out. Back in the early seventies, when Muhammad Ali told everyone he was "The greatest," it was a novelty. Now everyone is doing it.

The strong man may boast in his strength, but a physique is nothing to boast about. For one thing, the strength of a man is not to be compared with the strength of God. The Apostle Paul addressed this topic as well. In fact, he seems to have had Jeremiah 9 in mind when he wrote to the Corinthians.

After saying that "The foolishness of God is wiser than men," he goes on to say that "The weakness of God is stronger than men" (1 Corinthians 1:25). Furthermore, man's strength, as weak as it is, diminishes with age. At the 1996 Olympics in Atlanta it was everything Muhammad Ali could do to stand in silence and lift the Olympic torch.

The rich are as boastful as the wise and the strong. Jesus told the story of a rich man who had so many possessions, he had no place to keep them all.

> "And he said, 'I will do this: I will tear down my barns and build larger ones, and there I will store all my grain and my goods. And I will say to my soul, "Soul, you have ample goods laid up for many years; relax, eat, drink, be merry."' But God said to him, 'Fool! This night your soul is required of you, and the things you have prepared, whose will they be?'" (Luke 12:18–20)

Jesus then explained the point of the story: "So is the one who lays up treasure for himself and is not rich toward God" (v. 21). In other words, you can't take it with you.

The Puritan Thomas Fuller pointed out the two problems with wealth: "Riches may leave us while we live, we must leave them when we die." Earthly riches are no lasting treasure.

Wisdom, strength, riches—these things are nothing to boast about. Neither is anything else apart from God himself. John Calvin explained:

> Not only condemned in these words is the boasting of human power, and the glorying in wisdom and in wealth, but that men are wholly stripped of all the confidence they place in themselves, or seek from the world, in order that the knowledge of God alone may be deemed enough for obtaining perfect happiness.[7]

You may be smart. You may be strong. You may be rich. But you have nothing to boast about:

> The race is not to the swift, nor the battle to the strong, nor bread to the wise, nor riches to the intelligent, nor favor to those with knowledge, but time and chance happen to them all. (Ecclesiastes 9:11)

The limitations of mere talent were illustrated by the misfortune of the brilliant economist William Vickery. In October 1997, at the age of sixty-two, he was awarded the Nobel Prize for Economics. Twenty-four hours later he was dead.

Jeremiah discovered that neither mind nor body can give ultimate security in this life. Or the next. Death and destruction overtake everyone who trusts in worldly wisdom, human strength, or earthly treasure. When people are scattered among the nations, houses lie in ruins, Death climbs in through the window, and the Grim Reaper takes his sickle to the grain; then all boasting must come to an end. The dead do not boast.

Boast about This

The Christian, however, does have one thing to boast about:

> Let him who boasts boast in this, that he understands and knows me, that I am the LORD who practices steadfast love, justice, and righteousness in the earth. For in these things I delight. (9:24)

If you must boast—as all human beings must, because we were made to boast—then boast about the understanding and knowledge of God. Your boast is not that you understand and know God. The only reason you know God is because he has revealed himself through his Word and his world. But you may boast about God himself. The Christian's proper boast is in a Godward direction.

So boast about this, that God is the Lord who made Heaven and earth, the Lord God of Abraham, Isaac, and Jacob. He is the Lord who met Moses at the burning bush and brought the children of Israel out of their bondage in Egypt. He is the Lord who helped Joshua conquer the Promised Land, and whom David praised when he said "The LORD is my shepherd" (Psalm 23:1). He is the Lord who sent fire to consume Elijah's altar when all the people said, "The LORD, he is God; the LORD, he is God" (1 Kings 18:39). And he is the same Lord who brought his people back from their captivity in Babylon.

To boast in the Lord is also to boast in Jesus Christ. A boast about the Godness of God is a boast about the Lordship of Jesus Christ. The Lord God of the Old Testament is one and the same with God the Son in the New Testament.

> Therefore God has highly exalted him and bestowed on him the name that is above every name, so that at the name of Jesus every knee should bow, in heaven and on earth and under the earth, and every tongue confess that Jesus Christ is Lord, to the glory of God the Father. (Philippians 2:9–11; cf. Isaiah 45:22–25)

Now *that* is something to boast about. Jesus Christ is the risen Lord who must receive all praise, glory, and worship. The Lordship of Jesus Christ is the Christian's best boast.

Since you, as a human being, will boast from time to time, boast also about this, that the Lord exercises "steadfast love" on earth (9:24). This "steadfast love" means more than being nice, like feeding the dog or helping a little old lady across the street. The Hebrew word for *steadfast love* is so rich that it takes a half dozen English words to convey its meaning. It means covenant loyalty, unfailing devotion, and merciful affection. The *King James* and *New American Standard* versions translate it best as "lovingkindness." Kindness is the love of God expressed through Jesus Christ in the eternal covenant of God's grace.

God speaks of his kindness in the Ten Commandments when he promises to show "lovingkindness to thousands, to those who love Me and keep My commandments" (Exodus 20:6 NASB). God showed his lovingkindness to Moses on Mount Sinai when he passed in front of him and said, "The LORD, the LORD God, compassionate and gracious, slow to anger, and abounding in lovingkindness and truth, who keeps lovingkindness for thousands, who forgives iniquity, transgression and sin" (Exodus 34:6–7 NASB).

The lovingkindness of God—that is something worth boasting about. Psalm 136 is one long boast about God's kindness. Twenty-six times God's people utter this refrain: "His lovingkindness is everlasting" (NASB).

To boast about loving-kindness includes boasting in the lavish gift of God's Son, Jesus Christ. "For God so loved the world, that he gave his only Son, that whoever believes in him should not perish but have eternal life" (John 3:16). It is also to boast about the obedience of Christ when he suffered and died for our sins on the cross. "By this we know love, that he laid down his life for us" (1 John 3:16).

Boast about this, too, that the Lord exercises "justice" on earth. An unjust God is no more to be worshiped than an unkind God. Who would worship a God who lets righteousness go unrewarded or allows wickedness to go unpunished?

The God of the Christian's boast is no such God. He is a God of justice. He condemns the wicked and punishes them with eternal judgment. He vindicates the righteous and rewards them with pleasures forevermore. He will bring every deed to judgment, whether open or secret. God is slow to anger, it is true, but he will not leave the guilty unpunished. He is known for his justice (Psalm 9:16); he "loves righteous deeds" (Psalm 11:7); he gives justice to all the oppressed (Psalm 103:6). A God of such perfect and exacting justice is not to be trifled with. But he is worth boasting about!

Finally, boast about this, that the Lord exercises "righteousness" on earth. *Righteousness* is uprightness, rectitude, and integrity. It is moral perfection. To say that God is righteous is to say that he is "holy, holy, holy" (cf. Isaiah 6:3). He is upright in all his ways and perfect in all his actions.

To boast about the righteousness of God is really to boast about the righteousness of Jesus Christ. For in the righteousness of Christ, God's loving-kindness and justice embrace. As Jeremiah has already boasted, God is love, and God is just. Because of his justice God could not simply overlook sin. Although that might be loving, it would not be just. Because of his love God did not simply damn us for our sins. Although that would be just, it would not be a full expression of God's love. But love and justice embrace in the righteousness of Christ.

Jesus Christ gave himself up for us all—that is God's loving-kindness. Jesus Christ satisfied the justice of God by paying the price for our sins—that is God's justice. The righteousness of Christ makes God to be both just and the justifier of the ungodly (Romans 3:26). That is so far beyond anything mortals could improvise that it calls for a boast.

Paul proposes such a boast at the end of his exposition of Jeremiah 9. He moves from worldly wisdom (which is nothing to boast about) to the righteousness of Christ (which is everything to boast about):

> But God chose what is foolish in the world to shame the wise; God chose what is weak in the world to shame the strong; God chose what is low and despised in the world, even things that are not, to bring to nothing things that are, so that no human being might boast in the presence of God. And because of him you are in Christ Jesus, who became to us wisdom from God, righteousness and sanctification and redemption, so that, as it is written, "Let the one who boasts, boast in the Lord." (1 Corinthians 1:27–31)

Yes, let everyone who boasts boast in the Lord, "who practices steadfast love, justice, and righteousness in the earth."

Do you know this boastable Lord? If not, then you have nothing to boast about. If so, then boast all you want. You have so many reasons to boast you will be boasting away for all eternity.

16

The Scarecrow in the Melon Patch

JEREMIAH 9:25—10:16

JEREMIAH 10 IS A DUET in which two voices are woven together into one song. First one voice sings, then the other, and then the first sings again.

Derek Kidner describes the duet as a polemic and a psalm.[1] A *polemic* is an attack, objection, argument, critique, or refutation of something false. The polemical voice in this song speaks out against the idols of the nations and attacks them because they are worthless. A *psalm* is a song of praise for the matchless God of the universe.

Only Skin-Deep

Jeremiah's duet began with dark, ominous words, like chords from an organ at the beginning of a suspense film. With a foreboding sense of impending doom, God promised to punish all the nations of the world that refused to worship him: "Behold, the days are coming, declares the Lord, when I will punish all those who are circumcised merely in the flesh—Egypt, Judah, Edom, the sons of Ammon, Moab, and all who dwell in the desert" (9:25, 26a). It was a preview of coming destructions: "Coming soon to a nation near you . . . the God of justice!" The prophecy also served as a precursor of the end of Jeremiah's book, which contains six chapters of judgment against these very nations (chapters 46—51).

Divine judgment should come as no surprise, because "These nations are uncircumcised" (9:26b). They did not belong to God, nor did they bear in their bodies the sign of belonging to him.

The shocking thing was that God judged Israel along with these unholy nations, saying, "All the house of Israel are uncircumcised in heart" (9:26b; cf. Deuteronomy 10:16, 17; Jeremiah 4:4). God tossed the sacred in with the profane, the circumcised in with the uncircumcised, the clean laundry in with the dirty clothes. His people had become little more than pagans.

The problem was that Israel's religion was merely external. The people were just going through the motions. They practiced all the outward traditions of the Law of Moses, but they did not love God with an undying love. They circumcised their bodies, but not their hearts, so their faith was only skin-deep.

This reminds the Christian of the necessity of living a baptized life. The Westminster *Larger Catechism* calls this "improving our baptism" (Q & A 167). New Testament baptism—like Old Testament circumcision—marks the Christian's entrance into the family of God. It is a sign and a seal of God's grace. But the act of water baptism does not save. The believer must be baptized in the heart as well as in the flesh, with the Holy Spirit as well as with water (cf. Acts 11:16). Anyone who has been baptized with water but does not live like a Christian is still a pagan.

Why Idols Attract

The reason Jeremiah lumped the people of Judah in with the nations was because they had been acting like pagans. The point of his polemic is that God's people had been worshiping idols.

Contemporary Christians face a problem when they encounter Old Testament idols. Most have seen enough pictures of ancient Near Eastern artifacts to know that idols are little wooden statues or clay figurines standing on a shelf. They do not impress. They seem more like cultural relics than deities. They are not the kind of things postmoderns are tempted to worship.

Understanding how idols work, however, requires sensing their attraction. Calvin worried about this danger in his *Institutes of the Christian Religion*: "Let us learn how greatly our nature inclines toward idolatry, rather than, by charging the Jews with being guilty of the common failing, we, under vain enticements to sin, sleep the sleep of death."[2] To put it another way, take the two-by-four out of your own eye before taking the sawdust out of Israel's eye (cf. Luke 6:41, 42).

What made idol worship so attractive? First, "everybody was doing it." Idolatry was supported by the weight of public opinion. Jeremiah described idol worship as one of the ways of the nations, a custom of the peoples:

Hear the word that the LORD speaks to you, O house of Israel.
Thus says the LORD:

"Learn not the way of the nations,
    nor be dismayed at the signs of the heavens
    because the nations are dismayed at them,
for the customs of the peoples are vanity." (10:1–3a)

Israel was under international peer pressure. The Babylonians were so successful that everything they did seemed glamorous, even their religion. When the Babylonians read "The signs of the heavens" (v. 2), the Israelites wanted to check their horoscopes too. If idolatry was good enough for Babylon, it was good enough for Jerusalem.

Israel was fascinated with foreign religion: "Beaten silver is brought from Tarshish, and gold from Uphaz" (v. 9a). Idol worship was "in." It was trendy and fashionable. There were articles about it in the magazines at the grocery store. Idol worship was also exotic. It had all the sophistication of faraway lands. Peer pressure does not end with puberty. The social pressures to worship the wrong things can squeeze entire nations of adults. They might even squeeze you.

The other reason idols attract is aesthetic. In Jeremiah's day idolatry was beautiful. Ancient idols were adorned with precious metals and overlaid with silver and gold. "They are the work of the craftsman and of the hands of the goldsmith; their clothing is violet and purple; they are all the work of skilled men" (v. 9b). The idols were richly clothed, like so many mannequins in a department store. They were dressed in purple, the color of royalty. The craftsmanship was excellent.

Before laughing at the Israelites for bowing down before blocks of wood, feel the tug of idolatry in your own heart. Consider how attractive the idols of this age often seem. Consider the appeal of rich desserts. Or the satisfaction of managing the lives of others. Or the allure of sexual pleasure. Or the comfort of being well liked. Or the exhilaration of making it to the top of your profession. Or the relaxation of a luxury vacation. Or the security of good insurance coverage.

All these things can become idols. Origen (c. 185–254)—the great African theologian of the third century—said, "What each one honors before all else, what before all things he admires and loves, this for him is God." So food, control, sex, popularity, success, leisure, and financial security can all become like gods. They can occupy the place in life that God alone should occupy.

Theologian David Wells defines idolatry as "Trusting some substitute for God to serve some uniquely divine function. . . . These substitutes need not be supernatural; money, power, expertise, the location of the planets on the astrological charts, and a belief in Progress are among the most popular idols of Our Time."[3] Such idols attract. They seem good. The trouble comes when they take God's place.

Then add to the natural attraction of idolatry the fact that "everybody's doing it." It seems like everyone is eating like a glutton, fooling around, people pleasing, climbing the corporate ladder, using people to complete an agenda, living a life of ease, or basing his or her net worth on his or her net worth. Contemporary Christians face as much pressure to be idolaters as Jeremiah's friends did. Maybe more, since more idols are available.

If I Only Had a Brain

As attractive and popular as idols are, they are still worthless. Three times Jeremiah told the people of Israel that idols were "worthless" (NIV). "The customs of the peoples" (v. 3), wooden idols (v. 8), and images (v. 15) are all said to be "worthless." The word translated "worthless" is the same word repeated so often in Ecclesiastes. Idolatry is vanity. Idols are absolute nothings, total zeroes.

Why are idols so completely worthless? Here is the argument that forms Jeremiah's polemic. First, idols were man-made.

> [F]or the customs of the peoples are vanity.
> A tree from the forest is cut down
> and worked with an axe by the hands of a craftsman.
> They decorate it with silver and gold;
> they fasten it with hammer and nails
> so that it cannot move. (vv. 3, 4)

This is the prophet's do-it-yourself kit for making idols: Choose a sturdy tree in the forest, chop it down, and drag it back to your workbench. Next, take a hammer and some carving tools and shape it to look like an animal or a person. Then adorn it with silver and gold.

One more thing: Nail the idol down. Idols usually go up on the shelf; however, the kind of god that can be shelved runs the risk of toppling over and breaking. There is something embarrassing about a wobbly god, something unseemly about a deity who falls off the shelf and lands on his face. Better get out the hammer and nail him into place.

In this way Jeremiah showed how ridiculous it is to worship idols. His point was that idols are man-made. This is equally true within the human heart, which Calvin called "a perpetual factory of idols."[4]

The problem with such man-made idols is that they are impotent, powerless, unable to do anything. They are "like scarecrows in a cucumber field" (v. 5).

Jeremiah's analogy suggests that idols are much like the scarecrow in *The Wizard of Oz*. As Dorothy followed the Yellow Brick Road on her way to the Emerald City, she passed a scarecrow who was very sad. A tear ran down the poor fellow's cheek.

The reason the scarecrow was such a sad sack was because he was a few bales short of a haystack. He wistfully tells all the things he would be able to do, think, and say if he only had a brain: "My head I'd be scratchin' while my thoughts were busy hatchin' if I only had a brain."

False gods are "like scarecrows in a cucumber field." They do not have any brains (or anything else, for that matter):

> Their idols are like scarecrows in a cucumber field,
>   and they cannot speak;
> they have to be carried,
>   for they cannot walk.
>
> Do not be afraid of them,
>   for they cannot do evil,
>   neither is it in them to do good. (v. 5)

False gods cannot speak, think, walk, do any harm, or do any good. They cannot save from sin and death. They cannot do anything at all. The most that can be said for idols is that they are portable. "Jeremiah pictures a tame god, a user-friendly god, who exists by human manufacture, is at human disposal, and is under human control. This god would never rebuke, warn, threaten, or talk back."[5]

Idols appear lifelike, but they are actually lifeless:

> Every man is stupid and without knowledge;
>   every goldsmith is put to shame by his idols,
> for his images are false,
>   and there is no breath in them. (10:14)

Idolaters are as false as their idols. Even the wise men of the nations "are both stupid and foolish; the instruction of idols is but wood!" (v. 8).

This is Jeremiah's satiric polemic against idolatry: Idols are man-made, impotent, false, and generally worthless. The tone is scornful and sarcastic, which is typical of the way Old Testament prophets treat idols. Elijah was just as scornful on Mount Carmel, where he taunted the prophets of Baal (1 Kings

18). Isaiah was equally sarcastic when he ridiculed gods made of wood. Truly, idols "are worthless, a work of delusion" (10:15a).

The idols in your own heart deserve similar treatment. The first step is to identify them. Dick Keyes points out that most Christians have dozens of idols:

> In this society, our idols tend to be in clusters. They are inflationary, have short shelf lives, and change, adapt, and multiply quickly as if by mitosis, or cell-division. An idol can be a physical property, a person, an activity, a role, an institution, a hope, an image, an idea, a pleasure, a hero—anything that can substitute for God.[6]

This leaves plenty of scope for idolatry. A piece of merchandise in a mail-order catalog. A potential mate. Collecting antiques. Rollerblading. Popular music. A better-looking body. Your ministry in the church. All these things can become idols.

To identify your own idols, ask questions like these: What things take the place of God in my life? Where do I find my significance and my confidence? What things make me really angry? (Anger usually erupts when an idol gets knocked off the shelf.)

Once the idols on your shelf have been identified, see them for what they really are. Recognize that they are like the scarecrow in the melon patch: man-made, impotent, false, and worthless. Then scorn them the way Jeremiah scorned the idols of his day.

What would a prophet say about our private idolatries? He might say, "Do you mean to tell me that you worship television? You must be joking! The images on your TV screen are not even real. The characters in the soap opera do not deserve your pity; the characters in the sitcom do not deserve your laughter. When you pull the plug, they all vanish."

Or a prophet might say: "You worship your work? You must be out of your mind! Your career cannot give you lasting satisfaction. No one ever says, at a retirement dinner or from a death bed, 'I wish I had spent more time at the office.'"

Or maybe he would say, "You have to be kidding! You worship . . ." There are not enough pages in this book to list every example. But the Holy Spirit can help you identify your own idols and figure out what kind of derision they deserve.

God, the One and Only

The polemical part of Jeremiah's duet came wrapped in a psalm exceedingly rich in its praise of God's attributes. Everything Jeremiah praised about God's character stands in direct contrast to everything he criticized about pagan idols. While the polemic jangles against the worthlessness of every idol, the psalm sweetly praises the matchlessness of the only God.

Together the polemic and the psalm comprise an effective strategy for apologetics. Apologetics is a fancy term for explaining why you are a Christian. Biblical apologetics often employs a one-two punch—first a polemic and then a psalm. First an attack on false gods and then a vindication of the true God.

This was Elijah's strategy on Mount Carmel—the refutation of Baal before the demonstration of the Lord God of Israel (1 Kings 18). It was also Jeremiah's theme for his duet. Having proven the worthlessness of idols, he proceeded to show the matchlessness of God. This basic strategy is useful whenever you explain why you are a Christian. Start by revealing the weakness of a post-Christian worldview and end by boasting about salvation in Jesus Christ.

Jeremiah began his boast with the uniqueness of God. God is one-of-a-kind, incomparable: "There is none like you, O LORD; you are great, and your name is great in might" (10:6). Idols are a dime a dozen. There are as many idols as there are scarecrows in all the melon patches in the world. But there is only one God, whom Jeremiah presented as the One and Only. Idols are worthless, vain, empty. They cannot even stand on their own two feet without wobbling. But God is great. Even his name is mighty in power.

Furthermore, God is the King: "Who would not fear you, O King of the nations? For this is your due" (v. 7a). An idol can only be in one place at a time. Once the scarecrow gets put in the melon patch, it stays there until it gets moved. But God is everywhere. There is no limit to the extent of the kingdom of Jesus Christ. He deserves reverence from all peoples and nations.

Then add wisdom to God's greatness and sovereign rule. "Among all the wise ones of the nations and in all their kingdoms there is none like you" (v. 7b). All the wise men in all the nations would not begin to approach the wisdom of God. This is because God is True, with a capital T. "The LORD is the true God" (v. 10). The idols are false, witless, a total sham. Behind their fancy costumes and shiny jewels they are nothing but blocks of wood. But God is the genuine article. He is true to his character, true in all he says and does. The one God is the true God.

Moreover, he is "The living God" (v. 10). The trouble with scarecrows is that they are not alive. Their heads are full of stuffin'. "There is no breath in them" (v. 14). But the one, great, true God is the living God.

It is vastly preferable to have a God who is alive. Consider what an advantage it is that Jesus Christ has been raised from the dead. When you pray to him, he can answer. When you are sick, he can heal you. When you are in trouble, he can save you. When you sin, he can forgive you. And when you are dead, he can bring you back to life.

Jeremiah's psalm also praises God as "The everlasting King" (v. 10). Idols have short shelf lives. "At the time of their punishment they shall perish" (v. 15b). But the kingdom of God is no temporary monarchy. God is never in danger of being voted out of office. Jesus Christ will be King over Heaven and earth forever and forever. "Of the increase of his government and of peace there will be no end, on the throne of David and over his kingdom . . . forevermore" (Isaiah 9:7).

Then consider the justice of God's wrath: "At his wrath the earth quakes, and the nations cannot endure his indignation" (10:10b). Idols do not make people tremble. At best, scarecrows only frighten blackbirds. But the anger of God against sin will make all nations tremble. Who can withstand his wrath?

Perhaps the most important difference between mere scarecrows and the living God is that scarecrows are manufactured. Idols are always man-made. They do not make themselves and cannot make anything else. "Thus shall you say to them: 'The gods who did not make the heavens and the earth shall perish from the earth and from under the heavens'" (v. 11).

God is not man-made. On the contrary, God made man. God—the one and only, the true and living Lord, the eternal King—made human beings and gave life to all that is:

> It is he who made the earth by his power,
>> who established the world by his wisdom,
>> and by his understanding stretched out the heavens. (v. 12)

This is God's work of creation, his making the world and everything in it, and all of it very good. That is what God *did*.

Add what God *does* to what he did. His providence is as much his work as creation is. God did not just wind up the world and then let it wind down, like some cosmic watchmaker. He not only created the world but continues to sustain it by the word of his power.

> When he utters his voice, there is a tumult of waters in the heavens,
>> and he makes the mist rise from the ends of the earth.
> He makes lightning for the rain,
>> and he brings forth the wind from his storehouses. (v. 13)

The providence of God extends to the rain, the clouds, the lightning, and the wind.

This is a beautiful psalm written to praise a beautiful God. In it Jeremiah provided an outline for an entire Sunday school class on the doctrine of God, covering the uniqueness, power, sovereignty, wisdom, truth, eternity, creation, and providence of God.

A Healthy Portion

It might be tempting to think that an almighty God is out of reach. But Jeremiah saved the best for last, dismissing any doubts about having a friendship with an omnipotent and eternal God with a beautiful title: "Not like these is he who is the portion of Jacob" (v. 16a).

True, God is "The one who formed all things" (v. 16a). But what he made includes "Israel . . . the tribe of his inheritance; the LORD of hosts is his name" (v. 16b). So in addition to making the heavens and the earth, God made a people for himself. As the Scripture says, "The LORD's portion is his people" (Deuteronomy 32:9). A "portion" is a share or allotment of an inheritance. When the children of Israel entered the Promised Land, they each received a portion of the land (Joshua 13—19). To say that God's people are his portion is to say that they belong to him. His people are his by right. Jeremiah even calls them God's "inheritance," as if they were God's prized possession (which they are!).

At the same time, God belongs to his people. He has entered into a mutual friendship with them through Jesus Christ. Jesus is our allotment, our inheritance. In Christ we help ourselves to a portion of divinity. It is almost as if we can grab a piece of God. He is our possession. We are entitled to him. He is ours by grace.

To have a healthy portion of God is to have the ultimate inheritance. If God is your portion, you will not need any seconds. Jeremiah knew this from his own experience. The weeping prophet was often in deep distress. He wrote about being afflicted, having his heart pierced, becoming a laughingstock, having his teeth broken, and being downcast (Lamentations 3:1–20). But in the midst of his distress Jeremiah remembered that he had the ultimate inheritance: "'The LORD is my portion,' says my soul, 'therefore I will hope in him'" (Lamentations 3:24; cf. Psalm 73:26; 119:57). Jeremiah never let go of his portion of God.

It is hard to find such intimacy in the melon patch. Scarecrows are not much comfort. Consider the scarecrow in Mr. McGregor's Garden. In Beatrix Potter's *Peter Rabbit*, Peter gets into all kinds of trouble. After he runs into Mr.

McGregor "round the end of a cucumber frame," the old farmer chases him all over the garden. Along the way Peter loses his entire wardrobe. He loses one shoe in the cabbages and another among the potatoes. He gets caught in a gooseberry net by his buttons and has to wriggle out of his new jacket to get free.

Later, when Peter ventures back into the garden, he discovers that the enterprising McGregor has appropriated his clothes and turned them into a scarecrow. That is how a scarecrow is made. Nail a few pieces of wood together, throw on a jacket and a pair of shoes and voilà—a scarecrow. This is precisely why it is impossible to develop a relationship with an idol. Sane people do not carry on conversations with their wardrobes.

Jesus Christ is no scarecrow. He came to this world so his people could enter into friendship with God. Jesus says, "You are my friends if you do what I command you. No longer do I call you servants, for the servant does not know what his master is doing; but I have called you friends, for all that I have heard from my Father I have made known to you" (John 15:14, 15). What a friend we have in Jesus! He is the Christian's allotment and inheritance. The Lord Almighty, who made Heaven and earth, is our portion forever!

17

This Is (Not) Your Life

JEREMIAH 10:17–25

LET'S GO! LET'S GO! Get your things together! Grab your bags and start packing! It is time to get out of town!" God is sending Jerusalem packing. "Gather up your bundle from the ground, O you who dwell under siege!" (10:17). The command is startling. In the words of Derek Kidner, "Suddenly there is the sheer drop from the pinnacle to the depths: from the thought of Israel as God's own treasure to the pathetic sight of her as a refugee leaving the ruins for the road."[1]

Jeremiah seems to be writing in the middle of a siege, perhaps when Jerusalem was surrounded in 597 BC. He is preparing the people of God for deportation, and he knows that refugees are their own bellhops. Murals from the ancient Near East depict long trains of captives being led into exile, often shackled together at the ankle. Each prisoner carried all his earthly possessions on his head, wrapped in a bundle.

There is no time to lose:

For thus says the LORD:
"Behold, I am slinging out the inhabitants of the land
    at this time,
and I will bring distress on them,
    that they may feel it." (v. 18)

This is a prophecy of sudden and violent judgment. The word translated "slinging" is actually the word for "slingshot." God is going to catapult his people into captivity.

Everything left behind will be devastated. The Babylonian forces are beginning to mobilize. "Behold, it comes!—a great commotion out of the north country" (v. 22a). Soon the army will come and scorch the earth. It will "make the cities of Judah a desolation, a lair of jackals" (v. 22b). When the people of Judah march off to Babylon with their bundles on their heads, the towns they leave behind will only be suitable for wild hyenas.

Vicarious Suffering

What about Jeremiah? He was a righteous man. Did the Lord judge him along with the rest of his people?

Yes, Jeremiah did suffer. As a righteous prophet, he chose to suffer for the sake of God's people. He was one of the prophets the apostle James had in mind when he wrote, "As an example of suffering and patience, brothers, take the prophets who spoke in the name of the Lord" (James 5:10).

Jeremiah had already sworn absolute solidarity with his people: "For the wound of the daughter of my people is my heart wounded" (8:21). Now he is crushed. God's judgment against the nation of Israel has been brought down to the personal level. Jeremiah must endure his people's sufferings as his own. He does not speak for himself alone, but for the whole nation. What he says about his sons ("My children have gone from me, and they are not," v. 20) does not quite fit his personal circumstances since he was commanded not to marry or have sons (see 16:1–4). But Jeremiah identified so closely with the people of God that it was hard to know where their sufferings ended and his began.

Jeremiah faced three crushing afflictions. First, he was crushed *physically*. His own body was racked with illness and disease: "Woe is me because of my hurt! My wound is grievous. But I said, 'Truly this is an affliction, and I must bear it'" (v. 19; cf. 30:12). The life of faith is not always a life of health and happiness. Even though he was righteous, Jeremiah was afflicted with an incurable wound.

Second, Jeremiah was crushed *domestically*. His household was destroyed:

> My tent is destroyed,
>   and all my cords are broken;
> my children have gone from me,
>   and they are not;
> there is no one to spread my tent again
>   and to set up my curtains. (v. 20; cf. 4:20b)

Jeremiah thus described himself—or perhaps the city of Jerusalem—as a nomad under attack. Enemies have come and cut his ropes. His tent has collapsed on top of him. Worst of all, the invaders have taken away his sons. Now he is homeless. There is no one to help him set up his tent again. Jeremiah's house and household have been destroyed.

Third, Jeremiah was crushed *socially*. He suffered because the leaders of his nation were foolish and immoral:

> For the shepherds are stupid
>   and do not inquire of the LORD;
> therefore they have not prospered,
>   and all their flock is scattered. (v. 21)

Ancient priests and political leaders were supposed to be shepherds for their people. They were to gather, protect, and feed their sheep. But these shepherds were little better than stupid brutes because they did not follow the Law of God. Jeremiah may have had in mind kings like Manasseh and Jehoiakim, who deliberately rejected God. Or perhaps he was thinking of the false priests and prophets of Israel who denied that God would judge his people for their sins. Probably he was referring to both, since "shepherd" denotes both royal and religious leadership. Jeremiah suffered because the leaders of his nation and his church were incompetent and immoral.

The reason shepherds always need to be sensible is that sheep are always wayward. Without sound political or spiritual leadership, people do whatever they please. When shepherds do not shepherd, the flock is scattered.

Jeremiah was crushed physically, domestically, and socially along with the people of God. His calling as a prophet of God did not deliver him from suffering—it destined him for it.

Jeremiah's sufferings are not unfamiliar. Everyone has physical troubles. Everyone gets sick or injured. Many have near-fatal accidents or face life-threatening diseases. Some live under the threat of a serious illness that may recur at any time. Others have chronic infirmities that will torment them until death.

Then there are domestic troubles. Some people are not sure where they will live next, or with whom. Some are or have been homeless. Others feel alone in the world after losing loved ones through death. They have lost sons and daughters or have attended the funerals of many friends from their own generation.

Other people are abandoned by their families, or they become so alienated from them that they might as well be dead. They have no family to turn to in times of trouble, no one to help pitch a tent. In his book *Families at the Crossroads*, Rodney Clapp writes that we live in a society in which "The common Western framework of values about marriage, divorce, acceptable popular entertainment and so forth has broken down." As a result, "The postmodern world is a fragmented world, more and more populated with isolated and drifting individuals."[2]

There are social troubles as well. Society seems to be heading in the wrong direction. The shepherds seem senseless. Are there any politicians who exercise courage, wisdom, integrity, and justice? Leadership in the church is often just as weak. Many people are hindered spiritually by incompetent or ungodly ministers. Some have unresolved conflicts with elders in the church. Others nurse open wounds from divided churches.

The physical, domestic, and social problems Jeremiah faced are not unfamiliar. With the weeping prophet we say, "Woe is me because of my hurt! . . . my children have gone from me, and they are not . . . the shepherds are stupid."

The Providence of God

Imagine Jeremiah 10 containing only twenty-two verses. If so, then Jeremiah would continue to wallow in his despair. We would be able to empathize with him, but not to learn from him. We would never see him looking beyond his troubles to the Lord. In the words of R. E. O. White, we would only have "a fatalistic acceptance of terminal sickness or injury, a single desert traveler wrestling with a storm, a helpless flock abandoned by incompetent shepherds."[3]

But Jeremiah was no fatalist. A fatalist believes "That what will happen will happen, and nothing we do or do not do will make any difference."[4] So a fatalist stops at 10:22. A fatalist gives up on life. A fatalist lives without hope. A fatalist does not trust that God is good or that life has any meaning.

Jeremiah was not a fatalist because in the last three verses of chapter 10 he goes to the Lord in prayer. He carries his physical, domestic, and social troubles to the throne of grace. He still weeps, but he is not feeling sorry for himself. He casts himself upon the providence and merciful justice of God.

Jeremiah begins his prayer by throwing himself upon God's providence: "I know, O LORD, that the way of man is not in himself, that it is not in man who walks to direct his steps" (v. 23). There are echoes here from the book of Proverbs: "The heart of man plans his way, but the LORD establishes his steps" (Proverbs 16:9). "A man's steps are from the LORD; how then can man understand his way?" (20:24). Jeremiah is saying something like this: "This is not my life. The life that I live does not belong to me; it belongs to God."

The life you live is not your own. Even your footsteps are directed by God. Like Jeremiah, you follow the pathway marked out for you by the Lord. You follow divine dance steps, like a student at an Arthur Murray dance school: "One and two and step and four and one and two and slide and . . ."

Jeremiah did not always know where he was dancing. It is often the case that we see how God has directed our footsteps most clearly when we look back over our shoulders. Then we can see the pattern of our footprints behind us along the trail. Every Christian can testify how God guided his or her footsteps to faith in Christ, or to a spouse, or to a calling in life.

Jeremiah trusted that God was guiding his footsteps. Even when it seemed like he was out on the dance floor with two left feet, he trusted that his dance partner knew what he was doing. He recognized that his physical, domestic, and social troubles were under God's control. In the words of the great Puritan Matthew Henry, "The prophet here acknowledges the sovereignty and dominion of the divine Providence, that by it, and not by their own will and wisdom, the affairs both of nations and particular persons are directed and determined."[5]

The great Swiss Reformer Ulrich Zwingli (1484–1531) defined the providence of God like this: "All things are so done and disposed by the providence of God that nothing takes place without His will or command."[6] Is there anything in Heaven or earth that stands outside the control of God? No, nothing takes place without his will or command.

Zwingli partly based his doctrine of providence on the teaching of Jesus: "Are not two sparrows sold for a penny? And not one of them will fall to the ground apart from your Father" (Matthew 10:29). Zwingli reasoned that if the providence of God extends to sparrows, then it must extend to the smallest of creatures:

> It is evident, therefore, that God . . . is . . . such wisdom, knowledge, and foresight that nothing is hidden from Him, nothing unknown to Him, nothing beyond His reach, nothing disobedient to Him. Hence not even the mosquito has its sharp sting and musical hum without God's wisdom, knowledge, and foresight. His wisdom, then, knows all things even before they exist, His knowledge comprehends all things, His foresight regulates all things.[7]

Jeremiah took the doctrine of the providence of God and brought it down to the personal level. If God disposes all things by his will, then he also disposes the life of a single person. If nothing takes place without God's command, then nothing takes place in the life of the believer apart from God's command. Your life is not your own. Your every step is directed by God.

A firm trust in the providence of God is a great comfort in the midst of all kinds of suffering. First, God's providence extends to physical suffering. When you have an illness, throw yourself on the providence of God. Say,

"I know, O Lord, that my life is not my own; it is not for me to direct my steps. I do ask that you heal me, according to your will. In the meantime, I receive this illness as a gift from you and ask that you use it for my sanctification and the glory of Christ."

That is exactly what Ulrich Zwingli did. The doctrine of providence he learned from the Scriptures was confirmed by his experience of illness. In 1519 the plague swept through Zurich, stopped at the reformer's door, and nearly carried him off to an early grave. While Zwingli was lying on what he was sure was his deathbed, he came to a fresh conviction that he was under the providential care of God. He trusted that God was in such complete control of his situation that he had nothing to fear, whether he lived or died.

When Zwingli recovered, he wrote a poem about his ultimate resignation to the providence of God. It begins with these lines:

Help, Lord God, help
In this trouble!
I think Death is at the door.
Stand before me, Christ;
For Thou hast overcome him!
To thee I cry:
If it is Thy will
Take out the dart,
Which wounds me
Nor lets me have an hour's
Rest or repose!
Will'st Thou however
That Death take me
In the midst of my days,
So let it be!
Do what thou wilt;
Me nothing lacks.
Thy vessel am I;
To make or break altogether.[8]

The poem is a model of absolute trust in the providence of God in physical troubles.

The same trust in God's providence can be exercised during domestic troubles. You may not know where you will live or who will live with you. Nevertheless, you can say, "I know that my life is not my own; it is not for me to direct my steps. I trust you, Lord, to provide the housing I need."

The same providence extends to the family. There may be things in your family that you cannot fix. Some families are so badly broken, it is hard to know where all the pieces are, let alone how to glue them back together. But take the broken pieces to God in prayer and rest in his providence because he can fix all the broken places.

Start by asking God to forgive you, through Jesus Christ, for the wrongs you have done to other members of your family. It may be that you are more sinned against than sinning. Then ask God to heal you, through Jesus Christ, for the wrongs that have been done to you. Ask God for the grace to forgive and forget the sins of your father and mother, or your brothers and sisters, or your husband or wife. Then throw your family onto the providence of God. Entrust the salvation of your family to him. Place all those lives and relationships into God's care, and ask him to make right all the missteps.

Do the same thing with social difficulties. There are times in the life of a nation when the shepherds seem senseless and the sheep are scattered. But the life of a nation is not its own; a state does not direct its own steps. Accept the providence of God for your country. If that providence includes unprecedented judgment, then blessed be the name of the Lord. If it includes undeserved favor, then blessed be the name of the Lord. Throw the life of your nation onto the providence of God.

Do the same thing with troubles in the church. Admittedly, this is hard to do. It may be easy to accept the providence of God for an illness, but not for troubles in the church. When the shepherds are senseless, their sheep usually try to bite them.

What sheep ought to do is acknowledge that the life of a church is not its own and that the Lord directs its steps. Whenever possible, seek reconciliation with your brothers and sisters in Christ by confessing your sins. On occasion, speak the truth in love in order to help others see their need for reconciliation. Then throw your ecclesiastical difficulties onto the providence of God. Do not run from one church to the next, looking for a church that does not have any problems. Rather, love the church as it is, and pray for it to become what Christ wants it to be.

The Merciful Justice of Christ

Jeremiah did one more important thing. When he threw his troubles on the providence of God, he threw also himself on God's merciful justice. He said, "Correct me, O Lord, but in justice; not in your anger, lest you bring me to nothing" (10:24).

Two kinds of justice are mentioned here. One kind is destructive; the other is corrective. Jeremiah did not want to be judged with the angry justice of God. He prayed the way King David prayed: "O Lord, rebuke me not in your anger, nor discipline me in your wrath" (Psalm 6:1). This does not mean that God is so subject to his emotions that he gets into an uncontrollable rage. Rather, the anger of God is his pure and righteous determination to punish sin. Jeremiah recognized that if God were to judge him in the righteousness of his anger, he would be reduced to nothing. Strict justice demands the destruction of the sinner.

Destructive justice is what Jeremiah demanded for the nations of the world:

Pour out your wrath on the nations that know you not,
    and on the peoples that call not on your name,
for they have devoured Jacob;
    they have devoured him and consumed him,
    and have laid waste his habitation. (10:25)

His words were taken from Psalm 79:6, 7. They show what will happen to those who hate God and his people. God is a God of justice. He must punish sin. Jeremiah did not step back from destructive justice for the nations; he embraced it. He prayed that God's people would be vindicated from all their enemies.

But that is not the kind of justice Jeremiah wanted for himself. Instead he asked God for corrective justice. He asked for the kind of discipline a good father gives to his child. He asked to be chastised with loving discipline, not to be destroyed, but to be built up and helped to become obedient. He asked for merciful justice.

Jeremiah asked for the kind of justice King David received: "The LORD has disciplined me severely, but he has not given me over to death" (Psalm 118:18). The Lord did not judge David in anger, nor did he reduce him to nothing. David was chastened but not destroyed.

Jeremiah was willing to be corrected the same way. He was willing to be chastised for his own benefit. He was willing to have God purify his faults. He was willing to be disciplined through suffering with the people of God. So he begged for the merciful justice of God, the justice that corrects but does not destroy.

The basis for this corrective judgment is the death and resurrection of Jesus Christ. God's justice is tempered with mercy through the cross of Christ. If Christ had not died for our sins, we would deserve the justice of destruction. But Christ did die for our sins; so now he gives us only the justice of correction.

Jeremiah's sufferings are a reminder of the grace of the cross. They show the way Jesus took our destruction upon himself. Jeremiah said, "I belong to the people of God, so I will suffer whatever they deserve to suffer. I will be disciplined however they must be disciplined. I will be crushed when they are crushed."

Jesus Christ said much the same thing. When Jesus agreed to die for the sins of his people, he said, "I belong to the people of God, so I will suffer whatever they deserve to suffer. I will be disciplined however they must be disciplined. I will be crushed when they are crushed." Jesus Christ identified so closely with his people that their sufferings became his sufferings, their judgment his judgment, their punishments his punishments. "The chastisement of our peace was upon him" (Isaiah 53:5 KJV).

Jesus Christ suffered in precisely the ways Jeremiah suffered. He suffered physically. Woe was upon him because of his injury. The wounds that he received on the cross of Calvary were incurable. Jesus Christ suffered physically unto death.

Jesus Christ suffered domestically. He was a wandering preacher with nowhere to lay his head and nowhere to pitch his tent. He was driven out of his hometown (Luke 4:14–30). There was conflict within his own family concerning his ministry (Matthew 12:46–50).

Jesus Christ also suffered socially. He was despised by Jews and Gentiles alike. Both the religious and the political leaders of his day conspired to put him to death. The Pharisees plotted to kill him, and Pontius Pilate sentenced him to death.

These physical, domestic, and social sufferings were what the people of God deserved for their sins. They are what we deserve for our sins as well. We deserve to be wounded, abandoned, and scattered for our sins. We deserve the justice of destruction.

But in Christ we find only correction. Jesus Christ was wounded, abandoned, and scattered for our sins. His sufferings have satisfied the destructive justice of God against our wickedness. Therefore, whatever sufferings we still suffer are not for our destruction. They are only for our correction.

This is how we are to receive the mercy of God's corrective justice:

It is for discipline that you have to endure. God is treating you as sons. For what son is there whom his father does not discipline? If you are left without discipline, in which all have participated, then you are illegitimate children and not sons. Besides this, we have had earthly fathers who disciplined us and we respected them. Shall we not much more be subject to the Father of spirits and live? For they disciplined us for a short time as it seemed best to them, but he disciplines us for our good, that we may share his holiness. For the moment all discipline seems painful rather than pleasant, but later it yields the peaceful fruit of righteousness to those who have been trained by it. (Hebrews 12:7–11)

18

Amen, Lord!

JEREMIAH 11:1–17

SOMETIMES IT IS NOT JUST WHAT YOU SAY THAT MATTERS, but when you say it. Take the words *I* and *do*, for example. These two simple words are used all the time. They do not seem to matter very much. One time they really do matter is when they are used in a wedding. With those two simple words—"I do"—a husband and wife enter into a lifelong, life-or-death covenant with one another, binding themselves to one another for poverty as well as prosperity, illness as well as health, sorrow as well as joy.

The prophet Jeremiah utters two simple words in the first half of Jeremiah 11: "Amen" (NIV) and "Lord." Both words are sometimes used so casually that they hardly seem to matter. But when Jeremiah used them to say, "Amen, LORD," they were momentous.

Amen and Amen and Amen

Amen is a word of agreement. It means "Yes," or "That's right," or "Let it be so." It is not a word to be taken lightly because it is especially a word of agreement with the purposes of Almighty God. *Amen* means "Yes, Lord," or "So be it, Lord," or "Your will be done."

If *amen* is a word of agreement with the will of God, then it must be used carefully. When Jeremiah said "amen," what was he saying? "The word that came to Jeremiah from the LORD: 'Hear the words of this covenant, and speak to the men of Judah and the inhabitants of Jerusalem. You shall say to them, Thus says the LORD, the God of Israel: Cursed . . .'" (vv. 1–3a).

At this point Jeremiah's lawyer ought to stand up and raise an objection. God is proposing a covenant. He is giving Jeremiah his terms. Contracts are always serious business. To assume a mortgage, to set up a schedule for car payments, or to co-sign for a large loan is to undertake a weighty responsibility. The terms of such contracts must be considered carefully, especially the fine print.

In this case the contractual difficulty was not in the fine print. The problem was printed in big letters right at the top: "Cursed." One does not have to be a legal genius to realize that a covenant beginning with a curse is serious business.

Watch out, Jeremiah! Don't sign anything yet! Read the whole contract carefully: "Cursed be the man who does not hear the words of this covenant that I commanded your fathers when I brought them out of the land of Egypt, from the iron furnace" (vv. 3b, 4a). The contract came with stiff penalties for noncompliance. Jeremiah was not getting blanket coverage—he was getting a blanket curse. Failure to keep this covenant with God would result in malediction. A curse would go into effect the moment Jeremiah violated any of the terms of the contract.

What were the terms exactly? Dubious though the contract sounds, perhaps the terms were so easy that Jeremiah would not have to worry about the threats. Perhaps his covenant obligations were so minimal that he was in no danger of falling under the curse.

These are the terms: "Listen to my voice, and do all that I command you" (v. 4). Uh oh! The covenant demands nothing less than universal obedience to the will of God. But what human being is capable of rendering unfailing obedience? No mere human being—since the fall of Adam into sin—is capable of doing everything God commands, "for all have sinned and fall short of the glory of God" (Romans 3:23).

Surely Jeremiah could not accept the covenant God proposed. The demands are too strict, the penalties too extreme. The covenant requires perfect obedience to the Law of God. Once the Law is broken, God will curse Judah and Jerusalem, and Jeremiah with them. Surely Jeremiah could not accept this covenant, even though it holds out the promise of unhindered blessing for God's people. The covenant contains ample evidence of the goodness of God. It includes a reminder that he is the God of salvation. Its terms were first given when God brought Israel "out of the land of Egypt, from the iron furnace" (11:4). In other words, the covenant is offered by a God who has already shown mercy to his people. He has brought them out of captivity into freedom.

If God's people could obey the terms of the covenant, they would be God's people, and he would be their God. God puts it like this: "Listen to my voice, and do all that I command you. So shall you be my people, and I will be your God" (v. 4b). This is the most blessed of all the promises of Scripture, the promise of union, fellowship, and intimacy with God. God proposes the kind of romance described in the Song of Songs: "My beloved is mine, and I am his" (2:16a). There is no greater security than to belong to God. There is no greater inheritance than for God to belong to us. Thus there is no greater promise than the match made in Heaven: God will be our God, and we will be God's people.

Add to that great promise the blessings of material prosperity. God promises, "Listen to my voice, . . . that I may confirm the oath that I swore to your fathers, to give them a land flowing with milk and honey" (11:4, 5). It would be enough for the people to have God, but God promises even more. He promises his people a piece of the land of milk and honey.

Would you accept the covenant God proposes? The blessings described are so wonderful that one could almost urge Jeremiah to accept God's terms. Yet remember that the covenant begins with a curse. Remember also that it contains one unbearable term: "Do all that I command you."

Nevertheless, Jeremiah countersigned the contract. "I answered, 'Amen, LORD'" (v. 5b NIV). Very likely the prophet's mouth went dry and his blood ran cold when he found those simple words on his lips. Sometimes it is not just what you say that matters, but when you say it. "Amen, Lord. Yes, Lord. So be it. Your will be done." Jeremiah said "Yes" to the demand for perfect obedience, "Yes" to all the punishments that come from disobedience, and "Yes" to all the promises that come from obedience. Yes to the terms, yes to the curses, and yes to the blessings. Amen and amen and amen.

Jeremiah did not just say "amen" for himself; he said "amen" for all God's people. God told Jeremiah, "Hear the words of this covenant, and speak to the men of Judah and the inhabitants of Jerusalem" (v. 2). He commanded Jeremiah, "Proclaim all these words in the cities of Judah and in the streets of Jerusalem: Hear the words of this covenant and do them" (v. 6). Jeremiah was to publicize the covenant throughout the land because the covenant was for the whole people of God.

God's command to Jeremiah may be related to King Josiah's rediscovery of the Book of the Law and the renewal of Israel's covenant with God:

> Then the king sent, and all the elders of Judah and Jerusalem were gathered to him. And the king went up to the house of the LORD, and with him all the men of Judah and all the inhabitants of Jerusalem and the priests and the prophets, all the people, both small and great. And he read in their hearing all the words of the Book of the Covenant that had been found in the house of the LORD. And the king stood by the pillar and made a covenant before the LORD, to walk after the LORD and to keep his commandments and his

testimonies and his statutes with all his heart and all his soul, to perform
the words of this covenant that were written in this book. And all the people
joined in the covenant. (2 Kings 23:1–3; cf. 2 Chronicles 34)

When Josiah read the words of the Book of the Covenant, he undoubtedly
read the words of Deuteronomy 27, the great amen-to-the-covenant passage of
the Old Testament. Moses gathered all the people of Israel together at Mount
Ebal and said, "Obey the voice of the LORD your God, keeping his commandments and his statutes, which I command you today" (Deuteronomy 27:10).
The people recited the commands of God as a great antiphonal choir. The Levites pronounced the curses of the covenant and all the people said, "Amen":

"Cursed be the man who makes a carved or cast metal image." . . . "Amen."
(v. 15)

"Cursed be anyone who dishonors his father or his mother." . . . "Amen."
(v. 16)

"Cursed be anyone who perverts the justice due to the sojourner, the fatherless, and the widow." . . . "Amen." (v. 19)

"Cursed are those who commit sexual sin" (paraphrased summary). . . .
"Amen." (vv. 20–23)

"Cursed be anyone who strikes down his neighbor." . . . "Amen." (v. 24)

"Cursed be anyone who does not confirm the words of this law by doing
them." . . . "Amen." (v. 26)

Cursed, cursed, cursed. Amen and amen and amen.

The people of God were not asking for trouble. They were not gluttons
for punishment. But they recognized that the Law of God is good and right.
Their "amens" affirmed that God had a right to their obedience. When God
demanded worship, honor, justice, and chastity, they could only say, "Amen,
Lord."

Jeremiah's "amen" was an echo of the "amens" from Deuteronomy 27.
Like the children of Israel, the prophet could not help but say "Amen, Lord."
In the words of F. B. Meyer:

. . . as he utters the terrible curses and threatenings of divine justice and
predicts the inevitable fate of his people, he is so possessed with the sense
of the divine rectitude, so sure that God could not do differently, so convinced that, judged by the loftiest moral standards, the sins of Israel could

not be otherwise dealt with—that his soul rises up; and though he must pronounce the doom of Israel, he is forced to answer and say, "Amen, O Lord!"[1]

All we can say is "Amen, Lord." We must join with the children of Israel and with Jeremiah in saying "amen" to the covenant. We say "amen" to the Law and "amen" to the curse. We cannot do otherwise because we know that the covenant is just. We say, "Yes, Lord, your law is good. We agree that it is right for you to demand perfect obedience from us. Moreover, we accept your curse upon us if we fail to render perfect obedience to you. Amen, Lord."

Broken Covenant

When Jeremiah said, "Amen, Lord!" he agreed to the terms of the covenant, both for blessing and for curse. How did it turn out? Was it blessing or curse for Jeremiah and his people? Did they meet the terms of the covenant? Hardly. Verse after verse, chapter after chapter, the Weeping Prophet laments the sins of Israel.

In chapter 11 Jeremiah rounds up the usual suspects. First, there is the *hard-heartedness* of God's people. God says, "For I solemnly warned your fathers when I brought them up out of the land of Egypt, warning them persistently, even to this day, saying, Obey my voice" (11:7). Right up to the days of Jeremiah, God sent his prophets to warn them again and again to obey him. "Yet they did not obey or incline their ear" (v. 8a).

This is a strong warning to the hard-hearted. Perhaps your mind is skeptical about the Bible. Perhaps your conscience is hardened to your sins. Perhaps your heart is closed to God's message. But the Spirit of God is warning you to believe in his Word, repent for your sins, and open your heart up to him. If not, you are liable to God's curse.

Second, God's people were *idolatrous*.

Again the LORD said to me, "A conspiracy exists among the men of Judah and the inhabitants of Jerusalem. They have turned back to the iniquities of their forefathers, who refused to hear my words. They have gone after other gods to serve them. The house of Israel and the house of Judah have broken my covenant that I made with their fathers." (vv. 9, 10)

There was so much idolatry in the land that it seemed like a conspiracy. The people went right back into the sins of their forefathers. They broke covenant by following alternative gods.

One of those gods was Baal, of course: "The Lord of hosts . . . has decreed disaster against you, because of the evil that the house of Israel and the house of Judah have done, provoking me to anger by making offerings to Baal" (v. 17). But Baal was not the only idol on the shelf: "For your gods have become as many as your cities, O Judah, and as many as the streets of Jerusalem are the altars you have set up to shame, altars to make offerings to Baal" (v. 13; cf. 2:28). If one were to take the Jerusalem A-Z Travel Guide and count the number of streets in the city, the result would give a rough estimate of how many false idols there were in Judah.

What John Calvin said is true: The human heart is a factory for idols. Idols tend to multiply. They have short shelf lives. Worshiping a false god soon becomes tiresome or disappointing, and it is time to get another god.

The one thing all idols have in common is that they cannot offer salvation from God's judgment. "Then the cities of Judah and the inhabitants of Jerusalem will go and cry to the gods to whom they make offerings, but they cannot save them in the time of their trouble" (v. 12). Idols are "like scarecrows in a cucumber field" (see 10:5). They cannot see, speak, hear, or think, so they cannot save.

The people of Judah were also guilty of *false worship*. Idolatry is the worship of false gods, but it is not the only form of false worship. The people of Judah worshiped the true God in a false way. God says:

> What right has my beloved in my house, when she has done many vile deeds? Can even sacrificial flesh avert your doom? Can you then exult? (11:15)

The audacity of it all! God could hardly believe it! The temple had become the headquarters for sin in Jerusalem! Even while the people went through the motions of temple worship, they were plotting evil. They used the grace of God as an excuse to sin. Thus the sacrifices they offered were completely worthless.

Hard-heartedness. Idolatry. False worship. These were not just hairline fractures in the covenant—they were chasms. Frankly, by this point in Jeremiah's ministry the covenant-breaking of Israel is becoming tiresome. It is tedious to list their sins over and over again. During the course of fifty years of ministry, Jeremiah tired of it as well. But if Israel's sins make for tiresome reading, this gives a clue what it must be like for God when we commit the same sins over and over again. It is exceedingly tiresome.

The consequences of habitual sin are predictable. Once the terms of the covenant are stipulated, and once it is evident that the terms have not been kept, it is certain what the punishment will be. God always keeps his word. "Therefore I brought upon them all the words of this covenant, which I commanded them to do, but they did not" (v. 8b). Therefore this is what the Lord says: "I am bringing disaster upon them that they cannot escape" (v. 11). Judgment was so inevitable that God actually told Jeremiah, "Therefore do not pray for this people, or lift up a cry or prayer on their behalf, for I will not listen when they call to me in the time of their trouble" (v. 14; cf. 7:16).

Jeremiah then gives a vivid picture of what it is like to be under God's curse.

> The LORD once called you "a green olive tree, beautiful with good fruit." But with the roar of a great tempest he will set fire to it, and its branches will be consumed. The LORD of hosts, who planted you, has decreed disaster against you. (vv. 16, 17a)

When God called Jeremiah into the ministry, he set him over nations and kingdoms "To pluck up" and "To plant" (1:10). These verses are a reminder that uprooting and planting are God's prerogatives. God planted Israel, and God can dig her up. God planted Israel to be a beautiful and fruitful olive tree, but now he is sending a storm of judgment against her. Lightning will strike, and the tree will be torched, leaving nothing but ashes. Such is the curse of God against sin.

We stand under the same curse. All of us are obligated to keep perfectly the Law of God. Yet all of us fail to do so. Everyone has broken the covenant. The curse for covenant breaking is pronounced in Galatians 3. It is the same curse found in Deuteronomy 27 and Jeremiah 11: "Cursed be everyone who does not abide by all things written in the Book of the Law, and do them" (Galatians 3:10). The curse allows no exceptions. Cursed is *everyone*—every man, woman, and child—who does not do *everything* written in the Law. Cursed is everyone who is hard hearted, or who worships idols, or who offers God false worship. Cursed is everyone.

A Curse for Us

There is no way around this curse. Since we cannot help but say "Sorry" to God for our sins, we cannot help but say "Amen" to the curses of his covenant. Furthermore, we must accept the verdict that the Bible gives to those who break the covenant. There is no way around the curse.

But there is a way through the curse. That way passes through the cross of Christ. "Christ redeemed us from the curse of the law by becoming a curse for us—for it is written, 'Cursed is everyone who is hanged on a tree'" (Galatians 3:13).

Jeremiah was not the last prophet to say "Amen" to the curse of God. In the same night Jesus Christ was betrayed—after sharing a covenant meal with his disciples—he said "Amen" to the covenant between God and his people. His soul was "very sorrowful, even to death" (Matthew 26:38). He shrank back from the cursed cup. But he said to his Father, "Your will be done" (v. 42). Jesus was saying, "Yes, Father. So be it, Father." He was saying, "Amen" to the covenant and its curses.

When Jesus Christ said, "Your will be done," he was inviting all the curses of the covenant to fall upon his own head. When he went willingly to the cross, he was saying "Amen!" to the curse against you and me for not loving God, for idolatry, for taking God's name in vain, and for not resting in God. Jesus was saying "Amen!" to the curse against us for not honoring our parents, for murderous intentions, for sexual sin, for theft, for lying, and for coveting. Jesus took all of those righteous curses upon himself. Cursed, cursed, cursed. Amen and amen and amen.

How appropriate it was, then, for Jesus to die on a cross. The Law of God stipulated crucifixion as an accursed death: "And if a man has committed a crime punishable by death and he is put to death, and you hang him on a tree, his body shall not remain all night on the tree, but you shall bury him the same day, for a hanged man is cursed by God" (Deuteronomy 21:22, 23a). There is no way around the curse, but this is the way through it. God did not overlook the curses of the covenant; he poured them out on his own Son. The death of Christ on a cross proved that he was accepting upon himself the curse we deserved. "Christ redeemed us from the curse of the law by becoming a curse for us—for it is written, 'Cursed is everyone who is hanged on a tree'" (Galatians 3:13).

Amen to the Glory of God

Just two little words. "Amen, Lord!" How momentous they were for Jesus, as they were for Jeremiah. But how magnificent they are when Christians take them upon their own lips!

Once, as the Apostle Paul discussed his travel plans with the Corinthians, he interrupted himself to write, "For all the promises of God find their Yes in him. That is why it is through him that we utter our Amen to God for his glory" (2 Corinthians 1:20). All the promises of God are yes in Christ. When Jeremiah said "Amen," he was affirming the whole covenant, both for curse and for blessing. The same is true of Jesus Christ. When Jesus said, "Your will be done," he affirmed the whole covenant, both for curse and for blessing. Jesus said yes to the curses of the covenant in his death, but he also says yes to the promises of the covenant in his resurrection. In Christ, it is yes to the terms, yes to the curses, and yes to the blessings.

I imagine Jesus Christ saying yes to the blessings of the covenant like this. I imagine Jesus Christ—risen and ascended—sitting down upon his throne at the right hand of God. I imagine hosts of angels coming to his throne carrying great stacks of papers and placing them on his lap, each paper inscribed with one of the promises of God. Then I imagine the Lord Jesus Christ using one hand to sign his own name at the bottom of every promise to guarantee that it must be fulfilled. And I imagine him using his other hand to stamp every promise with his own personal "Yes!"

> "I will not leave you or forsake you." (Joshua 1:5b)

"Yes!"

> Surely goodness and mercy shall follow me all the days of my life, and I shall dwell in the house of the Lord forever. (Psalm 23:6)

"Yes!"

> "To me every knee shall bow, every tongue shall swear allegiance." (Isaiah 45:23b)

"Yes!"

> "I will remove the iniquity of this land in a single day." (Zechariah 3:9b)

"Yes!"

> "Whatever you ask the Father in my name, he may give it to you." (John 15:16b)

"Yes!"

> Angel after angel after angel. Page after page after page. Blessing after blessing after blessing. Yes after yes after yes. "For all the promises of God find their Yes in him" (2 Corinthians 1:20a).

And with every "Yes" of Christ to every promise of God, a great "Amen" goes up from God's people. "That is why it is through him [Christ] that we utter our Amen to God for his glory" (2 Corinthians 1:20b). "Amen" to the atonement, "Amen" to eternal life, "Amen" to the universal rule of God, "Amen" to the permanent presence of God, and "Amen" to answered prayer. Blessing, blessing, blessing. Yes, yes, yes. Amen and amen and amen.

Even the promises of Jeremiah 11 are "Yes" and "Amen" in Christ. The promise that God will be our God and that we will be his people is "Yes" in Christ. Through the death of Jesus Christ we were purchased to belong to God. Through fellowship with Christ, God is our God and we are his people. Likewise, the promise of a land flowing with milk and honey is "Yes" in Christ. Jesus promised that his meek children would inherit the whole earth (Matthew 5:5).

All the covenant promises of Jeremiah 11 will be confirmed in glory. There we will belong to God, God will belong to us, and we will take possession of the Promised Land. When the apostle John saw his great vision of the Heavenly City, the New Jerusalem, he heard a loud voice saying, "Behold, the dwelling place of God is with man. He will dwell with them, and they will be his people, and God himself will be with them as their God" (Revelation 21:3). We say "Amen!" to these promises because they are "Yes" in Christ.

> Blessed be the LORD, the God of Israel,
>   from everlasting to everlasting!
> And let all the people say, "Amen!"
>   Praise the LORD! (Psalm 106:48)

19

How Can You Run with Horses?

JEREMIAH 11:18—12:6

JEREMIAH NEVER SAW IT COMING. He was caught totally off guard. He was like the quarterback who gets blindsided while he is looking downfield. Or the corporate executive who suffers a hostile takeover while he is on vacation in the Bahamas. Or the mother who hears her toddler smash a vase on the floor while her back is turned. Jeremiah did not realize that men were plotting against him. He was "like a gentle lamb led to the slaughter" (11:19).

The Conspiracy

This portion of the book of Jeremiah reads like a spy novel. At the end of chapter 11 Jeremiah is caught up in a web of intrigue. The enemies plotting to assassinate him say, "Let us destroy the tree with its fruit, let us cut him off from the land of the living, that his name be remembered no more" (v. 19b).

These conspirators were out to get Jeremiah. They were seeking his life (v. 21). They did not want to leave any trace of him behind. They wanted to destroy the tree *and* its fruit. In other words, they wanted to kill Jeremiah before he had any offspring, so his name would vanish from the earth.

Who were Jeremiah's enemies? The men plotting against him were "The men of Anathoth" (v. 21). Jeremiah was "The son of Hilkiah, one of the priests who were in Anathoth in the land of Benjamin" (1:1). Little wonder, then, that he was taken by surprise. The men plotting against him were citizens of his hometown! They were friends of the family! Some were even members of his own household:

For even your brothers and the house of your father,
  even they have dealt treacherously with you;
  they are in full cry after you;
do not believe them,
  though they speak friendly words to you. (12:6)

Jeremiah was a despised and rejected prophet. He was without honor in his hometown.

Why the conspiracy? The men of Anathoth did not like Jeremiah's preaching. They were not happy with his homiletics. "Therefore thus says the LORD concerning the men of Anathoth, who seek your life, and say, 'Do not prophesy in the name of the LORD, or you will die by our hand'" (11:21). It sounds like a tough congregation. Their motto was "shut up or die."

The conspiracy of the men of Anathoth is a lesson in how *not* to respond to the Word of God. A minister stands or falls by the faithfulness of his preaching. And if a minister is faithful, then his congregation stands or falls by its response to his preaching, because his message comes from God.

The men of Anathoth did not care to hear God's voice, and it is not hard to guess why. Anathoth was a town of priests, and Jeremiah had some strong opinions about the priesthood. He was always making unpopular statements like these:

The prophets prophesy falsely,
  and the priests rule at their direction;
my people love to have it so. (5:31)

For from the least to the greatest of them,
  everyone is greedy for unjust gain;
and from prophet to priest,
  everyone deals falsely. (6:13)

It was not the kind of preaching to endear a young man to his elders. Jeremiah seemed like a traitor in his hometown. Not only did he criticize the priests, but he condemned the idol worship that made up such a large part of the local economy. Jeremiah's reformation preaching threatened the whole religious, social, and economic structure of his hometown. He was practically putting the priests of Anathoth out of work. When they gathered at their local pub to have a few beers and talk about temple politics, they did not exactly rise up and call Jeremiah blessed. They had heard just about enough out of him.

Biblical preaching can be a dangerous business. Once I was reading Bible stories with a three-year-old friend. Over the course of several weeks we read together about Joseph, Jeremiah, Peter, Paul, Stephen, and Jesus. We read how each one of those men was thrown into a pit, put in prison, stoned, or crucified. My young friend often asked me, "Why did they throw him in the pit?" "Why did they put him in prison?" "Why did they kill him?" I always gave the same answer: "It was because he was preaching God's Word." On one occasion there was a long pause. "Dad," he said, "are they going to kill you?"

It was a good question. It showed an effective use of inductive logic. It reasoned from a series of historical examples to a contemporary application. The Bible is full of stories about men who were persecuted for preaching the good news of God's free grace. Bold Biblical preaching is dangerous business.

This danger is acknowledged in *the Form of Government of the Presbyterian Church in America* (27–5). When a gospel minister is ordained, he answers this question: "Do you promise to be zealous and faithful in maintaining the truths of the Gospel and the purity and peace of the Church, whatever persecution or opposition may arise unto you on that account?" Jeremiah made and kept essentially the same vow. He was zealous and faithful in maintaining Biblical truth, however the enemies of the gospel conspired against him.

The Commitment

Jeremiah was able to honor the vows of his calling because he was committed to God. His commitment remained strong even in the middle of the conspiracy. He had no idea what his enemies were planning to do to him. But as soon as he found out, he placed himself under God's protection.

> But, O LORD of hosts, who judges righteously,
>   who tests the heart and the mind,
> let me see your vengeance upon them,
>   for to you have I committed my cause." (11:20)

From time to time Christians find themselves under attack. They may be ridiculed for their faith, criticized for their doctrine, or attacked for the way they conduct some ministry. Our first reaction in such cases is usually to defend ourselves. We want to stick up for our rights. We want to get mad, or better yet, to get even.

Jeremiah did not get mad. He did not seek to defend his preaching or vindicate his ministry. He did not blame God for the messages he had to preach on God's behalf. Rather, he committed his cause to the Lord. He asked the Lord to take up his case and be his advocate.

Jeremiah's commitment was well placed because God had already proven his loyalty to him. It was the Lord who revealed the conspiracy to him in the first place: "The LORD made it known to me and I knew; then you showed me their deeds. . . . I did not know it was against me they devised schemes" (vv. 18, 19b). It was also the Lord who warned him that his own family sought to betray him (12:6). Jeremiah had the world's greatest intelligence operative working full time for him—the God of the universe.

By keeping Jeremiah safe, God fulfilled the promise he had made when he first called Jeremiah to the ministry: "Do not be afraid of them, for I am with you to deliver you" (1:8). When the men of Anathoth plotted against Jeremiah, the Lord himself sounded the alarm. Jeremiah's commitment was well placed because God was committed to him.

It was also well placed because of God's character. Jeremiah put his trust in the Lord Almighty, who is all-powerful. No one can overcome the Lord—or anyone under his protection, for that matter. Jeremiah put his trust in the Lord who is the righteous Judge. God's decisions are always fair because he always has his facts straight. He tests the heart and mind. So if you are innocent—as Jeremiah was—God is your best possible judge. The Dutch theologian Geerhardus Vos (d. 1949) notes the quiet confidence of Jeremiah's prayer: "But you, O LORD, know me; you see me, and test my heart toward you" (12:3a; cf. 15:15; 18:23). This is a prayer, notes Vos, "for relief and unburdening of soul, such as derives from the simple drawing near to God." Jeremiah's "prayer-attitude" was one of "supreme confidence in God." "The prophet would have no secrets from Jehovah. And the mere pouring into the ears of God the disquietudes of the heart would bring calm and refreshment."[1]

It is hard to think of Jeremiah's commitment in the midst of conspiracy without also thinking of Jesus Christ. Like Jeremiah, Jesus was the victim of a conspiracy. The scribes and Pharisees plotted against him to take his life (Matthew 26:3, 4). Like Jeremiah, Jesus was betrayed by a close companion, his execution sealed with a kiss (Luke 22:47, 48). Like Jeremiah, Jesus was rejected by friends and family for preaching in the name of God (Luke 4:14–30). He was a gentle lamb led to the slaughter. Thus Jeremiah was one of the prophets who foretold how the Christ would suffer (see Acts 3:18).

There was one difference between Jeremiah and Jesus, however, the difference between a sinner and the Savior. Jeremiah asked God for vengeance upon his enemies. The Scriptures do not condemn him for doing so, perhaps because his legal case against the men of Anathoth was a legitimate one. But the Scriptures also point toward the greater mercy of the Lord Jesus Christ. Jesus committed his cause to God without pleading for vengeance against his enemies. When he was accused before the Sanhedrin, "he remained silent and made no answer" (Mark 14:61).

> He was oppressed, and he was afflicted,
>   yet he opened not his mouth;
> like a lamb that is led to the slaughter,
>   and like a sheep that before its shearers is silent,
>   so he opened not his mouth. (Isaiah 53:7)

Even when he was hanging on the cross of Calvary, Jesus simply said, "Father, forgive them, for they know not what they do" (Luke 23:34).

This is the mercy of Christ—to suffer and to die, but not to speak . . . only to forgive. The Bible teaches us to follow the example of Jesus at this point, rather than the example of Jeremiah:

> But if when you do good and suffer for it you endure, this is a gracious thing in the sight of God. For to this you have been called, because Christ also suffered for you, leaving you an example, so that you might follow in his steps. He committed no sin, neither was deceit found in his mouth. When he was reviled, he did not revile in return; when he suffered, he did not threaten, but continued entrusting himself to him who judges justly. (1 Peter 2:20b–23; cf. Isaiah 53:9)

The Condemnation

One reason to commit every cause to the Lord is that vengeance belongs to him alone (cf. Romans 12:19). Once Jeremiah had made his commitment, he received word of God's condemnation of the men of Anathoth.

> Therefore thus says the LORD of hosts: "Behold, I will punish them. The young men shall die by the sword, their sons and their daughters shall die by famine, and none of them shall be left. For I will bring disaster upon the men of Anathoth, the year of their punishment." (11:22, 23)

We noted earlier that congregations stand or fall by their reception of the Word of God. The same is true for towns and cities (cf. Matthew 10:14, 15). The children of Anathoth would fall by sword and by famine simply because the men of the town would not listen to the voice of God. Not even a remnant would remain. A town that will not stand under God's Word will fall under the weight of divine judgment.

This is a reminder to everyone—and especially to fathers—that God will judge every sin. Even the secret conspiracies of the men of Anathoth were exposed by the judgment of God. So it will be with our sins, even the secret ones.

One of my college philosophy professors—who taught ethics, appropriately enough—had a sign on the wall behind his desk that read, "I SAW WHAT YOU DID." The sign usually made me feel guilty for some sin or another. We may try to hide our sins, but our conscience reminds us that we cannot hide them from God. God saw what you did. He always does. And he "will bring every deed into judgment, with every secret thing, whether good or evil" (Ecclesiastes 12:14).

This is why we must throw ourselves upon the mercy of Christ, who died on the cross for our sins. If we do not ask for God's mercy on the basis of the death and resurrection of Jesus Christ, we will join the men of Anathoth in receiving God's eternal condemnation.

The Complaint

God's condemnation seems to be the last word. Once God pronounces his sentence of doom, what more can be said? The men of Anathoth hatched their plot, God foiled their plans, and Jeremiah committed his cause to the Lord. Now God has rendered his verdict against Jeremiah's enemies. Case closed.

Jeremiah, however, wanted to have the last word. He was committed to the Lord, but he still wanted to quibble with him. Jeremiah heard the condemnation. He knew that God would defend his cause. He knew that God is a righteous judge who always punishes his enemies. But Jeremiah still had a complaint he wanted to register: "Righteous are you, O Lord, when I complain to you; yet I would plead my case before you" (12:1a). In other words, "Could I have a word with you, Lord? Can we set up an appointment or something? I just want to make a few comments about the way you are handling this situation. I hope you don't mind if I offer some constructive criticism." Here is the gist of his criticism: "Why does the way of the wicked prosper? Why do all who are treacherous thrive?" (v. 1b). In other words, Jeremiah wanted to know why good things happen to bad people.

There are at least two plausible but wrong answers to the prophet's question. One way to explain why good things happen to bad people is to say that God is not in control. If God were not in control, it would be easy to explain the success of the wicked. Their success or failure would be entirely due to their own efforts. It would have nothing to do with God at all.

That answer is not an option for Jeremiah, however. He knows that God is in control. His answer is that God is not good. Since God is in control when the wicked do well, God must be to blame: "You plant them, and they take root; they grow and produce fruit" (v. 2a). Jeremiah did not question God's sovereignty, but his goodness. He knew that planting and uprooting are God's prerogatives. He admitted that the wicked prosper only because God allows them to do so. And that is precisely what made him mad. How can a good God allow the wicked to prosper, even for a little while? He must not be good after all.

Jeremiah's complaint is the reverse of Psalm 1. In Psalm 1 it is the righteous man who "is like a tree planted by streams of water that yields its fruit in its season" (v. 3). In Psalm 1 the wicked are just "chaff that the wind drives away" (v. 4). Here in Jeremiah 12, the opposite is happening. The wicked are well watered and flourishing. They are bearing fruit in their season. Worst of all, they profess to be believers. God is always "near in their mouth and far from their heart" (v. 2b). Why would God allow such hypocrites to prosper?

Jeremiah may sound as if he is raising the objection that Asaph raised:

> Truly God is good to Israel,
> to those who are pure in heart.
> But as for me, my feet had almost stumbled,
> my steps had nearly slipped.
> For I was envious of the arrogant
> when I saw the prosperity of the wicked.
> For they have no pangs until death;
> their bodies are fat and sleek.
> They are not in trouble as others are;
> they are not stricken like the rest of mankind. . . .
> Behold, these are the wicked;
> always at ease, they increase in riches. (Psalm 73:1–5, 12)

Asaph's complaint was about the prosperity of the wicked. He kept on complaining until he went to the temple to worship. There Asaph remembered that the wicked are destined for destruction. "Those who are far from you shall perish," he testifies; "you put an end to everyone who is unfaithful to you" (v. 27). It was enough for Asaph to know that God would judge the wicked in the end.

That was not enough for Jeremiah. He heard God promise to destroy the men of Anathoth, but he wanted judgment to come sooner rather than later. Though Asaph was content, Jeremiah continued to complain. He wanted God to write the final chapter on human evil RIGHT AWAY!

Many Christians feel the same way. We have heard that God will judge every deed, whether open or secret. We know that all the enemies of God will be put to shame at the final judgment. Still, we are discouraged by the triumph of evil in our times. We long for the day when murderers, rapists, racists, child molesters, persecutors of the church, and perpetrators of genocide will face divine judgment. In our darker moments we may even be tempted to ask for the kind of summary execution Jeremiah asked for:

> Pull them out like sheep for the slaughter,
>   and set them apart for the day of slaughter.
> How long will the land mourn
>   and the grass of every field wither?
> For the evil of those who dwell in it
>   the beasts and the birds are swept away,
>   because they said, "He will not see our latter end." (12:3b, 4)

The Contest

What is the answer? Why do good things happen to bad people? Why do the wheels of divine justice turn so slowly?

There are good answers to those questions, and no doubt Jeremiah expected to get some of them. When he complained about the slow justice of God, no doubt he expected God to defend his timetable. He expected an answer to the problem of evil, a philosophical explanation of the relationship between divine sovereignty and human depravity. Human beings often demand that kind of explanation from God. Like Jeremiah, we want some answers. We want to know why the innocent suffer while the wicked flourish. We want to know why good things happen to bad people.

But God does not always answer our questions. Usually he doesn't. In fact, in Jeremiah's case he came back with a few questions of his own:

> If you have raced with men on foot, and they have wearied you,
>   how will you compete with horses?
> And if in a safe land you are so trusting,
>   what will you do in the thicket of the Jordan? (v. 5)

God's answer ends with a question mark. This is God's usual strategy when his creatures try to place him on the witness stand. In the words of Derek Kidner, "God's answer is never philosophical, as though he owed us explanations, but always pastoral, to rebuke us, reorientate us or reassure us."[2]

Similarly, when Job wanted to question God about his suffering, God's answer was a question:

> Who is this that darkens counsel by words without knowledge?
> Dress for action like a man;
>   I will question you, and you make it known to me. (Job 38:2, 3)

Likewise, when Paul posed a hypothetical question about predestination, the Spirit answered with a couple of queries: "Who are you, O man, to answer back to God? Will what is molded say to its molder, 'Why have you made me like this?'" (Romans 9:20). If there is going to be an interrogation, God is going to ask the questions. We do not question God. God questions us. We do not place God under our microscope. God places us under his.

When God questioned Jeremiah, part of his point was that Jeremiah had no business demanding answers. But he made another point as well. To say that Jeremiah cannot run with the horses is a fancy way of saying, "You ain't seen nothin' yet." He took Jeremiah down to the racetrack and let him run in a few footraces. The 1500 meters perhaps. Maybe followed by a 4 x 400 relay. Then as Jeremiah stood on the infield, doubled over in exhaustion, so tired he could hardly drink his Gatorade, God said, "And now for the equestrian events. Are you ready for the derby? Jeremiah, you're over there in lane 6, next to the palomino. Sorry, all the bobtail nags ran in the last heat!"

"If you have raced with men on foot, and they have wearied you, how will you compete with horses?" (12:5a). It was no contest. Thoroughbreds were way out of Jeremiah's league. The horses of his day were smaller and perhaps slower than the horses of our own, but they were still at least twice as fast as Jeremiah. How can anyone who gets worn-out chasing Jesse Owens keep up with Secretariat?

God's second question makes the same point: "And if in a safe land you are so trusting, what will you do in the thicket of the Jordan?" (v. 5b). If Jeremiah stumbled on easy terrain—like the open country near Anathoth—then how could he possibly cope with the thick, lion-infested jungle that surrounded the Jordan River? To put it in an American context, how will someone who falls down on the Iowa plains ever make it across the Rocky Mountains?

Scholars have offered various interpretations of these questions. Perhaps the men who gave Jeremiah a run for his money were the false prophets, since God later says, "I did not send the prophets, yet they ran" (23:21). Perhaps the mention of the Jordan is a hint that Jeremiah will soon have a wider ministry within Israel. Perhaps the horses are from the Babylonian army, hinting that eventually Jeremiah will exercise an international ministry.

In any case, the point is that Jeremiah hadn't seen anything yet. The troubles he was having in Anathoth were nothing compared to the troubles he would later have in Jerusalem, Babylon, or Egypt. Things were bad but not the worst. If Jeremiah thought he had trouble today, he needed to wait until tomorrow. Anyone who gets discouraged, downtrodden, and defeated over little things will never fulfill his divine calling. If even little disappointments tempt Jeremiah to leave his calling, how will he cope with real persecution? God had great things in store for Jeremiah. But he would never achieve them unless he was willing to persevere in the little things. He had to be willing to race with men before he could compete with horses.

The same is true for every Christian. If you complain about the simple things God has already asked you to do, then you lack the spiritual strength to do what he wants you to do next. If your troubles keep you from doing the Lord's work now, you will never have the strength to do it later. If you want to do some great thing for God, then you must begin by doing the little things for God. And the only way to do little things for God is to do them by the strength of the Holy Spirit.

How can you run with horses? The best answer is the one Isaiah gave:

> Have you not known? Have you not heard?
> The LORD is the everlasting God,
>   the Creator of the ends of the earth.
> He does not faint or grow weary;
>   his understanding is unsearchable.
> He gives power to the faint,
>   and to him who has no might he increases strength.
> Even youths shall faint and be weary,
>   and young men shall fall exhausted;
> but they who wait for the LORD shall renew their strength;
>   they shall mount up with wings like eagles;
> they shall run and not be weary;
>   they shall walk and not faint. (Isaiah 40:28–31)

The Lord gives the strength to keep pace. Even when you run with horses.

20

Paradise Regained

JEREMIAH 12:7–17

THE SCOTTISH POET ROBERT BURNS (1759–1796) wrote a poem about "a faithless woman's broken vow." The woman he loves has left him. Yet the poet longs for his fickle lover and wonders if she will ever return. He fears for her safety on life's unsmooth path, since he will no longer be able to protect her.

> Encircled in her clasping arms,
> How have the raptur'd moments flown! . . .
> And, must I think! is she gone,
> My secret heart's exulting boast?
> And does she heedless hear my groan?
> And is she ever, ever lost?
> Oh! can she bear so base a heart,
> So lost to honour, lost to truth,
> As from the fondest lover part,
> The plighted husband of her youth?
> Alas! life's path may be unsmooth!
> Her way may lie thro' rough distress!
> Then, who her pangs and pains will soothe,
> Her sorrows share, and make them less?[1]

Love Lost

Robert Burns called his poem "The Lament." The book of Jeremiah is full of laments, most of them uttered by the prophet himself. Time and again the Weeping Prophet sheds hot tears of sorrow, repentance, and loneliness.

The lament in chapter 12 is different. Here the lover in the agonies of love is God himself. It is God's turn to wonder if his love is "ever, ever lost," and to wonder if she is "So lost to honour, lost to truth, As from the fondest lover part."

First, God lamented the loss of his love:

> I have forsaken my house;
>   I have abandoned my heritage;
> I have given the beloved of my soul
>   into the hands of her enemies. (v. 7)

These are not angry words; they are the words of a wounded lover. How lovingly God describes his people! Although they are wicked and wayward, they are still *his* people. They are his prized possession. Again and again God uses the first-person singular possessive pronoun: "*my* house," "*my* heritage" (v. 7); "*my* heritage" (v. 9); "*my* vineyard," "*my* pleasant portion" (v. 10).

These verses echo Deuteronomy 32, where God "gave to the nations their inheritance" (v. 8), a portion of land for each people. But he also retained an inheritance for himself, for "The LORD's portion is his people, Jacob his allotted heritage" (v. 9). This is why God can speak so emphatically about *his* house, *his* heritage, *his* pleasant portion. God maintains a righteous jealousy over his people. He has a claim upon us by inalienable right.

What God said in Jeremiah about his inheritance is shocking: He said he would forsake his people. He would abandon them and give them into the hands of their enemies (v. 7). He went so far as to say, "I hate her" (v. 8). Elizabeth Achtemeier writes, "That verse always sends chills up my spine. What would it mean if God hated us? To turn Paul's statement in Romans 8 upside down, 'If God be against us, who can be for us?'"[2] Jeremiah does not mean "hate" in the sense of a violent, angry emotion. What it means is that God intended to perform an act of rejecting his people (cf. Romans 9:13), at least for a time. He was going to disinherit them.

It is not hard to figure out why God intended to forsake and abandon his beloved. Her behavior had been beastly: "My heritage has become to me like a lion in the forest; she has lifted up her voice against me" (12:8). This is the Biblical version of the proverb about biting the hand that feeds you.

Judah was supposed to be God's lion. When Jacob blessed his sons he said:

> Judah is a lion's cub;
>   from the prey, my son, you have gone up.
> He stooped down; he crouched as a lion
>   and as a lioness; who dares rouse him? (Genesis 49:9)

In Jeremiah's day, however, the lion of Judah roared at the God who created her. She was hostile, antagonistic. She turned on God and roared back at him in rebellion. As God reached out to his people in love, a mighty roar filled the jungle.

Therefore, God threatened to abandon Judah and hand her over to her enemies. The expression in verse 7 is similar to the one found in Matthew 27:2, where the Jews "delivered him [Jesus] over to Pilate." But God still loved his people: "I have given the beloved of my soul into the hands of her enemies" (12:7). Not "The beloved," past tense, as if the love relationship was over. Rather, "The beloved of my soul." Judah was still beloved of God, still the one he loved.

Back in chapter 2 God actually filed for divorce from his beloved. But he never went through with it. Nor did he end his marital relationship on this occasion. He simply let his beloved reap the consequences of her sin, so she would return to him in love. But it pained him to do it:

> Has not my inheritance become to me
>> like a speckled bird of prey
>> that other birds of prey surround and attack?
> Go and gather all the wild beasts;
>> bring them to devour. (12:9 NIV)

Jeremiah imagines something like an ugly duckling, a speckled bird with unusual markings. Because it is remarkable, it is singled out for attack. Other birds gather to peck the speckled bird into submission.

I once watched seagulls squabble over a piece of dead fish. One gull was pecked in the skirmish and began to bleed. When the other gulls noticed the wounded gull they went after it, pecking away at the bloody spot. The same thing often happens in human relationships. Children who have a physical deformity or a unique talent are ridiculed by their friends. People who wear odd clothing are pressed to conform to the public dress code.

Jeremiah prophesied that the same thing would happen to Israel. The Jews were like the speckled bird. They were different. They stood out among the nations, perhaps because God's favor rested upon them. So the other nations will move in for the kill, like wild beasts who come and devour. Reluctantly God will let them attack, because his inheritance has become like a lion in the forest.

What lessons can be learned from God's lamentation? First, that our sins are painful to God. Our grumblings, complaints, moanings, rebellions, and arguments are like so many roarings in God's ears. Because our relationship with God is a love relationship, our sins wound his heart.

Second, no matter what we go through, God has been through worse. God's lament follows hard on the heels of Jeremiah's complaint at the beginning of chapter 12. Conspirators were plotting against the prophet to kill him. Even his own family sought to betray him. But God has been through all that. His own household, his own inheritance, his own beloved has roared against him.

God understands your sufferings. Have you been abandoned? Have you been deserted by your spouse? Have your sons and daughters defied you? Is your life filled with ungrateful, hostile people? God understands. He has been through it all before. He knows your pain.

God has also sent his Son Jesus Christ to suffer and to die for your sins. If God the Father was able to know Jeremiah's pain, how much more can God the Son feel your pain? You do not have a Savior who is unable to sympathize with your weaknesses, but you have one who has suffered in every way, just as you have, yet was and is without sin. "Let us then with confidence draw near to the throne of grace, that we may receive mercy and find grace to help in time of need" (Hebrews 4:16).

Paradise Lost

God also lamented the loss of his land (12:10–13). When God brought the children of Israel into the promised land, he planted them like a vineyard. They were "a choice vine, wholly of pure seed" (2:21).

But God's vine was about to be trampled underfoot. "Many shepherds [in other words, many kings from many nations] have destroyed my vineyard; they have trampled down my portion; they have made my pleasant portion a desolate wilderness" (12:10). When foreign armies invade, they often destroy the fruit of the land. Jeremiah prophesies that when the pagan nations come to Israel, they will trample out the vineyards where the grapes of wrath are stored.

Paradise will be lost. The promised land will become a wasteland:

> They have made it a desolation;
>   desolate, it mourns to me.
> The whole land is made desolate,
>   but no man lays it to heart. (v. 11)

Most English translations use several words to describe the devastation: "desolate," "wasteland," "parched." In Hebrew, however, the same word occurs over and over again: "Wasted, wasted, wasted." The whole land will be laid waste.

The wasting of Israel will be caused by an enemy attack: "Upon all the bare heights in the desert destroyers have come" (v. 12a). These outlaws can be connected to the events described in 2 Kings 24. In 602 BC, several years before the Babylonians captured Jerusalem and took the Jews into exile, roving bands of marauders attacked Judah from every direction: "The Lord sent against him [Jehoiakim] bands of the Chaldeans and bands of the Syrians and bands of the Moabites and bands of the Ammonites" (2 Kings 24:2).

These nations were the birds of prey who pecked the speckled bird. They destroyed everything. According to the prophecy, they would devour "from one end of the land to the other; no flesh has peace" (12:12b). This confirmed Jeremiah's frequent warnings about prophets who say "'Peace, peace,' when there is no peace" (6:14; 8:11). When the invasion came, there was no peace.

Not only would the invaders trample the vineyard, but they would also destroy the crops: "They have sown wheat and have reaped thorns; they have tired themselves out but profit nothing" (12:13a). The people of Israel sowed their wheat; but when the attack came, they would be unable to tend their crops. There would be nothing to reap but thorns. They would be worn out from farming, but they would have nothing to show for it.

All these things came to pass as a result of divine judgment: "They shall be ashamed of their harvests because of the fierce anger of the LORD" (v. 13b). When the nations came to lay the land to waste, they were weapons in God's hand. It was "The sword of the LORD" (v. 12) that devoured the land.

Modern archaeology confirms these Biblical prophecies. All the towns of Judah that have been excavated were destroyed around 600 BC, many of them twice over. God lost his beloved, and his beloved lost her paradise.

Paradise Regained

Brace yourself! Nothing prepares us for what comes next. Jeremiah often does this. Suddenly he shifts from first gear into overdrive. The gears of his message grind, and the prophecy lurches forward. One moment it is all judgment, and the next moment it is all grace. The promise of salvation comes unexpectedly, abruptly. Nothing prepares us for God's surprising grace.

Liberal Bible scholars do not appreciate the way Jeremiah jostles them around when he changes prophetic gears. They take a passage like this one and say, "These verses don't fit in here. They are prose rather than poetry. They are full of hope rather than despair. They promise return rather than exile. They extend grace to the nations and not just to Israel. Therefore they cannot come from Jeremiah. Someone must have added these verses later."

There is a reason the book of Jeremiah is arranged the way it is. Jeremiah was a preacher. He did not leave his hearers in despair longer than they could bear. Instead he often surprised them with divine grace. Jeremiah scattered his prophecies of hope like so many shooting stars against the black night of divine judgment. One never knows when the next promise will appear, but it will not be long.

The unexpected promise of 12:14–17 is the promise of paradise regained. The great English poet John Milton (1608–1674) began his great poem about the recovery of paradise with these words:

I who ere while the happy Garden sung,
By one man's disobedience lost, now sing
Recoverd Paradise to all mankind,
By one man's firm obedience fully tri'd
Through all temptation, and the Tempter foild
In all his wiles, defeated and repulst,
And Eden rais'd in the wast Wilderness.[3]

Jeremiah sang the same song. Paradise was to be recovered. Eden was to be raised in the waste wilderness.

In keeping with his ministry of uprooting nations and planting kingdoms (1:10), Jeremiah uttered four prophecies concerning paradise regained: 1) The wicked neighbors of Israel would be uprooted from their lands (12:14a). 2) The house of Judah would be rescued from exile (v. 14b). 3) God would have compassion on the wicked nations and bring them back to their own countries (v. 15). 4) Depending upon its response to God, each nation would either be saved or destroyed (vv. 16, 17).

To understand these prophecies, it is helpful to know how Biblical prophecy works. A Biblical prophecy is like a slide in a slide projector. It is possible to project a slide onto a screen as small as a 3 x 5 note card held close to the projector lens. Nearly the entire picture will fit on the note card. Yet the image will be a small one. There is more to the picture; some shafts of light spill over the edges of the note card and shed light on the darkness beyond.

When the note card is removed, the slide can be projected onto an ordinary projection screen. The image on the screen is bigger, fuller, and richer than the image on the note card. It can be seen from a greater distance, and more of its details can be recognized.

The image on the screen gives the big picture but not the biggest picture. Although the image fills the screen, there are still some shafts of light streaming away around the edges. It is not until the screen is taken away that the entire picture covers the whole wall of the auditorium. The same image can be projected onto the note card, the screen, and the wall. Each time the picture is created by the same rays of light shining through the same slide, but each time the picture is bigger and better.

The same prophecy can be fulfilled several times, each fulfillment bigger and better than the last. First, a prophecy shines on a 3 x 5 note card, so to speak. There is a near fulfillment in the life of the nation of Israel. Some time close to the giving of the prophecy, many of its details come to pass among God's people.

But there is always more to a prophecy than a note card can hold. Once the note card is pulled away, the deeper significance of the prophecy appears on the screen, which can be compared to Jesus Christ. In the New Testament, the Old Testament promise becomes "Yes" in Christ (2 Corinthians 1:20). When Jesus spoke to his disciples on the Emmaus road (Luke 24:13–35), he pulled away the note card and allowed all the promises of the Old Testament to shine upon the screen of his life. "Beginning with Moses and all the Prophets, he interpreted to them in all the Scriptures the things concerning himself" (v. 27).

Not every promise of the Old Testament was completely fulfilled in the first coming of Jesus Christ. Many of the promises of Scripture spill over beyond the first coming of Jesus and shine onto his second coming. When the screen of the life of Jesus Christ is removed, a Biblical prophecy shines against the backdrop of the end of human history.

These three stages of the fulfillment of a Biblical prophecy can be called *literal fulfillment*, *messianic fulfillment*, and *eschatological fulfillment*. *Literal fulfillment* is like the note card. It is the near fulfillment of a prophecy in the life of the Old Testament nation of Israel. *Messianic fulfillment* is like the screen. It is the intermediate fulfillment of a prophecy in the life of Jesus Christ. *Eschatological* (which simply means "last") *fulfillment* is the back wall of the auditorium. It is the final fulfillment of a prophecy for all eternity. Each time the picture is bigger and better, until Christ is all and is in all.

How do these principles apply to Jeremiah 12? First, they apply to Israel at a literal (note card) level. God promised to send Israel into captivity and to bring her back again. This promise began to be fulfilled when the Babylonians came and took Israel into captivity in 586BC. Later the exiles returned to Israel under Zerubbabel in 537 BC, and again under Ezra and Nehemiah in the fifth century. They regained their earthly paradise.

The promise of the restoration of Israel spilled over beyond the return from exile to shine on the ministry of Jesus Christ (messianic, screen fulfillment). When Jesus Christ came, he proclaimed that he is the Vine (John 15:5). That was a way of saying that Jesus is the new Israel. Although God's vineyard was trampled down by many foreign kings, God replanted his vineyard in Jesus Christ. All those who are joined to Jesus Christ become God's vineyard, God's inheritance.

When the screen is taken away, the promise of paradise regained shines on the end of human history (eschatological, final, wall fulfillment). Heaven brings a permanent end to all the exiles of the people of God. Revelation 21, 22 describes the eternal paradise where the people of God will find their eternal home.

The same three stages of fulfillment can be applied to the prophecies concerning Israel's neighbors:

> Thus says the LORD concerning all my evil neighbors who touch the heritage that I have given my people Israel to inherit: "Behold, I will pluck them up from their land, and I will pluck up the house of Judah from among them. And after I have plucked them up, I will again have compassion on them, and I will bring them again each to his heritage and each to his land." (12:14, 15)

God promised that after he uprooted his enemies from their lands, he would have compassion on them and bring them back to their own countries. How and when were these promises fulfilled?

There were near (literal, note card) fulfillments in the days of Jeremiah. Israel was not the only nation taken captive by Babylon. The nations that attacked Israel like a speckled bird—Aram, Moab, and Ammon—were uprooted from their lands and carried off into captivity. But eventually they had a homecoming. The Lord had compassion upon them and brought them back to their lands.

Jeremiah's promises to the nations also spilled over into the coming of Jesus Christ (messianic, screen fulfillment). God had always considered it too small a thing for the Messiah to save Israel alone; he wanted to bring "salvation . . . to the end of the earth" (Isaiah 49:6). Consider the several Gentiles who came to Jesus to confess his name. Wise men came from the east (Matthew 2). The Samaritan woman at the well was saved, with all her neighbors (John 4). The Roman soldier at the cross testified that Jesus was "innocent" (Luke 23:47).

Then the nations gathered at Pentecost. Each heard the message of the gospel in its own tongue, so that all might swear by the name of Jesus Christ.

> "Parthians and Medes and Elamites and residents of Mesopotamia, Judea and Cappadocia, Pontus and Asia, Phrygia and Pamphylia, Egypt and the parts of Libya belonging to Cyrene, and visitors from Rome, both Jews and proselytes, Cretans and Arabians—we hear them telling in our own tongues the mighty works of God." And all were amazed and perplexed, saying to one another, "What does this mean?" (Acts 2:9–12)

What it meant was that Jeremiah's promises concerning the salvation of the nations were being fulfilled in Jesus Christ.

The day will come when the screen will be taken away and God's promise to the nations will fill the whole wall. That day is yet to come, but the shafts of light are heading in the direction of an eschatological or final fulfillment. At the end of history the angels of Heaven will say, "The kingdom of the world has become the kingdom of our Lord and of his Christ, and he shall reign forever and ever" (Revelation 11:15).

A Final Warning

Jeremiah gave many wonderful promises concerning the nations. He offered the hope of redemption for the worst of God's enemies.

However, these promises also came with a condition. If the nations of the world are to be saved, they must forsake their foreign gods and worship the God of Israel. "If they will diligently learn the ways of my people, to swear by my name, 'As the Lord lives,' even as they taught my people to swear by Baal, then they shall be built up in the midst of my people" (12:16). The nations cannot be saved on their own terms or by their own gods. They must take the trouble to come and learn how to worship the one true God.

Jeremiah's prophecies contradict contemporary notions of religious pluralism. In 1996 the *New York Times* reported on a controversy in the Reformed Church in America. A pastor in Spring Lake, Michigan, no longer believed that Jesus Christ is the only way to salvation. In the words of one member of his congregation, "We do not know the limits of God's grace, and not knowing that, how can we possibly say we know these people are going to heaven, and these are not?"

The pastor of the church compared universal salvation to a great cathedral lined with stained-glass windows: "Inside stand groups of Jews, Christians and Muslims. Each group reads the story of its faith in a particular window. All the windows," he wrote, "are illuminated by the light of God."[4]

This is a popular view in post-Christian America, the view that there are many windows to divine light. The New Testament, of course, denies this view of salvation. Jesus Christ testified that he is the only way, the only truth, and the only life (John 14:6). But universal salvation was already ruled out in the Old Testament. Even in Jeremiah 12, a prophecy about the salvation of all nations, salvation was not for everyone. God's mercy is given freely but not universally. His salvation is wide, but it is not boundless.

Can unbelievers be saved? Yes, but only if they become believers! The condition for entering into blessing with the people of God is swearing by

God's name. The grace of God is available to all the nations of the world. Yet it is only given to those who come to the one true God and confess his name.

What will happen if the nations do not swear by the name of God? Quite simply, they will not be saved. They will not be given an everlasting inheritance. "If any nation will not listen, then I will utterly pluck it up and destroy it, declares the LORD" (v. 17).

It is not hard to see how these verses apply in the gospel age. Outside the path of the light streaming from the slide projector there is only darkness. Outside of faith in Christ there is only eternal judgment. Anyone who does not confess the name of Jesus Christ will not be saved unto eternal life. Jesus Christ will welcome you back into his paradise. But you must swear by his name. Otherwise, you will lose paradise forever.

21

Corruptio Optimi Pessima

JEREMIAH 13:1–27

THE FIRST LATIN PHRASE I ever learned was *corruptio optimi pessima*. It was printed on a battered, old, athletic T-shirt someone gave to my father, a shirt riddled with holes. *Corruptio optimi pessima* means, "The better the thing, the worse the abuse." Or, "Corruption in the best is the worst corruption." Or, "The corruption of the best becomes the worst." A garment that was once used for the best of all sports—namely, basketball—was in the worst of shape.

Corruptio optimi pessima became a popular Latin slogan, but it was perhaps first used in Aristotle's *Nichomachean Ethics*: "Tyranny being the corruption of the best form [of government] is therefore the worst."[1] Aristotle believed that society is best governed by a good king. However, if the king is immoral, then society will have the worst of all forms of government—namely, tyranny. A corrupt king becomes a dictator. The corruption of the best becomes the worst. *Corruptio optimi pessima*.

William Shakespeare expressed the same principle in Sonnet 94: "For fairest things grow foulest by foul deeds; lilies that fester smell far worse than weeds." The decay of the fairest flower creates the foulest odor. *Corruptio optimi pessima*.

The Linen Belt

In Jeremiah 13 five of the best things become the worst. The first is a linen belt, or loincloth (vv. 1–11). The Lord told Jeremiah to make a shopping trip: "This is what the LORD said to me: 'Go and buy a linen belt and put it around your waist, but do not let it touch water.' So I bought a belt, as the LORD directed, and put it around my waist" (vv. 1, 2 NIV). Jeremiah went down to his local department store, bought a linen belt, and tied it around his waist. The prophet was the proud owner of a brand-new belt. It was the best. It hadn't even been prewashed.

Jeremiah's bright new belt was a visual aid. Everyone would notice it right away because it would have been wrapped around the prophet's grubby old robes. Furthermore, a linen belt was not part of the prophetic wardrobe. It was a priestly accessory (Leviticus 16:4), or perhaps a kingly one. When Jeremiah put on his new belt, he became a public spectacle. It would be like a business-man wearing a bright new tie with jeans and a T-shirt.

Then Jeremiah did something even stranger than wearing the belt. He buried it. "Then the word of the LORD came to me a second time: 'Take the belt you bought and are wearing around your waist, and go now to Perath and hide it there in a crevice in the rocks.' So I went and hid it at Perath, as the LORD told me" (vv. 3–5 NIV).

Some Bible scholars offer a clever explanation for the location of Perath. They say Perath is really Parah, which was a village about four miles from Jeremiah's hometown (Anathoth). However, what the Scripture says is Perath, which everywhere else in the Old Testament simply means "Euphrates" (cf. 46:2), the great river of the Middle East. Some scholars object that the Euphrates River was some 300 miles away, but this is not a real difficulty. The long trek would have taken the prophet several months, but that was not an uncommon journey in those days.

If Jeremiah's belt was supposed to be an object lesson, then it made perfect sense for him to go all the way to the Euphrates. Imagine all the questions his neighbors would have asked when he came back—three months later—without his celebrated belt. It would have given Jeremiah the perfect opportunity to ex-plain his prophecy. Furthermore, Jeremiah waited a while before going back to the Euphrates to dig up his belt. "Many days later the LORD said to me, 'Go now to Perath and get the belt I told you to hide there.' So I went to Perath and dug up the belt and took it from the place where I had hidden it, but now it was ruined and completely useless" (vv. 6, 7 NIV). Enough time had elapsed for the belt to be ruined. Its fibers were threadbare and dirty. The belt was good for nothing.

God used the linen belt to make the spiritual point that the best had be-come the worst. God wanted his people to be the best. "For as the loincloth [or "belt" NIV] clings to the waist of a man, so I made the whole house of Israel and the whole house of Judah cling to me, declares the LORD, that they might be for me a people, a name, a praise, and a glory, but they would not listen" (v. 11). The linen belt was meant to be a beautiful picture of God's relation-ship with his people. God wants us to be bright and clean. He wants to wrap us around his waist like an embrace.

The new linen belt is an apt depiction of the first answer in the Westminster *Shorter Catechism*: "Man's chief end is to glorify God, and to enjoy him forever." The chief purpose and ultimate goal of human beings is to be wrapped around God's waist like a fashion accessory. When we are at our very best, we adorn God with glory.

The people of God were not at their best in Jeremiah's day, and the corruption of the best is the worst: "This evil people, who refuse to hear my words, who stubbornly follow their own heart and have gone after other gods to serve them and worship them, shall be like this loincloth, which is good for nothing" (v. 10). It sounds as if God is going to take his heavyweight title belt and dump it in the trash.

This may be a prophecy about the exile. Toward the end of Jeremiah's ministry the people of Judah were carried off into captivity in Babylon. When Jeremiah carried his belt to the Euphrates and buried it—near Babylon—it may have symbolized God's people being carried off into exile. There are prophecies of exile later in the chapter: "All Judah is taken into exile, wholly taken into exile" (v. 19b). "I will scatter you like chaff driven by the wind from the desert" (v. 24). The trouble with this view is that the exile did not spoil Israel but saved her. The Exile did not ruin Israel but cured her of her sin and restored her to faithfulness to God.[2]

A better interpretation of the linen belt has to do with foreign alliances. After the battle of Carchemish in 605 BC, Jehoiakim, king of Israel, pledged allegiance to Nebuchadrezzar, king of Babylon. The alliance displeased God greatly. God wanted his people, rather than trusting in kings and princes, to trust in him alone. "What will you say when they set as head over you those whom you yourself have taught to be friends to you?" (v. 21a).

The parable of the linen belt thus reminds us to glorify God and trust in him alone. If your whole life is devoted to the service of Jesus Christ, you are like a linen belt around God's waist. You look great! But if you are trusting in money, ability, family, government, or anything besides God, then what you are doing is useless. If your life is not dedicated to bringing honor and renown to God, then it is worth about as much as a belt buried in a pile of dirt. You are worthless when it comes to your primary purpose—giving glory to God. You were made to be the brightest ornament in all creation, but the corruption of the best becomes the worst. *Corruptio optimi pessima.*

The Full Bottle

Another best that has become the worst is the fruit of the vine (vv. 12–14). What drink is better than wine, which makes glad the hearts of men? "You shall speak to them this word: 'Thus says the LORD, the God of Israel, "Every jar shall be filled with wine"'" (v. 12a).

This was probably one of the few occasions when people actually listened to Jeremiah. He was quoting the chorus from an old drinking song. The people had heard this slogan before: "Do we not indeed know that every jar will be filled with wine?" (v. 12b). "Everybody knows that, Jerry! What are wine jars for? Pour us another round! Every wine jar should be filled with wine!"

Before all the laughter could die down, Jeremiah knocked their drinks right out of their hands: "Thus says the LORD: Behold, I will fill with drunkenness all the inhabitants of this land" (v. 13a). Jeremiah took a familiar proverb and turned it into a riddle. In the words of Calvin, "They indeed all knew that bottles were made for wine; but they did not understand that they were the bottles."[3] The people of Judah were not the drinkers—they were the jars of wine. This was a prophecy of God's judgment against sin. "I will not pity or spare or have compassion, that I should not destroy them" (v. 14b). If his people will not wrap their praise around him, he will pour the wine of his wrath into them.

Will anyone escape? No; God's bitter wine will be poured into "all the inhabitants of this land: the kings who sit on David's throne, the priests, the prophets, and all the inhabitants of Jerusalem. And I will dash them one against another, fathers and sons together" (vv. 13b, 14a). Jerusalem will be turned into one big fraternity party. Kings, priests, and prophets will roll out the barrel together. Fathers and sons will drink together and then smash into one another in drunken demolition.

This passage is not primarily about drinking, but it does summarize the Biblical teaching about the use of alcohol. It is good for every wineskin to be filled with wine. All things are permissible for the Christian, including a glass of wine. However, drunkenness is evil and destructive. Inebriation brings upon itself the judgment of God. Anyone who cannot have a drink without having a second and a third must not drink at all. To become drunk on wine is to corrupt the best, which becomes the worst. *Corruptio optimi pessima.*

The Dark Mountain

Another of the best things in life is daylight (vv. 15–17). Jeremiah imagines the people of God going up on the hills at twilight or just before dawn. They hope for even a few rays of light to shine on their path and help them find shelter.

Instead of getting more light, however, they get more darkness. God himself is making it dark earlier than they expect.

Give glory to the LORD your God
  before he brings darkness,
before your feet stumble
  on the twilight mountains,
and while you look for light
  he turns it into gloom
  and makes it deep darkness. (v. 16)

God's people face the kind of darkness described in Milton's *Samson Agonistes*:

O dark, dark, dark, amid the blaze of noon,
Irrevocably dark, total eclipse
Without all hope of day. (lines 80–82)

The beauty of the mountains has become a terror. As the people of God stumble on the darkening hills, the best has become the worst.

This is a prophecy about the captivity of King Jehoiachin in 597 BC. Ten years prior to Judah's great exile (587 BC), the king of Judah and his mother were carried off to Babylon. There was a little exile before the big exile, twilight before deep darkness.

The reason for the darkness is that the people of God were proud. God promised to "spoil the pride of Judah and the great pride of Jerusalem" (v. 9). Now Jeremiah warns them, "Hear and give ear; be not proud, for the LORD has spoken" (v. 15). Those who give glory to God will get all the light they need to find their way in life. But the proud will stumble in the darkness. If they refuse to listen to the Word of God, then even the little light they have will be taken away. This is Jeremiah's version of the proverb that pride goes before a fall (Proverbs 16:18). In this case, God's people were liable to fall right off the mountain.

It is best to respond to God's judgment against pride with humility and with tears. Jeremiah did not scold or berate the people of God. Instead he wept for them.

But if you will not listen,
  my soul will weep in secret for your pride;
my eyes will weep bitterly and run down with tears,
  because the LORD's flock has been taken captive. (13:17)

Jeremiah had the strongest sympathies for the people of God. His heart was full of tender compassion for their miserable condition. Their pride brought out his pity because he was a preacher of real gospel temperament. Jeremiah was willing to suffer with the people of God, even in their sin.

The Royal Disgrace

Jeremiah described a fourth best that became a worst—the royal family (vv. 18–21):

> Say to the king and the queen mother:
>   "Take a lowly seat,
> for your beautiful crown
>   has come down from your head." (v. 18)

The king and his mother—who was an important figure in ancient Israel—will be knocked off their thrones. Their crowns will topple from their heads.

This prophecy of royal disgrace is another specific prophecy about exile. When Jehoiachin was taken into captivity by the Babylonians, his mother Nehushta was taken with him (2 Kings 24:15; cf. Jeremiah 22:26). In fact, the Scripture records how all of the treasures from the royal palace were taken to Babylon. That booty undoubtedly included the crowns of the king and the queen mother (v. 13).

Jeremiah's prophecy about this sounded an ominous note: "The cities of the Negeb are shut up, with none to open them" (v. 19a). The Negeb is the vast desert south of Jerusalem. It is such a desolate area that people rarely travel there, if they can help it. Under normal circumstances an invading army would conquer Jerusalem and a few big towns in the north and would ignore the Negeb altogether. Why bother to attack a desert? But in this judgment, no one would be safe. Judah's defeat would be absolute.

> All Judah is taken into exile,
>   wholly taken into exile.
> "Lift up your eyes and see
>   those who come from the north.
> Where is the flock that was given you,
>   your beautiful flock?" (vv. 19b, 20)

The king and the queen mother were supposed to shepherd the people of God, but they would lose their sheep.

It is hard to read these verses without thinking of the near-collapse of the English Royal Family during the 1990s. In her annual speech on Christmas Day 1994, Queen Elizabeth told the British people that she had had a bad year. It was an *annus horribilis*, she said, a horrible year. If she had really wanted to show off her Latin, she could have quoted Aristotle: *Corruptio optimi pessima*. When a royal wedding is followed by adultery, deception, divorce, and death, the best has become the worst.

The royal disgrace in Judah is a reminder that God is no respecter of persons. Even the kings and queens of earth are subject to his rule. From the least to the greatest, God holds everyone accountable for his or her sins.

A Loose Woman

The last best that becomes the worst is a young maiden:

> And if you say in your heart,
>   "Why have these things come upon me?"
> it is for the greatness of your iniquity
>   that your skirts are lifted up
>   and you suffer violence. (v. 22; cf. Lamentations 1:9)

> I myself will lift up your skirts over your face,
>   and your shame will be seen.
> I have seen your abominations,
>   your adulteries and neighings, your lewd whorings,
> on the hills in the field.
>   Woe to you, O Jerusalem!
> How long will it be before you are made clean? (vv. 26, 27)

Once again, Israel had been spiritually unfaithful.

> This is your lot,
>   the portion I have measured out to you, declares the LORD,
> because you have forgotten me
>   and trusted in lies. (v. 25)

Israel had been flirting with false gods, even sleeping around with them. Jeremiah uses such lewd imagery because some of Israel's idol worship at the high places involved having sex with temple prostitutes.

All the sins of Israel would be uncovered. Perhaps Jeremiah was describing the way Babylonian soldiers would violate Israel. Or perhaps these verses describe the stripping of an adulteress, like the one described in Hosea 2. When the maiden's dress is pulled up, the shameful garments of her prostitution are exposed.

There is a similar scene in Edmund Spenser's (c. 1552–1599) epic poem *The Faerie Queene*. The hero of *The Faerie Queene* is Red Cross Knight, who represents the young Christian in search of holiness. He has been deceived by the charms of the beautiful Duessa, who seems fair but has a false heart. Underneath her fancy dress she is ugly and grotesque. Red Cross Knight cannot see Duessa for what she really is until her robes are stripped away:

> . . . that witch they disarrayed,
> And robbed of royal robes and purple pall
> And ornaments that richly were displayed;
> Ne spared they to strip her naked all.
> Then when they had dispoiled her tire and caul,
> Such as she was their eyes might her behold,
> That her misshaped parts did them appall—
> A loathly, wrinkled hag, ill favored, old,
> Whose secret filth good manners biddeth not be told. . . .
> Which when the knights beheld, amazed they were
> And wondered at so foul deformed wight.
> 'Such then,' said Una, 'as she seemeth here,
> Such is the face of falsehood, such the sight
> Of foul Duessa, when her borrowed light
> Is laid away and counterfeasance known.'[4]

Jeremiah 13 teaches the same lesson. Our fancy clothes cannot hide our false hearts. God sees our sins in all their monstrosity. Can you imagine what your heart would look like if God were to strip away all your defenses, all your hypocrisy, all your pious talk, and all your self-righteous actions? The sinful human heart is the most frightful thing in the whole universe.

The best has become the worst. The linen belt, the full bottle of wine, the twilight on the mountainside, the royal family, and the shaming of the prostitute all teach the same lesson. These are five pictures of total depravity. They show what sin looks like and what kind of judgment it deserves. They show what human beings become when they fall short of the glory of God. *Corruptio optimi pessima.*

How Long Will You Be Unclean?

Jeremiah closes with a haunting question: "How long will it be before you are made clean?" (v. 27). Sometimes the Old Testament gives us the answers. Sometimes it at least hints at God's final answer to the problem of human sin. But this is one of the times when it simply asks a question: "How long will it be before you are made clean?"

The answer is that you will remain unclean for as long as you insist on cleaning yourself. As long as you try to reform your own life you will remain unclean. There is nothing a sinner can do to change his or her sinful nature.

The point of Jeremiah's famous proverb is that you are a dyed-in-the-wool sinner: "Can the Ethiopian change his skin or the leopard his spots?" (v. 23a).

This verse is sometimes misunderstood in the context of race relations. The point is not that black skin is evil or that black spots are stains. In fact, black spots are the distinctive beauty of the leopard. Black is beautiful. The point is that skin color—like a sin nature—cannot be changed. As Jeremiah goes on to say, "Neither can you do good who are accustomed to doing evil" (v. 23b NIV).

It made sense for Jeremiah to use Ethiopians as an example because they were relatively rare in Israel. The Ethiopian Jeremiah meets in chapter 38 is uncommon enough for Jeremiah to mention his ethnic heritage. If Jeremiah had been prophesying to Ethiopians, perhaps he would have put it the other way around: "Can the Israelite change his skin?"

The answer is no. No human being can change the color of his or her skin. No animal can change its markings. And you can no more cleanse your own heart from sin than you can change the color of your skin.

"How long will it be before you are made clean?" You will be unclean until Jesus Christ makes you clean. The ultimate answer to Jeremiah's question is the work of Jesus Christ on the cross. His shed blood is the all-purpose cleanser for sin. Only Jesus Christ can take the worst in the human heart and make it the best.

The Bible shows how Jesus Christ has taken each of the worsts in Jeremiah 13 and turned it into a best. Start with linen spoiled by sin. The Bible promises that new linen will be given to the saints to wear in glory, "fine linen, bright and pure," which "is the righteous deeds of the saints" (Revelation 19:8). The worst will become the best.

Next, take the wine of God's wrath. Jesus drank down the cup of God's wrath on the cross of Calvary (Matthew 26:42). Now he offers his children the wine of salvation, the cup of the new covenant in his blood (Luke 22:20). The worst has become the best.

Or take darkness. Jesus Christ turns it into light. He is the light of the world (John 8:12). In Christ, "The darkness is passing away and the true light is already shining" (1 John 2:8). Things are not getting darker and darker— they are getting brighter and brighter for the people of God. The worst is becoming the best.

The same is true with royalty. Jesus Christ has come into the world to set the crown of dominion back on the head of humanity. The New Testament teaches that every believer will receive an eternal crown. Paul calls it a "crown of righteousness" (2 Timothy 4:8) and an "imperishable" wreath

(1 Corinthians 9:25). Peter calls it an "unfading crown of glory" (1 Peter 5:4). James calls it a "crown of life" (James 1:12; cf. Revelation 2:10). John calls it a crown of gold (Revelation 4:4). The worst will become the best.

Finally, consider the shameful prostitute. Jesus Christ turns the harlot into a virgin bride. Former prostitutes were among his most faithful followers when he walked upon this earth. His ultimate purpose is to present his people to his Father "as a bride adorned for her husband" (Revelation 21:2).

If you are still unclean, you do not need to be unclean any longer. Take all the things in your life that are soiled, spoiled, shattered, stained, and shameful and Jesus will make them right. Not *corruptio optimi pessima*, but *redemptio pessimi optima*: The redemption of the worst is the best. The worst will become the best. For those who come to Christ for salvation, it is all clean linen, fine wine, broad daylight, golden crowns, and bridal gowns.

22

For God's Sake, Do Something!

JEREMIAH 14:1–22

JEREMIAH 14 opens so matter-of-factly it is hard to appreciate what great suffering it represents: "The word of the Lord that came to Jeremiah concerning the drought" (v. 1). A drought is the continuous absence of rain. A drought happens when it does not rain day after day after day.

In the novel Cry, the Beloved Country, Alan Paton describes a drought in the South African valley of the Umzimkulu:

> The morning was already hot beyond endurance, but the skies were cloudless and held no sign of rain. There had never been such a drought in this country. The oldest men of the tribe could not remember such a time as this, when the leaves fell from the trees till they stood as though it were winter, and the small tough-footed boys ran from shade to shade because of the heat of the ground. If one walked on the grass, it crackled underfoot as it did after a fire, and in the whole valley there was not one stream that was running. Even on the tops the grass was yellow, and neither below nor above was there any ploughing. The sun poured down out of the pitiless sky, and the cattle moved thin and listless over the veld.[1]

Sword, Famine, and Pestilence

The drought Judah endured in the days of Jeremiah was equally severe. In fact, the Bible actually describes it as "The droughts" (v. 1 NKJV), since Jeremiah lived through more than one.

This is how he describes their devastating effects in Lamentations 4:

> The tongue of the nursing infant sticks
>   to the roof of its mouth for thirst;

the children beg for food,
    but no one gives to them.
Those who once feasted on delicacies
    perish in the streets;
those who were brought up in purple
    embrace ash heaps. . . .
Now their face is blacker than soot;
    they are not recognized in the streets;
their skin has shriveled on their bones;
    it has become as dry as wood. (Lamentations 4:4, 5, 8)

It was a terrible time to be alive. Jeremiah actually thought people were better off dead:

Happier were the victims of the sword
    than the victims of hunger,
who wasted away, pierced
    by lack of the fruits of the field. (Lamentations 4:9)

The drought caused such great distress that the whole nation gathered together to fast and to pray. There was weeping and wailing all over the country:

Judah mourns,
    and her gates languish;
her people lament on the ground,
    and the cry of Jerusalem goes up. (Jeremiah 14:2)

The nation mourned. All the flags were at half-mast. The only sound was crying.

The reason for the distress was no secret. Drought afflicted every level of society, from the top down:

Her nobles send their servants for water;
    they come to the cisterns;
they find no water;
    they return with their vessels empty;
they are ashamed and confounded
    and cover their heads. (v. 3)

Apparently the famine did not bother to check what tax bracket people were in. The rich could command their servants, but they could not create water. The cisterns ran dry. In their dismay the servants flipped their empty jars over to hide underneath them.

The farmers did the same thing:

Because of the ground that is dismayed,
  since there is no rain on the land,
the farmers are ashamed;
  they cover their heads. (v. 4)

The ground was so hard that it was impossible to plow or to plant.

Even the wild animals were afflicted by the drought. Jeremiah went out into the fields and watched a mother abandon her child. "Even the doe in the field forsakes her newborn fawn because there is no grass" (v. 5). Usually deer make the tenderest of mothers; yet this doe had no milk because she had no grass.

Then Jeremiah detected the telltale signs of starvation in the wild donkeys on the hills.

The wild donkeys stand on the bare heights;
  they pant for air like jackals;
their eyes fail
  because there is no vegetation." (v. 6)

Jeremiah watches the donkeys sniff the wind for moisture. Their eyesight has failed from lack of nourishment. Drought torments all creatures great and small. The whole creation groaned under the weight of Judah's sin (cf. Romans 8:22).

The drought was bad, but it was not Judah's only problem. The nation faced a triple threat: sword, famine, and pestilence (14:12). As Jeremiah complained:

If I go out into the field,
  behold, those pierced by the sword!
And if I enter the city,
  behold, the diseases of famine!
For both prophet and priest ply their trade through the land
  and have no knowledge. (v. 18)

When the prophet went out into the countryside he saw the corpses of the dead, butchered by the sword. When he returned to the city he saw the corpses of the living, ravaged by drought. His colleagues in ministry were beginning to vanish.

When God Does Nothing

What would you do if you had to witness such horrors? Jeremiah did three things: He wept, he argued, and he prayed.

It is no surprise that Jeremiah wept when he saw the people of God suffer.

He was the Weeping Prophet. For Jeremiah, the suffering of God's people was always an occasion for lamentation:

> Let my eyes run down with tears night and day,
>   and let them not cease,
> for the virgin daughter of my people is shattered with a great wound,
>   with a very grievous blow. (v. 17)

Jeremiah wept incessantly, the way a man would weep for his daughter if she had been wounded in war.

But Jeremiah did more than just weep. He argued with God, and he started by laying down this challenge: "For God's sake, do something!" The English Standard Version puts it slightly differently, but it amounts to the same thing: "Though our iniquities testify against us, act, O LORD, for your name's sake" (v. 7a). Jeremiah saw extreme human suffering all around him, and he wanted God to get up and do something about it. People were starving to death! Why didn't God do something?

We often feel the same way about human suffering. During the week I am writing this I have had several reminders of the sufferings of the world. I received a letter from a missionary asking me to pray for the children of a young Iranian evangelist who was executed for preaching the gospel. I saw a picture in the newspaper of refugees in Zaire desperately scrabbling for food from a relief truck. I heard an appeal to send shoes to war victims in Bosnia who face the prospect of walking barefoot through the cold winter. I read an article about a woman who burned herself to death on the campus of the University of Pennsylvania.

Add to the sufferings of the world the sufferings of your own friends and family. The unexpected pink slip. The sudden illness. The tragic accident. To say nothing of your own burdens. Your disappointment in life. Your loneliness. Your loss. Your pain.

These misfortunes deserve some answers! The sufferings of the world demand an explanation. God simply must respond to the kinds of questions Jeremiah posed to him:

> Have you utterly rejected Judah?
>   Does your soul loathe Zion?
> Why have you struck us down
>   so that there is no healing for us?
>
> We looked for peace, but no good came;
>   for a time of healing, but behold, terror. (v. 19)

Jeremiah was baffled by suffering. What was God up to? Why didn't he do something?

The trouble was that God did not seem to be doing *anything*. After all his promises about never forsaking his people, he was absent without leave.

> O you hope of Israel,
>> its savior in time of trouble,
> why should you be like a stranger in the land,
>> like a traveler who turns aside to tarry for a night? (v. 8)

Where is God when you really need him? To Jeremiah, he seemed like a bystander, a passer-by, an accidental tourist. You could never count on him. He was never around when you needed him. He showed up every now and then and stayed in the guest bedroom, but he did not dwell with his people. He was practically a stranger! Jeremiah thus came back to the question C. S. Lewis once posed: "Why is he so present a commander in our time of prosperity and so very absent a help in time of trouble?"[2]

Not only does God seem absent, but he also seems impotent: "Why should you be like a man confused, like a mighty warrior who cannot save?" (v. 9a). To Jeremiah, God seemed like an army recruit on his first mission who wanders into an ambush unawares and is taken captive. The prophet has called him a "savior" and a "warrior," but it turns out that he "cannot save."

By comparing God to a "stranger" and to a soldier taken by surprise, Jeremiah called into question two of God's eternal attributes—omnipresence and omnipotence. By definition, God is all present and all powerful. Where is God? God is everywhere. Can God do all things? Yes, God can do all his holy will. God is omnipresent and omnipotent.

But a God who drops by every now and then is hardly omnipresent. And if God is powerless to save, then he is not all powerful. Furthermore, if God is a stranger, then he is not all present after all. And a God who can be tied up by thugs is far from omnipotent. When Jeremiah saw the mess the world was in, his understanding of God came under attack. Could God really live up to his press clippings?

God proved quite capable of defending himself against these accusations. The problem was not that he was absent or impotent. The problem was that his people were recalcitrant.

> Thus says the LORD concerning this people:
> "They have loved to wander thus;
>> they have not restrained their feet;

therefore the LORD does not accept them;
    now he will remember their iniquity
and punish their sins. (v. 10)

God's people were suffering because of their sins. Drought is the proper punishment for covenant breaking (Deuteronomy 11:16, 17; 28:23, 24). In this case, judgment was so certain that God again told Jeremiah, "Do not pray for the welfare of this people" (14:11). There was nothing Jeremiah could do to save them.

Not even being religious could save them: "Though they fast, I will not hear their cry, and though they offer burnt offering and grain offering, I will not accept them. But I will consume them by the sword, by famine, and by pestilence" (v. 12).

Sword, famine, and pestilence. There was no going back on God's judgment against this generation. They had to suffer the punishment due for their sins. If God seemed absent, it was because he had withdrawn his favor. If he seemed impotent, it was because his people had to suffer the consequences of their sin.

Sin is the explanation for most of the suffering in the world. Sin always leads to suffering. Some people suffer because of their own addictions to sin. More often, people suffer because of the sins of others. Take the frequent famines in Central Africa as an example. They are partly caused by dry weather, but they are mainly caused by war and corruption. Even natural disasters ultimately flow from the curse of God against sin (see Genesis 3:17–19; Romans 5:12).

People sometimes use "The problem of evil" as an objection against the existence of God. That objection is aimed in the wrong direction. Evil is a problem, but it is not a problem for God. The problem of evil must be placed at the doorstep of humanity.

The problems we have with God are our own fault. Does God seem distant? Does he seem too far away to hear your prayers? If you feel estranged from God, it is worth asking who the real stranger is. Sin estranges the believer from God. If you do not feel as close to God as you did before, then you are the one who moved, not God. "Draw near to God, and he will draw near to you" (James 4:8). If you draw near to God in faith and repentance, he will come close to you again.

When Preachers Lie

Jeremiah accepted God's argument that his people deserved to be punished for their sins, but he still wanted to offer a rebuttal. "Then I said: 'Ah, Lord GOD, behold, the prophets say to them, "You shall not see the sword, nor shall you have famine, but I will give you assured peace in this place"'" (14:13).

Some scholars suggest that Jeremiah was simply making an excuse for Israel. They think he was saying something like, "Yes, God, your people have wandered, but it is not their fault. They are misguided. They are getting such bad preaching, they cannot really be held responsible for their sins."

A more likely explanation is that Jeremiah was getting confused. He had been listening to too much religious broadcasting. The more he heard the other prophets, the more plausible they sounded. They said everything was going to be okay. They claimed to have received a word from the Lord. They mixed in a little Scripture to make it sound as if God endorsed their message.

Meanwhile Jeremiah was the only prophet in Israel who was prophesying a judgment to come. Did he really have it right after all? Maybe something was wrong with his hearing. Maybe he had misunderstood what God was saying. Was it really true that God intended to punish his people for their sins?

Gospel ministers in the contemporary church sometimes wonder the same thing. Divine judgment has become increasingly unpopular. D. P. Walker's book *The Decline of Hell* shows how the doctrine of eternal punishment came under attack during the seventeenth century.[3] If Hell was in decline back then, it has all but disappeared since. Liberal theology gave up on the idea at the start of the twentieth century. At the dawn of the twenty-first century, eternal judgment is on its way out in the evangelical church as well. It is not so much that the doctrine of eternal punishment is under attack—it is just that the subject never comes up. As John Blanchard expressed it in the title of his book, *Whatever Happened to Hell?*[4] What indeed? Doctrines that cease to be taught in the church die a long, slow death.

The Bible does teach the doctrine of endless punishment for sin. In fact, most of the Biblical teaching about Hell comes from the lips of Jesus Christ (see, e.g., Matthew 25:41–46; Luke 16:19–31). Jesus wanted to be sure there would be no doubt about the wages of sin. Anyone who denies God's judgment to come is preaching lies, even if he speaks in the name of Christ.

God reassured Jeremiah that when it came to judgment, he had the message right: "And the LORD said to me: 'The prophets are prophesying lies in my name. I did not send them, nor did I command them or speak to them. They are prophesying to you a lying vision, worthless divination, and the deceit of their own minds'" (14:14).

He also warned of the fate of those who prophesy such lies. They will not even receive a decent burial:

Therefore thus says the LORD concerning the prophets who prophesy in my name although I did not send them, and who say, "Sword and famine shall not come upon this land": By sword and famine those prophets shall be consumed. And the people to whom they prophesy shall be cast out in the streets of Jerusalem, victims of famine and sword, with none to bury them—them, their wives, their sons, and their daughters. For I will pour out their evil upon them. (vv. 15, 16)

It is crucially important to pray for the minister. False preachers are liable to the judgment of God, and their congregations with them. Pray that preachers who know Christ will remain faithful to God and his Word. Pray that those who do not know Christ in a personal way will be converted and convinced of the truth of God's Word. May God have mercy upon them!

A Powerful Prayer

By the end of chapter 14 Jeremiah had run out of tears and arguments. There was only one thing left for him to do—pray. Since he is one of the prayer warriors of Scripture, there is much to be learned from his prayer.

Jeremiah's prayer comes in three parts. The first is a full confession of sin.

> We acknowledge our wickedness, O LORD,
>   and the iniquity of our fathers,
>   for we have sinned against you. (v. 20)

Full confession means confessing all kinds of sins. This verse contains three different words for sin: "wickedness," "iniquity," and "sinned." A similar variety of vocabulary appears earlier in the chapter: "For our backslidings are many; we have sinned against you" (v. 7). Jeremiah did not simply ask God to forgive one or two sins, but all sins of all kinds.

Full confession is also corporate confession. Jeremiah began with his own sins, but he did not stop there. He acknowledged the sins of his fathers. His prayer brought together all the sins of his people and presented them before God. Jeremiah repented on behalf of the whole nation.

It seems unnatural to Americans to repent for national or familial sins. We are used to taking responsibility for our own sins, and our own sins only. If our ancestors did something unfair we say, "That was before my time." When our company does something immoral we say, "I just work here." When our denomination does something un-Biblical we say, "That has nothing to do with my local congregation." When our country does something unjust we say, "I just live here." But Biblical repentance extends to the sins of family, church, and nation. Since we share in the guilt of corporate sins, we must confess the sins of our group.

The second part of Jeremiah's prayer is a plea for God's mercy for the sake of God's glory:

> Do not spurn us, for your name's sake;
>   do not dishonor your glorious throne;
>   remember and do not break your covenant with us. (v. 21)

This prayer echoes some of the prayers Jeremiah offered earlier in the chapter:

> Though our iniquities testify against us,
>   act, O LORD, for your name's sake. (v. 7a)

> Yet you, O LORD, are in the midst of us,
>   and we are called by your name;
>   do not leave us. (v. 9b)

Jeremiah was not selfish when he prayed. His primary motive was not to be delivered from his own suffering, or even to see others delivered from their sufferings. Rather, his prayer was motivated by a vision of the glory that redounds to God when prayer is answered: "For *God's* sake, do something! *Thine* be the glory! *Thy* kingdom come!"

The persuasive power of Jeremiah's prayer comes through its demonstration that God himself has a vested interest in saving his people. The credibility of God's name, the honor of God's throne, and the stability of God's covenant depend upon his salvation of his people. If he does not forgive his people, his name will be brought into disrepute, his throne will be dishonored, and his covenant will be broken. God cannot be God unless he saves his people.

Calvin points out that here Jeremiah assumed "That the grace of God cannot be wholly obliterated."[5] He assumed that God *must* exercise his grace. When God saves his people, his name will be exalted, his throne honored, and his covenant confirmed. Salvation will bring glory upon glory to God.

The glory of God should always be the primary motive for prayer. Instead of asking God to do something for your sake, ask him to do something for *his* sake. Prayers offered for the sake of God's glory are powerful prayers. What can be more persuasive to God than the opportunity to magnify his own glory? As F. B. Meyer has argued, "Whenever we so lose ourselves in prayer as to forget personal interest, and to plead for the glory of God, we have reached a vantage ground from which we can win anything from Him."[6]

Keeping prayer fixed on the glory of God helps us avoid trivial prayers.

It is easy to pray to the glory of God when praying for the salvation of neighbors or for the worldwide progress of the gospel. It is much harder to pray to the glory of God when praying about your favorite football team or the pain in your pinkie. If it proves difficult to put God's glory into the same sentence with a prayer request, then it is time to find something more important to pray about.

The last part of Jeremiah's prayer is an affirmation that only God can answer prayer. The prophet ends where this chapter began—with the drought in Israel. What the people of God really needed was some rain.

> Are there any among the false gods of the nations that can bring rain?
>   Or can the heavens give showers?
> Are you not he, O LORD our God?
>   We set our hope on you,
>   for you do all these things. (v. 22)

Jeremiah rejected every other solution to his problems except trusting in God. He rejected turning to other gods or getting back to nature. He rejected trusting in anyone or anything else but God. "No," he said, "only you, O Lord our God, can help us!"

Do you need forgiveness? Healing? Wisdom? Encouragement? Friendship? Put your hope in the living God. He is the only one who can give all these things. When you ask him to do something for his own sake, he will surely do it.

23

When God Lets You Down

JEREMIAH 15:1–21

SOMETIMES JEREMIAH WAS DISCOURAGED. He experienced periods of depression. At times he was filled with feelings of desperation and even doom.

Jeremiah was transparent about all these feelings. In the past several chapters he has exposed the dark depths of his soul, where doubt and dread resided. Scholars sometimes refer to these personal speeches as the "Confessions of Jeremiah." They appear in chapters 11, 12, 17, 18, and 20.

A better word for Jeremiah's speeches might be *soliloquies*. A soliloquy is a dramatic speech uttered when no one else is on stage. All the other characters in a play go off-stage so a leading actor can pour out his soul to the audience. A soliloquy is a private speech expressing the innermost feelings of a tragic figure, which is precisely what Jeremiah's confessions are. All the other characters in Israel go off-stage so he can put his tragic sufferings into words.

If Jeremiah's speeches are soliloquies, then chapter 15 is his "To be or not to be" soliloquy. By the third act of William Shakespeare's play *Hamlet*, Hamlet is starting to think about taking his own life:

> To be, or not to be, that is the question:
> Whether 'tis nobler in the mind to suffer
> The slings and arrows of outrageous fortune,
> Or to take arms against a sea of troubles
> And by opposing end them. To die: to sleep. (III.i.56–60)

Like Hamlet, Jeremiah called the value of his existence into question: "Woe is me, my mother, that you bore me, a man of strife and contention to the whole land!" (v. 10a).

The prophet had not quite hit rock bottom, but he was getting close. He hits absolute bottom in chapter 20, where he goes beyond lamenting his birth to cursing it (vv. 14–18). For the moment, however, he was as discouraged as can be. One of the first things we learned about Jeremiah (1:5) was that God had appointed him to be a prophet from his mother's womb. But there were times he wished he had never been born at all. He wanted to abort his mission.

Unanswered Prayer

God seemed to let Jeremiah down in three ways: He did not answer Jeremiah's prayers (15:1–14), he sent him sufferings he did not deserve (vv. 10b, 15), and he failed to reward him for his obedience (vv. 16–18).

Chapter 14 ended with a powerful prayer on behalf of God's people. The prayer was flawless. Jeremiah made full confession for all the sins of the nation. He pleaded for God's mercy for the sake of God's glory. He affirmed that only God can answer prayer. It was the best of prayers, offered from the purest of motives.

So God answered Jeremiah's prayer, right? Wrong. "Then the LORD said to me, 'Though Moses and Samuel stood before me, yet my heart would not turn toward this people. Send them out of my sight, and let them go!'" (15:1). God refused to answer Jeremiah's prayer (or anybody else's, for that matter).

Jeremiah's intercession proved to be a spectacular failure. In response, God promised to send judgment instead of blessing:

And when they ask you, "Where shall we go?" you shall say to them, "Thus says the LORD:

'Those who are for pestilence, to pestilence,
    and those who are for the sword, to the sword;
those who are for famine, to famine,
    and those who are for captivity, to captivity.'" (v. 2)

The judgment God threatens sounds like the Four Horsemen of the Apocalypse (Revelation 6:1–8). It also sums up about half the book of Jeremiah—death, sword, starvation, and captivity.

God was about to empty his arsenal. "I will appoint over them four kinds of destroyers, declares the LORD: the sword to kill, the dogs to tear, and the birds of the air and the beasts of the earth to devour and destroy" (15:3). The hyenas and the vultures will drag away and devour anyone the soldiers fail to kill.

The people of God would become total outcasts. "And I will make them a horror to all the kingdoms of the earth" (v. 4a). The international community will totally ignore what happens to them: "Who will have pity on you, O Jerusalem, or who will grieve for you? Who will turn aside to ask about your welfare?" (v. 5; cf. Lamentations 1:2). Literally, the Scripture says that no one will ask if there is peace (shalom) in the city. All along the other priests and prophets have promised "peace, peace" (cf. 6:14; 8:11). But when judgment comes, no one will even ask about peace.

God was planning to toss Israel into the air like a pile of grain from a threshing floor:

> I have winnowed them with a winnowing fork
>   in the gates of the land;
> I have bereaved them; I have destroyed my people;
>   they did not turn from their ways. (15:7)

The wheat would stay at the city gates, but the chaff would be scattered and blown into exile. Families would be destroyed.

> I have made their widows more in number
>   than the sand of the seas;
> I have brought against the mothers of young men
>   a destroyer at noonday;
> I have made anguish and terror
>   fall upon them suddenly.
> She who bore seven has grown feeble;
>   she has fainted away;
> her sun went down while it was yet day;
>   she has been shamed and disgraced.
> And the rest of them I will give to the sword
>   before their enemies,
>   declares the LORD. (vv. 8, 9)

So many men would die that widows would be more numerous than the sand of the sea. The mother of the perfect family (seven sons) would lose her children and die from shock.

When judgment came, there would be no resisting it:

> Can one break iron, iron from the north, and bronze? Your wealth and your treasures I will give as spoil, without price, for all your sins, throughout all your territory. I will make you serve your enemies in a land that you do not know, for in my anger a fire is kindled that shall burn forever. (vv. 12–14)

"Iron from the north"—in other words, Babylon, which gained strength from the iron of the Black Sea—cannot be broken. All Judah's wealth and treasures would be plundered as booty by the Babylonians. Judah herself would be taken into captivity in an unknown land. When the Lord said, "Those . . . [destined] for captivity, to captivity" (v. 2), he meant business!

The reason all these calamities came about was because God's people had sinned. Judgment came "because of what Manasseh the son of Hezekiah, king of Judah, did in Jerusalem" (v. 4b; cf. 2 Kings 21). Manasseh was the kind of political leader who sought prosperity at the cost of integrity. Davidson explains that he "kept Judah at peace for most of the first half of the seventh century BC by faithfully licking the boots of his Assyrian imperial overlord. He bought security and peace at a price, the price of encouraging the worship of many gods, including Assyrian gods, in Jerusalem."[1]

But Manasseh was not the only sinner in Judah.

> You have rejected me, declares the LORD;
>   you keep going backward,
> so I have stretched out my hand against you and destroyed you—
>   I am weary of relenting. (v. 6)

Jeremiah taught the same lesson over and over and over again: "The wages of sin is death" (Romans 6:23a). That is the literal truth. Those who do not love God deserve to die. The unchangeable law of the universe is that the proper punishment for sin is eternal death.

Thus the people of Judah were under a death sentence. They did not have a prayer. Jeremiah tried to pray for them, but his prayers were rejected. It was a spectacular intercessory failure! God promised to do exactly the opposite of what Jeremiah prayed for.

Jeremiah's unanswered prayer teaches two important spiritual lessons. First, God does not always answer prayer by giving godly people what they ask for. Even the best of prayers offered from the purest of motives may not receive an affirmative answer. Some prayers are hindered by the sins of the intercessor. Some are hindered by the sins of others, which is what happened to Jeremiah's prayers. Sometimes God intends to glorify himself in ways that go beyond or against our prayers. Whatever the reason, God does not always give godly people what they ask for. Do not be surprised by seemingly unanswered prayer.

Someone to Intercede

A second lesson to be learned from Jeremiah's failure is that every sinner needs the prayers of Jesus Christ. Who else can stand in the gap to save a sinner from the wrath of God? Not Jeremiah. His prayer for God's mercy was rejected.

What about Moses (15:1)? Moses certainly was a great man of prayer. While he was up on Mount Horeb to receive the Law of God, the children of Israel began to worship the golden calf they had built (Exodus 32; cf. Deuteronomy 9:11–29). So God said to Moses, "Now therefore let me alone, that my wrath may burn hot against them and I may consume them" (Exodus 32:10). But Moses stepped between God and his sinful people to plead for their salvation. "O LORD, why does your wrath burn hot against your people, whom you have brought out of the land of Egypt with great power and with a mighty hand?" (v. 11). And God heard Moses' prayer. He relented and did not bring on his people the disaster he had threatened (v. 14).

The same thing happened when the Israelites refused to enter the promised land (Numbers 14). God threatened to destroy them and make Moses into a great nation. Once again Moses stood in the gap between God and sinners, begging God to spare them for the sake of his glory. If anyone could stand before God to intercede for God's people, it was Moses! He was two-for-two in saving prayer.

Or what about Samuel? He was another man of great prayer. When the Israelites were threatened by the Philistines at Mizpah, Samuel interceded with the Lord on their behalf (1 Samuel 7). He offered a sacrificial lamb and "cried out to the LORD for Israel, and the LORD answered him" (v. 9b). Much the same thing happened when God was angry with the people because they asked for a king (2 Samuel 12:19–25). Samuel's track record was as good as Moses'. Maybe Samuel could have stood in the gap to save sinners.

Yet God told Jeremiah that even if Moses *and* Samuel had stood before him, he would not have answered their prayers (Jeremiah 15:1; cf. Psalm 99:6). This is a powerful admission of the limitations of the Old Testament prophets. They could not save their people from their sins. They could pray for sins, but they could not atone for them. They could beg for God's mercy, but they could not demand it.

Sinners need someone, not just to pray for them, but to offer a perfect sacrifice for their sins. They need intercession plus atonement. Jesus Christ offers both. Jesus made a perfect sacrifice for sin when he died on the cross of Calvary. On the basis of that perfect sacrifice he now persuades his Father to have mercy on poor sinners. "Consequently, he is able to save to the uttermost those who draw near to God through him, since he always lives to make intercession for them. For it was indeed fitting that we should have such a high priest, holy, innocent, unstained, separated from sinners, and exalted above the heavens . . . he did this [sacrificed for our sins] once for all when he offered up himself" (Hebrews 7:25–27a).

Get back, Moses! Step aside, Samuel! Move over, Jeremiah! Let Jesus Christ stand before his Father to plead for the salvation of lost sinners. His prayers will never fail! When Jesus prays, God's heart goes out to his people, and he invites them into his presence. Because of the intercession of Jesus Christ, at least one prayer—the greatest prayer of all, the prayer for the forgiveness of sins—will not go unanswered.

Undeserved Suffering

Jeremiah also complained about his undeserved suffering (15:10b, 15). He was a marked man. He was not just paranoid; everyone really was out to get him! He was public enemy number one. As he said in his soliloquy, he was "a man of strife and contention to the whole land" (v. 10a).

One thing seemed especially unfair: "I have not lent, nor have I borrowed, yet all of them curse me" (v. 10b). Jeremiah could have understood being cursed if he had outstanding debts or was defaulting on his loans. He even could have understood being cursed if people owed *him* a lot of money. Moneylenders and extortionists rarely win popularity contests. But Jeremiah did not owe anybody anything. Neither a borrower nor a lender, yet he was an accursed outcast.

Jeremiah acknowledged that God knew all about his situation. He took his suffering to the Lord in prayer, asking God to remember him and care for him: "O Lord, you know; remember me and visit me, and take vengeance for me on my persecutors" (v. 15a). This was more than a personal vendetta. Jeremiah was asking for divine vengeance. He needed God's protection because he was God's prophet.

However, a note of self-pity creeps into Jeremiah's prayer: "In your forbearance take me not away; know that for your sake I bear reproach" (v. 15b). The prophet wanted God to remember that his sufferings were undeserved. He almost seemed to think that his trials were God's fault, that he deserved something better. Jeremiah did not ask to be a prophet, and he did not want to preach judgment. In fact, he kept praying for God to do just the opposite.

Do you ever complain to God about your sufferings? Do you ever tell God that you deserve better than this, or that it is all his fault?

Unrewarded Obedience

Before God could answer his questions, Jeremiah lodged a third complaint: God was letting him down by not rewarding his obedience (vv. 16–18).

All Jeremiah's labor seemed like wasted effort. At this point, the prophet sounds very much like the elder brother in the parable of the prodigal father who squandered his love on his wayward son: "Look, these many years I have served you, and I never disobeyed your command, yet you never gave me a young goat, that I might celebrate with my friends" (Luke 15:29). All those years of following God, and Jeremiah had nothing to show for it.

Jeremiah had indeed been very obedient. He was a keen student of God's Word.

> Your words were found, and I ate them,
>   and your words became to me a joy
>   and the delight of my heart,
> for I am called by your name,
>   O Lord, God of hosts. (v. 16)

Francis Bacon (1561–1626)—one of the leading figures of the English Renaissance—observed that some books are to be tasted, some are to be chewed, and some are to be thoroughly digested. Jeremiah understood that the Bible is the one book to be devoured. Like the prophet Ezekiel, he gobbled up God's Word (Ezekiel 3:3). He understood that the Word of God is more than just hors d'oeuvres. When God spoke, Jeremiah bellied up to the banqueting table and started packing it in.

This is a reminder of the tastiness of God's Word. Jeremiah thought of God's Word as his "joy" and his heart's "delight." Reading and studying the Bible is a very delightful thing to do.

Jeremiah also obeyed God during his free time. He was not a partier. He said, "I did not sit in the company of revelers, nor did I rejoice" (15:17a). This verse echoes the first Psalm:

> Blessed is the man
>   who walks not in the counsel of the wicked,
> nor stands in the way of sinners,
>   nor sits in the seat of scoffers. (Psalm 1:1)

Jeremiah did not waste his time sitting on a bar stool and laughing at the world. Instead he spent his Friday nights at home. This was not because he was a party pooper, but because he had a passion for purity: "I sat alone, because your hand was upon me, for you had filled me with indignation" (15:17b). Sinful revelry filled him with indignation. He needed to separate himself from the secular environment around him.

Believers must give up some things to follow God. Serving God means giving up the (apparent) pleasures of idleness, drunkenness, gluttony, greed, mockery, and sexual immorality. Jeremiah gave up all those things, which is why he found himself spending so many quiet evenings at home.

But Jeremiah wanted something back. If he was so righteous, then why wasn't God blessing him?

> Why is my pain unceasing,
>   my wound incurable,
>   refusing to be healed?
> Will you be to me like a deceitful brook,
>   like waters that fail? (v. 18)

Jeremiah felt like he deserved something better from God. He moved from righteousness to self-righteousness.

Jeremiah's question about the failing spring is especially pointed. It is another echo from Psalm 1, which describes the blessed man like this:

> He is like a tree
>   planted by streams of water
> that yields its fruit in its season,
>   and its leaf does not wither.
> In all that he does, he prospers. (v. 3)

Jeremiah met all the criteria for the blessed man, yet he did not prosper. So perhaps the problem was not Jeremiah at all, but God. Back in chapter 2, God was described as "The fountain of living waters" (v. 13). But now he seemed more like a wadi that runs full after a rainstorm, but is a dry riverbed the rest of the year. Was God a deceptive brook? In other words, had God let Jeremiah down?

The God Who Never Lets You Down

God never lets his people down. He never has, and he never will. Jeremiah had it all wrong. Believers always have it wrong when they feel that God is letting them down. Sometimes we come to God with unanswered prayers, undeserved sufferings, and unrewarded obedience, and we want him to get his act together. We want God to change what he is doing. But the truth is that God *never* lets his people down.

There is an old story about a battleship lost in a fog at sea. The ship's captain could see the lights of another ship in the distance. So he radioed ahead, "Heading for collision. Turn 15 degrees north."

The reply came back almost immediately: "Heading for collision. Turn 15 degrees south."

The captain was not one to have his orders countermanded, so he sent a stronger message: "No, you turn 15 degrees north!"

Again came the reply: "No, you turn 15 degrees south!"

The captain was so angry that he decided to throw his weight around: "This is a battleship. Turn 15 degrees north."

The last message was a short one: "This is a lighthouse."

God is like the lighthouse. He is right where he is supposed to be, doing what he is supposed to be doing. He cannot and will not move. Jeremiah was like the battleship. His faith was heading for a shipwreck unless he changed direction.

The first thing God told Jeremiah to do was to turn around, to repent. If anyone was letting anyone down, Jeremiah was letting God down:

> Therefore thus says the LORD:
> "If you return, I will restore you,
>   and you shall stand before me.
> If you utter what is precious, and not what is worthless,
>   you shall be as my mouth." (15:19a)

Jeremiah came to God saying, "I did this, that, and the other thing for you." But God said, "Wait a minute. Hold it right there. Back up. Try again. Start over. And this time start by confessing your sins."

There may have been some truth in Jeremiah's soliloquy, but it was not the whole truth. Some of the things he said were "worthless" rather than "precious." Jeremiah was still a sinner, and sinners cannot approach God with a long list of credits. They can only come with their debts. They cannot pray on the basis of their merits; they can only beg on the basis of God's mercy.

It is ironic that God had to tell Jeremiah to repent. For years Jeremiah had been telling the people of Israel to turn back in repentance. But he had some repenting of his own to do. He needed to turn back from his self-righteousness and return to his calling.

If it *seems* as though God is letting you down, is he *really* letting you down? It is much more likely that you are the one doing the letting down.

The second thing God did for Jeremiah was to repeat his promises to him:

> The LORD said, "Have I not set you free for their good? Have I not pleaded for you before the enemy in the time of trouble and in the time of distress?" (v. 11)

"They shall turn to you,
    but you shall not turn to them.
And I will make you to this people
    a fortified wall of bronze;
they will fight against you,
    but they shall not prevail over you,
for I am with you
    to save you and deliver you,
    declares the LORD.
I will deliver you out of the hand of the wicked,
    and redeem you from the grasp of the ruthless." (vv. 19b–21)

If any of these words sound familiar, it is because God here repeats the promises he made when he first called Jeremiah to be a prophet: "I make you this day a fortified city, an iron pillar, and bronze walls, against the whole land, against the kings of Judah, its officials, its priests, and the people of the land. They will fight against you, but they shall not prevail against you, for I am with you, declares the LORD, to deliver you" (1:18, 19). When God promised not to let Jeremiah down, it was not a new promise. It was the same old promise promised all over again. God promised to make Jeremiah strong in the face of the danger and to save his life in the end.

This is a profound lesson about God's remedy for discouragement in the Christian life. Spiritual depression often compels the Christian to seek some new revelation from God, some new truth about God, or some new experience of God. God rarely gives such things because they are not what the believer needs. What the discouraged Christian needs most is to remember the promises of the Bible. Every last one of God's promises is still true. Spiritual renewal comes from hearing again the promises God has already made in Jesus Christ—that he will rescue us, save us, and redeem us.

Christians sometimes rehearse soliloquies in their minds. They prepare dramatic speeches about how God is letting them down, speeches about unanswered prayer and undeserved suffering. However, a Christian never can perform a true soliloquy. A soliloquy is a private speech. But Christians do not give any private thoughts because God is their playwright, and the playwright always gets the last word. Here is the last word on every Christian soliloquy:

If you return, I will restore you,
    and you shall stand before me . . .
for I am with you
    to save you and deliver you. (15:19a, 20b)

24

Jeremiah, the Pariah

JEREMIAH 16:1—17:4

JEREMIAH SPENT HIS FRIDAY NIGHTS AT HOME, ALONE. There were three things he did not do—go out on dates, send sympathy cards, or sit down to fancy dinners.

Jeremiah did not do these things because he was following God's orders. "You shall not take a wife, nor shall you have sons or daughters in this place" (16:2). "Do not enter the house of mourning, or go to lament or grieve for them" (v. 5). "You shall not go into the house of feasting to sit with them, to eat and drink" (v. 8). The prophet's job limited his social life. He could not go to weddings, funerals, or dinner parties. He was "Forbidden to Marry, Forbidden to Mourn, Forbidden to Mingle."[1]

Odd Man Out

Jeremiah was a pariah, a misfit, a social outcast. When people saw him coming down the sidewalk in Anathoth, they held their children close and crossed to the other side of the street. "Oh, no," they must have said, "here comes old Jeremiah. Strange chap. Not a bad man, really; just a little unusual. Never got married, you know. Never been one for socializing. Never comes to holiday gatherings. Always been something of a disappointment to the family."

In the context of an ancient Near Eastern village, Jeremiah's behavior was disgraceful. *Everyone* got married in those days. "Celibacy was not an ideal, it was an abnormality."[2] There was no singles ministry at Jeremiah's synagogue. The Law of God said it was not good for man to be alone (Genesis 2:18). So people married young, and confirmed old bachelors were scarce. In fact, Biblical Hebrew does not even have a word for "bachelor."[3]

Everyone went to funerals in those days, too. When someone died, the whole village would gather at the home of the deceased to mourn. Later the neighbors would bring food to share, since it would be unclean to prepare a meal in the same house with a dead body. The mourners would break bread and drink a cup of consolation together.

Everyone also went to feasts in those days. Whenever there was a religious holiday or a family celebration, everyone would join in the party. Everyone got married, everyone grieved, everyone partied . . . except for Jeremiah, the pariah. He was always conspicuous by his absence. He defied the social conventions of his day. He did not follow Emily Post or Miss Manners.

No Time for Matrimony, Sympathy, or Revelry

Jeremiah was a pariah because he was God's prophet. A prophet is a living sermon. Even his social life reveals something about the character and purposes of God. Jeremiah's refusal to participate in matrimony, sympathy, and revelry was a warning of the judgment to come.

By this point in the book of Jeremiah, we have heard as much as we care to hear about the wrath of God. It hardly seems necessary for Jeremiah to describe, again, what the day of judgment will be like. But it must be necessary because these things were written for our instruction. The Holy Spirit uses Jeremiah to engrave this lesson on the conscience: The God who hates sin will surely bring sinners to justice.

For the Israelites, being brought to justice meant being evicted from their place of residence. "I will hurl you out of this land into a land that neither you nor your fathers have known, and there you shall serve other gods day and night, for I will show you no favor" (16:13). God's people were hurled from Jerusalem to Babylon. In effect, God was saying something like this: "Look, if worshiping other gods is what you really want to do, then by all means, go to Babylon, where you can worship idols to your hearts' content!"

Like fishermen, the Babylonians would cast their nets over Jerusalem and drag the Israelites off to the north. Like so many hunters, they would track them down:

> Behold, I am sending for many fishers, declares the LORD, and they shall catch them. And afterward I will send for many hunters, and they shall hunt them from every mountain and every hill, and out of the clefts of the rocks. For my eyes are on all their ways. They are not hidden from me, nor is their iniquity concealed from my eyes. (vv. 16, 17)

There would be no escape, either from God or the Babylonians, either by land or by sea.

The people of God would be mugged:

> Your wealth and all your treasures I will give for spoil as the price of your high places for sin throughout all your territory. (17:3)

They would be kidnapped and become slaves:

> You shall loosen your hand from your heritage that I gave to you, and I will make you serve your enemies in a land that you do not know, for in my anger a fire is kindled that shall burn forever. (17:4)

That verse ends with a promise of eternal punishment. Wrath is one aspect of God's eternal justice.

Jeremiah's message ought to be getting through: God hates sin. He *hates* it. God is so holy and so just that he cannot overlook sin. Every sin deserves the wrath and curse of God, both in this life and in the life to come.

It was because judgment was so close at hand that Jeremiah had become a pariah. No doubt people asked him why his behavior was so bizarre. Too often people ask singles unwelcome questions like "How come you're not married yet?" Was Jeremiah ever ready for that question!

> For thus says the LORD concerning the sons and daughters who are born in this place, and concerning the mothers who bore them and the fathers who fathered them in this land: They shall die of deadly diseases. They shall not be lamented, nor shall they be buried. They shall be as dung on the surface of the ground. They shall perish by the sword and by famine, and their dead bodies shall be food for the birds of the air and for the beasts of the earth. (16:3, 4)

Jeremiah's singleness was symbolic of the judgment to come. It showed how much families would suffer on the day of judgment. Since parents and children alike would be reduced to carrion, it would be better for Jeremiah not to marry at all.

Doubtless the people asked why Jeremiah refused to grieve with the grieving: "Come on, Jerry, can't you at least send a sympathy card?" But the prophet's apparent lack of love and pity was symbolic of the judgment to come. They showed that God had withdrawn his blessing (shalom), his covenant love (*hesed*), and his compassion: "I have taken away my peace from this people, my steadfast love and mercy, declares the LORD" (v. 5b).

Jeremiah's refusal to go to funerals was also symbolic. In the day of battle, custom would be set aside, and the dead would not receive a proper burial. "They shall not be buried, and no one shall lament for them or cut himself or make himself bald for them. No one shall break bread for the mourner, to comfort him for the dead, nor shall anyone give him the cup of consolation to drink for his father or his mother" (vv. 6b, 7). The curse of indecent burial would fall on rich and poor alike: "Both great and small shall die in this land" (v.6a).

Jeremiah could not even go to dinner parties. What could be wrong with anniversary banquets or retirement dinners? The prophet's refusal to sit down at a table of thanksgiving was another symbol of the judgment to come. His friends would not have the favor of his presence because Israel did not have the favor of God's presence. "For thus says the LORD of hosts, the God of Israel: Behold, I will silence in this place, before your eyes and in your days, the voice of mirth and the voice of gladness, the voice of the bridegroom and the voice of the bride." (v. 9). The approach of judgment is no time for feasting.

Jeremiah's socially unacceptable behavior was a constant warning of the judgment to come. Even the great events of life—weddings and funerals and holidays—lost all meaning when society was about to come to a crashing halt. As Brueggemann rightly observes, "Celebrative social life depends on God's steadfast love and mercy."[4] When God is about to come in wrath and glory, forget about finding a spouse. Save your tears. Don't mail those party invitations.

This is a strong warning for everyone who has not entered into a personal friendship with Jesus Christ. The Day of Judgment approaches.

> For as were the days of Noah, so will be the coming of the Son of Man. For as in those days before the flood they were eating and drinking, marrying and giving in marriage, until the day when Noah entered the ark, and they were unaware until the flood came and swept them all away, so will be the coming of the Son of Man. (Matthew 24:37–39)

Do not walk down the aisle or go to a funeral or throw a party before you get right with God.

First Things First

Jeremiah's behavior may seem a little extreme. God's judgment may seem a little harsh. It certainly seemed that way to the people of Israel. "And when you tell this people all these words, and they say to you, 'Why has the LORD pronounced all this great evil against us? What is our iniquity? What is the sin that we have committed against the LORD our God?'" (16:10).

This is the way human beings usually respond when they are threatened with the punishment they deserve. "Who, me? What did I do? I didn't do it! And even if I did, it wasn't that bad! Who does God think he is, threatening me like that?"

In this case, of course, the people of God *had* done it. They had committed the worst of all sins: They did not worship God alone. They put other gods before him. "Then you shall say to them: '[It is b]ecause your fathers have forsaken me, declares the LORD, and have gone after other gods and have served and worshiped them, and have forsaken me and have not kept my law'" (v. 11). This verse teaches the principle of corporate responsibility. Everyone bears guilt for the sins of the fathers. Plus, everyone bears guilt for his or her own sins: "You have done worse than your fathers, for behold, every one of you follows his stubborn, evil will, refusing to listen to me" (v. 12).

The people of God did not keep the first commandment God ever gave them: "You shall have no other gods before me" (Exodus 20:3). As Kidner puts it, "The first commandment was the last to be considered."[5] The sin of idolatry was deeply ingrained. "The sin of Judah is written with a pen of iron; with a point of diamond it is engraved on the tablet of their heart" (17:1). The sins of God's people were not just written in pencil—they were chiseled into their stone-cold hearts with an adamantine stylus. (Incidentally, in 1979 archaeologists discovered two small silver scrolls, dating from the seventh or sixth century BC, in burial caves outside Jerusalem. The scrolls were engraved with a sharp instrument in a process similar to the one Jeremiah described.[6])

As for the children, they too were into goddess worship.

> Their children remember their altars and their Asherim, beside every green tree and on the high hills (v. 2)

It is universally true that children sin the way their parents sin.

Not worshiping God alone is a very great sin. Because God is the King of the whole universe, he deserves all praise, honor, and worship. To worship anyone or anything else is to deny the Godness of God. To give him anything less than one's whole heart, soul, and mind is to commit the greatest of sins.

Not worshiping God is such a great sin that it deserves double repayment for sin. "I will doubly repay their iniquity and their sin, because they have polluted my land with the carcasses of their detestable idols, and have filled my inheritance with their abominations" (16:18). Because God's people bore God's own name and lived in God's own land, it was doubly wicked for them not to worship him alone. Perhaps a better translation goes like this: "I will repay them exactly what they deserve for their wickedness and their sin." Their punishment was not so much double as it was proportional.[7] The punishment fit the crime. God gave his people exactly what they earned: death, sword, starvation, and captivity.

Since Jeremiah lived at such a time, among such a people, it is no wonder that he did not date, send sympathy cards, or sit down to fancy dinners. It was better for Jeremiah to be a pariah.

Salvation from and for the Nations

Suddenly there is grace! We have been stumbling down the corridors of divine judgment in the dark, reading prophecy after prophecy of punishment for sin. Then, quick as a flash, the Spirit of God switches on all the searchlights, and we are nearly blinded by promises of salvation. There is no way gradually to ease from judgment into grace; we can only stand blinking our eyes and shielding ourselves from the light.

God drops two promises into Jeremiah 16 like lightning bolts. The first lightning bolt is a promise of salvation from the nations:

> Therefore, behold, the days are coming, declares the LORD, when it shall no longer be said, "As the LORD lives who brought up the people of Israel out of the land of Egypt," but "As the LORD lives who brought up the people of Israel out of the north country and out of all the countries where he had driven them." For I will bring them back to their own land that I gave to their fathers. (vv. 14, 15)

This is a promise of homecoming. After the exile there was to be a return. After the people were dragged off to Babylon they would march back to Jerusalem. That return will be so wonderful that it will (almost) make the Israelites forget everything else God has ever done for them.

They will hardly be able to remember the exodus anymore. The exodus was *the* great act of salvation in the Old Testament. The children of Israel were slaves of Pharaoh in Egypt until the Lord appointed Moses to lead them out, sending great plagues upon the Egyptians, bringing the Israelites through the Red Sea on dry land, and leading them into the Promised Land. The Israelites looked back to their exodus as *the* defining moment in their history as a nation.

But when the Lord would bring the Israelites back from exile—saving them from all the terrible judgments Jeremiah prophesied—then they would *really* have something to shout about. They would hardly even mention the exodus anymore. Salvation from Babylon would be so amazing that they would praise God for a new and greater exodus. In the words of the prophet Isaiah, they would "remember not the former things" (Isaiah 43:18).

The same must be said about salvation in Jesus Christ. Each step in the plan of redemption is more glorious than the step before. Yes, the exodus was miraculous. Yes, the return from exile was marvelous. But Christians rarely remember to thank God for those mighty acts of salvation. That is because they have a much greater salvation to celebrate. Forget the former things! God has really outdone himself this time! Salvation from Egypt and Babylon cannot be compared with eternal salvation from sin, death, and the devil in Jesus Christ. When Christ died on the cross and rose from the dead, he saved his people once and for all.

Then comes a second lightning bolt—*salvation for the nations* (16:19–21). Jeremiah looked beyond his own people and praised God for the salvation of the nations.

> O LORD, my strength and my stronghold,
>   my refuge in the day of trouble,
> to you shall the nations come
> from the ends of the earth. (v. 19a; cf. Psalm 18:2)

It was a staggering promise! Jeremiah had become a pariah in order to show what terrible things the pagans would do to God's people. God would not only save his people *from* those nations, however. His salvation is *for* those very nations!

It is hard enough for God's own people to learn to worship God alone. But one day the nations will testify that they, too, have learned to obey the first commandment:

> Our fathers have inherited nothing but lies,
>   worthless things in which there is no profit.
> Can man make for himself gods?
>   Such are not gods! (vv. 19b, 20)

Even the most wicked of nations would come to God in repentance and faith. They would put away their false gods and confess that there is no god but God. They would admit that their idols were nothing more than "scarecrows in a cucumber field" (10:5).

Unbelievable! Only God himself could accomplish such a great salvation:

> "Therefore, behold, I will make them know, this once I will make them know my power and my might, and they shall know that my name is the LORD." (16:21)

In this promise, God took upon himself the responsibility for the salvation of all nations. *He* has promised to teach them his power and his might. This is what happens whenever the Spirit of God comes into the heart of a sinner. Only God can teach a sinner to obey.

Jeremiah's two great promises have been fulfilled. I see the sparks from the lightning bolts every time I preach at Tenth Presbyterian Church in Philadelphia, where Jewish and Gentile Christians worship in one congregation. If God had not saved Israel *from* the nations, then the Jews would still be in Babylon. If God had not provided salvation *for* the nations, then the Gentiles would still be worshiping false gods. But the promises have come true. God is gathering Jews and Gentiles from the ends of the earth to worship Jesus Christ.

A Time to Marry, a Time to Grieve, and a Time to Party

Since the promises of God have now come true, this is no time to be a pariah. God's commands for Jeremiah are not his commands for the Christian church. The gospel age is a time for matrimony, a time for sympathy, and a time for revelry.

Christians are not forbidden to marry. The gospel age is a good time to get married. Jeremiah 33 promises that in the streets of Jerusalem "There shall be heard again the voice of mirth and the voice of gladness, the voice of the bridegroom and the voice of the bride" (vv. 10, 11). This promise has come true in Jesus Christ. It is no accident that the first miracle Jesus performed was to turn water into wine at a wedding (John 2:1–11). When the Savior comes, it is time for wedding and for song.

If judgment is expected, then it is better to be a bachelor like Jeremiah. But Christian marriage is an act of hope. It looks forward to the return of Jesus Christ. However much trouble there is in the world, Christians keep on getting married and starting families. They know that God is building his eternal kingdom.

Do Christians have to get married? Of course not. Marriage is a temporary condition anyway. Jesus taught that when we get to Heaven there will be no more marriage (Matthew 22:30), for all the saints will be married to Christ (Ephesians 5:32). Christians who remain single do so because they are engaged to be married to Christ. In fact, the Scriptures teach that single Christians have a spiritual advantage. Because they are not distracted by family affairs they can live in "undivided devotion to the Lord" (1 Corinthians 7:32–35). Thus both marriage and singleness are blessed by God. This is a time to marry and a time to be single because it is a time to be married to Christ.

What about funerals? The gospel age is a time to weep with those who weep, as well as to rejoice with those who rejoice (Romans 12:15). Here again Christians follow the example of the Lord Jesus Christ. When Jesus saw Mary mourning the death of Lazarus, and all her friends mourning with her, "he was deeply moved in his spirit and greatly troubled" (John 11:33). When he came to the tomb itself, "Jesus wept" (v. 35). He did so even though he knew that Lazarus would be raised from the dead just moments later. Jesus was filled with sympathy for the pain and loss that come from death. To grieve with the grieving in the hope of the resurrection is to be like Christ.

Christian grief is bittersweet: "But we do not want you to be uninformed, brothers, about those who are asleep, that you may not grieve as others do who have no hope" (1 Thessalonians 4:13). The apostle assumes that Christians will grieve, but not like those who are without hope. The people of Jeremiah's day were grieving like pagans; they were even cutting themselves, which was forbidden by the Law of God (see Leviticus 19:28; Deuteronomy 14:1). Today pagans laugh about death, take tranquilizers to dull its pain, or simply get drunk. Christians grieve, but not like pagans. They do not dismiss or dull their grief. They taste their grief and find it bittersweet because they hope in the resurrection.

I was especially aware of the difference between Christian grief and pagan grief after the death of a childhood friend. She was killed in the prime of life, leaving behind a young husband and a thriving youth ministry. On the afternoon we gathered at the funeral parlor, our talking was hushed at first, then increasingly boisterous. Our love for one another and our hope in the resurrection was so strong that we could not help but be joyful in our grief.

The director of the funeral parlor marveled to me about the difference between that visitation and one he had hosted the week before. The two deaths were nearly identical; both involved young people killed in traffic accidents. Yet the other young man did not die in hope, and his friends and family could not grieve in hope. The silence, said the undertaker, was deathly. Knowing Christ makes all the difference when you die. To know Christ is to have a joyful, joyful funeral.

Finally, what about dinner parties? The gospel age is an age for holy revelry. Theologian Robert Hotchkins of the University of Chicago explains it well:

> Christians ought to be celebrating constantly. We ought to be preoccupied with parties, banquets, feasts, and merriment. We ought to give ourselves over to celebrations of joy because we have been liberated from the fear of life and the fear of death. We ought to attract people to the church quite literally by the sheer pleasure there is in being a Christian.[8]

The church's best feast is the Lord's Supper, which looks back to the victory Jesus won on the cross and looks forward to "The marriage supper of the Lamb" (Revelation 19:9). But that is not the only time Christians feast. Christians feast often to celebrate the joy of life in Christ. We feast because Jesus is coming very soon, and when he comes, we will all sit down at his banqueting table. "So, whether you eat or drink, or whatever you do, do all to the glory of God" (1 Corinthians 10:31). Eat, drink and be merry, for tomorrow we live!

25

Like a Tree

JEREMIAH 17:5–18

THE LAND THAT LIES to the southwest of the Sea of Galilee is dry. The soil is rocky and dusty. Vegetation is sparse, except where farmers irrigate. There is little or no grass. The trees are little more than shrubs.

Right in the middle of this wilderness is one of the most beautiful places on the face of the earth. It is called Gan Hasheloshah, "Garden of the Three Springs." Gan Hasheloshah is so beautiful that some rabbis say it was the location of the Garden of Eden. The pools and waterfalls in the garden are filled with deep, cool, emerald-blue water, continually refreshed by underground springs. It is a wonderful place for swimming and diving. Flowers and bushes crowd the banks of the pools, with giant palm trees overhead for shade.

The Bible teaches that a person who trusts in God is like a tree planted at Gan Hasheloshah. To know God is to be refreshed continually by his grace, like a tree watered by underground springs.

This is what the psalmist writes about the man who loves God:

> He is like a tree
>   planted by streams of water
> that yields its fruit in its season,
>   and its leaf does not wither.
> In all that he does, he prospers. (Psalm 1:3)

Jeremiah must have known his psalter (or perhaps the psalmist knew his Jeremiah!). Psalm 1 and Jeremiah 17 offer the same benediction for godliness. They both say that the one who trusts in God is like a well-watered tree.

In Self We Trust

Not only do Psalm 1 and Jeremiah 17 offer the same benediction, but they also pronounce the same curse. Unlike the psalmist, Jeremiah begins with the curse upon those who trust in themselves rather than in God:

> Thus says the LORD:
>   "Cursed is the man who trusts in man
> and makes flesh his strength,
>   whose heart turns away from the Lord." (v. 5)

This verse is a direct assault on American culture. It would be hard to imagine a statement that is more un-American, at least in the twenty-first century: "Cursed is the man who trusts in man." In other words, anyone who trusts in technology, economics, psychology, medicine, government, the military, the arts, or any other aspect of human culture is under God's curse. Yet these are exactly the things Americans trust for meaning and security in life. American money says "In God We Trust," but what Americans really mean is "In Self We Trust."

To understand the way Americans think, the author to read is Ralph Waldo Emerson (1803–1882). Emerson's philosophy is summarized in the title of one of his essays: "Self-Reliance" (1841).[1] In the essay, Emerson tells his readers to be completely self-reliant. He tells them not to care for the poor, love their families, or listen to preachers. "Insist on yourself," he writes, "never imitate." "Whoso would be a man, must be a nonconformist." "Nothing is at last sacred but the integrity of your own mind." "Nothing can bring you peace but yourself." Emerson's ideas are so contemporary that quotations from his writings were used to sell sneakers on television during the early 1990s. His motto is the creed of our times: "Trust thyself."

Jeremiah says just the opposite: Do not trust yourself. To trust in yourself is to turn away from God. Anyone who trusts in man will be cursed. Self-reliance does not bring peace but terror.

Three curses befall the self-reliant—loneliness, poverty, and death. First, loneliness:

> He is like a shrub in the desert,
>   and shall not see any good come.
> He shall dwell in the parched places of the wilderness,
>   in an uninhabited salt land. (v. 6)

It makes one thirsty to think of it. Jeremiah imagines a shrub in a salty land, like the dwarf juniper, which has a shallow root system.[2] The man who trusts in himself is like that lonely bush. His roots are not deep enough to get water from the ground. He is not planted by the living water of God's grace. So even when the rains finally come, they will not do him any good. When the showers of blessing come, they will simply disappear into the sand. When the Holy Spirit falls upon the people of God in the power of revival, he will miss it because he will be somewhere else. The man who trusts in himself will be left parched and lonely.

No one likes to be lonely. One thinks of the Phyllis Hyman song "I Refuse to Be Lonely." "I've got a right to take care of myself," she sings. "I realize that I come first, before anybody else." The Bible teaches you cannot have it both ways. You cannot put yourself first and refuse to be lonely. Once you decide that you come first, before anybody else, you are choosing to be lonely. You will be cut off from God, first of all, and then from other human beings. You will be like a dwarf juniper in the desert.

Second, those who trust in their own strength will become poor:

> Like the partridge that gathers a brood that she did not hatch,
>   so is he who gets riches but not by justice;
> in the midst of his days they will leave him,
>   and at his end he will be a fool. (v. 11)

Jeremiah was a keen student of nature. He had observed the partridge behave like a surrogate mother, going into another bird's nest to hatch another bird's eggs. The chicks hatched, but since they were not partridges, they soon flew away.

The same thing happens to those who amass fortunes by taking advantage of people. The money never belonged to them in the first place, so it will leave them in the end. One thinks of John Bennett, the founder of New Era Philanthropy. In the mid–1990s, Bennett set up a charitable foundation to provide funding for nonprofit organizations. Dozens of museums, universities, seminaries, and mission agencies signed up for matching grants. But when the scheme turned out to be a scam, dozens of institutions were bilked out of millions of dollars.

John Bennett was disgraced and imprisoned. He turned out to be a partridge. He gained riches by unjust means; so when his life was half gone, they deserted him. A man who trusts in his own strength turns out to be a fool. And a poor one at that, for a fool and his money are soon parted.

The third curse to befall men and women who trust in themselves is death:

O LORD, the hope of Israel,
   all who forsake you shall be put to shame;
those who turn away from you shall be written in the earth,
   for they have forsaken the LORD, the fountain of living water. (v. 13)

Leaving the oasis to wander out into the desert brings death. Where there is no water, there is no survival. In the same way, there is no spiritual life without the living water of God's grace. God had already warned his people about this: "My people . . . have forsaken me, the fountain of living waters" (2:13). But some people would rather die of thirst than turn to God; so die they must. Like names written in the dust, they will vanish without a trace. There is no water and no life apart from the Lord.

Down by the Riverside

Jeremiah knew that to have life, you must stop trusting in yourself. You must put your trust somewhere else:

Blessed is the man who trusts in the LORD,
   whose trust is the LORD.
He is like a tree planted by water,
   that sends out its roots by the stream. (17:7, 8a)

Like the curse, the blessing is a matter of trust. The contrast is absolute: "Cursed is the man who trusts in man" (v. 5), but "blessed is the man who trusts in the LORD" (v. 7). Kidner observes that the pivotal word in these verses "is *trust*, for everything will turn on where one's heart is."[3]

Everything turns on where one's heart is. So where is your heart? Where is your confidence? Do you rely on yourself most of the time, or do you trust in the Lord all the time? God only blesses those who trust in him. If you want life, you must depend on God the way a tree depends on a river. Total trust in God brings life.

The life God gives cannot be taken away. The blessed man or woman is "like a tree planted by water." Will such a tree become parched when there is a heat wave? No, because it is planted by streams of living water. Its leaves will stay green when the weather is hot. Will the tree wither during a year of drought? No, because it has a constant water supply. The tree by the river will be in full bloom when the bush in the desert dies.

Jeremiah was speaking from personal experience. He had been through a spiritual drought, a time when God seemed far away and his prayers seemed to go unanswered. He had tried to live the life of the blessed man from

Psalm 1; he "did not sit in the company of revelers" or "rejoice" with them (15:17a). But he was not experiencing God's blessing. So he complained to God, "Will you be to me like a deceitful brook, like waters that fail?" (15:18b).

By chapter 17, Jeremiah was able to answer his own questions. God is not "a deceitful brook." He does not fail like a spring that dries up. He is a stream of living water. So the tree planted by his banks

> does not fear when heat comes,
> for its leaves remain green,
> and is not anxious in the year of drought,
> for it does not cease to bear fruit. (17:8b)

This is Jeremiah's personal testimony of the faithfulness of God in a year of drought.

Jeremiah practiced what he preached at the end of this passage. He testified that the man who trusts in the Lord does not fear when heat comes. Suddenly he found himself on the hot seat. He became an object of ridicule; everyone was making fun of his message. "Behold, they say to me, 'Where is the word of the LORD? Let it come!'" (v. 15).

The people wanted Jeremiah to put up or shut up. They wanted him to prove that his prophecies were really true. He kept preaching about all the curses God would send. Well, where were they? If those who trust in themselves are cursed, then they wanted to see some loneliness, poverty, and death as proof.

Jeremiah was starting to feel the heat, but he kept cool because he was "like a tree planted by water." He stayed right where the Lord put him and said whatever the Lord told him to say:

> I have not run away from being your shepherd,
> nor have I desired the day of sickness.
> You know what came out of my lips;
> it was before your face. (v. 16)

Jeremiah did not desert the Lord or the Lord's message. He did, of course, pray for help. "Be not a terror to me," he begged; "you are my refuge in the day of disaster" (v. 17). This prayer was similar to the praise he had already offered: "A glorious throne set on high from the beginning is the place of our sanctuary" (v. 12). Jeremiah found his refuge and sanctuary in God. He was blessed because he put his confidence in the Lord.

Finally, Jeremiah asked the Lord to bless him and curse his enemies, just as he had promised:

> Let those be put to shame who persecute me,
>   but let me not be put to shame;
> let them be dismayed,
>   but let me not be dismayed;
> bring upon them the day of disaster;
>   destroy them with double destruction! (v. 18)

Jeremiah's example is a reminder to stay close to the Lord during the dry seasons of the soul. Christians who are under spiritual attack or who have lost the joy of their salvation sometimes withdraw from God. They decide they are not going to pray, read their Bibles, or go to worship until their desire for God returns. But that is like leaving a spring of living water to die in a spiritual desert.

Do not leave the water's edge. Keep trusting in God. Keep reading your Bible. Keep praying even if you are not sure God is listening. The tree planted by the water does not just stand there—it "sends out its roots by the stream" (v. 8a). The tree is alive; it stretches and strains toward the grace that is available through God's Word, through prayer, and through the sacraments. Keep sending your roots toward the stream of God's grace and reaching out for the water of life. God will refresh you. He will keep your leaves green when the heat comes and will bring forth abundant fruit in the year of drought.

The great Scottish preacher Thomas Boston made these helpful comments about the dry periods of the Christian life:

> A tree, that has life and nourishment, grows to its perfection, yet it is not always growing; it grows not in the winter. Christians also have their winters, wherein the influences of grace, necessary for their growth, cease. . . . What then will become of the soul? Why, there is still one sure ground of hope. The saint's faith is not as the hypocrite's like a pipe laid short of the fountain, whereby there can be no conveyance: it still remains a bond of union between Christ and the soul; and therefore, because Christ lives, the believer shall live also. . . . In the worst of times, the saints have a principle of growth in them. . . . Therefore, after decays, they revive again: namely, when the winter is over, and the Sun of righteousness returns to them with his warm influences.[4]

The tree planted by the water's edge is a picture of the Christian living close to Christ. After a day of feasting, Jesus stood up in Jerusalem and said in a loud voice, "If anyone thirsts, let him come to me and drink. Whoever believes in me, as the Scripture has said, 'Out of his heart will flow rivers of living water'" (John 7:37, 38).

To live like a tree is to live close to Christ. He is the water of life. In Jesus Christ there is water during times of drought for thirsty souls. In Jesus Christ there is water for cleansing from sin. Every tree planted close to Christ will have green leaves and rich fruit, and everyone who drinks from his fountain will never die.

The Tell-Tale Heart

How will you live? Will you be a shrub or a tree? Will you choose curse or blessing? Will you trust in man or trust in God? Will you wander in the desert or plant yourself by the river? Will you die or live?

It seemed obvious that Jeremiah would choose the life of blessing. He would plant himself by the river and send deep roots toward the streams of God's mercy. But then his heart betrayed him.

Edgar Allan Poe wrote a story about a man betrayed by his heart. The story is called "The Tell-Tale Heart." It begins with the murder of an old man with an evil eye. The murderer has just buried the old man's corpse beneath the floorboards when the police arrive. A neighbor has heard a scream in the dark, and they have come to investigate.

The murderer calmly invites the police to search the house. They find nothing. But as they investigate, the murderer begins to hear "a low, dull, quick sound—such a sound as a watch makes when enveloped in cotton." The story continues in the murderer's own words:

> I gasped for breath—and yet the officers heard it not. I talked more quickly—more vehemently; but the noise steadily increased. I arose and argued about trifles, in a high key and with violent gesticulations; but the noise steadily increased. . . . I paced the floor to and fro with heavy strides . . . but the noise steadily increased. . . . I swung the chair upon which I had been sitting, and grated it upon the boards, but the noise arose over all and continually increased. It grew louder—louder—*louder*! . . . "Villains!" I shrieked, "dissemble no more! I admit the deed!—tear up the planks!—here, here!—it is the beating of his hideous heart!"[5]

The murderer was betrayed by his tell-tale heart—not by the heart of the dead man, but by his own heart beating and beating with guilt.

Jeremiah had a tell-tale heart of his own. He knew that if he trusted in himself he would be cursed, and that if he trusted in the Lord he would be blessed. But his heart betrayed him: "The heart is deceitful above all things, and desperately sick; who can understand it?" (17:9). These words are true whether they came from Jeremiah himself or from the Lord. The human heart cannot be trusted, cannot be healed, cannot be understood. It is devious, incurable, and inscrutable. It cannot be trusted to live like a tree.

"The heart is deceitful above *all* things." This is one of the most powerful statements of human depravity in all of Scripture. The doctrine of total depravity means that every human being is sinful through and through. No part of the human person remains untouched by sin. The mind, the will, the emotions, and the conscience are all corrupt. So is the heart, which is the innermost core of the human person. It, too, is depraved.

Nothing is more deceitful than the human heart. The sin of our first parents was a sin of the heart. When Adam and Eve ate the forbidden fruit, their hearts were turning away from God to trust in man. From that one sin have come all the rest of the sins of the human heart. All the lies, conspiracies, betrayals, and murders in the history of the world have sprung from the deception of the human heart.

Every human being has a tell-tale heart. One thinks of the filmmaker Woody Allen, trying desperately to justify his sexual relationship with a young girl. "The heart wants what it wants," he explained.[6] So it does, but what it wants is often deceptively evil. In the introduction to the second edition of his Screwtape Letters, C. S. Lewis wrote:

> Some have paid me an undeserved compliment by supposing that my *Letters* were the ripe fruit of many years' study in moral and ascetic theology. They forgot that there is an equally reliable, though less creditable, way of learning how temptation works. "My heart"—I need no other's—"showeth me the wickedness of the ungodly."[7]

Truly, the heart is deceitful above all things, as anyone can confirm from personal experience.

If the heart is full of deceit, and it is, then the verse that follows is terrifying:

> I the LORD search the heart
>   and test the mind,
> to give every man according to his ways,
>   according to the fruit of his deeds. (v. 10)

God knows what is inside every heart. The tell-tale heart tells all its secrets to God.

How alarming it is that these two verses should stand next to one another in Holy Scripture: "The heart is deceitful above all things"—"I the LORD search the heart." Human depravity is pressed up against divine justice. How alarming it is to know that the deceitful-above-all-things heart falls under the seeing-all-things gaze of Almighty God. How frightening to know that the unknowable heart is known to God. How terrifying to know that God judges the heart, rewarding each person "according to the fruit of his deeds." "Human fickleness and divine accountability together lead to an inevitable judgment."[8] It may be that no one else knows your secret sins, how you have turned away from God in the privacy of your own heart. But God knows!

Jeremiah's heart betrayed him. He had long preached against the sins of his people. He had listed their transgressions in full, speaking out against the idolatry, adultery, and immorality of his day. But his own heart condemned him. The innermost core of his own being was deceitful beyond cure. This is true about every heart. You, too, have a devious, incurable, inscrutable heart.

Save Me, Lord!

The only thing to do with a tell-tale heart is cry to God for mercy. That is what Jeremiah did when he prayed, "Heal me, O LORD, and I shall be healed; save me, and I shall be saved, for you are my praise" (v. 14). That is the incurable heart's prayer for a cure, the unsavable heart's prayer for salvation.

Jeremiah had often pleaded with God for the salvation of his nation. He had often prayed that God would turn the hearts of his people back to him. But he also had to plead with God for the healing of his own heart.

Somehow Jeremiah must have known that God is able to cure an incurable heart. God not only searches the heart, he knows how to mend it. This is part of the mysterious work of the Holy Spirit. The Spirit takes a deceitful heart and makes it true to God. He comes into an incurable heart and heals it from sin. That is what happens when a sinner comes to Christ. A Christian is someone whose heart has been cured by the grace of God, for "with the heart one believes and is justified" (Romans 10:10a).

The closing verse of a hymn by George Croly (1780–1860) expresses the heart's prayer for the healing work of the Holy Spirit:

Teach me to love thee as thine angels love,
One holy passion filling all my frame;
The baptism of the heav'n descended Dove,
My heart an altar, and thy love the flame.

That is the same prayer Jeremiah offered. It is a prayer for the Holy Spirit to take a sinful heart and fill it with passion for God.

Acts 16 tells a wonderful story about the way God answered a similar prayer and cured an incurable heart. It is the story of Lydia, a businesswoman who dealt in purple cloth at Philippi. Like every son or daughter of Adam, she was born with a deceitful and incurable heart. But when she heard the apostles preach the good news about Jesus Christ, "The Lord opened her heart to pay attention to what was said by Paul" (Acts 16:14). That is a beautiful way to describe what happens when a sinner comes to Christ: "The Lord opened her heart." A heart cannot be mended on its own. But the Lord can send his Holy Spirit to open, mend, fix, and heal the heart. And his cure is total.

Has the Lord cured your deceitful, incurable, inscrutable heart? If he has, then be like a tree planted close to the water of life. Stretch your roots toward the grace that is yours in Jesus Christ. If the Lord has not yet cured your heart, then pray Jeremiah's prayer: "Heal me, O Lord, and I shall be healed; save me, and I shall be saved" (17:14).

26

Keep the Lord's Day Holy

JEREMIAH 17:19–27

AS PETER LOOKED at the notice posted in the locker room, he could hardly believe his eyes. "There must be some mistake!" he thought. Peter played rugby for the University of Oxford. The Blues had a match the following Sunday, their final tune-up before meeting Cambridge in the Varsity Match. As he stood in the locker room, he was dismayed to find his name in the starting lineup. Dismayed because he had informed the rugby coach at the start of his career that he would not play rugby on Sunday. Peter was a Christian. For him the first day of the week was a day for worship but not a day for rugby.

Peter went to his coach and said, "I'm sorry, but I will not play in the match on Sunday." The coach removed him from the lineup. But then he gave him the bad news: "You will not play against Cambridge next Saturday either." It was a crushing blow. The rugby match between Oxford and Cambridge is a major sporting event in England, like the Rose Bowl and the Army-Navy football game all rolled into one. Plus, the only way for an Oxford athlete to win a Blue—a prize something like a varsity letter—is to play in the Varsity Match.

Sure enough, when the Oxford team was announced for the Varsity Match Peter had lost his place in the lineup. Although he was listed as a substitute, he did not have much chance of getting into the game. Substitutes are only allowed in rugby for near-fatal injuries. But as he watched from the sidelines, one of his teammates went down with an injury. In the providence of God, the player had broken his ankle and needed to be carried off the pitch. The Oxford coach turned to the bench and called for Peter, who ran onto the field to help beat Cambridge and win his Blue. Did the Lord bless him because he had kept the Lord's Day holy?

Keep the Sabbath Holy

The end of Jeremiah 17 is about the blessings that come to God's people when they honor the Sabbath. God told Jeremiah to go to the shopping mall—or the city gate, as it was called back then—to deliver a message:

> Thus said the LORD to me: "Go and stand in the People's Gate, by which the kings of Judah enter and by which they go out, and in all the gates of Jerusalem, and say: 'Hear the word of the LORD, you kings of Judah, and all Judah, and all the inhabitants of Jerusalem, who enter by these gates. Thus says the LORD: Take care for the sake of your lives, and do not bear a burden on the Sabbath day or bring it in by the gates of Jerusalem. And do not carry a burden out of your houses on the Sabbath or do any work, but keep the Sabbath day holy, as I commanded your fathers.'" (vv. 19–22)

On the seventh day of the week it was business as usual in Jerusalem. The people were coming and going with loads of goods for sale. They had turned the Sabbath day into market day. They were treating the day of rest as a day for shopping.

Nehemiah faced the same problem in his day:

> I saw in Judah people treading winepresses on the Sabbath, and bringing in heaps of grain and loading them on donkeys, and also wine, grapes, figs, and all kinds of loads, which they brought into Jerusalem on the Sabbath day. (Nehemiah 13:15)

In the words of John Calvin, "It was as though they wished publicly to reproach and despise God."[1]

What better way to get ahead in the business world than to work seven days a week instead of six? But God did not intend his people to be slaves to their work. He wanted them to rest on the seventh day, as stipulated in the fourth commandment:

> Remember the Sabbath day, to keep it holy. Six days you shall labor, and do all your work, but the seventh day is a Sabbath to the LORD your God. On it you shall not do any work, you, or your son, or your daughter, your male servant, or your female servant, or your livestock, or the sojourner who is within your gates. For in six days the LORD made heaven and earth, the sea, and all that is in them, and rested on the seventh day. Therefore the LORD blessed the Sabbath day and made it holy. (Exodus 20:8–11)

The Sabbath was part of God's covenant with Israel. Like circumcision, it separated God's people from the rest of the world. According to one scholar, "This pattern of a continuous week of seven days and the interruption of work on the last day of the week is quite unique in the ancient Near East and has to be seen as a genuinely Israelite phenomenon."[2]

Yet the scholar errs when he goes on to say, "The origin and the original purpose of this unique division of the week is unknown."[3] The Hebrew Sabbath had its origin in the command of God. While everyone else was working, the people of God were to rest. Negatively, they were not to do any work. Positively, they were to keep the Sabbath holy. They were to set the seventh day apart for God because they themselves were set apart for God.

To keep the Sabbath holy was to follow God's own example. The fourth commandment was unique among the Ten Commandments in the way it went back to creation for its justification. God did the work of creation in six days, but he rested on the seventh day. Therefore God blessed the seventh day and called it holy (Genesis 2:3; Exodus 20:11). The Sabbath looked back to creation, back to the rest God took after his work of creation. Keeping the Sabbath was a way of sharing in God's rest.

Like the rest of God's laws, the Sabbath command was ignored only at the nation's peril. It had been ignored in the past. God's lament is that "They did not listen or incline their ear, but stiffened their neck, that they might not hear and receive instruction" (17:23). People were just as stubborn in Jeremiah's day, and just as unwilling to keep the Lord's day holy. So God made this threat: "If you do not listen to me, to keep the Sabbath day holy, and not to bear a burden and enter by the gates of Jerusalem on the Sabbath day, then I will kindle a fire in its gates, and it shall devour the palaces of Jerusalem and shall not be quenched" (v. 27). Here is one more transgression to add to Jeremiah's list of the sins that bring the fires of judgment—failure to keep the Sabbath holy.

Great blessing came to God's people whenever they remembered the Sabbath. God promised three blessings in particular. First, a *royal* blessing:

> But if you listen to me, declares the Lord, and bring in no burden by the gates of this city on the Sabbath day, but keep the Sabbath day holy and do no work on it, then there shall enter by the gates of this city kings and princes who sit on the throne of David, riding in chariots and on horses, they and their officials, the men of Judah and the inhabitants of Jerusalem. And this city shall be inhabited forever. (vv. 24, 25)

The people of Jerusalem had decided that keeping the Sabbath was not very important to them. But it was important to God. According to him, the very survival of the monarchy rested upon Sabbath-observance. The fourth commandment was a spiritual barometer, a test of covenant loyalty. Did Israel love God enough to set aside a day for his glory? There would only be a king on David's throne as long as they did. Even the strength of the king's army—his princes, his horses, and his chariots—depended on keeping the Sabbath holy.

Second, God promised a *civic* blessing. If Jerusalem would honor the Lord's day it would be "inhabited forever" (v. 25b). The gates of the city would remain open for people to come and go with their goods. Jerusalem would become a permanent dwelling place for God's people.

Third, God promised a *national* blessing. The blessings of the Sabbath would extend beyond the walls of Jerusalem to embrace the entire nation.

> And people shall come from the cities of Judah and the places around Jerusalem, from the land of Benjamin, from the Shephelah, from the hill country, and from the Negeb, bringing burnt offerings and sacrifices, grain offerings and frankincense, and bringing thank offerings to the house of the LORD. (v. 26)

Worship is contagious. There is something infectious about a congregation that worships God with joy and reverence. Other people start to hear about it. When they hear about it, they want to come and see it. And when they see it, they want to become part of it. That is what Jeremiah promised would happen in Israel. The whole nation would come home to give praise and honor to God . . . if only Jerusalem would keep the Sabbath holy.

Everything depends on the Sabbath. Keeping the Sabbath would "lead to a prosperous and independent state with its own royal family and court, with its capital city Jerusalem the religious centre of the nation's life."[4] It would bring blessing upon blessing to the people of God.

From Sabbath to Lord's Day

Can a Christian still receive the blessings of the Sabbath?

The question arises because Christians do not keep the Sabbath. The word Sabbath refers to the seventh day of the week. But Christians do not worship the Lord on the seventh day of the week; they worship him on the first day of the week. When Paul gave the Corinthians instructions about taking a collection for God's people he wrote, "On the first day of every week, each of you is to put something aside and store it up, as he may prosper" (1 Corinthians 16:2a). The collection was taken on the first day because that was the day Christians gathered for worship.

Not only did the first Christians move their day of rest and worship to the first day of the week, they also stopped calling it the Sabbath. Instead they called it "The Lord's day." When John recorded the revelation he had on the island of Patmos he wrote, "I was in the Spirit on the Lord's day" (Revelation 1:10).

The reason for these changes was the coming of Jesus Christ. The Sabbath was not the final resting place for the people of God; it was only "a shadow" of things to come (Colossians 2:17). The Sabbath pointed forward to the reality of the rest found in Jesus Christ. Jesus is the Sabbath rest. With his coming, the people of God moved from the Sabbath to the Lord's Day. Christians do not keep the Sabbath, but they do celebrate the Lord's Day. The reason they celebrate it on the first day of the week is because that was the day of resurrection, when Jesus Christ rose from the dead to conquer sin and death once and for all.

It is perhaps unfortunate that the Westminster Standards speak of a "Christian Sabbath" since that term is not used in the New Testament. Yet the Westminster Confession of Faith does recognize the transformation of the Sabbath that has occurred in Jesus Christ: "[God] hath particularly appointed one day in seven, for a Sabbath, to be kept holy unto him: which, from the beginning of the world to the resurrection of Christ, was the last day of the week; and, from the resurrection of Christ, was changed into the first day of the week, which, in Scripture, is called the Lord's Day" (26.7). In Christ the church has moved from the Sabbath to the Lord's Day.

A Day of Worship

How should Christians keep the Lord's Day holy?

First, Christians should honor Sunday as a day of worship. As the Puritans loved to say, the first day of the week is "The market day of the soul."

In his commentary on the book of John, James Boice lists no fewer than eleven events that happened on the first day of the week.[5] Here are some of them: On the first day of the week Jesus rose from the dead and ascended into Heaven. On the first day the risen Christ first appeared to the disciples, broke bread with them, and opened their minds so that they could understand all the Scriptures concerning him. On the first day Jesus commissioned the disciples for the task of world evangelization and imparted the Holy Spirit to them. It was also on the first day that Peter preached the gospel to all the nations of the world.

The Lord's Day is a day for all these kinds of worship. It is a day for celebrating the resurrection of Jesus Christ. For the Christian every Sunday is Easter Sunday. The Lord's Day is also a day for sharing the sacrament of the Lord's Supper. It is a day for opening up the Scriptures and preaching the gospel. It is not simply a day of rest—it is a day for the activities of worship, fellowship, Bible study, and evangelism.

Christians sometimes complain that they do not have enough time to pray, study their Bibles, or read Christian books. The Lord's Day is a wonderful day for all kinds of private worship. It is also a good day to memorize Scripture, or to study the catechism, as I did when I was a child.

The Lord's Day is also a wonderful day to invite others to worship. Your neighbors already know where you are going when you leave your home on Sunday morning. They know where you have been when you return. They know you have been to church. No doubt some have wondered what it is like to go to your church or have even said to themselves, "I really ought to go to church sometime." Do not make them wait for an invitation. Ask them to come with you. Then the same thing can happen in your church that happened in Jerusalem. Sinners will hear the gospel and "worship God and declare that God is really among you" (1 Corinthians 14:25).

A Day of Mercy

A second way for Christians to keep the Lord's Day holy is to show mercy. This is what Jesus kept trying to teach the Pharisees. The Pharisees were legalists. They were more concerned with what people *couldn't* do on the Sabbath than what they could do. It is easy to imagine some of them listening to Jeremiah and asking what he meant by "a burden" (v. 27). How much does a burden weigh? How big is it? The Pharisees would want to know so they could condemn anyone who was carrying a burden.

In fact, this is exactly the kind of reasoning the Pharisees used when Jesus healed a lame man on the Sabbath by the pool of Bethesda. Jesus told him, "Get up, take up your bed, and walk" (John 5:8). But the Pharisees said, "It is the Sabbath, and it is not lawful for you to take up your bed" (v. 10). They said, "Nope. Can't do that. See, it's right here in Jeremiah: 'Be careful not to carry a burden on the Sabbath.' That mat is a burden if we ever saw one!"

Jesus took the opposite point of view. He showed believers what they can do to bring glory to God on the Lord's Day. That is why Jesus performed miracles on the Sabbath—to bring glory to God by showing that the Lord's Day is a day for mercy.

Matthew tells about the time Jesus went into a synagogue, and "a man was there with a withered hand. And they [the Pharisees] asked him, 'Is it lawful to heal on the Sabbath?'—so that they might accuse him" (Matthew 12:10). That is the attitude of the legalist, always wanting to tell people what God forbids. But "[Jesus] said to them, 'Which one of you who has a sheep, if it falls into a pit on the Sabbath, will not take hold of it and lift it out? Of how much more value is a man than a sheep! So it is lawful to do good on the Sabbath'" (vv. 11, 12).

One wonders if Jesus had seen some Pharisees do exactly what he described. Perhaps he was out walking one Sabbath and passed a group of them huddled at the edge of a pit, anxiously grabbing hold of a sheep and pulling it to safety. Whether Jesus saw something like that or not, his question nailed the Pharisees right in the conscience. Would they rescue a sheep on the Sabbath? You bet they would! But how much better to show mercy to a man than to rescue a beast. "[Jesus] said to the man, 'Stretch out your hand.' And the man stretched it out, and it was restored, healthy like the other" (v. 13).

The Lord's Day is a day for mercy. The Westminster *Shorter Catechism* says that in addition to public and private worship, the Lord's Day "is to be taken up in the works of necessity and mercy" (Q & A 60). Similarly, the Puritan Ezekiel Hopkins wrote, "Notwithstanding this rest and cessation from labour which is required on the Lord's day, yet three sorts of works may and ought to be performed . . . these are works of *piety*, works of *necessity*, and works of *charity*."

Poverty, illness, depression, and brokenness are all around us, especially in our cities. The Lord's Day is a day for mercy. It is a wonderful day to visit older members of the church who are unable to come to worship with God's family. It is a wonderful day to visit a nursing home to share the love of Christ. It is a wonderful day to invite the poor and the needy into your home for a meal, especially those who do not know Christ. It is a wonderful day to feed the hungry and house the homeless. To do mercy on the Lord's Day is to be like the Lord Jesus himself.

A Day of Rest

A third way for Christians to keep the Lord's Day holy is to rest. Human beings are not made to work seven days a week. The rhythm of six days of labor followed by one day of rest was established by God at the creation of the world: "Whoever has entered God's rest has also rested from his works as God did from his" (Hebrews 4:10).

The Westminster divines claimed that the Sabbath is not a day for "recreations" (Q & A 60). They meant that the Lord's Day is not a day for entertaining oneself, but in a sense they chose the wrong word to say it. The Sabbath is a day for re-creation, in the proper sense. Christians are re-created by using the Lord's Day for rest. Like the Old Testament people of God, they look back to creation for their rest.

Christians also look back to redemption for their rest. Since Jesus Christ fulfilled the whole Law, we are now free from fulfilling the Law by our own works. We rest in the finished work of Christ seven days a week. Donald Grey Barnhouse rightly observed: "When we are thus free, the Lord will possess our Mondays and Tuesdays, our Wednesdays and Thursdays, our Fridays, Saturdays and Sundays, and all our days and weeks and months and years because he has bought us and possesses our hearts in simple grace."[6]

Christians look back to creation, back to redemption, and forward to eternity for their rest. Hebrews reminds us that "There remains a Sabbath rest for the people of God . . . Let us therefore strive to enter that rest" (Hebrews 4:9, 11; cf. Revelation 14:13). This refers to the glorious return of the Lord Jesus Christ. It is only when Christ returns that we will enter our everlasting rest. But as we wait for the second coming of Jesus Christ, we can already start to enjoy his rest by keeping the Lord's Day holy. "Sabbath rest for the people of God" "is evidently an experience which they do not enjoy in their present mortal life, although it belongs to them as a heritage, and by faith they may live in the good of it here and now."[7]

Rest is part of what Jesus meant when he said, "The Sabbath was made for man, not man for the Sabbath" (Mark 2:27). Legalists think man was made for the Sabbath. In other words, they think of the Sabbath as a religious duty they owe to God. For them it becomes a chore and a burden. They are like the people in the days of Amos who said, "When will the new moon be over, that we may sell grain?" (Amos 8:5). They are like the Pharisees who were always finding ways to get out of keeping the Sabbath. Some rabbis concluded that if you tied something to your body instead of carrying it in your arms, it did not count as a load. You can guess what they did: They strapped themselves down like pack mules.

Jesus taught instead that "The Sabbath was made for man." The Lord's Day is not something you owe to God—it is God's gift to you. As Moses said to the children of Israel, "The LORD has given you the Sabbath" (Exodus 16:29). The Lord's Day is for your benefit, your blessing, and your rest. In the middle of all your work God gives you the gift of one day of rest.

I was reminded of the value of that gift during my doctoral studies. As I prepared to return to the United States after nearly three years at Oxford, other students (and especially their long-suffering wives!) asked how I had managed to complete my degree. Most expected to take years more to finish. I explained how my academic preparation and choice of topic had helped me in my research. But then I said, "I also rest from my work on the Lord's Day, which has helped me stay productive without getting worn out." This surprised some people because Sunday seemed like a good day to write, even to Christians. But I learned from my experience that resting from work brings God's blessing.

You will receive the same blessing if you use the Lord's Day for rest as well as for worship and mercy. Each Christian needs to figure out how to honor the Lord's Day in his or her own life. Some have jobs—especially in the medical profession—that must be done on Sunday. This is what the Puritans meant by "works of necessity." If possible, change your schedule so you can celebrate the Lord's Day. If not, then work in the strength of the Lord, and with his blessing.

Others have heavy responsibilities on Monday morning and will have to plan for their rest. A college student, for example, might need to begin keeping the Lord's Day on Saturday night, leaving Sunday night free to prepare for Monday classes. However you do it, you will be blessed if you keep the Lord's Day holy. It is made for you.

Some years ago I made a commitment to honor the Lord by not playing competitive basketball on the Lord's Day. That decision may not be necessary for every Christian, but for me it did not seem right to work at basketball on a day of rest. My commitment was tested when I played at Oxford. I told the coach I had made a commitment to the Lord not to play basketball on Sunday. I did it with some trepidation because the Varsity Match with Cambridge was always played on Sunday, and it might have cost me my Blue. Happily, we were able to change the match from Sunday to Saturday during my years at the university.

What we were unable to change was the date of the British University Championships. During my last season we advanced to the finals in Cardiff with seven other teams. I played throughout the other matches, but the championship game itself was played on Sunday.

In the providence of God, on the day of the championship I came in my devotions to Jeremiah 17, where I read these words: "Keep the Sabbath day holy, as I commanded your fathers" (v. 22). Joy and thanksgiving filled my heart as I went to worship with the Lord's people that morning.

During the worship service the minister invited me to share my testimony. He made a special point of asking why I was in church rather than at the arena. The minister had a special reason for asking. He was a solidly built fellow who used to play rugby. He even won an Oxford Blue, in fact. His name was Peter, and he knew from his own experience that those who keep the Lord's Day holy are blessed by God.

27

In the Potter's Hands

JEREMIAH 18:1–23

IT WAS TIME FOR JEREMIAH to take another field trip. God had already taken him up and down the streets of Jerusalem (5:1) and around the ruins of Shiloh (7:12). This time he wanted to take him to a pottery workshop:

> The word that came to Jeremiah from the LORD: "Arise, and go down to the potter's house, and there I will let you hear my words." So I went down to the potter's house, and there he was working at his wheel. And the vessel he was making of clay was spoiled in the potter's hand, and he reworked it into another vessel, as it seemed good to the potter to do. (18:1–4)

What Jeremiah saw happens all the time in a pottery shop. First, the potter slapped a lump of clay in the middle of his stone wheel. Spinning the wheel with his feet, he deftly began to shape the clay with his hands, forming it into a pot. But then something went wrong. The pot was not shaping up properly. There was a flaw in the clay, or perhaps it was inferior for delicate work. So the potter skillfully formed it into a different kind of vessel altogether. He turned a pitcher into a bowl or a lamp into a cup, whatever seemed best to him.

The potter's wheel is a lesson in the absolute sovereignty of God. It puts an end to pride and silences every boast. "Then the word of the LORD came to me: 'O house of Israel, can I not do with you as this potter has done? declares the LORD'" (vv. 5, 6a).

God's question needs no answer. It is one of the great rhetorical questions of the Bible. "Can I not do with you as this potter has done?" Who would dare to answer such a question in the negative? "Behold, like the clay in the potter's hand, so are you in my hand, O house of Israel" (v. 6b).

He Is the Potter, We Are the Clay

The doctrinal point of this passage can be stated very simply: God can do whatever he wants with you. This is what it means for him to be God. Because God is God, he is free to do whatever he pleases. In his hands rest all power, rule, control, authority, kingdom, government, and dominion.

This is the doctrine of the sovereignty of God. Some people do not care for this doctrine. Others tremble at it. Some may even try to oppose it. But it cannot be denied. Human beings are not on equal terms with God. He is the Creator; we are the creatures. God is the absolute sovereign; all others are totally subservient. "Does the clay say to him who forms it, 'What are you making?'" (Isaiah 45:9). Of course not.

The picture of potter and clay is doubly appropriate to describe God's relationship to us. First, we are made of clay. *The Catechism for Young Children* asks, "Of what were our first parents made?" (Q. 17). The answer begins like this: "God made the body of Adam out of the ground" (A. 17). The words are taken straight from Scripture: "The Lord GOD formed the man of dust from the ground" (Genesis 2:7). God was the potter; Adam was the clay. The word Jeremiah used for "potter" comes from the word translated "formed" in Genesis 2. The first thing we learn about our position in the universe is that God is the potter and we are the clay.

If this was true at Creation, it is all the more true after the fall. When Adam sinned, God cursed humanity:

> By the sweat of your face
>   you shall eat bread,
> till you return to the ground,
>   for out of it you were taken;
> for you are dust,
>   and to dust you shall return. (Genesis 3:19)

God turned the dust into clay to form a pot. After a little while the pot will return to dust. "Ashes to ashes, dust to dust."

Since the beginning of the world, human beings have known that they are but dust. King David wrote, "You lay me in the dust of death" (Psalm 22:15). When Hamlet knelt beside a grave to hold poor Yorick's skull, he imagined the great emperors of the world reduced to dust, with their dirt then put to some common use:

> Alexander died, Alexander was buried, Alexander returneth into dust;
> the dust is earth; of earth we make loam; and why of that loam,

whereto he was converted, might they not stop a beer-barrel?
Imperious Caesar, dead and turn'd to clay,
Might stop a hole to keep the wind away:
O, that that earth, which kept the world in awe,
Should patch a wall to expel the winter's flaw![1]

The dustiness of humanity is recognized to the present day. "Dust in the wind," sang the popular group Kansas, "all we are is dust in the wind." On the television program *Star Trek: The Next Generation*, human beings were referred to as "carbon units." It may sound insulting, but it is sound theology, not to mention good science. The bodies of human beings are made from the dust of the ground. We are but clay.

The picture of the potter and the clay is also appropriate because a potter can do whatever he wants with clay. Wet clay is malleable. A skilled craftsman can shape it into almost anything. Just the slightest adjustment of the thumb or fingers changes the contours of a pot. The potter has complete mastery over the clay.

Have you ever seen a potter's arms? I once saw a potter challenge anyone in a large congregation to an arm-wrestling match. Although she was a small woman, she did not get any takers. Not after she flexed her massive forearms, anyway! Her muscles were strong from years of shaping pots. In the strong hands of a potter, clay is pounded and shaped however the potter pleases.

If we are only clay, then we are at the Potter's mercy. Calvin wrote, "Until men are brought to know that they are so subject to God's power that their condition can in a single moment be changed, according to his will, they will never be humble as they ought to be."[2] God can do whatever he wants with us.

Clay in the Hands of an Angry Potter

Though familiar, Jeremiah's image of the potter and the clay is often misunderstood. Some scholars say the potter was limited by his clay:

> The quality of the clay determined what the potter could do with it. He could make something else from the same clay, but not the particular vessel he had hoped for. The clay could thus frustrate the potter's original intention and cause him to change it. Yahweh the potter was dealing with a clay that was resistant to his purpose. The quality of the people in some way determined what God might do with them.[3]

This viewpoint gives too much credit to the clay, and too little to the Potter. It forgets that this potter *made* his clay in the first place. It allows the clay to control its own destiny, as if mere human beings could change the mind of God.

The prophet Isaiah had a good answer for people who exalt humanity at the expense of deity:

> You turn things upside down!
> Shall the potter be regarded as the clay,
> that the thing made should say of its maker,
>   "He did not make me";
> or the thing formed say of him who formed it,
>   "He has no understanding"? (Isaiah 29:16)

If God is the Potter, then let him be the Potter!

Others assume that the picture of God as Potter is comforting. They take these verses to mean something like this: "God isn't finished with me yet. He is making me into something beautiful." As we shall see, there is some truth in this idea. But it was not Jeremiah's main point.

Jeremiah's message is about judgment. The pot on the potter's wheel is not meant to be comforting. Like much modern art, it is meant to be disturbing. Jeremiah's message is about clay in the hands of an angry potter. If God can do whatever he wants, then he has the right to destroy you for your sins. God is the one who brought you into this world, and he can take you out of it. Until you recognize this, you have not fully reckoned with the sovereignty of God.

The reason God took Jeremiah down to the potter's house was to warn Israel about the wrath of God. He began with the ultimate reason for the rise and fall of nations:

> If at any time I declare concerning a nation or a kingdom, that I will pluck up and break down and destroy it, and if that nation, concerning which I have spoken, turns from its evil, I will relent of the disaster that I intended to do to it. And if at any time I declare concerning a nation or a kingdom that I will build and plant it, and if it does evil in my sight, not listening to my voice, then I will relent of the good that I had intended to do to it. (18:7–10)

These are general principles for the way God deals with the kingdoms of this world. God does not just make a wine jar here and a flowerpot there. Entire nations are shaped upon his wheel. He brings prosperity or disaster as he pleases. His prophet Jeremiah was appointed "over nations and over kingdoms, to pluck up and to break down, to destroy and to overthrow, to build and to plant" (1:10). A kingdom heading for destruction will be saved if it repents of its sins. On the other hand, a nation once blessed by God will be destroyed for its wickedness.

During the Irish crisis of 1641, Jeremiah's words were applied to the English Parliament. In a sermon preached before the House of Commons, the Puritan Edmund Calamy (1600–1666) developed the following points:

1. That God hath an independent and illuminated Prerogative over all Kingdoms and Nations to build them, or destroy them as he pleaseth.
2. Though God hath this absolute power over Kingdoms and Nations, yet he seldome useth this power, but first he gives warning.
3. That National turning from evil, will divert National judgments, and procure National blessings.
4. That when God begins to build and plant a Nation; if that Nation do evil in God's sight, God will unbuild, pluck up, and repent of the good he intended to do unto it.[4]

Jeremiah's words also serve as a warning for America in this new millennium. The United States is an empire in decline, seemingly headed for destruction. When will it be uprooted, torn down, and destroyed? In the 1990s Harold O. J. Brown observed somewhere that "It would take someone with a supernatural gift of prophecy to tell us the number of days or weeks or years that the American commonwealth can be expected to endure without . . . being overthrown. . . . But it does not take a prophetic gift to see that . . . disaster on a national scale is inevitable."

According to Jeremiah, the only way to escape such disaster is to turn away from sin. The only way to get God to relent is for Americans to repent of their hatred and violence, wastefulness and sloth, racism and injustice, selfishness, materialism, and sexual immorality. According to the Word of God, a sinful nation must either repent or perish.

What is especially sad about America's spiritual condition is that it was once a nation built up and planted by God (cf. 18:9). Christians often exaggerate the extent to which ours has been a Christian nation, but there is no doubt that God has shed his grace on America. The first colonists came to the New World to establish a Christian community living in covenant with God. The Constitution of the United States is based largely upon Biblical principles. God rewarded that solid foundation by making America a blessing to the world, using the nation to bring tyrants to justice and to pioneer in the work of worldwide missions. But the United States is mere clay, and God is the Potter. He will mold or mar as he pleases, according to the righteousness and repentance of the nation.

God gave the same message to Jerusalem in the days of Jeremiah. After setting forth his general principles for ruling the nations, he applied them to his own people: "Behold, I am shaping disaster against you and devising a plan against you. Return, every one from his evil way, and amend your ways and your deeds" (v. 11). The people of God were clay in the hands of an angry Potter.

Let's Get Jeremiah!

Given the choice between repenting or perishing, one might expect Israel to repent. Sadly, this clay rejected God's message: "That is in vain," they replied. "We will follow our own plans, and will every one act according to the stubbornness of his evil heart" (v. 12). Like most toddlers, the children of Israel had their own agenda. Once they had made their plans, there was little hope of getting them to submit to God's will.

The reason God's people were so stubborn was that they had forgotten God. They had a case of national amnesia. No one had ever heard anything like it: "Ask among the nations, Who has heard the like of this?" (v. 13a). It was like a freak of nature. "Does the snow of Lebanon leave the crags of Sirion?" (v. 14a). Not at that altitude. "Do the mountain waters run dry, the cold flowing streams?" (v. 14b). No, because they are fed by living springs.

> But my people have forgotten me;
>   they make offerings to false gods;
> they made them stumble in their ways,
>   in the ancient roads,
> and to walk into side roads,
>   not the highway. (v. 15)

Here Jeremiah returns to two of his favorite themes. Earlier he had compared Israel to a bride who forgets her wedding ornaments (2:32). That would be unthinkable; yet God's people forgot their love for God. He also stood at the crossroads and mapped out the best path for his people (6:16; cf. 12:5). But then they decided to take a shortcut, leaving God's highway, careening out of control down the back roads of idolatry. Jeremiah was shocked by their behavior. He sensed that "virgin Israel [had] done a very horrible thing" (18:13b).

These verses contain a strong warning for anyone who was raised in the church but has wandered away from God. Once you claimed to be a Christian. Once you read your Bible and prayed. Once you acted like a follower of Jesus Christ. But now you have spiritual amnesia. You did not mean to end up so far away from God, but look where you are! It is time to wake up before it is too late.

For Jerusalem, it was too late. Amnesia soon turned into enmity. "Then they said, 'Come, let us make plots against Jeremiah, for the law shall not perish from the priest, nor counsel from the wise, nor the word from the prophet. Come, let us strike him with the tongue, and let us not pay attention to any of his words'" (v. 18). Those who begin to forget God end up hating him.

First the Israelites rejected God's message; then they attacked his messenger. The leaders hatched another conspiracy. They tried to shut Jeremiah up. "Other priests can teach the law," they said in essence. "Other wise men can give good counsel. Other prophets can speak the Word of the Lord. But we have no use for Jeremiah." Though the prophet had done them good, they repaid him with evil.

> Hear me, O LORD,
>   and listen to the voice of my adversaries.
> Should good be repaid with evil?
>   Yet they have dug a pit for my life.
> Remember how I stood before you
>   to speak good for them,
>   to turn away your wrath from them. (vv. 19, 20)

Though Jeremiah often prayed for his enemies, they dug a pit to capture him.

What happens to people who reject God's message and attack his messenger? They are just clay, remember; so God has the right to do whatever he wants with them:

> [They have made] their land a horror,
>   a thing to be hissed at forever.
> Everyone who passes by it is horrified
>   and shakes his head.
> Like the east wind I will scatter them
>   before the enemy.
> I will show them my back, not my face,
>   in the day of their calamity. (vv. 16, 17)

Ashes to ashes, dust to dust. God will blow them away and turn his back on them.

Jerusalem received the terrible judgments for which Jeremiah prayed:

> Therefore deliver up their children to famine;
>   give them over to the power of the sword;

let their wives become childless and widowed.
    May their men meet death by pestilence,
    their youths be struck down by the sword in battle.
May a cry be heard from their houses,
    when you bring the plunderer suddenly upon them!
For they have dug a pit to take me
    and laid snares for my feet. (vv. 21, 22)

All these things happened when the Babylonians attacked Israel. A cry went up from the houses in Jerusalem at the sudden invasion. The children went hungry; the wives became widows; the men were put to death; and the young men were slain in battle.

Was it right for Jeremiah to ask for these things? Was it charitable to pray,

Yet you, O LORD, know
    all their plotting to kill me.
Forgive not their iniquity,
    nor blot out their sin from your sight.
Let them be overthrown before you;
    deal with them in the time of your anger. (v. 23)

Jeremiah went beyond seeking vindication to being vindictive. At the least he did not display the mercy of the Lord Jesus Christ, who prayed for his enemies and forgave his executioners.

Jeremiah may have been in the wrong, but God has the right to do all the things for which the prophet prayed. He has the right to repay evil with evil. He has the right to put his enemies to the sword. He has the right to let them fall into their own traps. He is not obligated to forgive those who plot against him. After all, he is the Potter.

Jeremiah 18 should strike holy fear into the heart of every mortal. You are only a lump of clay, spinning and spinning on the Potter's wheel. The God who made you can destroy you without a moment's notice. Any potter will smash a pot in an instant if it bears the slightest defect.

Are there any defects in your life? Any sinful attitudes? Any evil deeds? God has just cause to collapse you upon the wheel. Yet before he turns his back forever—in "The time of . . . anger," as Jeremiah calls it in verse 23—he gives an opportunity to turn back to him.

Ask the Potter for mercy. Beg God to forgive your sins. Trust in Jesus Christ for salvation, believing he died on the cross for you, for

As a father shows compassion to his children,
    so the LORD shows compassion to those who fear him.

For he knows our frame;
he remembers that we are dust. (Psalm 103:13, 14)

God knows that you are formed from dust, and sinful dust at that. He has compassion on all who fear him.

Work in Progress

The main reason God took Jeremiah down to the potter's house was to warn about judgment. But the picture of the potter and the clay also gives comfort. If God is the Potter, then he can make something out of the most unpromising blobs of clay. This also is part of his sovereignty.

Eugene Peterson writes:

> No one has ever been able to make a clay pot that is *just* a clay pot. Every pot is also an art form. Pottery is always changing its shape as potters find new proportions, different ways to shape the pots in pleasing combinations of curves. There is no pottery that besides being useful does not also show evidence of beauty. Pottery is artistically shaped, designed, painted, glazed, fired. It is one of the most functional items in life; it is also one of the most beautiful. . . . Useful and beautiful. Functionally necessary and artistically elegant at one and the same time with no thought that the two elements could be separated.[5]

It takes a patient artist to make a pot that is beautiful as well as useful. It takes the kind of potter Jeremiah watched, one who refuses to give up on his work. When there was a flaw in the clay, he did not throw it away; he worked it into something else. F. B. Meyer calls that pot "a memorial of the potter's patience and long-suffering, of his careful use of material, and of his power of repairing loss and making something out of failure and disappointment."[6]

The same could be said of God's people Israel. Though they were crushed for a time, as Jeremiah prophesied, God remade them into a beautiful kingdom.

The same could also be said of every Christian. We come into this world like so many clay pots. Our lives are pitted with blemishes and impurities. We are neither useful nor beautiful. As clay goes, we are not all that easy to work with. We need to be created all over again, which is what the Holy Spirit does in the life of a sinner who trusts in Christ. He makes him or her into something useful and beautiful. If you know Christ, then you are a memorial to God's patience and long-suffering, his careful use of material, and his power of making something out of failure.

Are you happy with the way God is shaping your life? God often makes something out of us that we do not have in mind. We have disappointments in love. There are diseases in our bodies. We have discouragements in our work and desperations in our families. For one reason or another, we are often unhappy with the way life is shaping up. Very likely, if you were behind the potter's wheel, you would make yourself differently. Would you then fashion yourself into the Potter and unseat God from the wheel?

You are not the Potter. You are only clay. The proper thing for clay to do is trust the Potter and yield to his skillful hands. The Swiss Reformer Ulrich Zwingli (1484–1531) once wrote to a friend: "I beseech Christ for this one thing only, that he will enable me to endure all things courageously, and that he break me as a potter's vessel or make me strong, as it pleases him."[7]

Are you willing to trust the Potter? Do you believe that he knows best, designs best, shapes best, and fashions best? If you have given your heart to God, you can trust him to transform you into something useful and beautiful. If that seems hard to believe, it is because he is not even close to being finished yet. He is taking the time to work on the parts of your life that are still lumpy and off-centered. Some parts he may need to smash down and raise up all over again. Will you trust him—really trust him—to do what is best?

Adelaide Pollard (1862–1934) wrote a hymn for willing clay, the kind of clay that stays on the wheel to be shaped in the Potter's hands:

> Have thine own way, Lord! Have thine own way!
> Thou art the potter; I am the clay.
> Mold me and make me after thy will,
> While I am waiting, yielded and still.
>
> Have thine own way, Lord! Have thine own way!
> Hold o'er my being absolute sway!
> Fill with thy Spirit till all shall see
> Christ only, always, living in me!

28

Vessels of Wrath

JEREMIAH 19:1-15

IN HIS ARCHAEOLOGICAL COMPANION to the book of Jeremiah, Philip J. King lists some things a potter needs to perform his craft:

> Associated with the potter's workshop were the potter's wheel, a space for treading, a kiln, a field for storing vessels, a dump for the discards, and a source of water, either a cistern or a stream. As Henk Franken comments: "The potters were living and working near the clay sources and where water was available. They needed a lot of space."[1]

One of these requirements is especially relevant for Jeremiah 19—"a dump for the discards."

Beyond Repair

Jeremiah 19 is the story of Jeremiah's trip to the dump. First God sent the prophet back to the potter's shop to buy a clay jar: "Thus says the LORD, 'Go, buy a potter's earthenware flask'" (v. 1a). The flask was a *baqbuq*, a jar or decanter with a wide body, a narrow neck, and a handle for pouring water. Its name came from the gurgling sound water made when it passed through its narrow opening—*baqbuq, baqbuq, baqbuq.*

Next God sent Jeremiah outside the city: "Take some of the elders of the people and some of the elders of the priests, and go out to the Valley of the Son of Hinnom at the entry of the Potsherd Gate, and proclaim there the words that I tell you" (vv. 1b, 2). So Jeremiah took the leaders of the Jerusalem establishment with him on his shopping trip. And when he had purchased his *baqbuq*, the entire party went straight to the garbage dump on the outskirts of the city, in the Valley of the Son of Hinnom (also known as Topheth), where the rubbish was left to burn. They stood near the Potsherd Gate, where the potters tossed the shards of their broken pottery.

As Jeremiah stood in the potter's field, he began to preach, for the Lord had said, "Proclaim there the words that I tell you. You shall say, 'Hear the word of the LORD, O kings of Judah and inhabitants of Jerusalem. Thus says the LORD of hosts, the God of Israel: Behold, I am bringing such disaster upon this place that the ears of everyone who hears of it will tingle'" (vv. 2b, 3). The tingly feeling Jeremiah described was the kind one gets upon hearing news of a sudden death or tragic accident. The force of the disaster can be felt all the way up to one's ears.

Then Jeremiah did something to make the ears of the elders ring. His instructions from God were these: "Then you shall break the flask in the sight of the men who go with you" (v. 10). So right in the middle of his sermon Jeremiah dashed his new pottery to the ground and said, "'Thus says the LORD of hosts: So will I break this people and this city, as one breaks a potter's vessel, so that it can never be mended'" (v. 11a). The elders looked down and saw Jeremiah's *baqbuq* shattered into a thousand pieces.

Jeremiah 18 was an object lesson in God's sovereignty. Jeremiah 19 is an even more dramatic lesson in God's wrath. The difference between the two lessons is the difference between wet clay and broken pottery. Clay can be reshaped. As long as clay is still on the potter's wheel, something can be done with it. Even if a pot is nearly finished, all the potter needs to do is add water, smash it down, and reshape it as he sees fit. But once a pot has been fired, burnished, and broken, it is beyond repair. Once a *baqbuq* has been smashed, it cannot be remade; its narrow neck is too delicate to be mended. From chapter 18 to chapter 19 Jeremiah moves from the potter's clay to a vessel of wrath.

Jeremiah explained the point of his demonstration by giving a frightening description of God's wrath.

> And in this place I will make void the plans of Judah and Jerusalem, and will cause their people to fall by the sword before their enemies, and by the hand of those who seek their life. I will give their dead bodies for food to the birds of the air and to the beasts of the earth. And I will make this city a horror, a thing to be hissed at. Everyone who passes by it will be horrified and will hiss because of all its wounds. And I will make them eat the flesh of their sons and their daughters, and everyone shall eat the flesh of his neighbor in the siege and in the distress, with which their enemies and those who seek their life afflict them. (vv. 7–9)

God's wrath would include death by sword and indecent burial. The city would be desecrated. Passersby would whistle between their teeth when they saw the ruins. When Jerusalem was besieged and its inhabitants were starving, God's wrath would even include parents eating their children.

The whole city would be destroyed. There scarcely would be room to bury the dead. Indeed, says God, "Men shall bury in Topheth because there will be no place else to bury. Thus will I do to this place, declares the LORD, and to its inhabitants, making this city like Topheth. The houses of Jerusalem and the houses of the kings of Judah . . . shall be defiled like the place of Topheth" (vv. 11b–13). The houses would become like so many shards of broken pottery.

These gruesome things all happened when Jerusalem was besieged by Babylon, right down to the cannibalism. As Jeremiah was later to lament, "The hands of compassionate women have boiled their own children; they became their food during the destruction of the daughter of my people" (Lamentations 4:10). What Jeremiah did with his *baqbuq* was more than just a drama. It was a symbol of judgment that became a reality.

Jeremiah 19 is also an object lesson in the wrath to be revealed at the final judgment. When the prophet preached this sermon, he was standing in the Valley of Ben Hinnom. In the New Testament Ben Hinnom is called Gehenna, usually translated as "hell" (see Matthew 23:33; Mark 9:45; Luke 12:5). Jeremiah's broken *baqbuq* is a symbol of the Hell reserved for all of God's enemies at the end of history.

This vessel of wrath teaches at least three lessons about divine judgment. The wrath of God is just, glorious, and fearsome. To these lessons we must add a fourth based on the good news of the gospel: Jesus Christ is the way to flee from the wrath to come.

The Justice of God's Wrath

To begin with, God's wrath is most just. In this passage, as in almost every other passage we have studied so far, Jeremiah lists the sins of his people. God's wrath was just punishment for their misdeeds.

First, God says, "The people have forsaken me" (19:4a). They had forgotten all about serving the one true God. They had not learned the lesson of the potter and the clay. They were not worshiping the sovereign Lord.

Second, they worshiped false gods: "The people have . . . profaned this place by making offerings in it to other gods whom neither they nor their fathers nor the kings of Judah have known" (v. 4). Their idolatrous practices were widespread. Jeremiah reminded them of "all the houses on whose roofs offerings have been offered to all the host of heaven, and drink offerings have been poured out to other gods" (v. 13b). The people of Jerusalem performed the rituals of pagan astrology right out in the open.

Third, they murdered their children. "They have filled this place with the blood of innocents, and have built the high places of Baal to burn their sons in the fire as burnt offerings to Baal, which I did not command or decree, nor did it come into my mind" (vv. 4b, 5). The leaders of Israel knew very well what Jeremiah was talking about. He had preached about it before. Back in chapters 7 and 8 he had condemned the child sacrifices being performed in the Valley of Slaughter. Now he was standing in the very place where these atrocities occurred. The valley reeked of sin.

All these accusations could be sustained against postmodern America. We, too, have forsaken God. We, too, have followed after other gods. Not just one god but dozens—money, sex, power, pleasure, food, beauty, success, comfort, self. We, too, have shed the innocent blood of children through abortion and infanticide. If Jeremiah were alive today, he would stand outside the clinics to condemn the abortions being done inside.

The point of Jeremiah's message is that there is justice in God's wrath. Every sin deserves the wrath and curse of God. To break even one commandment is to break the whole Law of God (James 2:10). But these sins especially deserve divine judgment. Is there a sin more heinous than forsaking God? More foolish than worshiping other gods? More vile than murdering one's own children?

God's punishment would fit these crimes. "Therefore, behold, days are coming, declares the LORD, when this place shall no more be called Topheth, or the Valley of the Son of Hinnom, but the Valley of Slaughter" (19:6). Those who slaughtered their children became cannibals. Those who observed pagan rites on their rooftops had their homes destroyed. For God to pour out his wrath against such sins, and such sinners, in such a way, was most just.

America's greatest theologian, Jonathan Edwards (1703–1758), once preached a sermon called "The Justice of God in the Damnation of Sinners."[2] In it he argued that it would be just for God to destroy every sinner. First, "If God should forever cast you off, it would be exactly agreeable to your treatment of him." You have not loved God, have not served God, and have not thanked him for all his goodness. Why, then, should you receive eternal life?

Edwards went on to show that you also deserve judgment for the way you have treated Jesus, others, and yourself. Your sins offend Christ, harm your neighbor, and wound your own soul. Edwards concludes: "Thus I have proposed some things to your consideration which, if you are not exceeding blind, senseless, and perverse, will stop your mouth and convince you that you stand justly condemned before God."[3]

The Glory of God's Wrath

If God's wrath is just, it must also be glorious. By that I mean that it brings glory to God. Justice is one of his glorious attributes. It is right and good for him to punish his enemies. Their destruction demonstrates his power, his holiness, and his sovereignty. God is as just as he is merciful, and his justice is no less glorious than his mercy.

The glory of God's wrath is explained in Romans 9, the great chapter about God's sovereignty in electing his people. Here Paul wrestles with the fact that God loved Jacob but hated Esau (Romans 9:13). He recognizes what this means about the sovereignty of the grace of God, that salvation "depends not on human will or exertion, but on God, who has mercy" (v. 16). Although God has mercy on some, he hardens others in their sin (v. 18).

How can this be? No sooner does Paul teach the sovereignty of God's grace than our minds are filled with questions: How can the will of God overrule my freedom? "You will say to me then, 'Why does he still find fault? For who can resist his will?'" (v. 19). If God determines whom he will save and whom he will destroy, then how can he hold me responsible for my sin?

The Scripture answers these questions by referring to what Isaiah said on the subject of clay pots: "But who are you, O man, to answer back to God? Will what is molded say to its molder, 'Why have you made me like this?'" (v. 20). Paul is actually quoting from two passages at once—Isaiah 45:9 and 29:16. His point is that God is the Creator and we are only creatures. It is God's prerogative to show mercy to us or to harden us as he pleases. We may not understand the ways of God, but we have no right to question them. God is the potter; we are the clay. The vessels he makes are his to create, his to protect, and his to destroy.

As Paul proceeds to defend God's right to destroy his creatures, he calls to mind the prophecies of Jeremiah 18, 19:

> Has the potter no right over the clay, to make out of the same lump one vessel for honorable use and another for dishonorable use? What if God, desiring to show his wrath and to make known his power, has endured with much patience vessels of wrath prepared for destruction, in order to make known the riches of his glory for vessels of mercy, which he has prepared beforehand for glory? (Romans 9:21–23)

These are not hypothetical questions. They are not questions that may be answered one way or the other. They demand a yes, which is why verse 21 begins with "Has the potter no right?"

Here the Scripture teaches that God's wrath is for God's glory. The potter has the right to destroy as well as to create. God is glorified when he reshapes a pot on his wheel to make it beautiful. He is glorified when he places earthenware on the shelves of his workshop to preserve it for all eternity. But he is also glorified when he dashes a *baqbuq* to the ground. God is glorified by the ignoble pottery as well as the noble. He is glorified in his wrath as well as in his mercy.

The Fear of God's Wrath

The justice and the glory of God's wrath ought to produce holy fear. God's enemies are not the only ones whose ears tingle when they hear of God's sovereign judgment. It seems fearsome even to his friends.

The Apostle Paul worshiped God for his justice as well as for his mercy. He recognized the way in which wrath revealed the glory of God. But the prospect of judgment still filled him with distress. "I am speaking the truth in Christ—I am not lying; my conscience bears me witness in the Holy Spirit—that I have great sorrow and unceasing anguish in my heart. For I could wish that I myself were accursed and cut off from Christ for the sake of my brothers, my kinsmen according to the flesh" (Romans 9:1–3). Paul was filled with holy fear by the wrath of God and with anguish for those still subject to it.

Jeremiah had the same holy fear. He could hear the rapidly approaching hoofbeats of divine judgment. In previous chapters he had revealed the impression this knowledge had made upon his soul. For example, "Nor have I desired the day of sickness" (17:16). That short phrase speaks volumes about Jeremiah's experience as a prophet of judgment. He is often called the Weeping Prophet, but he might as well be called the Reluctant Prophet. What anguish it must have been for him to deliver so many fearful prophecies of divine judgment. With every sinew of his being, he longed for his people to be delivered from the wrath of God.

Jeremiah did not desire "The day of sickness." In fact, he prayed against it. Several times God commanded him not to intercede on behalf of his people: "Do not pray for this people, or lift up a cry or prayer on their behalf" (11:14; cf. 14:11; 15:1). But Jeremiah did it anyway. He could not help himself. He loved his people so much that he had to pray for them: "Remember how I stood before you to speak good for them, to turn away your wrath from them" (18:20b). Jeremiah stood in the gap for the people of God. He prayed against the judgment of God, but it came anyway. Despite Jeremiah's many pleadings, his people simply would not listen.

So God had the last word. He did exactly what he always said he would do. For when the prophet was finished with his object lesson, "Jeremiah came from Topheth, where the LORD had sent him to prophesy, and he stood in the court of the LORD's house and said to all the people: 'Thus says the LORD of hosts, the God of Israel, behold, I am bringing upon this city and upon all its towns all the disaster that I have pronounced against it, because they have stiffened their neck, refusing to hear my words'" (19:14, 15). The wrath of God is as inevitable and as just as it is fearsome.

"Fly from the Wrath to Come"

Is it really true that there is a place of endless torment for the wicked? Has God indeed prepared a lake of fire for the devil and all his servants? The best way to begin answering questions about the reality of Hell is to remember that most of the Biblical teaching on the subject comes from the lips of Jesus Christ. Jesus is the chief Biblical proponent of the doctrine of Hell. Whenever we recite the Apostles' Creed and confess that Jesus Christ "descended into hell," we are reminded that he has been through hell himself. Surely the reason he teaches us about it in his Word is so we will make all possible haste to escape eternal judgment.

For Jesus Christ has himself provided a way—the *only* way—to escape the wrath of God. He gives a clue about the way of escape at the beginning of Matthew 26. There he has just finished his discourse on the sheep and the goats. He has explained that when the Son of Man comes in his glory, "Before him will be gathered all the nations, and he will separate people one from another as a shepherd separates the sheep from the goats" (25:32). He has explained how the King will invite his sheep (his friends) into "The kingdom prepared for [them] from the foundation of the world" (v. 34). And Jesus has just finished saying that the King will banish the goats (his enemies) to everlasting punishment (v. 46).

Notice what comes next: "When Jesus had finished all these sayings, he said to his disciples, 'You know that after two days the Passover is coming, and the Son of Man will be delivered up to be crucified'" (Matthew 26:1, 2). Jesus passed immediately from the threat of wrath to the promise of his own crucifixion. He went straight from hell to the cross. And rightly so! For it was on the cross that Jesus Christ endured the wrath and curse of God. It was on the cross that he suffered the hell that we deserve for our sins. It was on the cross that he became like the *baqbuq* in the Valley of Slaughter, shattered by the judgment of God. It was on the cross that Jesus Christ became for us a vessel of wrath.

This is why we must not lose our grip on the reality of divine judgment. We cannot understand what Christ was doing on the cross unless we believe in the justice, the glory, and the fearsomeness of the wrath of God. Only when we know what our sins deserve can we know the full extent of the love of Christ. Only then can we testify, with the Apostle Paul, that we "were by nature children of wrath, like the rest of mankind. But God, being rich in mercy, because of the great love with which he loved us, even when we were dead in our trespasses, made us alive together with Christ—by grace you have been saved" (Ephesians 2:3b–5).

Accepting the doctrine of judgment is crucial not only for our faith, but also for our evangelism. Escaping the wrath of God may not be a "felt need" for many people, but it is most certainly a real need. When you tell friends and family what the Lord has done for you, make sure you tell them this: "Jesus has saved me from the wrath to come." If we are weak in evangelism, could it be that we do not fully appreciate the justice or the fearsomeness of God's wrath?

The oldest member of the Westminster Assembly, Oliver Bowles, wrote a wise book about evangelical preaching. In it he observed that the doctrine of the wrath of God is preached "unto edification, not unto destruction."[4] This is as true for evangelism as it is for evangelistic preaching. We do not teach about the eternal judgment of God so that people will be destroyed; we teach it so they might be saved. The wrath of God is just and fearsome, but not inevitable. Jesus Christ provides the way—the only way—to escape the wrath of God. If you are frightened of becoming a vessel of wrath, then trust in Christ for salvation.

John Bunyan (1628–1688) wrote a beautiful story about a man who feared the wrath of God so greatly that he went running to Christ. Bunyan's book, called *The Pilgrim's Progress*, begins like this:

> I dreamed, and behold I saw a man clothed with rags, standing in a certain place, with . . . a book in his hand, and a great burden upon his back. I looked, and saw him open the book, and read therein; and as he read he wept and trembled, and not being able longer to contain, he brake out with a lamentable cry, saying, "What shall I do?"
>
> In this plight . . . he could not be silent long, because that his trouble increased. Wherefore at length he brake his mind to his wife and children; and thus he began to talk to them. "O my dear Wife," said he, "and you, the children of my bowels, I your dear friend am in myself undone, by reason of a burden that lieth hard upon me; moreover, I am for certain informed that this our city will be burned with fire from heaven, in which fearful overthrow both myself, with thee, my wife, and you, my sweet babes, shall miserably come to ruin; except (the which, yet I see not) some way of escape can be found, whereby we may be delivered." At this his relations were sore amazed; not for that they believed that what he had said to them

was true, but because they thought that some frenzy distemper had got into his head. . . .

Now, I saw upon a time, when he was walking in the Fields, that he was reading in his book and greatly distressed in his mind; and as he read, he burst out, as he had done before, crying, "What shall I do to be saved?" . . .

I looked then and saw a man named Evangelist coming to him and asked, "Wherefore doest thou cry?" He answered, "Sir, I perceive, by the book in my hand, that I am condemned to die and after that to come to judgement; and I find that I am not willing to do the first, nor able to do the second."

Then said Evangelist, "Why not willing to die? since this life is attended with so many evils?" The man answered, "Because I fear that this burden that is upon my back will sink me lower than the grave; and I shall fall into Tophet. And, sir, if I be not fit to go to prison, I am not fit (I am sure) to go to judgement and from thence to execution; and the thoughts of these things make me cry."

Then said Evangelist, "If this be thy condition, why standest thou still?" He answered, "Because I know not whither to go." Then he gave him a parchment roll, and there was written within, "Fly from the wrath to come." . . .

So I saw in my dream that the man began to run. Now he had not run far from his own door, but his wife and children perceiving it, began to cry after him to return. But the man put his fingers in his ears and ran on crying, "Life, life, eternal life."[5]

The man became a pilgrim. He entered the narrow gate and followed the narrow path to salvation. He went first to the cross, where the great burden of his sins was rolled away, then ran on and on until he reached God's heavenly city.

Pilgrim's Progress is really the story of every Christian. Christians begin their lives in a city doomed to destruction, weighed down by the burden of their sins. There they remain until some evangelist tells them to flee from the wrath to come. And then they run, with all possible haste, into the arms of Jesus Christ. They run to the narrow gate that leads to eternal life. They run to the cross where they can lose their burden of sin. They run and run down God's narrow path until they reach his glory.

If you have already started your own pilgrimage, do not turn back. If not, then you are in danger of becoming a vessel of wrath. It is time to start running, with your fingers in your ears, shouting, "Life, life, eternal life."

29

Dark Night of the Soul

JEREMIAH 20:1–18

THE WRITER KATHLEEN NORRIS once spent a year and a half with the Benedictine monks of St. John's Abbey in Minnesota. During her stay she discovered that an important part of monastic life is the continuous reading of entire books of the Bible, section by section, during morning and evening prayer.

By the end of her sabbatical Norris had heard the entire New Testament and large portions of the Old. She writes:

> The most remarkable experience of all was plunging into the prophet Jeremiah at morning prayer in late September one year, and staying with him through mid-November. We began with chapter 1, and read straight through, ending at chapter 22:17. Listening to Jeremiah is one . . . way to get your blood going in the morning; it puts caffeine to shame.[1]

Norris went on to explain how Jeremiah's sufferings became the agonies of her own soul:

> Opening oneself to a prophet as anguished as Jeremiah is painful. On some mornings, I found it impossible. . . . The voice of Jeremiah is compelling, often on an overwhelmingly personal level. One morning, I was so worn out by the emotional roller coaster of chapter 20 that after prayers I walked to my apartment and went back to bed. This passionate soliloquy, which begins with a bitter outburst on the nature of the prophet's calling, moves quickly into denial. Jeremiah's anger at the way his enemies deride him rears up, and also fear and sorrow. His statement of confidence in God seems forced under the circumstances, and a brief doxology feels more ironic than not, being followed by a bitter cry. The chapter concludes with an anguished question.[2]

Jeremiah 20 gives plenty of reasons to dive back under the covers. It is the low point of Jeremiah's ministry, his dark night of the soul. In it he blames God, rejects his calling, and curses the day he was born.

Jeremiah Does Time

The man to blame for Jeremiah's despair was a priest named Pashhur. As chief of security at the temple, Pashhur was in charge of the prophecy police. He heard Jeremiah had dashed a clay pot to the ground in the Valley of the Son of Hinnom (19:1–15). He also heard the gist of the prophecy Jeremiah uttered in the precincts of the temple, that Jerusalem was about to be smashed to smithereens. That sounded like treason; so Pashhur had God's prophet arrested and tortured: "Now Pashhur the priest, the son of Immer, who was chief officer in the house of the LORD, heard Jeremiah prophesying these things. Then Pashhur beat Jeremiah the prophet, and put him in the stocks that were in the upper Benjamin Gate of the house of the LORD" (20:1, 2). "Post-Christian" regimes are not always congenial to God's disciples.

Jeremiah had been threatened before, but this time the authorities took action. First they thrashed him, and then they tortured him. Putting Jeremiah in "stocks" meant more than just locking him up. The Hebrew word refers to twisting. They put Jeremiah on the rack, clamping his wrists and twisting his body into painful contortions.

What Pashhur did was very wicked. Apparently he felt some remorse because he freed Jeremiah the next morning. But the damage had already been done. Pashhur had beaten the Lord's anointed, and opposing faithful ministers always brings God's curse.

Upon his release, Jeremiah greeted Pashhur with a message of judgment—not from himself, but from the Lord:

> The next day, when Pashhur released Jeremiah from the stocks, Jeremiah said to him, "The LORD does not call your name Pashhur, but Terror on Every Side. For thus says the LORD: Behold, I will make you a terror to yourself and to all your friends. They shall fall by the sword of their enemies while you look on. And I will give all Judah into the hand of the king of Babylon. He shall carry them captive to Babylon, and shall strike them down with the sword. Moreover, I will give all the wealth of the city, all its gains, all its prized belongings, and all the treasures of the kings of Judah into the hand of their enemies, who shall plunder them and seize them and carry them to Babylon. And you, Pashhur, and all who dwell in your house, shall go into captivity. To Babylon you shall go, and there you shall die, and there you shall be buried, you and all your friends, to whom you have prophesied falsely." (vv. 3–6)

This prophecy is significant for what it says about Judah. Jeremiah often warned that judgment would come from the north, but until this point he had not mentioned the invader by name. Here, for the first time, we learn that Babylon will be the instrument of divine judgment. From this point on Jeremiah will mention that fierce city more than two hundred times.

The prophecy also had significance for Pashhur. Jeremiah's back was still throbbing, and his wrists were still chafing from his imprisonment. But Pashhur's punishment would be even more severe. His friends would fall by the sword or die in captivity, a prophecy that must have put a damper on his social life. His lies would be exposed and his crimes repaid with death. Jeremiah even had the satisfaction of giving Pashhur a nickname that was bound to stick: Magor-Missabib. Pashhur means "fruitful on every side," but Magor-Missabib means "Terror on Every Side" (v. 3).

Take It to the Lord in Prayer

That is the story, but not the whole story. It does not tell what went through Jeremiah's mind during his night in jail. Jeremiah 20 is best understood as the prophet's account of his night in the stocks, his dark night of the soul.

There are at least four valuable lessons about suffering in these verses. They are relevant for all times because God's people always suffer, but they are especially relevant for our own post-Christian times.

The first lesson is perhaps the most important: *Suffering may be taken to the Lord in prayer.* Jeremiah had good reason to be discouraged. For one thing, he was in danger.

> For I hear many whispering.
> > Terror is on every side!
> "Denounce him! Let us denounce him!"
> > say all my close friends,
> > watching for my fall.
> "Perhaps he will be deceived;
> > then we can overcome him
> > and take our revenge on him." (v. 10)

The priests gathered in the corners of the temple. Jeremiah heard their nasty whispers and saw their bony fingers pointed in his direction. Even his friends waited for him to take a false step so they could pounce on him. He already had been beaten and locked up. What would they do to him next? Jeremiah's persecution was perhaps only beginning.

The prophet was also discouraged, because he had become a laughingstock: "I have become a laughingstock all the day; everyone mocks me" (v. 7b). The comedians in Jerusalem were getting their funniest material at Jeremiah's expense. "There goes that crazy old Jeremiah. Did you hear what he did yesterday? He took a brand-new pot and smashed it outside the city walls. The guy needs a straitjacket. He keeps babbling about enemies coming to destroy the city."

One insult was especially vicious. They called Jeremiah Magor-Missabib, "Terror on every side" (v. 10). In other words, they took his rebuke of Pashhur and used it against him. Verbal abuse may not seem very serious compared to a good beating, but eventually ridicule starts to take its toll. Jeremiah was despised and rejected.

Jeremiah's friends betrayed him—even, he thought, the closest friend of all: "O Lord, you have deceived me, and I was deceived; you are stronger than I, and you have prevailed" (v. 7a). Jeremiah started to doubt whether God's Word was really true after all. God forced him to prophesy, and he prophesied, but where was the promised judgment? Had Jeremiah become a false prophet? He thought he had been speaking the Word of the Lord, but maybe the Lord had deceived him (cf. 1 Kings 22:22, 23; Ezekiel 14:9).

The only thing Jeremiah could do with his doubts and sufferings was take them to the Lord in prayer. He offered the prayer of a suffering believer. One can imagine him in solitary confinement, exhausted by physical and emotional pain. Yet the very first words out of his mouth formed an invocation: "O Lord," he cried.

God gives us permission to take our sufferings directly to him. This is what godly people have done throughout history. It is what Job did on the ash heap, when he lamented the loss of his family (Job 3). It is what Elijah did under the broom tree when he wanted the Lord to take his life (1 Kings 19:4). It is what David did in the cave when he fled from Saul (Psalm 57). It is what Jonah did in the belly of the great fish, when he ran away from God (Jonah 2). It is even what Jesus Christ did on the cross when he was crucified to atone for his people's sins: "My God, my God, why have you forsaken me?" (Matthew 27:46).

Take your sufferings to that secret place where you meet God in prayer. That is where you must take them. Where else can you unburden your heart so freely? Who else will comfort you so tenderly? There is no need to hide your troubles. Take them to the Lord in prayer, the way Jeremiah did.

Fire in the Bones

The second lesson Jeremiah 20 teaches about suffering is that *believers sometimes suffer for God's sake.*

Jeremiah knew why people hated him. The needle seemed to be stuck in the same place on his record album. People were getting sick of hearing him preach judgment all the time.

> For whenever I speak, I cry out,
>   I shout, "Violence and destruction!"
> For the word of the LORD has become for me
>   a reproach and derision all day long. (v. 8)

God was to blame for Jeremiah's problems. It was not the prophet's fault that he was insulted all day long. He just said whatever God told him to say. Although people like Pashhur blamed the messenger, their real problem was with the message. Jeremiah suffered for God's sake.

As Jeremiah reflected on his problem, he came up with a possible solution: "I will not mention him, or speak any more in his name" (v. 9a). He said, "That's it. I'm through. I'm going to hang up my sandals and get a real job. I will not speak the Word of the Lord any longer."

There was only one problem with trying to keep God's Word bottled up inside. As Vance Havner comments, "Jeremiah announces the impossible; he resigns and then declares immediately that he cannot resign; he quits but he cannot quit."[3]

> If I say, "I will not mention him,
>   or speak any more in his name,"
> there is in my heart as it were a burning fire
>   shut up in my bones,
> and I am weary with holding it in,
>   and I cannot. (v. 9)

This is another familiar text from Jeremiah that is usually taken out of context. It is often used as an inspirational verse for preachers. And so it is. The Word of God *is* like an unquenchable, uncontainable fire in the bones of the gospel minister. I sit at my desk with the Scriptures open before me, longing for the return of the Lord's Day. I labor during the week with a holy impatience for the call to worship to be read, the hymns to be sung, and the offering to be collected so the sermon can begin. There are times when the Word of God weighs upon me so heavily that preaching is a catharsis, the release of a burden seemingly too great to bear a moment longer.

When Jeremiah spoke about the fire in his bones, however, he was not speaking about the pleasures of ministry. He was not testifying to the delights of preaching in the Holy Spirit. He was not saying that his heart was aflame with the gospel. Rather, his heart burned with judgment. The fiery word in his bones was law rather than grace. He was not eager to preach but reluctant, for he knew that judgment would pour out as soon as he opened his mouth. Jeremiah would have given anything to have a mute ministry, but the Word of God would not allow him to remain silent. The fire in his bones inevitably blazed forth from his lips.

This reminds those who teach to say only what God says in his Word. This is one of the great lessons of Jeremiah's ministry. He was surrounded by false prophets who said whatever people wanted to hear. They said, "Peace, peace" even when there was no peace (6:14; 8:11). But Jeremiah was a true prophet. The distinguishing mark of a true prophet is that he preaches nothing except God's Word. When there was peace Jeremiah said, "Peace"; but when there was no peace, he said, "No peace." Faithful ministers preach law as well as grace, justice as well as mercy, judgment as well as salvation. Authentic preaching disturbs as well as comforts.

Sometimes preaching leads to suffering. Proclaiming the true Word of God may lead to opposition, hostility, and even persecution, as it did for Jeremiah. Sometimes believers suffer for the sake of God's Word, especially if they live in a culture that has turned its back on God.

At such times the Christian lives by God's calling. Jeremiah needed to take courage from the promises God had made when he first commissioned him to be a prophet: "I make you this day a fortified city, an iron pillar, and bronze walls, against the whole land, against the kings of Judah, its officials, its priests, and the people of the land. They will fight against you, but they shall not prevail against you, for I am with you, declares the LORD, to deliver you" (1:18, 19). That commission made it clear that Jeremiah would suffer for God's sake. Yet the Lord promised more than suffering; he promised that his prophet would be saved.

Jesus Christ makes the same promise to his disciples. Once he explained how they would suffer for his sake. They would be mistreated and hated by the world. For Christ's sake they would even be put to death, as events later confirmed. But Jesus ended with a promise: "I have said these things to you, that in me you may have peace. In the world you will have tribulation. But take heart; I have overcome the world" (John 16:33).

That is a wonderful verse to commit to memory and apply to daily life. Christians have many troubles in this world. We are sometimes depressed, often disheartened, frequently discouraged. Sometimes we ask, "Why is this happening to me?" Jesus teaches that suffering for God's sake is not a surprise. In this world you will have trouble. But take heart! Christ has overcome the world.

Call to Worship

Jeremiah took heart during his dark night of the soul. Suddenly he interrupted his complaint to hold a mini worship service. He was alone and afraid, depressed and discouraged, but he offered a short psalm of praise to God (20:11–13). From this a third lesson is to be learned: *God is always to be praised, even in the midst of suffering.*

Jeremiah's worship service was short but complete. His psalm contained three elements—a confession of faith, a prayer for deliverance, and a hymn of praise.

His confession of faith reads like this:

> But the LORD is with me as a dread warrior;
>   therefore my persecutors will stumble;
>   they will not overcome me.
> They will be greatly shamed,
>   for they will not succeed.
> Their eternal dishonor
>   will never be forgotten. (v. 11)

Jeremiah did not understand what was happening to him. Even the Lord seemed to be against him. Yet he continued to testify to what he knew to be true about God's character. In Calvin's judgment, "Here the Prophet sets up God's aid against all the plottings formed against him. However, then, might perfidious friends on one hand try privately to entrap him, and open enemies might on the other hand publicly oppose him, he yet doubted not but that God would be a sufficient protection to him."[4]

Jeremiah knew that the Lord was with him even though it *felt* as though God was far away. The prophet knew that the Lord is strong even if he seems powerless. He knew that the wicked would be defeated even when they appeared triumphant. So the prophet boldly confessed that the Lord would save him.

Next, Jeremiah prayed for help:

> O LORD of hosts, who tests the righteous,
>   who sees the heart and the mind,
> let me see your vengeance upon them,
>   for to you have I committed my cause. (v. 12)

Jeremiah did not take matters into his own hands but committed his cause to the Lord. He prayed that he would be vindicated, while his enemies were punished.

Jeremiah closed his worship with a hymn of praise. He burst into song:

Sing to the LORD;
   praise the LORD!
For he has delivered the life of the needy
   from the hand of evildoers. (v. 13)

One can imagine Jeremiah bent over in his stocks as he sang. He may not have had breath to sing a long hymn, but he could manage at least a short song of praise. Like Paul and Silas after him (Acts 16:25), he praised the Lord from prison.

It is also possible that Jeremiah added this stanza to his song *after* he was released from prison. It is striking that his psalm refers to the needy person in the singular. Literally, the Lord "delivered the life of the needy" (20:13), meaning the prophet himself. He came through his doubts to a place of strong confidence in the Lord. Jeremiah thus shows how to praise God during the dark night of the soul.

Like Jeremiah, the German theologian Dietrich Bonhoeffer (1906–1945) was imprisoned for the sake of God's Word. Bonhoeffer endured his dark night of the soul in a Nazi concentration camp. Yet he did not stop praising God: "I am lonely, but Thou leavest me not. I am restless, but with Thee there is peace."[5]

It is always good to praise the Lord, but especially when one is suffering. The best thing to do when discouraged is to go to worship. Keep confessing, keep praying, keep singing. Even when you have a complaint to make to God, confess your faith in him, pray for deliverance, and praise his name.

The Final Question

It is tempting to end with Jeremiah's psalm of praise, but that is not how the prophet himself ended. The Bible must be taken as it comes, and this time it ends on a downer:

Cursed be the day
   on which I was born!
The day when my mother bore me,
   let it not be blessed!
Cursed be the man who brought the news to my father,
"A son is born to you,"
   making him very glad.
Let that man be like the cities
   that the LORD overthrew without pity;
let him hear a cry in the morning
   and an alarm at noon,
because he did not kill me in the womb;

so my mother would have been my grave,
and her womb forever great. (vv. 14–17)

Instead of celebrating his birthday, Jeremiah cursed it. He wanted to reach back into history and curse everything and everyone who had anything to do with his birth. He wished the man who brought his father the good news had strangled him instead. He wished, in fact, that God would treat him as harshly as he treated Sodom and Gomorrah.[6]

Jeremiah's mood swung from praising to cursing with dizzying speed. One verse is a paean of high praise; the next is an imprecation of utter despair. Some scholars have thus concluded that verse 14 "can hardly belong after verse 13."[7] They view chapter 20 as a hodgepodge of Jeremiah's sayings. Even Calvin was mystified; to him it seemed "a levity unworthy of the holy man to pass suddenly from thanksgiving to God into imprecations, as though he had forgotten himself."[8]

Perhaps Jeremiah *had* forgotten himself, but these verses do belong together. They may not belong together by logic, but who says the life of the soul is always logical? Jeremiah's curses follow his praises because that is the way it was during his dark night of the soul.

We must recognize the confusing, almost schizophrenic nature of the Christian life. We are at one and the same time saints and sinners. Although our sins are forgiven, we continue to sin. One minute we praise, and the next we curse; one moment we rejoice in God's plan, and the very next we resist his will.

Jeremiah's curses form a bitter lament, the bitterest in the book of Jeremiah, if not in all of Scripture. Derek Kidner observes that they are intended "To bowl us over. Together with other tortured cries from him and his fellow sufferers, these raw wounds in Scripture remain lest we forget the sharpness of the age-long struggle, or the frailty of the finest overcomers."[9]

Jeremiah stopped just short of cursing God or his parents, both of which were capital offenses in Israel (Leviticus 20:9). He did not actually think about ending it all, but he did wish it had never started:

Why did I come out from the womb
   to see toil and sorrow,
   and spend my days in shame? (20:18)

Jeremiah knew the trouble of persecution, the sorrow of watching his people reject God's Word, and the shame of public humiliation. All this suffering placed a giant question mark over his existence. Though he was strong in his faith, there were times when he had more questions than answers. On this occasion he questioned his creation, his salvation, and his vocation.[10]

Jeremiah's queries teach a final lesson about suffering: *Although suffering can place a question mark over existence, it never has the last word.* Chapter 20 ends with a question that Jeremiah himself was in no shape to answer, but for which Scripture provides a good answer. Why did Jeremiah come out of the womb to see trouble and sorrow?

As we have seen, God had already given Jeremiah the answer when he first called him into the ministry. The prophet needed to be reminded of the first thing the Lord ever said to him:

> Before I formed you in the womb I knew you,
> and before you were born I consecrated you;
> I appointed you a prophet to the nations. (1:5)

Jeremiah traced his troubles back to the womb. But he did not go back far enough! God could trace his promises back *before* the womb. He'd had a purpose for Jeremiah's life since before the beginning of time. The prophet needed to be reminded that from all eternity, the Lord had set him apart for salvation and ministry.

Perhaps you need the same reminder. Are you suffering? Are you ridiculed by your friends or family? Are enemies waiting to trip you up? Are you weighed down by the ungodliness of contemporary society? Are there times when you wonder why you ever came out of your mother's womb?

This is why. God set you apart for salvation and for ministry. Before the beginning of time he planned to save you in Christ: "He chose us in him before the foundation of the world" (Ephesians 1:4). Then he set you apart to do his work. "For we are his workmanship, created in Christ Jesus for good works, which God prepared beforehand, that we should walk in them" (Ephesians 2:10). Suffering can place a giant question mark over our lives, but the grace of God always has the last word.

30

No King but Christ

JEREMIAH 21:1—22:30

WHO IS YOUR KING, and how does he rule?

Everyone has a king. In the words of that popular theologian Bob Dylan, "You're gonna have to serve somebody." Dylan is right. You do have to serve somebody, even if that somebody is only yourself. Who is your king, and how does he (or she, for that matter) rule?

The chief priests of Israel chose their king at the trial of Jesus of Nazareth before Pontius Pilate:

> He [Pilate] said to the Jews, "Behold your King!" They cried out, "Away with him, away with him, crucify him!" Pilate said to them, "Shall I crucify your King?" The chief priests answered, "We have no king but Caesar." (John 19:14b, 15)

With those chilling words the leaders of Israel rejected the High King of Heaven and embraced the kings of the earth. They wanted to serve Caesar rather than Christ. They preferred the harsh rule of tyranny to the gentle reign of God's kingdom.

Who is your king, and how does he rule?

A Royal Disaster

The message of Jeremiah 21, 22 is that there is no good king but Christ. These two chapters—which close the book on the kings of Judah—reveal that kingship had turned out to be a royal disaster. Each of the last four Judean monarchs was a bad king, and each met a horrible fate. As Jeremiah prophesied, "The wind shall shepherd all your shepherds, and your lovers shall go into captivity" (22:22a). The last kings of Judah were gone with the wind.

First came Josiah's young son Shallum, also known as Jehoahaz. Shallum was the people's choice when Josiah died in battle at Megiddo (2 Chronicles 36:1), but he lasted only three months (until 609 BC). At the time of Jeremiah's writing he had already been deposed by Pharaoh Neco and carried off to Egypt (2 Kings 23:30–33). Jeremiah performed a eulogy for Shallum because he would never, ever return:

> Weep not for him who is dead,
>   nor grieve for him,
> but weep bitterly for him who goes away,
>   for he shall return no more
>   to see his native land.

For thus says the LORD concerning Shallum the son of Josiah, king of Judah, who reigned instead of Josiah his father, and who went away from this place: "He shall return here no more, but in the place where they have carried him captive, there shall he die, and he shall never see this land again." (Jeremiah 22:10–12; cf. 2 Kings 23:34)

Then came wicked Jehoiakim (609–598 BC), another of Josiah's sons (vv. 18–23). He never even made it into captivity:

> With the burial of a donkey he shall be buried,
>   dragged and dumped beyond the gates of Jerusalem. (22:19)

That is exactly what happened when Nebuchadrezzar marched on Jerusalem in December of 598 BC. Jehoiakim was given a donkey's burial. His body was treated like an animal carcass. The historian Josephus records that it was "Thrown before the walls, without any burial."[1] In keeping with the words of the prophet, the nation did not even mourn his passing:

Therefore this is what the LORD says about Jehoiakim son of Josiah king of Judah:

> "They shall not lament for him, saying,
>   'Ah, my brother!' or 'Ah, sister!'
> They shall not lament for him, saying,
>   'Ah, lord!' or 'Ah, his majesty!'" (v. 18)

This is the Biblical version of "Don't Cry for Me, Argentina." Jehoiakim's family and subjects were not sorry to see him go.

Then came Jehoiachin (598–597 BC), son of Jehoiakim, who ascended

the throne when he was still a teenager (vv. 24–30; cf. 2 Kings 24:10–17).
Even if he had been a ring on God's finger, he would have been yanked off:

> As I live, declares the LORD, though Coniah [or Jehoiachin] the son of Je-
> hoiakim, king of Judah, were the signet ring on my right hand, yet I would
> tear you off and give you into the hand of those who seek your life, into the
> hand of those of whom you are afraid, even into the hand of Nebuchadnez-
> zar king of Babylon and into the hand of the Chaldeans. I will hurl you and
> the mother who bore you into another country, where you were not born,
> and there you shall die. But to the land to which they will long to return,
> there they shall not return. (vv. 24–27)

These prophecies also have become facts of history. A tablet in the Berlin
Museum lists Jehoiachin along with the oil and the barley the Babylonians
carried back to their capital.[2] He was treated like a piece of broken pottery:

> Is this man Coniah [or Jehoiachin] a despised, broken pot,
>   a vessel no one cares for?
> Why are he and his children hurled and cast
>   into a land that they do not know? (v. 28)

Last came Zedekiah, although Jeremiah told his story first (21:1–8). Zedekiah was the vassal who vacillated. The Babylonians installed him as their
interim king in Jerusalem (598–587 BC). For a decade he danced like a marionette on Babylonian strings. But when he tried to cross his overlords, they
moved in for the kill (cf. Jeremiah 52). As Jeremiah 21 opens, the Babylonians
are at the gates. They have come to take Zedekiah away.

Expect a Miracle?

The kings all failed. Then, at last, the nation turned to God in prayer. It would
have been almost comical had it not been so pathetic. For forty long years
Jeremiah prophesied the judgment to come. He warned and warned his people
that God would punish them for their sins. Had they listened? Had they repented? Had they changed their ways?

This is how the Lord summarized Jeremiah's forty years of fruitless
ministry:

> Go up to Lebanon, and cry out,
>   and lift up your voice in Bashan;
> cry out from Abarim,
>   for all your lovers are destroyed.
> I spoke to you in your prosperity,

but you said, 'I will not listen.'
This has been your way from your youth,
  that you have not obeyed my voice. (22:20, 21)

That is an apt summary of the first twenty chapters of Jeremiah. The prophet warned the people when they felt secure, but they would not listen. They said, "Who shall come down against us, or who shall enter our habitations?" (21:13b). They had more important things to do than make time for God. Decade after decade the prophet's warnings fell on deaf ears.

Suddenly, with the Babylonians at the gates and death climbing over the walls, Jeremiah was in high demand. He became the most sought after man in the kingdom. The people were willing to listen, finally ready to hear what he had to say. To this point Jeremiah had been a pariah, a laughingstock, a whipping boy. Now he was their last resort. "Where is good old Jeremiah?" Zedekiah wanted to know. The prophet always seemed to be hanging around where he wasn't wanted. Now that everyone needed him, where was he?

With hypocritical piety, Zedekiah sent for the prophet, hoping he could work wonders: "This is the word that came to Jeremiah from the LORD, when King Zedekiah sent to him Pashhur the son of Malchiah and Zephaniah the priest, the son of Maaseiah, saying, 'Inquire of the LORD for us, for Nebuchadnezzar king of Babylon is making war against us. Perhaps the LORD will deal with us according to all his wonderful deeds and will make him withdraw from us'" (21:1, 2). The people of Jerusalem were not willing to listen to Jeremiah's good teaching when they felt secure, but now they expected a miracle.

Would they get one? Not a chance! "Then Jeremiah said to them: 'Thus you shall say to Zedekiah, "Thus says the LORD, the God of Israel: Behold, I will turn back the weapons of war that are in your hands and with which you are fighting against the king of Babylon and against the Chaldeans who are besieging you outside the walls. And I will bring them together into the midst of this city"'" (vv. 3, 4). Zedekiah's own weapons would be used against him, for he who lives by the sword dies by the sword.

Whatever wonders God perhaps had in store would be worked *against* Israel instead of for her: "I myself will fight against you with outstretched hand and strong arm, in anger and in fury and in great wrath. And I will strike down the inhabitants of this city, both man and beast. They shall die of a great pestilence" (vv. 5, 6). What is ironic about this is that Jeremiah uses the same language used elsewhere in the Old Testament to describe God's saving his people (e.g., Deuteronomy 5:15). But this time God's "outstretched hand" and "strong arm" would be used to strike his people down.

No one was to escape, least of all Zedekiah: "Afterward, declares the LORD, I will give Zedekiah king of Judah and his servants and the people in this city who survive the pestilence, sword, and famine into the hand of Nebuchadnezzar king of Babylon and into the hand of their enemies, into the hand of those who seek their lives. He shall strike them down with the edge of the sword. He shall not pity them or spare them or have compassion" (21:7). Jeremiah proceeded to prophesy that the city, the suburbs, and the palace would all be burned (v. 14; 22:7).

In the face of this onslaught, the people must either surrender or perish:

> And to this people you shall say: "Thus says the LORD: Behold, I set before you the way of life and the way of death. He who stays in this city shall die by the sword, by famine, and by pestilence, but he who goes out and surrenders to the Chaldeans who are besieging you shall live and shall have his life as a prize of war. For I have set my face against this city for harm and not for good, declares the LORD: it shall be given into the hand of the king of Babylon, and he shall burn it with fire." (vv. 8–10)

God can perform miracles, but Zedekiah did not deserve one and would not get one.

Zedekiah was a fool. He thought he could ignore God his whole life and still get saved at the last minute. His example is a strong warning to everyone who feels secure but has not yet accepted Jesus Christ as King. Do you feel that God will accept you just the way you are? Unless you have told God that you are sorry for all your sins and trust that Jesus died on the cross for you, you have a false security. When the Babylonians pound the gates and death climbs over the wall, you will not feel so secure.

Sometimes God does perform miracles. Sometimes he saves people on their deathbeds. But don't count on it, especially if you do not heed God's warnings in the meantime. Do not expect God to hear you *then* if you refuse to repent *now*. Many people who refuse to sit in a pew for the preaching of the gospel call for a minister when they lie on their deathbeds. Many who will not pray diligently for daily bread plead desperately for a life-saving miracle. But they do not always get one.

The people of Jerusalem did not get a miracle. On the day the Babylonians stormed the gates, Jeremiah's prophecy was fulfilled:

> Then you will be ashamed and confounded
>   because of all your evil . . .
> how you will be pitied when pangs come upon you,
>   pain as of a woman in labor! (22:22b, 23b)

The pains will be just as sudden at the last judgment. On that day every human being who has ever lived will be gathered before the throne of God to account for every sinful thought, every evil word, and every wicked deed. On that dreadful day many sinners will pray like saints. But Jesus says, "Not everyone who says to me, 'Lord, Lord,' will enter the kingdom of heaven, but the one who does the will of my Father who is in heaven. On that day many will say to me, 'Lord, Lord' . . . And then will I declare to them, 'I never knew you; depart from me, you workers of lawlessness'" (Matthew 7:21–23).

Zedekiah said, "Lord, Lord," but the Lord never knew him. Do not be such a fool. If the Lord is warning you while you feel secure, you would be a fool not to listen. The only real security in life and death is to know Jesus Christ.

Luxury by Tyranny

Some might wonder why God treated the final quartet of Jewish kings so harshly. They certainly wondered during Jeremiah's times. "And many nations will pass by this city, and every man will say to his neighbor, 'Why has the LORD dealt thus with this great city?'" (22:8). The reason for the royal disaster was that the kings of Judah were as fallen as they were foolish. "And they will answer, 'Because they have forsaken the covenant of the LORD their God and worshiped other gods and served them'" (v. 9).

The kings of Judah had two vices in particular, vices shared by most kings of this world—luxury and tyranny.

Like the other kings of the ancient world, the Judean kings had an appetite for the finer things in life. Their tastes ran to the extravagant. Jehoiakim wanted a palace with a view:

> [He] says, "I will build myself a great house
>   with spacious upper rooms,"
> [he] cuts out windows for it,
>   paneling it with cedar
>   and painting it with vermilion. (v. 14)

Jehoiakim was so ostentatious that Derek Kidner compares him to a peacock.[3] His court is referred to as those "inhabitant[s] of Lebanon, nested among the cedars" (v. 23a; cf. 1 Kings 7:2–5). In other words, there was so much cedar in his palace that he was practically living in one of the great cedar forests of Lebanon.

God has a question for those who live a life of luxury: "Do you think you are a king because you compete in cedar?" (v. 15a). The worldly person answers "Yes, it does make me a king to have more and more cedar." This is because the world measures the worth of a king by his pompous circumstance. But that is not what the Lord values in a king, or in anyone else for that matter. All a king really needs is daily bread and to do the will of God. The Lord reminds Jehoiakim of the simple reign of his father, the righteous king Josiah:

> Did not your father eat and drink
> and do justice and righteousness?
> Then it was well with him." (v. 15b)

These verses are a reminder not to live for things. This is hard to remember in a culture based almost entirely upon the accumulation of things. Already in the nineteenth century Ralph Waldo Emerson warned that "Things are in the saddle and ride mankind." Today storefronts, billboards, magazines, and television commercials all clamor for the consumer's attention: "Get this. Buy this. Have this. You need this. This will make you feel good."

The core value of American society is summed up by the bumper sticker that reads, "He Who Dies with the Most Toys Wins." Peter Menzel's book *Material World* shows photographs of average families from thirty countries standing next to a pile of all their worldly possessions.[4] Guess who has the most toys? Does that make us the winners? Not exactly.

The trouble with toys is that they get broken. And the trouble with things is that they cannot withstand the fires of divine judgment:

> ". . . lest my wrath go forth like fire,
> and burn with none to quench it,
> because of your evil deeds.
> Behold, I am against you, O inhabitant of the valley,
> O rock of the plain,
> declares the LORD." (21:12b, 13a)

> "I will kindle a fire in her forest,
> and it shall devour all that is around her." (v. 14b)

For thus says the LORD concerning the house of the king of Judah:

> "You are like Gilead to me,
> like the summit of Lebanon,
> yet surely I will make you a desert,
> an uninhabited city.
> I will prepare destroyers against you,
> each with his weapons,
> and they shall cut down your choicest cedars
> and cast them into the fire. (22:6, 7)

Luxury will not last. When the Lord Jesus is "revealed from heaven with his mighty angels in flaming fire," no earthly treasure will survive the flames (2 Thessalonians 1:7, 8; cf. Matthew 6:19–21). Whoever has the most toys will have the biggest bonfire. That is why Jesus warns, "Lay up for yourselves treasures in heaven" (Matthew 6:20a).

The second sin of the kings of Judah was tyranny, and it was their appetite for luxury that led to their tyranny:

> Woe to him who builds his house by unrighteousness,
>   and his upper rooms by injustice,
> who makes his neighbor serve him for nothing
>   and does not give him his wages. (22:13)

The rule of the Judean kings was oppressive.

> But you have eyes and heart
>   only for your dishonest gain,
> for shedding innocent blood,
>   and for practicing oppression and violence. (22:17)

The kings would not pay fair wages for honest work, which was a violation of the Law of God (Leviticus 19:13). The peacocks had become vultures.[5]

This is the way despots usually operate. The great structures of the ancient world were built on the backs of slaves. The Pharaohs constructed their pyramids by gathering common laborers into giant work gangs. They bound them and beat them until they erected great monuments to their oppressors. The Chinese emperors built the Great Wall of China the same way. To keep out foreign invaders they conscripted peasants to pile massive stones along their northern border.

Tyranny is how the Communist rulers propped up their hollow empires. Joseph Stalin built the White Sea Canal at the cost of several million Russian lives. Throughout the 1970s and 1980s the Soviets boasted about the gas pipeline they were building to Siberia. But in 1983 the British Broadcasting Company discovered that the pipeline was being built by forced labor. Some four million Vietnamese and other prisoners were working and dying in the ice to pump oil to Moscow.[6]

What kings usually do is rule by tyranny in order to gain luxury. Caesar rules for personal gain at his people's expense. God warned his people about this when they first asked him for a king. Speaking through the prophet Samuel, he explained that kings bring oppression, violence, taxation, and slavery. "You will cry out because of your king, whom you have chosen for yourselves, but the LORD will not answer you in that day" (1 Samuel 8:18).

The King Who Comes in the Name of the Lord

What king have you chosen? How does he rule?

The last four kings of Judah are brought together into one passage to demonstrate the futility of having any king but Christ. Other kings live for luxury and rule by tyranny. The same thing happens whenever we turn away from the rule of God to serve anyone or anything else. All other kings are tyrants. In the words of J. Gresham Machen (1881–1937), "Emancipation from the blessed will of God always involves bondage to some worse taskmaster."[7] There is no good king but Christ.

That is why the last verses of Jeremiah 22 pose such a problem. There Jeremiah writes Jehoiachin's epitaph:

O land, land, land,
   hear the word of the LORD!
Thus says the LORD:
"Write this man down as childless,
   a man who shall not succeed in his days,
for none of his offspring shall succeed
   in sitting on the throne of David
   and ruling again in Judah." (vv. 29, 30)

That epitaph doubles as an obituary for the house and line of David. With the exile to Babylon, Israel seems to have come to the end of the legitimate monarchy.

How can that be? The Lord had promised David, "Your house and your kingdom shall be made sure forever before me. Your throne shall be established forever" (2 Samuel 7:16). Did the Lord break his promise? Did he foreclose on his pledge to his people? Had the covenant and kingdom come to an end? How could God say that "none" of Jehoiachin's offspring would ever prosper or sit on the throne of David?

This is one time it is important to keep reading. Jeremiah goes on in chapter 23 to clarify what he means:

Behold, the days are coming, declares the LORD, when I will raise up for David a righteous Branch, and he shall reign as king and deal wisely, and shall execute justice and righteousness in the land. (23:5)

When Jeremiah said that none of Jehoiachin's children would sit on the throne of David (22:30), he was talking about his immediate offspring. True, Jehoiachin's sons did not rule the people of God in Jerusalem (cf. 1 Chronicles 3:17, 18). But the family line continued, and the rightful king did come to reign.

This is also a time to follow one of the great Reformation principles for studying the Bible: Let Scripture interpret Scripture. First seek to understand a difficult Bible verse on its own terms and in its own context. Then allow the Holy Spirit to explain it from another passage.

In this case, Ezekiel makes the meaning clear. Like Jeremiah, Ezekiel prophesied that the monarchy would come to an end: "O profane wicked one, prince of Israel, whose day has come, the time of your final punishment, thus says the Lord GOD: Remove the turban and take off the crown" (Ezekiel 21:25, 26). Yet Ezekiel warned that the crown should not be thrown away! A king was still coming, the rightful heir to the throne of David. The crown would "not be [restored], until he comes, the one to whom judgment belongs, and I [God] will give it to him" (v. 27). God was saving the crown for Christ.

Jesus Christ is the King to whom the crown belongs: "As he [Jesus] was drawing near—already on the way down the Mount of Olives—the whole multitude of his disciples began to rejoice and praise God with a loud voice for all the mighty works that they had seen, saying, 'Blessed is the King who comes in the name of the Lord!'" (Luke 19:37, 38).

Blessed, blessed, blessed is King Jesus. How does he rule? Not by tyranny. Not for luxury. He rules with humility. His humility is evident in his approach. He does not come riding the white stallion of oppression, but the gray donkey of servanthood: "'Behold, your king is coming to you, humble, and mounted on a donkey, on a colt, the foal of a beast of burden'" (Matthew 21:5; cf. Zechariah 9:9).

Jesus Christ is no tyrant. Wherever he rules, there is justice and righteousness, which is how God's king is supposed to rule. Solomon prayed,

Give the king your justice, O God,
    and your righteousness to the royal son!
May he judge your people with righteousness,
    and your poor with justice! (Psalm 72:1, 2)

Jeremiah longed for that kind of rule to return to Judah. In his palace sermons he pleaded over and over for a just and righteous king:

And to the house of the king of Judah say, "Hear the word of the LORD, O house of David! Thus says the LORD:

> 'Execute justice in the morning,
>   and deliver from the hand of the oppressor
> him who has been robbed.'" (21:11, 12a)

Thus says the LORD: "Go down to the house of the king of Judah and speak there this word, and say, 'Hear the word of the LORD, O king of Judah, who sits on the throne of David, you, and your servants, and your people who enter these gates. Thus says the LORD: Do justice and righteousness, and deliver from the hand of the oppressor him who has been robbed. And do no wrong or violence to the resident alien, the fatherless, and the widow, nor shed innocent blood in this place. For if you will indeed obey this word, then there shall enter the gates of this house kings who sit on the throne of David, riding in chariots and on horses, they and their servants and their people. But if you will not obey these words, I swear by myself, declares the LORD, that this house shall become a desolation.'" (22:1–5; cf. Exodus 22:21–26)

The righteousness Jeremiah was looking forward to can only be found in the reign of King Jesus. He rescues the poor from their enemies. He delivers slaves from their bondage. He rescues sinners from their captivity to Satan. He welcomes strangers to live among his people. He takes particular notice of children without fathers. He takes special care of wives without husbands. He settles all his children into his family of love in the church. Jesus Christ is the best of kings.

Who Is Your King?

Is Christ your King?

One man who served Christ as King was Polycarp, the bishop of Smyrna (c. 70–155/160 AD). When the Romans demanded that every citizen worship Caesar as God, Polycarp refused. He was captured, tied to a stake, and prepared for the flames. "Come now," his captors urged, "where is the harm in just saying Caesar is Lord, and offering the incense, when it will save your life?"

Polycarp replied, "Eighty and six years have I served him, and he has done me no wrong. How then can I blaspheme my King and my Savior?"[8] In the face of persecution, he proved faithful to Christ the King.

Persecution is one way to tell if you have made Christ your King. There is another way, however. Concerning Josiah, Jeremiah writes,

> Did not your father . . . do justice and righteousness?
>   Then it was well with him.
> He judged the cause of the poor and needy;
>   then it was well.

Is not this to know me?
  declares the LORD. (v. 15b, 16)

To know the King of kings, as Josiah did, is to do what is right and just.

To know Christ as King is to defend the poor and needy. The Scripture does not say that doing justice is one good way to get to know God. Nor does it say that once I know God, one way I can serve him is to defend the poor. What it says is that doing justice and knowing God *are the same thing*. It says that defending the poor equals the knowledge of God. This is not to say that works of social justice are the basis of salvation. But it is to say that if we do not do justice and do not defend the poor, we do not know Christ. No one can serve an unknown king.

If Christ is King, then you must defend the poor. That means more than just not oppressing the poor; it means being an advocate for them by satisfying their spiritual and material needs. If Christ is your King, you must seek out the fatherless and minister to them as your own children. If Christ is your King, you must notice widows and honor them as your own mothers. If Christ is your King, your home must be a safe haven for aliens, the homeless, internationals, and all sinners who are strangers to God. Is that not what it means to know God? Is that not what it means to serve Christ as King? Where there is no justice, there is no true knowledge of God.

In *The Narrative of William W. Brown, a Fugitive Slave*, William Wells Brown makes a powerful statement about the connection between doing justice and knowing God:

> One Sabbath, as we were driving past the house of D. D. Page, a gentleman who owned a large baking establishment . . . I saw Mr. Page pursuing a slave around the yard, with a long whip, cutting him at every jump. . . . The same gentleman, but a short time previous, tied up a woman of his, by the name of Delphia, and whipped her nearly to death; yet he was a deacon in the Baptist church, in good and regular standing. Poor Delphia! I was well acquainted with her, and called to see her while upon her sick bed; and I shall never forget her appearance. She was a member of the same church with her master.[9]

Brown's point is that the church is no place for injustice, especially among the leadership. Righteousness and justice must prevail wherever Christ is King.

If Christ is your King, then you know how humbly, justly, and rightly he rules. If you are his royal subject, you must live the same way.

31

Music for the Messiah

JEREMIAH 23:1–8

THE BOOK OF JEREMIAH is like an orchestra concert. A concert always begins with the orchestra tuning up. First the oboist plays a single A on her oboe, a note taken up in turn by the strings, the woodwinds, and the brass. Then all chaos breaks loose as each musician plays his or her own notes. The sound of an orchestra tuning up is not music but discord. The Philadelphia Orchestra has yet to release a recording of its great orchestral warm-ups.

The first twenty-eight chapters of Jeremiah sound like an orchestra tuning up. They are full of the discord of sin and judgment. We hear plenty of notes but not very much beautiful music. We are still waiting to hear the great symphony of the new covenant, which begins in Jeremiah 29.

Sometimes, however, if you listen very carefully, you can hear a little music while an orchestra is tuning up. The leading cellist will play a scale. The bassoonist will play a few measures from his solo. One of the French horns will run through a tricky little section from the third movement. In the middle of all the discord there is some real music.

Jeremiah 23 is real music. After twenty-two chapters of sin and judgment, finally come some grace notes. It is the best music of all—music for the Messiah. Chapter 23 contains two catchy tunes—a song for the Good Shepherd and a melody for the Righteous Branch. We only hear the tunes for a moment and then they are gone. But the music will come back later in the book of Jeremiah and again at the coming of Jesus Christ.

Why Pastor, What Big Teeth You Have!

The song for the Good Shepherd (vv. 3, 4, 7, 8) comes in the middle of the discord of sin and judgment. Jeremiah 23 actually begins with woe: "'Woe to the shepherds who destroy and scatter the sheep of my pasture!' declares the LORD" (v. 1).

This is vintage Jeremiah. Even when he wants to play some music, he begins with the word "woe." We have heard him sing this tune before. Dangerous shepherds have been one of the prophet's main motifs. By "shepherds" he meant both the political and religious leaders of his day. Time and again he had warned of the greed and deceit of Jerusalem's priests and prophets (6:13). "The prophets prophesy falsely, and the priests rule at their direction" (5:31). And in chapter 22 he had pronounced woe against the kings for all their luxury.

Jeremiah's critique of the religious establishment of his day can be summarized like this: "The shepherds are stupid" (10:21). They have turned against the sheep of God's own pasture. As John Guest says, they have been "fleecing the flock."[1] It is hard for sheep to trust a shepherd who eats mutton chops for dinner, is it not? With shepherds like these, who needs wolves?

From one perspective, the history of humanity is largely the story of bad shepherding. So many political leaders have enslaved their own people. So many religious leaders have ministered to the spiritual detriment of their followers.

The religious leaders of postmodern America are no exception. God's sheep are scattered and destroyed on every side. People used to marvel at how many people attended church in the United States. Not anymore. One report showed that church attendance in America dropped from 49 percent to 37 percent during the first half of the 1990s.[2] The sheep are beginning to scatter.

Sometimes the sheep are even destroyed. A new Christian in Philadelphia once made a horrifying discovery. He picked up a flyer advertising a Christian student group on his university campus, a group sponsored by a number of Philadelphia churches. The leaders of the group call God "Mother" and celebrate their gay or lesbian sexuality. They also claim to be loyal to the message of Jesus Christ "as proclaimed in non-Christian faith traditions." In other words, they claim to have Christianity without Christ, which is bad logic as well as bad theology. The new Christian made no attempt to disguise his disbelief as he read their literature: "Why, they aren't teaching anything that's found in the Bible!"

Jeremiah speaks about shepherds who "care for" or "Take care of" God's people. "Take care of" has more than one meaning. It can mean to tend and nourish, as in "I will take care of your cat while you go on vacation." It can also mean to devour, as in "Let me take care of that bowl of ice cream for you." That was the kind of caretaking Jeremiah was worried about. Because of the way shepherds are "Taking care of" God's sheep, some are afraid, and others are missing altogether (cf. 23:4).

When the sheep are destroyed and scattered, the shepherds are to blame. A declining church is a sign of a declining ministry. How many ministers are personally unacquainted with the living Christ? How many do not have absolute confidence in the perfection of God's Word? How many have compromised their teaching or their morals according to the spirit of the present age? In other words, how many shepherds "have scattered [God's] flock and have driven them away, and . . . have not attended to them" (v. 2a)? Sometimes shepherds behave more like wolves. "Why, pastor," one might say, "what big teeth you have!"

God loves the sheep of his pasture; so he keeps an eye on his shepherds. He holds pastors accountable for their shepherding. If they will not take care of God's flock, God will take care of them. "Therefore thus says the LORD, the God of Israel, concerning the shepherds who care for my people: 'You have scattered my flock and have driven them away, and you have not attended to them. Behold, I will attend to you for your evil deeds'" (v. 2). This is why the church needs to pray for its ministers. They are responsible to God not only for their own godliness, but also for the godliness of the church. One day God will punish every bad shepherd for malpractice.

The Good Shepherd

Whenever God's people are surrounded by bad shepherds, they beg for a good shepherd. They pray for a shepherd who will make them lie down in green pastures and lead them beside the quiet waters (Psalm 23:2). They cry out for a shepherd who will not destroy, scatter, neglect, terrify, or lose them.

Listen! Can you hear the music for the Messiah? In his prophecy Jeremiah played a few notes from the song of the Good Shepherd: "Then I will gather the remnant of my flock out of all the countries where I have driven them, and I will bring them back to their fold, and they shall be fruitful and multiply" (23:3).

God promises to shepherd the lost sheep of Israel. He wants the job done right; so he promises to do it himself. After God drives the sheep out into the nations, he will bring them back to his own pasture. He will be the Good Shepherd who gathers the remnant of his flock back from exile. When God brings his people back from exile, it will be such a wonderful salvation that they will practically forget their deliverance from Egypt:

Therefore, behold, the days are coming, declares the LORD, when they shall no longer say, "As the LORD lives who brought up the people of Israel out of the land of Egypt," but "As the LORD lives who brought up and led the offspring of the house of Israel out of the north country and out of all the countries where he had driven them." Then they shall dwell in their own land. (vv. 7, 8)

The second exodus will be even greater than the first.

Once God's sheep return to God's pasture, God will look after them. He promises that "They shall be fruitful and multiply" (v. 3). This promise fulfills the command God first gave to Adam and Eve (Genesis 1:28). The land of Israel will be like a paradise regained, filled with the people of God.

These multitudes will be ruled by good shepherds, under the leadership of the Good Shepherd himself: "I will set shepherds over them who will care for them, and they shall fear no more, nor be dismayed, neither shall any be missing, declares the LORD" (23:4). These shepherds will behave themselves; they will tend God's sheep the way a shepherd should.

These promises were fulfilled when God brought his people back from exile in Babylon. The restoration of Israel began under King Cyrus in the sixth century and continued into the fifth century BC. God's people returned to their green pastures in large numbers. God appointed good shepherds over them, men like Ezra and Nehemiah, who actually cared for God's sheep. And not one of them was missing. Perhaps this is why the books of Ezra and Nehemiah have complete lists of the exiles who returned from captivity (see Ezra 8; Nehemiah 7). It was to show that God's promise came true.

Like most of Jeremiah's promises, these promises had a double fulfillment. They were fulfilled again in the coming of Jesus Christ. When Jesus said, "I am the good shepherd" (John 10:11, 14), he was claiming to fulfill everything the Old Testament promised about good shepherds, including all the promises of Jeremiah 23.

Jesus Christ is the Good Shepherd who gathers the remnant of his sheep from the nations. His sheep listen to his voice. "He calls his own sheep by name and leads them out. When he has brought out all his own, he goes before them, and the sheep follow him, for they know his voice" (John 10:3b, 4).

Jesus Christ is the Good Shepherd who has placed shepherds over his sheep to tend them. First he appointed the twelve apostles, like Peter, whom Jesus commanded to feed his lambs (John 21:15–17). Jesus was reminding Peter that a pastor's job is to shepherd the people of God. When Peter was approaching death, he passed that responsibility on to all the elders of the church: "Shepherd the flock of God that is among you, exercising oversight" (1 Peter 5:2).

Jesus Christ is the Good Shepherd who makes sure that none of his sheep is missing. What a remarkable promise! Think for a moment how difficult it is to keep track of people in postmodern society. When I think of struggling to keep track of people, I think of the Membership Directory at Tenth Presbyterian Church in Philadelphia. Because of the size of the congregation and the number of people who move in and out of the city, we print a new directory every week. Often it is partially obsolete almost as soon as it is published.

Or consider the mail that keeps showing up in your mailbox—letters addressed to former residents, extra copies of catalogs with your name slightly misspelled, or advertisements simply labeled *Occupant*. When my family lived in England, we often received mail (including threatening letters from banks) for four or five former residents. After we returned to Philadelphia we started getting mail addressed to "Joshua Ryken, President, Ryken Wrecking Company." It had a nice ring to it, but our little corporate executive was only three years old at the time!

How great God must be to keep perfect track of every man, every woman, and every child who belongs to him. When God writes down your name in the Book of Life, he writes down your name, and it will stay written down for all eternity. Jesus says, "I am the good shepherd. I know my own" (John 10:14).

A shepherd who knows his sheep is careful not to lose any of them. This is what Jesus taught in his parable about the found sheep. Not "The lost sheep," as it is so often called, but "The found sheep," because the whole point of the parable is that the sheep will and must be found: "What man of you, having a hundred sheep, if he has lost one of them, does not leave the ninety-nine in the open country, and go after the one that is lost, until he finds it? And when he has found it, he lays it on his shoulders, rejoicing" (Luke 15:3–5). Jesus Christ is that Good Shepherd. He keeps careful count of all his sheep. If one is missing, he will not rest until he finds it.

This is strong encouragement for the work of missions and evangelism. Jesus Christ will not lose even one of his own sheep. If they are lost, he will find them. Jesus told his disciples, "I have other sheep that are not of this fold. I must bring them also" (John 10:16). This is the doctrine of irresistible grace. Jesus does not say that other sheep "may" come in, or "should" come in, or "can" come in if they feel like it, but that they *must* come in.

If the lost sheep must come in, then why are Christians such timid evangelists? Christians often look at their secular friends and have trouble imagining how they could ever come to Christ. The work of evangelism seems so impossible. The work of missions sometimes seems equally impossible, especially in the Muslim world. The world seems to be full of unlikely candidates for spiritual conversion.

That is not how the Good Shepherd looks at the world, however. Jesus sees in the world many lost souls who absolutely, positively *must* come in. They must come because Jesus must bring them. Jesus is the Good Shepherd who makes sure that none of his sheep is missing. On the day of resurrection all will be present and accounted for. So speak in the name of Christ whenever you have the chance. His sheep will "listen to [his] voice. So there will be one flock, one shepherd" (John 10:16).

Some of the lost sheep who must come belong to a nomadic tribe in Togo, North Africa. The tribesmen are known as "The blue men of the Sahara" because they wear long blue robes to protect them from the desert sun. They are called the Touareg, an Arabic name that means "The forgotten ones of God."

Forgotten of God? Impossible! One of the Touareg tribesmen graduated from a Christian university and began to broadcast a gospel radio program into the tents of his people scattered across the desert. Among the half million Touareg there were soon several dozen Christians.[3] Surely more will follow. They are not forgotten of God, because the Good Shepherd knows his sheep and they must come in.

The Righteous Branch

When God's sheep come into his fold, he rules them wisely and well. This is Jeremiah's second melody for the Messiah, the melody of the Righteous Branch:

> Behold, the days are coming, declares the LORD, when I will raise up for David a righteous Branch, and he shall reign as king and deal wisely, and shall execute justice and righteousness in the land. In his days Judah will be saved, and Israel will dwell securely. And this is the name by which he will be called: "The LORD is our righteousness." (vv. 5, 6)

Whenever David's name is mentioned in the lyrics of the Old Testament, our ears should prick up because we know that the Messiah will be David's son. The King coming to rule over the people of God will be David's rightful heir. He will be an offshoot from David's family, a branch off the old tree.

Isaiah made the same promise. He prophesied that a Son would be given to the people of God—"Wonderful Counselor, Mighty God, Everlasting Father, Prince of Peace." He foretold that this coming King would reign "on the throne of David and over his kingdom" (Isaiah 9:6, 7). Not only would he reign on David's throne, but he would also come from David's family: "There shall come forth a shoot from the stump of Jesse, and a branch from his roots shall bear fruit" (Isaiah 11:1; cf. Zechariah 3:8; 6:12).

This is why the Gospels take such an interest in the genealogy of Jesus Christ (see Matthew 1:1–17; Luke 3:23–38). If Jesus is the Messiah, then he must be "of the house and lineage of David" (Luke 2:4). And so he is! The genealogy of Jesus Christ is more than just a list of names. It proves that Jesus Christ is the son of David, the rightful heir of Israel's throne.

Jeremiah's melody for the Righteous Branch helps explain what kind of a king he will be. It lists the several excellencies of the kingship of Jesus Christ. The King would "deal wisely" (23:5). He would follow a wise policy, and wise sayings would be found on his lips. This is just what we find in the teaching of Jesus Christ. He is the wisdom of God (1 Corinthians 1:30), the wisest teacher who ever lived.

The Righteous Branch would also be a just king. He would "execute justice and righteousness in the land" (23:5). He would pull down the proud and the arrogant; he would lift up the poor and the downtrodden. He would defend the cause of the widow and the orphan. He would do right by his sheep.

This is precisely what we will find on the day when Jesus Christ comes to judge the earth. He will do what is just and right. He will gather his servants to be with him forever, but he will turn his back on his enemies and cast them into the outer darkness (Matthew 25:31–46).

The Righteous Branch would also be a safe king. He would save his people (23:6a). He would rescue, deliver, and liberate the children of Israel. His very presence would keep them safe from danger. After all the horrors of military conquest, the nation would return to domestic tranquillity.

Best of all, the Righteous Branch would be a righteous King. He would be a man of perfect integrity. He would not only *do* what is right, but he would also *be* what is right. "And this is the name by which he will be called: 'The Lord is our righteousness'" (v. 6b). The coming King would be synonymous with righteousness.

A righteous King was exactly what God's people needed. They needed a righteous King for two reasons. First, their own king was unrighteous. The end of verse 6 is actually a Hebrew pun (Jeremiah was a great one for puns). Jeremiah prophesied during the reign of King Zedekiah, which means "righteousness of the Lord." That is nearly how verse 6 ends: "The Lord is our righteousness."

King Zedekiah, however, was anything but righteous. He reigned in Jerusalem for eleven years, during which "he did what was evil in the sight of the Lord" (2 Kings 24:19). As we will discover, Jeremiah later prophesied divine judgment against Zedekiah (see 29:15–19). Among other things, God gave him this warning to deliver to Zedekiah: "I am giving this city into the hand of the king of Babylon, and he shall burn it with fire. You shall not escape from his hand but shall surely be captured and delivered into his hand. You shall see the king of Babylon eye to eye" (34:2, 3). The Scripture records how Zedekiah was captured and bound in bronze shackles. He did see the king of Babylon, but not for long, and the last thing he saw before his eyes were gouged out was the slaughter of his sons (39:6, 7).

The people of Jeremiah's day were looking for wise, just, and righteous leadership. Instead they had a king—Zedekiah—who was foolish, capricious, and wicked. He sounds like many of the political leaders of our own day. Like the Israelites, we long for judges and senators who will govern righteously.

Jeremiah's prophecy about the Messiah, therefore, is music to our ears. The coming King would be called "The LORD is our righteousness" (23:6b). In other words, he would be exactly the opposite of the kind of ruler we have come to expect in this world. That is why Jeremiah switched Zedekiah's name around to make his pun. Zedekiah was called "Righteous is the Lord," but the Messiah would be called "The LORD is our righteousness." He would be the antithesis of men like Zedekiah.

Unlike the last kings of Judah, the Righteous Branch would be the kind of king who obeys God's commands for how a king ought to behave. He would do what is just and right. He would bring restitution to the victims of theft. He would protect the alien, the fatherless, and the widow. He would not shed innocent blood. He would be a righteous king in every respect.

The Lord Our Righteousness

There is another reason the people of God needed a Righteous Branch. True, their king was unrighteous. But they also needed a righteous king because *they* were unrighteous. For twenty-two chapters Jeremiah has documented the sins of God's people in careful detail. They were no more righteous than their kings were. They broke every one of God's commandments.

Back in chapter 5, God promised that he would forgive his people if Jeremiah could find just one good man. The prophet searched high and low. He walked up the streets and down the alleys, but he could not find even one man to be righteous for the people.

In chapter 23 Jeremiah finally finds his man. This Good Shepherd, this Son of David, this Wise King, will be righteous for his people. In some way— perhaps even beyond Jeremiah's comprehension—the goodness, integrity, and moral perfection of the Righteous Branch would belong to God's people. His righteousness would be credited to their account.

All these promises have been fulfilled in the Lord Jesus Christ. When we hear the melody of the Righteous Branch, we know that Jeremiah is playing Christ's song. Jesus Christ is righteous for his people. His righteousness belongs to them. All his righteous deeds fulfill the Law that they could never keep. All his righteous sufferings satisfy the atonement they could never pay. If you trust in Jesus Christ, then his righteousness belongs to you, and you will be righteous in God's sight forever.

The Righteous Branch was the answer to the Apostle Paul's great problem in Romans 3. He looked around at all the sins of humanity (including his own!) and wrote:

> None is righteous, no, not one;
>   no one understands;
>   no one seeks for God.
> All have turned aside; together they have become worthless;
>   no one does good,
>   not even one. (vv. 10–12)

Paul reached exactly the same conclusion Jeremiah reached. He looked high and low, but he could not find even one righteous person.

If no one is righteous, then what hope is there for the human race? What hope is there for you? None at all, it would seem. "But now the righteousness of God has been manifested apart from the law, although the Law and the Prophets bear witness to it" (Romans 3:21; cf. 1 Corinthians 1:30). Wonderful news! A righteousness from God has been made known, exactly the kind of righteousness that Jeremiah promised. "The righteousness of God [comes] through faith in Jesus Christ for all who believe" (Romans 3:22).

The righteousness of God himself belongs to you if you put your trust in Jesus Christ. You can have the righteousness of God if you believe in Jesus Christ. "And this is the name by which he will be called: 'The LORD is our righteousness'" (23:6b).

Coda

This is wonderful music! And it is a great encouragement to know that Jeremiah knew some music about Christ. The Weeping Prophet suffered many dark days of despair, but he did not live without hope. He knew some music for the Messiah. He had a couple of catchy tunes to hum whenever he was discouraged—a song for the Good Shepherd and a melody for the Righteous Branch. If you know this Good Shepherd, this Righteous Branch, this Jesus, then you can sing them too.

32

I Had a Dream!

JEREMIAH 23:9–40

ANYONE WHO HAS HEARD Felix Mendelssohn's (1809–1847) *Elijah* cannot doubt that God's Word has a burning, breaking power. After God sends fire from Heaven to consume Elijah's sacrifice on Mount Carmel, and after the Israelites put the prophets of Baal to death at the Kishon River, Mendelssohn's Elijah asks this question: "Is not His word like a fire; and like a hammer that breaketh the rock in pieces?"

Curiously, these words come from the prophet Jeremiah. The text for *Elijah* was compiled by Mendelssohn's friend Julius Schubring. At first it seems strange to hear Jeremiah's words on Elijah's lips. Why include this verse from Jeremiah? Was Schubring just trying to expand the libretto?

The answer is that Schubring knew his Bible. His inclusion of Jeremiah 23:29 is not inadvertent but inspired. He understood that 1 Kings 18 and Jeremiah 23 make the same point. Like Elijah, Jeremiah was surrounded by hundreds of false prophets. And like Elijah, Jeremiah learned that God's Word will consume every false prophecy.

Consider the Source

What is so false about the prophets who opposed Jeremiah? First of all, the sources of their prophecies were false. Some came from the devil himself:

> In the prophets of Samaria
>   I saw an unsavory thing:
> they prophesied by Baal
>   and led my people Israel astray. (v. 13)

The children of Israel should have learned their lesson back at Mount Carmel. Baal does not hear and cannot answer. He is no god, for there is no god but God. Yet the prophets of Israel turned back to Baal.

Another source of false prophecy is a prophet's own mind.

> Thus says the LORD of hosts: "Do not listen to the words of the prophets who prophesy to you, filling you with vain hopes. They speak visions of their own minds, not from the mouth of the LORD." (v. 16)

> How long shall there be lies in the heart of the prophets who prophesy lies, and who prophesy the deceit of their own heart, who think to make my people forget my name by their dreams that they tell one another, even as their fathers forgot my name for Baal? (vv. 26, 27)

These false prophets were frauds and impostors. They were not sent by God; they were self-appointed. They were only prophets in their own minds, and they made things up as they went along:

> Behold, I am against the prophets, declares the LORD, who use their tongues and declare, "declares the LORD." Behold, I am against those who prophesy lying dreams, declares the LORD, and who tell them and lead my people astray by their lies and their recklessness, when I did not send them or charge them. So they do not profit this people at all, declares the LORD. (vv. 31, 32)

The false prophets were nothing but dreamers and liars; their sermons were the products of wishful thinking rather than divine revelation.

The dreamers and liars of Jeremiah's day have become the televangelists of our day. The Violent Femmes sang a song about lying prophets back in the 1980s: "On the motel T.V. I dig the evangelist, he'll tell you all about that, and then he tell you all about this . . . he's mixin' up the truth with something funny." And then came the chorus: "He's telling lies, lies, lies, lies, lies, lies, lies. . . ."[1]

There may even be a lying prophet at your local church. These are the days Jesus warned about, when "many false prophets will arise and lead many astray" (Matthew 24:11). A man once told me that to inoculate himself against the bad preaching at his home church he tuned in to Dr. James Montgomery Boice on *The Bible Study Hour* every Sunday morning. On one occasion a guest preacher stood in the pulpit at that man's church and began a sermon with these words: "The Bible has no authority." Hardly a promising beginning.

Derek Kidner compares false teachers to reporters who gather outside a room where a political meeting is being held.[2] The analogy is a good one.

Journalists make reports about cabinet meetings that take place behind closed doors. Thus their reports depend largely on conjecture. They are based on rumor rather than revelation. Sometimes the reporters are just guessing. Often they are wrong.

About such preachers God says:

> I did not send the prophets,
>   yet they ran;
> I did not speak to them,
>   yet they prophesied. (23:21)

The prophet who runs with his own message soon will be outpaced by the swift heralds described in Isaiah:

> How beautiful upon the mountains
>   are the feet of him who brings good news,
> who publishes peace, who brings good news of happiness,
>   who publishes salvation,
>   who says to Zion, "Your God reigns." (Isaiah 52:7)

A preacher who rejects the authority of God's Word preaches by his own authority, and what authority is that? His teaching is just his opinion. God's people do not go to God's house to hear what a man has to say; they go to hear what God has to say.

A third source of false prophecy is the false words of other false prophets. "Therefore, behold, I am against the prophets, declares the LORD, who steal my words from one another" (23:30). This is a strong statement against plagiarism. Some false prophets are not even clever enough to think up something false on their own. They get their material secondhand. They quote other popular preachers without bothering to mention their sources. They probably think they are just "borrowing," but the correct word for it is stealing.

A 1995 survey by the Center for Academic Integrity showed that more than 50 percent of university students cheat in school. Even at colleges with honor codes, the percentage of cheaters exceeded 40 percent. But plagiarism and all other forms of cheating are sins. They are offenses against both God and one's neighbor. It is a sin to copy someone else's words onto one's own paper. Outside sources must be acknowledged properly. It is a sin to fudge lab results or to look at notes during an exam or to consult last year's midterm (unless the instructor allows for this). The only work that is pleasing to God is the very best of one's own work.

To Tell the Truth

There are plenty of sources for false prophecy, but only one source for true prophecy. What makes a true prophet true is that he gets his prophecy straight from God. If a prophet wants to know God's revealed will, he must go to God to get it.

Concerning the false prophets, Jeremiah asked, "For who among them has stood in the council of the LORD to see and to hear his word, or who has paid attention to his word and listened?" (v. 18). The prophet was speaking about the heavenly council described by the psalmist:

> For who in the skies can be compared to the LORD?
>   Who among the heavenly beings is like the LORD,
> a God greatly to be feared in the council of the holy ones,
>   and awesome above all who are around him? (Psalm 89:6, 7)

The difference between true prophecy and false is that the true prophet has been there and seen that. He has been in the council of the holy ones to hear God's Word from God's own mouth.

Jeremiah was a true prophet. He appeared before the mighty council of God when he was first called to the ministry (1:7–10). The Lord sent him to be a prophet. The Lord reached out and touched Jeremiah to put his words right into his mouth. The Lord appointed him to be a prophet to the nations. So whenever Jeremiah said, "This is what the Lord says," he knew what he was talking about.

The words of Scripture are the words of men who have been in God's heavenly council. They are the words of men like Moses, who talked with God on the mountain (Exodus 33, 34); or men like Isaiah, who "saw the LORD sitting upon a throne, high and lifted up" (Isaiah 6:1); or men like Paul, who "was caught up to the third heaven" (2 Corinthians 12:2); or men like John, who was taken "in the Spirit" to see the glories of the kingdom of God (Revelation 1:10). And they are men like the writers of the Gospels, who saw "his glory, glory as of the only Son from the Father" (John 1:14). The prophecies of Scripture come directly from the throne room of the Most High God.

What a vast difference there is between the burning, breaking Word of God and the chatterings of mere mortals. Martin Luther testified that spiritual truth did not come from himself or from any of the great teachers in the history of the church, but from God himself:

> Let none think that God's Word cometh to earth of man's device. If it is to be God's Word, it must be sent. . . . Therefore we should neither utter nor

hear aught, save the Word of God alone. Is it invented by man's choice and device, avoid it. It cometh not except it be sent from heaven. . . . Without God's sending cometh no Word into the world. Hath it grown out of my heart, cling I to Chrysostom, Augustine, and Ambrose, still 'tis not God's Word. For 'tis a vast difference 'twixt the Word that is sent from heaven and that which of my own choice and device I invent.[3]

A Likely Story!

False prophets not only get their information from false sources, but they also preach a false message. First, they deny the sinfulness of sin. They do not turn God's people "from their evil way, and from the evil of their deeds" (23:22b). Instead they tell people whatever they want to hear (cf. 2 Timothy 4:3).

This is often the problem with false theology, especially liberal theology. It teaches something less than total depravity. It condones immorality rather than condemning it. It does not take sin as seriously as God takes it. In other words, it does not take sin seriously enough! The proof that our own culture does not take sin seriously is the way that sin has been redefined. Moral failings are treated as bad habits or honest mistakes or pathological diseases or psychological disorders—anything except what they actually are: sins.

The false prophets of Jeremiah's day were soft on one sin in particular:

> But in the prophets of Jerusalem
>   I have seen a horrible thing:
> they commit adultery and walk in lies;
>   they strengthen the hands of evildoers,
>   so that no one turns from his evil;
> all of them have become like Sodom to me,
>   and its inhabitants like Gomorrah. (23:14)

Given the popularity of Canaanite fertility cults in those days, Jeremiah was probably referring to adultery, both in the spiritual sense of worshipping other gods and in the physical sense of sexual sin. The prophets were repeating one of Satan's favorite lies, the lie that there is no harm in sex outside of marriage.

In this case the prophets themselves were part of the problem. They were guilty of false conduct. They were living a lie, saying one thing and doing another. They were guilty of sexual sin, and as the prophets sin, so sin the people. What Jeremiah says is not surprising: "The land is full of adulterers" (v. 10a; cf. 5:7, 8). Whenever spiritual leaders are soft on sin, they are endorsing iniquity. As Jeremiah put it, they "strengthen the hands of evildoers" (v. 14b).

To mention just one contemporary example, consider the way that permissive attitudes toward divorce promote adultery in North America.

Jeremiah's reference to Sodom and Gomorrah suggests that part of the problem in Jerusalem was homosexual sin. The men of Sodom and Gomorrah wanted to have sex whenever they wanted, wherever they wanted, and with whomever they wanted. When angels came to visit Lot in Sodom, the neighbors surrounded his house and demanded, "Where are the men who came to you tonight? Bring them out to us, that we may know them" (Genesis 19:5). The Sodomites and "Gomorralists" (as Garrison Keillor calls them) reveled in all kinds of sexual sin.

This is a warning to any follower of Christ who continues to struggle with homosexual sin, or with any other sexual sin for that matter. To think that it is safe to dabble in lust, pornography, or adultery is to listen to a false message. The lie of pro-gay theology is that homosexual fantasy and intercourse have the blessing of God. That is a false message from a false source. The Bible teaches that all sexual fantasies and actions outside of Biblical marriage are sin. Of course, there is forgiveness for every sin in Christ. But the full extent of God's grace cannot be learned by minimizing the sinfulness of sexual sin. A sin must be called a sin so that grace can be grace all the way through the Christian's sexuality.

Not only were the false prophets soft on sin, but they were also silent about God's wrath. Once they denied the sinfulness of sin, it made perfect sense to deny the justice of judgment. One false message leads to the other. Along with "easy views of sin go rosy views of judgment."[4]

> Do not listen to the words of the prophets who prophesy to you, filling you with vain hopes. . . . They say continually to those who despise the word of the LORD, "It shall be well with you"; and to everyone who stubbornly follows his own heart, they say, "No disaster shall come upon you." (23:16a, 17)

The false prophets held out "vain hopes," like the "vanities" of Ecclesiastes. Contrary to Jeremiah, they told people that Jerusalem would not be destroyed and that God would not punish their sins. Like a tiresome ad campaign, they kept on broadcasting "peace, peace" when there was no peace, "shalom, shalom" when there was no shalom.

The false prophets in the postmodern church say the same thing. They teach that God is not angry with sinners, just disappointed. H. Richard Niebuhr put it best when he described the old liberal theology as that system of doctrine in which "a God without wrath brought men without sin into a kingdom without judgment through the ministrations of a Christ without a Cross."[5] If there is no wrath, no sin, and no judgment, then who needs a cross?

Truth or Consequences

The sad truth is that sin always brings divine judgment. For false prophets who get false messages from false sources and live false lives, salvation will turn out to be a false hope. They have a false sense of security. Jeremiah has been right all along. God *will* destroy the city of Jerusalem.

Jeremiah 23 is filled with various references to God's terrible judgment against false ministers and the people who listen to them. Their land was to be destroyed; "because of the curse the land mourns, and the pastures of the wilderness are dried up" (v. 10a). The people were starting to slide down the slippery slope to destruction:

Therefore their way shall be to them
    like slippery paths in the darkness,
    into which they shall be driven and fall,
for I will bring disaster upon them
    in the year of their punishment,
    declares the LORD. (v. 12)

The Lord would make them eat wormwood and drink gall:

Therefore thus says the LORD of hosts concerning the prophets:
"Behold, I will feed them with bitter food
    and give them poisoned water to drink,
for from the prophets of Jerusalem
    ungodliness has gone out into all the land." (v. 15)

The storm clouds of God's wrath had gathered and were about to break:

Behold, the storm of the LORD!
    Wrath has gone forth,
a whirling tempest;
    it will burst upon the head of the wicked.
The anger of the LORD will not turn back
    until he has executed and accomplished
    the intents of his heart.
In the latter days you will understand it clearly. (vv. 19, 20)

In the end, God would forget all about the people of Jerusalem: "Therefore, behold, I will surely lift you up and cast you away from my presence, you and the city that I gave to you and your fathers. And I will bring upon you everlasting reproach and perpetual shame, which shall not be forgotten" (vv. 39, 40). Yet even were God to forget them, they would be unable to escape his wrath:

> Am I a God at hand, declares the LORD, and not a God far away? Can a man hide himself in secret places so that I cannot see him? declares the LORD. Do I not fill heaven and earth? declares the LORD. (vv. 23, 24; cf. Psalm 139:7–12)

In other words, false prophets can run, but they cannot hide.

There is no escape from the wrath of God. History has vindicated everything Jeremiah ever said about divine judgment. Furthermore, eternity will vindicate everything the Bible says about the judgment to come. The wrath of God is about to be revealed against every false person. You will not get saved by escaping God's notice, or assuming you are just good enough to get by, or hoping that God will not judge your sins after all. You are a sinner who deserves judgment. The only way to escape is to trust Jesus Christ for salvation, believing that he died on the cross for your sins.

Lament for a Ministry

Jeremiah 23 is about the difference between lies and the truth. When false prophets discount and downgrade God's Word, how can a Christian give the truth its proper value?

First, by lamenting what is false. Jeremiah did not get mad at false prophets, or get even with them; he wept for them. He indicted his fellow prophets with tears:

> Concerning the prophets:

> My heart is broken within me;
>   all my bones shake;
> I am like a drunken man,
>   like a man overcome by wine,
> because of the LORD
>   and because of his holy words. (v. 9)

Jeremiah was overcome by the holiness of God's Word. So when he heard what other people were saying about God, he was deeply disturbed. He experienced "almost uncontrollable emotional agitation."[6] The falseness of the other clergy in his city did not make him smug about his own ministry. It filled him with sadness and dismay. Jeremiah sang a lament for ungodly ministers.

Faithful preaching ought to expose the errors of the contemporary church. It is right and good to warn the people of God about the dangers of false teaching. Good preaching both declares Biblical truth *and* refutes doctrinal error. There is no way to do one without doing the other. The truth must be explained and defended without reservation or compromise.

However, Biblical truth must not be defended without charity or humility. The decline of the church is nothing to be smug about. As I look around the city of Philadelphia, I see many churches that have either departed from the Word of God or closed their doors altogether. Jeremiah saw the same thing when he looked around at his colleagues in ministry. He was heartbroken about it. He said, "Concerning the prophets: My heart is broken within me; all my bones shake" (v. 9a). Contemporary Christians should be saying the same thing. "Concerning the mainline church: my heart is broken. . . . Concerning the evangelical church: all my bones tremble."

A good model to follow when simultaneously warning and mourning the church is the great apologist Francis Schaeffer. D. A. Carson writes:

> One of the reasons for Francis Schaeffer's influence was his ability to present his analysis of the culture with a tear in his eye. Whether or not one agrees at every point with his analysis, and regardless of how severe his judgments were, one could not responsibly doubt his compassion, his genuine love for men and women. Too many of his would-be successors simply sound like angry people. Our times call for Christian leaders who will articulate the truth boldly, courageously, humbly, knowledgeably, in a contemporary fashion, with prophetic fire—and with profound compassion. One cannot imagine how the kind of gospel set forth in the Bible could be effectively communicated in any other way.[7]

It is not surprising to learn that Schaeffer had made Jeremiah a subject for careful study.[8]

More Than a Feeling

A second way to value truth is to be careful how you talk about getting messages from the Lord. Some Christians speak very casually about receiving private revelation from the Lord. "I feel led," they say. "The Lord has laid it on my heart." "God told me thus and so." Or more alarmingly, "God told me to tell *you* to do thus and so."

The false prophets of Jerusalem said the same kinds of things, although they used their own clichés to do it: "I have heard what the prophets have said who prophesy lies in my name, saying, 'I have dreamed, I have dreamed!'" (v. 25). (One way to remember this chapter is to think of it as Jeremiah's

"I Had a Dream" sermon.) On other occasions the prophets said, "Declares the LORD" (v. 31b). Here is another of their favorites: "The burden of the LORD" (v. 34).

Like most clichés, these phrases were used over and over again. The prophets kept on saying these things (vv. 35, 37). God grew so tired of it that he reached the point where he never wanted to hear someone say he had "a word from the Lord" again:

> When one of this people, or a prophet or a priest asks you, "What is the burden of the LORD?" you shall say to them, "You are the burden, and I will cast you off, declares the LORD." And as for the prophet, priest, or one of the people who says, "The burden of the LORD," I will punish that man and his household. Thus shall you say, every one to his neighbor and every one to his brother, "What has the LORD answered?" or "What has the LORD spoken?" But "The burden of the LORD" you shall mention no more, for the burden is every man's own word, and you pervert the words of the living God, the LORD of hosts, our God. Thus you shall say to the prophet, "What has the LORD answered you?" or "What has the LORD spoken?" But if you say, "The burden of the LORD," thus says the LORD, "Because you have said these words, 'The burden of the LORD,' when I sent to you, saying, 'You shall not say, "The burden of the LORD . . ."'" (vv. 33–38)

There are several Biblical examples of God revealing his will through dreams. Joseph, Daniel, and the Magi come immediately to mind. Yet the Bible tends to minimize the value of dreams for revelation. Indeed, Moses warned about giving them too much weight:

> If a prophet or a dreamer of dreams arises among you and gives you a sign or a wonder, and the sign or wonder that he tells you comes to pass, and if he says, "Let us go after other gods," which you have not known, "and let us serve them," you shall not listen to the words of that prophet or that dreamer of dreams. For the Lord your God is testing you, to know whether you love the Lord your God with all your heart and with all your soul. (Deuteronomy 13:1–3)

Dreams do not interpret themselves. Not all signs and wonders come from God. Prophets must be tested to see if they obey God and submit to what God has already revealed in his Word. If they live unholy lives or contradict the teaching of Scripture, they are false prophets.

In order to claim to receive a word of knowledge from the LORD, one must be able to answer God's question: "For who among them has stood in the council of the LORD to see and to hear his word, or who has paid attention to his word and listened?" (23:18).

This was the kind of experience Isaiah had when he "saw the LORD sitting upon a throne, high and lifted up" and heard the voices of the seraphim saying, "Holy, holy, holy is the LORD of hosts" (Isaiah 6:1, 3). When Isaiah saw and heard all that, he did not go around saying, "I had a dream! I had a dream!" He said, "Woe is me! For I am lost; for I am a man of unclean lips, and I dwell in the midst of a people of unclean lips; for my eyes have seen the King, the LORD of hosts!" (v. 5).

In order to claim to have received a revelation from God, one also must be able to answer the rest of God's questions: "Let the prophet who has a dream tell the dream, but let him who has my word speak my word faithfully. What has straw in common with wheat? declares the LORD. Is not my word like fire, declares the LORD, and like a hammer that breaks the rock in pieces?" (23:28, 29).

This was the kind of experience Elijah had on Mount Carmel when he defeated the prophets of Baal. When the people of Israel saw fire descend from Heaven, they did not go around shouting, "The oracle of the LORD! The oracle of the LORD!" Instead they lay down face first in the dust and worshiped God (1 Kings 18:39).

The true Word of God is like fire. It refines God's people and consumes everyone else. The true Word of God is "like a hammer that breaks the rock in pieces." The difference between the true Word of God and the false words of men is the difference between wheat and chaff. False dreams and empty Christian clichés are just straw. They may provide good bedding for livestock, but they do not nourish the soul. The best that can be said for straw is that it is easy to burn, which is part of Jeremiah's point.

Jeremiah 23 is a warning not to make false claims of receiving revelation from God. To do so is to take God's name in vain. Remember that Jesus said, "I tell you, on the day of judgment people will give account for every careless word they speak, for by your words you will be justified, and by your words you will be condemned" (Matthew 12:36, 37). Notice that Jesus was speaking about careless words, not evil words. Yet Christian jargon mostly consists of careless words!

It is true that the Holy Spirit guides and directs the Christian's thoughts. The Spirit gives wisdom for life's decisions. But now that he has spoken in Jesus Christ, the Spirit has said everything that needs to be said. He does not give a new chapter and a new verse for every new day, nor does he need to. Dick Keyes, who directs the L'Abri fellowship near Boston, points out that what people really mean when they say, "The Lord is telling me thus and so" is, "I have a warm spiritual hunch."[9]

Sometimes Christians do get warm spiritual hunches. But if what you have is a warm spiritual hunch, then by all means call it a warm spiritual hunch. It is much better to say something like, "I am still asking the Lord for guidance, but I sense that he may be leading me in this direction." Otherwise you are in danger of taking God's name in vain.

If the Lord ever takes you into his throne room for an audience, you will not need to say, "I had a dream! I had a dream!" If you live to tell about it, people will be able to tell by the whites of your eyes!

Worth a Listen

A third way to apply the message of Jeremiah 23 is to listen to Jesus Christ, God's true prophet.

The message of chapters 21, 22 was that all the kings of Israel have failed. There can be no king but Christ for the people of God. Jeremiah 23 builds on that message by teaching that all the prophets and priests of Israel have failed as well. "Their course is evil, and their might is not right. 'Both prophet and priest are ungodly; even in my house I have found their evil, declares the LORD'" (vv. 10b, 11). In other words, the three pillars of Israelite society— prophet, priest, and king—have all toppled. What the people of God need is someone to teach them God's truth. They need a true prophet as well as a true king and a true priest.

Jesus Christ is the only true prophet for the people of God. Jeremiah said that what distinguishes a true prophet is that he has met with God. "If they had stood in my council, then they would have proclaimed my words to my people" (v. 22a). Jesus Christ meets these qualifications. He has been in the council room of the Most High God to see and to hear the Word of God. When the false prophets of his own day threatened to put him to death he said, "You seek to kill me because my word finds no place in you. I speak of what I have seen with my Father . . . but now you seek to kill me, a man who has told you the truth that I heard from God" (John 8:37b, 38, 40a).

Jesus Christ both saw and heard the truth from God the Father. Then he confirmed that visible, audible truth by his death and resurrection. He is God's true prophet. Listen to him.

33

Two Baskets of Figs

JEREMIAH 24:1—25:14

WHEN I WAS IN THE SIXTH GRADE my grammar school embarked on a massive fund-raising project. Armed with flyers and clipboards, hundreds of elementary students were unleashed on an unsuspecting suburban public. Our merchandise was an easy sell in the dead of a Chicago winter—large boxes of Florida oranges and grapefruit.

Once the orders had been safely placed, we waited for the fruit to arrive. I can still remember the thrill that ran through the school the day the trailer-truck with Florida plates backed up to the building. Noses were pressed hard against classroom windows all along the end of the school. Carpool moms with station wagons lined up as far as the eye could see, waiting to receive the boxes of fruit and deliver them to hungry neighbors.

Then the back of the truck opened, and excitement turned to dismay. The refrigeration system had failed, the fruit was blighted, and a putrid stench emanated from the truck. The oranges and the grapefruit were so bad they could not be eaten.

Spoiled Rotten

The prophet Jeremiah had seen some rotten fruit in his time, but nothing to compare with the basket of figs he saw in the produce department one fine day in 597 BC. It had been a disastrous year: "Nebuchadnezzar king of Babylon had taken into exile from Jerusalem Jeconiah [or, Jehoiachin] the son of Jehoiakim, king of Judah, together with the officials of Judah, the craftsmen, and the metal workers, and had brought them to Babylon" (24:1a). The Babylonians had skimmed the cream off Jewish society. All the courtiers, soldiers, civil servants, doctors, lawyers, priests, honor students, and Eagle Scouts had been taken captive. Nebuchadnezzar "carried away all Jerusalem and all the officials and all the mighty men of valor, 10,000 captives, and all the craftsmen and the smiths. None remained, except the poorest people of the land" (2 Kings 24:14).

In that fateful year the Lord took Jeremiah to the fruit stand by the temple, where people were supposed to offer their firstfruits to the Lord. In the prophet's own words:

> The LORD showed me this vision: behold, two baskets of figs placed before the temple of the LORD. One basket had very good figs, like first-ripe figs, but the other basket had very bad figs, so bad that they could not be eaten. And the LORD said to me, "What do you see, Jeremiah?" I said, "Figs, the good figs very good, and the bad figs very bad, so bad that they cannot be eaten." (24:1b–3)

Jeremiah may not have been a greengrocer, but he knew a bad fig when he smelled it. These figs were terrible.

The news was even worse. The basket of spoiled figs was a symbol that something was rotten in Jerusalem:

> But thus says the LORD: Like the bad figs that are so bad they cannot be eaten, so will I treat Zedekiah the king of Judah, his officials, the remnant of Jerusalem who remain in this land, and those who dwell in the land of Egypt. I will make them a horror to all the kingdoms of the earth, to be a reproach, a byword, a taunt, and a curse in all the places where I shall drive them. And I will send sword, famine, and pestilence upon them, until they shall be utterly destroyed from the land that I gave to them and their fathers. (vv. 8–10; cf. chapter 39)

This was a promise of judgment against those who had disobeyed God. Back in chapter 21 God gave his people a choice between "The way of life and the way of death" (v. 8). "The way of life" was to go into exile in Babylon. Surrender was their only hope of survival. "The way of death" was to remain in Jerusalem with Zedekiah, the puppet king of the Babylonians. God had determined to do the city "harm and not . . . good." The king of Babylon would "burn it with fire" (21:10), and whoever stayed in the city would "die by the sword, by famine, and by pestilence" (21:9a). It was turn or burn for the citizens of Jerusalem.

The bad figs represented the people who stayed in Jerusalem. They thought that they were the favored sons, that they still had the blessings that belonged to God's chosen people. They also thought that they would be safe in Jerusalem. What God had told them to do was to go to Babylon instead of staying in Jerusalem. But they were unwilling to do this because they knew exile would involve suffering. The irony is that by staying in Jerusalem rather than going to Babylon they suffered much worse in the end, which is generally what happens when people disobey God.

Once God's people realized that they were cursed, they wanted to run off to Egypt (24:8). But God had made them an object of ridicule and cursing to the nations. Once fruit is rotten, it stays rotten. It stays spoiled even if it gets put into the refrigerator. That principle holds true for spiritual things as well. If God's people stayed in Jerusalem, they would be rotten. If they went down to Egypt, they would be rotten there too. Wherever they went on the face of the globe, the smell of their disobedience would be just as rank.

Israel had been spoiling for a long time. Chapter 25 is a prophecy Jeremiah had made some years before, in 605 BC, the year the superpowers clashed at Carchemish and the Babylonians defeated the Egyptians. The prophecy appears at this point in Jeremiah's book because it explains how the bad figs got spoiled in the first place. It was not for lack of warning:

> The word that came to Jeremiah concerning all the people of Judah, in the fourth year of Jehoiakim the son of Josiah, king of Judah (that was the first year of Nebuchadnezzar king of Babylon), which Jeremiah the prophet spoke to all the people of Judah and all the inhabitants of Jerusalem: "For twenty-three years, from the thirteenth year of Josiah the son of Amon, king of Judah, to this day, the word of the LORD has come to me, and I have spoken persistently to you." (25:1–3a)

The prophet had been warning the people incessantly for decades.

And Jeremiah was not the only one.

> You have neither listened nor inclined your ears to hear, although the LORD persistently sent to you all his servants the prophets, saying, "Turn now, every one of you, from his evil way and evil deeds, and dwell upon the land that the LORD has given to you and your fathers from of old and forever. Do not go after other gods to serve and worship them, or provoke me to anger with the work of your hands. Then I will do you no harm." (vv. 4–6)

God understands the value of repetition. In the Bible he repeatedly warns his people about the things he hates. This is part of God's grace. He does not keep people guessing about how to please him. He gives his instructions over and over. However, God also holds people responsible for every warning they ignore.

Perhaps there is value in repeating the warnings God has given again and again throughout the book of Jeremiah: Do not worship other gods. Do not forget your love for the Lord. Do not fool around with sexual sin. Do not love your-selves more than your children. Do not ignore the poor. Do not listen to false teaching. Do not boast in your wisdom, your strength, or your riches. Do not dishonor the Lord's Day. Do not live for things. Do not serve any king but Christ.

The consequences of ignoring such warnings are always devastating. In the case of the people of Jerusalem, judgment was to include invasion, humili-ation, ruination, and desolation (25:8, 9, 11). God would finally send Nebu-chadnezzar to deliver a message his people could not ignore:

> Therefore thus says the LORD of hosts: Because you have not obeyed my words, behold, I will send for all the tribes of the north, declares the LORD, and for Nebuchadnezzar the king of Babylon, my servant, and I will bring them against this land and its inhabitants, and against all these surround-ing nations. I will devote them to destruction, and make them a horror, a hissing, and an everlasting desolation. Moreover, I will banish from them the voice of mirth and the voice of gladness, the voice of the bridegroom and the voice of the bride, the grinding of the millstones and the light of the lamp. (vv. 8–10)

There would be no more joy in Jerusalem. Everyday life as the people knew it would come to an end. The activities of daily life—work and wed-dings—would cease.

It may have been tempting to blame Nebuchadnezzar for these troubles. Yet the judgment he brought came from the Lord, which is why Nebuchad-nezzar is referred to as God's "servant" (v. 9). If Nebuchadnezzar was God's servant, it must have been even more tempting to blame God for the troubles of Jerusalem. Yet those who refused to listen to God had only themselves to blame. "Yet you have not listened to me, declares the LORD, that you might provoke me to anger with the work of your hands to your own harm" (v. 7).

Why does God punish people for their sins? Usually part of the answer is that people bring themselves under judgment. Most of the wounds people suffer for disobedience are self-inflicted. To choose sin is also to choose its consequences.

The unregenerate pay their own way to Hell. In *The Great Divorce* C. S. Lewis argued:

> There are only two kinds of people in the end: those who say to God, "Thy will be done," and those to whom God says, in the end, "Thy will be done." All that are in Hell, choose it. Without that self-choice there could be no Hell. No soul that seriously and constantly desires joy will ever miss it. Those who seek find. To those who knock it is opened.[1]

Do not ignore God's warning. Do not choose to go your own way. If you want to escape the wrath of God, you must leave your sins behind and come to Christ. You must admit that you are an idolater, an adulterer, and an oppressor. You must confess that you are boastful, selfish, and loveless. Then you must ask God to accept the sacrifice Jesus made when he died on the cross for your sins.

If you do not accept Jesus Christ, Jeremiah has pronounced your doom already; it will be "To your own harm" (v. 7). You will end up like a rotten fig at the bottom of the basket. Or even worse, you will end up like the fig tree Jesus cursed on his way into Jerusalem (Matthew 21:18, 19).

Fresh Fruit

The message of the bad figs was that the people who stayed in Jerusalem were rotten in their sin and needed to be thrown out. However, as John Guest observes, "There are two kinds of basket cases."[2] One of the baskets Jeremiah saw at the market "had very good figs, like first-ripe figs" (24:2a; cf. Hosea 9:10a).

The figs the prophet saw looked terrific. In fact, their skin looked so fresh they could hardly be ripe. Yet they were ripe! They matured early and tasted as good as they looked. What delicacies! The good figs were very good indeed.

The news was even better:

> Thus says the LORD, the God of Israel: Like these good figs, so I will regard as good the exiles from Judah, whom I have sent away from this place to the land of the Chaldeans. I will set my eyes on them for good, and I will bring them back to this land. I will build them up, and not tear them down; I will plant them, and not pluck them up. I will give them a heart to know that I am the LORD, and they shall be my people and I will be their God, for they shall return to me with their whole heart. (vv. 5–7)

The prophet had waited a long, long time to deliver such wonderful news. When God first called Jeremiah into the ministry, he appointed him "over nations and over kingdoms, to pluck up and to break down, to destroy and to overthrow, to build and to plant" (1:10). God's choice of verbs on that occasion made it apparent that curse ("pluck up, break down, destroy, overthrow") would outweigh blessing ("build, plant") by a ratio of two to one. That explains why Jeremiah has had so much to say about overthrowing and uprooting.

Now finally, in chapter 24, the prophet has something to say about building and planting. The people of God could do something besides just sitting in a basket and rotting. Exile in Babylon was more than a curse. By the grace of God, the exiles could become fresh and fruitful figs.

The promises God made to the exiles from Judah were all covenant promises. He offered them nothing less than the chief blessing of the covenant—personal knowledge of himself. In his book *Knowing God*, J. I. Packer begins a chapter entitled "Knowing and Being Known" like this:

> What were we made for? To know God. What aim should we set ourselves in life? To know God. What is the "eternal life" that Jesus gives? Knowledge of God. "This is life eternal, that they might know thee, the only true God, and Jesus Christ, whom thou hast sent" (John 17:3). What is the best thing in life, bringing more joy, delight, and contentment than anything else? Knowledge of God. "Thus saith the LORD, Let not the wise man glory in his wisdom, neither let the mighty man glory in his might, let not the rich man glory in his riches; but let him that glorieth glory in this, that he understandeth and knoweth me" (Jeremiah 9:23 f.). What, of all the states God ever sees man in, gives Him most pleasure? Knowledge of Himself. "I desire . . . the knowledge of God more than burnt offerings," says God (Hosea 6:6).[3]

To know God is the best knowledge of all, which is why the promise of the good figs is the best of all possible news: "I will give them a heart to know that I am the LORD" (24:7a).

Before seeing how much there is to know of God, we must realize that such knowledge often comes through suffering. Unlike the bad figs, the good figs followed God right into suffering. They did not go down with the city. There was a way of escape for them. But the way of escape led through Babylon. The good figs were exiles and slaves who had to endure a lifetime of servitude to the Babylonians. They were forced to sit down by the rivers of Babylon, hang their harps on the poplars, and weep for Zion (Psalm 137:1, 2). In order to know God, they had to pass through the refining fires of suffering.

Perhaps I can put it like this: If you want to make Fig Newtons, you have to crush a few figs along the way! This is the usual pattern of the Christian life. Knowing God does not come by avoiding suffering—it comes *through* suffering. Suffering brings increased knowledge of God. Remember what Paul wrote to the Philippians about the overriding passion of his life, namely, "That I may know him and the power of his resurrection, and may share his sufferings, becoming like him in his death, that by any means possible I may attain the resurrection from the dead" (Philippians 3:10, 11). Paul did not expect to know God except through suffering. He understood that the Christian life is often equal parts suffering and glory.

The great London minister Charles Haddon Spurgeon (1834–1892) also understood the way suffering promotes the knowledge of God. Spurgeon said:

It is of no use our hoping that we shall be well-rooted if no March winds have passed over us. The young oak cannot be expected to strike its roots so deep as the old one. Those old gnarlings on the roots, and those strange twistings of the branches, all tell of many storms that have swept over the aged tree. But they are also indicators of the depths into which the roots have dived.[4]

The Old Testament people of God could not come to know God to the very depths except through exile. Their captivity in Babylon was no accident; it was part of God's sovereign plan of redemption. The Israelites would not come to know God in spite of their suffering, but *because* of their suffering.

Grace, Grace, God's Grace

Jeremiah described four ways the exiles would know God through their captivity.

The first was to know God through his *justifying* grace. Through their suffering, God's people would learn that God counts them as good: "Thus says the LORD, the God of Israel: Like these good figs, so I will regard as good the exiles from Judah" (24:5). This is the justifying grace of God. The exiles from Judah were not good. They were just as rotten as the rest of God's figs. Like the others, they had ignored God's warnings to turn away from sin. But God was going to regard them as good anyway. He was going to consider or reckon them good, not based on their merits, but because of his grace.

This is the sheer grace of God in justifying sinners. We are not good. We have broken the whole law of God. But God regards us as good because of the work of Jesus Christ. Whoever trusts in Christ for salvation looks good to God. According to this gracious reckoning, everyone who trusts in Christ is counted among the righteous. As Scripture says, "Abraham 'believed God, and it was counted to him as righteousness'" (Galatians 3:6).

Second, God's people would know God's *protecting* grace. Through their sufferings they would learn that God watches over his people for good: "I will set my eyes on them for good" (24:6a). God would take care of his people. Even when the exiles went all the way to Babylon, they did not escape God's field of vision. He did not abandon them to suffer alone.

The proof that God watched over his people for good in Babylon can be seen in his care for Daniel's friends Hananiah, Mishael, and Azariah. These three young men were carried off by Nebuchadnezzar to Babylon, where they were put in the service of the king. They were even given Babylonian names—Shadrach, Meshach, and Abednego (Daniel 1:1–7).

The eyes of God watched over Shadrach, Meshach, and Abednego for good. He even protected them when they defied Nebuchadnezzar by refusing to worship his golden idol (3:1, 12). Nebuchadnezzar commanded them to either worship his image or be thrown into a blazing furnace. They replied:

> O Nebuchadnezzar, we have no need to answer you in this matter. If this be so, our God whom we serve is able to deliver us from the burning fiery furnace, and he will deliver us out of your hand, O king. But if not, be it known to you, O king, that we will not serve your gods or worship the golden image that you have set up. (Daniel 3:16–18)

Shadrach, Meshach, and Abednego trusted the promise God made to his people through the prophet Jeremiah. They knew he was watching over them for good, even in Babylon.

It was a good thing, too, because their words made Nebuchadnezzar blaze with anger:

> He ordered the furnace heated seven times more than it was usually heated. And he ordered some of the mighty men of his army to bind Shadrach, Meshach, and Abednego, and to cast them into the burning fiery furnace. Then these men were bound in their cloaks, their tunics, their hats, and their other garments, and they were thrown into the burning fiery furnace. Because the king's order was urgent and the furnace overheated, the flame of the fire killed those men who took up Shadrach, Meshach, and Abednego. And these three men, Shadrach, Meshach, and Abednego, fell bound into the burning fiery furnace. (vv. 19b–23)

God did not abandon his servants to suffer alone. As Nebuchadnezzar peered into the furnace he saw not three men, but four. The fourth man looked "like a son of the gods" (v. 25). God sent an angel to protect his servants from the flames. When Shadrach, Meshach, and Abednego came out of the furnace, "The fire had not had any power over the bodies of those men. The hair of their heads was not singed, their cloaks were not harmed, and no smell of fire had come upon them" (v. 27). Even in the fiery furnace, God kept his promise to watch over them for good.

God makes the same promise to all his servants. Those who know Christ are under God's watchful care wherever they go. The *Catechism for Young Children* asks, "Can you see God?" "No, I cannot see God, but he always sees me." Somewhere the Spanish poet Unamuno has expressed the same idea in verse: "The eye is, Not because you see it, But because It sees you."

The unblinking, all-seeing eye of God is a threat to all his enemies. As God warned in the previous chapter, "Am I a God at hand . . . and not a God far away? Can a man hide himself in secret places so that I cannot see him?" (23:23, 24). Yet God is always watching out for his people. As the prophet

Hanani said to King Asa, "The eyes of the LORD run to and fro throughout the whole earth, to give strong support to those whose heart is blameless toward him" (2 Chronicles 16:9).

Home Is Where the Heart Is

To know God is also to know his *overcoming* grace. The exiles would know this grace when they would finally see God overcome their enemies, deliver them from captivity, and bring them home for good. They would suffer, but not forever.

This portion of Jeremiah's prophecy ends with a promise of judgment for the Babylonians:

> Then after seventy years are completed, I will punish the king of Babylon and that nation, the land of the Chaldeans, for their iniquity, declares the LORD, making the land an everlasting waste. I will bring upon that land all the words that I have uttered against it, everything written in this book, which Jeremiah prophesied against all the nations. For many nations and great kings shall make slaves even of them, and I will recompense them according to their deeds and the work of their hands. (25:12–14; cf. chaps. 50, 51)

With typical Scottish understatement, Gordon McConville notes that the Babylonians were to be "discomfited."[5] To put it another way, "What goes around comes around." Israel is not the only nation God watches. He also has his eye on the Babylonians, so he can punish their evil deeds.

It is a great comfort to know that God will overcome all his enemies. It is more comforting still to know that he will bring his friends back home. Concerning the exiles, he promised, "I will bring them back to this land" (24:6). God even told his friends when their sufferings would come to an end: "This whole land shall become a ruin and a waste, and these nations shall serve the king of Babylon seventy years" (25:11).

It is hard to know how the Bible counts these seventy years. They may represent the span of a normal lifetime, as they do in the Psalms: "The years of our life are seventy, or even by reason of strength eighty" (Psalm 90:10). Or perhaps seventy is a round number to represent the time between 605 BC, when the Babylonians won the battle of Carchemish, and 536 BC, when the first exiles returned to Jerusalem.[6] In any case, the point is that the sufferings of God's people would not last forever. Seventy years sounds like a long time, but at least it was only seventy!

For the Christian, all troubles are temporary. Most of them will not even last seventy years, although some may last a lifetime. The apostle Peter had a wonderful way of talking about the limits of tribulation. He was completely honest about the griefs, sufferings, and trials of the Christian life. But he insisted on saying that these things would last only "a little while." "In this you rejoice, though now for a little while, if necessary, you have been grieved by various trials" (1 Peter 1:6). "After you have suffered a little while, the God of all grace . . . will himself restore, confirm, strengthen, and establish you" (1 Peter 5:10). Peter shrank sufferings down to size by placing them next to the yardstick of eternity. Thanks to God's overcoming grace, they will only last "a little while." Soon Christ will come to take us home for good.

A Change of Heart

Another way to know God is by his *regenerating* grace. God not only counts his people as good, watches over them for good, and brings them home for good—he also makes them good.

If there is one thing to be learned from the first twenty-three chapters of Jeremiah, it is that God's people are not very good. In those days, their problem was that they did not have good hearts. In fact, they had "stubborn and rebellious" hearts (5:23). They "stubbornly follow[ed] their own evil heart" (3:17; cf. 11:8). Jeremiah was in such despair about his own heart that he cried out, "The heart is deceitful above all things, and desperately sick; who can understand it?" (17:9).

If you have ever looked into the depths of your own heart, you know it is just as stubborn, rebellious, evil, and deceitful as Jeremiah's was. And a bad heart is like a basket of rotten figs. Once it is spoiled, it will not get ripe again on its own. Who can cure the heart? Who can even understand it?

God understands the human heart. And he not only understands it, he can cure it. This is the promise of his regenerating grace: "I will give them a heart to know that I am the LORD, and they shall be my people and I will be their God, for they shall return to me with their whole heart" (24:7). This promise of a new heart was not just for the exiles in Babylon. It is for every sinner who turns to God in faith and repentance.

Returning wholeheartedly to God requires more than just a change of heart. So if you have not had one yet, may I suggest that you undergo a heart transplant? The human heart is so desperately wicked that what you need—what everyone needs, really—is a spiritual heart transplant.

I can also recommend a good surgeon. The God who made your heart in the first place specializes in heart transplants. I even have a donor lined up for you—the Lord Jesus Christ. When Jesus gives you his heart, you will come to know God in the most intimate way. Your new heart is ready. All you need to do is ask for it.

34

"Take from My Hand This Cup"

JEREMIAH 25:15–38

SOMETIMES THE BIBLE compares God to a shepherd, a father, a judge, or a king. But in this passage of Scripture God compares himself to a bartender. "Take from my hand this cup," he says to Jeremiah.

When God dispenses his wines, he has two casks from which to draw. He pours two wines into two cups, and he offers everyone a drink. "Take from my hand one of these cups," he says. Everyone must drink one cup or the other. Thus it is important to see which wine has the best appearance, to smell which wine has the most aromatic bouquet, and to taste which wine has the richest flavor. See, smell, taste . . . and then choose which wine you will drink.

A Bitter Cup for the Nations

First, God offers a cup to his enemies, a cup full of divine judgment. It is the bitter cup of God's wrath prepared for the nations.

God mixed strong drink, poured it into a cup, and handed it to Jeremiah. The wine had been prepared for all the nations of the world. "Thus the LORD, the God of Israel, said to me: 'Take from my hand this cup of the wine of wrath, and make all the nations to whom I send you drink it'" (25:15).

First to drink the wine of God's wrath were the kings of Judah, with all the officials of Jerusalem. Jeremiah explains what happened: "So I took the cup from the LORD's hand, and made all the nations to whom the LORD sent me drink it: Jerusalem and the cities of Judah, its kings and officials, to make them a desolation and a waste, a hissing and a curse, as at this day" (vv. 17, 18). God did not overlook sin among his own people, for judgment always begins with the house of God.

Then Jeremiah passed the cup to the other nations of the world. He went as God's ambassador, but not to pursue quiet diplomacy. When God called Jeremiah to be a prophet, he appointed him "over nations and over kingdoms, to pluck up and to break down, to destroy and to overthrow" (1:10). Jeremiah was set over the nations to serve them with divine judgment.

The nations Jeremiah served are listed in his prophecy. The united nations gathered around a banqueting table for an unholy communion of bitter wine:

> Pharaoh king of Egypt, his servants, his officials, all his people, and all the mixed tribes among them; all the kings of the land of Uz and all the kings of the land of the Philistines (Ashkelon, Gaza, Ekron, and the remnant of Ashdod); Edom, Moab, and the sons of Ammon; all the kings of Tyre, all the kings of Sidon, and the kings of the coastland across the sea; Dedan, Tema, Buz, and all who cut the corners of their hair; all the kings of Arabia and all the kings of the mixed tribes who dwell in the desert; all the kings of Zimri, all the kings of Elam, and all the kings of Media; all the kings of the north, far and near, one after another, and all the kingdoms of the world that are on the face of the earth. (25:19–26a)

It was the Olympics of divine judgment, and all the nations of the earth were there.

Jeremiah saved the big surprise for last: "And after them the king of Babylon [or Sheshach, NIV] shall drink" (v. 26b). Even Sheshach, which is a code word for Babylon, the mightiest empire of Jeremiah's day, would have to drink the cup of God's wrath. *Babel* is spelled with the second and the twelfth letters of the Hebrew alphabet (the second letter is repeated). If one starts from the back of the alphabet, however, and takes the second and the twelfth letters of the alphabet, it spells *Sheshach*. Even mighty Babylon would be compelled to drink the wine of God's judgment. No person, no nation, no empire could escape the wrath to come.

Can the nations refuse to drink? Can they abstain from this alcohol? No, they cannot: "And if they refuse to accept the cup from your hand to drink, then you shall say to them, 'Thus says the LORD of hosts: You must drink!'" (v. 28; cf. 49:12).

When God serves the drinks, no one is allowed to be a teetotaler. When God says, "Take from my hand this cup," it is not just an invitation; it is a command. The nations must drink the judgment of God.

If any proof of this divine compulsion is required, look no further than Jerusalem, the city that bears God's name, where God's own people dwell. Even that city would come under judgment. "For behold," God says, "I begin to work disaster at the city that is called by my name, and shall you go unpunished?" (v. 29a). And if disaster would befall Jerusalem, how could Uz and Buz or Ashdod and Ashkelon possibly escape? "You shall not go unpunished, for I am summoning a sword against all the inhabitants of the earth, declares the Lord of hosts" (v. 29b). If God's own children suffer, then everyone must suffer.

What is it like to drink the wine of God's judgment? What does the bitter cup of God's wrath taste like? "They shall drink and stagger and be crazed because of the sword that I am sending among them" (v. 16).

This is strong drink indeed, a bitter brew. It is a goblet of staggering and madness. The word translated "stagger" suggests there is something venomous or poisonous in the cup. The cup of God's wrath does not just intoxicate and inebriate; it staggers and stupefies. "Drink, be drunk and vomit," the Lord says again in verse 27; "fall and rise no more, because of the sword that I am sending among you."

I have seen such staggering and such falling. When I was twelve or so, the boy across the street staggered across the road and careened across our front yard. He was dazed and unsteady, and his eyes were glazed over. There was a good reason for this: He had just downed sixteen shot glasses of whiskey! One of his drinking buddies was pushing him toward the sprinkler in our front yard, trying desperately to revive him. The boy fell to the ground like a stone, flat on his face. When my mother ran out to save his life he was out cold, lying face-down in his own vomit. He had been drinking from the cup of God's wrath, the bitter wine of divine judgment.

Here in Jeremiah we see the bitter cup of God's wrath in the hands of the nations. Such unholy intoxication will befall the world because of its sins. The nations will drink the cup filled with the wine of God's wrath; they will drink the cup of God's wrath against sin. Jeremiah was not speaking primarily about the effects of alcohol—although he does suggest that drunkenness is a foretaste of the judgment to come—but about God's wrath against sin.

God rules the nations, and he will bring them to justice for their sins. Someday the nations will stagger and reel under the weight of God's judgment. They will stagger, reel, and retch, and then they will fall to rise no more. The cup of wrath they drink will come from the hand of God, and God is the one who will make them drink it.

A Bitter Cup for Every Sinner

The bitter cup of God's wrath has been mixed for every sinner who does not repent. A cup of judgment has been prepared for every sinner who rejects God and his Son Jesus Christ.

As we have already noticed, Jeremiah's prophecy makes it clear that divine judgment is not simply for the nations of his own day, but for all the nations of the earth. This becomes even more clear at the end of the chapter, where God says:

> You, therefore, shall prophesy against them all these words, and say to them:
>
>> "The LORD will roar from on high,
>>   and from his holy habitation utter his voice;
>> he will roar mightily against his fold,
>>   and shout, like those who tread grapes,
>>   against all the inhabitants of the earth.
>> The clamor will resound to the ends of the earth,
>>   for the LORD has an indictment against the nations;
>> he is entering into judgment with all flesh,
>>   and the wicked he will put to the sword,
>>   declares the LORD."
>
>> Thus says the LORD of hosts:
>> Behold, disaster is going forth
>>   from nation to nation,
>> and a great tempest is stirring
>>   from the farthest parts of the earth! (vv. 30–32)

Jeremiah's vision of judgment widens out from Jerusalem to the Middle East, and from the Middle East to the whole world.

When the Old Testament speaks of God's worldwide judgment, it often describes it as a cup of wrath prepared for sinners. This theme comes up in the Psalms: "For in the hand of the LORD there is a cup with foaming wine, well mixed, and he pours out from it, and all the wicked of the earth shall drain it down to the dregs" (Psalm 75:8). It also appears in the prophets: "Wake yourself, wake yourself, stand up, O Jerusalem, you who have drunk from the hand of the LORD the cup of his wrath, who have drunk to the dregs the bowl, the cup of staggering" (Isaiah 51:17). Jeremiah used the image again in his lamentations: "Rejoice and be glad, O daughter of Edom, you who dwell in the land of Uz; but to you also the cup shall pass; you shall become drunk and strip yourself bare" (Lamentations 4:21).

A cup of strong wine is one Biblical symbol for divine judgment. But the cup of wrath was not just for Jeremiah's day. It is not just an Old Testament figure of speech. A cup of wrath is stored away for *every* sinner who does not repent. The wine of God's judgment is a present threat for those who do not know Jesus Christ as Savior and Lord.

Jeremiah describes judgment in such vivid detail that it almost becomes a picture of the final judgment:

> And those pierced by the LORD on that day shall extend from one end of the earth to the other. They shall not be lamented, or gathered, or buried; they shall be dung on the surface of the ground.

> "Wail, you shepherds, and cry out,
>   and roll in ashes, you lords of the flock,
> for the days of your slaughter and dispersion have come,
>   and you shall fall like a choice vessel.
> No refuge will remain for the shepherds,
>   nor escape for the lords of the flock.
> A voice—the cry of the shepherds,
>   and the wail of the lords of the flock!
> For the LORD is laying waste their pasture,
>   and the peaceful folds are devastated
>   because of the fierce anger of the LORD.
> Like a lion he has left his lair,
>   for their land has become a waste
> because of the sword of the oppressor,
>   and because of his fierce anger." (25:33–38)

In the book of Revelation, at the end of the New Testament, the apostle John describes the judgment that awaits the man who rejects Christ: "He also will drink the wine of God's wrath, poured full strength into the cup of his anger, and he will be tormented with fire and sulfur in the presence of the holy angels and in the presence of the Lamb. And the smoke of their torment goes up forever and ever" (14:10, 11a). There is an eternal drinking of the cup filled with the wine of God's wrath, and that cup is bitter all the way down.

Would you choose this cup? Would you drink the wine of divine judgment? Would you drink the foaming bowl of God's wrath? Does your hand not tremble at the very thought of grasping the cup of staggering? Do your lips not quiver at the very thought of drinking the cup of God's wrath down to the last drop? What person would dare to drink the bitter cup of God's wrath and swallow up divine judgment?

A Bitter Cup for Christ

In Isaiah's prophecy about the bitter cup (chapter 51) something remarkable happens. One minute the sons of Jerusalem were lying about in a drunken stupor, staggering around and collapsing in their own vomit because of the Lord's judgment upon their sin, just as in Jeremiah's prophecy. But then in the middle of Jerusalem's drunken stupor, without any warning or explanation, we read this verse: "Thus says your LORD, the LORD, your God who pleads the cause of his people: 'Behold, I have taken from your hand the cup of staggering; the bowl of my wrath you shall drink no more'" (v. 22).

The Sovereign Lord thus snatches the cup of wrath right out of the hands of his people, so that the bitter cup of God's wrath is no longer in the hands of sinners. Isaiah foresees a day when the captivity in Babylon will be over, when God will remove his chastisement from Jerusalem, when God's people will return to their land, and when the cup of wrath will be removed from their lips.

Isaiah, Jeremiah, and the rest of the Old Testament prophets longed to understand these things. They longed to see how God would take away the bitter cup he had once given. They longed to see how a just and righteous God could forgive his people for all their sins. They longed to see the Messiah redeem the nations. In some ways they *did* see these things, but not the way we can, for we can see how God has taken the cup of wrath away from the sinner and placed it into the hands of Jesus Christ.

It is in the gospel that the bitter cup of God's wrath ends up in the hand of Christ. At first Jesus Christ shrank back from the awful cup. Anyone who has smelled the bitter aroma of the cup in Jeremiah can understand why this was so, why Jesus was almost afraid to drink it. It is little wonder that Christ should draw back from the horrid cup of God's wrath, or that he should endure a dark hour of trial in the garden of Gethsemane, or that he should say, "My soul is very sorrowful, even to death" (Matthew 26:38).

Jesus was overwhelmed with sorrow because he knew the terror of God's wrath. He knew the Old Testament prophecies about the cup of God's wrath. He knew how bitter that cup would be. He knew it to be the cup that makes men stagger and go mad, the cup that makes men lie facedown in their own vomit. More than that, Jesus knew it to be the cup from which men fall and do not rise. He knew it to be the cup of death. He knew it was the cup of suffering, even of the sufferings of the cross.

It was because Jesus knew the cup of God's wrath to be a cup of staggering unto death that he said, "My Father, if it be possible, let this cup pass from me" (Matthew 26:39). Here we see Jesus at the point where he did not want to die, at the point where he did not want to drink the cup of wrath against our sin. Here, therefore, we see how terrible our sins really are. Like the disciples, we are often asleep in the garden, dozing through the Christian life, ambivalent about our sin. But were we to watch and pray, to kneel beside our Savior in the grass, to hear his cries of anguish, and to see the bloody sweat upon his brow, then we would see the fearfulness of God's wrath. And then we would know the sinfulness of our sin.

Jesus took the bitter cup of God's wrath into his hands, and he shrank from it. If you want proof of the sinfulness of sin, here it is. If you want proof of the reality of divine judgment, here it is. And if the Son of God himself hesitated to drink such a cup, will you be so bold as to drink it for yourself?

The amazing thing is that Jesus took the cup of God's wrath into his hands and drank it down, down to the very dregs. Note the courageous words of the Lord Jesus Christ: "My Father, if this cannot pass unless I drink it, your will be done" (Matthew 26:42). This is the willing, active, courageous obedience of Jesus Christ.

Notice also the slight but important difference between his two prayers to his Father. Back in verse 39 Jesus said, "My Father, if it be possible, let this cup pass from me." Later on, in verse 42, he said, "My Father, if this cannot pass unless I drink it . . ." At first it was "if it be possible," but then it was "if this *cannot* pass." The difference shows the Son's growing acceptance of the Father's will. If it was not possible—indeed, *since* it was not possible—Jesus Christ was willing to drink the cup. The Son of God knew the will of his Father. He knew that the Father was saying, "Take from my hand this cup." He knew that he had to endure the cross set before him. And he knew that there was no way to save his people from this bitter cup except to drink it. Therefore, he said, "Your will be done."

The bitter cup *must be* consumed. If Jesus Christ was to win salvation for his people, God's wrath had to be turned aside. God's anger against our sin had to be propitiated, for his righteousness cannot tolerate any of our sins. So Christ came to take those sins upon himself. He came to suffer the punishment for our sins. He came to drink the bitter cup of the wrath of God that our sins deserved.

When Jesus Christ came to drink that cup, then the bitter cup of God's wrath was no longer in the hands of a sinner. Quite the contrary. The bitter cup of God's wrath was in the hands of the sinless one, Jesus Christ, the Son of God.

But the cup did not stay in Christ's hands for long, because Jesus Christ drained it. He drank the bitter wine of God's wrath down to the very dregs.

This is why the sufferings of Christ were the ultimate sufferings—he drank the full measure of God's wrath, down to the last drop. Jesus endured every imprint of every thorn upon his forehead, every stripe beaten upon his back, and every nail driven into his hands.

Jesus endured all those things until the very moment when he cried out, "It is finished" (John 19:30). Finished indeed, for when the cup filled with the wine of God's wrath passed into the hands of Christ, it became an empty cup.

If you know that you are a sinner, then know also that there is no need for you to drink the cup of God's wrath. If your hand trembles, if your lips quiver at the thought, then give the cup to Christ. Pass the bitter cup to Christ, for he has drunk down the wrath of God. Let Jesus drink the cup of God's wrath in your place.

A Sweet Cup for the Christian

Jesus Christ drank down the cup of God's wrath in the place of every sinner who trusts in him. Because Christ drank the cup of wrath in the place of his people, there is no bitter wine left for them to drink. It is on the basis of the work of Christ that God can say, "The bowl of my wrath you shall drink no more" (see Isaiah 51:22).

But there is one cup left to drink. We have seen the bitter cup of God's wrath in the hands of the sinner and on the lips of Christ. That is the cup we deserve, the wine of staggering. But there is another cup that comes from the hand of God, a cup that contains the sweet, sweet wine of God's love. It is the cup that stands on the Lord's Table.

Remember what Jesus did for his disciples before going to the garden of Gethsemane: "And he took a cup, and when he had given thanks he gave it to them, saying, 'Drink of it, all of you, for this is my blood of the covenant, which is poured out for many for the forgiveness of sins. I tell you I will not drink again of this fruit of the vine until that day when I drink it new with you in my Father's kingdom'" (Matthew 26:27–29).

Now Jesus offers all his disciples a new cup, the cup of the new covenant in his blood. The cup of wrath has been taken away from the Christian, never to be tasted again. But there is a new cup to replace it, and Jesus says, "Take this cup from my hand."

The new cup is the cup of salvation from sin. It is the cup of victory over death. It is the cup that represents Jesus' own blood, the precious blood he spilled on Calvary when he drank the cup of God's wrath. It is the cup that pours out forgiveness, the forgiveness Christ earned for us when he completely drained the bitter cup of divine judgment.

There could be no cup like this, no new cup, unless Christ had been willing to drink the wine of divine wrath. But he did drink it, and now that God's wrath has been swallowed by Christ, you may hold out your hand to receive the sweet, sweet cup of God's love. In the words of George Herbert (1593–1633), "Love is that liquor sweet and most divine/Which my God feels as blood; but I, as wine."[1]

God's Word assures us that there are no dregs in the cup of God's love. You can drink and drink and drink. You can drink and it will be sweet all the way down. It will be sweet all the way down because it has been made sweet with Christ's own blood. One Puritan preacher in London put it like this: "Christ's treading the Wine-press, leads you into the Wine-Celler; though to him it was very painful, to you it is very comfortable; that which he felt as blood, Believers may taste as wine."[2]

It is a beautiful picture. Imagine Christ leading you down into the wine cellar, where there are great casks of the wine of God's love as far as the eye can see. There is enough to drink forever and ever in the eternal kingdom of God. And drink as long as you may, drink as deeply as you may, gulp down as many of the rich draughts of God's mercy as you may, you will never taste God's wrath. Come, take this cup from the hand of God, and drink. Come taste how sweet it is!

35

Delivered from Death

JEREMIAH 26:1–24

IN THE 1920S IT WAS THE SCOPES TRIAL, when William Jennings Bryan and Clarence Darrow squared off to debate creation versus evolution. In the 1930s it was the Lindbergh case, which tried to convict the kidnapper and killer of Charles Lindbergh's young son. In the 1970s it was Watergate, and the American presidency was on trial. In the 1990s it was O. J. Simpson. Every generation has its "Trial of the Century" to capture the public imagination.

The same was true during Biblical times. One famous case began with a true prophet preaching an unpopular message in the city of Jerusalem. Among other things, the prophet predicted that God's temple would be destroyed. The citizens of the city were so hostile to his message that they angrily formed a mob, hastily put him on trial, and eagerly demanded the death penalty. Because the man was a true prophet, putting him to death would have brought the guilt of shedding innocent blood on every inhabitant of the city.

The (Alleged) Crime

The trial in question was the trial of Jeremiah, of course, and Jeremiah 26 contains a complete record of the criminal proceedings. The prophet committed an alleged crime (vv. 1–6). He was arrested (vv. 7–9) and then charged (vv. 10, 11). He made his plea (vv. 12–15), and a vigorous defense was mounted in his behalf (vv. 16–23), after which a verdict was rendered (v. 24).

The trial occurred in the troubled years before the Babylonians attacked Jerusalem, probably in 609 BC "In the beginning of the reign of Jehoiakim the son of Josiah, king of Judah, this word came from the LORD" (v. 1). Jeremiah's only crime was preaching God's Word. His message seems to have been a shorter version of his famous Temple Sermon from chapter 7. There the focus was on the sermon itself. Here attention is drawn to the reaction it provoked. Perhaps chapter 7 records the full text, and chapter 26 just contains the sermon notes. Or perhaps, like most good preachers, Jeremiah repeated his best sermons more than once.

The sermon was a good one. To begin with, it had good content. It had the two elements every faithful sermon must have—law and grace. Good preaching both explains the Law of God, which exposes sin, and proclaims the grace of God, which forgives sin.

Jeremiah began with the Law, and he did not hold back. He followed the instructions he was given: "Thus says the LORD: Stand in the court of the LORD's house, and speak to all the cities of Judah that come to worship in the house of the LORD all the words that I command you to speak to them; do not hold back a word" (v. 2). As we noticed in our study of the fuller version of this sermon (7:1–15), Jeremiah preached nearly every one of the Ten Commandments. He explained in detail how the people were failing to keep covenant with their God.

Jeremiah did not preach the Law to condemn, but to convict. God hoped that this preaching of the Law would turn people away from sin. "It may be they will listen," God thought, "and every one turn from his evil way, that I may relent of the disaster that I intend to do to them because of their evil deeds" (26:3). There was still hope. Jeremiah preached the possibility of grace. If the people of Jerusalem repented, God would be faithful and just to forgive their sin. Even the preaching of the Law has the gracious intention of turning God's people away from sin.

Law and grace must be preached together. There was a vivid illustration of this at Wrigley Field during the late 1980s. Mark Grace had just come up to the majors and was playing first base for the Chicago Cubs. Playing third base, on the opposite corner of the baseball diamond, was Vance Law.[1] Grace and Law. Law and Grace. They belong together.

The Law of God shows us our sins, and then the grace of God forgives them. "Now the law came in to increase the trespass, but where sin increased, grace abounded all the more, so that, as sin reigned in death, grace also might reign through righteousness leading to eternal life through Jesus Christ our Lord" (Romans 5:20, 21).

Law without grace is legalism. Grace without law is license. The Puritan John Sedgwick observed:

> Such as preach not the Law at all may make dead and loose hearers, and
> such as preach the Law too far may make desperate hearers. The golden

mean is to be observed. (1) I would not have the Law to be preached alone by itself, without a mixture of some of the promises of the Gospel. (2) I would have the Law to be preached, as it was published, for evangelical and merciful intentions and purposes; not for destruction and desperation, but for edification.[2]

Not only did Jeremiah's sermon have good content, it also had strong application. Jeremiah preached the consequences of failing to keep the Law. If the people of Jerusalem failed to obey God, then their city and their temple would be destroyed.

> You shall say to them, "Thus says the LORD: If you will not listen to me, to walk in my law that I have set before you, and to listen to the words of my servants the prophets whom I send to you urgently, though you have not listened, then I will make this house like Shiloh, and I will make this city a curse for all the nations of the earth." (26:4–6)

If the people of Jerusalem wanted to see what would happen to them, all they needed to do was go to Shiloh (7:12–15). Shiloh was the city where God used to dwell. Before Solomon built the temple in Jerusalem, the ark of the covenant rested in the temple of meeting at Shiloh (Joshua 18). But the ark did not remain there. When the people broke God's commands, the ark was carried off by the Philistines, and Shiloh was made a ruin (1 Samuel 4; Psalm 78:58–64). Therefore, when God threatened to make the temple like Shiloh, he was threatening to tear it down brick by brick.

Shiloh represents the departure of God's living Spirit. A Shiloh is anyplace where God once lived but lives no longer. Many church buildings have become Shilohs. I saw some of them when I was living in England. Just a short walk down the Cowley Road in Oxford was an enormous Methodist church that used to host revival meetings. People used to go there to get saved. Now people go there to get lucky: The hall has become a full-time bingo parlor. There was another Shiloh on Headington Road, where a Baptist church had become an Islamic mosque.

If these things can happen to Baptists and Methodists, they can happen to anyone. Keep God's commandments. Serve him in the power of the Holy Spirit. Otherwise your church building may become a bingo parlor. Or a mosque.

The Arrest

One man's sermon turned out to be another man's criminal offense (26:7–9). Jeremiah was just trying to preach law and grace the way God told him to preach it. But his congregation did not see it that way. They made him a victim of public endangerment.[3]

By way of contrast consider the cartoon that depicts a seminarian sitting at a desk piled high with books and papers. He is not studying. He is daydreaming about what it will be like to be a pastor. He fantasizes about preaching the best of all possible sermons. In his imagination he can hear the congregation shout his praises and see the elders hoist him on their shoulders and carry him out of the sanctuary in triumph. (A word to seminary students: This will not happen often.)

Jeremiah was not carried out like a champion at the end of his Shiloh sermon, to say the least. "The priests and the prophets and all the people heard Jeremiah speaking these words in the house of the LORD. And when Jeremiah had finished speaking all that the LORD had commanded him to speak to all the people, then the priests and the prophets and all the people laid hold of him, saying, 'You shall die!'" (vv. 7, 8). The people grabbed him all right, but not in triumph. Jeremiah was a victim of mob violence. The Scripture goes on to say that "all the people gathered around Jeremiah in the house of the LORD" (v. 9b). They were not crowding around him to get his autograph. They were out to get him.

This ugly scene undoubtedly would have ended in murder had not the authorities rushed in to break things up. "When the officials of Judah heard these things, they came up from the king's house to the house of the LORD and took their seat in the entry of the New Gate of the house of the LORD" (v. 10). They followed all the proper legal procedures. They took Jeremiah from God's house to the courthouse.

The Charge

As soon as the judges sat down in the city gates, the court was in session. The legal experts did not give in to mob rule. Instead they gave Jeremiah something that has become increasingly rare—a speedy trial.

Jeremiah's trial began with a reading of the charges. The murderous intentions of the plaintiffs were revealed when they called for the death penalty, even before they stated their charge or made their case! "Then the priests and the prophets said to the officials and to all the people, 'This man deserves the sentence of death, because he has prophesied against this city, as you have heard with your own ears'" (v. 11). The facts of the case were clear. The prosecution hardly saw the need to present any evidence. According to them, all the people had heard Jeremiah's sermon with their own ears.

In the minds of the lying prophets and the false priests, the temple sermon was a capital offense. It was blasphemous and treasonable. Jeremiah preached against both God's house and God's city. They had made their complaint about this as soon as the prophet had finished his sermon: "Why have you prophesied in the name of the LORD, saying, 'This house shall be like Shiloh, and this city shall be desolate, without inhabitant'?" (v. 9a).

The prophets and the priests were not interested in repentance. They completely ignored Jeremiah's message of law and grace. They were more concerned with what he had said about the temple. Speaking against the temple seemed like treason, for they considered the temple inviolable. It had become a national shrine, a sort of lucky charm to protect them from the need to obey God. Thus they were offended when Jeremiah warned that God was going to destroy their precious temple.

Whenever a church becomes preoccupied with its buildings or its finances, it is in spiritual danger. I once visited a church pastored by a slovenly man who had little confidence in either the Bible or the gospel it contains. Yet when he saw me leaning against the Communion rail during a wedding rehearsal he was outraged. He gave me a public rebuke. To him, the Communion rail was sacrosanct. Sadly, although he treated sacred things as if they were profane, he treated indifferent things as if they were holy.

Church buildings need to be maintained, of course, as do the more mundane matters of church life. But first a congregation needs to listen to God's Word and confess their sins.

The Plea

Once the charges had been read, it was up to the defendant to make his plea. In effect Jeremiah pled "not guilty by reason of obedience." "Then Jeremiah spoke to all the officials and all the people, saying, 'The LORD sent me to prophesy against this house and this city all the words you have heard . . . in truth the LORD sent me to you to speak all these words in your ears'" (vv. 12, 15b). Jeremiah explained that he had not been preaching on his own behalf. The people of Jerusalem were blaming the messenger, but their real complaint was with the message.

Human nature being what it is, ministers often come under criticism. Sometimes criticism is justified, in which case a minister must receive correction with all humility. But many complaints a faithful minister receives are not complaints against him at all—they are complaints against God. That was certainly the case in this trial, and Jeremiah was not afraid to point it out. The people thought they were contending with Jeremiah, but actually they were contending with God. If they had a grievance they would have to take it up with God himself, for he was the one warning them about judgment and calling them to repentance.

While Jeremiah was making his legal plea, he took advantage of the opportunity to repeat his message: "Now therefore mend your ways and your deeds, and obey the voice of the LORD your God, and the LORD will relent of the disaster that he has pronounced against you" (v. 13). Jeremiah was a good preacher, and good preachers repeat their sermons as often as they can get away with it.

Then Jeremiah explained the reasoning behind his plea. Although he pled "not guilty," he was not really interested in defending himself: "But as for me, behold, I am in your hands. Do with me as seems good and right to you" (v. 14). Jeremiah submitted to the jurisdiction of the court. His chief concern—his only concern—was to be God's faithful messenger. He would not lift a finger to save his life. But he would defend God to the death.

When I was in high school I spent a summer at a debate workshop at Northwestern University in Evanston, Illinois. In the middle of the summer we took a break from our usual routine and spent two days discussing ethical case studies. During one of our discussions we were asked what we would be willing to die for. With some trepidation I raised my hand and volunteered that I (gulp!) might be willing to die for my faith in Jesus Christ, or words to that effect.

The environment was not conducive to Christian conviction, and afterwards several Christian students thanked me for my courage. "However," they wondered, "wouldn't it be okay to deny God to save your life, as long as you believed him in your heart?" No! The believer testifies, with Peter and all the apostles, "We must obey God rather than men" (Acts 5:29). To do anything else is to be unfaithful to God.

There is an example of such unfaithfulness in the story of Uriah, son of Shemaiah, a story Jeremiah recounts at the end of chapter 26. Uriah's story started out much like Jeremiah's: "There was another man who prophesied in the name of the LORD, Uriah the son of Shemaiah from Kiriath-jearim. He prophesied against this city and against this land in words like those of Jeremiah" (v. 20). Uriah's message made people just as mad too. "And when King Jehoiakim, with all his warriors and all the officials, heard his words, the king sought to put him to death" (v. 21a).

What made Uriah's story different was its tragic ending: "But when Uriah heard of it, he was afraid and fled and escaped to Egypt" (v. 21b). His life is not an example for us, but a counterexample. Two things were wrong with what Uriah did. First, he ran away scared. He did not trust the Lord to deliver him from death. He feared men rather than God. Second, Uriah was a fugitive to Egypt, and God warned his people against the temptation of turning to the Egyptians for salvation (2:36; chapters 42, 43). Uriah's flight was a sign of apostasy.

Some scholars say Uriah's story was told to show that Jeremiah was in mortal danger. True, Uriah proves that preaching can be hazardous to your health. But the proper literary term for Uriah is that he serves as Jeremiah's *foil*. He shows up in Jeremiah 26 for contrast. Uriah's cowardice reveals Jeremiah's courage. Jeremiah is the good example to follow. He obeyed the commission he received when God first called him into the ministry: "Do not be dismayed by them, lest I dismay you before them" (1:17). Jeremiah was willing to seem like a traitor to his people as long as he did not commit treason against God.

The tragic irony is that in the end Uriah failed to deliver himself from death. "Then King Jehoiakim sent to Egypt certain men, Elnathan the son of Achbor and others with him, and they took Uriah from Egypt and brought him to King Jehoiakim, who struck him down with the sword and dumped his dead body into the burial place of the common people" (26:22, 23). Jehoiakim had Uriah extradited and executed. Then he was given an ignominious burial. Thus Uriah illustrates the paradox uttered by Jesus Christ: "Whoever finds his life will lose it, and whoever loses his life for my sake will find it" (Matthew 10:39).

The Defense

Jeremiah did not lose his life. He found it. He found his life not by delivering himself from death, but with the help of advocates who took up his case.

Some people listened when Jeremiah said, "Only know for certain that if you put me to death, you will bring innocent blood upon yourselves and upon this city and its inhabitants" (26:15). As soon as they realized they were in danger of putting an innocent man to death, they leapt to his defense. "Then the officials and all the people said to the priests and the prophets, 'This man does not deserve the sentence of death, for he has spoken to us in the name of the LORD our God'" (v. 16). Robert Davidson points out how fickle the mob was, "one minute howling for blood, the next defending the decision to acquit him."[4]

Fickle or not, a number of them came up with a clever line of defense. They understood that legal cases are adjudicated on the basis of precedent. Lawyers and judges want to know if a similar case has ever been tried before. If someone else in a similar situation has been charged with a similar crime, that past case may have some bearing on the present trial.

Jeremiah's defenders came up with a perfect legal precedent. They remembered that someone else, in a similar situation, had been charged with a similar crime:

> And certain of the elders of the land arose and spoke to all the assembled people, saying, "Micah of Moresheth prophesied in the days of Hezekiah king of Judah, and said to all the people of Judah: 'Thus says the LORD of hosts,
>
> "'Zion shall be plowed as a field;
> Jerusalem shall become a heap of ruins,
> and the mountain of the house a wooded height.'" (vv. 17, 18)

The elders were quoting Micah 3:12, which shows how well some Old Testament believers knew the Scriptures.

Nearly a century before, Micah had prophesied against the city of Jerusalem and the temple at Zion. What had happened to him? "Did Hezekiah king of Judah and all Judah put him to death? Did he not fear the LORD and entreat the favor of the LORD, and did not the LORD relent of the disaster that he had pronounced against them? But we are about to bring great disaster upon ourselves" (26:19). Micah was a rare prophet in Israel. People actually heeded his warnings! When the Assyrians besieged Jerusalem in 701 BC, Hezekiah repented, and the Lord delivered his city.

The lesson was obvious: Jeremiah must not be put to death. More importantly, the people should listen to his message and repent of their sins. Then perhaps Jerusalem would be saved.

This defense shows how important it is for believers to be strong in their knowledge of the Bible. When spiritual leaders stray from Scripture, the laypeople must call them back to Biblical truth. The clergy of Jeremiah's time were not thinking or acting Biblically. Jeremiah would not get any help from them. But he was saved by a Bible verse kept safe in the hearts of God's people.

The Verdict

In the end, Jeremiah was delivered from death. He was acquitted of all the charges against him. The tide of public opinion started to turn in his favor when he warned the people about the guilt of innocent blood. But the verdict was not certain until "The hand of Ahikam the son of Shaphan was with Jeremiah so that he was not given over to the people to be put to death" (v. 24).

Shaphan was the scribe who first read the Book of the Law when it was discovered during the reign of King Josiah (2 Kings 22:8–13). Shaphan had at least three sons, and they were all men of God. Soon we will meet Gemariah, who tried to prevent King Jehoiakim from burning the scroll of the Lord (36:25). We will also meet Gedaliah, who saved Jeremiah's life when Jerusalem fell to the Babylonians (39:14). Here we meet Ahikam, who helped deliver Jeremiah from death.

Wrongful Death

The words of the verdict in Jeremiah's case are bound to remind us of another prophet who was handed over to the people to be put to death. For like Jeremiah, Jesus Christ was tried in the city of Jerusalem. Like Jeremiah, he was seized by a fickle band of angry men who crowded him on every side. And like Jeremiah, he was charged with treason against the temple. When Jesus appeared before the Sanhedrin at his religious trial, two false witnesses came forward "and said, 'This man said, "I am able to destroy the temple of God, and to rebuild it in three days"'" (Matthew 26:61).

Like Jeremiah, Jesus Christ was innocent of the charges brought against him. Indeed, he was innocent of all charges. Jesus Christ was without sin. Yet, like Jeremiah, he did not defend himself. At his religious trial "The high priest stood up in the midst and asked Jesus, 'Have you no answer to make? What is it that these men testify against you?' But he remained silent and made no answer" (Mark 14:60, 61).

The same thing happened at Jesus' political trial. Pontius Pilate asked, "'Where are you from?' But Jesus gave him no answer" (John 19:9b). This was to fulfill the words of the prophet Isaiah:

> He was oppressed, and he was afflicted,
>   yet he opened not his mouth;
> like a lamb that is led to the slaughter,
>   and like a sheep that before its shearers is silent,
>   so he opened not his mouth. (Isaiah 53:7)

When the trial of Jeremiah is placed beside the trial of Jesus Christ, one finds obvious similarities in the charge, arrest, accusation, and defense. When some people said the Son of Man was the second coming of Jeremiah (Matthew 16:14), they were more accurate than they realized.

There is, however, one great difference between the trial of Jeremiah and the trial of Jesus Christ—the verdict. At the trial of Jesus, no one heeded the warning that his death would bring the guilt of innocent blood upon his executioners. No official insisted, "This man should not be sentenced to death!" No elder stepped forward to argue that Micah, or even Jeremiah himself, offered a legal precedent in Jesus' defense. No one saved Jesus the way Ahikam saved Jeremiah. Jesus Christ was not delivered from death—he was delivered *unto* death. He was handed over to be executed (Matthew 27:26). Jesus Christ was arrested, charged, convicted, and crucified.

The trial of Jeremiah reveals what a wicked thing it was to hand Jesus over to death. As immoral as people were in the days of Jeremiah, they were horrified by the prospect of bringing the guilt of the blood of an innocent man upon themselves and their city. When Jeremiah warned them of the danger of bearing guilt for a wrongful death, they instantly changed their minds.

The Jews and Gentiles who crucified Jesus had no such scruples. Indeed, they invited guilt upon themselves and their children (Matthew 27:25). Thus when Jesus was crucified, the guilt for his blood came to rest on all humanity. Our sins sent Christ to the cross as much as the sins of anyone else.

Final Appeal

There is one other difference between the trial of Jeremiah and the trial of Jesus. The verdict against Jesus Christ was overturned on appeal. In his dying moments Jesus appealed to the highest court in the whole universe. "Then Jesus, calling out with a loud voice, said, 'Father, into your hands I commit my spirit!'" (Luke 23:46). He not only appealed his own case—he appealed our case as well. He said, "Father, forgive them, for they know not what they do" (Luke 23:34).

And God the Father accepted those appeals. The guilty verdict given to Jesus by sinful men was overruled by holy God. The proof of the success of that appeal is the empty tomb on Easter Sunday. The Resurrection proves that Jesus Christ was innocent of all charges. Since Jesus was wrongly executed, the moral law of the highest court in the universe demanded that he be returned back to life.

Furthermore, the Resurrection proves that the sacrifice Jesus offered for sin has been accepted by God. The appeal Jesus made for God to overturn the verdict against you has been just as successful as his own appeal. Once he paid for your crimes, the verdict against you was no longer able to stand. If you trust that Jesus died on the cross for your sins, and if you believe that he was raised from the dead, then you too will be delivered from death.

36

Under the Yoke

JEREMIAH 27:1–22

JEREMIAH WOULD HAVE MADE a terrific children's Sunday school teacher. Teaching children involves showing as well as telling. A good teacher knows how to use the chalkboard or a poster or a flannelgraph or some other object to make a Bible story come to life.

Following God's instructions, Jeremiah knew how to use a prop to teach a spiritual lesson. Once he took off his linen belt, buried it in the ground, and dug it back up again to show how God would ruin Judah (13:1–11). Another time he bought a clay pot and smashed it outside the walls of the city to show how God would destroy Jerusalem (19:1–15). There was also the time he used two baskets of figs to show the difference between sweet submission and rotten rebellion to the will of God (24:1–10).

Then there was the time Jeremiah brought a farm implement for show-and-tell: "In the beginning of the reign of Zedekiah the son of Josiah, king of Judah, this word came to Jeremiah from the Lord. Thus the Lord said to me: 'Make yourself straps and yoke-bars, and put them on your neck'" (27:1, 2).

A yoke is what hitches a team of oxen to a plow. In Biblical times a long wooden crossbar was laid across the necks of two oxen. Four pegs were then driven through the crossbar, and ropes or thongs were tied around the necks of the beasts to anchor them to the pegs.[1] Once the oxen were under the yoke, they were ready to work.

Jeremiah was ready to go to work as well. He used his yoke to teach three great lessons about God's kingship: God rules over kingdoms (vv. 1–11); God rules over kings (vv. 6, 7); and, at the risk of excessive alliteration, God rules over his own kids (vv. 12–22).

God Rules over Kingdoms

Once Jeremiah finished making his yoke, he sent a message to all the foreign delegations in Jerusalem. His instructions were these: "Send word to the king of Edom, the king of Moab, the king of the sons of Ammon, the king of Tyre, and the king of Sidon by the hand of the envoys who have come to Jerusalem to Zedekiah king of Judah" (v. 3). The city was bustling with diplomats in those days. Special envoys from Edom, Moab, Ammon, Tyre, and Sidon had all gathered in Jerusalem for a summit meeting. They were having talks to form a military coalition and throw off the yoke of Babylonian oppression.

Back in 597 BC the Babylonians had downsized Jerusalem, carrying much plunder and many people back to Babylon. They set up Zedekiah as the puppet king of Judah. But at the time this chapter was written, in 594 BC or so, Nebuchadnezzar seemed vulnerable. The *Babylonian Chronicles* record that during this period he had to repel an attack by an enemy, put down a revolt among his own people, and launch a military campaign against the Syrians.[2] So with King Zedekiah as their ringleader, the downtrodden nations of the Middle East gathered in Jerusalem to plot the downfall of Babylon.

All the political analysts were in favor of armed resistance. Had the ambassadors been interviewed on late-night television, they would have pointed out that Nebuchadnezzar was nearly 1,000 miles away and that he had plenty of his own troubles to deal with. It was a perfect time for a revolution. There was only one problem. These politicians did not stop to seek the will of God.

So Jeremiah, wearing his yoke around his neck, went to them with a message from God:

> Give them this charge for their masters: "Thus says the LORD of hosts, the God of Israel: This is what you shall say to your masters: 'It is I who by my great power and my outstretched arm have made the earth, with the men and animals that are on the earth, and I give it to whomever it seems right to me. Now I have given all these lands into the hand of Nebuchadnezzar, the king of Babylon, my servant, and I have given him also the beasts of the field to serve him. All the nations shall serve him and his son and his grandson. . . . But any nation that will bring its neck under the yoke of the king of Babylon and serve him, I will leave on its own land, to work it and dwell there, declares the LORD.'" (vv. 4–7a, 11)

Jeremiah's style of diplomacy was not very diplomatic. His policy recommendation was total surrender. One commentator points out that because Jeremiah was using only half his yoke, there was still plenty of room for someone else to join him![3] In effect, he was inviting the kings of the earth to come beside him and submit to the Babylonian yoke.

The consequences of failing to surrender would be deadly. "But if any nation or kingdom will not serve this Nebuchadnezzar king of Babylon, and put its neck under the yoke of the king of Babylon, I will punish that nation with the sword, with famine, and with pestilence, declares the LORD, until I have consumed it by his hand" (v. 8). "Sword . . . famine, and . . . pestilence" is Jeremiah's typical description for total disaster. It means that his earlier prophecies of judgment would be fulfilled. "Behold, the days are coming, declares the LORD, when I will punish all those who are circumcised merely in the flesh—Egypt, Judah, Edom, the sons of Ammon, Moab, and all who dwell in the desert" (9:25, 26). Well, those days were closer than ever. Similarly, Jeremiah had described taking a cup of judgment to "Edom, Moab, and the sons of Ammon; all the kings of Tyre, all the kings of Sidon" (25:21, 22a). Try as they might, those nations would not be able to throw off the Babylonian yoke. According to the will of God, they must surrender or perish.

What do you suppose the ambassadors thought of Jeremiah's little demonstration? I imagine them wondering something like this: "Who does the God of Israel think he is? How can the God of this puny little nation claim the right to rule over us? What business does he have ordering us around? We are mighty nations!"

Jeremiah's point was that the one true and living God rules all the kingdoms of the world. The reason he rules them is that he made them in the first place. "It is I who by my great power and my outstretched arm have made the earth, with the men and animals that are on the earth, and I give it to whomever it seems right to me" (27:5). God made the earth and everything in it; therefore he rules the earth and everything in it. By virtue of the act of creation, God rules over all nations, whether they recognize it or not. He has the right to do whatever he wants with them.

Verse 5 ends with a remarkable statement of God's foreign policy: "I give it [the earth] to whomever it seems right to me." God is so powerful, and his rule is so absolute that he can speak about the momentous events of world affairs in the most casual way. He parcels out kingdoms the way people pass out sticks of gum. He is like the industrial magnate who used to do television commercials for an electric razor. "I liked this razor so much," he would say, "That I bought the company." Almighty God can speak with equal nonchalance about entire kingdoms. "Here," he says to Nebuchadnezzar, "have a kingdom. It's on me."

God's audacious claim to world power challenges our limited perspective on world events. Whenever there is a change in government the Lord is behind it. Early in 1997, for example, there was a change of leaders in the People's

Republic of China. Deng Xiaoping, the longtime ruler of the Communist Party, finally died. The journalists speculated about which new leader would seize political power. The photos of the leading candidates were plastered over the pages of the news magazines. No one could say for certain who would rule, for how long, and with what authority. But God could say. He gives the kingdoms of the earth—with all their people and all their animals—to anyone he pleases. He sets the presidents, the premiers, and the prime ministers in their places.

Kingdom Concerns

If God rules over kingdoms, then kingdoms are our concern. Many years ago Daniel Fleming wrote a book called *Marks of a World Christian*.[4] By "world Christian," Fleming meant someone who recognizes that God rules the kingdoms of the world. A world Christian is someone who takes a vital interest in the worldwide work of God and prays for the unbroken advance of God's kingdom. To put it another way, "World Christians are day-to-day disciples for whom Christ's global cause has become the integrating, overriding priority."[5]

Throughout the history of the church, Biblical Christians have always been world Christians. Their ministries have been like Jeremiah's ministry, which spanned the globe. He was appointed "over nations and over kingdoms, to pluck up and to break down, to destroy and to overthrow, to build and to plant" (1:10).

John Chrysostom (347–407 AD) was a world Christian. The great preacher of Constantinople long prayed for the conversion of the Barbarians in the Balkans. When he sent missionaries to evangelize that region he said, "We have a whole Christ for our salvation; a whole Bible for our staff; a whole Church for our fellowship; and a whole world for our parish."[6]

I lived among world Christians during my internship at Gilcomston South Church in Aberdeen, where Reverend William Still served as minister for over half a century (1945–1997). For two hours every Saturday night sixty or seventy Christians gathered at Gilcomston to pray for the worldwide progress of the gospel. They began by praying all the way around Scotland, then through the British Isles, and then off to some other continent. Even after two hours of prayer, Mr. Still often closed the meeting lamenting that some continent or another had been left unprayed for.

Back in 1992 it was typical for a member of that church to thank God for the way he had brought down the Iron Curtain of Communism in eastern Europe. From the way that they prayed, it was clear that they believed that *their* prayers had something to do with the collapse of the Soviet Empire. I was tempted to pull one of them aside and say, "You know, it was a little more complicated than that. The global economy had something to do with it, not to mention the arms race and the spiritual bankruptcy of Communism. It took more than your prayers to pull down the Berlin Wall."

I was tempted to say such things, but I knew better. Who is to say what part a praying church actually plays in world affairs? To go to Gilcomston on a Saturday night was to know what was going on in the world. The prayers of God's people really are at the heart of what God is doing. When the true history of the world is finally written, we will discover that Christians like the ones in Aberdeen had a profound influence on world events.

The missionary statesman David Bryant defines a world Christian as someone who believes that "God has a worldwide PURPOSE in Christ that encompasses all history, all creation and all peoples everywhere, especially those yet to be reached by the gospel."[7] Do you believe that? Do you believe that God has a global purpose for all history and all peoples in Christ?

If you are not a world Christian, you need to become one. Start by choosing a missionary or a part of the world to pray for in your family or Bible study. Obtain a copy of Patrick Johnstone's *Operation World* to help you know what to pray for.[8] Teach children how to traverse the globe in prayer. Take a vital interest in world news. Read the newspaper and listen to the nightly news with an eye and an ear for the church. Pay special attention to news from countries where missionaries you know are serving. You may not have the time to master global politics, but you can still become a world Christian.

Remember the bold claim of our Lord Jesus Christ: "All authority in heaven and on earth has been given to me. Go therefore and make disciples of all nations" (Matthew 28:18, 19a). Jesus Christ is Lord of Afghanistan and Albania. He is King of Zaire and Zimbabwe. There is no place on this globe where Christ is not King.

God Rules over Kings

If God rules over kingdoms, he must also rule over kings. After all, he is the King of kings. Notice how he describes one of the greatest kings in the history of the world: "Now I have given all these lands into the hand of Nebuchadnezzar, the king of Babylon, my servant" (v. 6).

That statement is remarkable for two reasons. First, it is a most condescending way to speak about the most powerful man on the face of the earth: "Nebuchadnezzar . . . my servant" (cf. 25:9; 43:10). It is the kind of language an ancient king would use to describe one of his vassals. Nebuchadnezzar was

God's lapdog. How powerful must God be to speak so casually about a world superpower?

Second, this statement is remarkable because Nebuchadnezzar was a cruel and wicked king. He was an erratic despot, the Saddam Hussein of his day. Nebuchadnezzar ruled the kingdom of Babylon with an iron fist. He crushed and devoured God's people (see chapters 50, 51). Nevertheless, God counted this fierce king as one of his servants. Even his most powerful enemies are instruments to accomplish his will.

Eventually even Nebuchadnezzar realized he was God's servant. One night he took a stroll "on the roof of the royal palace of Babylon" (Daniel 4:29). With smug satisfaction he surveyed his kingdom, including the famed Hanging Gardens, one of the Seven Wonders of the Ancient World. He said, "Is not this great Babylon, which I have built by my mighty power as a royal residence and for the glory of my majesty?" (v. 30).

The answer was no! Nebuchadnezzar did not build great Babylon by his power and for his majesty. According to Jeremiah, the kingdom of Babylon had nothing to do with him at all—it was a gift from God.

No sooner had Nebuchadnezzar made his boast than God humiliated him. "While the words were still in the king's mouth, there fell a voice from heaven, 'O King Nebuchadnezzar, to you it is spoken: The kingdom has departed from you, and you shall be driven from among men, and your dwelling shall be with the beasts of the field. And you shall be made to eat grass like an ox'" (vv. 31, 32a). The braggy king of Babylon needed to learn the lesson of Jeremiah 27:5. He needed to admit that "The Most High rules the kingdom of men and gives it to whom he will" (Daniel 4:32b).

Nebuchadnezzar ended up learning the hard way. "Immediately the word was fulfilled against Nebuchadnezzar. He was driven from among men and ate grass like an ox, and his body was wet with the dew of heaven till his hair grew as long as eagles' feathers, and his nails were like birds' claws" (vv. 33, 34).

How ironic for Nebuchadnezzar to become a beast! Jeremiah promised that even the wild beasts would be subject to him (27:6). And so they were. When Daniel appeared before Nebuchadnezzar, he said, "You, O king, the king of kings, to whom the God of heaven has given the kingdom, the power, and the might, and the glory, and into whose hand he has given, wherever they dwell, the children of man, the beasts of the field, and the birds of the heavens . . ." (Daniel 2:37, 38). But when Nebuchadnezzar gloried in his own might, he became like a beast himself, overruled by animal instincts.

Nebuchadnezzar's punishment was not only ironic, it was also appropriate. In his commentary on the book of Daniel, James Montgomery Boice explains why his punishment fit his crime:

> It is not a case of God merely going down a list of the various punishments available and saying, "Let's see now . . . Eeny, meeny, miney, moe—let's take this one: *insanity.*" God does not operate that way. Everything God does is significant. So when God caused Nebuchadnezzar to be lowered from the pinnacle of pride to the baseness of insanity and to be associated with the beasts and behave like a beast, God was saying by that punishment that this is the result when men give the glory of God to themselves. They become beastlike.[9]

Nebuchadnezzar stands as a warning against the pride of Western culture. We have big homes, tall buildings, and fat bank accounts. But at the same time we live in a society marked by physical violence and sexual license. In other words, we commit the very sins that make us seem most like animals.

In the mid 1990s a Scandinavian zoo created an exhibit of human beings. Not an exhibit *for* human beings, understand, but *of* human beings. A man and a woman were put on display in a glass enclosure. The point was that human beings are animals, which is the basic premise of the evolutionary worldview. And what makes that worldview plausible is the beastly way we behave toward one another.

Nebuchadnezzar also stands as a warning to everyone who is a success in life. Perhaps your career is going better than you expected. Perhaps you are making decent money or have received a promotion. Perhaps, beyond all expectation, your children are doing well in school. Or perhaps your ministry is being blessed. Do not take any credit for your triumphs. Everything you are and have comes from God. Humble yourself before him.

King Nebuchadnezzar discovered that "Those who walk in pride he [God] is able to humble" (Daniel 4:37). That was the king's testimony after he came back to his senses. His pride was a sort of temporary insanity. He was out of his mind to take credit for his kingdom. He stayed out of his mind until he admitted "That the Most High rules the kingdom of men and gives it to whom he will" (Daniel 4:32):

> At the end of the days I, Nebuchadnezzar, lifted my eyes to heaven, and my reason returned to me, and I blessed the Most High, and praised and honored him who lives forever,
>
> > for his dominion is an everlasting dominion,
> >   and his kingdom endures from generation to generation;
> > all the inhabitants of the earth are accounted as nothing,

> and he does according to his will among the host of heaven
> and among the inhabitants of the earth;
> and none can stay his hand
> or say to him, "What have you done?" . . .

> Now I, Nebuchadnezzar, praise and extol and honor the King of heaven, for all his works are right and his ways are just. (Daniel 4:34, 35, 37)

That is the testimony of a man who learned well the lessons of Jeremiah 27. To regain your spiritual sanity, acknowledge that the God who rules over kings and kingdoms also rules over you.

God Rules over His Kids

God also rules over his own children. Jeremiah had exactly the same message for Zedekiah as he had for his colleagues.

Jeremiah reports, "To Zedekiah king of Judah I spoke in like manner: 'Bring your necks under the yoke of the king of Babylon, and serve him and his people and live. Why will you and your people die by the sword, by famine, and by pestilence, as the LORD has spoken concerning any nation that will not serve the king of Babylon?'" (27:12, 13). God gave Zedekiah the same choice he gave the other nations: surrender or perish. Like everyone else, God's people had to come under the yoke of Babylon.

The reason for their punishment was that they had thrown off the yoke of obedience to God. Near the beginning of his ministry, Jeremiah had conveyed this message from the Lord: "Long ago you broke off your yoke and tore off your bonds; you said, 'I will not serve you!'" (2:20 NIV; cf. 5:5). By now it was becoming increasingly apparent that breaking away from obedience to God never brings freedom; instead it brings slavery to some harsh taskmaster. The gentle yoke of obedience was to be replaced by the brutal yoke of oppression, service to God by servitude to Nebuchadnezzar.

As usual, Jeremiah's message was unpopular. Even though the Babylonian captivity had already begun, the rest of the prophets were still claiming that they would not end up in captivity:

> So do not listen to your prophets, your diviners, your dreamers, your fortune-tellers, or your sorcerers, who are saying to you, 'You shall not serve the king of Babylon.' For it is a lie that they are prophesying to you, with the result that you will be removed far from your land, and I will drive you out, and you will perish. . . . Do not listen to the words of the prophets who are saying to you, 'You shall not serve the king of Babylon,' for it is a lie that they are prophesying to you. I have not sent them, declares the LORD,

but they are prophesying falsely in my name, with the result that I will drive you out and you will perish, you and the prophets who are prophesying to you. (27:9, 10, 14, 15)

The false prophets were lying through their teeth, and they were not to be listened to.

Because the prophets were lying, Jeremiah had to appeal directly to the people. He gave them the right answer to one of the great political and theological questions of their times: What would become of the temple furnishings? When the Babylonians first attacked Jerusalem in 597 BC they did something scandalous—they ransacked the treasury and carried off most of the temple accessories (2 Kings 24:13). Would the people of Israel ever get their national treasures back?

The false prophets said they would. However, good news is not always God's news. "Then I spoke to the priests and to all this people, saying, 'Thus says the LORD: Do not listen to the words of your prophets who are prophesying to you, saying, "Behold, the vessels of the LORD's house will now shortly be brought back from Babylon," for it is a lie that they are prophesying to you. Do not listen to them'" (27:16, 17a).

In fact, things were going to get worse before they got better. The situation was very much like the one that led Jesus to say, "From the one who has not, even what he has will be taken away" (Matthew 25:29b). Catch the sarcasm in Jeremiah's response: "If they are prophets, and if the word of the LORD is with them, then let them intercede with the LORD of hosts, that the vessels that are left in the house of the LORD, in the house of the king of Judah, and in Jerusalem may not go to Babylon" (27:18).

In other words, if the prophets really wanted to make themselves useful, they should spend some time praying that the rest of their stuff would not get stolen. Even the pieces of equipment Nebuchadnezzar left behind the first time—the pillars (in front of the temple; 1 Kings 6:15–22), the Sea (for priestly washings; 1 Kings 7:23–26), and the movable stands (for washing animals; 1 Kings 7:27–37)—were going to be taken away:

> For thus says the LORD of hosts concerning the pillars, the sea, the stands, and the rest of the vessels that are left in this city, which Nebuchadnezzar king of Babylon did not take away, when he took into exile from Jerusalem to Babylon Jeconiah the son of Jehoiakim, king of Judah, and all the nobles of Judah and Jerusalem—thus says the LORD of hosts, the God of Israel, concerning the vessels that are left in the house of the LORD, in the house of the king of Judah, and in Jerusalem: They shall be carried to Babylon and

remain there until the day when I visit them, declares the LORD. Then I will
bring them back and restore them to this place. (27:19–22)

Every last word of that prophecy came true. Zedekiah refused to come
under the yoke. He rebelled and was captured by the Babylonians (2 Kings
25:1). "They slaughtered the sons of Zedekiah before his eyes, and put out
the eyes of Zedekiah and bound him in chains and took him to Babylon"
(2 Kings 25:7). They also broke down the rest of the temple furnishings and
carried them off to Babylon (Jeremiah 52:17–23; cf. 2 Kings 25:13–17). When
God tells people to bow under the yoke, they must either bow or face the
consequences.

But God is still a God of grace. He placed a time limit on Babylonian rule:
"All the nations shall serve him and his son and his grandson, until the time of
his own land comes. Then many nations and great kings shall make him their
slave" (27:7). The Babylonian yoke turned out to be God's yoke. God's yoke
is always gentle, and Jeremiah 27 ends with a promise about the end of the
exile. "They [the temple furnishings] shall be carried to Babylon and remain
there until the day when I visit them, declares the LORD. Then I will bring
them back and restore them to this place" (v. 22). God kept this promise. The
Bible records that the temple furnishings did not remain in Babylon but were
returned to Jerusalem in 539 BC (Ezra 1:7–11).

This is a reminder that the sufferings of God's people will not last forever.
Even the sufferings of the exile did not last forever. As long as the yoke is
God's yoke, it is a good yoke to be under, especially for the Christian. If you
have given your heart to Jesus Christ, then even your heaviest burdens are
made light by the grace of God. Jesus says, "Come to me, all who labor and
are heavy laden, and I will give you rest. Take my yoke upon you, and learn
from me, for I am gentle and lowly in heart, and you will find rest for your
souls. For my yoke is easy, and my burden is light" (Matthew 11:28–30).

37

A Yoke of Iron

JEREMIAH 28:1–17

JEREMIAH DID what God told him to do. He made the kind of yoke a farmer uses to hitch oxen to a plow. He made it out of straps and crossbars, hung it around his neck, and paraded about the temple (27:2). The point of his object lesson was that all nations must come under the yoke of the king of Babylon.

Several months passed, and Jeremiah was still under the yoke. He must have made quite a spectacle around Jerusalem in those days. Seeing someone wear a big yoke around his neck is like seeing someone with a pierced eyebrow. It is hard to ignore. Even if you do not want to look at it or talk about it, you know it is there. And that was the point. Jeremiah's yoke was supposed to attract attention. "OK, Jeremiah," people would say, "what is it this time? Tell us what the yoke is for." Then the prophet would explain that the people of Judah must bow their necks under the yoke of Babylon (27:12). They must come under the yoke of captivity or they would be destroyed.

A Prediction

Soon everyone in Jerusalem had seen and heard Jeremiah. Hananiah, for one, had seen and heard enough. He went head-to-head with Jeremiah at the temple. "In that same year, at the beginning of the reign of Zedekiah king of Judah, in the fifth month of the fourth year, Hananiah the son of Azzur, the prophet from Gibeon, spoke to me in the house of the LORD, in the presence of the priests and all the people" (28:1).

Hananiah confronted Jeremiah by making a prediction. In his opinion, the exile in Babylon was almost over. So he put this prophecy into God's mouth:

> Thus says the LORD of hosts, the God of Israel: I have broken the yoke of the king of Babylon. Within two years I will bring back to this place all the vessels of the LORD's house, which Nebuchadnezzar king of Babylon took away from this place and carried to Babylon. I will also bring back to this place Jeconiah the son of Jehoiakim, king of Judah, and all the exiles from Judah who went to Babylon, declares the LORD, for I will break the yoke of the king of Babylon. (vv. 2–4)

The king, the people, and the temple furnishings that had been taken into captivity in 598 BC would be brought back in a couple of years, he said.

The problem with Hananiah's prediction was that it contradicted the prophecies of Jeremiah. Hananiah thought the exile would be over in two years at the most. But Jeremiah had already prophesied quite otherwise. Concerning King Jehoiachin, he had repeated this message from the Lord: "I will hurl you and the mother who bore you into another country, where you were not born, and there you shall die. But to the land to which they will long to return, there they shall not return" (22:26, 27). Concerning the duration of the exile, he had said, "This whole land shall become a ruin and a waste, and these nations shall serve the king of Babylon seventy years" (25:11). Concerning the temple furnishings, Jeremiah had said, "They shall be carried to Babylon and remain there until the day when I visit them" (27:22).

Hananiah was wrong about God's plans. God did not intend to bring the king back to Jerusalem. Plus he was wrong about God's timetable. Way wrong—he was off by sixty-eight years. Hananiah thought the exile would be short-term, but Jeremiah knew Israel was in Babylon for the long haul.

Then things started to get personal. "Then the prophet Hananiah took the yoke-bars from the neck of Jeremiah the prophet and broke them" (28:10). After predicting that God was going to break the yoke of the king of Babylon, Hananiah dramatized his message by breaking Jeremiah's yoke. "And Hananiah spoke in the presence of all the people, saying, 'Thus says the LORD: Even so will I break the yoke of Nebuchadnezzar king of Babylon from the neck of all the nations within two years'" (v. 11a).

No doubt Hananiah's message was very popular. It was bold, patriotic, and uplifting. Whose church would you rather go to? With Jeremiah it would be gloom and doom for the next seven decades. Hardly the message for a seeker-sensitive church! Hananiah, on the other hand, would tell you what you wanted to hear. In soothing tones he promised you would be free from all your troubles before you knew it. Even his name sounded nice; it means "The Lord is gracious."

The trouble with Hananiah was that his message was as false as it was popular. Perhaps this is what one would expect from a prophet born in Gibeon. The Gibeonites were the ones who lied to Israel in the days of Joshua (Joshua 9:1–15). Hananiah was doing the same thing. As the Lord said to him, "You have made this people trust in a lie" (28:15). In fact, the words "lie" or "lying" are repeated half a dozen times in chapters 27, 28. Hananiah's prediction was just plain false. He was telling the big lie of liberalism—that God is a God of love but not a God of justice.

How should Jeremiah respond? Hananiah was a false prophet who contradicted his message and laid violent hands upon him. So what should Jeremiah do? More to the point, what should we do when people in our own culture reject the hard truths of God's Word? Francis Schaeffer explains that the situation has not changed very much, if at all, since the days of Jeremiah:

> For a man to think that he can preach the Word of God today and not experience the true price of the cross of Christ in the sense of not being accepted by the culture—for a man to think that he can be a teller, whether he be a teacher, a minister, a Christian artist, poet, musician, movie-maker, or dramatist—any man who thinks he can speak truly of the things of God today into such a culture as our own and not have such words spoken against him is foolish. It is not possible. It is not possible whether one is the teller with his music or with his voice, whether one plays an instrument or speaks out behind a pulpit, whether one writes a book or paints a picture. To think that one can give the Christian message and not have the world with its monolithic, post-Christian culture bear down on us is not to understand the fierceness of the battle in such a day as Jeremiah's or such a day as our own.[1]

If Schaeffer is right, how should we then live?

A Prayer

Jeremiah responded to Hananiah's false teaching in four ways. First, he prayed about it:

> Then the prophet Jeremiah spoke to Hananiah the prophet in the presence of the priests and all the people who were standing in the house of the LORD, and the prophet Jeremiah said, "Amen! May the LORD do so; may the LORD make the words that you have prophesied come true, and bring back to this place from Babylon the vessels of the house of the LORD, and all the exiles." (vv. 5, 6)

It was a remarkable prayer. It seems so unexpected that some scholars think it is sarcastic. They suggest that Jeremiah says "Amen!" only to mock

Hananiah. In that case Jeremiah would be saying something like, "Right! Sure, Hananiah. Whatever you say."

The trouble with that view is that "Amen" is a word of spiritual acceptance. It expresses agreement with someone else's prayer or praise. It means "So be it!" or "Yes, Lord!" Surely Jeremiah was too holy a man to make a mockery out of prayer. Instead his prayer must have come from the heart. He truly wished that Hananiah's prophecy would come true, that the exile would end within two years.

That is remarkable! Jeremiah actually prays that his own prophecy would turn out to be false. John Calvin paraphrases his prayer like this: "I wish I were a false prophet; I would willingly retract, and that with shame, all that I have hitherto predicted, so great is my care and anxiety for the safety of the public; for I would prefer the welfare of the whole people to my own reputation."[2]

Sometimes when people hear Christians speak about divine judgment they get the wrong idea. We Christians do speak about divine judgment—Hell and all the rest of it. We explain that every sin deserves the wrath and curse of God. We teach that sin leads to death. We testify that God has reserved a place of endless torment for everyone who refuses to repent of his sins. But Christians do not talk about God's judgment because they enjoy it. The only reason we teach these things is because the Lord Jesus Christ himself teaches them in the Bible.

Jeremiah had the same attitude. He did not preach judgment because he enjoyed it. He did not take perverse pleasure in prophesying the fall of Jerusalem. He only preached judgment because God told him to preach it. His testimony was that he did not desire "The day of sickness" (17:16). Indeed, he stood in the presence of God to intercede on behalf of his people, begging God to turn away his wrath (18:20). So when Hananiah predicted that God's mercy would preempt God's justice, Jeremiah hoped he was right. In front of all the people he prayed, "Amen! May the Lord do so."

When someone tries to minimize the judgment of God, it is appropriate for the Christian to say, "I hope you're right." Given the choice between praying for mercy and praying for justice, we pray for mercy. This is what motivates us to share the good news about Jesus Christ. We know it is perfectly just for God to condemn sinners and banish them into eternal darkness. But we also know that "it is a fearful thing to fall into the hands of the living God" (Hebrews 10:31). So we desire all men, all women, and all children to be saved. We desire it because God desires it. He "desires all people to be saved and to come to the knowledge of the truth" (1 Timothy 2:4).

On Probation

Nevertheless, no sooner had Jeremiah prayed that Hananiah's prediction would come true than he said, "Yet hear now this word that I speak in your hearing and in the hearing of all the people" (28:7).

Jeremiah desired everyone to be saved. Nevertheless, he knew that human beings are sinners who deserve the wrath and curse of God. However nice it may seem to think that everything will turn out all right in the end, Jeremiah took God's justice seriously, which is why he put Hananiah on probation, saying, "The prophets who preceded you and me from ancient times prophesied war, famine, and pestilence against many countries and great kingdoms. As for the prophet who prophesies peace, when the word of that prophet comes to pass, then it will be known that the LORD has truly sent the prophet" (vv. 8, 9).

Jeremiah and Hananiah were in diametric disagreement about the will of God. Hananiah said God's people would receive mercy. Jeremiah said they would receive judgment first. So who was right? And how could one know for sure? They were both prophets. They were both sincere. They both claimed to speak in the name of the Lord. And they both made demonstrations to back up their prophecies. So how could one tell who was telling the truth?

Jeremiah proposed a Biblical test. It comes from the job description of a prophet: "When a prophet speaks in the name of the LORD, if the word does not come to pass or come true, that is a word that the LORD has not spoken; the prophet has spoken it presumptuously" (Deuteronomy 18:22). Jeremiah knew the best way to tell if a prophecy is true or false is to wait and see what happens. Fulfillment is the proof of prophecy.

This is especially true if a prophet predicts peace. If he prophesies war, plague, and disaster, he is usually right, which tells us something about human nature. Most individuals, families, and nations deserve judgment most of the time. So one can usually count on a prophecy of disaster coming true. But if a prophet prophesies peace, that is a different story. Peace is a condition so rare among human beings that it can only be prophesied correctly on the basis of divine revelation. Since Hananiah had predicted peace, he would remain on probation until peace actually broke out.

The same test can be used to prove that Jesus Christ is a true prophet. Jesus made many prophecies of war, disaster, and plague: "Do not think that I have come to bring peace to the earth. I have not come to bring peace, but a sword" (Matthew 10:34). Jesus promised wars and rumors of wars, nations rising against nations, kingdoms clashing against kingdoms, plagues, famines, and earthquakes (Matthew 24:6, 7). He can be taken at his word for all of it because the sad course of human history has confirmed that he was right.

But Jesus also promised peace: "Peace I leave with you; my peace I give to you" (John 14:27). "In me you may have peace" (John 16:33b). What about these promises? Can Jesus make good on them? If a prophet promises peace, only peace can confirm the truth of his prophecy.

Jesus is a true prophet because he gives true peace. He has made peace between us and God, first of all. Although we were once at war with God because of our sin and rebellion, we are now at peace. Jesus Christ is *the* peacemaker. His death on the cross turned away God's wrath against our sin. "Therefore, since we have been justified by faith, we have peace with God through our Lord Jesus Christ" (Romans 5:1). Everyone who trusts in Jesus is at peace with God. Furthermore, everyone who is at peace with God is at peace in the world. To know Christ is to discover that "The peace of God, which surpasses all understanding, will guard your hearts and your minds in Christ Jesus" (Philippians 4:7).

The surpassing peace of Christ is strongest in the very worst moments of life. Five young missionaries were killed by headhunters in 1956—Jim Elliot, Peter Fleming, Ed McCully, Nate Saint, and Roger Youderian. These men took their families into the jungles of Ecuador to share the gospel with the Auca Indians. After several weeks of friendly contact with the natives, the men decided to leave their families for a short while and camp by a river near the village. Not long after they arrived they were savagely murdered.

One of the remarkable things about what happened to those men was the way their wives responded the day they heard the terrible news. Radio contact had been broken off, so the women already feared the worst. Then a military unit was sent to see if the men were still alive. As the reports came in, the women gradually discovered that all of their husbands had been martyred. This is how Barbara Youderian described that sad experience in her diary:

> Tonight the Captain told us of his finding four bodies in the river. One had a tee-shirt and blue-jeans. Roj was the only one who wore them. . . . God gave me this verse two days ago, Psalm 48:14, "For this God is our God for ever and ever; He will be our Guide even unto death." As I came face to face with the news of Roj's death, my heart was filled with praise. He was worthy of his home-going. . . . I wrote a letter to the mission family, trying to explain the peace I have. I want to be free of self-pity. It is a tool of Satan to rot away a life. I am sure that this is the perfect will of God. . . . The Lord has closed our hearts to grief and hysteria, and filled in with His perfect peace.[3]

To know Christ is to have surpassing peace. Even in the moments of greatest suffering, the perfect peace of Christ fills the Christian's heart and closes it to grief and hysteria. Such peace is the proof that Jesus is a true prophet sent by God.

A Parting of the Ways

The third way Jeremiah responded to Hananiah's attack was to part company with him. After Hananiah broke the yoke that had taken all that time and trouble to make, Jeremiah simply walked away. As the Scripture says, "But Jeremiah the prophet went his way" (28:11b).

This parting of the ways must have required great restraint on the part of Jeremiah. After all, Hananiah laid angry hands on him. Breaking the yoke was an act of aggression that could easily have led to further violence. The British have a wonderful expression for this kind of altercation. They call it an "argy-bargy." "The prophets had a bit of an argy-bargy up at the temple," they would say.

Philadelphia, where I live and minister, is better known for its argy-bargies than for its brotherly love. Philadelphians have argy-bargies in their homes, neighborhoods, stadiums, and offices. It is not uncommon for me to see argy-bargies when I walk to and from Tenth Presbyterian Church. A delivery truck will block traffic perhaps, and two motorists will end up trying to occupy the same space in the same lane at the same time. Certain words and gestures will be exchanged, none of them charitable. Sometimes there are even argy-bargies in the church. At any given moment there may be dozens of conflicts—both large and small—within any community of believers.

Jeremiah's example demonstrates that sometimes the most courageous and godly thing to do is to walk away from an argy-bargy. He did not defend himself or stick up for his rights; he went graciously on his way.

The prophet knew how to apply those wonderful verses in Proverbs that, though adjacent, seem to contradict one another:

Answer not a fool according to his folly,
   lest you be like him yourself.
Answer a fool according to his folly,
   lest he be wise in his own eyes. (Proverbs 26:4, 5)

So which is it? "Answer not a fool" or "Answer a fool"?

It depends on the situation, and it takes spiritual wisdom to know the difference. Sometimes answering a fool will bring you down to the fool's level.

On such occasions a fool ought to be ignored. Other times a fool needs to be answered so he knows he is in the wrong. There is "a time to keep silence, and a time to speak" (Ecclesiastes 3:7).

In his relationship with Hananiah, Jeremiah did both. He answered, and then he did not answer. When Hananiah first made his prophecy, Jeremiah answered him according to his folly. But when Hananiah tore off the other prophet's yoke, Jeremiah did not answer him according to his folly. The first time he spoke, and the second time he walked away. But on both occasions Jeremiah did what was pleasing to the Lord.

There is spiritual wisdom in knowing when to walk away from a dispute. One spring I was playing in a hotly contested basketball game on a Philadelphia playground, and feelings were starting to run high (as they often do). As I was fighting for a rebound, someone took a swing at me. It made me mad, but I did what Jeremiah did: I walked away. I knew I needed to get off the court right away, before I said anything or did anything to dishonor the Lord. I suppose Jeremiah would have done the same thing. He knew the wisdom of walking away from some battles. Not walking away in anger or pride, but in peace, offering full and free forgiveness to his opponent. Such forgiveness is all the more necessary if one's "enemy" turns out to be a brother or sister in Christ.

The Punishment

The last thing Jeremiah did was pronounce Hananiah's punishment. Sometime later he went back to speak with him privately. When Jeremiah was attacked, he did not see the need to defend himself. But he was still God's spokesman, and God had a message for him to deliver. For the nation of Israel there would be a yoke of iron.

> Sometime after the prophet Hananiah had broken the yoke-bars from off the neck of Jeremiah the prophet, the word of the LORD came to Jeremiah: "Go, tell Hananiah, 'Thus says the LORD: You have broken wooden bars, but you have made in their place bars of iron. For thus says the LORD of hosts, the God of Israel: I have put upon the neck of all these nations an iron yoke to serve Nebuchadnezzar king of Babylon, and they shall serve him, for I have given to him even the beasts of the field.'" (28:12–14)

It was one thing for Hananiah to break Jeremiah's wooden yoke, but it is another thing to throw off God's judgment. Resistance only makes punishment more severe. The yoke of exile in Babylon was made of iron, not wood, and it could not be broken.

For Hananiah, the punishment was even more severe. His probation was over:

> And Jeremiah the prophet said to the prophet Hananiah, "Listen, Hananiah, the LORD has not sent you, and you have made this people trust in a lie. Therefore thus says the LORD: 'Behold, I will remove you from the face of the earth. This year you shall die, because you have uttered rebellion against the LORD.'" In that same year, in the seventh month, the prophet Hananiah died. (vv. 15–17)

Soon everyone would know who the true prophet was, for God's Word always comes true. Just a month or two later they gathered to throw flowers on Hananiah's grave.

Hananiah's example shows how deadly false prophecy is. In particular, it is deadly to deny God's justice. No doubt Hananiah seemed very sincere when he said, "I have a word from the Lord." But his sincerity is precisely what made his message so dangerous. As Derek Kidner points out, "What we might describe as wishful and unorthodox teaching, God more briefly calls a lie (15) and rebellion (16)."[4] Thus the proper judicial sentence for a lying prophet is death (Deuteronomy 18:20). The battle between the false prophet and the true turned out to be a battle to the death.

However sincere it is, false teaching is always deadly, both for the teacher and for his students. False teachers usually mean well. Often they are nice people. They call themselves Christians. They seem genuine. They claim to speak in the name of the Lord. But Jesus says, "Not everyone who says to me, 'Lord, Lord,' will enter the kingdom of heaven" (Matthew 7:21).

There are many Hananiahs in the contemporary church, false teachers who discount God's justice and deny the judgment to come.[5] As Lesslie Newbigin accurately states, "It is one of the weaknesses of a great deal of contemporary Christianity that we do not speak of the last judgment and of the possibility of being finally lost."[6]

The lies about which Newbigin warns will be repeated right up until the very moment Jesus Christ returns to judge the earth: "While people are saying, 'There is peace and security,' then sudden destruction will come upon them as labor pains come upon a pregnant woman, and they will not escape" (1 Thessalonians 5:3). "There is peace and security," the Hananiahs will say. "Everything is going to be OK. Everyone will be saved. God will not punish us for our sins."

"There is peace and security," they will say, but there will be neither peace nor security. The truth is that God is a righteous judge. Anyone who does not repent of his or her sins will be fitted for a yoke of iron. The only way to throw off that iron yoke is to come to Jesus for salvation. He is always waiting with open arms. His welcome is so inviting that it bears repeating: "Come to me, all who labor and are heavy laden, and I will give you rest. Take my yoke upon you, and learn from me, for I am gentle and lowly in heart, and you will find rest for your souls. For my yoke is easy, and my burden is light" (Matthew 11:28–30).

38

Seek the Welfare of the City

JEREMIAH 29:1–9, 24–32

IT FINALLY HAPPENED. For decades Jeremiah had prophesied judgment upon God's people. Over and over he said God would punish them with sword, famine, and captivity. He turned out to be right. Jeremiah knew what he was prophesying about. In the year 597 BC the Babylonians swooped down and attacked Jerusalem, killing many and carrying most of the rest into captivity.

When judgment finally arrived, something remarkable happened. Jeremiah changed his tune. The next several chapters are filled with some of the most wonderful promises in all of Scripture. After twenty-eight chapters of gloom and doom, Jeremiah came bearing tidings of grace and glory. He promised that God would bring his people back from captivity (30:3). He would love them "with an everlasting love" (31:3) and "Turn their mourning into joy" (31:13). He would make a new covenant with them (31:31) and give them "one heart and one way" (32:39). God would even "cleanse them from all the guilt of their sin" (33:8).

Jeremiah summarized all these blessings in one wonderful promise: "For I know the plans I have for you, declares the LORD, plans for welfare and not for evil, to give you a future and a hope" (29:11). The promise meant that God knew what he was doing. He had known it all along, as he always does. God makes his plan, and then he carries it out. Everything he does is for the ultimate good of his people.

The promise of Jeremiah 29:11 is precious to me because it is the theme verse for my family. We take an illuminated copy of it wherever we live and mount it on the wall.

I used to think I understood the promise well, but there was something I did not understand about it until we moved to Philadelphia. One evening I stood in the Delancey Lobby of the Tenth Presbyterian Church paging through Robert Linthicum's book *City of God, City of Satan*. My eye was arrested by his exposition of Jeremiah 29:

> My daughter and her family live near Detroit, Michigan. Recently when I was there to visit, I noticed a rather intriguing plaque hanging on the wall of their home. It was a photograph with golden lettering on it. The photograph was any camera buff's dream—pine trees near the foreground framing the picture, a crystal-clear lake mid-scene, and in the background a majestic snowcapped mountain against a cloudless sky. Across that plaque was inscribed the promise from Scripture:
>
> "I know the plans I have for you," declares the LORD, "plans to prosper you and not to harm you, plans to give you hope and a future."
>
> It is a magnificent Biblical promise that is engraved on the photograph of that plaque—in fact, one of my favorite promises of Scripture. But that promise was not made among pine trees and crystal-clear lakes and snow-capped mountains. Instead, this was a promise made in a city and given to an urban people of God.[1]

After I recovered from shock, I pulled out a Bible and turned to Jeremiah 29. Of course! How could I have missed it? God's promise for the future is for God's people in the city! "For I know the plans I have for you" (v. 11) comes just a few verses after "Seek the welfare of the city" (v. 7). The promises of Jeremiah 29 are for urban exiles.

Gaining this insight was like coming home. It was as if the Lord was saying, "See? This is why I pressed this Scripture into your heart. I have called you to seek the welfare of the city."

The City of Man

It is not always easy to live, work, or worship in the city. Thomas Jefferson viewed cities "as pestilential to the morals, the health, and the liberties of men."[2] Back in the 1830s the Reverend John Todd warned, "Let no man who values his soul, or his body, ever go into a great city to become a pastor."[3] Todd knew what he was talking about—his church was located in my adopted city, Philadelphia. Ralph Waldo Emerson was even harsher in his infamous judgment: "If all the world was Philadelphia, suicide would be extremely common."

Things were even worse in Babylon. In 597 BC King Nebuchadnezzar carried the best and brightest of Judah off to Babylon. The chapter begins: "These are the words of the letter that Jeremiah the prophet sent from Jerusalem to the surviving elders of the exiles, and to the priests, the prophets, and all the people, whom Nebuchadnezzar had taken into exile from Jerusalem to Babylon" (v. 1). The reference to "surviving elders" shows how badly things had gone. The survivors were the lucky ones, so to speak: "This was after King Jeconiah and the queen mother, the eunuchs, the officials of Judah and Jerusalem, the craftsmen, and the metal workers had departed from Jerusalem" (v. 2). The Babylonians had done terrible things to the Jews. They had destroyed their city, ransacked their temple, ruined their economy, removed their leaders, and enslaved their populace. Babylon had done its worst to Jerusalem.

It is not surprising, then, that Saint Augustine (354–430) viewed Babylon as a symbol of evil. In his classic work *The City of God*, the great North African theologian described human history as a conflict between two great cities—the city of God and the city of Man.

> This race we have distributed into two parts, the one consisting of those who live according to man, the other of those who live according to God. And these we also mystically call the two cities, or the two communities of men, of which the one is predestined to reign eternally with God, and the other to suffer eternal punishment with the devil.[4]

Augustine later identified Babylon as the Biblical symbol of the city of Man.

James Montgomery Boice's book *Two Cities, Two Loves* applies Augustine's insights to the post-Christian world:

> According to St. Augustine, who gave us the distinction between "The two cities" . . . Scripture unfolds the history of two distinct groups of people, each having a distinct origin, development, characteristics and destiny. These are two cities or societies. The earthly society has as its highest expression the city cultures of Babylon and . . . Rome. The other is the church, composed of God's elect. The former is destined to pass away. The latter is blessed by God and is to last forever.[5]

To read Jeremiah 29 with the two cities in mind is to recognize that God's people were prisoners in the city of Satan. They were refugees in Babylon, which represents everything hateful and odious to God.

Most postmodern cities are like Babylon. They are Cities of Man, ruled by Satan, and Satan is doing all he possibly can, all in line with his condemnation, to turn them into suburbs of hell. One can see it in the abandoned buildings, the graffiti, the tired faces of the prostitutes, the racial altercations, the slow shuffle of the poor, and the great buildings built for human pride. Satan has been very busy.

The Dutch Christian Pieter Bos has devoted his life to the city. He was trained as an architect and city planner before becoming a full-time missionary in Amsterdam. This is how he explains the work of Satan in the city:

> In modern cities decisions are often made haphazardly and with no regard for God. As a result, the city falls under the influence of the principalities and powers of Satan. Satan uses the anonymous nature of the city as an environment which encourages the growth of evil. People flock to the cities seduced by the lie that there they will survive. The results are evident in the environment, in the economy, in social problems and in resistance to the gospel.[6]

These problems should concern Christians who do not live in the city as well as those who do. The future of the world is urban. More than half the world's population now lives in the city, and the figure will rise to 80 percent during the next half century.[7] The global village is fast becoming a global megalopolis.

The City of God

What should God's people do when their zip code places them in Satan's precincts? When God's people were captives in Babylon, they might have expected God to tell them to run away. Or revolt. What he did instead was tell them to make themselves at home. The gist of Jeremiah's prophecy was that God was going to build *his* city in the middle of Satan's city.

Jeremiah was still living back in Jerusalem, perhaps because the Babylonians did not consider him important enough to deport. Thus he needed to fax this prophecy to the exiles in Babylon. Actually, the letter was written on papyrus and carried in a diplomatic mailbag.

> The letter was sent by the hand of Elasah the son of Shaphan and Gemariah the son of Hilkiah, whom Zedekiah king of Judah sent to Babylon to Nebuchadnezzar king of Babylon. It said: "Thus says the LORD of hosts, the God of Israel, to all the exiles whom I have sent into exile from Jerusalem to Babylon: Build houses and live in them; plant gardens and eat their produce. Take wives and have sons and daughters; take wives for your sons, and give your daughters in marriage, that they may bear sons and daughters; multiply there, and do not decrease. But seek the welfare of the city where I have sent you into exile, and pray to the LORD on its behalf, for in its welfare you will find your welfare." (vv. 3–7)

God practically sounded like the ad man for Babylonian Realty. Anyone who has tried to buy a house knows how realtors tend to exaggerate.

"Charming," the ad will say, which means the house is roughly the size of a telephone booth. "Needs some work" translates as "Bring your own wrecking ball." "Luxurious library," said the real estate fact sheet. I imagined myself sitting in a leather armchair beside a fireplace reading a richly ornamented copy of *Paradise Lost*. Then I learned that in the city "luxurious library" means a walk-in closet with bookshelves.

Imagine the reaction when Jeremiah's prophecy was read in the Jewish ghetto in Babylon. There God's people were, languishing in captivity, bemoaning their fate, complaining about the crime rate and the wretched Babylonian city school system. But God gave them the hard sell. "You're going to love this place," he said. "Wonderful place to raise a family! Exciting opportunities for small business! Great location, right in the heart of the Fertile Crescent!" One senses God's passion for urban planning. Yet he was talking about the city of Babylon, of all places. His surprising plan for the redemption of the city meant building the City of God smack-dab in the middle of the City of Man.

No doubt when the captives discussed their sojourn in Babylon they used words like "abandoned" or "banished" or "condemned" to describe what God had done to them. But that is not how God saw things. He viewed the exile as a mission. Literally what he said was, "Seek the peace and prosperity of the city to which I have *sent* you." Nebuchadnezzar did not take them to Babylon. God sent them there. The exiles were not captives—they were missionaries.

Establish a Presence in the City

What did God send his people to the city to do? First, he sent them to *establish a presence in the city*.

God wanted them to get involved in community development: "Build houses and live in them" (v. 5a). That sounds like a good slogan for Habitat for Humanity. God wanted to establish a presence in the city, which meant living in the city. God's people were resident aliens. *Aliens* because they were not living in their hometown anymore. But also *residents* because they lived where God wanted them to live. Since God had planned an extended stay for them, there was no sense renting; they might as well build.

God also wanted his people to get involved in agriculture: "Plant gardens and eat their produce" (v. 5b). This is a reminder that when God first called Jeremiah, he appointed him "over nations and over kingdoms, to pluck up and to break down, to destroy and to overthrow, to build and to plant" (1:10). After twenty-eight chapters of uprooting and overthrowing, Jeremiah finally got around to building and planting.

God wanted his people to do some matchmaking as well, maybe even start a singles group at the local synagogue: "Take wives and have sons and daughters; take wives for your sons, and give your daughters in marriage" (29:6a). Then he wanted them to start families. They should marry off their kids, "That they may bear sons and daughters; multiply there, and do not decrease" (v. 6b). In short, God wanted his people to go about their business as usual. Despite the fact that they were living in a godless city, he wanted them to lead normal lives. Furthermore, he wanted them to build for the future.

These verses teach the importance of daily family life for the redemption of the post-Christian city. The construction of the house, the planting of the garden, and the raising of the family all build the City of God. The most important thing a Christian parent can do in his or her lifetime is to raise a godly family. And nowhere is the godly family more valuable than in the city.

For some, though not for all, establishing a presence in the city will mean more than just worshiping and ministering in the city. It will mean answering God's call to *live* in the city. For too long, evangelical Christians have abandoned the city to establish the kingdom of God in suburbia. God's plan for the redemption of the city calls Christians to do just the opposite. Ronald J. Sider, who teaches theology at Eastern Baptist Theological Seminary in Philadelphia, argues:

> Evangelicals must reverse the continuing evangelical flight from the cities. . . . Tens of thousands of evangelicals ought to move back into the city. . . . If one percent of evangelicals living outside the inner city had the faith and courage to move in town, evangelicals would fundamentally alter the history of urban America.[8]

To this it should be added that if 1 percent of evangelical *families* would move into the city, the impact would be all the greater.

The Lord does not just call people to jobs and to spouses—he also calls them to churches and to cities. I sometimes challenge people to ask the Lord if he is calling them to make a lifetime commitment to Tenth Presbyterian Church. If he is, then I challenge them to ask if God is also calling them to live in the city. When it comes to urban ministry, "being there" makes all the difference. An outsider can seldom know the needs of the community well enough to know how best to respond to them. Rarely, if ever, can an outsider effectively lead the community in finding solutions to its own problems. The kind of leadership that empowers people comes from insiders.[9]

Becoming an urban insider was no more popular in Jeremiah's time than it is in the twenty-first century. The exiles thought their exile would end any minute, so they still had their bags packed to go back to Jerusalem. They were working part-time jobs. They were renting rather than buying. They were not committed to the city.

As soon as Jeremiah told people to settle down in Babylon, he ran into fierce opposition. The patriots were infuriated. Shemaiah the Nehelamite was so angry that he attacked Jeremiah via correspondence. He mailed letters—in his own name, not God's—back to Jerusalem. But God knew about the letters and instructed Jeremiah to deal with Shemaiah:

> To Shemaiah of Nehelam you shall say: "Thus says the LORD of hosts, the God of Israel: You have sent letters in your name to all the people who are in Jerusalem, and to Zephaniah the son of Maaseiah the priest, and to all the priests, saying, 'The LORD has made you priest instead of Jehoiada the priest, to have charge in the house of the LORD over every madman who prophesies, to put him in the stocks and neck irons. Now why have you not rebuked Jeremiah of Anathoth who is prophesying to you? For he has sent to us in Babylon, saying, "Your exile will be long; build houses and live in them, and plant gardens and eat their produce."'" (vv. 24–28)

Shemaiah understood Jeremiah's message well enough to summarize it; he just didn't like it. Since he was sure Jeremiah was crazy, he wanted him locked up in the loony bin (cf. 20:2, 3). One translation has Shemaiah refer to Jeremiah in 29:26 as that "crazy fellow who takes himself for a prophet."[10] Settle down in Babylon, you say? You mean, raise a family in the city of Satan? Jeremiah had to be out of his mind!

What Shemaiah failed to understand was God's loving plan for the city. He did not understand that God wanted his people to love the city, not leave it. According to the French social critic Jacques Ellul, "We have our job to do in the city. We have seen that down through history God's answer to the construction of man's closed world was to move in just the same. And if he is there by his hidden presence, he is also there by those whom he sends. Our task is therefore to represent him in the heart of the city."[11]

Fortunately, Zephaniah had the good sense to show his mail to Jeremiah, who knew better than to listen to the propaganda of lying prophets. Jeremiah had already corresponded with the exiles about the dangers of false prophecy: "For thus says the LORD of hosts, the God of Israel: Do not let your prophets and your diviners who are among you deceive you, and do not listen to the dreams that they dream, for it is a lie that they are prophesying to you in my name; I did not send them, declares the LORD" (vv. 8, 9).

This, therefore, was the message Jeremiah sent back to Babylon posthaste:

Zephaniah the priest read this letter in the hearing of Jeremiah the prophet. Then the word of the LORD came to Jeremiah: "Send to all the exiles, saying, 'Thus says the LORD concerning Shemaiah of Nehelam: Because Shemaiah had prophesied to you when I did not send him, and has made you trust in a lie, therefore thus says the LORD: Behold, I will punish Shemaiah of Nehelam and his descendants. He shall not have anyone living among this people, and he shall not see the good that I will do to my people, declares the LORD, for he has spoken rebellion against the LORD.'" (vv. 29–32)

Because Shemaiah was not indeed a prophet, he would have no posterity.

Shemaiah's sin was to rebel against God's call to establish a presence in the city. If God calls you to work, worship, or live in the city, do not resist his call. God loves the city. If you love God, then his heart for the city must become your heart for the city.

Seek the Peace of the City

A second reason God sent his people to the city was to "seek [its] welfare" (v. 7). Here the English Standard Version best captures the sense of the Hebrew: "Seek the welfare of the city where I have sent you into exile, and pray to the LORD on its behalf, for in its welfare you will find your welfare." The recurrent word for "welfare" is the word shalom. "Seek the shalom of the city; its shalom is your shalom."

Shalom is comprehensive peace. "More than the absence of conflict and death," says Clifford Green, "This rich term fills out the word community by embracing well-being, contentment, wholeness, health, prosperity, safety, and rest."[12] Shalom means order, harmony, and happiness. It means that all is right with the city.

God hereby commands Christians to do anything and everything to further the public good. Seeking the peace of the city means being a good neighbor. It means shoveling the sidewalk. It means cleaning the street. It means planting a tree. It means feeding the poor. It means volunteering at the local school. It means greeting people at the store. It means driving safely and helping people with car trouble. It means shutting down immoral businesses. It means embracing people from every ethnic background with the love of Christ.

Still, a church could do all those things and fail to bring shalom to the city. By themselves, random acts of kindness cannot bring enduring peace. The only basis for real and lasting shalom is the work of Christ on the cross. The city cannot be at peace until the city knows Jesus Christ, and him crucified. In its sin, the whole city is at war with God. It deserves the wrath and curse of God. But Jesus Christ came to make peace between God and humanity. The

Bible says that "we have peace with God through our Lord Jesus Christ" (Romans 5:1). Anyone who believes in the Lord Jesus Christ has peace with God.

Whatever shalom the Hebrews offered to Babylon, Christians are able to offer a much greater peace to the postmodern city. What we offer is eternal peace with God through the work of Christ on the cross. That peace is the basis for everything else we do in the city. It is what makes us neighborly, compassionate, and charitable. When the city finds peace with God, all will be well with the city.

Pray for the Prosperity of the City

Once they had established a presence in the city and had begun to seek its peace, God's people were to pray for its prosperity. Jeremiah urges the exiles, "Pray to the LORD for it, because if it prospers, you too will prosper" (29:7 NIV). This is the Biblical version of the proverb, "A rising tide lifts all boats." Christians have a vested interest in the welfare of the city. When the city prospers, the church prospers.

That is not how Christians usually think about the city. Many Christians write the city off. At most, they try to establish their own fortress within the city. But God does not tell his people to seek peace in the city; he tells them to seek the peace of the city. God is not trying to establish a ghetto but a government.

One of the best ways to seek the peace of the city is through prayer. Prayer is the Christian's civic duty. It must have been hard for the Jews to pray for the peace of Babylon. The shalom of Babylon? It sounds like an oxymoron, a contradiction in terms. Sometimes God's people were even instructed to pray against the peace of Babylon. For example:

> O daughter of Babylon, doomed to be destroyed,
>   blessed shall he be who repays you
>   with what you have done to us!
> Blessed shall he be who takes your little ones
>   and dashes them against the rock! (Psalm 137:8, 9)

In fact, Jeremiah 29:7 is the only verse in the entire Old Testament in which God's people are explicitly told to pray for their enemies.[13] Prayer for the Babylonians is a foretaste of the forgiveness of Jesus Christ, who teaches, "Love your enemies and pray for those who persecute you" (Matthew 5:44).

When the Jews in Babylon were at a loss to know how to pray for Babylon, one psalm should have come immediately to mind:

Pray for peace in Jerusalem:
  "Prosperity to your houses!
Peace inside your city walls!
  Prosperity to your palaces!"
Since all are my brothers and friends,
  I say, "Peace be with you!"
Since Yahweh our God lives here,
  I pray for your happiness. (Psalm 122:6–9 JB)

The language of Jeremiah 29:7 echoes the vocabulary of Psalm 122. The people of God had long prayed for the peace and prosperity of Jerusalem. But when they went into exile, he commanded them to use the same liturgy for Babylon.

The same prayer should be offered for the post-Christian city. Notice four things to pray for.[14] First, pray for the *economy* of the city ("Prosperity to your houses!"). Pray for the "common wealth" of the city, asking God to bring justice to the poor and prosperity for everyone within the economic systems of the city.

Second, pray for the *safety* of the city ("Peace inside your city walls!"). Pray that citizens will be kept safe from harm and violence on the streets. And pray that criminals themselves will be transformed by the love of Christ.

Third, pray for the *politics* of the city ("Prosperity to your palaces!"). Ask the Lord to grant wisdom and integrity to the authorities who govern the city. Pray for the restoration of virtue to public office.

Fourth, pray for the *people* of the city ("Peace be with you!"). Pray for the Lord's blessing on all people and all people groups in the city. Pray neighborhood by neighborhood, church by church, business by business, and house by house for the welfare of the city.

Three times a year Christians gather in Center City Philadelphia to take a Prayer Walk in the neighborhood near Tenth Presbyterian Church. We walk the streets of the city asking the Holy Spirit to guide our prayers. We stop at apartment buildings and pray for the salvation of those who live in them. We stop at schools and pray for the teachers. We stop at businesses to pray for their owners. We stop at churches to pray for their ministers. We stop at the street corners and pray for the prostitutes. And we stop at the homes of Christians and pray for their ministry in the city. Prayer should not be kept within the four walls of the church or the home. Get out into the streets to pray for the shalom of your neighborhood. The prosperity of the city comes through prayer.

Once someone gave me notes from a sermon by Charles Spurgeon called "Blessing in the City." It was based on the text, ". . . if thou shalt hearken unto the voice of the LORD thy God. Blessed shalt thou be in the city" (Deuteronomy 28:2, 3 KJV). Although Spurgeon's message was meant for a modern city (London) at the dawn of the twentieth century, it is just as appropriate for the postmodern city at the dawn of the twenty-first century:

> The city is full of care, and he who has to go there from day to day finds it to be a place of great wear and tear. It is full of noise, and stir, and bustle, and sore travail; many are its temptations, losses, and worries. But to go there with the divine blessing takes off the edge of its difficulty; to remain there with that blessing is to find pleasure in its duties, and strength equal to its demands.
> A blessing in the city may not make us great, but it will keep us good; it may not make us rich, but it will preserve us honest. Whether we are porters, or clerks, or managers, or merchants, or magistrates, the city will afford us opportunities for usefulness. It is good fishing where there are shoals of fish, and it is hopeful to work for our Lord amid the thronging crowds.

May the Lord bless the city, and the church in the city.

39

The Best-Laid Plans

JEREMIAH 29:10–23

DO YOU EVER WONDER WHAT GOD IS UP TO? A friend of mine once parked his car overnight in Center City Philadelphia. Someone broke into his car and stole some belongings. Nothing of tremendous value was taken, just some odds and ends. But then my friend noticed that the thief also had stolen a series of lecture tapes on—of all subjects!—the sovereignty of God. The crook must have been either a Calvinist or a humorist.

Why does God allow stuff like that to happen? What is he up to? What is he doing with your life? Why won't he answer the request you keep praying? Why is he letting you suffer? Why are there so many difficult people in your life? Why are you still struggling with the same stubborn sin? Why are you still stuck in the same boring job? What, if anything at all, is God doing with your life?

The people of God asked the same kinds of questions during the days of Jeremiah. They had been deported to Babylon. They were exiles living in a ghetto a thousand miles from home. Many had watched in horror as friends and family were murdered. So they wanted to know where God was in all of that. Why was he allowing them to suffer? Some prophets said this, and others said that, but nobody seemed to know for sure what God was up to. Why were bad things happening to God's people?

Jeremiah 29 was written to answer that question. The chapter contains a letter from home written by Jeremiah, who was still living back in Jerusalem. The main point of the letter is that God knows what he is doing, even when it does not seem that way. His plans are always the best-laid plans.

Known Plans

One reason God's plans are best is because God knows all about them. "For I know the plans I have for you, declares the LORD" (v. 11a). God's plans are known plans.

Paul Simon's song "Slip Slidin' Away" has this to say about God's planning ability: "Well God only knows, and God makes his plan, and the information's unavailable to the mortal man." The last part of that lyric is not sound doctrine. Some information *is* available to the mortal man, including "all things that pertain to life and godliness" (2 Peter 1:3). But the first part contains some good theology. "God only knows, and God makes his plan" is Jeremiah's message.

God makes and God knows God's plan. This fact is stressed by the grammar of Jeremiah 29:11, where the "I" is repeated in Hebrew for emphasis: "I, I know the plans I have for you." We do not know what the plans are, but God does. These are God's plans for us, not our plans for God, or even our plans for us. God insists on his right to know and fulfill his plans, which is why the plans are so good. They are God's plans rather than ours.

The God who knows the plans also carries them out. In the verses that follow, Jeremiah proceeds to list all the things God will do. "I will be found by you." "I will restore your fortunes." "I will . . . gather you." "I will bring you back to the place." God will do the finding, the gathering, and the bringing back. (To discover how God did all of this, read the books of Ezra and Nehemiah.) Since God made the plans and knows the plans, it makes sense for him to fulfill the plans.

When God says he knows the plans he has for you, it is important to understand whom he means by "you." Christians often apply Jeremiah's promise to themselves individually. "Terrific!" they say. "God knows the plans he has for me." This shows how self-centered Bible reading can be. Jeremiah's promise should not be taken individualistically. It is not a private promise. It is for the entire church. The "you" in "I know the plans I have for you" refers to the whole people of God. Before thinking about what the promise means for you, think about what it means for us.

In Jeremiah's case, the promise of return was for the whole community of exiles. In the case of the church, the promise of salvation in Christ is for the whole community of believers.

He chose us in him before the foundation of the world, that we should be holy and blameless before him. In love he predestined us for adoption as sons through Jesus Christ, according to the purpose of his will. . . . In

him we have redemption through his blood, the forgiveness of our trespasses, according to the riches of his grace. . . . In him we have obtained
an inheritance, having been predestined according to the purpose of him
who works all things according to the counsel of his will. (Ephesians 1:4,
5, 7, 11)

This passage shows how well-known salvation in Christ has been from
all eternity. God chose us and redeemed us according to plan. Actually, everything God does is according to plan, since he "works all things according
to the counsel of his will." But God especially knows every step of salvation,
from beginning to end, which is why it is sometimes called "The plan of
salvation."

Ephesians 1 also shows that the plan of salvation is for the whole church.
Rather than writing about his own personal predestination and redemption, the
Apostle Paul continually refers to "we" and "us." The best-laid plan of salvation in Christ is something all believers share in common. God's well-known
plans are for the redemption of all his people in Jesus Christ.

If God knows his plans for the church, then he also knows his plans for
the Christian. Although we should not take Jeremiah's promise individualistically, we can apply it individually. God does know his plans for each and every
Christian.

In the previous chapter I mentioned that 29:11–13 is a theme passage for
my family. I sometimes think of all the times we have trusted this promise
together—and all the times the Lord has kept it. I think of the time Lisa and I
had only a couple of days to find a home during seminary. On our last day of
looking, we found the perfect apartment. The only reason it was still available
was because the landlord's phone number had been misprinted in the newspaper the week before. The Lord knew the plans he had for us.

Or I think of the time I needed to choose a topic for doctoral research.
I did not have a clue which theologian to study. In frustration I sat down to
pray about it in the library of Westminster Theological Seminary. Within the
next hour the Holy Spirit called to mind the name of a pastor I had barely
encountered—Thomas Boston of Ettrick. Boston's ministry, piety, and theology ended up making him the perfect figure for me to study. In the providence
of God, my subsequent travels to Scotland for ministry led me to Aberdeen,
where I rediscovered some of Boston's original sermon manuscripts. It was a
surprise to me, but God knew it all along. He always knows what he is about.

Or I think of the time we moved into our apartment in England. After we
moved in, we discovered that we were an answer to prayer. Our new neighbors

showed us the line in their family prayer journal where they had prayed for a Christian family to move into that very apartment.

Then I think of the time I stood in front of a red English mailbox, holding a letter addressed to Dr. James M. Boice. I prayed, "Lord, if you want me to go to Tenth Presbyterian Church, help them to know." Somehow they did know, and it must have been because God knew.

I share these experiences not because they are unusual, but because they show the way God works out his plan in the lives of ordinary Christians. If you are a Christian, then surely you have found the same thing to be true in your own life. You can look back and see how God's hand has guided you every step of the way. You know from your own experience that "for those who love God all things work together for good, for those who are called according to his purpose" (Romans 8:28). That promise is not trite—it is the truth. God really does work all things for the good of those who love him. He knows the plans he has for you, and he always has.

Promising Plans

The second thing Jeremiah 29 says about God's plans is that they are promising. Very promising.

The exiles thought they had every reason to be pessimistic about their plight. They were being held captive, and they had no way of escape. But God had plans "To give [them] a future and a hope" (v. 11b).

Here was the plan: "I will restore your fortunes and gather you from all the nations and all the places where I have driven you, declares the LORD, and I will bring you back to the place from which I sent you into exile" (v. 14b). The exiles would not have to live in Babylon forever. Theirs was a fixed-term captivity. "For thus says the LORD: When seventy years are completed for Babylon, I will visit you, and I will fulfill to you my promise and bring you back to this place" (v. 10). At the end of seventy years they would get to celebrate homecoming (cf. 25:11–14).

Jeremiah may have used seventy years to represent a typical lifespan, the way Moses did: "The years of our life are seventy" (Psalm 90:10a). Or perhaps he was using seventy years more literally. That is what Daniel assumed when he was sitting around in Babylon trying to figure out when his exile would come to an end (Daniel 9:2). The exile did last seventy years. R. K. Harrison counts seventy years from the Babylonian victory at Carchemish in 605 BC to the return of the first exiles in 536 BC.[1] In any case, the point is that the exile was not to last forever. Even though God's people were going through the worst of times, things were still promising because God knew the plans he had for them.

If God's plans are for the future, the Christian must not complain about the present. One of the dangers of grumbling about what God is doing is that, whatever it is, God probably is not finished doing it. By its very nature, a plan is something that will not be completed until sometime in the future. And once it is completed, it will not be a plan anymore; it will be history. If God has plans for hope and a future, you must give him enough time to work them out.

This is why the Christian always lives by faith. A Christian is someone who trusts the promises of God for the future and acts upon them in the present. In other words, the Christian acts on God's promises *before* they are fulfilled. "Now faith is the assurance of things hoped for, the conviction of things not seen" (Hebrews 11:1). To draw comfort from God's plans for the future, one must take them by faith.

The refugees in Babylon had to live by faith. During the seventy long years of their captivity, they had to trust the promises of God. They had to live for God in the city by faith. They had to build houses, plant gardens, raise families, and pray for the welfare of the city by faith (29:5–7). Things looked promising, but only as long as they trusted God to do what he had said he would do.

Not all the exiles lived by faith. Jeremiah told the sad story of two men who did not—Ahab son of Kolaiah and Zedekiah son of Maaseiah:

> Hear the word of the LORD, all you exiles whom I sent away from Jerusalem to Babylon: "Thus says the LORD of hosts, the God of Israel, concerning Ahab the son of Kolaiah and Zedekiah the son of Maaseiah, who are prophesying a lie to you in my name: Behold, I will deliver them into the hand of Nebuchadnezzar king of Babylon, and he shall strike them down before your eyes." (vv. 20, 21)

These false prophets, named after two evil kings, were impatient. They were unwilling to wait seventy years for God to work his plan. They wanted him to work it out *now*; so they took matters into their own hands. They started a seeker-sensitive synagogue, telling people what they most wanted to hear, that the exile was almost over. They were also guilty of several outrageous sins—"folly, fornication and fraud," one commentator calls them.[2] "They have done an outrageous thing in Israel, they have committed adultery with their neighbors' wives, and they have spoken in my name lying words that I did not command them. I am the one who knows, and I am witness, declares the LORD" (v. 23).

Most likely, the reason Nebuchadnezzar had Ahab and Zedekiah put to death is that they tried to lead a rebellion against Babylon. They were treated so disgracefully that they became swearwords among the exiles. "Because of them this curse shall be used by all the exiles from Judah in Babylon: 'The LORD make you like Zedekiah and Ahab, whom the king of Babylon roasted in the fire'" (v. 22). Nebuchadnezzar "roasted" them, which was the proper punishment for treason in Hammurabi's Code. But the biggest sin Ahab and Zedekiah committed was not treason against Babylon, but treason against God. They were not willing to live by faith in God's promises.

If you have decided to live for Jesus, then your future looks very promising. Jesus has promised to forgive your sins, to make you a child of the living God, to send his Holy Spirit to comfort you, to prepare a place for you, and to come back so you can live with him forever. It all sounds most promising, but you must live by faith in those promises.

An inscription in an old church in Yorkshire, England, reads as follows: "In the year 1652 when through England all things sacred were either profaned or neglected, this church was built by Sir Robert Shirley, whose special praise it is to have done the best of things in the worst of times and to have hoped them in the most calamitous."[3] That is a wonderful epitaph for a Christian. Robert Shirley did and hoped for the best in the worst of times. He did so because he knew how promising God's plans were for the future of his people.

Good Plans

One can imagine the exiles hearing about God's plans and thinking that, however promising they were, they were not very good, especially that part about the seventy years. Seventy years is a long, long time to wait for God to work things out. Most people would like God to work out their problems by the end of the week, not the end of the century. The exiles probably knew enough arithmetic to figure out that they would be dead by the time the exile would be over. "Seventy years, you say, Jeremiah? Sounds great for my grandchildren, but what about me?"

The answer is that God's plans were not only promising—they were also good. There is a hint of the goodness of these plans in verse 10, where God speaks of fulfilling his "gracious promise" (NIV). Grace is the unmerited favor of God. To receive something by grace is to receive something one does not deserve. What God's people deserved in this case was to stay in captivity as long as God was pleased to keep them there. But God promised to give them something they did not deserve. By his grace he would bring them back home.

The Christian cannot think about gracious promises without thinking about the grace that comes through the Lord Jesus Christ. The Bible teaches that all of us are guilty sinners who deserve to be damned for our sins. God has every right to give us the death penalty. Yet "God, being rich in mercy, because of the great love with which he loved us, even when we were dead in our trespasses, made us alive together with Christ—by grace you have been saved" (Ephesians 2:4, 5). Now that is a good plan. It is God's plan for saving sinners. We do not deserve to be rescued from sin or delivered from death. But by his grace God sent his only Son, Jesus Christ, to die on the cross for our sins. Salvation is God's "abundance of grace . . . through the one man Jesus Christ" (Romans 5:17).

God's plans are not only gracious for the future, they are also gracious for the present. "For I know the plans I have for you, declares the LORD, plans for welfare and not for evil" (29:11). God's grace is available right now. The exiles in Babylon did not have to wait seventy years for God to do them any good. His plans included their present welfare. The word "welfare" is the same word Jeremiah used when he said, "Seek the welfare of the city . . . for in its welfare you will find your welfare" (v. 7). It is the Hebrew word shalom, meaning order, stability, health, and safety. Shalom is all-encompassing peace. God promised that he would begin to give his people that kind of peace right away. He not only wanted them to work for shalom (vv. 5–7), he wanted to give it to them.

This good plan stands in contrast to God's plan for the people who stayed back in Jerusalem. His plans for them were not good, for they were judged for their holier-than-thou attitude toward the exiles:

> Because you have said, "The LORD has raised up prophets for us in Baby-
> lon," [namely, the lying prophets who said the exile was almost over; see
> vv. 8, 9] thus says the LORD concerning the king who sits on the throne of
> David, and concerning all the people who dwell in this city, your kinsmen
> who did not go out with you into exile: "Thus says the LORD of hosts, be-
> hold, I am sending on them sword, famine, and pestilence, and I will make
> them like vile figs that are so rotten they cannot be eaten. I will pursue them
> with sword, famine, and pestilence, and will make them a horror to all the
> kingdoms of the earth, to be a curse, a terror, a hissing, and a reproach
> among all the nations where I have driven them, because they did not pay
> attention to my words, declares the LORD, that I persistently sent to you by
> my servants the prophets, but you would not listen, declares the LORD."
> (vv. 15–19)

This goes back to what Jeremiah prophesied about the good figs and the bad figs in chapter 24. The people who stayed in Jerusalem were like bad figs to be thrown away. But the exiles in Babylon were good figs, and God's plans for them were good.

A perfect example of God's good plans for his people in Babylon is the prophet Daniel. Daniel prospered in exile. Because of his faith in God he was a star pupil in the Babylonian school system. He was not only "better in appearance and fatter in flesh" than the pagan students, but he also had "learning and skill in all literature and wisdom" (Daniel 1:15, 17). When Daniel was able to interpret King Nebuchadnezzar's dreams, "The king gave Daniel high honors and many great gifts, and made him ruler over the whole province of Babylon and chief prefect over all the wise men of Babylon" (2:48). Much the same thing happened when Daniel interpreted Belshazzar's dream. "Then Belshazzar gave the command, and Daniel was clothed with purple, a chain of gold was put around his neck, and a proclamation was made about him, that he should be the third ruler in the kingdom" (5:29).

Then Daniel's career took a turn for the worse. Notice that Jeremiah said God's plans were good, not easy. Christians usually want life to be easy, but often the good God wants to do can only come through suffering. That is the way it was for Daniel. God's plans for him were not easy. They included being attacked by his coworkers, persecuted for his faith, and thrown into a den of hungry lions.

But God delivered Daniel from all his troubles, and after he emerged unscathed from the lions' den, Jeremiah's promise was fulfilled. "So this Daniel prospered during the reign of Darius and the reign of Cyrus the Persian" (6:28). Daniel was a success. He thrived in Babylon. Of course he did! God knew the plans he had for Daniel, plans to prosper him and not to harm him.

From beginning to end, God's plans for his people are altogether good.

> His plans concerning his people are always thoughts of good, of blessing. Even if he is obliged to use the rod, it is the rod not of wrath, but the Father's rod of chastisement for their temporal and eternal welfare. There is not a single item of evil in his plans for his people, neither in their motive, nor in their conception, nor in their revelation, nor in their consummation.[4]

Do you believe that? Do you believe there is not one single item of evil in God's plans for his people? Do you believe that whatever God does is all for the best and could not possibly be any better?

Some Christians harbor a lingering suspicion that God is out to get them. When things go well, they secretly think God eventually will make them pay for their prosperity. Perhaps that is why God makes a point of saying that his plans are not harmful. "Plans for welfare and not for evil," he calls them

(29:11b). God's plans for his children are only good. Even if God sends suffering their way, it will be for their good. Christians who live in fear or worry need to grab hold of the goodness of God. If you are God's child, God is not going to hurt you.

Personal Plans

The last thing Jeremiah teaches about God's plans is that they are personal. God's purpose in all his plans is to bring his people into intimate relationship with himself. "Then you will call upon me and come and pray to me, and I will hear you. You will seek me and find me, when you seek me with all your heart. I will be found by you, declares the LORD" (vv. 12–14a). God's plans are not just for you—they are for you in relation to him.

This relationship was to begin right away. In this respect, the "Then" at the beginning of verse 12 is somewhat misleading.[5] It makes it sound as if God's people will not find him until the end of their exile. What the Bible actually says is, "*And* you will call upon me." The exiles in Babylon did not have to wait seventy years to have a relationship with God. He invited them into a personal relationship right away, in Babylon, in their suffering.

The lesson is easy to apply. We do not need to wait to call upon God. He is available to us right now. Whenever we call, he will listen. Whenever we pray, he will answer. Whoever seeks will find.

Seeking God sometimes seems like playing spiritual hide-and-seek. God's ways are so mysterious that we sometimes despair of ever finding him. But if we do play hide-and-seek with God, it is the kind of hide-and-seek one plays with a toddler. Toddlers get scared if they have to look for very long. For a toddler, the joy of hide-and-seek is not the hiding or the seeking, but the finding. God knows how scary it is to be alone in the world without him. So his good plans are personal plans. They draw his children into the heart of a relationship with him.

Jeremiah 29:13 is a wonderful verse for anyone on a spiritual quest. God says, "You will seek me and find me, when you seek me with all your heart." Anyone who seeks God sincerely and wholeheartedly will find him. What the seeker is really looking for (even if he or she does not yet realize it) is Jesus Christ. Jesus is the way to God, the Savior of the world, and the answer to all of life's questions.

Jesus repeats the same wonderful promise first made in Jeremiah 29. He says, "Ask, and it will be given to you; seek, and you will find; knock, and it will be opened to you. For everyone who asks receives, and the one who seeks finds, and to the one who knocks it will be opened" (Matthew 7:7, 8). God's plans really are the best-laid plans. What could be better than good, gracious, well-known plans that lead to a wonderful friendship?

In his book *Spiritual Leadership*, Oswald Sanders quotes this poem about the way God works out his plans:

How He bends but never breaks
When our good He undertakes;
How He uses whom He chooses
And with every purpose fuses him;
By every act induces him
To try His splendor out—
God knows what He's about.[6]

Do you ever wonder what God is up to? Of course. We all do. But whatever it is, God knows what he's about. He knows the plans he has for you. Plans to prosper and not to harm you. Plans for hope and a future.

40

"And Ransom Captive Israel"

JEREMIAH 30:1-17

IT IS SURPRISING how rarely Jeremiah is preached at Christmas. It is not that preachers ignore the Old Testament. Isaiah gets plenty of airtime—"Behold, a virgin shall conceive, and bear a son, and shall call his name Immanuel" (Isaiah 7:14 KJV), "For unto us a child is born, unto us a son is given" (Isaiah 9:6a KJV), and so forth.

Even minor prophets like Micah come into their own in late December:

But you, O Bethlehem Ephrathah,
    who are too little to be among the clans of Judah,
from you shall come forth for me
    one who is to be ruler in Israel. (Micah 5:2)

Nothing against Isaiah or Micah, but it is unfortunate that Jeremiah's teaching about the Messiah remains so unfamiliar.

"That Mourns in Lonely Exile Here"

Most of Jeremiah's Messianic prophecies come in chapters 30—33. These chapters are filled with such hope and joy they are sometimes called "The Book of Consolation" or "The Book of Comfort." E. W. Hengstenberg identifies them as "The grand hymn of Israel's deliverance."[1] R. E. O. White calls them "An Anthology of Hope" and says they are characterized by "moving poetry, solid argument, and eloquent descriptions of the coming restoration."[2]

The consolation begins with the promise that the Messiah will ransom his people—both Judah and Israel—from their captivity.

> The word that came to Jeremiah from the LORD: "Thus says the LORD, the God of Israel: Write in a book all the words that I have spoken to you. For behold, days are coming, declares the LORD, when I will restore the fortunes of my people, Israel and Judah, says the LORD, and I will bring them back to the land that I gave to their fathers, and they shall take possession of it." (30:1–3)

This is a reminder of something Jeremiah's people could never forget: They were captives, living as exiles in Babylon. The Lord gave this word to Jeremiah not long after King Jehoiachin and all his officials were dragged off to Babylon (597 BC; cf. 29:2). The wounds of captivity were still fresh. Throughout the passage there are hints of how greatly God's people suffered at the hands of their enemies.

What was captivity like for God's people? Captivity meant, of course, slavery. Jeremiah described the yoke that hung around the necks of God's people. He admitted that they had been enslaved to "foreigners" (v. 8). He referred to "The land of their captivity" (v. 10; cf. 46:27). He said they had been devoured, plundered, and despoiled (v. 16).

Captivity meant misery, which Jeremiah portrayed in the most vivid terms:

> These are the words that the LORD spoke concerning Israel and Judah:
>
> "Thus says the LORD:
> We have heard a cry of panic,
>   of terror, and no peace.
> Ask now, and see,
>   can a man bear a child?
> Why then do I see every man
>   with his hands on his stomach like a woman in labor?
> Why has every face turned pale?" (vv. 4–6)

The scenes of battle were fresh in Jeremiah's mind as he wrote. He could still hear the desperate cries of the vanquished. He could see warriors clutching their stomachs in agony, their faces turning green, like women in the throes of childbirth. Yet for all their pain, they delivered nothing but misery.

Captivity also meant anxiety. God told his people not to be afraid or "dismayed" (v. 10), which means, of course, that they were afraid and dismayed. They were afraid of Babylon, afraid of servitude, afraid of suffering, afraid of being separated from their loved ones, and afraid of death.

Captivity meant slavery, misery, and anxiety. It also meant loss of identity. The people of God were alone in the world. They felt rejected. In fact, they *were* rejected, first of all by their enemies: "They have called you an outcast," the Lord said, "Zion, for whom no one cares!" (v. 17b). This was not surprising. One cannot expect to be loved by one's enemies.

Yet the people of Israel were also rejected by their friends, which was more devastating. "All your lovers have forgotten you; they care nothing for you" (v. 14a; cf. 22:20). When the days of trouble came and the Babylonians were on the march, Jerusalem tried to make unholy alliances with pagan kings. Instead of trusting the Lord, the Jews invited Edom, Moab, Ammon, Tyre, and Sidon to make treaties of war (27:1–7).

Their trust was misplaced. Jeremiah accused them of looking for love in all the wrong places. Turning to pagan kings for safety was a way of committing spiritual adultery. In the end, their "lovers" would abandon them, and they would be left completely alone. No one would care what happened to them.

Slavery, misery, anxiety, loss of identity—these are common experiences. We must not trivialize the sufferings of the exiles. Yet there are times when we ourselves are miserable or anxious. There are many kinds of misery—physical suffering, family strife, unfulfilled desire, shattered expectations, daily drudgery, abject failure. Then we are anxious, uncertain what the future may bring. We wonder about our job security, or about how our children are turning out, or about whether we have enough money for retirement.

Then, like the exiles in Babylon, we may feel alone in the world. We have lost the people we love most. Or we never had them in the first place. Our families oppose our faith. We have little in common with our coworkers. At times we feel so forsaken and rejected—even in the church—that we wonder if there is any place where we belong.

So Great, So Many

There is a reason we are sometimes held captive by these emotions. It is the same reason the exiles were held captive in Babylon—iniquity. Most of all, captivity means bondage to sin, both our own sins and the sins of others.

This is how God explained the exile:

> . . . I have dealt you the blow of an enemy,
>   the punishment of a merciless foe,
> because your guilt is great,
>   because your sins are flagrant.
> Why do you cry out over your hurt?
>   Your pain is incurable.
> Because your guilt is great,
>   because your sins are flagrant,
>   I have done these things to you. (30:14b, 15)

God's actions were just. If he turned against his people, it was only because of their sin. They had been sent to Babylon not because God is weak, unloving, or spiteful, but because they were sinners.

All their misery, anxiety, and loss of identity came ultimately from their captivity to sin. Bondage to sin is the greatest of all captivities. Sin will not be satisfied until it achieves total domination. It seizes the mind to think sinful thoughts. It grabs the body to perform wicked deeds. It poisons the imagination to crave unholy fantasies. It bends the will to its own design. In the end it steals the heart, so that the sinner loves what is evil and hates what is good.

Notice how captive God's people were to sin. Their guilt was "great." Their sins were "flagrant" (v. 14). God reminded his people that they were very great sinners. Instead of being filled with self-pity, the exiles should have been filled with self-accusation. The reason they were so miserable was because they were flagrant sinners.

Do you believe the same thing to be true about yourself? Do you admit that you are a sinner who deserves the wrath and curse of God? You will never become a growing Christian until you confess that your guilt is great and your sins are many. You must know the sinfulness of sin before you can know the graciousness of God's grace.

If you have trouble remembering how great a sinner you are, ask the kinds of hard questions the Puritans asked about their love for God. I have a list that begins like this:

Have I been fervent in prayer? Was there warmth?
Have I practiced God's presence, at least every hour?
Have I, before every deliberate action or conversation, considered how it might
    be turned to God's glory?

Had enough yet? Usually I only need to ask one or two questions before I have to get out the dust and ashes. But there is more to the list:

Have I sought to center conversations on the other person's interest and needs
    and ultimately toward God, or did I turn it toward my own interests?
Have I given thanks to God after every pleasant occurrence or time?
Have I thought or spoken unkindly of anyone?
Have I been careful to avoid proud thoughts or comparing myself to others?
Have I done things just for appearances?
Have I been sensitive, warm, and cheerful toward everyone?

Our guilt is great. Our sins are many. May God have mercy on us.

"O Come, O Come, Emmanuel"

What we need is a Savior. We need someone to deliver us from bondage, which is exactly what the people of Israel needed. They needed someone to ransom them from their captivity to Babylon.

The end of captivity is what Jeremiah 30 promises: "For behold, days are coming, declares the LORD, when I will restore the fortunes of my people, Israel and Judah, says the LORD, and I will bring them back to the land that I gave to their fathers, and they shall take possession of it" (v. 3). Again and again he promised to save them. "It is a time of distress for Jacob; yet he shall be saved out of it" (v. 7b). "I will save you from far away, and your offspring from the land of their captivity" (v. 10b). "I am with you to save you, declares the LORD" (v. 11a).

History shows that God saved his people Israel the way he promised. He gathered them from Babylon and all the northern lands and brought them back to Jerusalem. Their exile lasted seventy years, and then it was over. They came home to their land:

> Nations would come and nations would go; they would strut their stuff across the stage of human history. Israel, however, was different from all of them. She would come, but she would never go. Yes, she would be punished and developed by wars and tribulations. She would look like any other nation, but unlike any other nation she was under the preserving hand of the Almighty.[3]

As the priest says in Walker Percy's novel *The Thanatos Syndrome*, "Since the Jews were the original chosen people of God, a tribe of people who are still here, they are a sign of God's presence which cannot be evacuated."[4]

Jeremiah's promise meant salvation for Israel, but not just for Israel. There are clues he was promising something much bigger than the end of the Babylonian Captivity:

> Throughout this God-given dream of things to come, the language and the landscape are those of Jeremiah's day, dominated by the theme of exile and restoration. Nevertheless a vaster ingathering than the modest one of 538 is foretold; and the covenant with Israel and Judah would, in the event, embrace the world-wide 'sons of the living God', 'not from the Jews only but also from the Gentiles'.[5]

In other words, Jeremiah was one of the first to bring news of a coming Messiah "That will be for all the people" (Luke 2:10).

To begin with, Jeremiah introduced his prophecy with favorite Messianic phrases. "Days are coming" (30:3). "In that day" (v. 8). Furthermore, he was talking about a day that would be utterly unprecedented: "Alas! That day is so great there is none like it" (v. 7a). A better way to translate this verse is, "How great that day will be,"[6] or "how awesome."

The day Jeremiah envisioned would be an awesome day. It would bring deliverance not only for Jeremiah's people, but also for their descendants: "I will save you from far away, and your offspring from the land of their captivity" (v. 10b). It would bring deliverance not only for a time but forever, and from all foreign powers, not simply from Babylon:

> And it shall come to pass in that day, declares the LORD of hosts, that I will break his yoke from off your neck, and I will burst your bonds, and foreigners shall no more make a servant of him. (v. 8)

This verse hearkens back to the days when Jeremiah wandered around Jerusalem with a yoke around his neck (27:1–15). More importantly, it makes promises that are much larger than simply the end of the exile in Babylon.

Jeremiah went on to make a promise about the house and line of David:

> But they shall serve the LORD their God and David their king, whom I will raise up for them. (30:9; cf. 23:5, 6)

This prophecy was not fulfilled at the end of the exile. Under the leadership of Nehemiah, Jerusalem was rebuilt. But no king was put back on the throne.

Jeremiah's promises, therefore, were not fulfilled until the coming of Jesus. Jesus of Nazareth was born a king, a true son of David. This is why the Gospels place so much emphasis on his genealogy. Even to qualify as a candidate for Messiah, he had to be a direct descendant of King David. And so he was. On both sides of the family! Matthew shows that his father Joseph was of the house and line of David (Matthew 1:1–17), while Luke seems to trace his Davidic bloodline through Mary, his mother (Luke 3:23–38). Jesus is the king God promised to raise up for his people.

Jeremiah's prophecy even seemed to hint that the coming king would be God himself. When this Savior comes, this Messiah, this King, then God's people "'shall serve the LORD their God and David their king'" (30:9). Serving God and serving David are placed in parallel. To serve David is to be a servant of God, and vice versa.[7] It is easy to see how the coming of Jesus Christ makes sense of this verse. He is the promised son of David. He is also the Son of God. He is God as well as man. Therefore, to serve Jesus is to serve God, and vice versa.

All this shows that Jeremiah was waiting for the Messiah. His hope is summarized in the words of a well-known Latin hymn from the twelfth century:

> O come, O come, Emmanuel,
> And ransom captive Israel,
> That mourns in lonely exile here,
> Until the Son of God appear.
> Rejoice! Rejoice!
> Emmanuel shall come to thee, O Israel.

"And Ransom Captive Israel"

When the king finally came, what would he do? What kind of Messiah did Jeremiah promise?

The Messiah was to be a liberator. He would ransom his people from their captivity (cf. Isaiah 61:1; Luke 4:18, 19). He would be a Savior, which is why his mother called him "Jesus"—he would save his people from their sins (Matthew 1:21).

The Messiah would be a peacemaker. Isaiah called him the "Prince of Peace" (Isaiah 9:6). Jeremiah promised, "Jacob shall return and have quiet and ease, and none shall make him afraid" (30:10c). We have already seen that the captives were afraid and dismayed. But when Messiah came, they would have lasting peace.

Because the Messiah to come was a peacemaker, God gave his people this command: "Then fear not, O Jacob my servant, declares the LORD, nor be dismayed, O Israel" (v. 10a). This is the most frequently repeated command in Scripture: "Fear not!" And it was this command, remember, that the angel first gave to the shepherds: "Fear not: for, behold, I bring you good tidings of great joy, which shall be to all people" (Luke 2:10 KJV). Then all the angels shouted, "On earth peace, good will toward men" (v. 14 KJV). Jesus Christ has brought peace to the earth. If you trust in him, you have peace with God, peace with man, peace with the world, and peace with yourself.

Then Jeremiah promised that the Messiah would be God with us: "I [God] am with you to save you" (30:11a). Jeremiah piled one Messianic promise on top of another. This is the same promise Isaiah made: "The virgin shall conceive and bear a son, and shall call his name Immanuel" (Isaiah 7:14). Immanuel—that is to say, "God with us."

To know that God is with us has been the greatest comfort to believers throughout all ages of history. It was a comfort to Jacob in the wilderness at Bethel when God said, "I am with you and will keep you wherever you go" (Genesis 28:15). It was a comfort to Moses at the burning bush when God commissioned him to contend with Pharaoh, saying, "I will be with you" (Exodus 3:12). It was a comfort to Joshua after the death of Moses. God appointed Joshua to lead his people and commanded him, "Do not be frightened, and do not be dismayed, for the LORD your God is with you wherever you go" (Joshua 1:9). It was a comfort to Jeremiah when he was first called to the ministry. God said the whole land would oppose him but promised, "I am with you . . . to deliver you" (1:19).

The promise of God with us was a comfort to Mary and Joseph at the manger. This was the meaning of the first Christmas: Jesus is our Immanuel, God with us. When Jesus was born at Bethlehem, God became man. Jesus of Nazareth was God as well as man, fully man and fully God. He thus entered into our humanity, becoming like us in every way, yet without sin. This is the mystery of the incarnation. God is with us because Jesus came to be one of us.

This is our comfort as well, for God is still with us. Before the Lord Jesus Christ ascended to his Father in Heaven, he made one last promise to his disciples: "And behold, I am with you always, to the end of the age" (Matthew 28:20b). Jesus meant that he would remain with us by his Holy Spirit.

Jesus is often considered God's Christmas gift to humanity. He is the gift that keeps on giving. Now that God has come to be with us, we have salvation, freedom, peace, comfort, and every other spiritual blessing in Christ.

We also have protection. Jeremiah promised that the Messiah would be a righteous judge:

I will make a full end of all the nations
    among whom I scattered you,
    but of you I will not make a full end.
I will discipline you in just measure,
    and I will by no means leave you unpunished.
        (30:11b; cf. 17:23; 32:33; 46:28)

Here, Jeremiah speaks of "discipline." When the Messiah came, he would discipline his people the way a father disciplines his children.

When God judges his people, it is for their own good. This is the kind of chastisement described in the book of Proverbs: "The fear of the LORD is the beginning of knowledge; fools despise wisdom and instruction" (Proverbs

1:7). Or again, from the New Testament, "He disciplines us for our good, that we may share his holiness" (Hebrews 12:10b). God judges his people, not for retribution, but for correction.

In Jeremiah's day, God's enemies were not so fortunate:

> Therefore all who devour you shall be devoured,
>> and all your foes, every one of them, shall go into captivity;
> those who plunder you shall be plundered,
>> and all who prey on you I will make a prey. (30:16)

These verses show the perfect justice of God. When the Messiah would come, he would set everything to rights. The destroyer would be destroyed. The devourer would be devoured. The exiler would be exiled. The plunderer would be plundered. The spoiler would be despoiled. The Messiah would expose every sin, tear down every tyrant, and bring every criminal to justice.

The Ultimate Cure

Only one problem remained. It was a problem so serious that apparently nothing could be done about it. Jeremiah described it in medical terms:

> For thus says the LORD:
> Your hurt is incurable,
>> and your wound is grievous.
> There is none to uphold your cause,
>> no medicine for your wound,
>> no healing for you. . . .
> Why do you cry out over your hurt?
>> Your pain is incurable. (vv. 12, 13, 15a)

What do you think of Jeremiah's bedside manner? Tactlessly, he came right out and said that Israel's spiritual condition was terminal.

Jeremiah had brought up the idea of an incurable wound before:

> Is there no balm in Gilead?
>> Is there no physician there?
> Why then has the health of the daughter of my people
>> not been restored? (8:22; cf. 14:19)

The prophet himself suffered from the same ailment.

> Why is my pain unceasing,
>> my wound incurable,
>> refusing to be healed? (15:18a)

There was no known cure for this mysterious malady. Even the most advanced medical remedies of Jeremiah's day were powerless against it.

So much for the prognosis. What about the diagnosis? What mortal wound, what infectious disease laid the people of God on their deathbed? The answer, of course, was sin:

> Why do you cry out over your hurt?
>   Your pain is incurable.
> Because your guilt is great,
>   because your sins are flagrant,
>   I have done these things to you. (30:15)

As Walter Brueggemann puts it, "The cause of the illness is no mystery. Sickness unto death is the outcome of sin, disobedience, and flagrant disregard of God."[8]

You too suffer from this incurable malady. You are in captivity to iniquity. You have a bad case of sin, and you will not—cannot—recover on your own. It will take more than a couple of days in bed and a few bowls of chicken soup to put you back on your feet.

Apart from the grace of God, sin is an incurable disease. The General Confession from *The Book of Common Prayer* expresses it well: "We have left undone those things which we ought to have done; And we have done those things which we ought not to have done; And there is no health in us."[9] Sin is like a vicious strain of bacteria that has grown resistant even to the most powerful antibiotic. It spreads in the soul until it carries the sinner to the grave.

How can sin ever be cured? In November 1997, a forum called "Sin and the Art of Zen Archery" was held at a synagogue in New Jersey. The forum, which featured panelists from several world religions, was on the topic of sin. In the discussion that followed, one woman objected to the whole idea of sin, saying, "I don't know whether there is any proper place for evil in human nature. If I believe part of me is evil, how will I ever overcome evil?"

That haunting question expresses what Jeremiah meant when he said Israel's wound was incurable. If sin is within me, how can I ever escape it? Sin is such a part of us that we cannot get rid of it. But God can. He is the Great Physician, as Jeremiah promised: "For I will restore health to you, and your wounds I will heal, declares the LORD" (v. 17a).

Jeremiah 30 makes two statements that seem irreconcilable. Some scholars say they "blatantly contradict each other."[10] First God says a wound is incurable; then he promises to cure it. First he declares that an injury cannot be healed; then he vows to heal it. We are tempted to wonder how this can be, until we remember that Jesus said, "Those who are well have no need of a physician, but those who are sick" (Matthew 9:12), and "With man this is impossible, but with God all things are possible" (Matthew 19:26).

In Jeremiah 30 God promises to do the impossible. He promises to cure what is incurable and to heal what is beyond healing. The promise of healing is a promise to make new flesh grow over an old wound. Imagine if skin cells did not have the power to regenerate. Imagine if wounds never healed. Imagine how hideous people would look if every cut, scrape, bruise, or blemish were permanent.

Then imagine how hideous a soul looks in which sin has been allowed to fester, untouched by the grace of God. Imagine idolatry added to immorality, compounded by selfishness and ungodliness. If you could look inside your own soul, you would see a malignant evil. Who could ever heal such a spiritual cancer?

Only God, and only through the death of his Son on the cross. For there is only one curative for iniquity, only one remedy for guilt, only one atonement for sin, and that is the blood of Jesus Christ shed on the cross. We ourselves cannot overcome evil, but Jesus Christ won the victory over sin through his death and resurrection. The work of Christ on the cross was done to cure the incurable wound of sin. Do you believe this?

The exiles in Babylon believed it. They were waiting, hoping, longing for their Messiah to come. They prayed that he would deliver them from all the misery of their captivity. We look to the same Messiah to ransom us from our bondage to sin. We believe that he has come, and we have hope that he will come again. "Rejoice! Rejoice! Emmanuel shall come to thee, O Israel."

41

Messiah in the City

JEREMIAH 30:18—31:6

CECIL FRANCES ALEXANDER (1818–1895) wrote many good hymns for the children in her Sunday school class. Two of her best make reference to the city. One reminds us that the Messiah was born in the city:

> Once in royal David's city
> Stood a lowly cattle shed,
> Where a mother laid her baby
> In a manger for his bed:
> Mary was that mother mild,
> Jesus Christ her little child.

The words of this carol are in keeping with Scripture. "And Joseph also went up from Galilee . . . to the city of David, which is called Bethlehem" (Luke 2:4). The angels said the same thing to the shepherds: "For unto you is born this day in the city of David a Savior, who is Christ the Lord" (Luke 2:11). The word used in these verses is *polis*, the standard Greek word for city.

Mrs. Alexander also wrote a well-known hymn about the Messiah's death in the city:

> There is a green hill far away,
> Outside a city wall,
> Where the dear Lord was crucified,
> Who died to save us all.

She was inspired to write these words by a green hill outside the old walls of Derry, the city in Northern Ireland where she lived.[1] This, too, is in keeping with Scripture, for the Gospel of John emphasizes that "The place where Jesus was crucified was near the city" (19:20).

Urban Renewal

The Messiah was born and died in the city. Jeremiah teaches that he also came to build a city. True, most of his prophecies were about urban decay, which is why Francis Schaeffer called his exposition of Jeremiah *Death in the City*. But the prophet also promised life for the city. He was called "To build and to plant" as well as "To destroy and to overthrow" (1:10). Jeremiah promised that when the Messiah came, he would rebuild the city of God.

As we have already seen, in chapter 30 Jeremiah introduced the coming Messiah, the Davidic king God would raise up for his people. The end of that prophecy was about urban renewal, beginning with a blueprint for a housing development:

> Thus says the LORD:
> Behold, I will restore the fortunes of the tents of Jacob
>   and have compassion on his dwellings;
> the city shall be rebuilt on its mound,
>   and the palace shall stand where it used to be. (30:18)

> Again I will build you, and you shall be built,
>   O virgin Israel! (31:4a)

Jeremiah promised that God would reverse the fortunes of his people. A new city would arise from the ruins of the old, which is generally the way cities were rebuilt in those days. "In ancient times when the earthen homes were destroyed by war, erosion, or age, new dwellings and entire new cities were built on the ruins of the old, forming a new level of occupation on top of the old."[2]

God's strategy for urban redevelopment would touch every level of society. The reference to "Tents" shows God's compassion for the general population, including the poor. But not only for the poor. Homes would go up for the middle class. The business district would be gentrified. And since the king should have a kingly place to live, the Lord would rebuild his palace. From the slums to the mansions, God promised to rebuild his city.

A city is more than its buildings, however. The citizens of God's new city would be filled with joy. There were to be great civic festivals, full of singing and dancing, music, and all kinds of merriment: "Out of them shall come songs of thanksgiving, and the voices of those who celebrate" (30:19a; cf.

33:10, 11); literally "The sound of laughter." Once God had promised to "silence . . . the voice of mirth and the voice of gladness" (7:34; cf. 16:9; 25:10), but here he was promising to turn the volume back up.

Way up. "Again you shall adorn yourself with tambourines and shall go forth in the dance of the merrymakers" (31:4b). This is the way maidens danced on their wedding day. Once Jeremiah had condemned God's people for their spiritual prostitution (3:2, 3; 4:30). But the day would come when they would dance their way through the city like virgin brides on a fine wedding morning, singing and dancing before the Lord.

Imagine how wonderful it would be to live in a city where all the great civic events centered on the worship of Almighty God. Imagine a city where all the memorials, monuments, fairs, parades, parties, concerts, and fireworks were directed ultimately to the glory of God. That is God's ultimate plan for his city.

His urban planning included room for expansion. The Babylonians had been carrying wave after wave of Jews into captivity. But when the Messiah came, he would make the city grow. There would be a population boom: "I will multiply them, and they shall not be few" (30:19b; cf. 29:6). Wherever God's people have God's blessing, they grow in size as well as in maturity.

The prestige of the city would be enhanced. This is important because people are sensitive about their civic reputation. Everybody loves a good Cleveland joke—except native Clevelanders. Today cities spend millions of dollars on marketing. In some cases the money is wasted, as it was during the infamous "Philadelphia—The City That Loves You Back" campaign. But the city of God does not need an ad campaign. God himself will guarantee its reputation: "I will make them honored, and they shall not be small" (30:19c).

The economy of the city would flourish, its prosperity spreading to the surrounding countryside. God intended to plant as well as to build (cf. 1:10):

Again you shall plant vineyards
    on the mountains of Samaria;
the planters shall plant
    and shall enjoy the fruit. (31:5)

The mention of "Samaria" is significant. God's strategy for urban renewal was actually a strategy for regional development. It was a plan for the suburbs as well as the city.

The mention of "vineyards" is also significant. A nation must be at peace before it can produce fine wine. It takes at least four years for a new vine to produce a good crop of grapes. According to the Levitical laws, a vine's fourth crop belonged to the Lord (Leviticus 19:23–25). It was not until the fifth year that farmers could enjoy their fruit, as Jeremiah promised they would.

Jeremiah also promised that the Messiah's city would be safe. "Their children shall be as they were of old, and their congregation shall be established before me" (30:20a). As a father, I long to live in a city where my children can play safely in the streets. We live on a quiet one-way street in Center City Philadelphia. After school we often put a portable sign at the end of the street to slow down the cars: "Play Street—No Thru Traffic." But we still need to watch the children as they play, especially the little ones. They are not safe there, and a city is not safe until its children are safe.

The reason Jeremiah could promise safety in the city was because the Messiah would personally ensure its safety: "I will punish all who oppress them" (v. 20b).

> Behold the storm of the LORD!
>   Wrath has gone forth,
> a whirling tempest;
>   it will burst upon the head of the wicked.
> The fierce anger of the LORD will not turn back
>   until he has executed and accomplished
>   the intentions of his mind. (vv. 23, 24a; cf. 23:19, 20)

Pamela Scalise calls this a "storm warning."[3] The city of the Messiah would be protected from outside enemies like Babylon. The threat of evil would not be ignored, but punished and destroyed.

The Messiah's heart for his city included protection from the enemy within. He would do something about Israel's gang problem. "At that time, declares the LORD, I will be the God of all the clans of Israel, and they shall be my people" (31:1). The tribes from the north and the tribes from the south would be united as one nation.

Then God's city would be so safe that a police force would be unnecessary.

> For there shall be a day when watchmen will call
>   in the hill country of Ephraim:
> "Arise, and let us go up to Zion,
>   to the Lord our God." (31:6; cf. 3:18)

The policemen would become pilgrims. They would turn in their badges, leave their posts, and go to worship. If the watchmen needed to watch out for anything, it was only to join the festal procession dancing up to the temple.

Jeremiah, Nehemiah, and the Messiah

God's plan for urban renewal was ambitious. It touched every aspect of civic life—housing, entertainment, population, business, community development, and public safety.

When the Messiah came, he would rebuild everything that had been broken down.

> The poem of restoration recapitulates God's provision for ancient Israel in the wilderness, the settlement of the land, and the choice of Zion as the place of worship in a portrayal of the promised future. This restoration reverses at least six aspects of the judgment suffered by Israel and Judah: no resting place in exile, a nation torn down, celebrations silenced, vines and plants uprooted, watchmen announcing the invading conqueror, and the temple destroyed. The poem also introduces an Israel transformed from a desperate adulteress (4:30) to a joyful maiden on her way back to God.[4]

Who would not want to live with the Messiah in the city? His metropolis has everything most modern cities lack—good housing, vibrant celebrations, a growing population, a booming economy, and a strong sense of community. When will such a city ever be built?

Jeremiah's promises were partly fulfilled in the life and ministry of Nehemiah. Nehemiah went back to the city of Jerusalem to serve as its governor. Under his leadership, God's people rebuilt a new city on the ruins of the old (Nehemiah 3, 4, 6). They were protected from their enemies (4, 6). They cared for the poor (5). They grew in number (7, 10—12). They worshiped God and had feasts of thanksgiving (8).

Nehemiah fulfilled many of Jeremiah's prophecies, but not all of them. God's people did not remain faithful. The time of blessing did not last forever. Most importantly, the palace was never rebuilt. Jeremiah promised that the Messiah would sit on his throne in his palace. He said God would raise up a son of David to be king (30:9). But Nehemiah was no son of David and could never be king. Therefore, Jeremiah's promises about the city were waiting for the Messiah to come.

Perhaps this is part of what Jeremiah meant when he wrote, "In the latter days you will understand this" (30:24b). Someday, when the Messiah came, everything would be made clear. What was hidden would be revealed. Back in Jeremiah's day, hearing Old Testament prophecy was like stumbling around in a dark room. People could see some of the furniture, but they couldn't always tell where they were going. Then Jesus came, the Light of the World who makes everything as bright as day. Knowing the Messiah shines the light onto the Old Testament.

The Messiah has come. He was born in the city of David; he died and rose again in the city of Jerusalem. And the coming of the Messiah makes sense of Jeremiah's prophecy of urban renewal. Now Jesus Christ is at work to build his city. It is not an earthly city, but a spiritual city. Its citizens are all those who love him and believe that he died for their sins. They come with "songs of thanksgiving, and the voices of those who celebrate" (30:19a). They will not decrease (30:19b) but will grow as they did in the days of the early church, when "The Lord added to their number day by day those who were being saved" (Acts 2:47b). They are not made "small" (30:19c). They are called Christians and thus have the honor of bearing Christ's own name. "Their congregation," the church, is being "established" (30:20). The Messiah is building his spiritual city.

One of the places the Messiah is building his city is in the middle of every earthly city. God's people help build God's city in their own cities. Wherever Christians build houses, attend worship, celebrate feasts, increase in number, and establish safe communities, they are working to build God's city.

Margaret Clarkson has written a hymn about doing God's work in the city. She is honest about the problems of the city, but hopeful about God's plan for urban renewal.

> Our cities cry to you, O God, from out their pain and strife;
> You made us for yourself alone, but we choose alien life.
> Our goals are pleasure, gold and power; injustice stalks our earth;
> In vain we seek for rest, for joy, for sense of human worth.
>
> Yet still You walk our streets, O Christ! We know your presence here
> Where humble Christians love and serve in godly grace and fear.
> O Word made flesh be seen in us! May all we say and do
> Affirm You God, Incarnate still, and turn men's hearts to you.
>
> Your people are your hands and feet to serve your world today,
> Our lives the book our cities read to help them find your way.
> O pour your sov'reign Spirit out on heart and will and brain;
> Inspire your Church with love and pow'r to ease our cities' pain!
>
> O healing Savior, Prince of Peace, salvation's Source and Sum,
> For you our broken cities cry—O come, Lord Jesus, come!
> With truth your royal diadem, with righteousness your rod,
> O come, Lord Jesus, bring to earth the City of our God![5]

The Majestic One

Margaret Clarkson's hymn affirms that only the Messiah can rebuild God's city. A strong city requires strong leadership, which is what Jeremiah promised:

Their prince shall be one of themselves;
    their ruler shall come out from their midst;
I will make him draw near, and he shall approach me,
    for who would dare of himself to approach me?
declares the LORD. (30:21)

Jeremiah had already explained that the Messiah would be a king like David (30:9). Here in verse 21 he does not call him a king, but he does use royal vocabulary. He calls him a "prince," which comes from a verb that means "To be majestic." Jeremiah promised a leader who would rule in majesty.

Jeremiah's prophecy mentioned two great facts about this majestic leader, one about his person and the other about his work. First, the leader would be one of his own people. He would not be a stranger or a foreigner. Nor would he be a Babylonian overlord. This is in keeping with the command of Moses: "You may indeed set a king over you whom the LORD your God will choose. One from among your brothers you shall set as king over you" (Deuteronomy 17:15). The Majestic Ruler would be a full-blooded native. He would come from the ranks of his own people.

This is exactly the kind of majestic ruler Jesus Christ came to be. He did everything possible to identify with his people. He was eternal God, yet he became a man. He was a Hebrew among Hebrews and a man among men. He had the same kind of body his people had, a body that could grow tired and hungry and die.

Jesus lived the way his people lived. He was born into a poor family. He was wrapped in swaddling clothes and laid in a manger, a common child. In her Christmas hymn Cecil Frances Alexander put it like this:

He came down to earth from heaven
Who is God and Lord of all,
And his shelter was a stable,
And his cradle was a stall:
With the poor, and mean, and lowly,
Lived on earth our Savior holy.

Jesus worked the way his people worked, doing hard, honest labor with his hands. He worshiped the way his people worshiped. Every year he went up to Jerusalem for the great religious festivals (see Luke 2:41; John 7). He went to the synagogue week by week (Luke 4:16), where he sang psalms with his people. In the book of Hebrews Jesus says, "I will tell of your name to my brothers; in the midst of the congregation I will sing your praise" (2:12). This is a beautiful testimony of Jesus Christ as the sweet singer of Israel, praising his Father in song with the rest of his people.

Jesus was tempted the way his people are tempted. The Bible says, "We do not have a high priest who is unable to sympathize with our weaknesses, but one who in every respect has been tempted as we are, yet without sin" (Hebrews 4:15). Then, finally, Jesus identified himself with our sins. He wrapped himself in the guilt of his people and died on the cross. He became one of us to save us. Somewhere the great fourth-century theologian Athanasius (295–373) explained it like this: "He became what we are that He might make us what He is." The Messiah, the Majestic Ruler, is one of our own, and we are his. Therefore, "he is not ashamed to call [us] brothers" (Hebrews 2:11).

Jeremiah made a second promise about the Majestic Ruler. The first was about his person: He would be one with his people. The second was about his work: He would come close to God.

> I will make him draw near, and he shall approach me,
>   for who would dare of himself to approach me?
>   declares the LORD. (30:21b)

Jeremiah asks the question, "Who would *dare* to come close to God?" All through Old Testament times the people of God learned that coming unbidden into the presence of Almighty God meant death. Only the High Priest entered the Holy of Holies, and he only once a year. But this Messiah, this Majestic Ruler, would come close to God.

Jesus fulfilled this promise, for who could be closer to God the Father than God the Son? From eternity past the Father and the Son lived in the most intimate friendship and fellowship. They remained close even after the Son became a man. All through the Gospels Jesus speaks to his Father with the intimacy of a son to a father. They were so close that Jesus could say, "I and the Father are one" (John 10:30). Thus Jesus fulfilled Jeremiah's prophecy to a supreme degree. He was as near and as close to God as he could possibly be.

This is the priestly work of Jesus Christ. He is our Priest as well as our King. As our King he is our Majestic Ruler. As our Priest he brings us into close relationship with God:

Therefore, brothers, since we have confidence to enter the holy places by the blood of Jesus, by the new and living way that he opened for us through the curtain, that is, through his flesh, and since we have a great priest over the house of God, let us draw near with a true heart in full assurance of faith, with our hearts sprinkled clean from an evil conscience and our bodies washed with pure water. (Hebrews 10:19–22)

Furthermore, Jesus was devoted to the Father, which Jeremiah also promised. In verse 21 God literally asks, "Who is he who will devote his *heart* to me?" This is a reminder of how devoted King David was to God. He was "a man after his [God's] own heart" (1 Samuel 13:14).

Yet Jesus was even more devoted to the Father. He consecrated himself to the will of his Father. He said, "I have come down from heaven, not to do my own will but the will of him who sent me" (John 6:38). He was the epitome of the devoted son. His birth, his life, his death—he did it all in devotion to his Father. Jesus was obedient to his Father's every command, even unto his death on the cross.

Everlasting Love

Jeremiah promised a Messiah to build the city, a Majestic Ruler who would arise from his own people and come close to the heart of God. Jesus is that Messiah, and he is doing that work for one great purpose: "And you shall be my people, and I will be your God" (30:22).

"My people . . . your God." This is what God has promised his people throughout all the ages. It was the promise he made to Abraham: "And I will establish my covenant between me and you and your offspring after you throughout their generations for an everlasting covenant, to be God to you" (Genesis 17:7). It was the promise God made to his people under Moses: "I will take you to be my people, and I will be your God" (Exodus 6:7a; cf. Leviticus 26:12). It was the promise he repeated early in the ministry of Jeremiah: "Obey my voice, and I will be your God, and you shall be my people" (7:23). Ezekiel heard the same promise (Ezekiel 36:28), as did Hosea: "I will say to Not My People, 'You are my people'; and he shall say, 'You are my God'" (Hosea 2:23b).

This is God's promise of the covenant. It contains everything you have ever longed for and everything you could ever hope for. God will be your God, and you will belong to him. Everything you could ever need or desire in the whole universe is wrapped up in that one promise. Derek Kidner says the covenant promise has "The radical simplicity of a marriage vow."[6] In this promise

God is betrothing himself to his people in marital fidelity. He is saying, "You belong to me, and I belong to you—forever."

Like a marriage vow, God's covenant promise is for life and for love. God and his people belonged together in the past, and they will stay together in the future:

> "At that time, declares the Lord, I will be the God of all the clans of Israel, and they shall be my people."

> Thus says the LORD:
> "The people who survived the sword
>   found grace in the wilderness;
> when Israel sought for rest . . ." (31:1, 2)

The former verse is about the future; the latter is about the past. It mentions the two major events of the Old Testament—the exodus and the exile. "The people who survived the sword"—in other words, the exiles who escaped from Babylon and Assyria (cf. 51:50)—"found grace in the wilderness." This is a reminder of the exodus, when God saved his people in the wilderness. The point is that God will save his people in the future the way he saved them in the past. He did it before, and he will do it again, because his covenant vow is for life.

God will keep on keeping his covenant promise forever, as Jeremiah promised in one of the most moving verses in the Bible: "The LORD appeared to him from far away. I have loved you with an everlasting love; therefore I have continued my faithfulness to you" (31:3).

When God tells us that his love is "everlasting," he means that it will last forever. The kind of love he is talking about is covenant love, for the word "faithfulness" is the Old Testament word for covenant faithfulness. God's vow is like a marriage vow because it is a covenant for life and for love. Properly speaking, his vow is not even a promise. It is simply a statement of fact. This is God's unchanging attitude toward his people: He loves us with an everlasting love.

What does love mean? In the words of Geerhardus Vos,

> The prophet means to describe by this term something quite extraordinary, something well-nigh inconceivable, a supreme wonder in that land of wonders which religion can never cease to be. Love is to him the highest form of the spiritual embrace of person by person. To ascribe it to God in connection with a creature is at the farthest remove from being a figure of speech. It means that in the most literal sense He concentrates all the light

and warmth of His affection, all the prodigious wealth of its resources, his endless capacity of delight, upon the heart-to-heart union between the pious and Himself. And what God for His part brings into this union has a generosity, a sublime abandon, an absoluteness, that, measured by human analogies, we can only designate as the highest and purest type of devotion. It is named love for this very reason, that God puts into it His heart and soul and mind and strength, and gathers all His concerns with His people into the focus of this one desire.[7]

Thus 31:3 takes us into the very heart of God. Jeremiah gave a glimpse into God's heart when he spoke of God accomplishing "The purposes of his heart" (30:24 NIV). One of the deep, deep desires of God's heart is to make a people for himself, a whole city of people.

Perhaps you have seen the bumper sticker that reads "I LOVE NY." God has a bumper sticker too. It reads "I LOVE ZION." He is building the city he loves for the people he loves.

One of the reasons God's love is certain to last forever is because God promises to keep both halves of the covenant himself. He promises to do our part as well as his. "And you shall be my people" (30:22)—that is God's promise about how he will treat us. "And I will be your God"—that is God's promise about how we will treat him.

God can make good on this promise because the Messiah, the Majestic One, will keep the covenant for us. "The Davidic king is the covenant mediator through whom all the promises and responsibilities of the covenant will become realities."[8] We receive the everlasting love of God through the blood-covenant made by Jesus Christ. Our security is not that we love God, but that he loves us with a love that will not, cannot let us go.

This is the everlasting love God showed to us when the Messiah was born in the city, when he died in the city, and when he was raised again in the city. It is the everlasting love God will show to us when the Messiah comes again to the city. The Bible promises that "The holy city, new Jerusalem, [will come] down out of heaven from God. . . . And I heard a loud voice from the throne saying, 'Behold, the dwelling place of God is with man. He will dwell with them, and they will be his people, and God himself will be with them as their God'" (Revelation 21:2, 3).

42

Rachel, Dry Your Tears

JEREMIAH 31:7–26

THERE IS A DARK SIDE TO THE CHRISTMAS STORY. My son discovered it when he was only three years old. His mother read him a paraphrase of the Christmas story from Madeleine L'Engle's book *The Glorious Impossible*.[1] The book is beautifully illustrated with full-color reproductions of Giotto's paintings of the life of Christ from the Scrovegni Chapel in Padua.

As they read, my wife and my little boy came to a painting entitled "The Massacre of the Innocents." In it Giotto depicts King Herod's soldiers searching for the baby Jesus and putting the infants of Judea to the sword. The results of their grisly labors lie underfoot, a naked jumble at the bottom of the page.

"What are those from, Mommy?" asked my son.

Rachel Weeping for Her Children

What is a mother to say? Told in all its gruesome detail, the Christmas story is hardly suitable for children. After being warned by God in a dream, "[the wise men] departed to their own country by another way. . . . Then Herod, when he saw that he had been tricked by the wise men, became furious, and he sent and killed all the male children in Bethlehem and in all that region who were two years old or under, according to the time that he had ascertained from the wise men" (Matthew 2:12, 16). This is the dark side of Christmas, the raw wound of the Nativity. Army boots tromped and stamped across the manger scene. Though Christ was born and rescued, the babes of Bethlehem were slaughtered and buried.

For Matthew, the tragedy brought to mind a prophecy from the Old Testament:

Then was fulfilled what was spoken by the prophet Jeremiah:

> "A voice was heard in Ramah,
>   weeping and loud lamentation,
> Rachel weeping for her children;
>   she refused to be comforted, because they are no more."
>   (Matthew 2:17, 18; cf. Jeremiah 31:15)

The quotation ends almost in despair. Rachel weeps while Mary rejoices. Her grief is inconsolable; she pushes away her comforters. Her children are gone, never to return, and she will weep the rest of her days.

Who was Rachel? The Biblical Rachel was the wife of Jacob (Genesis 29:28). While she was traveling from Bethel to Bethlehem she stopped near Ramah. There "Rachel went into labor, and she had hard labor" (Genesis 35:16). She delivered a son in anguish and named him with her dying breath—Ben-Oni, meaning "son of my trouble," although Jacob renamed him Benjamin (Genesis 35:18; cf. 1 Samuel 10:2).

In addition to Benjamin, Rachel's offspring among the tribes of Israel were Ephraim and Manasseh (sons of Joseph), the tribes of the north. On the southern edge of Ephraim's territory lies Bethlehem, or Ephrata. Therefore, Rachel represents every mother in Bethlehem. She died in Ephraim, just outside Bethlehem. When Herod killed the baby boys in the vicinity of Bethlehem, it reminded Matthew of Rachel, who went weeping to her grave at Ramah, not far away.

Rachel's story touches the heart of every mother who has ever suffered for her children, who has had a miscarriage, lost a newborn, or buried a child in the prime of youth. She stands for every mother who lies awake at night worrying about her wayward children.

The writer Jonathan Kozol met a woman named Rachel when he spent Christmas at a hotel for the homeless in New York City. She was a mother of four, and as she sat on the edge of her bed, crying softly and holding a Bible in her hands, she said:

> They laid him in a manger. Right? Listen to me. I didn't say that God forsaken us. I am confused about religion. I'm just sayin' evil overrules the good. So many bad things goin' on. Lot of bad things right here in this buildin'. It's not easy to believe. I don't read the Bible no more 'cause I don't find no more hope in it. I don't believe.[2]

When Kozol wrote a book about his visit, he borrowed his title from Jeremiah: *Rachel and Her Children.*

Why must the Rachels of the world suffer these inconsolable losses? In particular, why did the birth of Mary's Son mean the death of Rachel's sons? Why does a good God allow bad things to happen in his world?

A Voice in Ramah

The prophet Jeremiah did not have all the answers to the problem of suffering, but he did know where to turn for comfort. By the grace of God, his prophecy did not end in tears but laughter. Rachel would find comfort after all.

Matthew understood what comfort Jeremiah had to offer. When the writers of the New Testament quote from the Old, they do not just refer to a single verse. Usually a single verse is all they quote, but they refer to that verse in its context. The quotation is intended to call to mind an entire Old Testament passage.

Therefore, when Matthew quoted Jeremiah about Rachel weeping in Ramah, he also had in mind the verses that follow:

> Thus says the LORD:
> "Keep your voice from weeping,
>   and your eyes from tears,
> for there is a reward for your work,
>   declares the LORD,
> and they shall come back from the land of the enemy.
> There is hope for your future,
>   declares the LORD,
> and your children shall come back to their own country." (31:16, 17)

Calvin called this "a promise which moderates the grievousness of the calamity."[3] Sorrow and grief do not have the last word, either in Jeremiah or in Matthew. A mother may refuse to be comforted, but God will comfort her nonetheless. "Rachel's tears were not in vain and not for ever."[4]

Why was Mother Rachel disconsolate? To understand God's comfort, one must first understand Rachel's loss. Jeremiah could hear the sound of Rachel's sobbing in Jerusalem, coming all the way from Ramah. Ramah was a transit camp for refugees (cf. 40:1). The Babylonians dragged their prisoners five miles from Jerusalem to a staging area at Ramah, where they were chained together for the long march to Babylon.

It must have been a place of utter despair—fathers chafing against their chains and mothers lifting their voices in lamentation. Their children, their babies, were gone! Some had starved during the siege. Others had been put to the sword during the invasion. In the confusion of battle, still others had been ripped from their mother's breasts, never to be seen again.

With her children dead or lost, it was only natural for Rachel to weep. But eventually she must dry her tears. The Puritan Matthew Henry explained it like this: "We are not forbidden to mourn in such a case; allowances are made for natural affection. But we must not suffer our sorrow to run into an extreme, to hinder our joy in God, or take us off from our duty to him. Though we mourn, we must not murmur."[5]

This is the way God's Word teaches us to suffer. The Bible is honest about the misery of the human condition, but it never gives in to it. Even those losses that seem inconsolable can be consoled. Not in this life perhaps, for we carry some griefs to the grave. Yet by quoting Jeremiah, Matthew wanted us to know that the Messiah came to bring comfort and joy, even to the Rachels of the world.

Tidings of Comfort and Joy

Why should Rachel be comforted? Sometimes the difficulty with Jeremiah is finding the grace. Here the difficulty is keeping it all in. Since Rachel's grief is great, her comfort must be even greater; so Jeremiah 31 contains all kinds of comfort.

First, the prophet promised the comfort of *worship*. The joyful note of worship is sounded at the beginning, middle, and end of Jeremiah's prophecy. "For thus says the LORD: 'Sing aloud with gladness for Jacob, and raise shouts for the chief of the nations'" (31:7a). Jacob would become the most favored nation. "They shall come and sing aloud on the height of Zion" (v. 12a). Literally, "Their faces will be all aglow."[6] There would be dancing as well as singing and shouting. "Then shall the young women rejoice in the dance, and the young men and the old shall be merry" (v. 13a).

Jeremiah's prophecy was about the public worship of God. He had already invited God's people to worship on Mount Zion (v. 6). In this prophecy, he shows what it will be like when they do: "Thus says the LORD of hosts, the God of Israel: 'Once more they shall use these words in the land of Judah and in its cities, when I restore their fortunes: "The LORD bless you, O habitation of righteousness, O holy hill!"'" (v. 23). Jeremiah was quoting from Israel's hymnal, which described Zion as God's "holy mountain" (Psalm 48:1). His point was that God's people would come back to God's house to worship.

The joy of worship is among the greatest comforts of this life. It is the reason we were made in the first place—to praise and to glorify God. So public worship on the Lord's Day is the center of the Christian life. More than anywhere else, this is where we find comfort in our grief. After all the trials and sorrows of the week before, we begin the new week in the sanctuary. We enter God's house to hear God's voice and to be comforted by God's grace. Even in sorrow, we do not stop worshiping God.

Second, God promised to *answer prayer*. He began by commanding his people to pray: "Proclaim, give praise, and say, 'O LORD, save your people, the remnant of Israel'" (31:7b). Then he promised to answer their prayers: "Behold, I will bring them from the north country and gather them from the farthest parts of the earth" (v. 8a).

The prayer God promised to answer was a prayer for salvation. God's people were scattered in exile. All that remained of them was a "remnant" (cf. 6:9; 23:3). Yet one day God would gather his displaced people from the four corners of the earth and give them a great homecoming. He would do all this in answer to their prayers.

The Christian life begins the same way—with a prayer. If you have not prayed for salvation, you must not be saved, because salvation always comes as an answer to prayer. Becoming a Christian starts with a prayer like this: "Dear God, I confess that I am a sinner who deserves to perish for my sins. Only you can save me, and only through Jesus Christ. Please let his death on the cross count for the punishment of my sins. I trust in him for my salvation." When we cry out for God to save us from our sins by the death and resurrection of Jesus Christ, our prayer does not fall on deaf ears. God hears and answers.

Third, God promised *preservation*. When the exiles returned from Babylon, even the weak and the wounded would survive the return trip. "Among them [will be] the blind and the lame, the pregnant woman and she who is in labor, together; a great company, they shall return here" (v. 8b). Jeremiah made a point of mentioning the people who would never expect to survive captivity. How could the blind find their way back from Babylon to Jerusalem? How could the lame walk all that way? How could women in labor survive the wilderness? Yet everyone in the whole caravan would be saved.

This is a reminder that God takes special care of the blind, the lame, and the disabled. He also preserves pregnant mothers. Childbirth is a harrowing experience. When God said, "in pain you shall bring forth children" (Genesis 3:16), he knew what he was talking about. Yet he also promised to sustain his daughters in their distress. God's grace is sufficient for every weakness.

Father and Son

The fourth promise in this passage is *return*, and of course returning to God always involves repentance. When the exiles return, "With weeping they shall come, and with pleas for mercy I will lead them back" (31:9a). Scholars have wondered what kind of tears these might be. Tears of joy or tears of sorrow?

Most likely Jeremiah meant tears of repentance, especially since they were accompanied with prayer. In fact, there is a tearful prayer of repentance later in Jeremiah 31:

> I have heard Ephraim grieving,
> "You have disciplined me, and I was disciplined,
>   like an untrained calf;
> bring me back that I may be restored,
>   for you are the LORD my God.
> For after I had turned away, I relented,
>   and after I was instructed, I struck my thigh;
> I was ashamed, and I was confounded,
>   because I bore the disgrace of my youth." (vv. 18, 19)

This is the prayer of a wayward son on his homeward journey. The name "Ephraim" represents the northern tribes of Israel who were lost in their sins.

Ephraim's confession is a reminder that no suffering is completely innocent. The death of the babes of Bethlehem is often called "The Massacre of the Innocents." In one sense they were innocent; they had done nothing against King Herod or his soldiers. Yet is there any suffering in the world that is absolutely innocent? None save the sufferings of Christ on the cross. Every adult is a sinner, and every child is born in sin.

This is why coming to God always requires the kind of repentance Rachel's son Ephraim offered. Do not assume everything is all right between you and God. Unless you have come to God repenting for your sins, everything is not all right between you. You must ask God to forgive you for Jesus' sake. Personally. When Ephraim repented he came to God in a personal way, saying, "You are the LORD my God" (v. 18b).

Repentance demands a change of direction. The Hebrew word for *repentance* is repeated seven times in these verses. It means "To turn." Those who turn away must "return." They must do what the prodigal son did in the story Jesus told (Luke 15:11–32). After he squandered his father's fortune in a far country, he made up his mind to turn around and go back home.

Repentance includes recognition of sin. Rachel's son Ephraim "was instructed" that he had strayed (31:19). In other words, he finally recognized his sin as sin. In the same way, Jesus describes the prodigal son as "[coming] to himself" (Luke 15:17). Human beings are thinking most clearly and most sensibly when they recognize how sinful they are.

Since repentance is a matter of the heart as well as the mind, it also means being sorry for sin. There must be remorse as well as recognition. That is why the words of Ephraim's confession were moaned, and not spoken. He beat his breast. He was "ashamed, and . . . confounded" because of his sins. They were youthful sins, committed when he was undisciplined and lacked good judgment. Nevertheless, the sins themselves were disgraceful, and they required tearful repentance.

All this is required to get right with God. Repentance means a change of behavior and a full confession of sin, mixed with sorrow. True repentance is a gift from God. Ephraim never could have repented like this on his own. He prayed, "Bring me back that I may be restored" (31:18), because he knew that the initiative for his change of heart had to come from God.

Whenever a sinner confesses his sins, God welcomes him back home. Jeremiah's fifth comforting promise is *forgiveness*. God readily forgives every sinner who truly repents.

God forgave Ephraim because he was his own son. He said, "I am a father to Israel, and Ephraim is my firstborn" (v. 9c; cf. Hosea 11:8). How could God fail to forgive his own son? He could not; therefore he answers Ephraim's prayer:

Is Ephraim my dear son?
    Is he my darling child?
For as often as I speak against him,
    I do remember him still.
Therefore my heart yearns for him;
    I will surely have mercy on him,
    declares the LORD. (v. 20)

Imagine the scene: A tender father welcomes home his wayward son after years of separation. He uses every term of endearment in his vocabulary. God called Ephraim his "son," his "dear" son, and his "darling child." Even though he had been away for a long time, the son was well remembered. Here J. A. Thompson offers the best translation. It is not "As often as I speak against him," as if God were an embittered father, but "The more I speak of him, the more vividly I remember him."[7] Again we are reminded of the story of the prodigal son, in which the father recognized his son "while he was still a long way off" (Luke 15:20). God is the kind of father who never forgets his children.

God loves his children as well as he remembers them. In Jeremiah's prophecy, he is said to yearn for Ephraim with great "mercy." Jesus used the same kinds of words in his parable. He said the father "saw him and felt compassion, and ran and embraced him and kissed him" (Luke 15:20). In effect, Jesus was showing us the gut-reaction of God when we repent for our sins and come back home.

This is the New Testament doctrine of adoption. By faith in Christ we become God's darling children. When sinners repent, they become the sons and daughters of God. And Jeremiah mentioned the daughters. He used feminine vocabulary to describe Israel as a wayward daughter (31:22a: "How long will you waver, O faithless daughter?") who would become as pure as a virgin (v. 21). The fatherly affection of God is not just for prodigal sons, but also for backsliding daughters.

All this should have been of special comfort to Rachel. Her lament was that her children were no more. But it was not true! Jeremiah 31 is about the salvation of Rachel's children. Her sons were lost, but not forever. God would find them and bring them back home. Surely Matthew had this clearly in mind when he quoted Jeremiah's prophecy. He wanted to show that the coming of the Messiah meant salvation for God's people, even for the babes of Bethlehem.

More Comfort, More Joy

There was still more comfort for Rachel. The sixth kind of comfort God promised was *guidance*. He promised to help his people find their way home: "I will make them walk by brooks of water, in a straight path in which they shall not stumble" (v. 9b; cf. 6:16). Like a good shepherd, God would bring his people back by an easy road. Rest stops would be frequent, and there would be plenty to drink.

The idea of a good path returns later in the chapter. In effect, God tells his people to play Hansel and Gretel as they make their path on their way to Babylon.

> Set up road markers for yourself;
>   make yourself guideposts;
> consider well the highway,
>   the road by which you went.
> Return, O virgin Israel,
>   return to these your cities. (v. 21)

God booked his people on a round-trip passage to Babylon. They would return from exile exactly the same way they came. And since things often look different on the return voyage, they should mark their trail carefully.

Guidance is also promised for the Christian. God gives good directions.

His will for life is not found by opening a Christian fortune cookie or turning to a random passage of Scripture. Instead through prayer, circumstances, godly counsel, and obedience to his revealed will, God will be your guide.

Jeremiah's seventh promise was one he had made several times already (3:15; 23:4), the promise of *a good shepherd.*

> Hear the word of the LORD, O nations,
>   and declare it in the coastlands far away;
> say, "He who scattered Israel will gather him,
>   and will keep him as a shepherd keeps his flock." (31:10)

First the shepherd gathers his flock, which in this case was scattered among the nations. Then he watches over them with a shepherd's care.

This shepherd promise was fulfilled in the coming of Jesus Christ. He is the Good Shepherd who gathers his sheep, going out into the hills to find every last one (Luke 15:4). He also stands guard at the door of the sheepfold to prevent that wolf Satan from devouring them (John 10:7–10).

Jeremiah's eighth promise was actually a double promise: "For the LORD has ransomed Jacob and has redeemed him from hands too strong for him" (31:11). The prophet used two words to describe salvation—*ransom* and *redeem.*

> "Ransom" is a legal word; it describes what you pay in money or in kind to secure the release or return of something which has passed into someone else's possession (Exodus 13:13; Numbers 18:15ff.). "Redeem" is more closely tied up with the life of the family. The "redeemer" (*go-el*) is the nearest next of kin who had, among other things, the responsibility to secure the release of a member of the family who had fallen into debt slavery, or to keep a piece of family property from being sold with the family, or to marry the childless widow of a deceased brother to continue the family line (see the Book of Ruth).[8]

Ransom and redeem—in Hebrew both of these words were used to describe the exodus from Egypt (see Deuteronomy 9:26 and Exodus 6:6). The terms are equally apt to describe the end of the exile, and also salvation in Jesus Christ. The blood of Jesus is our ransom and redemption. "For there is one God, and there is one mediator between God and men, the man Christ Jesus, who gave himself as a ransom for all" (1 Timothy 2:5, 6). Jesus said, "The Son of Man came not to be served but to serve, and to give his life as a ransom for many" (Matthew 20:28). And when he died on the cross, Jesus was paying the ransom for our sins.

Another way to say it is that Jesus redeemed his people. "Christ redeemed us from the curse of the law" (Galatians 3:13a). Redemption is a family matter. According to Old Testament law, a redeemer had to be a near kinsman. So the Son of God became our close relative on the first Christmas. Although he was conceived by the Holy Spirit, he became our own flesh and blood by being born of the virgin Mary. He entered into a common human race with the babes of Bethlehem.

It is even possible that Jeremiah promised the virgin birth of Christ. His prophecy was this: "The LORD has created a new thing on earth: a woman encircles a man" (31:22b). This is a curious and disputed verse.[9] It may simply mean that the return from exile was as unexpected as women going to battle to protect their men.[10]

Notice, however, that Jeremiah promised that God would "create" something. The Hebrew verb for *create* usually refers to God making the world out of nothing, as in the first chapters of Genesis. Furthermore, what God creates will be completely unprecedented, something no one has ever seen before.

What is new is that a woman will surround not "a man" (ESV) but "a mighty one." Matthew Henry noted that Jeremiah later uses the same term to refer to God himself (32:18). It is identical to the word Isaiah used in his Messianic prophecy:

For to us a child is born,
    to us a son is given;
and the government shall be upon his shoulder,
    and his name shall be called
Wonderful Counselor, Mighty God,
    Everlasting Father, Prince of Peace. (Isaiah 9:6)

Thus Henry understood "This new thing created in that land to be the incarnation of Christ."[11]

How could a woman surround "a mighty one," especially if he is God himself? Jerome thought this referred to Mary holding the baby Jesus in her arms.[12] But perhaps Jeremiah was referring to the Christ-child in Mary's womb. There the mighty Son of God was surrounded or enclosed inside a woman's body. A new thing was created on the earth—Jesus Christ, man as well as God. Whether Jeremiah promised this or not—and there is no reason to suggest that he did not—this is how Christ came into the world to ransom and redeem his people.

The ninth and final promise was *provision*. God promised to provide all the fine foods and delicious drinks that were the staples of the Jewish diet (cf.

Deuteronomy 7:12–14). "And Judah and all its cities shall dwell there together, and the farmers and those who wander with their flocks" (31:24). "They shall be radiant over the goodness of the LORD, over the grain, the wine, and the oil, and over the young of the flock and the herd" (v. 12a). God's people would be well irrigated, like an oasis in the desert. "Their life shall be like a watered garden, and they shall languish no more" (v. 12b).

Even the priests, who depended on the generosity of God's people for their food, would have more than enough to eat: "I will feast the soul of the priests with abundance, and my people shall be satisfied with my goodness, declares the LORD" (v. 14). If you have ever wondered why so many church events involve good food, this is probably why. God is so good, so faithful, and so bounteous that he spreads a perpetual banquet before his people.

Blessed Are They Who Mourn

Nine promises. Nine reasons to be comforted. When God told Rachel to dry her tears, he was not just saying, "There, there, it's all right." He was promising to *make* things all right. The comfort God offers is real comfort, and the joy he promises is real joy. Weeping will last only for the night; then morning comes, full of song.

Matthew was honest about suffering. He did not conceal the dark side of the first Christmas. Jeremiah was equally honest. In his prophecy he used all the different Hebrew words for *grief* to show that the sufferings of life are many and various.

But the prophet and the evangelist both knew that those who mourn will be comforted (Matthew 5:4). Matthew quoted Jeremiah so Rachel would know God's grace in her suffering. It was his way of saying that the Messiah has come to bring all the comfort and joy Jeremiah promised.

Jesus came to make our worship joyful and to answer our prayers. He came to forgive us and preserve us. He came to make us sons and daughters of God. He came to guide us and provide for us. He came to redeem us, to give his life as a ransom for our sins, and to take us home.

Sometimes it is difficult to believe such promises, especially when life is hard and our sufferings seem great. There may even be times when we, like Rachel, refuse to be comforted. But God promises that the believer's sufferings will not last forever: "I will turn their mourning into joy; I will comfort them, and give them gladness for sorrow" (31:13b; cf. Psalm 30:11). "I will satisfy the weary soul, and every languishing soul I will replenish" (v. 25).

These promises must be received the way Jeremiah received them—by faith. Few of God's promises were realities for Jeremiah. They were only promises. At the end of his prophecy he said, "At this I awoke and looked" (v. 26a). Most likely, what Jeremiah saw when he looked around was that he was still in prison and that Jerusalem was still a shambles. Yet he went on to say, "My sleep was pleasant to me" (v. 26b). Jeremiah's vision of comfort and joy gave him the strength to keep on living for the Lord, even while he suffered.

It should be the same for us. We still see great suffering in the world. We still suffer ourselves. There may even be times when we refuse to be comforted. But God has comfort for us. The day will come when all will be made right with the world, when suffering will come to an end, and when even Rachel will dry her tears.

43

The New Covenant

JEREMIAH 31:27–40

A SIGN IN A SHOP WINDOW along Philadelphia's Antique Row reads: "Quality is a thing of the past." The sign is right; newer is not necessarily better. Many new products are flimsy, cheap, and inferior. "The new ones are not as good as the old ones," people say.

Once my mother tried to replace her forty-year-old kitchen faucet because it was starting to corrode. Our plumber counseled against it, saying, "I could give you a new one, but it wouldn't be as good as the old one. They just don't make them like they used to."

Jeremiah 31 ends with the promise of a new covenant. The promotional material states that it is better than the old covenant. But if quality is a thing of the past, it seems prudent to have a healthy suspicion of all things new. Is the covenant new and improved, or is it just new?

The Old Covenant

God has always dealt with humanity by way of covenant. The *Catechism for Young Children* teaches that a covenant is "an agreement between two or more persons" (Q. & A. 22). Covenant is often compared to contract, treaty, or alliance.

Many theologians downplay the contractual aspect of the Biblical covenants. They prefer to think of a covenant as a testament rather than as a bargain. In other words, like a "last will and testament," the blessings of the covenant are bequeathed as free gifts. Thus O. Palmer Robertson calls covenant "a bond in blood sovereignly administered."[1] Similarly, John Murray defines it as "a sovereign administration of grace and of promise."[2]

Even a gracious covenant, however, calls for a response on the part of

465

God's people. For this reason, Robert Davidson says that covenant is "a relationship rooted in God's initiative, in what he has done *for* the people, but it looks for a response *from* the people."[3] The classic covenant theologian Herman Witsius (1636–1708) also highlights man's responsibility to respond to God's grace: "A covenant of God with man, is an agreement between God and man, about the way of obtaining consummate happiness; including a commination of eternal destruction, with which the contemner of the happiness, offered in that way, is to be punished."[4] Perhaps a shorter definition is possible: A Biblical covenant is a binding relationship of eternal consequence in which God promises to bless and his people promise to obey.

The history of God's people is a story of covenants. In the covenant of works, Adam was bound to obey God perfectly. For his part, God promised to reward Adam with life if he obeyed and threatened to punish Adam with death if he disobeyed (Genesis 2:16, 17). God made a covenant of safety with Noah and every living creature (Genesis 9:8–17). The rainbow is a sign of God's covenant promise that he will never again destroy the world with a flood.

God made a covenant of destiny with Abraham (Genesis 12:1–3; 15:1–21; 17:1–27). He promised to give him a land populated with descendants as numerous as the stars (Genesis 15:5). God said, "Behold, my covenant is with you, and you shall be the father of a multitude of nations. . . . And I will establish my covenant between me and you and your offspring after you throughout their generations for an everlasting covenant" (Genesis 17:4, 7). He also promised that through Abraham's offspring all nations on earth will be blessed (Genesis 22:18; cf. 12:3). For his part, Abraham was bound to obey God by circumcising every male in his household (Genesis 17:9–14). Every one of these covenants was a personal bond in which God promised to bless and his people promised to obey.

In Jeremiah 31 God refers to "The covenant that I made with their fathers on the day when I took them by the hand to bring them out of the land of Egypt" (v. 32a). For Jeremiah, therefore, the old covenant meant the covenant God made with his people at Mount Sinai. The Mosaic Covenant was for a people already saved by grace. "And God spoke all these words, saying, 'I am the LORD your God, who brought you out of the land of Egypt, out of the house of slavery'" (Exodus 20:1, 2). Once they were saved, God's people had to keep God's covenant in order to receive God's blessing. They had to worship God alone, keep the Sabbath holy, preserve the sanctity of human life, tell the truth, and obey the rest of the Ten Commandments (Exodus 2:3–17). The Mosaic Covenant was a good and gracious covenant.

The Broken Covenant

There was only one problem with the old covenant—sin. The covenant was broken even before it could be ratified. By the time Moses came down from the mountain, the people had cast a golden idol in the shape of a calf. "And as soon as he came near the camp and saw the calf and the dancing, Moses' anger burned hot, and he threw the tablets out of his hands and broke them at the foot of the mountain" (Exodus 32:19).

So God reissued the covenant (Exodus 34), only to see his people break it all over again. The history of the Old Testament is one of idolatry, immorality, discontent, and disobedience. According to the Old Testament scholar Gerhard Von Rad, "The reason why a new covenant is to ensue on the old is not that the regulations revealed in the latter have proved inadequate, but that the covenant has been broken, because Israel has refused to obey it."[5] J. A. Thompson goes one step further: "They had not merely refused to obey the law or to acknowledge Yahweh's complete and sole sovereignty, but were incapable of such obedience."[6]

Jeremiah rightly identified sin as the problem with the old covenant: "My covenant . . . they broke, though I was their husband, declares the LORD" (31:32b). Robertson explains that here "Jeremiah does not condemn the old covenant. He condemns Israel for breaking the covenant."[7] And not just breaking it! The first twenty-eight chapters of Jeremiah are an exhaustive record of how Judah shattered the covenant and ground the fragments into dust.

The shocking thing was that this agreement was actually a marriage covenant. More than once Jeremiah stated that God was like a husband to his people. But the day finally came when the Almighty filed for divorce. Israel "fell out of love" and committed spiritual adultery "on every high hill and under every green tree" (2:20b). She stood up in court to deny the charges, but God made them stick. His virgin bride had become a spiritual whore.

Here is the real shocker, however: If every sin is an act of covenant breaking, then every sinner is a covenant breaker. Every time you sin, you are being unfaithful in your marriage to God. That is why sin is so tawdry, cheap, and degrading. As the Apostle Paul so carefully explained, there is nothing wrong with the Law, the commandment, or the old covenant (Romans 7:7–13). The problem is with *us*. We are covenant breakers by nature.

Failure to keep the covenant brings a curse (cf. 11:8, 10, 11). Jeremiah cited the conventional wisdom of his day: "The fathers have eaten sour grapes, and the children's teeth are set on edge" (31:29b). This must have been a popular saying because the prophet Ezekiel quoted it as well (Ezekiel 18:2). It is a memorable proverb. When a father bites into an unripe grape, the lips of his children pucker in disgust. This refers to the curse of the old covenant, in which God threatened to "[visit] the iniquity of the fathers on the children to the third and the fourth generation" (Exodus 20:5).

How the people of Judah resented that curse! "While in exile the people concluded out of self-pity and fatalistic despair that they were being punished unjustly for sins of previous generations."[8] They felt sorry for themselves. The sour grapes their fathers ate left a bitter taste in their mouths. Why should they suffer for the spiritual adultery of their parents?

What the prophet Jeremiah taught them, however, was that they deserved God's curse for their own sins as well as for those of their parents: "In those days they shall no longer say: 'The fathers have eaten sour grapes, and the children's teeth are set on edge.' But everyone shall die for his own iniquity. Each man who eats sour grapes, his teeth shall be set on edge" (31:29, 30). Corporately or individually, everyone who breaks covenant is under God's curse. This is also true for nations—including the United States of America—that have covenanted to live under God.

The New Covenant

If the old covenant ended in a curse, then the new covenant merits investigation. Jeremiah 31 is the place to start because it is the only passage in the Old Testament that promises "a new covenant." It is the one place in the old covenant that lists the promises of the new covenant. And since a covenant is also called a "Testament," it is the passage that gives the New Testament its name.

Jeremiah made seven promises in all. First, the new covenant promised *reconciliation*, the bringing together of all God's people into one redeemed race.

> Behold, the days are coming, declares the LORD, when I will make a new covenant with the house of Israel and the house of Judah. (v. 31)

Because of its emphasis on personal responsibility, Jeremiah's new covenant is sometimes viewed as the triumph of individualism. R. K. Harrison says:

> Probably the most significant contribution which Jeremiah made to religious thought was inherent in his insistence that the new covenant involved a one-to-one relationship of the spirit. When the new covenant was inaugurated by the atoning work of Jesus Christ on Calvary, this important development of personal, as opposed to corporate, faith and spirituality was made real for the whole of mankind.[9]

The trouble with this view is that the first promise of the new covenant was a corporate promise, not an individual promise. It promised to end the division between the northern and southern tribes. "Behold, the days are coming, declares the Lord, when I will sow the house of Israel and the house of Judah with the seed of man and the seed of beast" (v. 27). God promised to plant both houses in one land.

Jeremiah first promised this reconciliation at the beginning of his book:

> At that time Jerusalem shall be called the throne of the Lord, and all nations shall gather to it, to the presence of the Lord in Jerusalem, and they shall no more stubbornly follow their own evil heart. In those days the house of Judah shall join the house of Israel, and together they shall come from the land of the north to the land that I gave your fathers for a heritage. (3:17, 18)

He would repeat it at the end of his book:

> In those days and in that time, declares the Lord, the people of Israel and the people of Judah shall come together, weeping as they come, and they shall seek the Lord their God. They shall ask the way to Zion, with faces turned toward it, saying, "Come, let us join ourselves to the Lord in an everlasting covenant that will never be forgotten." (50:4, 5)

Jeremiah's promises were fulfilled with the coming of Christ. There is only one new covenant people of God. "There is neither Jew nor Greek, there is neither slave nor free, there is no male and female, for you are all one in Christ Jesus" (Galatians 3:28). In the new covenant community there is no black, no white, no brown. There is no rich, no poor. There is only one new covenant people in Christ.

Second, the new covenant promised *regeneration*, the transformation of God's people from the inside out:

> For this is the covenant that I will make with the house of Israel after those days, declares the Lord: I will put my law within them, and I will write it on their hearts. (31:33a)

The problem with the Mosaic Covenant was that it was written on tablets of stone (Exodus 31:18). If anything was written on the hearts of God's people, it was only their sin:

> The sin of Judah is written with a pen of iron; with a point of diamond it is engraved on the tablet of their heart. (17:1; cf. v. 9)

With the new covenant, however, God solved the problem of the sinful heart by giving his children new hearts and new minds. According to Calvin, the new covenant "penetrates into the heart and reforms all the inward faculties, so that obedience is rendered to the righteousness of God."[10]

It must be emphasized that the new covenant did not abolish the old. Christ did not come to abolish the Law, but to fulfill it (Matthew 5:17). Thus, "The *new* covenant is not so called because it is contrary to the first covenant."[11] Both covenants demand obedience to the Law. The difference is that the new covenant brings the Law from the outside to the inside. "The distinctiveness of the ministry of law under the new covenant resides in its inward character. Rather than being administered externally, the law shall be administered from within the heart."[12]

Thomas à Kempis (c. 1380–1471) wrote a beautiful prayer about his longing for this new heart:

> Write your blessed name, O Lord, upon my heart,
> There to remain so indelibly engraved
> that no prosperity or adversity
> shall ever remove me from your love.
> O Jesu, my only Savior!
> Write your blessed name, O Lord, upon my heart.[13]

The Law written on the heart is a promise about the coming of God's Spirit, for the book of Hebrews attributes Jeremiah's promise to the Holy Spirit:

And the Holy Spirit also bears witness to us; for after saying,

> "This is the covenant that I will make with them
>   after those days, declares the Lord:
> I will put my laws on their hearts,
>   and write them on their minds." (Hebrews 10:15, 16)

Only the Holy Spirit can change a heart. A Christian whose heart has been regenerated by God's Spirit knows how to please God and does not need to pull out a Bible every time a decision needs to be made. The Law written on the heart helps the Christian know what to do instantly and instinctively.

For the Christian, obedience to the Law is not a prior condition for entering the new covenant. Rather, it is one of the promised blessings of the new covenant. In his notes on this verse Jonathan Edwards (1703–1758) wrote, "I think the difference here pointed out between these two covenants, lies plainly here, that in the old covenant God promised to be their God upon condition of hearty obedience; obedience was stipulated as a condition, but not promised. But in the new covenant, this hearty obedience is promised."[14]

Third, the new covenant promised *possession*. God's people would have a claim on God, and he would have a claim on them: "And I will be their God, and they shall be my people" (31:33b). God's people would no longer be their own. They would belong to God, and God would belong to them.

The promise of belonging to God in a mutual love relationship is among the most frequently repeated promises of the Old Testament:

> I will take you to be my people, and I will be your God. (Exodus 6:7)

> You have declared today that the LORD is your God, and that you will walk in his ways, and keep his statutes and his commandments and his rules, and will obey his voice. And the LORD has declared today that you are a people for his treasured possession, as he has promised you, and that you are to keep all his commandments. (Deuteronomy 26:17, 18; cf. 29:12, 13; Ezekiel 11:20)

> My beloved is mine, and I am his. (Song of Songs 2:16a)

> I will say to Not My People, "You are my people"; and he shall say, "You are my God." (Hosea 2:23b; cf. Zechariah 8:8)

Whenever God makes a covenant with his people, what he is really giving them is himself. Thus the primary blessing of the new covenant is friendship and fellowship with the Triune God. This "is the crown and goal of the whole process of religion, namely, union and communion with God."[15]

The New Covenant Continued

A fourth aspect of Jeremiah's New Covenant promise was *evangelization*.

> And no longer shall each one teach his neighbor and each his brother, saying, "Know the Lord," for they shall all know me, from the least of them to the greatest, declares the LORD." (31:34a)

The Bible often commands believers to teach one another to know the Lord (Deuteronomy 6:1–9; Colossians 3:16). But Jeremiah promised a day when such teaching would no longer be necessary because everyone—from the youngest babe to the oldest saint—would know God. Here the word *know* "carries its most profound connotation, the intimate personal knowledge which arises between two persons who are committed wholly to one another in a relationship that touches mind, emotion, and will."[16]

To a limited degree, this promise has already come true in the Church. Every believer knows Jesus Christ. So although every Christian needs the gospel every day, every Christian does not need to be converted every day.

Yet the promise of the end of evangelization is especially for eternity. There will be no revival meetings in Heaven. No one will stand on the corner and pass out tracts. No one will share the Four Spiritual Laws. No one will knock on your door and ask, "If you were to die tonight, what would you say to God when he asks, 'Why should I let you into my Heaven?'" There will be no evangelism because there will be no need. Everyone will know God, from the least to the greatest.

Fifth, the new covenant promised *satisfaction for sin*: "For I will forgive their iniquity, and I will remember their sin no more" (31:34b). This is perhaps the best blessing of the new covenant. The old covenant tried to deal with the problem of sin through the sacrifices of the Law. But in the new covenant, sin would be dealt with once and for all. The price for sin would be paid in full; God not only forgives, but he also forgets.

The way the new covenant deals with the problem of sin is through the death of Jesus Christ on the cross. The sins of God's people were forgiven and forgotten at Calvary. When Jesus celebrated Passover with his disciples, he took "The cup after they had eaten, saying, 'This cup that is poured out for you is the new covenant in my blood'" (Luke 22:20; cf. 1 Corinthians 11:25). Jesus was claiming that all the promises of the new covenant find their fulfillment in him. Jesus *is* the new covenant. The new covenant is established by his blood shed on the cross for our sins. All the blessings of the new covenant are located in the crucified (and risen!) Christ.

The writer to the Hebrews was captivated by Jeremiah's vision of the new covenant. Again and again he speaks of "a better covenant" (7:22) or a superior covenant "enacted on better promises" (8:6). A better covenant was needed because there was a problem with the old one. It was the same problem Jeremiah identified: "For if that first covenant had been faultless, there would have been no occasion to look for a second. For he finds fault with them" (Hebrews 8:7, 8a). God found fault not with the covenant but with the people. A better covenant was needed to deal with the problem of sin.

The better covenant in Hebrews is one and the same as the new covenant in Jeremiah, for Hebrews quotes Jeremiah's entire promise (8:8–12). Then the writer to the Hebrews makes this significant statement: "In speaking of a new covenant, he [God] makes the first one obsolete" (v. 13a). We have already seen that the old covenant is not abolished but fulfilled in the new. The laws of the old covenant remain, now written on the heart. But the new covenant is so much better that it is *as if* the old has been done away with completely.

The reason the new covenant is so much better is because Christ "is the mediator of a new covenant, so that those who are called may receive the promised eternal inheritance, since a death has occurred that redeems them from the transgressions committed under the first covenant" (9:15; cf. 12:24). The new covenant offers full and final satisfaction for the curse of God against every kind of covenant breaking.

Sixth, Jeremiah promised that the new covenant would be *endless in duration*:

> Thus says the LORD,
> who gives the sun for light by day
>   and the fixed order of the moon and the stars for light by night,
> who stirs up the sea so that its waves roar—
>   the LORD of hosts is his name:
> "If this fixed order departs
>   from before me, declares the LORD,
> then shall the offspring of Israel cease
>   from being a nation before me forever."
>
> Thus says the LORD:
> "If the heavens above can be measured,
>   and the foundations of the earth below can be explored,
> then I will cast off all the offspring of Israel
>   for all that they have done,
>   declares the LORD." (31:35–37)

The God of creation is also the God of salvation. Therefore, the new covenant in Christ is as reliable as the fixed laws of nature, if not more so. It is irrevocable.

Jeremiah's pleas for God to remember his covenant have not gone unanswered (14:21). Not even the disastrous events of 587 BC (the ultimate fall of Jerusalem and the beginning of the Babylonian captivity) marked its end. The new covenant is as likely to fail as the entire universe is to grind to a halt. God will no more forget his people than humanity will unravel all the mysteries of interstellar space. The new covenant is an everlasting covenant.

Theologians have struggled to explain the eternal duration of the covenant. The Biblical covenants often sound like contracts, as if God does his part and we do our part. But of course we never keep our end of the bargain, and so the covenant ought to be null and void. Yet the mystery of God's grace is that he continues to keep covenant even when we break it.

The only explanation for the permanence of the covenant is that Jesus Christ keeps it on our behalf. His covenant keeping counts for us. The Westminster *Larger Catechism* asks, "With whom was the covenant of grace made?" Answer: "The covenant of grace was made with Christ as the second Adam, and in him with all the elect as his seed" (Q. & A. 30). In other words, the new covenant is not a bargain between God and us. If that were the case, the new covenant would be no better than the old. Rather, the new covenant is a blood bond between God the Father and God the Son on our behalf. Jesus Christ makes and keeps the covenant for us. We are in the covenant because we are in Christ.

The seventh and final promise of the new covenant was *urbanization*:

> Behold, the days are coming, declares the LORD, when the city shall be rebuilt for the LORD from the Tower of Hananel to the Corner Gate. And the measuring line shall go out farther, straight to the hill Gareb, and shall then turn to Goah. The whole valley of the dead bodies and the ashes, and all the fields as far as the brook Kidron, to the corner of the Horse Gate toward the east, shall be sacred to the LORD. It shall not be plucked up or overthrown anymore forever. (31:38–40)

Jeremiah's first calling was "To pluck up and break down, to overthrow, destroy, and bring harm" (v. 28a; cf. 1:10). After forty years of demolition work, his prophecies all came true. The Babylonians uprooted, tore down, overthrew, and destroyed Jerusalem.

That demolition work set the stage for Jeremiah to enter the second phase of his ministry to God's people as God began to "watch over them to build and to plant" (v. 28b). This was a promise of urban renewal. As Jeremiah went on a grand tour of the city, he noted its landmarks and described its boundaries. God was making real promises for a real city. There would be life after death for Jerusalem. The parts of the city that lay in ruins would be rebuilt. What had been cursed would be blessed. The profane would be made sacred. Even the Valley of Ben Hinnom—the Auschwitz of ancient Palestine, where children were cremated on pagan altars (7:30–32)—would become "sacred to the LORD" (31:40). The graveyard and the garbage dump would become holy ground.

All these promises came true. When Nehemiah rebuilt Jerusalem after the exile, his engineers started at "The Tower of Hananel" (Nehemiah 3:1) and worked their way around Jeremiah's map to make repairs "above the Horse

Gate" (Nehemiah 3:28). That was the earthly, physical fulfillment of Jeremiah's promise.

There is also a heavenly, spiritual fulfillment of the urban promise of the new covenant. God is building his people an eternal city. In the words of Oxford theologian Oliver O'Donovan, "No destiny can possibly be conceived in the world, or even out of it, other than that of a city."[17] When Christ returns, his people will see "The holy city, new Jerusalem, coming down out of heaven from God" (Revelation 21:2).

In the Covenant

Bible expositions often end by applying the promises and commands of God to daily life. But after hearing the seven promises of the new covenant, what still needs to be done?

There is nothing left to do—only believe. For all the promises of the new covenant are things God himself undertakes: "I will make a new covenant" (31:31). "I will put my law within them . . . I will be their God" (v. 33). "I will forgive their iniquity" (v. 34). He will not "cast off all the offspring of Israel" (v. 37). All the terms of the new covenant are promises. As the great covenant theologian Thomas Boston taught:

> What remains for sinners, that they may be personally and savingly in covenant with God, is not, as parties contractors and undertakers, to make a covenant with him for life and salvation; but only, to take hold of God's covenant already made from eternity, between the Father and Christ the second Adam, and revealed and offered to us in the gospel.[18]

44

Buyer's Market

JEREMIAH 32:1–25

SOME YEARS AFTER he reported God's promise of a new covenant, Jeremiah's faith was tested. God told him to buy a piece of property, even though buying it seemed like a complete waste of money.

The real estate principle that applied to Jeremiah's purchase is known as anticipation:

> According to the principle of *anticipation*, property value may be affected by expectation of a future event. . . . Real estate has historically proved to be a generally appreciating asset. . . . However, anticipation may also lower value if property rights are expected to be restricted or if the property somehow becomes less appealing to prospective buyers.[1]

In other words, how much a piece of real estate is worth depends on what is expected to happen to it in the future. If the government decides to run a superhighway through your dining room, for example, your property value will plummet.

A Bad Time to Buy

The principle of anticipation helps explain why Jeremiah's land deal seemed like such a bad investment. It was absolutely the worst time to buy. At the moment God told him to buy the property, "Jeremiah the prophet was shut up in the court of the guard that was in the palace of the king of Judah" (32:2b). Since Jeremiah was locked up in the stockade, it was no time to invest in real estate, especially out in the countryside. Even if the prophet bought the ranch, he would be unable to farm it.

Jeremiah had been sent to jail by the king himself:

For Zedekiah king of Judah had imprisoned him, saying, "Why do you prophesy and say, 'Thus says the LORD: Behold, I am giving this city into the hand of the king of Babylon, and he shall capture it; Zedekiah king of Judah shall not escape out of the hand of the Chaldeans, but shall surely be given into the hand of the king of Babylon, and shall speak with him face to face and see him eye to eye. And he shall take Zedekiah to Babylon, and there he shall remain until I visit him, declares the LORD. Though you fight against the Chaldeans, you shall not succeed'?" (vv. 3–5)

It is not hard to understand Zedekiah's anger. Jeremiah prophesied that the king would be defeated and humiliated. At best, his words were demoralizing; at worst, they were treason (cf. chapters 37, 38). Thus Jeremiah's life was in Zedekiah's hands. And buying *a* farm becomes less appealing when there is a good chance of buying *the* farm.

Then there was the war. As it says in the real estate textbooks, "Anticipation may also lower value if property rights are expected to be restricted or if the property somehow becomes less appealing to prospective buyers." Less appealing? Restricted? Jeremiah's property settlement took place shortly before the city of Jerusalem was destroyed. "The word that came to Jeremiah from the LORD in the tenth year of Zedekiah king of Judah" (v. 1). In other words, these events took place in 587 BC, the year "The army of the king of Babylon was besieging Jerusalem" (v. 2a).

During the last days before the fall of Jerusalem, the bottom fell out of the housing market. Things got so bad that entire houses and palaces were torn down in a desperate attempt to shore up the city walls (33:4). It hardly seemed like the time to buy. Imagine trying to persuade a bank to give you a loan when your city is surrounded by the most powerful army on earth!

In short, it was positively the worst time for Jeremiah to buy. The city was under siege, the prophet under arrest.[2]

A Long-Lost Cousin

Then Hanamel showed up to visit Jeremiah in prison. Long-lost cousin Hanamel is one of the great characters and all-time wheeler-dealers of the Old Testament. There is someone like Hanamel in most families. He is the cousin everyone avoids at family reunions because he is always trying to sell something. He hasn't been seen or heard from in years, but he slaps everyone on the back and says, "Listen, have I got a sweetheart of a deal for you! It's a once-in-a-lifetime opportunity!"

Fortunately, God had warned Jeremiah that Hanamel was coming. "Jeremiah said, 'The word of the LORD came to me: Behold, Hanamel the son of Shallum your uncle will come to you and say, "Buy my field that is at Anathoth, for the right of redemption by purchase is yours"'" (32:6, 7). It was nice of God to provide a warning; the prophet probably needed some time to brace himself. "Then Hanamel my cousin came to me in the court of the guard, in accordance with the word of the LORD, and said to me, 'Buy my field that is at Anathoth in the land of Benjamin, for the right of possession and redemption is yours; buy it for yourself'" (v. 8a).

The Bible does not say why Hanamel gave Jeremiah the option to buy. Maybe he was trying to make a fast shekel before the Babylonians took over. Perhaps he was in debt and needed the money to buy food. In any case, he appealed to the prophet's sense of family obligation. According to the Law of Moses (Leviticus 25:25–34), the promised land was a sacred inheritance. Property was not to leave the family. God did not want his people to go outside their bloodline to get help. If they fell into debt, one of their own kin was supposed to redeem their property. Hanamel was asking Jeremiah to be his kinsman-redeemer or *goel* (cf. Ruth 4:1–12).

No doubt Jeremiah's realtor would have counseled against accepting the offer. The old family farm was on the outskirts of Jerusalem, in Anathoth (cf. 1:1), which at that very moment was enemy-occupied territory. To put it bluntly, it was a dumb time to buy.

But Jeremiah bought the land anyway. He conducted the settlement by the book. He scraped together the money for a down payment, looked over the terms of the contract, signed the deed, had it notarized, and took it to the title office. Duplicate copies were made, one open for inspection and one sealed in case of a later dispute:

> And I bought the field at Anathoth from Hanamel my cousin, and weighed out the money to him, seventeen shekels of silver. I signed the deed, sealed it, got witnesses, and weighed the money on scales. Then I took the sealed deed of purchase, containing the terms and conditions and the open copy. And I gave the deed of purchase to Baruch the son of Neriah son of Mahseiah, in the presence of Hanamel my cousin, in the presence of the witnesses who signed the deed of purchase, and in the presence of all the Judeans who were sitting in the court of the guard. (vv. 9–12)

This is more or less how real estate transactions are settled to this very day, which is a reminder that the people of the Bible lived in the real world. Then, as now, buying property was too important to rely on a handshake.

A Good Reason to Buy

Once Jeremiah signed the deed, Hanamel probably laughed all the way to the bank. At first he couldn't even give the property away, but somehow he had managed to persuade Jeremiah to pay him seventeen shekels for it. It was not a large sum of money, but Hanamel was happy to take whatever he could get. The deed probably was not even worth the papyrus it was scratched on. Any price would have been too much to pay for a property under Babylonian occupation, purchased sight unseen. As Calvin wrote, "The Prophet must have appeared to have been beside himself when he bought a field in the possession of enemies."[3]

So why did Jeremiah do it? For one thing, because God told him to, which is the best reason to do anything. In the prophet's own words: "I knew that this was the word of the LORD. And I bought the field at Anathoth from Hanamel my cousin" (vv. 8b, 9a). But there was more to the deal than sheer obedience.

A similar purchase was made several centuries later, during the Second Punic War (between Carthage and Rome, 218–202 BC). Livy, the Roman historian, writes how Hannibal, the North African general, sailed across the Straits of Gibraltar, conquered Spain, crossed the Alps with his elephants, and marched on the city of Rome. It happened that when Hannibal arrived on the outskirts of Rome, the very piece of property on which he was camped came up for sale by auction. It was purchased by a Roman citizen "without any reduction in price." When Hannibal heard about it, he was outraged. Livy writes, "That a purchaser should have been found in Rome for the land he had taken by force of arms and of which he was now the occupier and owner seemed to him evidence of outrageous conceit."[4]

Jeremiah made the same kind of purchase, but not from outrageous conceit. Rather, it was audacious faith that led him to pay full market value: "For thus says the LORD of hosts, the God of Israel: Houses and fields and vineyards shall again be bought in this land" (v. 15). It may have been a bad time to buy, but Jeremiah had a good reason to buy. Eventually God was going to bring his people back home from their exile. Property values would go back up. Despite the war, the siege, the destruction the Babylonians were about to wreak on Jerusalem, and the seventy long years of captivity that would ensue, it was a buyer's market for those who trusted God's promise.

And Jeremiah believed. He was willing to take the long view. So he told his secretary to put his title in a safe deposit box: "I charged Baruch in their presence, saying, 'Thus says the LORD of hosts, the God of Israel: Take these deeds, both this sealed deed of purchase and this open deed, and put them in an earthenware vessel, that they may last for a long time'" (vv. 13, 14). This was standard practice for keeping a document safe in those days. It was a good system. For two millennia the famous Dead Sea Scrolls were protected by clay jars in the caves at Qumran. The Shrine of the Book, the museum in Jerusalem where some of those scrolls are housed, also exhibits property deeds like the ones Jeremiah's secretary held for Hanamel's property.

Preserving the title to the property was an act of faith. When Jeremiah signed and sealed the deed, he was banking on God's ability to deliver on his promises. By faith he was making an investment in the kingdom of God. Derek Kidner observes: "To buy land overrun by the world's conqueror, and then to take elaborate care of the title-deeds was a striking affirmation, as solid as the silver that paid for it, that God would bring his people back to their inheritance."[5] Even though Jeremiah would not live to see that day, he made sure the documents would be around to prove that God was faithful to his promise.

Do you have faith to act on God's promises, even if some of them will not be fulfilled until the end of history? Jeremiah had that kind of faith. He made a major life decision based on what God promised to do seven decades later.

Christians make the same kinds of decisions every day. They do strange things because they trust the promises of God. Some Christians get married. How odd! With the divorce rate so high, why would anyone want to get married? Christians get married because God tells them to do it and because they trust his faithfulness for the future.

Some Christians raise families. This, too, is becoming increasingly radical. A Christian woman went to see her dentist, whose wife was expecting a baby. The patient told him how wonderful it was to raise children. Afterward the dental hygienist told her she could tell whether or not people were Christians by what they said to the dentist about having a baby. Non-Christians talked about what a nuisance it is to have children, but Christians viewed them as gifts from the Lord.

Some Christians go to distant lands as missionaries, which is even stranger than raising a family. They leave behind all the conveniences of American culture. Why on earth would anyone do that? They do it because God calls them to take the gospel to the ends of the earth and because they trust his promise that he will go with them (Matthew 28:20).

The list goes on and on. Some Christians move into the city. On purpose. Some Christians feed the homeless or tutor the ignorant. Others reach across ethnic and economic barriers to form friendships. Still others give up one night a week to study the Bible and pray in small groups. Some Christians even give away 10 percent of their income—or more—for the work of the church.

All these behaviors seem strange to the post-Christian mind. The strongest countercultural movement in twenty-first-century America will be the church of the Lord Jesus Christ. There is only one good explanation for the strange things Christians do: They believe the promises of God. They trust what God has said about the family, or evangelism, or compassion, or stewardship, and they act accordingly.

A Prayer for the Bewildered

Living for God was as daunting a challenge in Jeremiah's times as it is in our own. As soon as the prophet put his money where his mouth was, he turned to the Lord in prayer: "After I had given the deed of purchase to Baruch the son of Neriah, I prayed to the LORD" (32:16). Calvin observes, "By this we are taught, that whenever thoughts creep into our minds, which toss us here and there, we ought to flee to prayer."[6]

What follows is a page from Jeremiah's prayer journal. It is a prayer for the bewildered. For forty years Jeremiah preached the destruction of Jerusalem. But when the city was finally about to be overrun, God told him to buy land. Jeremiah obeyed the Lord immediately, of course, but then he started to have second thoughts. So he took his doubts and his misgivings to the Lord in prayer. Derek Kidner says:

> It is a fine example of the way to pray in a desperate situation: concentrating first on the creative power (17) and perfect fidelity and justice (18–19) of God; remembering next his great redemptive acts (20–23a; to which the Christian can now add the greatest of them all)—and then with this background, laying before God the guilt of the past (23b), the hard facts of the present (24) and the riddle of the future (25).[7]

There are four parts to Jeremiah's prayer. The first is the groan. "*Ah,*" says Jeremiah (v. 17a), or "Alas!" He began his prayer with a cry from the soul.

Jeremiah often did this when he was in distress. Four of his prayers begin not with a word, but with an "Ah!" When God called him to the ministry, Jeremiah prayed, "Ah, Lord GOD! Behold, I do not know how to speak, for I am only a youth" (1:6). When the Lord announced that Jerusalem would be invaded, Jeremiah said, "Ah, Lord GOD, surely you have utterly deceived this people and Jerusalem, saying, 'It shall be well with you,' whereas the sword has reached their very life" (4:10). He prayed the same way when the other clergy were speaking against him. "Then I said, 'Ah, Lord GOD, behold, the prophets say to them, "You shall not see the sword, nor shall you have famine, but I will give you assured peace in this place"'" (14:13).

Whenever Jeremiah had a crisis—whenever he did not know what the Lord wanted him to do, was worried about the future, or was being attacked by enemies—his soul cried out to the Lord. Thus he experienced the truth of this wonderful promise:

> Likewise the Spirit helps us in our weakness. For we do not know what to pray for as we ought, but the Spirit himself intercedes for us with groanings too deep for words. And he who searches hearts knows what is the mind of the Spirit, because the Spirit intercedes for the saints according to the will of God. (Romans 8:26, 27)

It is appropriate to begin some prayers with a groan. When the only thing that comes out is "Arrrgh!" God knows what you mean. The Holy Spirit articulates the cries of the soul. He turns frustration into intercession.

Second, Jeremiah praises God for his mighty acts: "O great and mighty God, whose name is the LORD of hosts, great in counsel and mighty in deed . . ." (32:18b, 19a). He starts with God's mighty act of creation: "Ah, Lord GOD! It is you who have made the heavens and the earth by your great power and by your outstretched arm!" (v. 17a). The Lord God made everything there is. He made "The heavens and the earth," which is another way of saying he made the entire universe. He made all the moons, stars, planets, and galaxies. He made all the birds, bugs, and beasts. He made all the trees, bushes, flowers, and plants. Without God, nothing was made that has been made.

The Christian doctrine of creation stands against the philosophy of naturalism. Naturalism is one of the dominant worldviews of post-Christian culture. It is the belief—notice the word *belief*—that nature is all there is. There is no God, no soul, and no spirit, only matter in motion.

Since the days of Charles Darwin (1809–1882), evolutionary naturalism has told its own creation story. The Harvard paleontologist George Gaylord Simpson put it like this: "Man is the result of a purposeless and natural process that did not have him in mind."[8] In other words, the existence of human beings is an accident, the product of sheer chance.

In his critique of naturalism, University of California at Berkeley professor Phillip Johnson points out that naturalism reverses the Biblical doctrine of creation.[9] If the Bible is true, then God created mankind. But if naturalism is true, then mankind created God. God is just make-believe. He does not actually exist; he is the product of the human mind.

Naturalism thus denies God his proper place of rule over the universe. It denies him the worship and the praise that rightfully belong to him as the Creator of all that is. When God is praised for his mighty acts of creation, he is restored to his proper place. And his worshipers put themselves back in their proper place as well. God is the Creator; we are creatures God made by his "great power and . . . outstretched arm" (v. 17).

The other mighty act Jeremiah mentions in his prayer is redemption. He gives a short history lesson about how God brought his people out of Egypt: "You have shown signs and wonders in the land of Egypt, and to this day in Israel and among all mankind, and have made a name for yourself, as at this day" (v. 20). Jeremiah has in mind the miracles of Moses and the plagues on the Egyptians. He remembers that God not only brought his people out of Egypt, he also brought them into Canaan, the promised land: "You gave them this land, which you swore to their fathers to give them, a land flowing with milk and honey" (v. 22). Again, God did all this by his own strength: "You brought your people Israel out of the land of Egypt with signs and wonders, with a strong hand and outstretched arm" (v. 21).

God is to be praised as both Creator and Redeemer. When the Christian praises God as Redeemer, he praises God for salvation in Jesus Christ. Calvin emphasized this by the way he organized his *Institutes*.[10] The first book concerns "The Knowledge of God the Creator." The second teaches "The Knowledge of God the Redeemer in Christ." To redeem is to purchase or to buy back. God has redeemed his people from sin and death through the death and resurrection of Jesus Christ. "In him we have redemption through his blood, the forgiveness of our trespasses" (Ephesians 1:7, 8). Anyone who is made in the image of God can praise God as Creator. But everyone who believes in Jesus Christ for salvation can also praise him as Redeemer.

Third, Jeremiah worships God for his glorious attributes. He does not praise him simply for what he does, but also for who he is, cramming as many of God's characteristics as possible into two and a half verses.

The prophet starts with God's *omnipotence*: "Nothing is too hard for you" (32:17b). Whatever the task, God is up to it. He never meets his limitations. Nothing is too difficult for him.

Next Jeremiah worships God for his *covenant love*: "You show steadfast love to thousands" (v. 18a). Thousands upon millions of believers have been showered with the love of God in Christ throughout history and around the globe. Jeremiah's "love to thousands" echoes the second commandment, which speaks of God showing love to thousands of those who love and obey him (Exodus 20:6).

Jeremiah also echoes the second commandment when he praises God for his *justice*: "You show steadfast love to thousands, but you repay the guilt of fathers to their children after them" (32:18a). And again, "[Your] eyes are open to all the ways of the children of man, rewarding each one according to his ways and according to the fruit of his deeds" (v. 19b). God even judged his own people. "And they entered and took possession of it [the land]. But they did not obey your voice or walk in your law. They did nothing of all you commanded them to do. Therefore you have made all this disaster come upon them" (v. 23).

What these verses show is that the prophet remembered the Lord to be "a jealous God, visiting the iniquity of the fathers on the children to the third and the fourth generation of those who hate me" (Exodus 20:5). Postmoderns sometimes feel uneasy about God's justice, as if it is wrong for God to punish sin. It is not wrong; it is right! Since it is right, God is to be praised for maintaining his honor and his holiness by judging his enemies.

Next Jeremiah worships God for *knowing all* things: "[Your] eyes are open to all the ways of the children of man" (32:19b). Jeremiah had been reminded of God's universal knowledge, or omniscience, when his cousin Hanamel showed up at his prison cell. God knew all about the visit even before it happened, as he always does.

This prayer is rich in its praise of the attributes of God. Jeremiah worships God for his omnipotence and omniscience, for his love and justice. The prayer is highly theological, informed by his understanding of the rich doctrine of God.

The same thing ought to be true of the prayers of every Christian. You must have a theology before you can have a prayer life. Knowing the character of God precedes having intimacy with him through prayer. Too many prayers are superficial in their grasp of the character of God. Instead they ought to be saturated with the praise of his glorious attributes.

The final part of Jeremiah's prayer concerned his situation. It is worth noticing the proportions of his prayer. The prophet spent more time praising God than he did talking about his problems. John Guest says he "offered seven parts of praise to one part of puzzlement."[11]

Here was Jeremiah's puzzlement:

> Behold, the siege mounds have come up to the city to take it, and because of sword and famine and pestilence the city is given into the hands of the Chaldeans who are fighting against it. What you spoke has come to pass, and behold, you see it. Yet you, O Lord GOD, have said to me, "Buy the field for money and get witnesses"—though the city is given into the hands of the Chaldeans. (vv. 24, 25)

What was the point of Jeremiah's prayer? He did not actually make a request. He did not ask God for anything. He simply told God what God already knew—namely, that the Babylonian siege engines were at the gates and that he had just made the worst financial decision of his life.

Jeremiah's prayer sounds like a complaint. The word "Though" is not in the Hebrew text, but it properly captures the reproach in Jeremiah's voice: "Yet you, O Lord GOD, have said to me, 'Buy the field'" (v. 25). Jeremiah called attention to the fact that God told him to buy property even though it did not take a military genius to figure out that Jerusalem was on the verge of ruin. The prophet was perplexed by the whole thing, even flabbergasted. He did not understand what God was doing. So his prayer ends with a question mark. "You're really telling me to invest in real estate, Lord? Seriously?"

Or perhaps Jeremiah did not even make it to the question mark. It sounds as if he ran out of prayer before he figured out what to pray, which is the way bewildered prayers often end.

The only one who never gets bewildered is God: "The word of the LORD came to Jeremiah: 'Behold, I am the LORD, the God of all flesh. Is anything too hard for me?'" (vv. 26, 27). Literally, "Is anything too marvelous for me? Is anything too difficult, too wonderful, too extraordinary for me?" Of course not! In fact, Jeremiah said as much at the beginning of his prayer. With his own lips he had prayed, "Nothing is too hard for you" (v. 17b). So God's answer to his prophet's prayer was to say, "That's right, Jeremiah, you have the right God!"

If Jeremiah would only listen to his own prayer, he could answer his own question. Nothing is too difficult or wonderful for God. If God says he will rebuild Jerusalem, then rebuild it he will. And if God says it is a good time to buy, then it is a buyer's market for men and women of faith.

Jeremiah's example shows the value of praying with an informed view of God, especially during desperate times. Approach God with a proper sense of his power, love, justice, and knowledge and you will find the faith to trust him, even if he tells you to fork over seventeen shekels to Cousin Hanamel.

45

Is Anything Too Hard for God?

JEREMIAH 32:26-44

JEREMIAH HAD JUST SETTLED A LAND DEAL. Arguably, it was one of the worst real estate investments in the history of the Middle East. Jeremiah himself was in jail. Judah was at war. Jerusalem was surrounded by the Babylonians. Yet the prophet carefully counted out seventeen shekels of silver and bought the family farm from Cousin Hanamel. It was a bad time to buy, especially since the property in question lay in enemy-occupied territory.

The strangest thing about the whole transaction was that it was God's idea. Why would God tell Jeremiah to make such a risky investment? Jeremiah was willing to do it, of course, even to pray about it, but his prayer ends with more than a hint of reproach:

> Behold, the siege mounds have come up to the city to take it, and because of sword and famine and pestilence the city is given into the hands of the Chaldeans who are fighting against it. What you spoke has come to pass, and behold, you see it. Yet you, O Lord God, have said to me, "Buy the field for money and get witnesses"—though the city is given into the hands of the Chaldeans. (32:24, 25)

What Jeremiah offered was a "Lord, look what you're doing to my life" prayer. He worded it as a statement, but it sounds more like a suspicious question: "Lord, seriously, you're really telling me to buy this field? Are you sure? Is that your final answer?"

A Question for an Answer

The Lord took Jeremiah's question and immediately answered it with a question of his own: "The word of the LORD came to Jeremiah: 'Behold, I am the LORD, the God of all flesh. Is anything too hard for me?'" (vv. 26, 27). It was a rhetorical question, a question to which the answer is so obvious that it goes without saying. Literally God was asking if anything is "Too difficult" or "Too wonderful" for him. If God is the God of all mankind, then it follows that nothing is impossible for him.

Asking rhetorical questions seems to be God's favorite strategy for dealing with impertinent prayers. God had posed the same kind of question to Jeremiah once before, when the prophet tried to put him in the dock and make him answer the problem of evil.

> Righteous are you, O LORD,
>   when I complain to you;
>   yet I would plead my case before you.
> Why does the way of the wicked prosper? (12:1)

But if anyone is going to ask the questions, God is. So he answered Jeremiah with another question:

> If you have raced with men on foot, and they have wearied you,
>   how will you compete with horses? (12:5a)

The answer is obvious. If Jeremiah got worn out running the 100-yard dash, he would never be able to compete in the Kidron Derby. God's question silenced all his objections.

God used the same strategy with Job. Job and his friends spent thirty-odd chapters questioning the love of God. But then God came back with a question of his own: "Who is this that darkens counsel by words without knowledge?" (Job 38:2). That shut Job up in a hurry! Once God started asking the questions, there was nothing Job could say. "Therefore I have uttered what I did not understand," he admitted, "Things too wonderful for me, which I did not know" (Job 42:3).

God used the same strategy in the ninth chapter of Paul's letter to the Romans. Paul anticipated that when the Romans heard about the doctrine of election they would say, "Why does he still find fault? For who can resist his will?" (Romans 9:19). The Holy Spirit answered with his own list of questions—"But who are you, O man, to answer back to God?" and so forth (vv. 20–24).

Skeptics often have some questions for God. They think they have questions about his mercy and justice that he would be hard-pressed to answer. But the truth is that God has a few questions of his own, questions to silence every objection and shut every mouth. Sooner or later people who question the ways of God will have to answer some questions they will be too terrified to answer.

The point of the rhetorical question in 32:27 is that God is almighty. God was reminding Jeremiah of the lesson he taught Sarah, in the very same words. The Lord came to Abraham in his old age and said, "I will surely return to you about this time next year, and Sarah your wife shall have a son" (Genesis 18:10). It was such a joke that Sarah—ninety years old at the time—burst out laughing. But God silenced her laughter with a question: "Why did Sarah laugh and say, 'Shall I indeed bear a child, now that I am old?' Is anything too hard for the LORD?" (vv. 13, 14). It turned out that the answer was no; nothing is too hard for the Lord. Miraculously, God enabled Sarah to give birth to the son of promise.

Now Jeremiah was asking the same kind of question Sarah asked. He was wondering if God could really make good on his promise. So God answered him exactly the way he answered Sarah, using the same rhetorical question to teach the same lesson. Nothing is too hard, too difficult, too impossible, or too wonderful for God.

This is the doctrine of divine omnipotence. Is anything too hard for God? No, nothing is too hard for God. Jesus said, "With God all things are possible" (Matthew 19:26). There is no limit to God's ability to make or to do. He is infinite and eternal in his power. He is able to perform all his holy will. The Dutch theologian Herman Bavinck put it like this: "He possesses absolute power in regard to everything."[1] Enough said!

Power to Punish Sin

In the rest of Jeremiah 32 God reveals what he plans to do with all his power. The first thing he plans to do is *punish sin*. It is not too hard for God to judge his people for their sins.

Judgment was already at hand. Perhaps even from prison Jeremiah could hear the Babylonians pounding on the walls of the city. At the very least he had seen the siege ramps mounded up to the city gates. God had sent the Babylonians to attack, capture, and burn the city of Jerusalem.

This sounds harsh, until one remembers how sinful the city had been. The citizens of Jerusalem had been sinners from day one:

> For the children of Israel and the children of Judah have done nothing but evil in my sight from their youth. The children of Israel have done nothing

> but provoke me to anger by the work of their hands, declares the LORD. This
> city has aroused my anger and wrath, from the day it was built to this day,
> so that I will remove it from my sight. (vv. 30, 31)

There was sin at every level of society: "because of all the evil of the
children of Israel and the children of Judah that they did to provoke me to
anger—their kings and their officials, their priests and their prophets, the men
of Judah and the inhabitants of Jerusalem" (v. 32). The politicians were evil.
The pastors were evil. The people were evil. There was no one righteous; no,
not one.

Not only was there sin at every level, there was sin in every place, especially the sin of idolatry. Even from their rooftops, the people provoked God
to anger: "Offerings have been made to Baal and drink offerings have been
poured out to other gods" (v. 29b). They were making gods with their own
hands and then bowing down to them on top of their houses. Baal worship was
everywhere. The entire city was characterized by idolatry.

The same could well be said of the post-Christian West at the dawn of
the twenty-first century. True, not many people burn incense to Baal on their
roofs. But God would not have any trouble identifying the idols we worship
in our homes and on our streets—money, self, sex, and a pantheon of others.

What idols would God find in the church? The sins of Jeremiah's day were
not just the sins of secular people. Under King Manasseh, it was the religious
people who erected altars to Baal and all the starry hosts right in God's house
(2 Kings 21:1–9). Such worship was an affront to God. With an obvious sense
of horror, he said, "They set up their abominations in the house that is called
by my name, to defile it" (32:34).

Christians commit a similar abomination whenever they carry idols in
their hearts and bring them into the church. Many who claim to be servants
of the Lord Jesus Christ still worship fashion, intellect, luxury, and privacy.

The reason the evangelical church is so feeble is not because Christians
have ceased to worship God. Rather, its weakness comes from the desire to
worship God *plus* a few other things. Many Christians, in fact, are like the
Roman Emperor Alexander Severus (208–235). When Alexander heard about
Christianity, he wanted to adopt it as one of the Roman religions. So he set up
an image of Jesus Christ in his private chapel, adding the Christian God to the
gods he already worshiped.[2] But anyone who refuses to worship *God alone* is
an idolater. The true and living God will not stand for any rivals. He will not
share his glory, his worship, or his praise with any other god.

One form of idolatry was so despicable that Jeremiah singled it out for special mention. It symbolized the moral bankruptcy of the entire culture. Jeremiah preached a sermon on this sin when he was standing in "The Valley of Slaughter" (7:30—8:3). He mentioned it again in chapter 19 when he shattered a clay jar outside the Potsherd Gate. It was the sin of infanticide. "They built the high places of Baal in the Valley of the Son of Hinnom, to offer up their sons and daughters to Molech, though I did not command them, nor did it enter into my mind, that they should do this abomination, to cause Judah to sin" (32:35). In an attempt to appease Baal, Jeremiah's neighbors were offering human sacrifices. No wonder God wanted Jerusalem to get out of his sight! "This city has aroused my anger and wrath, from the day it was built to this day, so that I will remove it from my sight" (v. 31).

The moral worth of a culture is not determined by how it treats the strong, the rich, and the beautiful, but by how it treats the weak, the poor, and the vulnerable. What can one say about a culture that takes the lives of its own children, whether inside or outside the womb? Or about a culture that makes allowance for assisted suicide? What can one say, in other words, about the post-Christian culture of death in the new millennium?

In the spring of 1997 New Jersey residents were shocked to learn what one high school student did on her prom night. The girl left her glass by the punch bowl, went to the bathroom, gave birth, strangled her child, and then went back out on the floor to dance to her favorite song. A "post-term abortion," some called it. God calls it an abomination, a human sacrifice to the goddess of self.

If God is really God, then he hates sin and will punish it, both in this life and in the next. He is the Lord, the God of all mankind. Is it too hard for him to overthrow any person, city, or nation that sets itself up against his will? If nothing is too hard for God, then he will and must punish sin.

In the case of Jerusalem, God made sure the punishment fit the crime:

> Therefore, thus says the Lord: Behold, I am giving this city into the hands of the Chaldeans and into the hand of Nebuchadnezzar king of Babylon, and he shall capture it. The Chaldeans who are fighting against this city shall come and set this city on fire and burn it, with the houses on whose roofs offerings have been made to Baal and drink offerings have been poured out to other gods, to provoke me to anger. (vv. 28, 29; cf. 52:13)

The very rooftops on which incense was burned to Baal were later torched by the Babylonians.

The people of Jeremiah's day failed to heed God's warnings. Apparently they thought it was too hard for him to punish sin. "They have turned to me their back and not their face. And though I have taught them persistently, they have not listened to receive instruction" (v. 33). Do not turn your back on God. Instead turn your face toward him and ask him to forgive your sins for Jesus' sake.

Power to Save Sinners

Jeremiah's response to God's judgment seemed to be the logical one. As far as he could tell, there was no hope for Jerusalem. "By sword, by famine, and by pestilence," he said, "it is given into the hand of the king of Babylon" (v. 36a).

But then God changed the subject by saying something totally surprising and completely unexpected. Whereas verses 28–35 showed the power of God in the judgment of sin, verses 36–44 go on to show the power of God in the salvation of sinners. God moves from sin to salvation so quickly it is hard to keep up. Gordon McConville goes so far as to say that verse 36 is "unexpected and illogical."[3]

One hesitates to say that God is illogical, but McConville has a point. Verse 36 begins with the words "Now therefore." The word "Therefore" is omitted from most English versions because translators cannot bring themselves to keep it in the text. That is because the "Therefore" does not appear to make any sense. It does not add up. It is a non sequitur. "Verse 36 does not follow in any way from the argument of vv. 28–35. Indeed, in v. 36 the text makes an enormous leap away from vv. 28–35 to God's second impossibility."[4]

God's syllogism goes like this: "You are despicable sinners, and I am going to destroy you in my wrath; *therefore*, I will never stop doing good to you." But what does God mean by "Therefore"? How does it follow? Where is the logic in it? "How could a people guilty of offering incense, libations, and even their own children to other gods become the Lord's people again?"[5] Impossible!

Impossible? Well, is *anything* too hard for God? The "Therefore" of 32:36 is a reminder that there is something totally unexpected, almost illogical, about the grace of God for sinners. But not impossible. The great Bible teacher Donald Grey Barnhouse once said that Hell was the only logical doctrine in the Bible. Barnhouse was exaggerating, of course, but he was making an important point about the justice of God. The power of God in the punishment of sin makes perfect sense. What else could sinners who live in rebellion against God possibly deserve except to be banished from God's sight? It is perfectly logical for God to reject anyone who rejects the gift of eternal life he has offered through his son Jesus Christ.

But what is logical about the grace of God? Where is the logic in the free grace of the gospel for guilty sinners? Where is the logic in God sending his Son to die on the cross, or in adopting his bitter enemies as his own sons and daughters? Such grace seems illogical, almost impossible. The only reason it is not impossible is that nothing is impossible for God.

The rest of Jeremiah 32 is full of grace that seems illogical but is not impossible. It is God's agenda for saving sinners, his to-do list of grace.

First, God promised to bring his people home: "Behold, I will gather them from all the countries to which I drove them in my anger and my wrath and in great indignation. I will bring them back to this place, and I will make them dwell in safety" (v. 37). He promised the end of the exile. God's people Israel were scattered across the globe, but God would gather them together and bring them back home.

Second, God promised to make his people his own: "And they shall be my people, and I will be their God" (v. 38). God would enter into a beautiful romance with his people. They would belong to him, and he would belong to them. This is the central promise of the covenant. We have a God, and God has a people.

Third, God promised to give his people a new heart: "I will give them one heart and one way, that they may fear me forever, for their own good and the good of their children after them" (v. 39). This is the doctrine of the new birth, also known as conversion or regeneration. Anyone who becomes a Christian receives a new heart, and God is the one who performs the transplant. A heart for God does not grow on its own; it comes from the Holy Spirit. Everyone who turns away from sin and comes to Christ receives a new heart of love for God.

This new heart for God is something all God's people share. They become single-hearted. They become single-hearted, having "one heart and one way." This promise is fulfilled in the unity of the church, like the first church in Jerusalem, where "The full number of those who believed were of one heart and soul" (Acts 4:32). Wherever the hearts of God's people beat as one, and wherever they walk in the same direction, they experience the communion of the saints.

The opposite of being single-hearted is being double-minded, which was exactly the problem with the people of Israel. They were of two minds. They were trying to worship both God and Baal at the same time.

The contemporary church commits the same error. Too many people who call themselves Christians are double-minded. They want to be both godly *and* worldly. They want to live for the Lord *and* for their own pleasures. They are like the man who tried to step into a rowboat. As soon as he planted his foot in the boat, he felt it drifting away from the dock—fast! Before he could make up his mind whether to stand on the dock or float in the boat, he found himself at the bottom of the river. The same thing will happen to you if you cannot make up your mind about Jesus Christ. If Jesus Christ is the only Savior, then get in the boat and let him be your Captain. Otherwise you will find yourself drowning at the bottom of the river.

Fourth, God promised concerning his people, "I will make with them an everlasting covenant" (32:40a). The new covenant will never end. All God's almost illogical, almost impossible promises will last forever.

The reason God's covenant will last forever is that it is established by the blood of Jesus Christ, the blood he shed on the cross for sinners. Because Jesus was raised from the dead to live forever, the new covenant established in his blood will last forever. It will be an everlasting covenant, for this is God's promise: "I will make with them an everlasting covenant, that I will not turn away from doing good to them" (v. 40a).

Here is a fifth impossibility made possible by the finished work of Jesus Christ: God will hold on to his people. This is the doctrine of perseverance, which is simply a fancy way of saying that all God's children will make it to glory. Sometimes people say it like this: "Once saved, always saved."

That language is not found in the Bible, but the idea is found in Jeremiah 32, where God says, "And I will put the fear of me in their hearts, that they may not turn from me" (v. 40b). The same power by which God saves sinners is also at work to preserve the saints. The Christian perseveres with God to the very end because God perseveres with the Christian to the very end. Perseverance, wrote Calvin,

> is the gift of God and the work of the Holy Spirit. . . . [W]ere God only to form our hearts once . . . the devil might, at any moment, entice us, by his wiles, from the right way. . . . To rule us then for one hour would avail us nothing, except God preserved us through the whole course of life, and led us on to the end. It hence then follows, that the whole course of our life is directed by the Spirit of God, so that the end no less than the beginning of good works ought to be ascribed to his grace.[6]

Finally, God promised to rejoice over his people. Angels and saints are not the only ones who rejoice when God blesses his people. God himself rejoices! Sometimes he even sings about it, as the prophet Zephaniah promised:

> The LORD your God is in your midst,
>   a mighty one who will save;

> he will rejoice over you with gladness;
> he will quiet you by his love;
> he will exult over you with loud singing. (Zephaniah 3:17)

Like Zephaniah, Jeremiah saw that when God does the impossible to save sinners it brings joy to his heart: "I will rejoice in doing them good, and I will plant them in this land in faithfulness, with all my heart and all my soul" (32:41). The idea of planting goes back to Jeremiah's call to the ministry, when God appointed him "over nations and over kingdoms, to pluck up and to break down, to destroy and to overthrow, to build and to plant" (1:10). God, therefore, is like a happy farmer, planting his people in a good land and rejoicing when the planting is done. God is happy because he loves to do what seems to be impossible for the people he loves.

A Good Investment

The end of Jeremiah 32 brings the power of God's grace down to the personal level. His grace was not just for the whole nation of Israel; it was also for poor Jeremiah, still languishing in the Jerusalem jail.

Many believers trust that God can do all things. They believe in the power of God to save sinners. But when it comes to their own affairs they doubt the reality of God's omnipotence.

Jeremiah was like that. He believed in the power of God; at least, he believed it when he prayed. Back at the beginning of his prayer he praised God for his omnipotence: "Nothing is too hard for you" (v. 17b). But by the time he had finished praying, God had to come back and repeat Jeremiah's words, as if to say, "Jeremiah, do you really believe that? Do you actually believe I can do all things?" "Is anything too hard for me?" (v. 27b). The reason God had to ask was because he had detected the doubt in Jeremiah's prayer.

There was an ounce of rebuke in God's question, but more than a pound of grace in his answer. He knew that Jeremiah had just bought a field that seemed like a bad investment. So he reassured him that it was all for the best:

> For thus says the Lord: Just as I have brought all this great disaster upon this people, so I will bring upon them all the good that I promise them. Fields shall be bought in this land of which you are saying, 'It is a desolation, without man or beast; it is given into the hand of the Chaldeans.' Fields shall be bought for money, and deeds shall be signed and sealed and witnessed, in the land of Benjamin, in the places about Jerusalem, and in the cities of Judah, in the cities of the hill country, in the cities of the Shephelah, and in the cities of the Negeb; for I will restore their fortunes, declares the Lord. (vv. 42–44)

God promised that one day things in Jerusalem would return to normal. The economy would stabilize, property values would go back up, and it would become a seller's market once again. Then the seventeen shekels Jeremiah had plunked down for Hanamel's field would turn out to be the best investment he had ever made. The land deed that was signed and sealed would be delivered because God always delivers on his promises.

Do not doubt the power of God in your own life. You may doubt that your marriage can be saved, or that you can have victory over a particular sin, or that a family member will ever get saved, or that God will ever bless your work. As long as you try to solve your own problems, things will continue to be impossible. But not when you entrust them to the Lord, the God of all mankind. Is anything too hard for him?

Well?

46

"Pardon for Sin and a Peace That Endureth"

JEREMIAH 33:1–9

THEY WERE THE LAST, desperate days before Jerusalem fell into the hands of the Babylonians. After many months of siege the city was shaken to its very foundations. In a last-ditch effort to save their city, the citizens tore down their houses and palaces and threw them up against the city walls.

Jerusalem was becoming a desolate waste, as excavations along the eastern slope of the city have confirmed. The houses overlooking the Kidron Valley were built on terraces. "Under the assault of the Chaldean army considerable areas of the terraces and the houses which rested on them collapsed and slid down the slope, leaving an unbelievable mass of fallen masonry."[1] Jeremiah's Jerusalem was coming to an end.

Let Me Tell You a Secret

The prophet himself was still in jail. Yet right at this moment the Lord came to give him a little inside information. "The word of the LORD came to Jeremiah a second time, while he was still shut up in the court of the guard: 'Thus says the LORD who made the earth, the LORD who formed it to establish it—the LORD is his name'" (33:1, 2).

The information Jeremiah was about to get came from a reliable source. God guaranteed his credibility by reminding the prophet of his work of creation. The words he used for *making* and *forming* were first used in the creation account (Genesis 1, 2). God thus spoke to Jeremiah as the God who "made," "formed," and "establish[ed]" the earth. In other words, he knew what he was talking about.

God had a secret for Jeremiah, and everyone loves a secret. Children especially love to tell secrets and have them told. One of the joys of life is to take a small child on your lap and whisper in her ear that you love her. What God whispered to Jeremiah in that prison cell is one of the great promises of the Bible: "Call to me and I will answer you, and will tell you great and hidden things that you have not known" (33:3).

Next to secret love, secret knowledge is the most enticing of all secrets. I still remember the first time I walked into the Duke Humfrey's Library at the University of Oxford. The library dates back to the seventeenth century. Its walls and ceilings are richly carved and beautifully painted. Its shelves are lined with great folio volumes bound in calfskin, many of them locked with silver clasps. For C. S. Lewis—and for many other scholars before and since— the Duke Humfrey's was the best place to study in the world. To this day it is a complete repository of human knowledge from ancient times through the Reformation.

As I studied at the Duke Humfrey's day after day I was constantly reminded of how little I know. There I saw complete sets of Plato and Aristotle and all the ancient philosophers in their original languages. There I lifted enormous tomes written in Latin from the Medieval theologians—William of Ockham, Duns Scotus, and all the rest. There I perused the works of the Reformers and studied the commentaries of the great Puritans. The Duke Humfrey's is a library filled with great things it would take many lifetimes to know.

How much greater, how much more unsearchable, is the knowledge of God! The word "hidden" in verse 3 implies that the knowledge of divine things is inaccessible, incomprehensible, impregnable.[2] Later Jeremiah will use the same word to describe a fortified city (34:7). The things of God are out of reach. The things God has planned to do in the future, especially, are hidden from our sight. The Apostle Paul asked, "Who has known the mind of the Lord?" (Romans 11:34a). The answer, of course, is that no one has ever known the mind of God.

Yet God invited Jeremiah to search the divine mind. He promised to make known the unknowable things. He pledged to reveal the secrets of redemption. All Jeremiah had to do was call upon the Lord, for "everyone who asks receives" (Matthew 7:8).

God promised to reveal himself through prayer, for he loves to share the secret plan of redemption. Moses declared, "The secret things belong to the LORD our God, but the things that are revealed belong to us and to our children forever" (Deuteronomy 29:29). The biggest secret of all was the victory of God over sin through the death and resurrection of the Lord Jesus Christ. The

Apostle Paul called salvation in Christ the mystery "kept secret for long ages but has now been disclosed and through the prophetic writings has been made known" (Romans 16:25, 26).

Great and Unsearchable Justice

Jeremiah 33 reveals at least three great and unsearchable things Jeremiah did not know. The first was a great and unsearchable thing he probably didn't want to know—that God would destroy all his enemies. The prophecy was gruesome:

> For thus says the Lord, the God of Israel, concerning the houses of this city and the houses of the kings of Judah that were torn down to make a defense against the siege mounds and against the sword: They are coming in to fight against the Chaldeans and to fill them with the dead bodies of men whom I shall strike down in my anger and my wrath, for I have hidden my face from this city because of all their evil. (vv. 4, 5)

These verses are notoriously difficult to translate, but they convey the chaos and confusion that led up to the fall of Jerusalem. As Pamela Scalise argues:

> Despite the difficult syntax, three aspects of the experience of siege are evident in these verses: (1) the defensive action of demolishing houses in order to remove flammable material and to strengthen the wall at the point where the battering ram and other siege machines will attack; (2) the offensive activity of "The sword," which will fight against the Chaldeans; and (3) the victims of divine judgment who have already died inside the besieged city and who cannot be given a proper burial outside it.[3]

Even the strongest city cannot withstand the judgment of God. And in this case, the punishment fit the crime. Jeremiah had already condemned Jerusalem for burning incense to Baal on its rooftops (32:29). How appropriate, then, for those very same houses to be torn down!

The wrath of God against sin is great and unsearchable. The creature cannot understand the way the Creator works out his justice. Why are the wicked exalted and the righteous abased? Why does God allow one man to taste the pleasures of sin while another meets a bitter end? Why does one dictator remain in power while another is brought to justice?

Such questions cannot be answered because God's justice is beyond comprehension. The Apostle Paul put it best in his doxology: "How unsearchable are his judgments and how inscrutable his ways!" (Romans 11:33b).

God's judgments may be unsearchable, but there is something great about them too. One of the great things about God is that he will not tolerate evil. As he told Jeremiah, "I have hidden my face from this city because of all their evil" (33:5b).

God will do the same thing at the end of history. Then he will turn his back on the ungodly forever (Matthew 25:41). At the last day, every unholy thought, every wicked word, and every evil deed will be brought to judgment. That day of judgment will be a great day. It will be great because it will show how great God is. God will not besmirch his honor by allowing any sin to go unpunished. Every sin will and must be judged, including your own.

There are two things you can do with your sins. One is to hold on to them until the day of judgment, when you will suffer the punishment for them yourself. That is what Jeremiah's neighbors did. When the day of judgment came, therefore, they were jumbled together like so many corpses under the rubble of Jerusalem.

But thanks be to God, there is something else you can do with your sins! You can take them to the cross of Christ. When Jesus died on the cross, he was accepting the punishment you deserved for your sins. If you believe in Jesus Christ, then you do not have to die for your sins; Jesus has already died for them.

Know this: God will preserve his great justice one way or the other. Your sin must be punished, either in your own person or in the person of Jesus Christ. The best thing to do is to take your sin to the cross and let Jesus deal with it there.

Pardon for Sin

The second great and unsearchable thing God revealed to Jeremiah was pardon for sin: "I will cleanse them from all the sin they have committed against me and will forgive all their sins of rebellion against me" (33:8 NIV).

Here the Scripture makes a distinction between "sin" and "sins." God offers cleansing for sin (in the singular) and forgiveness for sins (in the plural). The difference is important. The Westminster Confession of Faith refers to it as the difference between "original sin" and "actual sins" (VII.ii-vi). The Scottish minister William Still (1911–1997) liked to call it the difference between the *root* and the *fruit* of sin.[4]

Original sin is the sin nature that every man, woman, and child inherits from Adam. The one sin of Adam is the root of all sin. The single sin that he committed in the garden of Eden brought sin and death upon all humanity.

This is the doctrine of original sin that Paul developed in the fifth chapter of Romans:

> Sin came into the world through one man. (v. 12)

> The judgment following one trespass brought condemnation. (v. 16)

> Because of one man's trespass, death reigned. (v. 17)

> One trespass led to condemnation for all men. (v. 18)

> By the one man's disobedience the many were made sinners. (v. 19)

The one sin of Adam made us all sinners. The guilt of Adam's sin is imputed to every human being who has ever lived, except the Lord Jesus Christ. As the Puritans loved to put it, "In Adam's fall, we sinned all."

The doctrine of original sin means that even before a child commits the first sin, he or she is already a sinner. In his comments on Romans, John Calvin explained it like this:

> The natural depravity which we bring from our mother's womb, although it does not produce its fruits immediately, is still sin before God, and deserves His punishment. This is what is called original sin. As Adam at his first creation had received for his posterity as well as for himself the gifts of divine grace, so by falling from the Lord, in himself he corrupted, vitiated, depraved, and ruined our nature—having lost the image of God, the only seed which he could have produced was that which bore resemblance to himself. We have, therefore, all sinned, because all are imbued with natural corruption, and for this reason are wicked and perverse.[5]

We sin because we are sinners; we are not sinners because we sin.

Original sin, the root of sin, is bad enough. Even by itself, the sinful nature we inherit from Adam deserves the wrath and curse of God. But then we bring further judgment upon ourselves by the sins we commit. We add actual sins—idolatry, murder, adultery, theft, coveting, and all the rest—to original sin. According to Thomas Boston, original sin is "The spawn which the great leviathan has left in the souls of men, from whence comes all the fry of actual sins and abominations."[6] Or in the language of the Westminster Confession of Faith, "From this original corruption, whereby we are utterly indisposed, disabled, and made opposite to all good, and wholly inclined to all evil, do proceed all actual transgressions" (VIII.v).

Although we come into life having already inherited an infinite debt to

God from Adam, we rack up further debt by the sins we commit each day. Actual sins pile up on top of original sin to create a credit nightmare, spiritually speaking. All the *sins* are added to all the *sin*. The root of sin produces the noxious fruit of sin.

But here is something great and unsearchable to know: God will cleanse his people from all the sin they have committed and will forgive all their sins of rebellion against him. This is pardon for sin, full and free. God promises atonement for sin and for sins. All original sin will be cleansed, and all actual sins will be forgiven. The root of sin will be dug up, and the fruit of sin will be destroyed.

To understand how great and how unsearchable that promise is, it helps to know how great and how offensive sin is. Jeremiah used three different Hebrew words to define sin (33:8). They are the same words God used on Mount Sinai when he promised to forgive "iniquity and transgression and sin" (Exodus 34:7). These words describe sin in all its variety.

The phrase "all the sin" (NIV) is sometimes translated as "iniquity," which refers to something twisted or bent. The phrase "all their sins" (NIV) means "missing the mark." Then there is the word that is rightly translated "rebellion." Sin is all those things. It is a twisting and bending of the person whom God created upright. It is a missing of the mark of God's perfect Law. And it is active rebellion against the kingdom of God.

Whatever you want to call it, the people of Jerusalem had done it. There is as much sin in the book of Jeremiah as in any other book of the Bible, if not more. Page after page, prophecy after prophecy, Jeremiah has identified the sins of his people. He has preached against forsaking God, worshiping idols, committing adultery, forgetting the Lord, practicing prostitution, ignoring the prophets, oppressing the poor, rejecting the truth, doubting God, abusing the weak, speaking lies, pursuing wealth, harming aliens, murdering the innocent, stealing goods, committing perjury, following Baal, breaking the Sabbath, slaughtering children, betraying friends, and breaking the covenant. It is quite a list. It adds up to an infinite debt of actual sins.

How great, how unsearchable is the promise that all these sins will be forgiven! How unsearchable it is that God offers forgiveness for backsliding, idolatry, adultery, hypocrisy, murder, theft, infanticide, and rebellion! How great God must be to devise a plan for the forgiveness of such sins!

At the center of God's unsearchable plan for the cleansing of sin is the cross of Jesus Christ. When Jesus Christ was crucified at the Place of the Skull, the blood dripped down from his hands, his feet, and his side. In that blood—that is, through his death—there is cleansing from all sin, original as well as actual. Jesus Christ bore all our sin and carried all our sins on the cross.

At the cross you will find pardon for your own sins. At the cross you will find cleansing from the guilt of original sin inherited from Adam. At the cross you will find forgiveness for all sins you have actually committed. Through the blood that Christ shed on the cross, everyone can receive what Jeremiah was promised—cleansing from sin and forgiveness of sins. "The blood of Jesus his Son cleanses us from all sin" (1 John 1:7). "In him we have redemption through his blood, the forgiveness of our trespasses" (Ephesians 1:7).

Theologians sometimes speak of the doctrine of *limited atonement*. The doctrine of limited atonement has its place. It teaches that Jesus Christ atoned for the sins of his people and his people only. But there is also a doctrine of unlimited atonement, as expressed in 33:8: "I will cleanse them from all the guilt of their sin against me, and I will forgive all the guilt of their sin and rebellion against me." The atonement Jesus Christ offered for sin is unlimited in its ability to wash away every kind of sin. It has unlimited ability to cleanse original sin and to forgive actual sins. What could be greater or more unsearchable than the unlimited atonement of Jesus Christ?

A Peace That Endures

A third great and unsearchable thing about God is beautifully expressed in a line from a great hymn—"pardon for sin and a peace that endureth." The line comes from "Great Is Thy Faithfulness," written by Thomas Chisholm (1866–1960) in 1923. Once Chisholm received pardon for his sins through Jesus Christ, he discovered that God gives enduring peace to his people.

God revealed the same secret to Jeremiah: "Behold, I will bring to it [Jerusalem] health and healing, and I will heal them and reveal to them abundance of prosperity and security. I will restore the fortunes of Judah and the fortunes of Israel, and rebuild them as they were at first" (vv. 6, 7). God promised to restore, renew, and rebuild Jerusalem. He promised to give his people peace as well as pardon.

One of the remarkable things about this promise of peace is that Jeremiah had spent most of his ministry prophesying just the opposite. He had often rebuked the false prophets for saying, "Peace, peace" when there was no peace (6:14; 8:11). Furthermore, he had often claimed that the spiritual wounds of his people were "incurable, refusing to be healed" (15:18). "There is none to uphold your cause," he said, "no medicine for your wound, no healing for you" (30:13).

In desperation he cried:

Is there no balm in Gilead?
  Is there no physician there?
Why then has the health of the daughter of my people
  not been restored? (8:22)

The answer to these questions is that as long as God's people are dead in their trespasses and sins, there is no health in them. But once their sin is cleansed and their sins are forgiven, then all of God's promises will come true.

One place to see how God brought peace to his people is in the book of Nehemiah. More than a century after Jeremiah's death, Nehemiah surveyed Jerusalem and found the city pretty much the way the Babylonians left it. He said, "You see the trouble we are in, how Jerusalem lies in ruins with its gates burned" (Nehemiah 2:17a). But Nehemiah did not leave the city in ruins. He said, "Come, let us build the wall of Jerusalem, that we may no longer suffer derision" (v. 17b). The book of Nehemiah goes on to describe how the city was rebuilt, gate by gate and stone by stone. God brought Judah and Israel back from captivity and rebuilt them "as they were at first," just as he promised (33:7).

God gives even greater peace to the Christian. Anyone who trusts in Jesus Christ for salvation has the peace of God. The Christian is at peace in the world because God is on his side. The Christian is at peace with himself because he is no longer troubled by a guilty conscience. And the Christian is at peace with God because Jesus Christ has accepted the punishment for sin and for sins.

The hymn Thomas Ken (1637–1711) wrote for the boys of the Winchester school—"All Praise to Thee, My God, This Night"—speaks of this peace:

Forgive me, Lord, for thy dear Son,
The ills that I this day have done.
That with the world, myself and Thee,
I ere I sleep at peace may be.

How great, how unsearchable is the peace of God. The Apostle Paul rightly called it "The peace of God, which surpasses all understanding" (Philippians 4:7).

If you have received "pardon for sin and a peace that endureth," there is only one thing left to do—praise God. The great and unsearchable plan of redemption deserves highest praise. It deserves the kind of praise God promises his people will give: "And this city shall be to me a name of joy, a praise and a glory before all the nations of the earth who shall hear of all the good that

I do for them. They shall fear and tremble because of all the good and all the prosperity I provide for it" (33:9).

Here Jeremiah testifies to the evangelistic value of a worshiping church. When the church worships God in all his unsearchable greatness, the world sits up to take notice. "Here surely we can see one of the most powerful continuing agents of evangelism; not merely preaching, nor an attack on other people for their sinfulness, but the vibrant life, the joy-filled character of the believing community."[7] If it is true that God grants "pardon for sin and a peace that endureth," then he deserves all the renown, joy, praise, and glory we can give him.

47

While Shepherds
Watched Their Flocks

JEREMIAH 33:10-16

EVERYONE KNOWS ABOUT the first Christmas shepherds. Everyone knows they were abiding in the fields near Bethlehem, "keeping watch over their flock by night" (Luke 2:8). Everyone knows that "lo, the angel of the Lord came upon them, and the glory of the Lord shone round about them." Everyone knows the shepherds were terrified to see such great glory; "They were sore afraid" (v. 9 KJV).

Everyone knows the shepherds were given good news. After telling them to "fear not," the angel said, "Behold, I bring you good tidings of great joy, which shall be to all people. For unto you is born this day in the city of David a Saviour, which is Christ the Lord" (vv. 10, 11 KJV). Everyone knows that the angel gave the shepherds a sign: "Ye shall find the babe wrapped in swaddling clothes, lying in a manger" (v. 12 KJV). Everyone knows, too, that the shepherds were greeted by a mighty chorus of angels. "And suddenly there was with the angel a multitude of the heavenly host praising God, and saying, 'Glory to God in the highest, and on earth peace, good will toward men'" (vv. 13, 14 KJV).

Some people even know that the shepherds were the first evangelists. They hurried off to Bethlehem to see this thing that had come to pass. They found the baby wrapped in swaddling clothes and lying in a manger. And after they had seen Jesus, they went into the streets and "made known abroad the saying which was told them concerning this child" (v. 17 KJV). Then they returned to their fields "glorifying and praising God for all the things they had heard and seen, as it was told unto them" (v. 20 KJV).

Why Shepherds?

The story of the shepherds is one of the most familiar stories in the Bible. But why was the birth of Jesus Christ first announced (not counting Mary and Joseph, of course) to the shepherds? Why *shepherds*? What is the significance of the appearance of the angels to the shepherds who watched their flocks by night?

The usual line of explanation goes something like this: Shepherds were among the lowest members of society. They were useful but not influential. God wanted them to be the first to welcome his Son to show that the gift of his Son was for all people, even for shepherds. It was as if a chorus of angels had appeared to auto mechanics or cab drivers or trash collectors. If the good news is for shepherds, it must be for all of us.

In his commentary on the book of Luke, Leon Morris observes:

> As a class shepherds had a bad reputation. The nature of their calling kept them from observing the ceremonial law which meant so much to religious people. More regrettable was their unfortunate habit of confusing "mine" with "Thine" as they moved about the country. They were considered unreliable and were not allowed to give testimony in the law-courts.[1]

Walter Liefeld is more generous in his view of shepherds, but reaches a similar conclusion:

> There may be several reasons for the special role of the shepherds in the events of this unique night. Among the occupations, shepherding had a lowly place. Shepherds were considered untrustworthy and their work made them ceremonially unclean. Thus the most obvious implication is that the gospel first came to the social outcasts of Jesus' day. . . . Finally, in both testaments shepherds symbolize those who care for God's people, including the Lord himself. The shepherds of Luke 2 may, therefore, symbolize all the ordinary people who have joyfully received the gospel and have become in various ways pastors to others.[2]

There may be some truth to what the commentators say. If the good news of great joy is for shepherds, then it really must be for all people. But Luke himself did not explain why the "good news of great joy that will be for all the people" was first given to the shepherds. Actually, the place to discover the meaning of the Christmas shepherds is Jeremiah 33.

Reversal of Fortune

Jeremiah's promise about the Messiah's birth could hardly have come at a better time. Things did not look promising for the people of God. Jeremiah himself was still in jail. Jerusalem was besieged by the Babylonians. Nebuchadnezzar and his armies were marching against the city to destroy it. All the judgments Jeremiah had been warning about for many years were about to come crashing down on God's people.

The land would be laid waste. "Thus says the LORD: In this place of which you say, 'It is a waste without man or beast . . .'" (33:10a). The towns of Judah and the streets of Jerusalem would be deserted, inhabited by neither man nor beast. No children would laugh and play in the streets. No stray cats would prowl the alleyways. Jerusalem would become a ghost town, and God's people would be skeptical about the future of God's city.

"What a waste!" the people would say. But the Lord knew the plans he had for his people, plans to prosper them and not to harm them. Jeremiah 33 began with God promising to tell Jeremiah "great and hidden things" he did not know (v. 3). Verses 10–16 explain what some of those great and unsearchable things are.

This section of Jeremiah's prophecy can be summarized like this: "For I will restore the fortunes of the land as at first, says the LORD" (v. 11c). With these words God promised a reversal of fortune. Literally he promised to "reverse their reversals" (this is another one of Jeremiah's puns). Sorrow would be turned into joy. Whatever had been undone in justice would be redone in mercy. God would put everything back in its place. Peace and safety would return to his people. The proof would come in three leading indicators of peace or shalom: Weddings, thanksgiving, and farming would return to the people of God.

First, there would be *weddings*: "In the cities of Judah and the streets of Jerusalem that are desolate, without man or inhabitant or beast, there shall be heard again the voice of mirth and the voice of gladness, the voice of the bridegroom and the voice of the bride" (vv. 10b, 11a). The blessing of marriage would return to God's people; the deserted towns and cities of Israel would be repopulated.

Time and again Jeremiah had prophesied the death of marriage. Jeremiah, the pariah, was himself forbidden to marry (16:2). A wedding is an investment in the future. But the people had no future, so how could they marry? God was about to judge them for their sins. He said, "I will silence in the cities of Judah and in the streets of Jerusalem the voice of mirth and the voice of gladness, the voice of the bridegroom and the voice of the bride, for the land shall become a waste" (7:34; cf. 16:9; 25:10).

God warned of a time when all social occasions would come to an end. The invitations would not be mailed, the vows would not be exchanged, and the cake would not be cut, for a society at war has no time for matrimony. Weddings only happen when people are at peace.

But one day peace would return. Happy days would come again for the people of God. Grace would triumph over judgment. God would redeem his people from captivity. Then marriage not only would be permitted, it positively would be encouraged. The bridal shops in Jerusalem would reopen. Once again brides would say, "I take you to be my lawful wedded husband," and grooms would say, "With this ring, I thee wed." Once again ministers would say, "I now pronounce you man and wife." Bands would crank out the oldies, wedding parties would take to the dance floor, and the happy sounds of celebration would return to the city.

This promise was fulfilled in Israel's history. The psalmist wrote:

When the LORD restored the fortunes of Zion,
    we were like those who dream.
Then our mouth was filled with laughter,
    and our tongue with shouts of joy. (Psalm 126:1, 2a)

Some of that laughter came from wedding receptions. Make the wedding gown! Send out the invitations! Bake the wedding cake! Propose a toast! Grace will triumph over judgment for the people of God.

Another leading indicator of shalom is *thanksgiving*. A society in which people interrupt their regular routine to give thanks to God is a good society. The Puritans taught, "Nothing is more to the praise and honour of a people than to have God praised and honoured among them."[3]

Sadly, when the Israelites were carried off to Babylon, they could no longer give thanks to God in Jerusalem. But God promised that thanksgiving celebrations would be reestablished at his temple. Once again the people of God would take the words of Psalm 136 on their lips. The citizens of Jerusalem would hear "The voices of those who sing, as they bring thank offerings to the house of the LORD: 'Give thanks to the LORD of hosts, for the LORD is good, for his steadfast love endures forever!'" (33:11b).

To understand the joy of these words, imagine being taken as a hostage. Or imagine your whole congregation being captured as slaves and forced to march to a faraway country. Imagine how you would long to go back to your home church to worship God. Then imagine regaining your freedom, returning from captivity, and going back home. Imagine rejoining God's people to sing "A Mighty Fortress Is Our God" or some other great hymn. How great your joy would be!

That is what it was like for the people of God in the Old Testament. Jeremiah prophesied that someday they would go back to the temple in Jerusalem and sing praise to God. And so they did. Ezra the scribe records how this specific prophecy was fulfilled when the children of Israel returned from exile:

> And when the builders laid the foundation of the temple of the LORD, the priests in their vestments came forward with trumpets, and the Levites, the sons of Asaph, with cymbals, to praise the LORD, according to the directions of David king of Israel. And they sang responsively, praising and giving thanks to the LORD,
>
> > "For he is good,
> > for his steadfast love endures forever toward Israel."
>
> And all the people shouted with a great shout when they praised the LORD, because the foundation of the house of the LORD was laid. (Ezra 3:10, 11)

The people of God returned to the same city to sing the same song to the same God in the same temple. Their fortunes were restored as they were before. Once again they gathered for services of public thanksgiving.

A third leading shalomic indicator is *farming*. Agriculture only works in a stable society, when a farmer knows that he will be living in the same place when the harvest comes. Warfare and captivity make farming impossible. When ancient armies invaded a land, the first thing they did was destroy the crops and livestock. It is impossible to defend your land and farm it at the same time. So when the Babylonians attacked, Israel became desolate, bereft of beasts as well as men.

But God had good news for farmers. He promised to restore the fortunes of the land:

> Thus says the LORD of hosts: In this place that is waste, without man or beast, and in all of its cities, there shall again be habitations of shepherds resting their flocks. In the cities of the hill country, in the cities of the Shephelah, and in the cities of the Negeb, in the land of Benjamin, the places about Jerusalem, and in the cities of Judah, flocks shall again pass under the hands of the one who counts them, says the LORD. (33:12, 13)

When sheep may safely graze, it is a sure sign of peace. The soldiers would become shepherds once again. They would watch their flocks by night. They would count the noses of their sheep passing into the sheepfold.

These are wonderful promises! "Behold, the days are coming, declares the LORD, when I will fulfill the promise I made to the house of Israel and the house of Judah" (v. 14). God would restore the fortunes of Israel. Weddings, thanksgiving, farming—these were unmistakable signs of a land at peace. When young men and maidens plan a wedding, when believers meet in the Lord's house to give thanks, and when shepherds watch their flocks by night, the whole land has been healed.

A Royal Promise

Peace in Israel was only the beginning. The most wonderful promise God made is that he would send his people a good King:

> In those days and at that time I will cause a righteous Branch to spring up for David, and he shall execute justice and righteousness in the land. In those days Judah will be saved, and Jerusalem will dwell securely. (vv. 15, 16a)

The King would be a branch off the old tree. He would come from the house and line of David to bring salvation to the people of God.

But when would this King come? The promise provided a clue: "In those days and at that time" (v. 15a). In what days? At what time? In the days and at the time Jeremiah had just described. The King would come when peace (shalom) had been restored to Israel. He would come when the sounds of the bride and bridegroom could be heard in the streets of Jerusalem. He would come when songs of thanksgiving were sung in the temple. The Messiah would not come at a moment of desperate crisis. He would come when peace had returned to Israel.

This promise is often missed in the genealogy of Jesus Christ. The Gospel of Matthew lists the names of all the grandfathers and great-great-grandfathers of Jesus Christ (Matthew 1:1–16). Then Matthew provides a short summary: "So all the generations from Abraham to David were fourteen generations, and from David to the deportation to Babylon fourteen generations, and from the deportation to Babylon to the Christ fourteen generations" (v. 17). The story of the first fourteen generations (between Abraham and David) is familiar. The Bible recounts the lives of men like Isaac, Jacob, Judah, and Boaz. The second fourteen generations (between David and the exile) are nearly as well known (Solomon, Hezekiah, Josiah, and others).

But scarcely anything is known about the men between the exile and Jesus Christ. Abiud? Akim? Matthan? Who were these guys? Yet all these generations were necessary for the coming of the King. The last fourteen generations were as important as the first twenty-eight. Each generation was necessary for the Christ to come in the fullness of time.

God promised to send the King when generations had restored peace to Israel. He promised to send the King when, for example, shepherds were abiding in the fields, keeping watch over their flocks by night. Why the shepherds? This is why! To show God's people that the time for the Messiah had come. "In those days and at that time I will cause a righteous Branch to spring up for David" (33:15). The Messiah would come when there were "habitations of shepherds resting their flocks" (v. 12). The Messiah would come when sheep would "again pass under the hands of the one who counts them" in "The cities of the hill country . . . [and] the places about Jerusalem, and in the cities of Judah" (v. 13).

The Christmas story in the Gospel of Luke fulfills these promises. A couple of newlyweds went up from Nazareth to a little town in Judea and gave birth to a son. Yes! Of course! They went to the hill country, to a village around Jerusalem, to one of the towns of Judah. "And in the same region there were shepherds out in the field, keeping watch over their flock by night" (Luke 2:8). Exactly! Just as Jeremiah had promised! The King came when there were shepherds in the hills giving rest to their sheep.

The announcement of the birth of Jesus Christ to *shepherds* was as necessary as his birth in the town of Bethlehem, or his belonging to the house and line of David, or his being born of a virgin. It was necessary because the Holy Spirit promised that the Messiah would come in a day of weddings, thanksgiving, and farming. The King would come when shepherds had peace enough to count the noses of their sheep. What better proof that Jesus is the Christ than a chorus of angels appearing by night to shepherds in the hill country of Judea? *Those* were the days, *that* was the time for the King to come.

Just as Advertised

What difference does Jeremiah's teaching about the shepherds make? First, it proves that Jesus is the Christ. The birth, death, and resurrection of Jesus Christ were a total fulfillment of the promises of the Old Testament. Down to the least detail, Jesus is the King whom God promised to send. The identity of Jesus Christ does not rest on one or two isolated passages, but on a host of prophecies from the Old Testament. The Old Testament is full of teaching about the person and work of Jesus Christ.

If you do not yet believe in Jesus, then examine what the Bible says about him. The Bible is the oldest and most reliable of religious documents. It records the spiritual wisdom of the oldest peoples of the world. It offers many convincing proofs that Jesus Christ is the Savior of the world. His birth, death, and resurrection were predicted long centuries before he walked on this earth.

He was born exactly the way the prophets always said he would be born, including the virgin birth and all the rest of it (see Isaiah 7:14; Matthew 1:23). Who except God himself could predict something centuries in advance and then make it come to pass? As you read the Bible, you will hear the voice of God himself speaking to your heart that Jesus is the Savior he promised to send.

Second, the shepherd promise in Jeremiah 33 assures us that Jesus is exactly the *kind* of king God promised to send. He came just as advertised. If this one promise about shepherds is true, then all the rest of Jeremiah's promises about his kingship must be true as well.

Jeremiah said the coming king would be a *rightful* king. God promised to "cause a righteous Branch to spring up for David" (33:15a). That promise came true. Jesus Christ was no usurper; he was David's rightful heir. He fulfilled the covenant God made with David—namely, that one of his sons would rule forever on the throne of Israel.

Jeremiah said the coming King would be a *just* king: "He shall execute justice and righteousness in the land" (v. 15b). That promise came true as well. Jesus Christ is a just king. He is "righteous in enacting laws, waging wars, and giving judgment, righteous in vindicating those that suffer wrong and punishing those that do wrong."[4]

Jeremiah said the coming king would be a victorious king: "In those days Judah will be saved, and Jerusalem will dwell securely" (v. 16a). This promise came true as well. Jesus Christ has conquered all the enemies of God. He reigns supreme over sin, death, and the devil. His kingship is a saving kingship, for he has come to save his people from their sins. He brings peace and safety to the people of God, protecting them from eternal judgment and the wrath of God.

If any of these promises sound familiar, it is because they were made back in 23:5, 6, where the prophet first played the Messiah's song. There is one difference, however. This time the prophecy states that "*Jerusalem* will dwell securely" (33:16a). Back in chapter 23, *Israel* was to live in safety (23:6). The promise for the nation is thus applied to the city. The coming of the Messiah is good news for the city. Jeremiah's promises about the coming Messiah were *urban* promises, for God has planned to build an eternal city for his people.

Finally, Jeremiah said the coming king would be a *righteous* king. His name would be "The LORD is our righteousness." But that name would also be given to the entire city: "And this is the name by which it will be called: 'The LORD is our righteousness'" (v. 16b). "It" refers to Jerusalem, the city of God. God's city would be as righteous as its King. Hence also the use of the possessive pronoun "our" in the name of the city: It is called "The LORD is *our* righteousness." The righteous name of the righteous King belongs to everyone who lives in the righteous city.

This promise, too, has been fulfilled in Jesus Christ. Jesus is the answer to the greatest problem of the human race—sin. Sinners do not have a righteousness of their own to protect them from the wrath and curse of God. But Jesus Christ is the King who gives his righteousness to his people. If you know Christ in a personal way, then "you are in Christ Jesus, who became to us wisdom from God, [our] righteousness" (1 Corinthians 1:30). The righteousness of Christ belongs to the Christian. *His* righteousness becomes *our* righteousness.

This is the "good news of great joy that will be for all the people" (Luke 2:10). When the shepherds ran from the hill country of Judea to Bethlehem to gaze upon the face of the baby Jesus, they went to worship the Lord, our righteousness. The coming of the righteous King was good news for the shepherds. It is also good news for you, but it had to come to the shepherds first.

> Glory to God in the highest,
> and on earth peace among those with whom he is pleased! (Luke 2:14)

48

God Never Fails

JEREMIAH 33:17-26

THE DEATH OF A KING is always reason for concern. In the C. S. Lewis novel *Till We Have Faces*, the King of Glome lies on his death bed.[1] The king has had an accident and is no longer capable of ruling his kingdom. Soon he will die. In the meantime, his advisors and his offspring huddle together by firelight in the passageways, worrying about the fate of their kingdom. An enemy army has just ridden across their borders. What is to be done? If the king is dying, who will save the kingdom?

The death of a king endangers his kingdom. This can be illustrated from the history of Israel. Under Solomon, Israel became a great and powerful kingdom. But when Solomon died, the northern tribes rebelled. The kingdom was divided between Rehoboam and Jeroboam, never to regain its former splendor (1 Kings 12).

The same thing happened to the Alexandrian Empire. At the height of his powers, Alexander the Great (356–323 BC) reigned supreme in the ancient Near East. He ruled provinces stretching from the Ionian Sea to northern India. Alexander was establishing a new capital in the city of Babylon when he contracted malaria and died. Four of his generals assumed command, but they started squabbling, and the empire was divided among them. The death of a king threatens to destroy his kingdom.

King of the Ages

According to Jeremiah, the kingdom of God will never face such a danger. Already he had made many bold promises about God's kingdom. The coming King would be David's rightful heir. He would do what was right and just. He would bring peace and safety to God's people.

To those earlier prophecies, Jeremiah added the promise of an unbroken kingship. "For thus says the LORD: David shall never lack a man to sit on the throne of the house of Israel" (33:17). The kingdom of David would continue in perpetuity. His dynasty would never end. The kingship would pass peacefully from one king to the next, until a king came to rule forever and forever.

The Lord first made this promise to David himself, through the prophet Nathan: "The LORD declares to you that the LORD will make you a house. . . . And your house and your kingdom shall be made sure forever before me. Your throne shall be established forever" (2 Samuel 7:11b, 16). The promise was reiterated by the psalmist:

> The LORD swore to David a sure oath
>   from which he will not turn back:
> "One of the sons of your body
>   I will set on your throne . . .
> their sons also forever
>   shall sit on your throne." (Psalm 132:11, 12)

The prophet Isaiah took the same promise and applied it to the coming Messiah:

> For to us a child is born,
>   to us a son is given;
> and the government shall be upon his shoulder. . . .
> Of the increase of his government and of peace
>   there will be no end,
> on the throne of David and over his kingdom . . .
>   from this time forth and forevermore. (Isaiah 9:6a, 7a)

Throughout the Old Testament, God promised to send a King whose kingdom would never, ever fail.

If the kingdom of David ever seemed in jeopardy, it was during the days of Jeremiah. The kingdom was in decline. By this point in Jeremiah's ministry only a few cities were still holding out against the Babylonians—Jerusalem, Lachish, and Azekah. "These were the only fortified cities of Judah that remained" (34:7b). The counselors huddled in the passageways. What would become of the king? What would happen to the kingdom?

The Lord told Jeremiah exactly what would happen: "Go and speak to Zedekiah king of Judah and say to him, 'Thus says the LORD: Behold, I am giving this city into the hand of the king of Babylon, and he shall burn it with fire. You shall not escape from his hand but shall surely be captured and delivered into his hand'" (34:2b, 3a). Not long afterward, Zedekiah's sons were slaughtered before his very eyes. Then his eyes were gouged out, and he was taken to Babylon in bronze shackles (39:6, 7). But how could God keep his promise of an everlasting kingdom if such terrible things were to happen to Zedekiah, son of Josiah, son of David?

The word on the street was that God had failed. So God called Jeremiah into his office for a conference. "The word of the LORD came to Jeremiah: 'Have you not observed that these people are saying, "The LORD has rejected the two clans that he chose"? Thus they have despised my people so that they are no longer a nation in their sight'" (33:23, 24). The people of Israel were saying that God had failed. They allowed their troubles to cast doubt on God's promises.

Do you ever think God has failed you? Do the troubles of life ever seem to cast doubt on God's promises?

The message of Jeremiah is that God *never* fails. David failed, and the sons of David may fail, but God himself never fails. Even Zedekiah would eventually learn that God never fails. Although he would be tortured, he would die in peace. The people of God would build a funeral pyre in his honor (34:4, 5). For the sake of his people and for the sake of his Son, God's promise to David did not and cannot fail.

The fact that God never fails explains the significance of the ending of Jeremiah's book. This is one time it is good to peek at the ending of the book before we get there. The last chapter of Jeremiah closes with this report on Jehoiachin, son of David, king of Judah:

> Evil-merodach king of Babylon, in the year that he began to reign, graciously freed Jehoiachin king of Judah and brought him out of prison. And he spoke kindly to him and gave him a seat above the seats of the kings who were with him in Babylon. So Jehoiachin put off his prison garments. And every day of his life he dined regularly at the king's table. (52:31–33)

This little epilogue is not quite "happily ever after," but it comes close. It shows that God never forgot his promise to David. Even though God's people were in captivity, David's rightful heir was alive and well. He was still known as the "king of Judah" (52:31), and he was flourishing in the courts of Babylon.

Thus the ending of the book of Jeremiah begs us to stay tuned to the history of redemption. Even when the kingdom of God seemed to be hanging by the barest thread of a promise, it was still hanging. Jeremiah's book thus demands a sequel. That sequel is the book of Matthew, where we read the name of this Jehoiachin—also known as Jeconiah—in the genealogy of Jesus Christ (Matthew 1:11, 12). Generation after generation, God preserved the succession of the kings of Israel. His promise to David did not fail.

In the fullness of time, Jesus Christ was born as a king. When the Magi came from the east to Jerusalem they asked, "Where is he who has been born king of the Jews?" (Matthew 2:2). The Magi came to the Christ in Bethlehem to offer worship and gifts suitable for a king—gold, frankincense, and myrrh (Matthew 2:11).

Jesus Christ suffered as a king. When the soldiers mocked him, they placed a crown of thorns on his head, draped a purple robe over his body, and shouted, "Hail, King of the Jews!" (John 19:2, 3). The soldiers spoke mockingly but truthfully; Jesus *is* the King of the Jews.

Then Jesus died as a king. Pontius Pilate had a notice made and nailed to the cross. It read: "Jesus of Nazareth, the King of the Jews" (John 19:19). That notice was so noteworthy that it was written in three languages and recorded in all four Gospels. In his Gospel, John wrote about the consternation Pilate's placard caused among the leaders of Jerusalem. "So the chief priests of the Jews said to Pilate, 'Do not write, "The King of the Jews," but rather, "This man said, I am King of the Jews"'" (John 19:21). But the chief priests could not obstruct the message of the Holy Spirit. What was written was written. And what the sign said was the gospel truth: Jesus is the King of the Jews.

To this very day Jesus sits on the throne of David, just as Jeremiah promised. He was raised a king to rule over the house of David forever. When the saints gather with the angels in glory, they sing praises to Jesus the risen King:

> Great and amazing are your deeds,
>   O Lord God the Almighty!
> Just and true are your ways,
>   O King of the nations! (Revelation 15:3: cf. 17:14; 19:16)

Jesus Christ is the King of the ages. He reigns and reigns and keeps on reigning. Thus the promise God made to David has been fulfilled in Jesus Christ: "David shall never lack a man to sit on the throne of the house of Israel" (33:17). The kingdom of Jesus Christ is no temporary monarchy. There will never be an interregnum in the kingdom of God. It is an eternal dynasty. Our King will never lie on his deathbed. We will never meet in the passageways by firelight to discuss the future of our kingdom. The kingly rule of Jesus Christ will never fail.

Do you believe this, or do you sometimes suspect that God has failed you? The troubles of life tempt us to believe that God fails. We experience some sudden loss. We are struck by some pang of grief. We pray, but our prayer remains unanswered. We think we know just how God is working things out for us, but then our situation changes and everything is up for grabs again. We are often tempted to think that God has failed us.

But God never fails. His rule over the events of life never fails. He is working out all things for his glory and for the good of those who love him (Romans 8:28). The kingdom of Jesus Christ is a fail-safe kingdom. Now that he has ascended his kingly throne, the King of the ages will reign supreme forever.

A Priest Forever

There is something else Jesus will do forever. Jeremiah's promise was a double promise, two for the price of one. He went on to say: "The Levitical priests shall never lack a man in my presence to offer burnt offerings, to burn grain offerings, and to make sacrifices forever" (v. 18). In other words, the Messiah's eternal kingship would be matched by his permanent priesthood.

The death of a priest can be nearly as devastating for a kingdom as the death of a king. If there is no priest to offer sacrifices, who will atone for the sins of the people?

During the Middle Ages, the popes in Rome sometimes took advantage of this fear. Whenever a pope had political difficulties with a king, he would threaten to place his entire kingdom under an "interdict." A papal interdict would ban all sacraments offered in that kingdom. Priests were not allowed to atone for the sins of their people in the sacrifice of the Mass. This was a national disaster. According to the theology of the day—which was false—a kingdom under interdiction was cut off from the grace of God.

Although no human being—let alone the pope—has the power to ban the means of grace, we can sympathize with the fears of people in medieval times. As far as they understood, a papal interdict cut them off from the grace of God. There was no one to offer a sacrifice for their sins or save them from the wrath of God.

This is the great problem with contemporary Judaism. Jews who do not accept Jesus of Nazareth as their Messiah have no one to atone for their sins. The temple in Jerusalem was destroyed in 70 AD and has not been rebuilt. No priests offer burnt offerings for the Jews. No Levites stand before God to make atonement for them. Unless Jesus is the Messiah, therefore, the promise of a permanent priesthood has failed.

The same may be said of the promise of an eternal King, since no descendant of David presently rules over the house of Israel. If Christ is not the King, there is no king of the Jews. If Christ is not the Priest, there is no priest for the Jews. So if Jesus is not the Messiah, the promises of God have failed.

Yet thanks be to God, the promises of God have *not* failed, either for Jews or Gentiles. It is striking that both of Jeremiah's promises were to be fulfilled in a *man*. In both promises (vv. 17, 18), the eternal King, the permanent Priest, is called "a man." This gives a hint of the incarnation of the Son of God. God promised that the King who would sit on David's throne and the Priest who would stand before his own throne was to be a human being.

Jesus Christ is that human being. He is man as well as God. He is Priest as well as King. In the one man Jesus Christ, both of Jeremiah's promises have been fulfilled. Jesus is both eternal King and permanent Priest for every Jew or Gentile who trusts in him.

The priesthood of Jesus Christ is most clearly explained in the book of Hebrews, where Jesus is portrayed as the perfect High Priest for God's people. His priesthood is superior in every way, but especially because he is "a priest forever, after the order of Melchizedek" (Hebrews 5:6). Incidentally, contrary to what some have said, the fact that Jesus is a priest in the order of Melchizedek rather than Levi is not a problem for Jeremiah's prophecy (see Hebrews 7:11). Jeremiah did not promise a priest *from* the Levites but a priest *for* the Levites (33:18).

Hebrews reaches its climax when it compares Jesus Christ to the rest of the priests of Israel: "The former priests were many in number, because they were prevented by death from continuing in office, but he holds his priesthood permanently, because he continues forever. Consequently, he is able to save to the uttermost those who draw near to God through him, since he always lives to make intercession for them" (Hebrews 7:23–25). The priesthood of Jesus Christ is no temporary priesthood. Therefore, Jesus can be trusted to provide salvation from sin. Jesus offered one sacrifice for sins on the cross. To this very day, he stands before the throne of his Father in Heaven, praying for all the sins of his people to be forgiven. His atonement and his intercession never fail; so our salvation never fails.

As a pastor, I am often approached by people with doubts about their salvation. "I am a very great sinner," they say. "No one has ever sinned the way I have sinned. After all the grace God has shown to me, I have turned my back on him. Is there any hope for me? Will God ever take me back? How can I be sure that I have not lost my salvation?"

The answer to all our doubts about salvation is that God never fails. Yes, we are very great sinners. True, no one has ever sinned quite the way we have sinned. And it cannot be denied that we fail. But our salvation depends upon

God—not upon us!—and God never fails. And because God never fails, we will "never lack a man in [God's] presence to offer . . . sacrifices" (33:18). That man, Jesus Christ, "is able to save to the uttermost those who draw near to God through him, since he always lives to make intercession for them" (Hebrews 7:25).

There is one more dimension to God's promises about kingship and priesthood. Through the prophet Jeremiah, God said, "As the host of heaven cannot be numbered and the sands of the sea cannot be measured, so I will multiply the offspring of David my servant, and the Levitical priests who minister to me" (33:22). This promise, which was an echo of the promise God made to Abraham long before (Genesis 15:5; 22:17), has now been fulfilled in the Church of Jesus Christ. Those who trust in Christ for salvation are the sons and daughters of Abraham. They are as countless as the stars in the sky and the sand on the seashore.

What is new in Jeremiah is the mention of the kingship and priesthood of all believers. To say that Christians are descendants of David is to say that they are like kings and queens in the kingdom of God. Every believer is a king or a queen, for someday every believer will rule with Christ over the universe (2 Timothy 2:12).

To speak of Christians as the descendants of Levi is to say that they are like priests in the temple of God. Every believer is a priest, for every believer shares the grace of God with others. Christians have been given these commands: "Let the word of Christ dwell in you richly, teaching and admonishing one another in all wisdom" (Colossians 3:16a). "[Address] one another in psalms and hymns and spiritual songs" (Ephesians 5:19a). In this way we minister to one another as God's priests.

Some Collateral!

If any proof is required for the eternal kingship and permanent priesthood of Christ, see what God put up as collateral:

> The word of the LORD came to Jeremiah: "Thus says the LORD: If you can break my covenant with the day and my covenant with the night, so that day and night will not come at their appointed time, then also my covenant with David my servant may be broken, so that he shall not have a son to reign on his throne, and my covenant with the Levitical priests my ministers." (33:19–21)

Some collateral! God placed the sun and the moon on the bargaining table. He offered the heavenly bodies as a security deposit for his covenant promise.

If God ever fails to provide an eternal King or a permanent priest, then the sun and the moon will be yours to keep!

This audacious bargain means that God's promise will never, ever fail. One could no more halt the glorious rule of Jesus Christ or diminish the efficacy of his atonement than one could stand on the eastern seaboard and forbid the sun to rise over the Atlantic Ocean. The very idea of God breaking his covenant with the day and the night is absurd, and so is the idea that he could break his covenant with David and Levi.

When people want to say that something will never happen, they sometimes say, "It will be a cold day in hell before that ever happens." That is not a phrase for Christians to use because it contains a hint of blasphemy. But the Christian can say this about the promises of God in Christ: "The sun will stop shining before Jesus stops reigning." God would have to un-God himself to bring the eternal kingship and permanent priesthood of Jesus to an end.

Science and Salvation

It should be noted, if only in passing, that these verses form part of the foundation for the modern study of science. They assert that the regularity of day and night is not the product of evolutionary chance. Rather, God has established a covenant with the sun and the moon. "Thus says the LORD: If I have not established my covenant with day and night and the fixed order of heaven and earth . . .'" (v. 25). This principle is not just for astronomy—it is for all the disciplines of science, for everything from astronomy to zoology.

The study of science depends upon the fixed laws of heaven and earth. If the natural world did not follow orderly patterns, scientific measurements would be unreliable and scientific investigation would be impossible. Science depends upon the fixed laws of heaven and earth, which in turn depend upon the will of God. This is why Christians were at the forefront of the development of the scientific method. They understood that the faithfulness of God is what makes science possible. Since knowledge of the created world is one part of the knowledge of God, Christianity has always led to the flourishing of the sciences.

Melvin Calvin, the Nobel Prize-winning biochemist, once tried to identify the basis for modern science. Recognizing that scientific investigation depends upon a belief in the regularity of nature, he wrote:

> As I try to discern the origin of that conviction, I seem to find it in a basic notion discovered 2000 or 3000 years ago, and enunciated first in the Western world by the ancient Hebrews: namely, that the universe is governed

by a single God, and is not the product of the whims of many gods, each governing his own province according to his own laws. This monotheistic view seems to be the historical foundation for modern science.[2]

A good example of the way science depends upon the fixed laws of nature comes from the work of the astronomer Johannes Kepler (1571–1630). Kepler found that there was a discrepancy of eight minutes between his calculations and his observations of the orbit of the planet Mars. Although the discrepancy was small, Kepler wrestled for years to resolve it because it seemed to deny that the laws of the heavens were fixed.

Kepler was such a devout Christian that he refused to abandon his belief in the regularity of nature. His dilemma was eventually resolved by his breakthrough discovery that the orbit of Mars was an ellipse rather than a circle. He later spoke of the eight-minute discrepancy that gave him his clue as a "gift of God."[3] The fixed laws of nature were part of God's gift to Kepler, for without them he never could have made his discovery.

Take any of the settled principles of science, like Boyle's law or Heisenberg's uncertainty principle or Planck's constant. These are among the fixed laws of heaven and earth that were established by divine covenant. Our understanding of these laws may change over time. Some universal laws that once seemed settled—such as the principles of Newtonian Physics—have been qualified by further research. But the laws themselves are fixed. The laws of heaven and earth always have been fixed, and they always will be. The only thing that is bound to change is our limited understanding of them.

The development of "Chaos Theory" at the end of the twentieth century provides an excellent example of the fixity of the laws of heaven and earth. Chaos Theory is sometimes misunderstood to teach that nature is ultimately unpredictable. In fact, it teaches nearly the opposite. It demonstrates how events in nature that seem chaotic actually follow an orderly pattern. In the prologue of his best-selling book *Chaos*, James Gleick observed:

> Now that science is looking, chaos seems to be everywhere. A rising column of cigarette smoke breaks into wild swirls. A flag snaps back and forth in the wind. A dripping faucet goes from a steady pattern to a random one. Chaos appears in the behavior of the weather, the behavior of an airplane in flight, the behavior of cars clustering on an expressway, the behavior of oil flowing in underground pipes. [But] no matter what the medium, the behavior obeys the same newly discovered laws.[4]

Gleick's last sentence is striking: Wherever you find them, chaotic events "obey the same newly discovered laws." The dimensions of nature that seem lawless actually behave lawfully. Even chaos obeys the fixed laws of nature!

New Every Morning

I mention these things in passing because Jeremiah was not trying to establish a foundation for modern science. He already knew that the "order of heaven and earth" were "fixed" by the decree of God. His point was that God's covenant with his people is just as certain as his covenant with heaven and earth.

The possibility of science thus reminds us of the certainty of salvation.

> Thus says the LORD: If I have not established my covenant with day and night and the fixed order of heaven and earth, then I will reject the offspring of Jacob and David my servant and will not choose one of his offspring to rule over the offspring of Abraham, Isaac, and Jacob. For I will restore their fortunes and will have mercy on them. (vv. 25, 26)

God has promised to restore the fortunes of his people. He has guaranteed that his Messiah will rule forever and ever, presenting his sacrifice as the once-for-all payment for their sins.

If you ever doubt whether or not these promises are true, all you need to do is look out the window. Every bright day and every dark night gives further proof of the eternal kingdom and permanent priesthood of Jesus Christ. Sunrise and sunset alike are reminders that God never fails.

Jeremiah looked for a reminder of God's never-failing love every day. He endured such great suffering that he sometimes doubted the rule and mercy of God. But he had heard that God's covenant with his people would last as long as his covenant with the sun and moon. So he looked for the proof of God's promise with the dawn of every new day. This was his testimony:

> The steadfast love of the LORD never ceases;
>   his mercies never come to an end;
> they are new every morning;
>   great is your faithfulness. (Lamentations 3:22, 23)

God's compassion never fails because God never fails.

49

The Emancipation Revocation

JEREMIAH 34:1-22

> On the first day of January, in the year of our Lord one thousand eight hundred and sixty-three, all persons held as slaves within any State, or designated part of a State . . . shall be then, thenceforward, and forever free. . . . And upon this act, sincerely believed to be an act of justice, warranted by the Constitution upon military necessity, I invoke the considerate judgment of mankind and the gracious favor of Almighty God.

Thus states the Emancipation Proclamation, the legal document that announced liberty for the African slaves of the United States. Its pronouncement by President Abraham Lincoln was one of the greatest moments in American history.

Another Emancipation Proclamation

There was a similar moment in the history of Judah. Under the leadership of King Zedekiah, the leaders of Jerusalem proclaimed freedom for the captives: "The word that came to Jeremiah from the LORD, after King Zedekiah had made a covenant with all the people in Jerusalem to make a proclamation of liberty to them, that everyone should set free his Hebrew slaves, male and female, so that no one should enslave a Jew, his brother" (34:8, 9).

The citizens not only freed their slaves, but they also canceled their debts and bound themselves by covenant before God to keep them "Then, thenceforward, and forever free." So all the officials and people who entered into this covenant agreed that they would free their male and female slaves and no longer hold them in bondage. "They obeyed and set them free" (v. 10).

The Bible does not explain why Zedekiah made his emancipation proclamation. At the time "Nebuchadnezzar king of Babylon and all his army and all the kingdoms of the earth under his dominion and all the peoples were fighting against Jerusalem and all of its cities" (v. 1). The strength of the Babylonian assault is indicated by the repetition of the word all: "*all* his army and *all* the kingdoms . . . against . . . *all* of its cities." At the end, only Jerusalem and two other garrisons were still holding out. "Then Jeremiah the prophet spoke all these words to Zedekiah king of Judah, in Jerusalem, when the army of the king of Babylon was fighting against Jerusalem and against all the cities of Judah that were left, Lachish and Azekah, for these were the only fortified cities of Judah that remained" (vv. 6, 7).

The terror of the Babylonian attack is captured in

> . . . the Lachish Letters, twenty-one in all, written on pieces of broken pottery which were found in a room filled with ashes from the fire that destroyed the city in 587 BC. They represent urgent messages from military commanders in outposts to the garrison commander at Lachish. Letter IV in particular contains the words, "And let my lord know that we are watching for the signals of Lachish according to all the indications which my lord has given, for we cannot see Azekah."[1]

This siege may explain why Zedekiah granted manumission to the slaves. Perhaps there was too little food to feed the slaves anyway. Perhaps he was trying to placate them so they would help their masters defend the city.[2]

Or perhaps Zedekiah freed the slaves in a last-ditch effort to appease God before the Babylonians sacked Jerusalem. The prophet Jeremiah had just given him a most unpleasant message.

> Thus says the LORD, the God of Israel: Go and speak to Zedekiah king of Judah and say to him, "Thus says the LORD: Behold, I am giving this city into the hand of the king of Babylon, and he shall burn it with fire. You shall not escape from his hand but shall surely be captured and delivered into his hand. You shall see the king of Babylon eye to eye and speak with him face to face. And you shall go to Babylon." (vv. 2, 3)

These threats were followed by the promise of a peaceful and honorable death:

> Yet hear the word of the Lord, O Zedekiah king of Judah! Thus says the LORD concerning you: "You shall not die by the sword. You shall die in peace. And as spices were burned for your fathers, the former kings who were before you, so people shall burn spices for you and lament for you, saying, 'Alas, lord!'" For I have spoken the word, declares the LORD. (vv. 4, 5)

This promise offered little comfort, and Zedekiah may have tried to avoid death altogether by freeing all the slaves.

Whatever his personal or political motivations may have been, emancipation was the best proclamation Zedekiah ever made. Slavery, as it was practiced among the people of God in those days, was scandalous. It was a violation of God's Law: "When you buy a Hebrew slave, he shall serve six years, and in the seventh he shall go out free, for nothing" (Exodus 21:2; cf. Deuteronomy 15:12). The same proclamation was made in Leviticus:

> If your brother becomes poor beside you and sells himself to you, you shall not make him serve as a slave: he shall be with you as a hired worker and as a sojourner. He shall serve with you until the year of the jubilee. Then he shall go out from you, he and his children with him, and go back to his own clan and return to the possession of his fathers. For they are my servants, whom I brought out of the land of Egypt; they shall not be sold as slaves. (25:39–42)

The Sabbath Year and the Jubilee Year granted freedom to the captives. Because the people belonged to God, they could not be sold to one another.

Remarkably, after centuries of not paying any attention to these laws, God's people finally listened, repented, and proclaimed freedom to their countrymen. They followed this divine command: "At the end of seven years each of you must set free the fellow Hebrew who has been sold to you and has served you six years; you must set him free from your service" (34:14a). They obeyed the text of Leviticus 25:10 that is inscribed on Philadelphia's most famous landmark: "Proclaim liberty throughout the land to all the inhabitants."

This is "The Gospel According to the Liberty Bell." Wherever it has been sounded, it has brought freedom for the oppressed and liberty for the captives. It brought liberty in the days of Zedekiah when the people agreed to free their slaves. It brought liberty when William Penn enacted his Charter of Liberties for the Commonwealth of Pennsylvania (1701). In fact, the reason Leviticus 25:10 was inscribed on the Liberty Bell was because the bell was cast on the fiftieth anniversary of Penn's Charter (1751). It was meant to remind people of the Levitical practice of freeing the captives in the Jubilee Year.

"The Gospel According to the Liberty Bell" also brought freedom in the days of Abraham Lincoln, when the Liberty Bell became a national symbol for the movement to abolish slavery. There was great joy when the slaves were emancipated in the United States. In the words of the black abolitionist Frederick Douglass (1818–1895), "We shout for joy that we live to record this righteous decree."[3]

Booker T. Washington (1856–1915) recounted the happy scene on the West Virginia plantation where he was raised:

> Finally the war closed, and the day of freedom came. It was a momentous and eventful day to all upon our plantation. We had been expecting it. Freedom was in the air, and it had been for months. . . . There was little, if any, sleep that night. All was excitement and expectancy. Early the next morning word was sent to all the slaves, old and young, to gather at the house. . . . The most distinct thing that I now recall in connection with the scene was that some man who seemed to be a stranger (a United States officer, I presume) made a little speech and then read a rather long paper—the Emancipation Proclamation, I think. After the reading we were told that we were all free, and could go when and where we pleased. My mother, who was standing by my side, leaned over and kissed her children, while tears of joy ran down her cheeks. She explained to us what it all meant, that this was the day for which she had been so long praying, but fearing that she would never live to see.[4]

It must have been the same way in Jerusalem when Zedekiah freed the slaves—mothers kissing their children, with tears of joy running down their cheeks. A day of emancipation is a day of celebration, not only for slaves, but also for their former masters. God exalts the nation that renounces injustice.

Emancipation Revocation

But then the leaders of Jerusalem changed their minds. They went back on their word. They announced the revocation of the proclamation of emancipation. "But afterward they turned around and took back the male and female slaves they had set free, and brought them into subjection as slaves" (34:11). Therefore, God made this accusation against them: "But then you turned around and profaned my name when each of you took back his male and female slaves, whom you had set free according to their desire, and you brought them into subjection to be your slaves" (v. 16).

Freedom turned out to be short lived. The leaders made a treaty, and then they violated it. They made a deal, and then they reneged on it. They established a covenant, and then they broke it. There had been no genuine repentance, so there was no permanent release. Unconditional release was followed by unexpected recapture.

It could be argued that much the same thing happened at the end of the Civil War. The Emancipation Proclamation held out the promise of real freedom. But it took a long time for that promise to even begin to be fulfilled. Slavery gave way to lynching. Lynching gave way to Jim Crow laws. Jim Crow laws gave way to segregation. Segregation gave way to prejudice. Americans can thank God for the great progress the United States has made toward racial reconciliation, but prejudice persists to the present day. Zedekiah's emancipation revocation teaches what a wicked thing it is to go back on the promise of freedom.

Like many immoral decisions, Zedekiah's emancipation revocation was politically motivated. The end of Jeremiah 34 offers a clue to what changed the king's mind. God said:

> And Zedekiah king of Judah and his officials I will give into the hand of their enemies and into the hand of those who seek their lives, into the hand of the army of the king of Babylon which has withdrawn from you. Behold, I will command, declares the LORD, and will bring them back to this city. And they will fight against it and take it and burn it with fire. I will make the cities of Judah a desolation without inhabitant. (vv. 21, 22)

Another clue to Zedekiah's policy reversal appears a few chapters later: "The army of Pharaoh had come out of Egypt. And when the Chaldeans who were besieging Jerusalem heard news about them, they withdrew from Jerusalem" (37:5).

This is what must have happened: Zedekiah freed the slaves when it seemed like Jerusalem was doomed. But then the Egyptians showed up to help in the summer of 588 BC. The Egyptians posed enough of a threat to give the Israelites respite from the Babylonian siege. Thus "The emancipation was revoked, the new covenant was forgotten, and the slaves reclaimed (vv. 11, 16)."[5] But when the danger had passed, and the dishes started to pile up again in the kitchen, the people of Jerusalem wanted their slaves back. After a brief manumission, they went right back to the sin of slavery.

This is how many ungodly people behave in life-or-death situations. In desperation they cry out to God to save them. They pledge to give him their undying devotion if he will only deliver them this once. But when God answers their prayers, they go right back into their former way of life. How many people in the hospital are scared enough to call for a minister but not sorry enough to call for the Savior? Anyone who has ever promised to give his or her whole life to Christ must be sure to live up to that promise.

The emancipation revocation was not the first time Zedekiah had acted in bad faith. In fact, the reason Nebuchadnezzar was paying such an unfriendly visit to Jerusalem was because Zedekiah had broken his promise. The prophet Ezekiel told the whole story:

> The king of Babylon came to Jerusalem, and took her king and her princes and brought them to him to Babylon. And he took one of the royal offspring [namely, Zedekiah] and made a covenant with him, putting him under oath

(the chief men of the land he had taken away), that the kingdom might be humble and not lift itself up, and keep his covenant that it might stand. But he [Zedekiah] rebelled against him by sending his ambassadors to Egypt, that they might give him horses and a large army. Will he thrive? Can one escape who does such things? Can he break the covenant and yet escape? (Ezekiel 17:12b–15)

The answer to Ezekiel's questions, of course, was "No way!"

As I live, declares the Lord GOD, surely in the place where the king dwells who made him king, whose oath he despised, and whose covenant with him he broke, in Babylon he shall die. Pharaoh with his mighty army and great company will not help him in war, when mounds are cast up and siege walls built to cut off many lives. He despised the oath in breaking the covenant, and behold, he gave his hand and did all these things; he shall not escape. (Ezekiel 17:16–18)

Zedekiah's example teaches what a wicked thing it is to go back on one's word. When Jeremiah told Zedekiah he would see the king of Babylon with his own eyes (34:3; cf. 2 Kings 25:6, 7), he was not trying to cheer him up. The ancient Jewish historian Josephus (AD 37–100) explained how unpleasant that face-to-face meeting turned out to be: "When he was come, Nebuchadnezzar began to call him a wicked wretch, and a covenant-breaker, and one that had forgotten his former words, when he promised to keep the country for him. He also reproached him for his ingratitude." Then Nebuchadnezzar said, "God is great who hateth that conduct of thine, and hath brought thee under us."[6] Nebuchadnezzar's theology was sound. To break faith with another human being is also to break faith with God.

According to God's verdict, Zedekiah's emancipation revocation was a sin against God as well as his neighbor. God said:

But your fathers did not listen to me or incline their ears to me. You recently repented and did what was right in my eyes by proclaiming liberty, each to his neighbor, and you made a covenant before me in the house that is called by my name, but then you turned around and profaned my name when each of you took back his male and female slaves, whom you had set free according to their desire, and you brought them into subjection to be your slaves. (vv. 14b–16)

God notices whenever sinners repent. Anyone who repents—who truly repents in the name of Jesus Christ—will receive mercy. But God also notices when sinners repent of their repentance. In this case God's people had broken the third commandment (Exodus 20:7). By violating a treaty made in God's house, they had profaned God's name, adding perjury to slavery.

These two sins—perjury and slavery—are both contrary to the character of God. "The word of the LORD came to Jeremiah from the LORD: 'Thus says the LORD, the God of Israel: I myself made a covenant with your fathers when I brought them out of the land of Egypt, out of the house of slavery'" (34:12, 13). This was a reminder that God always keeps his word. How can God's people be covenant breakers when their God is a covenant keeper?

By referring to Egypt, God was also reminding his people that they used to be slaves themselves. Thus the people of Jerusalem owed their very freedom to God. They had received their liberty "from the gratuitous mercy of God, who made them free, who brought them forth from tyranny in Egypt. It hence follows, that they could not be masters over others, since they themselves were servants."[7]

Slaveholding was such a great sin that it demanded a harsh punishment. "Therefore, thus says the LORD: You have not obeyed me by proclaiming liberty, every one to his brother and to his neighbor; behold, I proclaim to you liberty to the sword, to pestilence, and to famine, declares the LORD. I will make you a horror to all the kingdoms of the earth" (v. 17). According to God, the people did not actually proclaim liberty in the first place because they did not grant liberty in the end.

If liberty is what the people wanted, however, then God would give them "liberty" all right! This was perhaps the most ironic of Jeremiah's puns. God promised to give his people freedom—freedom to suffer war, disease, and starvation. In effect he was saying, "You did not release [your neighbors from their debts], so I will release—sword, pestilence, and famine!"[8] In the words of J. Gresham Machen, "Emancipation from the blessed will of God always involves bondage to some worse taskmaster."[9]

In this case the worse taskmaster was death. The city would be burned down, the towns would be laid waste, and the slaveholders would meet a bloody end. God said:

> And the men who transgressed my covenant and did not keep the terms of the covenant that they made before me, I will make them like the calf that they cut in two and passed between its parts—the officials of Judah, the officials of Jerusalem, the eunuchs, the priests, and all the people of the land who passed between the parts of the calf. And I will give them into the hand of their enemies and into the hand of those who seek their lives. Their dead bodies shall be food for the birds of the air and the beasts of the earth. (vv. 18–20)

To understand this punishment, it helps to know that Biblical covenants were not made, they were *cut*. Instead of signing a contract, the parties to a covenant took an animal and cut it in two. Then they walked between the severed halves of the carcass (cf. Genesis 15:9–17). They were taking a self-maledictory oath, calling down curses upon themselves should they violate the terms of the agreement. Anyone who violated the covenant—especially slaveholders—deserved to be dismembered and left to the dogs.

Because God is a covenant keeper, he hates covenant breaking. If you belong to God, you must keep your word, meet your obligations, fulfill your vows, satisfy your contracts, and keep your promises. After all, you are the child of a promise-keeping God.

Freedom for My People

The story of the emancipation revocation teaches about the evils of slavery and the necessity of keeping covenant. But like all Scripture, it is mainly intended to teach about salvation in Jesus Christ.

Freedom from slavery was the subject of the first sermon Jesus ever preached:

> And he came to Nazareth, where he had been brought up. And as was his custom, he went to the synagogue on the Sabbath day, and he stood up to read. And the scroll of the prophet Isaiah was given to him. He unrolled the scroll and found the place where it was written,
>
> > "The Spirit of the Lord is upon me,
> >   because he has anointed me
> >   to proclaim good news to the poor.
> > He has sent me to proclaim liberty to the captives
> >   and recovering of sight to the blind,
> >   to set at liberty those who are oppressed,
> > to proclaim the year of the Lord's favor."
>
> And he rolled up the scroll and gave it back to the attendant and sat down. And the eyes of all in the synagogue were fixed on him. And he began to say to them, "Today this Scripture has been fulfilled in your hearing." (Luke 4:16–21)

This was and is the emancipation proclamation of Jesus Christ. Jesus was quoting from Isaiah 61, which celebrates the release of captives every seventh year and every Jubilee Year. When Jesus sat down in the synagogue, he taught that he himself was the fulfillment of Isaiah 61. The Old Testament laws about freedom from slavery were meant to teach about the work of Christ in bringing freedom once and for all. Jesus *is* the Jubilee.

What kind of freedom does Jesus offer? Not, primarily, political freedom. This is why it would be a mistake to study Jeremiah 34 and think *only* about the politics of slavery. Remember, Jesus did not throw off the yoke of Roman rule. He did not free the Jews from their servitude. In fact, right up until his death Jesus had to keep reminding people that he was not offering political freedom.

When the soldiers came to seize Jesus in the garden of Gethsemane, his disciples said, "'Lord, shall we strike with the sword?' And one of them struck the servant of the high priest and cut off his right ear. But Jesus said, 'No more of this!'" (Luke 22:49–51a). Jesus Christ did not come to give political freedom. He understood that spiritual freedom is more important and longer lasting than any political freedom. It is better to be a slave and a Christian than a master and an enemy of Christ.

The freedom Jesus offers is the best of all freedoms—freedom from sin. There has never been any worse slavery than slavery to sin. Every child who comes into the world is born in bondage, already a captive of sin. From the very first moment of life, sin controls and dominates thoughts, desires, wills, hearts, imaginations, emotions, and actions. Jesus said, "everyone who practices sin is a slave to sin" (John 8:34). The Apostle Paul said, "I am of the flesh, sold under sin" (Romans 7:14; cf. 7:25). Slavery to sin brings guilt, grief, condemnation, and finally death.

If slavery to sin is the worst of all slaveries, then freedom from sin is the best of all freedoms. Freedom is what Christ won for his people on the cross. On the cross Jesus broke the power that sin once held over humanity. His lifeblood paid the price for sin. Once the price for sin had been paid, sin could no longer hold God's people in bondage. "Jesus . . . loves us and has freed us from our sins by his blood" (Revelation 1:5).

Now everyone who trusts in Christ is free, by the grace of the Holy Spirit, to live a life pleasing to God. "Thanks be to God, that you who were once slaves of sin have . . . been set free from sin, [and] have become slaves of righteousness" (Romans 6:17, 18).

If you have been set free from sin, then why would you ever want to go back into bondage? That would be as wicked as what Zedekiah did when he took free men and put them back into slavery.

Yet the sad truth is that many Christians still behave like slaves—not to sin, but to the Law. Although they understand they have been set free from sin, they still try to earn favor with God by their obedience. They measure their spirituality by what they do for God rather than by what Christ has done for them. They have not learned to rest in the grace of the Lord Jesus Christ. Therefore, they are in constant danger of slipping back into bondage to the Law.

Anyone who is bound to the Law needs to hear the warning Paul gave the Galatians: "For freedom Christ has set us free; stand firm therefore, and do not submit again to a yoke of slavery" (Galatians 5:1). What Paul meant by "a yoke of slavery" was anything added to the work of Christ to establish righteousness before God.

The Puritans are often accused of being legalists; yet they understood freedom in Christ better than most. Contemporary Christians often think of sanctification as what they do for Christ. But this is how the Puritans who wrote the Westminster Confession of Faith defined it:

> They, who are once effectually called, and regenerated, having a new heart, and a new spirit created in them, are further sanctified, really and personally, through the virtue of Christ's death and resurrection, by His Word and Spirit dwelling in them: the dominion of the whole body of sin is destroyed, and the several lusts thereof are more quickened and strengthened in all saving graces, to the practice of true holiness, without which no man shall see the Lord (XIII.i).

In that entire definition of sanctification, not one word is said about what the Christian does for Christ. It is all about what *Christ* does for the Christian. Christ creates a new heart and a new spirit, dwells in the Christian by His Word and Spirit, destroys the dominion of sin, and strengthens all saving graces. The Christian life is not a new form of slavery. Rather, through the cross we have been set free from sin and set free to live for Christ.

There is one more thing to know about the emancipation proclamation of Jesus Christ. It can never be revoked. Once Christ sets you free from sin and from bondage to the Law, you will remain free forever. "Truly, truly, I say to you, everyone who practices sin is a slave to sin. The slave does not remain in the house forever; the son remains forever. So if the Son sets you free, you will be free indeed" (John 8:34–36).

Charles Wesley (1707–1788) celebrated this irrevocable emancipation in the joyous words of one of his hymns:

> Ye slaves of sin and hell,
> Your liberty receive;
> And safe in Jesus dwell,
> And blest in Jesus live:
> The year of jubilee is come;
> Return, ye ransomed sinners, home;
> Return, ye ransomed sinners, home.[10]

50

Promise Keepers

JEREMIAH 35:1–19

EVERY SUMMER Wheaton College sends a group of students to the University of Oxford to study English literature. Anyone familiar with Wheaton will know that members of the college sign a "Statement of Responsibilities" to govern their conduct as brothers and sisters in Christ. Among other things, they pledge not to drink any alcoholic beverages.

One summer the Wheaton College study group was invited to a reception somewhere in Oxford. Although the English are tea drinkers they are not, by and large, teetotalers. So it was very natural for the hosts of the reception to serve their American guests wine and cheese. The table was covered with row upon row of goblets, already filled with red wine. According to the conventions of polite society, the wine simply *had* to be drunk. But according to a vow taken in the sight of God, the wine simply *could not* be drunk. What was to be done?

Teetotalers at the Temple

The Rechabites once found themselves in almost exactly the same situation. The Rechabites were a tribe of nomads who lived here and there in northern Israel. When roving bands of Babylonians started pillaging the Middle East, the Rechabites fled to Jerusalem for safety.

After the Rechabites arrived in the city, Jeremiah sent party invitations to everyone in their community:

> The word that came to Jeremiah from the LORD in the days of Jehoiakim the son of Josiah, king of Judah: "Go to the house of the Rechabites and speak with them and bring them to the house of the LORD, into one of the chambers; then offer them wine to drink." So I took Jaazaniah the son of

Jeremiah, son of Habazziniah and his brothers and all his sons and the
whole house of the Rechabites. (35:1–3)

The prophet threw a reception at the temple in honor of the Rechabites.
"I brought them to the house of the LORD into the chamber of the sons of
Hanan the son of Igdaliah, the man of God, which was near the chamber of
the officials, above the chamber of Maaseiah the son of Shallum, keeper of the
threshold" (v. 4).

When the Rechabites arrived at the reception, they undoubtedly noticed
the absence of finger food. Jeremiah did not serve any cheese, any crudités,
or any hors d'oeuvres. Just wine. Lots of it. "Then I set before the Rechabites
pitchers full of wine, and cups, and I said to them, 'Drink wine'" (v. 5). Jeremiah's party turned out to be one long cocktail hour.

It must have been awkward for the Rechabites. Because they were nomads, these grubby refugees probably seemed like country bumpkins to the
urban sophisticates in Jerusalem. They didn't even live in houses, let alone
drink wine. Their simple lifestyle was, to say the least, eccentric. R. E. O.
White describes them as follows:

> The Rechabites were a family guild who worshipped God strictly after
> the manner of the pilgrim patriarchs, living as nearly as possible in the
> nomadic fashion of Abraham, Isaac, and Jacob. Crops, vineyards, houses,
> towns, and cities all tied men to one place, they said, and so bred luxury,
> strife of possession, materialism, worship of fertility gods, and all manner
> of soft, lazy, extravagance, very different from the hard, disciplined life of
> herdsmen under the desert stars.[1]

The Rechabites were reactionaries; they were the counterculture movement of the Divided Kingdom. Perhaps they were something like a cross between the hippies of the 1960s and the old order Amish of Lancaster County,
Pennsylvania. Imagine straw hats and tie-dyed robes. Think horse-drawn
buggies decorated with giant pastel flowers. Like some hippies, they were a
tight-knit community constantly on the move. Like the Amish, they separated
themselves from the pleasures of popular culture.

Thus when Jeremiah put bowls of wine in front of the Rechabites, it was a
test of their whole way of life. They usually did not drink, but how could they
refuse this time? It would have been churlish of them to spurn Jeremiah's hospitality. "Many superficial reasons might have suggested to the Recabites com-
pliance with the prophet's tempting suggestion. The wine was before them;
there was no sin against God in taking it; the people around had no scruples

about it; and the prophet himself invited them."[2] "When in Jerusalem," they might have said, "do as the prophets do."

Yet the Rechabites remained true to their radical lifestyle. Together they recited their family catechism:

> But they answered, "We will drink no wine, for Jonadab the son of Rechab, our father, commanded us, 'You shall not drink wine, neither you nor your sons forever. You shall not build a house; you shall not sow seed; you shall not plant or have a vineyard; but you shall live in tents all your days, that you may live many days in the land where you sojourn.'" (vv. 6, 7)

They proceeded to explain that they always kept these vows to the letter.

> We have obeyed the voice of Jonadab the son of Rechab, our father, in all that he commanded us, to drink no wine all our days, ourselves, our wives, our sons, or our daughters, and not to build houses to dwell in. We have no vineyard or field or seed, but we have lived in tents and have obeyed and done all that Jonadab our father commanded us. (vv. 8–10)

In case anyone wondered what they were doing in a big city like Jerusalem, the Rechabites quickly explained that their visit was only temporary. "But when Nebuchadnezzar king of Babylon came up against the land, we said, 'Come, and let us go to Jerusalem for fear of the army of the Chaldeans and the army of the Syrians.' So we are living in Jerusalem" (v. 11). The Rechabites may have been odd, but they were not stupid. They would not be off on their nomadic way until Nebuchadnezzar left Israel for good.

The amazing thing is that the Rechabites had kept their promises for more than two centuries! Jonadab son of Rechab was one of the seven thousand in Israel who did not bow the knee to Baal during the days of Elijah (1 Kings 19:18). He was the mighty man who rode in the chariot when Jehu purged Ahab's palace in 842 BC, killing that evil king's entire family (2 Kings 10:15–17). So when the Rechabites showed up for happy hour at the temple, Jonadab had been dead for nearly 250 years.

How many families have scrupulously maintained a set of traditions from the eighteenth century to the present? Especially ascetic traditions like these! The Rechabite way of life had been out of fashion in Israel since the day Joshua crossed the Jordan River.

This I Swear

There are several practical lessons to learn from the example of the Rechabites. The first is the importance of keeping vows.

Jeremiah 34, 35 is a study in contrasts. Chapter 34 took place during the reign of Zedekiah, shortly before the Babylonians destroyed Jerusalem. Chapter 35 is a flashback to the reign of Jehoiakim at least a decade earlier (609–598 BC). This is one of the many places where the book of Jeremiah is arranged topically rather than chronologically. The contrast between the two chapters shows the difference between promise breaking and promise keeping.

Zedekiah was a promise breaker. First, he violated his treaty with Nebuchadnezzar (Ezekiel 17:12–18). Then, after freeing all the Hebrew slaves, he changed his mind and revoked his emancipation proclamation (34:11). The Rechabites, by contrast, were promise keepers. They understood that keeping covenant means keeping one's word, no matter what.

Some Christians believe it is un-Biblical to make vows. They base this view on the words of Jesus in the Sermon on the Mount:

> Again you have heard that it was said to those of old, "You shall not swear falsely, but shall perform to the Lord what you have sworn." But I say to you, Do not take an oath at all, either by heaven, for it is the throne of God, or by the earth, for it is his footstool, or by Jerusalem, for it is the city of the great King. And do not take an oath by your head, for you cannot make one hair white or black. Let what you say be simply "Yes" or "No"; anything more than this comes from evil. (Matthew 5:33–37)

Does Jesus completely forbid any form of oath-taking?

The answer seems to be no. Elsewhere the Bible teaches that there are proper times to make vows. There are many oaths, of course, in the Old Testament (Numbers 6; Deuteronomy 6:13; 10:20; Judges 10, 11; etc.). Vows are also taken or mentioned in the New Testament. On occasion the Apostle Paul said, "God is my witness" (Romans 1:9) or "I call God to witness" (2 Corinthians 1:23).

God himself swore an oath when he promised to bless all nations through Abraham (Genesis 22:15–18). Concerning this divine oath, the writer to the Hebrews says:

> For when God made a promise to Abraham, since he had no one greater by whom to swear, he swore by himself, saying, "Surely I will bless you and multiply you." And thus Abraham, having patiently waited, obtained the promise. For people swear by something greater than themselves, and in all their disputes an oath is final for confirmation. So when God desired to show more convincingly to the heirs of the promise the unchangeable character of his purpose, he guaranteed it with an oath, so that by two unchangeable things, in which it is impossible for God to lie, we who have

fled for refuge might have strong encouragement to hold fast to the hope set before us. (6:13–18)

These verses not only teach that God has sworn an unbreakable oath, they also assume that human beings sometimes take oaths. This is why the Westminster Confession of Faith contains an entire chapter titled "Of Lawful Oaths and Vows" (chap. XXII).

Jesus must not have intended, therefore, to eliminate oaths altogether. The Old Princeton theologian A. A. Hodge (1823–1886) offers this judicious explanation:

> It is evident, therefore, that the words of our Saviour (Matthew v. 33–37), "Swear not at all," cannot be intended to forbid swearing upon proper occasions in the name of the true God, but must be designed to forbid the calling upon his name in ordinary conversation and on trifling occasions, and the swearing by that which is not God.[3]

What Jesus forbids is silly, idle, or ungodly oath-taking. The people of his day had learned how to get away with lying. Rather than swearing in God's name, they swore "by heaven" or "by the earth" or even by the hairs of their heads. Then they would try to get out of their vows because they had not actually sworn in the name of God.

Silly oaths have maintained their popularity to the present day. "As God is my witness!" "I swear I'll never do that again!" "So help me God!" "I swear to God." "Cross my heart and hope to die." Jesus forbids the taking of these and any other idle oaths. Among Christians, especially, it is enough to say yes or no and to stand by one's word.

There are many occasions when a Christian properly may take an oath or a vow. One is in a court of law. In the name of God, a Christian may swear to tell the truth in a trial. Or a Christian who serves in government may take an oath of office. Another time Christians take vows is at weddings, which is why they get married in a church rather than in a chapel in Las Vegas. They take their vows in the presence of Almighty God. The same is true of ordination vows for elders and deacons, or of the membership vows taken when someone joins the church.

A Christian may also take vows of obedience to the Lord, like the "Seven Promises of a Promise Keeper" that became popular among Christian men in the 1990s. It is good for men to honor Christ, practice sexual purity, love their wives, nurture their children, pray for their pastors, confront racial prejudice, and reach the lost. It is good for men and women to make such promises, provided they make them in the name of God, in keeping with the Word of God, with a sense of the fear of God.

It is a solemn thing to swear an oath. To quote again from A. A. Hodge, "An oath is an act of supreme religious worship, since it recognizes the omnipresence, omniscience, absolute justice and sovereignty of the Person whose august witness is invoked, and whose judgment is appealed to as final."[4]

It is sometimes necessary to take an oath, but it is *always* necessary to keep one's word. That is what Jesus meant when he said, "Let what you say be simply 'Yes' or 'No'" (Matthew 5:37). In these post-Christian times, "No" often means "Maybe," and "Yes" usually means "Only if I feel like it when the time comes." It is hard to take people at their word because their words come so cheap. Some doctors no longer keep the Hippocratic Oath. Some Supreme Court justices violate their oath of office. Some ministers renounce their ordination vows. Some couples break their marriage vows. If people do not really mean it when they say, "'Til death do us part," when do their promises ever mean anything?

Christians are called to be different. They keep their promises—even to their own detriment. Booker T. Washington recounted a wonderful story about meeting a promise keeper. The man was an ex-slave from Virginia who

> had made a contract with his master, two or three years previous to the Emancipation Proclamation, to the effect that the slave was to be permitted to buy himself, by paying so much per year for his body; and while he was paying for himself, he was to be permitted to labour where and for whom he pleased. Finding that he could secure better wages in Ohio, he went there. When freedom came he was still in debt to his master some three hundred dollars. Notwithstanding that the Emancipation Proclamation freed him from any obligation to his master, this black man walked the greater portion of the distance back to where his old master lived in Virginia, and placed the last dollar, with interest, in his hands. In talking to me about this, the man told me that he knew that he did not have to pay the debt, but that he had given his word to his master, and his word he had never broken.[5]

Washington's friend sounds like a long-lost descendant of the Rechabites. Or maybe he was just a Christian.

Honor Your Father

A second lesson to learn from the Rechabites concerns giving honor to fathers.

The vows they had taken did not come from God—they came from Jonadab. God himself pointed this out in his commendation of the Rechabites:

"They drink none to this day, for they have obeyed their father's command" (35:14b). It was not un-Biblical for Jonadab to make all these commands, but it was not required either. As far as God was concerned, it was right and good for his people to drink wine, build houses, sow seed, and plant vineyards in the promised land. But once their founding father made these commands, the Lord was pleased with the Rechabites when they kept them.

God always blesses children who obey their parents. This is in keeping with the fifth commandment: "Honor your father and your mother, that your days may be long in the land that the LORD your God is giving you" (Exodus 20:12). The blessing Jonadab gave his children deliberately echoed that commandment: "That you may live many days in the land where you sojourn" (35:7b).

The best way for young people to honor their fathers is to love, serve, and obey them. Later in life, honoring one's father means respecting his counsel and caring for him in his old age. It means helping him whenever there is opportunity.

Every summer I visit the Summer Medical Institute, which is sponsored by the Medical Campus Outreach of Tenth Presbyterian Church. Medical students at the Institute give door-to-door immunizations and share the love of Christ with families in the troubled neighborhoods of North Philadelphia. During one of my visits, a medical student received a distressing telephone call from home. His parents were at the end of their rope, and his father begged him to come back home and help run the family store. Setting aside his own plans, the aspiring young doctor packed that very night and drove home. He was willing to sacrifice his own interests to honor his father.

God blesses sons and daughters who honor their fathers. He certainly blessed the Rechabites:

> But to the house of the Rechabites Jeremiah said, "Thus says the LORD of hosts, the God of Israel: Because you have obeyed the command of Jonadab your father and kept all his precepts and done all that he commanded you, therefore thus says the LORD of hosts, the God of Israel: Jonadab the son of Rechab shall never lack a man to stand before me." (vv. 18, 19)

God kept that promise. When the Israelites went back home after the exile, they started to rebuild the city of Jerusalem. The engineer in charge of that building project, Nehemiah, carefully recorded the names of his best workers. One of them was a Rechabite: "Malchijah the son of Rechab, ruler of the district of Beth-haccherem, repaired the Dung Gate" (Nehemiah 3:14a). That detail is recorded in Scripture as a reminder that God blesses sons who honor their fathers. God retained the sons of Rechab in his service. Curiously, Haccherem means "vineyard," which suggests that the Rechabites took new vows when they became God's servants. The nomads who had once renounced secular culture eventually helped to rebuild God's sacred city.

Alcohol and the Christian

A third lesson to learn from the Rechabites concerns the right use of alcohol. Admittedly, some commentators deny that this chapter has anything to teach about the use of alcohol. Davidson says, "At no point in the incident does Jeremiah commend the Rechabite *principles*. . . . It was not the principles of the Rechabites, but their faithfulness, Jeremiah commended."[6]

It is correct to say that the Rechabites were commended for their faithfulness. But surely God would not have held them up as an example *unless* their vows were at least permissible. So what does Jeremiah 35 teach about the use of alcohol?

God permits and even commends the drinking of wine. Apparently it was appropriate for Jeremiah to bring wine into the temple. Even great big bowls of it! As long as they were off-duty, temple priests were permitted to drink wine. This is in keeping with the rest of Scripture. The psalmist praised God for "wine to gladden the heart of man" (Psalm 104:15). The Lord Jesus himself was not above turning the odd jar of water into fine wine, especially at parties (John 2:1–11). Even young pastors, like Timothy, are instructed to have a little wine when they suffer from indigestion (1 Timothy 5:23). Anyone who claims that Christians are forbidden to use alcohol is adding a human law to the Law of God.

However, Christians are also free *not* to drink. Refraining from alcoholic beverages can be one expression of freedom in Christ. Not all abstinence is legalism. It is interesting to note that the nineteenth-century temperance movement in England adopted the name "Rechabites."[7] The name was appropriate because God commended the Rechabites for keeping their promise not to drink any wine. Nor were they the only teetotalers in the Bible. Abstaining from wine or other strong drink was one of the vows the Nazirites took when they devoted themselves to the Lord (Numbers 6:1–3; Judges 13:7, 14). Likewise, John the Baptist was instructed "not [to] drink wine or strong drink" (Luke 1:15). Even the good things of life can distract believers from their devotion to Christ. Thus, on occasion it is good for Christians to show their love to God by refraining from alcohol.

One more thing needs to be said about the right use of alcohol. Although the Bible does not altogether forbid drinking, it expressly forbids drunkenness.

The prophet Isaiah pronounced "woe to those who are heroes at drinking wine, and valiant men in mixing strong drink" (Isaiah 5:22). The Corinthians were warned not to "associate with anyone who bears the name of brother if he is . . . [a] drunkard" (1 Corinthians 5:11). An elder must "not [be] a drunkard" (1 Timothy 3:3).

The Bible forbids drunkenness because it leads to foolishness, immorality, violence, and sometimes death. Being filled with spirits and being filled with the Spirit are in direct conflict. "Do not get drunk with wine, for that is debauchery, but be filled with the Spirit" (Ephesians 5:18). Those who cannot drink without getting drunk must not drink. Instead, pray for the filling of the Holy Spirit.

To summarize: Some Christians should not drink. No Christian has to drink. Most Christians may drink. But all Christians *must* love one another. The use or the prohibition of alcohol has sometimes disturbed the unity of churches and nations. On occasion it has divided entire branches of Christianity.

Nor is alcohol the only issue that divides Christians, even though it is a matter of indifference to God. Do we keep the Sabbath holy this way or that way? Full-time ministry or secular job? Live in the suburbs or serve in the city? Home school, public school, Christian school, or private school? Paul's warning to the Romans applies to all such disputes:

> Therefore let us not pass judgment on one another any longer, but rather decide never to put a stumbling block or hindrance in the way of a brother. I know and am persuaded in the Lord Jesus that nothing is unclean in itself, but it is unclean for anyone who thinks it unclean. For if your brother is grieved by what you eat, you are no longer walking in love. By what you eat, do not destroy the one for whom Christ died. So do not let what you regard as good be spoken of as evil. For the kingdom of God is not a matter of eating and drinking but of righteousness and peace and joy in the Holy Spirit. (Romans 14:13–17)

The Master's Voice

There are valuable lessons to be learned from the Rechabites about vows, family relationships, and abstaining from strong drink. But the main point of Jeremiah 35 is to hear and obey the Lord.

God praised the sons of Jonadab primarily for their listening skills:

> Then the word of the Lord came to Jeremiah: "Thus says the Lord of hosts, the God of Israel: Go and say to the people of Judah and the inhabitants of Jerusalem, Will you not receive instruction and listen to my words?

declares the LORD. The command that Jonadab the son of Rechab gave to his sons, to drink no wine, has been kept, and they drink none to this day, for they have obeyed their father's command. I have spoken to you persistently, but you have not listened to me. I have sent to you all my servants the prophets, sending them persistently, saying, 'Turn now every one of you from his evil way, and amend your deeds, and do not go after other gods to serve them, and then you shall dwell in the land that I gave to you and your fathers.' But you did not incline your ear or listen to me. The sons of Jonadab the son of Rechab have kept the command that their father gave them, but this people has not obeyed me." (vv. 12–16)

The contrast between the fidelity of the sons of Jonadab and the infidelity of the sons of Judah was absolute. The Rechabites did what their founding father told them to do. But the Israelites refused to do the will of their heavenly Father. And God had grown weary of their disobedience. When would they ever learn their lesson?

The main problem with God's people was that they were poor listeners. Jonadab had given his commands hundreds of years before, and his sons were still keeping them. By contrast, God spoke to his people nearly every day. His prophets kept coming to them to warn them of the danger of following after other gods. Still, they refused to pay any attention. "Therefore, thus says the LORD, the God of hosts, the God of Israel: Behold, I am bringing upon Judah and all the inhabitants of Jerusalem all the disaster that I have pronounced against them, because I have spoken to them and they have not listened, I have called to them and they have not answered" (v. 17).

Few things are more frustrating to a parent than children who will not listen. I am forever telling my children to look me in the eye. I want to at least *feel* like genuine communication is taking place. God often feels the same way about his people. He commands them. He warns them. He rebukes them. But they do not pay any attention. So he commands them, warns them, and rebukes them again. And they say, "Sure, whatever, God." Then he commands them, warns them, and rebukes them all over again. Still they go right back into their sins! One of the great sins of God's people is not paying attention to God.

Every son or daughter of God must be a good listener. Listen to the Word of God to find wisdom for life. Listen to the Holy Spirit prompting your conscience to confess your sins. Listen to Jesus Christ when he tells you to believe in his name to receive salvation. Listen to God the Father when he tells you what he wants to do with your life. "Let every person be quick to hear," writes the apostle James. Then he adds, "But be doers of the word, and not hearers only, deceiving yourselves" (James 1:19, 22). If the Lord is trying to get your attention, listen up! If he is trying to tell you to do something, just do it!

The emblem of the old RCA Victor company depicted a dog sitting with his ear cocked toward a phonograph player. The slogan beneath the picture said, "His Master's Voice." The idea was that the sound of the phonograph was of such high quality that a dog could mistake it for the voice of his owner. The emblem was a picture of devotion—man's best friend straining to hear his master's voice.

It should also be a picture of the Christian. Those who sit with ears inclined to the Word of God speaking in Scripture will hear the Master's voice. Those who not only listen but actually do what he says will be his friends.

51

Book Burning

JEREMIAH 36:1–32

AMONG THE MANY REASONS TO TRUST THE BIBLE is its staying power. This was well stated by Thomas Watson:

> We may know the Scripture to be the Word of God by its miraculous preservation in all ages. The holy Scriptures are the richest jewel that Christ has left us; and the church of God has so kept these public records of heaven, that they have not been lost. The Word of God has never wanted enemies to oppose, and, if possible, to extirpate it . . . but God has preserved this blessed Book inviolable to this day. The devil and his agents have been blowing at Scripture light, but could never blow it out; a clear sign that it was lighted from heaven.[1]

As the Puritan Thomas Watson (d. 1690) rightly observed, the enemies of God have often tried—unsuccessfully!—to extinguish the light of Scripture.

Once God's enemies even tried to burn the Bible. During the days when Jehoiakim reigned in Judah, all Jeremiah's prophecies were written on a scroll and taken to the king in his winter apartment. As he sat warming himself by the fire, Jehoiakim used the Word of God for fuel.

Jehoiakim's wanton act of destruction placed Jeremiah's writings in jeopardy. If the king had succeeded, there would be no book of Jeremiah today. There would be no warnings about spiritual adultery (2, 3), no signpost at the crossroads pointing out the ancient path (6:16), no boasting in the knowledge of God (9:24), no taunting the scarecrow in the melon patch (10:5), no visiting the potter's house (18, 19), no seeking the peace and prosperity of the city (29:7), and no promise of the new covenant (31:31–34). Everything Jeremiah ever prophesied would have gone up in smoke.

Yet to this day the church holds the prophecies of Jeremiah as a sacred treasure. All of them. One reason the Scripture is known to be the Word of God is because of its miraculous preservation throughout all ages.

Writing the Word

Jeremiah 36 is about writing, receiving, rejecting, and preserving the Bible.

First, the *writing*: The Word of God passed from the mind of the Holy Spirit onto the pages of the Bible. "In the fourth year of Jehoiakim the son of Josiah, king of Judah, this word came to Jeremiah from the LORD: 'Take a scroll and write on it all the words that I have spoken to you against Israel and Judah and all the nations, from the day I spoke to you, from the days of Josiah until today'" (36:1, 2).

This transcription took place in 605 BC, the year the Babylonians won a momentous military victory over the Egyptians at Carchemish. God told Jeremiah to write down all the prophecies he'd received in his first twenty years of ministry.

It is often pointed out that Jeremiah's scroll had to be short enough to be read three times in one day. This is because the events of verses 8–26, which include three separate readings of the scroll, seem to have transpired in a single day. However, most scholars overestimate the amount of time such readings would take. It is reasonable to think that this scroll contained all (or nearly all) the prophecies that now comprise Jeremiah chapters 1—25 and 46—51.

The words Jeremiah wrote down were not his words—they were God's words. Although the book of Jeremiah reflects the personality and experiences of the man Jeremiah, its ultimate author is the Holy Spirit. When the writer to the Hebrews quoted from Jeremiah's prophecies, he wrote, "The Holy Spirit also bears witness" (Hebrews 10:15). Thus, what Peter wrote about Biblical prophecy in general applies specifically to Jeremiah: ". . . knowing this first of all, that no prophecy of Scripture comes from someone's own interpretation. For no prophecy was ever produced by the will of man, but men spoke from God as they were carried along by the Holy Spirit" (2 Peter 1:20, 21). In other words, the Word of God is the Word of *God*. The words in Jeremiah's book are not words about God—they are words *from* God, which is why they will never lose their power.

The reason God wanted his words written down was to save his people from their sins: "It may be that the house of Judah will hear all the disaster that I intend to do to them, so that every one may turn from his evil way, and that I may forgive their iniquity and their sin" (36:3). This verse helps explain Jeremiah's many terrible prophecies of divine judgment. They were not intended simply to terrify; they were also intended to save. "God wants to do more than convict; he wants to convert."[2] This is a hope Jeremiah shared, for he said, "It may be that their plea for mercy will come before the LORD, and that every one will turn from his evil way, for great is the anger and wrath that the Lord has pronounced against this people" (v. 7).

All God's threatenings have the gracious purpose of turning sinners away from their sins. As Derek Kidner asks, "Why else should he pour out threats rather than immediate actions, unless it is to bring us to our senses and to his feet?"[3] The preaching of final judgment and eternal punishment is founded upon the grace of God. The Word of God tells us that we deserve to be damned in order to make us run to Christ to be saved.

In order for Scripture to fulfill that saving purpose, it had to be written down. The divine words Jeremiah committed to memory needed to be put on paper. "Then Jeremiah called Baruch the son of Neriah, and Baruch wrote on a scroll at the dictation of Jeremiah all the words of the LORD that he had spoken to him" (v. 4). This is how many parts of the Bible were recorded. First, they were revealed; then they were remembered; finally, they were written down. The book of Jeremiah was revealed by the Holy Spirit, remembered by the prophet Jeremiah, and written down by the learned Baruch.

Baruch was more than a scribe; he was Jeremiah's executive secretary. In addition to taking dictation, he handled publicity.

> And Jeremiah ordered Baruch, saying, "I am banned from going to the house of the LORD, so you are to go, and on a day of fasting in the hearing of all the people in the LORD's house you shall read the words of the LORD from the scroll that you have written at my dictation. You shall read them also in the hearing of all the men of Judah who come out of their cities." (vv. 5, 6)

So Baruch went to the temple. It was now nearly a year after Jeremiah had first begun to work on his scroll (December, 604 BC). A fast had been proclaimed throughout Judah (see v. 9), probably because the Babylonian victory over the Philistines at Ashkelon had created a national panic. Jeremiah himself was barred from going to the temple. Either the Lord prevented him from going, or he was ceremonially unclean, or his notorious Temple Sermon had made him Public Enemy Number One (26:1–19; cf. 7:1—8:3). In any case, Baruch was the one chosen to risk his life for the sake of God's Word.

Receiving the Word

Baruch had some misgivings about serving as Jeremiah's "stunt double" (see chapter 45). Nevertheless,

And Baruch the son of Neriah did all that Jeremiah the prophet ordered him about reading from the scroll the words of the LORD in the Lord's house. In the fifth year of Jehoiakim the son of Josiah, king of Judah, in the ninth month, all the people in Jerusalem and all the people who came from the cities of Judah to Jerusalem proclaimed a fast before the LORD. Then, in the hearing of all the people, Baruch read the words of Jeremiah from the scroll, in the house of the LORD, in the chamber of Gemariah the son of Shaphan the secretary, which was in the upper court, at the entry of the New Gate of the LORD's house. (36:8–10)

When it was first "published," Jeremiah's book received mixed reviews. Baruch read it to everyone he could, but most people were too busy with the ritual of fasting actually to repent (cf. 7:2ff.)! One man, however, was hanging on Jeremiah's every prophecy. His name was Micaiah.

Micaiah demonstrates the proper receiving of the Word of God. First comes the *hearing* of the Word: "Micaiah the son of Gemariah, son of Shaphan, heard all the words of the LORD from the scroll" (36:11). He listened to God's Word in its entirety. He did not doze off in the middle of the reading or leave before Baruch was finished. Micaiah listened to Jeremiah's prophecies from beginning to end.

The members of Jehoiakim's royal cabinet also listened attentively to the whole counsel of God. When Micaiah told them about the scroll, they were not satisfied with a book report. They sent directly for Baruch: "Then all the officials sent Jehudi the son of Nethaniah, son of Shelemiah, son of Cushi, to say to Baruch, 'Take in your hand the scroll that you read in the hearing of the people, and come.' So Baruch the son of Neriah took the scroll in his hand and came to them. And they said to him, 'Sit down and read it'" (vv. 14, 15a). Like Micaiah, these officials were careful hearers of God's Word.

Receiving the Word begins with hearing it from beginning to end. This is why expository preaching is so necessary. It takes God's Word the way God gives it—verse by verse, chapter by chapter, book by book. This is also why systematic Bible reading is so valuable. One place the Bible needs to be read is in church. Since the nineteenth century, the Tenth Presbyterian Church in Philadelphia has read continuously through the Psalms and the New Testament during its morning worship services. At the end of Psalm 150 the congregation starts all over again with Psalm 1; the last chapter of Revelation is followed by the first chapter of Matthew.

Another place the Bible needs to be read is at home. Every Christian needs to make a regular practice of reading the Word of God. Get a Bible, get a bookmark, and start reading. Or use the monthly study guide produced by

The Bible Study Hour, God's Word Today.[4] Or get a copy of Robert Murray M'Cheyne's *Calendar for Daily Readings* and read the whole Bible in a year.[5] Receiving God's Word means hearing it, and the best way to hear it is to take it whole.

Next comes the *fearing* of God's Word. When Micaiah heard that God was angry against Judah's sin, he feared the Lord greatly. Immediately he went to tell his father and the other officials. "When they heard all the words, they turned one to another in fear" (36:16a). Literally, they trembled in front of one another. The cabinet realized that their nation was about to be judged.

It is one thing to hear God's Word. It is another to fear it, heeding all God's warnings, trusting all God's promises, and obeying all God's commands. To fear God's Word is to confess that you are a sinner, trust that Jesus died on the cross for your sins, and live the rest of your life according to God's will.

Then comes *sharing* God's Word. To receive it properly means to pass it on to others. When Micaiah heard words of divine judgment, he could not keep them to himself. "He went down to the king's house, into the secretary's chamber, and all the officials were sitting there: Elishama the secretary, Delaiah the son of Shemaiah, Elnathan the son of Achbor, Gemariah the son of Shaphan, Zedekiah the son of Hananiah, and all the officials" (v. 12). There "Micaiah told them all the words that he had heard, when Baruch read the scroll in the hearing of the people" (v. 13). The cabinet, in turn, wanted to tell the king. They "said to Baruch, 'We must report all these words to the king'" (v. 16b).

First, however, they were careful to make sure that the scroll was the authentic Word of God. "Then they asked Baruch, 'Tell us, please, how did you write all these words? Was it at his dictation?' Baruch answered them, 'He dictated all these words to me, while I wrote them with ink on the scroll'" (vv. 17, 18). Once they were sure the scroll was God's written Word, the officials pleaded with their king to receive it respectfully. "Elnathan and Delaiah and Gemariah urged the king not to burn the scroll" (v. 25).

These men were passionate evangelists. They were not content to hear the Word of God for themselves; they wanted others to hear it as well. And they wanted others to hear the whole thing. Micaiah told them "all" that he had heard (v. 13). The cabinet reported "all these words" to the king (v. 16). This is all the more impressive when it is remembered that what these men shared so thoroughly was not good news. It was all about God's judgment against sin.

Too much contemporary evangelism fails to take God's wrath seriously. Many Christians testify to the grace and goodness of God. Yet how often do they explain how much God hates sin and how severely he intends to deal with it? News of divine judgment has an essential place in evangelism. People have to hear the bad news about sin and death before they can receive the good news about forgiveness and new life in Christ.

Receiving God's Word means hearing it fully, fearing it greatly, and sharing it unstintingly. It is no surprise that Micaiah received the Word of God this way. After all, he was a grandson of Shaphan. Shaphan was the great man who served as Secretary of State under King Josiah. When the Book of the Law was rediscovered in the temple, Shaphan read it and reread it for the king (2 Kings 22; cf. 2 Chronicles 34).

Shaphan was also a good father. Great spiritual leaders do not always raise godly children. Often they do not. But Shaphan was a good father as well as a great leader. His sons were among the forgotten heroes of the Bible: "The hand of Ahikam the son of Shaphan was with Jeremiah so that he was not given over to the people to be put to death" (26:24). Elasah, the son of Shaphan, carried Jeremiah's letter to the exiles in Babylon (29:3). Gemariah, the son of Shaphan, was one of the officials who took Jeremiah's scroll to Jehoiakim (36:12).[6]

The godly influence of Shaphan also extended to his grandchildren. Micaiah, the son of Gemariah, the son of Shaphan, shared God's Word with the king's cabinet (vv. 11–14). His cousin Gedaliah, the son of Ahikam, the son of Shaphan, rescued Jeremiah and brought him into his own home when Jerusalem fell (39:14; cf. 40, 41). Eventually Gedaliah became governor of the Jewish remnant in Jerusalem (40:7).

The sons and grandsons of Shaphan were great men of God. They were national leaders and lovers of God's Word. Therefore, their patriarch is a model for Christian parents living in a post-Christian culture. Fathers like Shaphan raise sons and daughters to go anywhere and do anything to share God's Word.

Rejecting the Word

King Jehoiakim did exactly the opposite. He would not hear God's Word and did not fear it. In fact, he tried to make sure it would never be shared again. His private book burning shows the awful consequences of rejecting God's Word.

Jehoiakim had never been a godly king. His cabinet members rarely knew how he would react, so they were always prepared for the worst. This time they took the precaution of hiding the scroll and sending Baruch and Jeremiah underground:

> Then the officials said to Baruch, "Go and hide, you and Jeremiah, and let no one know where you are." So they went into the court to the king,

having put the scroll in the chamber of Elishama the secretary, and they reported all the words to the king. (36:19, 20)

These were necessary precautions. After all, Jehoiakim had been so angry with the prophet Uriah that he had him extradited from Egypt and executed (26:22, 23).

The scene for the third reading of Baruch's scroll is among the most memorable in the Bible:

Then the king sent Jehudi to get the scroll, and he took it from the chamber of Elishama the secretary. And Jehudi read it to the king and all the officials who stood beside the king. It was the ninth month, and the king was sitting in the winter house, and there was a fire burning in the fire pot before him. As Jehudi read three or four columns, the king would cut them off with a knife and throw them into the fire in the fire pot, until the entire scroll was consumed in the fire. (36:21–23)

Jehoiakim did not even wait for Jehudi to finish. As soon as Jehudi unrolled each section of the scroll, which was written on leather or papyrus and wrapped around wooden rollers, the king began his outrageous act of censorship. He methodically used a scribe's penknife to cut holy Scripture into pieces. Then he tossed the fragments into his brazier, the movable hearth that was probably wheeled up to his throne on a small cart.[7]

Perhaps Jehoiakim doubted the reality of divine judgment. God later rebuked the king for calling his prophet into question. God said to Jeremiah, "And concerning Jehoiakim king of Judah you shall say, 'Thus says the LORD, You have burned this scroll, saying, "Why have you written in it that the king of Babylon will certainly come and destroy this land, and will cut off from it man and beast?"'" (v. 29). Or perhaps Jehoiakim thought burning God's Word would prevent his doom from coming to pass. If so, he failed to recognize that the power of the Word flows from the power of God himself. J. I. Packer once commented, "Jehoiakim burns God's Word, ignoring its warnings. That's like getting out of a car to destroy a 'Bridge Out' sign: done at one's own peril."[8]

The shocking thing was not so much Jehoiakim's stupidity as his audacity. Jehoiakim was casual, almost nonchalant in his defiance of God's Word: "Yet neither the king nor any of his servants who heard all these words was afraid, nor did they tear their garments" (v. 24). The arrogance, the contempt, the insolence of the man! He should have rent his garments in repentance. Instead he turned a deaf ear to his counselors: "Even when Elnathan and Delaiah and Gemariah urged the king not to burn the scroll, he would not listen to them" (v. 25). Then he added injury to insult by calling for the arrest of God's prophet. "And the king commanded Jerahmeel the king's son and Seraiah the son of Azriel and Shelemiah the son of Abdeel to seize Baruch the secretary and Jeremiah the prophet, but the LORD hid them" (v. 26).

It had been a very different scene when the Book of the Law was rediscovered in the days of King Josiah. When that good king heard God's words, he did not tear the words but his clothes, as a sign of repentance (2 Kings 22:11). These are the only two ways to respond to God's Word—to receive it or to reject it, to hear it or to ignore it, to fear it or to forget it. Dwight L. Moody (1837–1899) described the difference between men like Josiah and men like Jehoiakim this way: "Either the Bible will keep you from sin, or sin will keep you from the Bible."

There are many sons and daughters of Jehoiakim in the world today. Sinners who will not sit still long enough to hear a Biblical sermon. Bible scholars who cut and paste the Bible rather than receiving it as the Word of God. Churchgoers who only open their Bibles in the pews on Sunday. Ministers who spend all their time thinking about how a passage will preach and never get around to figuring out how it applies to the preacher.

Most evangelicals consider themselves students of God's Word. Maybe we are. But could it be that we are more like Jehoiakim than Micaiah? Could it be that we spend as much time avoiding the implications of God's Word as we do studying it? J. I. Packer gives this wise warning: "The privilege of knowing God's truth with certainty and precision carries with it the responsibility of obeying that truth with equal precision."[9]

Preserving the Word

With so many enemies of God's Word in the world, it is a wonder there is any Bible left to read! Yet the Word of God is indestructible. No sooner had the first edition of Jeremiah been reduced to ashes than the second went into production.

> Now after the king had burned the scroll with the words that Baruch wrote at Jeremiah's dictation, the word of the LORD came to Jeremiah: "Take another scroll and write on it all the former words that were in the first scroll, which Jehoiakim the king of Judah has burned." . . . Then Jeremiah took another scroll and gave it to Baruch the scribe, the son of Neriah, who wrote on it at the dictation of Jeremiah all the words of the scroll that Jehoiakim king of Judah had burned in the fire. And many similar words were added to them. (36:27, 28, 32)

Notice that all the words from the first scroll were recorded on the second. Even if Jeremiah had forgotten what he prophesied, the Holy Spirit remembered.

One of the great ironies of the Bible is that Jehoiakim himself made an appearance in the expanded edition of Jeremiah's manuscript. For among the "many similar words" added were some that pertained specifically to the king:

> Therefore thus says the LORD concerning Jehoiakim king of Judah: He shall have none to sit on the throne of David, and his dead body shall be cast out to the heat by day and the frost by night. And I will punish him and his offspring and his servants for their iniquity. I will bring upon them and upon the inhabitants of Jerusalem and upon the people of Judah all the disaster that I have pronounced against them, but they would not hear. (vv. 30, 31; cf. 22:13–19)

Jeremiah's mention of David's throne did not mean that the Davidic line had come to an end. It meant that Jehoiakim's offspring would not rule in Jerusalem for long. Jehoiakim's son Jehoiachin reigned for only three months, and he was succeeded not by his son, but by his uncle (2 Kings 24).

For Jehoiakim himself there was to be another irony: One day the king who burned the Bible because he was so anxious to keep warm would be "cast out to the heat by day and the frost by night" (36:30b). His children, his attendants, and the whole nation would also be judged, for this reason—because "They would not hear" (v. 31b). God holds people responsible for what they do not do as well as for what they do.

God always has the last word. His words outlast their enemies. The endurance of the Bible attests to the remarkable, at times miraculous, preservation of the Word of God. Satan has done his worst to prevent the production, translation, and proclamation of God's Word. But he has completely and utterly failed.

Consider all the reliable manuscripts of the Bible. The books of the Bible are far and away the best-attested writings of the ancient world. Think of the great number of accurate translations now available in English. Or of the work of Bible translation going on this very moment all over the globe. Sometime in the twenty-first century the Gospels of Jesus Christ will be available in every one of the more than six thousand known languages in the world. Some time after that the prophecies of Jeremiah—the very words Jehoiakim cut from the scroll and burned in his firepot—will be read around the globe by every tribe and people and nation.

The Word of God may be despised, but it will never be destroyed. The

Westminster Confession of Faith remarks: "The Old Testament in Hebrew and the New Testament in Greek, being immediately inspired by God, by His singular care and providence" have been "kept pure in all ages" (I.viii).

There are many remarkable stories of the preservation of the Bible. One of the best comes from the early days of the English Reformation, when William Tyndale (c. 1494–1536) had just published the first translation of the New Testament into the English language from the original Hebrew and Greek (1528).

In his great rage against the Protestant gospel, Archbishop Wolsey began to burn copies of Tyndale's Testament at St. Paul's Cathedral in London. The Catholics needed a steady supply of Bibles to burn; so the bishop of London tried to buy as many as possible in Antwerp, where the Bibles were printed.

The historical account of the bishop's errand deserves to be repeated in full:

> And so it happened that one Augustine Packington, a mercer and merchant of London, and of a great honesty, the same time was in Antwerp, where the bishop then was, and this Packington was a man that highly favoured William Tyndale, but to the bishop utterly showed himself to the contrary. The bishop desirous to have his purpose brought to pass, communed of the New Testaments, and how gladly he would buy them.
>
> Packington then hearing that he wished for, said unto the bishop, My Lord if it be your pleasure, I can in this matter do more I dare say, than most of the merchants of England that are here, for I know the Dutch men and strangers that have brought them of Tyndale, and have them here to sell, so that if it be your lordship's pleasure, to pay for them, I will then assure you, to have every book of them, that is imprinted and is here unsold.
>
> The bishop thinking that he had God by the toe, when indeed he had (as after he thought) the Devil by the fist, said, gentle Master Packington, do your diligence and get them and with all my heart I will pay for them, whatsoever they cost you, for the books are erroneous and naughts and I intend surely to destroy them all, and to burn them at Paul's Cross.
>
> Augustine Packington came to William Tyndale and said, William I know thou art a poor man, and hast a heap of New Testaments, and books by thee, for the which thou hast both endangered thy friends, and beggared thyself, and I have now gotten thee a merchant, which with ready money shall dispatch thee of all that thou hast, if you think it so profitable for yourself.
>
> Who is the merchant said Tyndale?
>
> The bishop of London said Packington.
>
> O that is because he will burn them said Tyndale. Yea marry quoth Packington. I am the gladder said Tyndale, for these two benefits shall come thereon, I shall get money of him for these books, to bring myself out of debt, (and the whole world shall cry out upon the burning of God's word). And the overplus of the money, that shall remain to me, shall make

me more studious, to correct the said New Testament, and so newly to imprint the same once again, and I trust the second will much better like you, than ever did the first: And so forward went the bargain, the bishop had the books, Packington had the thanks, and Tyndale had the money.

Afterward, when more New Testaments were printed, they came thick and threefold into England, the bishop of London hearing that still there were so many New Testaments abroad, sent for Augustine Packington and said unto him: Sir how cometh this, that there are so many New Testaments abroad, and you promised and assured me, that you had bought all?[10]

Had the bishop bothered to look, he could have found his answer in the pages of Tyndale's New Testament: "The grass withereth, and the flower falleth away: But the word of the Lord endureth ever" (1 Peter 1:24b, 25a).

52

Benedict Jeremiah?

JEREMIAH 37:1–21

THE MOST FAMOUS TRAITOR in the history of the United States was Benedict Arnold (1741–1801). Like many traitors, Arnold began his career as a patriot. He joined the Revolutionary Army as a colonel in 1775 and led several successful military campaigns. He helped Ethan Allen and the Green Mountain Boys capture Fort Ticonderoga. He was one of General Washington's most trusted officers. Twice he was wounded in battle and acclaimed a hero.

Benedict Arnold failed to win a promotion to major general, however, a promotion he thought he deserved. Then he was accused of personal misconduct. Although he was cleared by the court-martial, Arnold was angry about the way he had been treated and began plotting revenge. After a year and a half of secret correspondence he found a way to betray his country. He would hand over the fortress at West Point, then under his command, to the British army. But some of his letters were intercepted, the conspiracy was uncovered, and Benedict Arnold was disgraced forever.

Jeremiah was accused of a similar act of treason. During a brief cease-fire between the Babylonians and the Jews, the prophet tried to slip out of Jerusalem unnoticed. He was captured, arrested, beaten, and imprisoned. But Jeremiah was no Benedict Arnold. He was a patriot for God and his people.

The Traitor Who Does Not Listen . . .

The real traitor was King Zedekiah. Zedekiah pretended to be true to God's people, but everything about him was false. He was not even the rightful king. "Zedekiah the son of Josiah, whom Nebuchadnezzar king of Babylon made king in the land of Judah, reigned instead of Coniah the son of Jehoiakim" (37:1). The Babylonians put him on the throne because he was willing to dance on their strings like a marionette. Later Zedekiah betrayed his overlords, which is why they attacked Jerusalem (cf. Ezekiel 17:11–15). But worst of all, he proved to be a traitor to the cause of God.

Zedekiah displayed three characteristics of a spiritual traitor. First, he did not listen to God's Word: "Neither he nor his servants nor the people of the land listened to the words of the LORD that he spoke through Jeremiah the prophet" (37:2). The Bible records pages and pages of Jeremiah's prophecies. Zedekiah ignored them all. So did his people. And the kingdom reflected the spiritual apathy of its king. If Zedekiah was not going to listen to God's Word, no one else was either. Thus the whole nation of Judah lived in ignorance of God's will.

Most Americans live in similar ignorance. At the dawn of a new millennium, the citizens of the United States do not know their Bibles. Church is almost the only place people have a chance to hear Scripture anymore. They rarely hear the Word of God on the street, at the marketplace, in the classroom, or especially on television. The worldview of an entire culture is being constructed with little or no input from the only reliable source for understanding the world. This famine of the hearing of God's Word extends even to the church, where Bible reading and Bible exposition are often the first things to go in the quest for contemporary worship.

Zedekiah is a politician for post-Christian times, when people have only a passing interest in God's Word. On rare occasions he was willing to hear what God had to say. From time to time he secretly wondered if perhaps Jeremiah's prophecies were true after all. For example, after Jeremiah had languished in the dungeon for a long time, "King Zedekiah sent for him and received him. The king questioned him secretly in his house and said, 'Is there any word from the LORD?'" (v. 17a).

The king could not quite get Jeremiah out of his system. Davidson comments that Zedekiah

> seems to have been haunted by the thought, or perhaps by the fear, that the true word for his day was to be found not on the lips of his political advisers or his official chaplains, but on the lips of that odd-ball Jeremiah. . . . He is like a patient returning again and again to a doctor in search of reassurance, yet unwilling to take the medicine prescribed.[1]

Zedekiah may have flirted with the Word of God, but he never obeyed it. When Jeremiah came to prophesy before the royal court, his words would go in one ear and out the other. Zedekiah was the kind of man who goes to church every now and then but *never* does anything about it. Gordon McConville observes, "For all his craven toying with the word of YHWH, he will never hear it."[2] The only time he actually listened to God, he freed all the slaves in Jerusalem; but then he changed his mind and took them right back into captivity (34:8–11). King Zedekiah was often accused of vacillating. A better word to describe his actions is treachery, since only a traitor would change sides midway through a battle.

People who take only a passing interest in the Bible cannot be patriots in the Lord's army. They have divided loyalties. In other words, they are turncoats. They are like King Herod, who put John the Baptist in prison. The Bible says Herod "feared John, knowing that he was a righteous and holy man, and he kept him safe. When he heard him, he was greatly perplexed, and yet he heard him gladly" (Mark 6:20).

The Apostle Paul met the same kind of man when he was imprisoned in Caesarea:

Felix [the governor] came with his wife Drusilla, who was Jewish, and he sent for Paul and heard him speak about faith in Christ Jesus. And as he reasoned about righteousness and self-control and the coming judgment, Felix was alarmed and said, "Go away for the present. When I get an opportunity I will summon you." (Acts 24:24, 25)

Like Herod and Felix, Zedekiah enjoyed dabbling in religion. He liked to hear what the minister had to say. He was interested in discussing religious affairs. But as soon as the prophet started to press his message to the point of personal faith and repentance, he refused to listen any longer.

How many Presidents of the United States have taken a similar approach to the Bible? They invite evangelical ministers to the White House. They speak vaguely about their faith in God. But Christians look in vain for signs of genuine repentance and faith in Jesus Christ.

How many churchgoers are just as wishy-washy when it comes to Scripture? They halfheartedly read their Bibles or listen to sermons, but their hearts and minds remain unchanged. You will not become the pure bride of Christ by flirting with the gospel. You must listen and believe the Word of God. If you claim to be a Christian, then failure to study and obey the Bible is an act of high treason.

. . . and Does Not Pray . . .

The second thing Zedekiah refused to do was pray. He did not have a personal relationship with the living God, so he could not speak to God about his troubles. Access to the King of kings through prayer is the unique privilege of the patriot, not the traitor.

Although Zedekiah was not a man of prayer, he almost believed in the power of prayer. When he was really in a jam he liked to cover his bases. So he asked people to intercede for him—people like Jeremiah, who actually knew the Lord in a personal way: "King Zedekiah sent Jehucal the son of Shelemiah, and Zephaniah the priest, the son of Maaseiah, to Jeremiah the prophet, saying, 'Please pray for us to the LORD our God.' Now Jeremiah was still going in and out among the people, for he had not yet been put in prison" (37:3, 4; cf. 21:1–2). Like many spiritual traitors, Zedekiah half-trusted the efficacy of prayer.

How ironic—after all the times Jeremiah had been ignored and abused—that the king should ask him to pray. It is more ironic still that in the next chapter Jehucal (here sent to ask for prayer) will insist that Jeremiah be put to death (38:1–4). Yet this often happens. The colleague who always mocks Christianity will come up and say, "Send up a little prayer for me." Or the neighbor who will never come to church will ask for prayer during a family crisis.

Inability to pray for one's self is a sign of desperate spiritual weakness. Yet those who pray should not look down upon those who do not. Instead they should offer to pray for them as often as possible. When a colleague is under stress, mention that you are praying for him. When your neighbor is in trouble, ask if you can pray with her. When a family member calls in the middle of a crisis, say, "Why don't we have a prayer about that right now?" Even most unbelievers find comfort in prayer. And because prayer is a spiritual activity, it opens a door for the Holy Spirit to work in a person's life.

What about the person who does not know how to pray? How should one begin? Say, "God, I don't even know how to pray, but here goes . . ." "God, help me!" "God, be merciful to me, a sinner." Ask God to forgive your sins for Jesus' sake. Say whatever is on your heart to say. God is the most patient of listeners. He already knows what you need! And your prayers will improve with practice. The more one prays, the better one prays.

. . . Will Not Be Saved

Zedekiah neither prayed nor listened to the Word of God. To put it another way, he rejected the means of grace. Prayer and the Word are sometimes called the means of grace because the Holy Spirit uses them to help believers grow in grace. According to the Westminster *Shorter Catechism*, "The outward and ordinary means whereby Christ communicateth to us the benefits of redemption, are his ordinances, especially the Word, sacraments, and prayer; all which are made effectual to the elect for salvation" (A. 88).

King Zedekiah had rejected the means of grace. As a result—and this is a third characteristic of a spiritual traitor—he would not be saved. All his hopes of escaping divine judgment would turn out to be false. Salvation is only for patriots, never for traitors.

Zedekiah thought he would be saved. He was hoping for the best. He had just won an unexpected military victory of sorts. The Babylonians had been besieging Jerusalem for months. F. B. Meyer describes how "every day the air was full of the cries of the combatants, the heavy thud of the battering rams against the walls, and the cries of wounded men born from the ramparts to the tendance [watchful care] of women."[3] But suddenly, in the late spring or early summer of 588 BC, "The army of Pharaoh had come out of Egypt. And when the Chaldeans who were besieging Jerusalem heard news about them, they withdrew from Jerusalem" (37:5; cf. 34:21, 22; the emancipation revocation took place at this time). The siege was lifted, and the whole city breathed a huge sigh of relief. Their prayers were answered.

Not so fast! The relief was only temporary. God sent Jeremiah back to Zedekiah with a most discouraging prophecy:

> Then the word of the LORD came to Jeremiah the prophet: "Thus says the LORD, God of Israel: Thus shall you say to the king of Judah who sent you to me to inquire of me, 'Behold, Pharaoh's army that came to help you is about to return to Egypt, to its own land. And the Chaldeans shall come back and fight against this city. They shall capture it and burn it with fire. Thus says the LORD, Do not deceive yourselves, saying, "The Chaldeans will surely go away from us," for they will not go away. For even if you should defeat the whole army of Chaldeans who are fighting against you, and there remained of them only wounded men, every man in his tent, they would rise up and burn this city with fire.'" (vv. 6–10)

All Zedekiah's hopes turned out to be false. God promised defeat, and defeat it would be. By the power of God, even a band of wounded, straggling Babylonians would outmatch Judah. This is a hyperbole, an exaggeration to make a spiritual point. The point was that God intended to punish the people of Judah for their sins.

The more Zedekiah thought about that prophecy, the more he wondered what would become of him. He was so worried, he sent for Jeremiah and asked, "Is there any word from the LORD?" (v. 17a). The king's simple question received a straightforward prophetic answer. "There is," Jeremiah replied. "You shall be delivered into the hand of the king of Babylon" (v. 17b; cf.

38:3). Zedekiah was not on the Lord's side. He would not believe God's Word or pray for God's help. Therefore he had no hope of salvation. Whatever hopes he had would prove to be false.

The same is true of everyone who refuses to come to God through Jesus Christ. Anyone who does not believe the gospel or pray for the forgiveness of sins is a traitor to God, and traitors will never be saved.

Although Tortured . . .

Jeremiah was no traitor. He was God's patriot. Still, it is easy to see why his enemies thought he was a turncoat.

For one thing, it seemed like years since Jeremiah had spoken a good word about the future of Jerusalem. He was critical of his political leaders, even during wartime, when everyone needed to pull together.

For another thing, Jeremiah always disagreed with conventional political wisdom. The leaders were in favor of normalizing relations with Egypt. In fact, one of the Lachish Letters refers to a Judean diplomat who was sent down to Egypt to ask for help in fighting the Babylonians.[4] But Jeremiah always had a way of undermining the official propaganda machine. He told people not to trust in Egypt. Nor was his prophecy about being defeated by wounded enemies exactly a boost for morale! The prophet even told the Jews they should surrender to the Babylonians (21:9; 38:2)!

The leaders had always suspected that Jeremiah was a Babylonian sympathizer. Now they had their proof: During a break in the hostilities, the prophet tried to leave Jerusalem:

> Now when the Chaldean army had withdrawn from Jerusalem at the approach of Pharaoh's army, Jeremiah set out from Jerusalem to go to the land of Benjamin to receive his portion there among the people. When he was at the Benjamin Gate, a sentry there named Irijah the son of Shelemiah, son of Hananiah, seized Jeremiah the prophet, saying, "You are deserting to the Chaldeans." (37:11–13)

Jeremiah had good reason to leave the city: He needed to take care of some personal business. Most likely he was going to discuss his family estate, including the field his cousin Hanamel was trying to sell him (cf. 32; the actual purchase was not made until after Jeremiah was in prison).[5] But he ran into trouble at Checkpoint Benjamin. The head of security misinterpreted Jeremiah's intentions. Irijah recognized him, accused him of desertion, and arrested him for treason.

The prophet protested, "It is a lie; I am not deserting to the Chaldeans"

(37:14a). Not only was the charge false, it was also outrageous. There was not a man in the whole city who had been more faithful to God's people than Jeremiah. For forty years he had pleaded with them to turn back to God. For forty years he had wept over their sins. Has a man ever cared more deeply for the spiritual condition of a nation than Jeremiah cared for his own people? His motto for ministry was, "For the wound of the daughter of my people is my heart wounded" (8:21a).

To charge such a true patriot with treason is an injustice; to subject him to police brutality is an inhumanity.

> But Irijah would not listen to him, and seized Jeremiah and brought him to the officials. And the officials were enraged at Jeremiah, and they beat him and imprisoned him in the house of Jonathan the secretary, for it had been made a prison. When Jeremiah had come to the dungeon cells and remained there many days . . . (37:14b–16)

Zedekiah's Secret Service put the prophet in a makeshift prison at the home of the Secretary of State. Apparently Jeremiah's prophecies were considered a security risk.

Then they lowered him into a dungeon, which was probably a cistern.

> Such cisterns were usually hewn out of limestone rock. Narrow at the top, they opened out into a bottle-shaped cavity in which water was stored. They were rather like the bottle dungeons that you find in old castles, such as the castle at St Andrews in Scotland; and they could serve the same purpose. There prisoners could be left to rot, to go mad or to die.[6]

Francis Schaeffer has shown how Jeremiah's enemies "gradually increased the punishment—from the stocks, to a prison, to a dungeon."[7] Finally, in the next chapter, they will leave him to die.

. . . the Patriot Remains True . . .

The sufferings of Jeremiah—like the sufferings of all the Old Testament prophets—teach about the Messiah.

When Stephen preached to the members of the Sanhedrin, he told them they were just like the officials who tried to kill Jeremiah:

> You stiff-necked people, uncircumcised in heart and ears, you always resist the Holy Spirit. As your fathers did, so do you. Which of the prophets did your fathers not persecute? And they killed those who announced beforehand the coming of the Righteous One, whom you have now betrayed and murdered. (Acts 7:51, 52)

The sufferings of Jeremiah are a type or a picture of the sufferings and death of Jesus Christ. Like Jeremiah, Jesus was a persecuted prophet. Like Jeremiah, he was tortured for his teaching and was considered an enemy of God's people.

However, also like Jeremiah, Jesus was no traitor. Jesus and Jeremiah proved they were patriots to God's cause by remaining true to the very end. The *Oxford English Dictionary* defines *patriot* as "a person who is devoted to and ready to support or defend his or her country." But one wonders if that definition is strong enough. A true patriot is willing not only to support and defend, but also to suffer and to die for his people.

Jeremiah proved he was a patriot by remaining true to God's Word, even when his life was at stake. Remember that it was God's Word that got Jeremiah into trouble in the first place. His prophecies put him in the dungeon. According to Schaeffer, the reason Jeremiah suffered so much was because he was preaching God's Word:

> [Jeremiah] is not giving an optimistic answer; he isn't saying everything is going to turn out well. He isn't saying there is an easy solution; all we need is a little more technical advance to make the grade. He is cutting down their humanistic optimism, saying that they are under the judgment of God, and thereby weakening the people, undercutting their morale. "For this man seeketh not the welfare of this people, but the hurt." Of course it is not true. Jeremiah is wanting their real welfare. He is saying, "You must be healed of the real disease, which is your revolt against God, and not merely of some superficial, external wound." But that didn't please the dignitaries.[8]

Schaeffer concludes that Jeremiah was sent to the dungeon "as a result of his faithful preaching of God's judgment to a 'post-Christian' world."[9]

Most people do not like to hear that God is angry with them for their sins. Often they will go to great lengths to silence preachers of divine justice. But the spiritual patriot continues to testify to the full truth of God's Word, including what it has to say about the Law, sin, and judgment. This is one difference between a patriot and a traitor. Traitors like Zedekiah refuse to listen to God's Word. Patriots like Jeremiah refuse to preach anything else.

If ever there was a time for Jeremiah to change his message or to fudge on a prophecy, it was when Zedekiah invited him to the palace to hear what the Lord had to say. If Jeremiah pleased the king, he might have a chance of getting out of the slammer alive. If not, back to the dungeon he would go.

Yet when the king asked if there was a word from the Lord, Jeremiah gave it to him straight: "There is . . . You shall be delivered into the hand of the king of Babylon" (37:17b). Such candor is the mark of a spiritual patriot, a man who speaks the Word of God to king and country, no matter what the cost. Traitors are always people-pleasers, prophets who only tell people what they want to hear.

It is not safe to be a patriot. Francis Schaeffer—who took a keen, personal interest in the sufferings of Jeremiah—stated that "if one really preaches the Word of God to a post-Christian world, he must understand that he is likely to end up like Jeremiah."[10]

Or worse. Because of his refusal to betray God's Word under trial, Jesus was accused of treachery: "And they began to accuse him, saying, 'We found this man misleading our nation'" (Luke 23:2). Jesus' patriotism to God's cause cost him his life, the life he gave on the cross for our sins.

. . . and Will Be Saved in the End

One more thing must be said about God's patriots: They will be saved in the end. Jeremiah and everyone else who remains true to God's Word will be delivered from death.

Although Jeremiah did not betray God's Word, he did beg Zedekiah for mercy. He argued that he was under false arrest:

> Jeremiah also said to King Zedekiah, "What wrong have I done to you or your servants or this people, that you have put me in prison? Where are your prophets who prophesied to you, saying, 'The king of Babylon will not come against you and against this land'? Now hear, please, O my lord the king: let my humble plea come before you and do not send me back to the house of Jonathan the secretary, lest I die there." (37:18–20)

The prophet appealed for clemency because, like any other human being, he did not want to die.

Jeremiah said two things to try to gain his freedom. He tried to prove his innocence and his truthfulness. He began by pointing out to Zedekiah that he had committed no crime. Furthermore, all his enemies had proven to be false. Where were all the prophets who used to disagree with Jeremiah? Good question. All Jeremiah's words were coming true. The Babylonians had attacked, just as he promised. But where were the false prophets? As Zedekiah well knew, most of them were languishing in exile in Babylon!

Deep down, the king must have known that Jeremiah was innocent, for "King Zedekiah gave orders, and they committed Jeremiah to the court of the guard. And a loaf of bread was given him daily from the bakers' street, until all the bread of the city was gone. So Jeremiah remained in the court of the guard"

(v. 21). It is a mystery why Zedekiah moved Jeremiah from the dungeon to the stockade. It was almost the right thing to do, but it failed to do the king much credit. One act of kindness hardly made up for all the times he had ignored and abused God's prophet!

The point is, however, that God did not desert Jeremiah. God knew that Jeremiah was no traitor; so he cared for his daily needs. Right up until the fall of Jerusalem, Jeremiah had a ration of bread baked fresh each day and delivered to his doorstep.

Do not overlook the importance of daily bread. The Lord Jesus tells all his disciples to ask God for it every day (Matthew 6:11). So every time we sit down to a meal we should praise God with genuine thanksgiving. Jeremiah's daily bread teaches "That God often so provides for his servants, that he appears to have forsaken them; and yet he then especially takes care of them and supplies them with what is needful for their support."[11]

Like Jeremiah, Jesus appealed for his life to be preserved. On the cross he said, "Father, into your hands I commit my spirit" (Luke 23:46). Jesus did not ask to be delivered *from* death; he asked to be delivered *through* death. And his petition was answered. Jesus was delivered when God the Father raised him from the dead.

The resurrection of Jesus Christ points to the biggest difference between traitors and patriots—what happens to them in the end. Benedict Arnold came to a bad end. Curiously, a historical marker outside his residence in London identifies him as "an American patriot." Not a British patriot, notice, but an American patriot. Perhaps this is because the British know American history about as well as Americans know British history.

Or perhaps it is because they never accepted Benedict Arnold as one of their own. The British army gave him less than a third of the salary they promised, and when he moved to London he was scorned by English high society. At the end of his life, Benedict Arnold was distrusted, indebted, and deeply discouraged. He died forsaken by the Americans and forgotten by the British.

King Zedekiah fared even worse. He was defeated in battle (39:1–4). Then, as Jeremiah promised, he was handed over to the king of Babylon (39:5). What Jeremiah did not mention was that Zedekiah would witness the slaughter of his own sons and suffer the gouging out of his eyeballs (39:6, 7). He lost his kingdom, his children, and his eyesight.

The moral is that traitors to the Lord's cause have no one to save them in the day of trouble. At the day of judgment many traitors will say, "Lord, Lord," as if they were patriots. "And then will I [Jesus] declare to them, 'I never knew you; depart from me, you workers of lawlessness'" (Matthew 7:23). Traitors always come to a bad end.

It will be much better on the day of judgment to be known as a patriot. All God's patriots will be saved in the end. Although they may be abused by men, they will be vindicated by God if they remain true to God's Word. Like Jeremiah, and like Jesus, they will be delivered from death.

53

In and Out of the Cistern

JEREMIAH 38:1–13

> Jeremiah has always a fascination to Christian hearts because of the close similarity that exists between his life and that of Jesus Christ. Each of them was "a man of sorrows, and acquainted with grief"; each came to his own, and his own received him not; each passed through hours of rejection, desolation, and forsakenness. And in Jeremiah we may see beaten out into detail, experiences which, in our Lord, are but lightly touched on by the evangelists.[1]

The truth of these words from F. B. Meyer is amply demonstrated in the first thirteen verses of Jeremiah 38, where Jeremiah's sufferings remind the Christian of the sufferings of Christ.

It may even be tempting to view this Scripture passage in terms of resurrection. After all, when Jeremiah went in and out of the cistern, he went in and out of the ground. Calvin went so far as to observe that the cistern was a sort of a grave.[2] However, Jeremiah's going in and out of the cistern is not presented in the New Testament as a type of the death and resurrection of Jesus Christ. Strictly speaking, Jeremiah 38 is not a resurrection passage.

It is, however, a story about what happens to a true prophet at the hands of ungodly men. It is a story about how God rescues his prophet from death. And it is a story about how salvation comes to those who trust in the prophet's word from God.

In other words, Jeremiah 38 has many similarities to the story of Easter Week. Jeremiah's experience going in and out of the cistern teaches the believer about Jesus Christ. It shows how he suffered at the hands of ungodly men, how God rescued him from death, and how salvation comes to those who trust in him.

The Prophet Rejected

The story goes like this: First, ungodly men reject the prophet's word. At the end of chapter 37, some of King Zedekiah's lobbyists were so angry with Jeremiah that they had him beaten and imprisoned. Zedekiah granted Jeremiah a limited pardon, but the prophet was still confined to the courtyard of the prison.

They locked Jeremiah up, but they couldn't shut him up. The reason he kept getting into trouble with the law was because he preached fearlessly the Word of God. Like the Apostle Paul (Philippians 1:12, 13), Jeremiah preached to everyone who passed through the prison.

Jeremiah basically had only one sermon:

> Now Shephatiah the son of Mattan, Gedaliah the son of Pashhur, Jucal the son of Shelemiah, and Pashhur the son of Malchiah heard the words that Jeremiah was saying to all the people, "Thus says the LORD: He who stays in this city shall die by the sword, by famine, and by pestilence, but he who goes out to the Chaldeans shall live. He shall have his life as a prize of war, and live. Thus says the LORD: This city shall surely be given into the hand of the army of the king of Babylon and be taken." (38:1–3)

To understand why Jeremiah's sermon made people mad, it helps to understand how desperate the situation was in Jerusalem. The city was under siege. The most powerful military force in the world—the Babylonian army—was camped outside its walls, cutting off all supplies. Bread rations were starting to run low, and there was no water left in any of the cisterns, only brackish mud.

Very likely, the Babylonians had started to attack the walls of the city, trying to undermine its towers or knock down its gates with battering rams. The prophet Ezekiel offered a grim military briefing about this siege: "The sword is without; pestilence and famine are within. He who is in the field dies by the sword, and him who is in the city famine and pestilence devour" (Ezekiel 7:15). One way or another, the citizens were doomed.

Given the city's weak tactical position, it is easy to see why Jeremiah's little sermon was bad for morale. He was announcing that victory was impossible, defeat inevitable. His message was "Surrender or Die." He was preaching that message not because the Babylonians were invincible, but because God himself was fighting on Babylon's side.

Even though Jeremiah spoke his message on God's behalf, Shephatiah, Gedaliah, Jucal, and Pashhur did not want to hear it. That "Gang of Four" (Zedekiah's policy analysts or cabinet members) wanted assurance of victory, not a dire prophecy of defeat. They wanted a message of peace, not ruin.

"Then the officials said to the king, 'Let this man be put to death, for he is weakening the hands of the soldiers who are left in this city, and the hands of all the people, by speaking such words to them. For this man is not seeking the welfare of this people, but their harm'" (38:4).

The persecution of God's prophet begins with the rejection of the prophetic word. Jeremiah's enemies were shutting their ears to his life-or-death message.

It is hard not to feel at least a little sympathy for the "Gang of Four" who opposed Jeremiah. The prophet *was* discouraging the soldiers. When the soldiers heard Jeremiah's message, their hands fell slack, and their weapons dropped from their hands. They were so discouraged that they could hardly lift a finger to defend Jerusalem.

Notice also the words "who are left" in the phrase "The soldiers who are left in this city." Apparently Judah had lost a few good men. No doubt some had fallen in battle while defending the city walls. Others were slipping out at night by ones and twos and going over to surrender to the Babylonians. After all, that is precisely what Jeremiah was encouraging them to do: "He who goes out to the Chaldeans shall live" (v. 2). One can guess how many deserters there had been by King Zedekiah's fear that the Jews who already had gone over to the Babylonians would mistreat him after he was captured (38:19).

Furthermore, Jeremiah was getting a wide hearing. The soldiers were not the only ones who were discouraged—*everyone* was discouraged. Jeremiah was confined to the prison courtyard, but people had been passing his sermon tapes all over the city. The word was getting out.

It is not hard to figure out why Shephatiah, Gedaliah, Jucal, and Pashhur were so upset. They were patriots trying to defend their homeland, but Jeremiah was hurting the war effort with his defeatist attitude. Not surprisingly, when they heard what Jeremiah was preaching, they cried "Treason!"

Here is the real question, however: Was their accusation true? Listen again to the charge the "Gang of Four" leveled against Jeremiah: "This man is not seeking the welfare of this people, but their harm" (v. 4). Was the accusation true? Was Jeremiah a traitor to God's people or not? Was he seeking their ruin or their good?

News of divine judgment is always bad news. It is unpleasant to hear that God punishes sin rather than overlooks it. But the only thing that really matters is whether or not the bad news of divine judgment is true. When the bad news is God's news, it needs to be heard.

In this case, Jeremiah was no traitor. He was speaking the very words of God. When God's prophet speaks God's judgment in God's name, he is no traitor to God's people. Furthermore, Jeremiah was preaching sweet grace as well as sure judgment. He was telling God's people how they could save themselves. The real traitors were the members of the "Gang of Four." When they rejected God's prophet, they were rejecting God himself, setting themselves up as the enemies of the living God. That was not courageous; it was foolhardy.

The accusation these coconspirators actually leveled against Jeremiah was that he was not seeking the peace, or shalom, of Judah. Ironically, Jeremiah had warned about leaders who make such claims:

> They have healed the wound of my people lightly,
>   saying, "Peace, peace,"
>   when there is no peace. (8:11)

"'Shalom, shalom,' they say, when there is no shalom."

Shephatiah, Gedaliah, Jucal, and Pashhur were the liberal theologians of their day. They wanted a God of mercy, but not a God of justice. They wanted a God who gives victory, but not a God who allows suffering. They wanted a Father of love, but not a Father of discipline. The "Gang of Four" were willing to sacrifice the lives of God's people for only half a god.

This story is a parable for post-Christian times. The church of Jesus Christ is like Jeremiah to a postmodern culture. We do not say, "There, there, everything will be all right." Instead we say, "It's *not* all right with you until you get right with God." We do not say, "Peace, peace." Instead, we say, "You will be troubled until you make peace with God." We proclaim God's judgment, speaking out against greed, pride, false worship, sexual immorality, and all kinds of sin. And we proclaim God's grace to this world, announcing free pardon from every sin in Jesus Christ.

How will the world respond to the church's message? Many will be like Shephatiah, Gedaliah, Jucal, and Pashhur. They will say, "What's your problem?" "You Christians are all a bunch of extremists." Or even, "You're a menace to society."

The postmodern attitude toward the church may be illustrated from a 1996 article in *Gentleman's Quarterly*.[3] At the time the Christian organization Promise Keepers was calling American men to be faithful to God, faithful to their families, and faithful to the church. *GQ* was terrified by that call. The magazine compared the director of Promise Keepers to Adolf Hitler, describing him as a "raving lunatic" and a "lop-eyed loon." It also likened evangelical Christians to Islamic terrorists.

Such words are a warning of persecution to come. But they should not come as a surprise. God's truth sounds dangerous to the post-Christian mind.

Jesus endured the same kind of opposition. When he preached repentance and the kingdom of God, he was rejected as a threat to society. The religious leaders of his day "were seeking how to put [Jesus] to death" (Luke 22:2). They said, "We found this man misleading our nation" (Luke 23:2a). God's enemies always reject the word of God's prophet.

The Prophet Executed

The next thing God's enemies want to do is put God's prophet to death. That is what the "Gang of Four" wanted to do with Jeremiah. They hated the message, so they tried to kill the messenger. They were tired of all the barking, so they wanted to shoot the watchdog. "There is only one thing to do with traitors," they told Zedekiah in essence. "Let this man be put to death" (38:4a).

King Zedekiah's response reveals that he was a coward, a slave to political pressure. In his commentary on this chapter, John Guest observes that there are three kinds of people—those who make things happen, those who let things happen, and those who say "What happened?"[4] In this case Zedekiah was letting things happen, but soon he would be asking, "What happened?"

Zedekiah seems to have been an alumnus of the same school of politics that Pontius Pilate later attended. "King Zedekiah said, 'Behold, he is in your hands, for the king can do nothing against you'" (v. 5). In effect he was saying, "My hands are tied. I'm not going to stop you."

That is what Pontius Pilate said as well. When the leaders of the Jews brought Jesus before Pilate and demanded his execution, "he took water and washed his hands before the crowd, saying, 'I am innocent of this man's blood; see to it yourselves'" (Matthew 27:24b). When wicked men conspire to murder God's prophets, the rulers of this world will do nothing to stop them.

Shephatiah, Gedaliah, Jucal, and Pashhur were conspiring to murder God's prophet, but they did not want his blood on their hands either. So they arranged for a bloodless execution. "So they took Jeremiah and cast him into the cistern of Malchiah, the king's son, which was in the court of the guard, letting Jeremiah down by ropes. And there was no water in the cistern, but only mud, and Jeremiah sank in the mud" (38:6).

A cistern, of course, is an underground cavity for storing rainwater. As was mentioned earlier, the cisterns of Jeremiah's day were usually bottle-shaped, with a narrow opening at the top and a large round cavern underneath. They were often fifteen feet deep or more. This cistern must have been a deep one, because Jeremiah needed to be lowered into it by ropes.

There was no water in this cistern, so Jeremiah was stuck in the mud. There is a strong connection between the prophet's experience and the experience of the Messiah in Psalm 69. Consider how appropriate these words would sound from the lips of Jeremiah:

> I sink in deep mire,
>   where there is no foothold . . .
> Deliver me
>   from sinking in the mire;
> let me be delivered from my enemies
>   and from the deep waters.
> Let not the flood sweep over me,
>   or the deep swallow me up,
>   or the pit close its mouth over me. (Psalm 69:2a, 14, 15)

The experiences of Jeremiah point forward to the sufferings of Jesus Christ. They remind us that he, too, was a prophet put to death by ungodly men.

The New Testament writers often observe that the treatment Jesus received from the scribes and Pharisees was the fulfillment of the treatment God's prophets received before him. Remember the words of Stephen before the Sanhedrin: "You stiff-necked people, uncircumcised in heart and ears, you always resist the Holy Spirit. As your fathers did, so do you. Which of the prophets did your fathers not persecute? And they killed those who announced beforehand the coming of the Righteous One, whom you have now betrayed and murdered" (Acts 7:51, 52). That description of the leaders who put Jesus to death is also an apt description of the "Gang of Four." They closed their hearts and their ears to the Word of God. Then they persecuted God's prophet Jeremiah, even to the brink of death.

The Prophet Delivered

Jeremiah was persecuted, but not to death. Although ungodly men sought to kill him, God delivered his prophet from death.

When God first called Jeremiah to the ministry, he promised to rescue him (1:8). At the time Jeremiah may well have wondered what dangers he would have to be rescued from. Eventually he found out. He fell out of prison and into the cistern. There he reached rock-bottom in his ministry, or perhaps one should say "sludge-bottom."

One of my parishioners once described Jeremiah as "The one prophet I would not want to be." Jeremiah may have felt that way himself from time to time. When he answered God's call—although he did not know it at the time—he was agreeing to stand up to his thighs in a pile of mud in a hole in the ground, waiting to die.

In that very place, however, and in all places, God was faithful to his prophet. Even in the cistern Jeremiah was not to be afraid because God was with him. Even from the mud he would be rescued, because God had promised to rescue him. God delivered his prophet from death. Therefore, Jeremiah could testify with the psalmist:

> I waited patiently for the LORD;
>   he inclined to me and heard my cry.
> He drew me up from the pit of destruction,
>   out of the miry bog,
> and set my feet upon a rock,
>   making my steps secure. (Psalm 40:1, 2)

Jesus Christ can give the same testimony. He, too, waited patiently for God. He, too, cried out to God, asking his Father to receive his spirit (Luke 23:46). He, too, was rescued from the pit. More than that, Jesus Christ triumphed over the pit of the grave, for he was raised up from the dead.

Saved by Faith

Everyone who trusts in Christ can share in his victory over death. How? By faith. The example of Ebed-melech in Jeremiah 38 teaches that God saves everyone who trusts in him.

Ebed-melech was a nobody. He was a Cushite, to begin with. Cushites were Gentiles, black Africans from Ethiopia. So Ebed-melech was an alien in Judah. Plus, he was a eunuch in the royal palace. Perhaps he was in charge of Zedekiah's harem, but in any case he was a slave, and very likely an emasculated slave. We may not even know his name, for "Ebed-melech" simply means "servant of the king." It was not much of a name. Even if it was the man's proper name, it shows that he had no identity of his own. His status as a human being was completely defined by his relationship to his owner.

Within the context of Hebrew culture, Ebed-melech counted for nothing. He was nameless. He was alienated from God's people by his ethnicity. And he was banned from God's temple by his sexual deformity (see Deuteronomy 23:1).

Ebed-melech did count, however, because he counted to God. Remember that Jeremiah was called to be a prophet to the nations. Ebed-melech was the fruit of that international ministry. Cushite though he was, he heard God's Word from Jeremiah and received it unto salvation.

See how courageous he became in God's service! In the first place, he left his post. "Ebed-melech went out of the palace" (38:8 NIV). This was not a good career move, especially for a slave.

Then Ebed-melech went to seek an audience with Zedekiah: "When Ebed-melech the Ethiopian, a eunuch who was in the king's house, heard that they had put Jeremiah into the cistern—the king was sitting in the Benjamin Gate— Ebed-melech went from the king's house and said to the king . . ." (vv. 7, 8). The slave did not speak to the king in some private corner of the palace but went and confronted him in public, while he was conducting the affairs of his state. In front of the whole court, he accused Jeremiah's accusers: "My lord the king, these men have done evil in all that they did to Jeremiah the prophet by casting him into the cistern, and he will die there of hunger, for there is no bread left in the city" (v. 9).

Because Ebed-melech was God's man, he was willing to take a stand for God's prophet. He could see that Jeremiah was as good as dead. But he valued the life of God's prophet as much as he prized the truth of God's Word. Even when the whole world seemed to be arrayed against him, he had the courage to do what was right.

Calvin observed that when one compares the courage of Ebed-melech with the cowardice of Zedekiah, "The wonderful constancy and also the singular meekness of God's servant shine forth gloriously."[5] Milton's description of the angel Abdiel in Paradise Lost might well be applied to Ebed-melech:

> Among the faithless faithful only he;
> Among innumerable false, unmoved,
> Unshaken, unseduced, unterrified,
> His loyalty he kept, his love, his zeal;
> Nor number, nor example with him wrought
> To swerve from truth, or change his constant mind,
> Though single.[6]

This single, brave man forced Zedekiah's hand. The king had washed his hands of the whole affair, but Ebed-melech put it right back into his hands. When he exposed Cisterngate on the floor of the Senate, Zedekiah could no longer plead ignorance. He was compelled to take responsibility for what was happening to Jeremiah.

In typical fashion, King Zedekiah decided to change his mind. "Then the king commanded Ebed-melech the Ethiopian, 'Take thirty men with you from here, and lift Jeremiah the prophet out of the cistern before he dies'" (v. 10). The fact that so many men were needed shows what a risk the slave had taken on behalf of the prophet. They were not needed to extricate Jeremiah from the cistern, most likely, but to protect the rescue operation from the prophet's enemies.

God never forgot Ebed-melech's courage, as subsequent events were to prove:

> The word of the LORD came to Jeremiah while he was shut up in the court of the guard: "Go, and say to Ebed-melech the Ethiopian, 'Thus says the LORD of hosts, the God of Israel: Behold, I will fulfill my words against this city for harm and not for good, and they shall be accomplished before you on that day. But I will deliver you on that day, declares the LORD, and you shall not be given into the hand of the men of whom you are afraid. For I will surely save you, and you shall not fall by the sword, but you shall have your life as a prize of war, because you have put your trust in me, declares the LORD.'" (39:15–18)

Ebed-melech's profile in courage is a perfect illustration of a principle Jesus taught his disciples: "The one who receives a prophet because he is a prophet will receive a prophet's reward, and the one who receives a righteous person because he is a righteous person will receive a righteous person's reward" (Matthew 10:41). Ebed-melech received the same reward as Jeremiah. When Jerusalem fell, both men were rescued, for God delivers all who trust in him. Like all true servants of the King, Ebed-melech was saved by faith.

The slave performed one further act of faith that deserves careful attention: "So Ebed-melech took the men with him and went to the house of the king, to a wardrobe in the storehouse, and took from there old rags and worn-out clothes, which he let down to Jeremiah in the cistern by ropes" (38:11). One can imagine Ebed-melech going to the palace linen closet, or perhaps to the "Lost-and-Found." He rummaged around for what he needed, sorting through old T-shirts and hand towels, picking them up, looking them over, and setting them down again until he found what he was looking for.

He took the softest rags he could find and threw them down the cistern. "Ebed-melech the Ethiopian said to Jeremiah, 'Put the rags and clothes between your armpits and the ropes.' Jeremiah did so. Then they drew Jeremiah up with ropes and lifted him out of the cistern. And Jeremiah remained in the court of the guard" (vv. 12, 13). It was a beautiful act of kindness that revealed the man's great love for God's prophet. For him, it was not enough simply to save Jeremiah's life. He wanted to honor the prophet by caring for his body.

One can hardly think of Ebed-Melech's rescue operation without also thinking of the care that was lavished on the body of Jesus Christ. Sadly, some scholars have suggested that the body of Jesus was eaten by wild dogs at the foot of the cross.[7] Shame on them for their blasphemy! The Scripture tells how Joseph of Arimathea went to Pilate to ask for the body of Jesus and how he "[took] him down, wrapped him in the linen shroud and laid him in a tomb that had been cut out of the rock" (Mark 15:46). Joseph exercised the same tender care for the body of Jesus that Ebed-melech showed for the body of Jeremiah. These men understood that bodies matter, especially the bodies of prophets.

The first witnesses of the empty tomb understood the same thing. "When the Sabbath was past, Mary Magdalene, Mary the mother of James, and Salome bought spices, so that they might go and anoint him" (Mark 16:1). They wanted to care for Jesus' body, but there was no need. God himself had cared for the body of his Son, the Prophet. He did not abandon Jesus to the grave. He did not let his "holy one see corruption" (Psalm 16:10). Rather, God raised him up from the dead, giving him a resurrection body that will endure for all eternity.

One day Jeremiah will get the same kind of body. Surely he was one of the prophets the writer of Hebrews had in mind when he wrote:

> And what more shall I say? For time would fail me to tell of . . . the proph-ets—who through faith conquered kingdoms. . . . Others suffered mock-ing and flogging, and even chains and imprisonment. . . . They went about in skins of sheep and goats, destitute, afflicted, mistreated—of whom the world was not worthy—wandering about in deserts and mountains, and in dens and caves of the earth. (11:32, 33a, 36, 37b, 38)

Many of those things were true of Jeremiah. He was flogged and put in prison; he was persecuted and mistreated; he was confined to a hole in the ground. But Hebrews goes on to say: "And all these, though commended through their faith, did not receive what was promised, since God had pro-vided something better for us, that apart from us they should not be made perfect" (11:39, 40).

Something better? Yes, the prophets had to wait for the resurrection. They were looking forward to eternal life in Jesus Christ, which is better by far than anything else they ever experienced. One day Jeremiah will receive that resur-rection life, just as we will receive it, in the risen Christ.

54

A Private Audience

JEREMIAH 38:14–28

IS ANY OF THIS starting to sound familiar? Jeremiah the prophet is in jail. His enemies among the leaders of Jerusalem have thrown him into the water cistern in a private home. There they have left him to die, as if in a dungeon. King Zedekiah is nervous. He is afraid of the Babylonian army that has attacked his city, and he wants to know what God is planning to do with him.

So Zedekiah has Jeremiah brought up from the dungeon for a private audience. When the prophet arrives, the king anxiously asks for a word from the Lord. Jeremiah gives it to him: Jerusalem will fall into the hands of the Babylonians; Zedekiah will not escape. At the end of the conversation, Jeremiah returns not to the dungeon, but to house arrest in the courtyard of the guard.

Déjà Vu?

If any of this sounds familiar, it is because what happened to Jeremiah in chapter 37 happens to him again in chapter 38. Jeremiah 38 is a case of déjà vu. The two stories share many of the same characters and events.

The similarities between these two chapters have led some scholars to argue that they are two (contradictory) reports of the same event. Douglas Rawlinson Jones, for example, provides a list of the "elements common to both accounts":

(1) The officials hear of Jeremiah's preaching, and cast him into a prison which is of such a kind that, if he is allowed to remain there, he will die.
(2) Zedekiah has him released and questions him secretly.
(3) Jeremiah's oracle is in each case twofold: Zedekiah will survive; Jerusalem will fall.

(4) Jeremiah pleads not to be returned to his former cell and is committed to the court of the guard.

(5) There he remains until the fall of the city.

Jones concludes that "There can be no reasonable doubt that these stories are duplicate traditions of the same event, each however providing something which the other omits."[1]

This is a favorite strategy of Bible scholars—deciding that two similar events are actually the same event. It is as if nothing in the world ever happens twice! In this commentary I have chosen not to answer all the criticisms lodged against Jeremiah's book, which has suffered much at the hands of many scholars. But this is one time when the history and artistry of the Bible must be defended.

For all their similarities, Jeremiah 37 and 38 describe two separate events. Consider all the differences: There are two charges. First Jeremiah is accused of desertion (37:13); then he is blamed for demoralizing the troops (38:4). There are two jails. In one chapter Jeremiah is imprisoned in Jonathan's dungeon (37:15), while in the other he ends up in Malchiah's cistern (38:6). There are two rescues. First Zedekiah orders Jeremiah to be removed from Jonathan's dungeon and held in the courtyard of the guard (37:21). Later Ebed-melech uses ropes to haul Jeremiah out of Malchiah's cistern (38:11–13). There are two meeting places. In one chapter Jeremiah is invited to the palace (37:17); in the next chapter he goes to the temple (38:14).

Finally, there are two conversations. In their first rendezvous, Jeremiah pronounces judgment upon the king and pleads for his own life (37:17–20). At their second secret meeting, the prophet tells Zedekiah to surrender to the Babylonians (38:18). Surrender was unnecessary in chapter 37 because the Babylonians had just lifted their siege, but by chapter 38 it is the city's only hope.

Thus a careful reading of Jeremiah 37 and 38 yields the following sequence of events:

1. Under threat of an Egyptian attack, the Babylonians lift their siege of Jerusalem (37:4, 5).
2. Zedekiah asks Jeremiah for prayer (v. 3) but receives a prophecy of judgment (vv. 6–10).
3. As he tries to leave Jerusalem on a business trip (vv. 11, 12), Jeremiah is arrested, beaten, and imprisoned in a dungeon at the house of Jonathan (vv. 13–15).
4. Some time later Zedekiah sends for Jeremiah. Once again Jeremiah prophesies disaster (vv. 16, 17).

5. Zedekiah grants Jeremiah's petition to leave the dungeon and has him placed in custody in the courtyard of the guard (vv. 18–21).
6. Tired of Jeremiah's preaching, a group of officials persuade the king to put the prophet to death (38:1–5). Presumably by this time the Babylonians have resumed hostilities (cf. 32:1–5).
7. The prophet is sent to a dungeon a second time. This time it is a cistern in the house of Malchiah, and Jeremiah is left to die (38:6).
8. Ebed-melech gets permission to rescue Jeremiah and return him to the courtyard of the guard (vv. 7–13).
9. Zedekiah sends for Jeremiah a second time (v. 14). Disaster is again foretold, with the possibility of escape if the king will surrender to Babylon (vv. 17–23).
10. Jeremiah returns to the courtyard of the guard, where he remains until the fall of Jerusalem (vv. 24–28).

Nothing in this chronology is at all implausible, particularly when it is remembered that these were days of utter chaos in Jerusalem.

The Fellowship of Suffering

Getting the facts straight about Jeremiah's incarceration is important. The facts show how greatly Jeremiah suffered for God and for God's Word. He was ignored, accused, beaten, imprisoned, and falsely charged with treason. He was hauled from prison to prison and dungeon to dungeon, dragged from one miserable place to another, until finally he was left to die in the mud.

Jeremiah's legal troubles were similar to those of the Apostle Paul, who claimed that he had worked

> with far greater labors, far more imprisonments, with countless beatings, and often near death. Five times I received at the hands of the Jews the forty lashes less one. Three times I was beaten with rods. Once I was stoned. Three times I was shipwrecked; a night and a day I was adrift at sea; on frequent journeys, in danger from rivers, danger from robbers, danger from my own people, danger from Gentiles, danger in the city, danger in the wilderness, danger at sea, danger from false brothers; in toil and hardship, through many a sleepless night, in hunger and thirst, often without food, in cold and exposure. And, apart from other things, there is the daily pressure on me of my anxiety for all the churches. (2 Corinthians 11:23b–28)

With the exception of being stoned or shipwrecked on the high seas, Jeremiah went through all of that, including the daily burden of his concern for God's people.

Paul and Jeremiah show how much a believer may suffer for the sake of

Christ. Suffering is the usual pattern of the Christian life. This is because suffering was the pattern of Christ's life. As the Westminster *Shorter Catechism* explains, Jesus Christ suffered "The miseries of this life, the wrath of God, and the cursed death of the cross" (A. 27). Just as Christ suffered, so the Christian must suffer. "We are children of God . . . provided we suffer with him in order that we may also be glorified with him" (Romans 8:16b, 17). Anyone who wants to share in Christ's exaltation must first share in his humiliation.

The Apostle Paul understood how necessary it is for the Christian to suffer. Amazingly, he even desired the trials of life. He wanted to know Christ "and the power of his resurrection, and . . . share his sufferings, becoming like him in his death, that by any means possible [he might] attain the resurrection from the dead" (Philippians 3:10, 11). Jeremiah had a passionate desire to know the same things. His place in the history of redemption prevented him from knowing Christ's resurrection power, but surely he knew the fellowship of sharing in Christ's sufferings.

When you suffer, it should not come as a surprise, especially if you suffer for the sake of Christ. Do you know the fellowship of sharing your sufferings with Christ? Do you sense his compassion as one who has tasted all the miseries of human life and death? Do you experience the sympathy of the Holy Spirit to comfort you in grief? Do you take strength from the hope of the resurrection? All this help is available to God's friends whenever they are in trouble.

Everyone who suffers with Christ receives strength through suffering. Dietrich Bonhoeffer (1906–1945), the German pastor who lost his life for resisting the Nazis, wrote:

> If we refuse to take up our cross and submit to suffering and rejection at the hands of men, we forfeit our fellowship with Christ and have ceased to follow him. But if we lose our lives in his service and carry our cross, we shall find our lives again in the fellowship of the cross with Christ. . . . To bear the cross proves to be the only way of triumphing over suffering. This is true for all who follow Christ, because it was true for him.[2]

By Fear or by Faith?

There is another reason it is important to know that Zedekiah had at least two meetings with Jeremiah: It shows what kind of king he was. The fact that he kept sending for Jeremiah shows that he could not make up his mind:

> Nothing lasted long with Zedekiah. The man was a marshmallow. He received impressions from anyone who pushed hard enough. When the pres-

sure was off, he gradually resumed his earlier state ready for the next impression. In contrast to Jeremiah, who was formed within by obedience to God and faith in God (an iron pillar!), Zedekiah took on whatever shape the circumstances required.[3]

Zedekiah was vulnerable to peer pressure. Whoever had the ear of the king steered the ship of state. When Nebuchadnezzar first came to capture Jerusalem in 597 BC, Zedekiah was all for the Babylonians. In fact, he became their puppet king over the city. But once they went back home, he started listening to the advisers who wanted to rebel (cf. Ezekiel 17:11–21). So Zedekiah reversed his foreign policy. He also vacillated in his domestic policy. First the abolitionists persuaded him to make an emancipation proclamation, but then the slaveholders talked him into revoking it (34:8–11).

The king had equal difficulty making up his mind about Jeremiah. He sent him to the dungeon (37:16), but then he took him out and placed him under house arrest (37:21). He refused to listen to him (37:2), but he also wanted to hear what he had to say (21:1, 2; 37:17). "King Zedekiah sent for Jeremiah the prophet and received him at the third entrance of the temple of the Lord. The king said to Jeremiah, 'I will ask you a question; hide nothing from me'" (38:14). The king was asking the prophet to speak "off the record."

Apparently Zedekiah still held out the hope that God might change his mind. But God insisted that if anyone needed to change his mind, it was Zedekiah himself:

> Then Jeremiah said to Zedekiah, "Thus says the LORD, the God of hosts, the God of Israel: If you will surrender to the officials of the king of Babylon, then your life shall be spared, and this city shall not be burned with fire, and you and your house shall live. But if you do not surrender to the officials of the king of Babylon, then this city shall be given into the hand of the Chaldeans, and they shall burn it with fire, and you shall not escape from their hand." (vv. 17, 18)

Jeremiah gave the king a choice: turn or burn. If he turned himself over to the Babylonians, he would be saved. If not, Jerusalem would be burned to the ground. This was the same choice God had given the whole city some time before (21:8ff.: "Behold, I set before you the way of life and the way of death"). "Surrender spells safety; resistance means ruin."[4]

The fact that God even gave Zedekiah a choice was a remarkable sign of his patience. Many times God warned the king that his sins would lead to judgment. Just as often, Zedekiah ignored the warnings. Yet the Lord still held out to him a way of escape. He still offered him grace, mercy, and peace.

God shows the same patience to every sinner. The Scripture makes this promise:

> But by the same word the heavens and earth that now exist are stored up for fire, being kept until the day of judgment and destruction of the ungodly. But do not overlook this one fact, beloved, that with the Lord one day is as a thousand years, and a thousand years as one day. The Lord is not slow to fulfill his promise as some count slowness, but is patient toward you, not wishing that any should perish, but that all should reach repentance. (2 Peter 3:7–9)

At this very moment God is exercising his patience toward sinners. The day of judgment is being held back because God does not want anyone to perish. He still offers every sinner a way of escape—eternal life through faith in Jesus Christ.

Sadly, Zedekiah rejected the way of salvation. God told him exactly what to do, but he was too afraid to do it. He may have been afraid of the Babylonians. "Rebel kings who surrendered were usually mutilated and put to death, so the prospects for Zedekiah were anything but pleasant."[5] He was especially afraid of the Jews who had deserted to the enemy. "King Zedekiah said to Jeremiah, 'I am afraid of the Judeans who have deserted to the Chaldeans, lest I be handed over to them and they deal cruelly with me'" (38:19; cf. 38:4). When Zedekiah used the phrase "deal cruelly," literally he was afraid that his own countrymen would "abuse" him.

By itself, Zedekiah's fear was not a sin. There are times when it is good to fear the Lord or even to be afraid of danger. Zedekiah's sin was living by his fears rather than by faith. His sin was not trusting God when he was afraid. His sin was keeping his fears to himself rather than taking them to the Lord. Once he admitted, "I am afraid," he found himself unable to do anything else. He was paralyzed with fear.

King David once found himself in the same kind of situation King Zedekiah was in. He was surrounded by enemies and finally captured by the Philistines. He described his troubles like this:

> Be gracious to me, O God, for man tramples on me;
>   all day long an attacker oppresses me;
> my enemies trample on me all day long,
>   for many attack me proudly. (Psalm 56:1, 2)

Although David was a man of great courage, he feared for his life. In the next verse he admitted that he was as afraid as Zedekiah was. But David did not remain frightened for long. Unlike Zedekiah, he knew how to trust and obey while he was still afraid:

> When I am afraid,
>   I put my trust in you.
> In God, whose word I praise,
>   in God I trust; I shall not be afraid.
> What can flesh do to me? (Psalm 56:3, 4)

As he wrote his psalm, David was still scared, but he would not stay that way. He knew how to live by faith in the middle of his fear. He was working through his fear to a place of confidence and trust in God.

As a pastor I often counsel people who are trying to decide whether to live by faith or by fear. They know the right thing to do, but they are afraid to do it. Here are some typical examples:

> A young Christian woman is involved in a romantic relationship with a man who is not a Christian. She knows she must break off the relationship because they cannot marry. Yet she is afraid to break up with him because of the pain and loneliness she will experience.
> A teenager has committed a petty theft. He knows it is not enough to confess his stealing to the Lord; he must go back and repay the party he has robbed. But he is afraid of what his parents will do when they find out.
> An addict knows that drugs and alcohol are destroying his life. He half wants to quit, but he is unable to leave behind the familiar comfort and security of his addictions.
> A wife is deep in credit card debt or a husband has fallen into the snare of pornography. Each is in such bondage to sin that escape seems impossible. Yet they are afraid to get spiritual help. Among other things, they know their spouses will be angry or devastated if they find out.

In such cases it is all too easy to say, "I know what I should do, but . . ." "But the situation is too far gone." "But I am afraid what people will think." "But I can't face the consequences." "But I don't know what will happen to me if I confess."

The truth is that it is always best to obey the Lord. No matter what. If you hold back from obeying the Lord, it will permanently weaken your spiritual condition. It is much worse to end up in an unequal marriage, to stay addicted to drugs, or to carry around a weight of guilt for secret sin than it is to face up to sin and pray for the grace to overcome it. Sin is like foul-smelling mold. When it stays in the dark it festers, but as soon as it is brought out into the light of God's grace it begins to die.

Once I received a telephone call from an officer in another church. He was in great distress because he was involved in a sin that threatened to destroy not only his family but also, in his opinion, his church. He knew he needed to go to his pastor and confess his sin so the process of reconciliation could begin. But he was afraid. He was afraid of what would happen to him, to the people he loved, and to his church.

I gave him the same counsel I would give to anyone who is afraid to do the right thing: You *must* do the right thing. The consequences of disobedience are always much worse than the consequences of repentance. God is so wise and gracious that he can bring great good out of a bad situation, provided there is genuine repentance.

Genuine repentance is what Zedekiah needed to give. God offered him a good way out of a bad situation. If only he would surrender, his life would be spared and his city would be saved! So Jeremiah pleaded with him to obey. "Jeremiah said, 'You shall not be given to them. Obey now the voice of the Lord in what I say to you, and it shall be well with you, and your life shall be spared'" (38:20).

What would Zedekiah, that marshmallow of a king, decide to do? The fate of an entire nation was hanging in the balance. Kidner says, "To see what hung on the king's yes or no, we have only to read the next chapter for the horror awaiting him and his sons, or to read Lamentations 4 for the living skeletons and cannibals of the city's last days."[6]

The German scholar B. Duhm paints a vivid portrait of the encounter:

> The scene is just as moving as it is historically interesting; on the one hand is the prophet, disfigured by mistreatment, the prison atmosphere and privations, but firm in his predictions, without any invective against his persecutors, without defiance, exaggeration or fanaticism, simple, physically mild and humble; on the other hand is the king who, obviously against his own will, had been led by his officials into the war venture, anxiously watching the lips of the martyr for a favorable word for himself, whispering secretly with the man whom his officials imprisoned for treason, weak, a poor creature but not evil, a king but much more bound than the prisoner who stands before him.[7]

As it turned out, this was the last interview Jeremiah and Zedekiah ever had. It was the king's last, best chance for salvation. John Guest writes: "This was Zedekiah's last chance to save the city, its walls, its warriors, its women and children. All he had to do was trust the prophet, to lift his head high, take up the flag of truce, walk past the princes and out to the Chaldean armies. This simple act of contrition would have saved the city."[8] Sadly, Zedekiah squandered his final opportunity for salvation. "Zedekiah dithered until Jerusalem burned."[9]

In the end Zedekiah was betrayed by his own officials. Jeremiah's prophecy about this was vivid. He portrayed the royal harem taunting the king while they were being carried off as prisoners of war.

> But if you refuse to surrender, this is the vision which the LORD has shown to me: Behold, all the women left in the house of the king of Judah were being led out to the officials of the king of Babylon and were saying,
>
> > "Your trusted friends have deceived you
> > and prevailed against you;
> > now that your feet are sunk in the mud,
> > they turn away from you."
>
> All your wives and your sons shall be led out to the Chaldeans, and you yourself shall not escape from their hand, but shall be seized by the king of Babylon, and this city shall be burned with fire." (vv. 21–23)

These verses are highly ironic. The king's "Trusted friends" are literally called "men of shalom." They are the ones, remember, who promised "peace, peace" when there was no peace. But the final irony is that Zedekiah—who let Jeremiah be thrown into the muddy cistern—will be stuck in the mud himself!

The Fearless One

It is not easy to live by faith rather than by fear. On occasion even a faithful man like Jeremiah can allow fear to lead him into sin.

After their last private audience:

> Then Zedekiah said to Jeremiah, "Let no one know of these words, and you shall not die. If the officials hear that I have spoken with you and come to you and say to you, 'Tell us what you said to the king and what the king said to you; hide nothing from us and we will not put you to death,' then you shall say to them, 'I made a humble plea to the king that he would not send me back to the house of Jonathan to die there.'" (vv. 24–26)

Zedekiah was more concerned about the political situation than about his spiritual condition. He was more worried about what people would think than about doing what was right. He was a man like King Herod, who preferred to commit murder than to be embarrassed in front of his dinner guests (Matthew 14:9, 10). Zedekiah did not want Jeremiah to tell on him. Like most unscrupulous politicians, he was afraid of leaks. So he told Jeremiah what kind of "spin" to put on their private meeting.

The surprise is that Jeremiah went along with him: "Then all the officials came to Jeremiah and asked him, and he answered them as the king had instructed him. So they stopped speaking with him, for the conversation had not been overheard. And Jeremiah remained in the court of the guard until the day that Jerusalem was taken" (38:27, 28). Jeremiah lied. There is no other way to put it. The prophet was given another opportunity to preach sin and grace to the leaders of Jerusalem, but he kept his mouth shut. Instead he gave them a clever story about an earlier audience with the king.

The fact that the king told Jeremiah to lie is no excuse. When it comes to a choice between serving the king and serving the King of kings, "We must obey God rather than men" (Acts 5:29).

Jeremiah's dishonesty is surprising because he had never been afraid before, especially of politicians. He rebuked them in the city. He opposed them in the temple. He braved their beatings. He defied their dungeons. Through it all he kept preaching God's Word without compromise. In keeping with God's promise, the prophet had always been "a fortified city, an iron pillar, and bronze walls, against the whole land, against the kings of Judah, its officials, its priests, and the people of the land" (1:18).

The walls started to crumble, however, and the pillar started to crack. Jeremiah's fears finally started to get the best of him. The last time he visited Zedekiah, he begged the king to rescue him from Jonathan's dungeon lest he should die (37:20). In this audience, he feared for his life once again.

First, he was afraid of the king himself: "Jeremiah said to Zedekiah, 'If I tell you, will you not surely put me to death? And if I give you counsel, you will not listen to me'" (v. 15). Jeremiah hesitated to prophesy because he feared (with some justification!) that the king would put him to death. He wanted Zedekiah to give him prophetic immunity, which he did: "Then King Zedekiah swore secretly to Jeremiah, 'As the LORD lives, who made our souls, I will not put you to death or deliver you into the hand of these men who seek your life'" (v. 16). Even after this reassurance, however, Jeremiah was still afraid. At the end of his audience with Zedekiah, he was so afraid that he lied to save his neck.

Jeremiah's fear is a reminder of his humanity. He was a hero of the faith, not a superhero. Like any other believer, Jeremiah had times of doubt, fear, weakness, and even sin. In his sinful nature he was no better than Zedekiah, who acted on his fears rather than by his faith. On this occasion at least, Jeremiah committed the very same sin. Twice God had delivered him from death, but this time Jeremiah fearfully tried to save himself.

It is dangerous to think that one has ever mastered a sin. Being faithful to God in the past is no guarantee of faithfulness in the future. Maybe you were very bold in your evangelism when you first became a Christian. Are you as outspoken now as you were then? Perhaps you are more humble than you were three years ago. Still, it would be very easy for you to slip back into pride. Maybe there was a time when you sold everything you had and gave it to the poor. But that does not prevent the weed of covetousness from ever sprouting in your spiritual garden. "Therefore let anyone who thinks that he stands take heed lest he fall" (1 Corinthians 10:12).

Jeremiah was a very great prophet. A careful study of his life and ministry places an indelible stamp on any Christian's life. He was passionate, faithful, long-suffering. He had a heart for God and a love for God's people. But Jeremiah was not perfect. There were even times when his fear overcame his faith and he disobeyed God. What Jeremiah needed was a Savior for his sins.

When people met Jesus of Nazareth, they were sometimes reminded of Jeremiah:

> Now when Jesus came into the district of Caesarea Philippi, he asked his disciples, "Who do people say that the Son of Man is?" And they said, "Some say John the Baptist, others say Elijah, and others Jeremiah or one of the prophets." He said to them, "But who do you say that I am?" Simon Peter replied, "You are the Christ, the Son of the living God." And Jesus answered him, "Blessed are you, Simon Bar-Jonah! For flesh and blood has not revealed this to you, but my Father who is in heaven." (Matthew 16:13–17)

The similarities between Jesus and Jeremiah were striking. Both men had a gift for teaching. Both men had a passion for rebuking sin. Both men had a love for God's people. But by the Spirit of God, Simon Peter spotted the crucial difference. Jesus was and is "The Christ, the Son of the living God." He was and is the perfect Son of God as well as a real human being.

Because Jesus is the Christ, he never committed a single sin. His fears never got the best of him. He always lived by faith, never by fear. Even when he was being led to his own crucifixion, he kept trusting his Father in Heaven. Jesus lived, died, and rose again by faith rather than by fear. He did it so he could be Jeremiah's Savior, and the Savior of all who trust in him.

55

Brands from the Burning

JEREMIAH 39:1–18

TRY TO PICTURE THIS SCENE:

The tongue of the nursing infant sticks
    to the roof of its mouth for thirst;
the children beg for food,
    but no one gives to them.

Those who once feasted on delicacies
    perish in the streets;
those who were brought up in purple
    embrace ash heaps. . . .

Happier were the victims of the sword
    than the victims of hunger,
who wasted away, pierced
    by lack of the fruits of the field.

The hands of compassionate women
    have boiled their own children;
they became their food
    during the destruction of the daughter of my people.

The LORD gave full vent to his wrath;
    he poured out his hot anger,
and he kindled a fire in Zion
    that consumed its foundations. . . .

They dogged our steps
    so that we could not walk in our streets;
our end drew near; our days were numbered,
    for our end had come. (Lamentations 4:4, 5, 9–11, 18)

These lines of poetry were written by the prophet Jeremiah. They form an eyewitness account of the last, desperate days leading up to the fall of Jerusalem. After eighteen long months of siege, the Babylonian army marched into Jerusalem for the last time in July of 587 BC

According to Josephus, "The battering ram took its last run at the walls. Darts from the enemy siege mounds arched into the midnight sky and struck their mark in flames. Famine had already claimed many lives inside the walls. Five Babylonian princes marched through the streets of Jerusalem, their faces illuminated by the flames of destruction."[1]

These historical reports have been confirmed by the archaeologist Katherine Kenyon, who has shown how the walls and houses of Jerusalem were reduced to rubble.[2] The fall of Jerusalem was an epochal event in world history. The city did not return to Jewish rule until the middle of the twentieth century, some twenty-five hundred years later.

Jerusalem Burning

The fall of Jerusalem was also an important event in redemptive history. It proved that all God's promises of judgment come true.

The prophet Jeremiah gave a sober, restrained account of Jerusalem's fall, explaining who occupied the city, when, and how:

> In the ninth year of Zedekiah king of Judah, in the tenth month, Nebuchadnezzar king of Babylon and all his army came against Jerusalem and besieged it. In the eleventh year of Zedekiah, in the fourth month, on the ninth day of the month, a breach was made in the city. Then all the officials of the king of Babylon came and sat in the middle gate: Nergal-sar-ezer of Samgar, Nebu-sar-sekim the Rab-saris, Nergal-sar-ezer the Rab-mag, with all the rest of the officers of the king of Babylon. (39:1–3; cf. 2 Kings 25:1–4)

This is how ancient generals claimed victory over a defeated city. The victors would take their seats in the city gates. In triumph they would claim the place of rule and governance. Jeremiah listed some Babylonian names to show that Judah's conquerors spoke a strange and unfamiliar tongue (cf. 5:15).

Once they took the city, "The Chaldeans burned the king's house and the house of the people, and broke down the walls of Jerusalem" (39:8; cf. 2 Kings 25:8–10). Palaces, houses, walls—everything was torched. Then the best and brightest of the Jews were deported to Babylon. "Then Nebuzaradan, the captain of the guard, carried into exile to Babylon the rest of the people who were left in the city, those who had deserted to him, and the people who remained" (v. 9).

These verses form the climax of Jeremiah's book—and the low point of Jeremiah's life. From the first verse of the first chapter, his prophecies have marched relentlessly toward the day of Jerusalem's destruction. Although in this passage he writes with the detachment of a historian, every word strikes like a hammer. The dreaded day has finally come.

On the day of judgment every promise God ever made about the fall of Jerusalem came true (cf. 2 Kings 25:1–26; Jeremiah 52:4–30). God said disaster would come from the north (1:14; 4:6; 6:22; 13:20), and disaster came from the north. God said a strange, foreign nation would attack (5:15), and a strange, foreign nation attacked. God said Jerusalem would be surrounded and besieged (4:17; 6:3, 6; cf. Ezekiel 4:1–3), and Jerusalem was surrounded and besieged. God said there would be famine in the land (14:1–6, 16, 18; 18:21; cf. Ezekiel 4:16, 17), and there was famine in the land. God said the whole land would be laid waste (25:11), and the whole land was laid waste. God said nations and kingdoms would be torn down (1:10; cf. 39:8), and the nation of Judah was torn down, stone by stone.

The list of fulfilled prophecy goes on and on. God said death would enter the city (9:21; cf. 15:7–9; 18:21), and death entered the city. God said kings would "come, and every one shall set his throne at the entrance of the gates of Jerusalem" (1:15). The kings came, they conquered, and they sat. God promised that the city would be burned (21:10, 14; 32:29; 34:2, 22; 37:8; 38:18, 23; cf. Ezekiel 5:1–4), and the city was reduced to ashes. God said his people would be taken into exile (10:17, 18; 13:17–19; 15:14; 17:4), and they were lined up in chains to be deported.

God even promised, through the prophet Ezekiel, "I will bring him [Zedekiah] to Babylon, the land of the Chaldeans, yet he shall not see it, and he shall die there" (Ezekiel 12:13). This curious prophecy was fulfilled when Zedekiah was blinded before his arrival in Babylon; he went to that great city, but he never saw it!

The fall of Jerusalem confirmed many specific promises of divine judgment. All Jeremiah's prophecies of destruction came true. Calvin thus referred to chapter 39 as "The proof of all his former doctrine."[3] Twice God told Jeremiah, "Behold, I am bringing upon Judah and all the inhabitants of Jerusalem all the disaster that I have pronounced against them" (35:17a; cf. 19:15). He meant what he said. God delivered every disaster he promised. Lest there be any doubt who brought these things to pass, he said, "I will fulfill my words against this city for harm" (39:16; cf. 40:2).

The Judgment to Come

Many of Jeremiah's contemporaries doubted that the day of judgment would ever come. The religious leaders were promising "peace, peace" rather than the sword (6:14; 8:11). By and large the people of Jerusalem did not believe in the wrath of God, despite many warnings to the contrary.

The same is true in these post-Christian times. The person on the street lives in ignorance of Christ's imminent return. The final judgment is generally treated as a humorous subject. The man carrying the sign that reads, "Repent—The End Is Near" is either mocked or ignored. The place Hell is most likely to be mentioned in American culture is on the comics page in the newspaper. Doubts about the reality of judgment and eternal damnation have also entered the church. As John Blanchard has asked, *Whatever Happened to Hell?*[4]

The apostle Peter promised this would happen. He said "That scoffers will come in the last days with scoffing, following their own sinful desires. They will say, 'Where is the promise of his coming? For ever since the fathers fell asleep, all things are continuing as they were from the beginning of creation'" (2 Peter 3:3, 4). Peter was right. The people of this generation do not believe in God's wrath, do not look for Christ's coming, and do not fear the day of judgment.

Therefore, the question must be asked and answered: What does the Bible say will happen on the day of judgment?

First, the Lord Jesus Christ will return. He will return *personally*. As the angel said to the disciples, "This Jesus, who was taken up from you into heaven, will come in the same way as you saw him go into heaven" (Acts 1:11). He will return *impressively*. "For the Lord himself will descend from heaven with a cry of command, with the voice of an archangel, and with the sound of the trumpet of God" (1 Thessalonians 4:16). And he will return *visibly*: "Behold, he is coming with the clouds, and every eye will see him" (Revelation 1:7a).

The personal, impressive, visible return of Jesus Christ will be sudden and cataclysmic:

> The heavens and earth that now exist are stored up for fire, being kept until the day of judgment and destruction of the ungodly. . . . But the day of the Lord will come like a thief, and then the heavens will pass away with a roar, and the heavenly bodies will be burned up and dissolved, and the earth and the works that are done on it will be exposed. . . . the heavens will be set on fire and dissolved, and the heavenly bodies will melt as they burn! (2 Peter 3:7, 10, 12)

No one knows when the day of judgment will come (Matthew 24:36). But when it does come, everything in the heavens and the earth will be destroyed. The conflagration in Jerusalem was a warning of what will happen to the entire cosmos at the end of history. The whole universe—with all its stars, planets, comets, and galaxies—will undergo instantaneous heat death.

Furthermore, the Bible says it will be a day of reckoning: "He [God] has fixed a day on which he will judge the world in righteousness by a man whom he has appointed" (Acts 17:31). The dead will be raised, and every man, woman, and child who has ever lived will be gathered before God's throne for judgment.

Then God "will render to each one according to his works" (Romans 2:6). "For we must all appear before the judgment seat of Christ" (2 Corinthians 5:10; cf. John 5:25–29). As Jesus himself has promised, "When the Son of Man comes in his glory, and all the angels with him, then he will sit on his glorious throne. Before him will be gathered all the nations, and he will separate people one from another as a shepherd separates the sheep from the goats" (Matthew 25:31, 32).

"Depart from Me, You Cursed"

There is a second question to be asked about the day of judgment. The first has already been asked and answered from Scripture: What will happen on the day of judgment? The second must be answered within every human heart: What will happen to me on the day of judgment?

Not everyone will meet the same end. There will be two different kinds of people on that day—the sheep and the goats; the righteous and the unrighteous. These two peoples will have two very different destinies. Some will be saved, while the rest will be lost forever. Some will walk through pearly gates into the heavenly city of gold (Revelation 21:21), while the rest will be condemned to an eternal hell of fire (Matthew 18:8, 9; cf. Revelation 20:11–15). Jesus promised that the unrighteous "will go away into eternal punishment, but the righteous into eternal life" (Matthew 25:46).

The burning of Jerusalem is a picture of the final judgment. There were also two kinds of people on that day—the righteous and the unrighteous. And they met two very different ends. Some were saved, and some were lost. Some were redeemed, and some were damned.

Zedekiah was lost. When the day of judgment came, the king who could never make up his mind whether he wanted to follow God or not had no one to save him but himself. The Bible gives a glimpse of his desperate attempt to escape by a secret route to the valley: "When Zedekiah king of Judah and all the soldiers saw them [the Babylonian generals], they fled, going out of the city at night by way of the king's garden through the gate between the two walls; and they went toward the Arabah" (39:4; cf. Ezekiel 12:12). Zedekiah abandoned ship like a coward instead of going down with it like a worthy captain.

Zedekiah did not get very far, however. Fugitives can run, but they cannot hide. "But the army of the Chaldeans pursued them and overtook Zedekiah in the plains of Jericho" (v. 5a). The soldiers captured them and brought them to Nebuchadnezzar's field headquarters, where Zedekiah received summary military justice:

> And when they had taken him, they brought him up to Nebuchadnezzar king of Babylon, at Riblah, in the land of Hamath; and he passed sentence on him. The king of Babylon slaughtered the sons of Zedekiah at Riblah before his eyes, and the king of Babylon slaughtered all the nobles of Judah. He put out the eyes of Zedekiah and bound him in chains to take him to Babylon. (vv. 5b–7)

Zedekiah received the punishment God had long promised for his sins. And worse. Jeremiah prophesied that the king of Judah would not escape (38:18) but would see the king of Babylon with his own eyes (34:3). What he did not prophesy was that Zedekiah would watch his sons, the princes of Judah, butchered before his very eyes. Or specifically that Nebuchadnezzar would blind him as well as bind him. In an act of cruel barbarity, Nebuchadnezzar tore out Zedekiah's eyes. In the words of one commentator: "The brutal death of his sons is the last thing he sees, the last thing he will ever see, the thing he will see as long as he lives."[5]

Zedekiah's fate finds an echo in the torture of Gloucester in William Shakespeare's *King Lear*. Taking knife to eyeball, his wicked daughter Cornwall says, "Out, vile jelly!" To which Gloucester responds, "All dark and comfortless."[6] For Zedekiah, as for Gloucester, all was dark and comfortless. How he must have longed for death on his long, slow, dark march to Babylon. The day of judgment turned out to be far worse than he could have ever imagined.

Like Zedekiah, many people hope to escape the day of judgment. They doubt the personal return of Jesus Christ to judge the world. They hope that the wrath of God has been exaggerated. They deny the existence of Hell. They think they are good enough to get to Heaven. They expect to have time to slip out the garden door and run for dear life.

Jeremiah 39 stands as a warning against every naive hope of escaping the judgment to come. Zedekiah suffered a fate worse than death. To his dismay, he discovered the day of judgment to be a living hell.

The saddest thing about the final chapter in Zedekiah's tragic story is that the king could have written a happy ending. Right up until the very end, God gave him every opportunity to repent for his sins (38:20). Jeremiah repeatedly went to Zedekiah and pleaded with him to turn to God in faith and repentance. But the king rejected every last entreaty.

If the Holy Spirit has warned you of divine judgment, do not be so foolish. At this very moment God is giving you the same chance he gave Zedekiah. It is the chance—perhaps your last—to confess your sins, believe in Jesus Christ, and escape the judgment to come.

"Come, You Who Are Blessed by My Father"

Happily, not everyone will be lost on the day of judgment. Although the fall of Jerusalem was a day of damnation for some, it was a day of salvation for others. The poor were made rich, and slaves received their freedom: "Nebuzaradan, the captain of the guard, left in the land of Judah some of the poor people who owned nothing, and gave them vineyards and fields at the same time" (39:10). Thus, after the grand deportation, the property of wealthy landowners was redistributed among the peasants.

It was also a day of salvation for God's servants. As the city burned, Jeremiah and Ebed-melech were delivered from death like brands snatched from the burning.

Jeremiah was saved from judgment because—somewhat unexpectedly—he had friends in high places: "Nebuchadnezzar king of Babylon gave command concerning Jeremiah through Nebuzaradan, the captain of the guard, saying, 'Take him, look after him well, and do him no harm, but deal with him as he tells you'" (vv. 11, 12). Even in the chaos of the fallen city, Jeremiah was not forgotten. Why Nebuchadnezzar took notice of him is a mystery. Perhaps, and there is some evidence for this (see the book of Daniel), he had respect for prophets. Perhaps some of the Jews who deserted to the Babylonians told him about the man who begged the city to surrender. In any case, by the providence of God, Jeremiah's life was spared.

God will not forget his friends on the day of judgment. It is easy to be overlooked in this world. Every day people get left behind by the bus. Birthdays are ignored, and anniversaries are forgotten. Applications get misplaced, and packages get lost in the mail. But God will not leave behind, ignore, forget, misplace, or lose a single believer on the day of judgment. Like Jeremiah, every child of God will be saved.

The contrast between Zedekiah and Jeremiah illustrates the teaching of Jesus Christ: "For whoever would save his life will lose it, but whoever loses his life for my sake will save it" (Luke 9:24). The king did everything he could to save his life and lost it. Jeremiah threw away his life for God and saved it.

God not only saved Jeremiah's life, but he also gave him a royal escort: "So Nebuzaradan the captain of the guard, Nebushazban the Rab-saris, Nergal-sar-ezer the Rab-mag, and all the chief officers of the king of Babylon sent and took Jeremiah from the court of the guard" (39:13, 14a). Then Jeremiah was received into the care of godly friends. "They entrusted him to Gedaliah the son of Ahikam, son of Shaphan, that he should take him home. So he lived among the people" (v. 14b).

Gedaliah, as we have seen, was a good man. He was a member of one of the godliest families left in Jerusalem. He was the grandson of Shaphan, who brought the Book of the Law to King Josiah (2 Kings 22:3–20). And he was the son of Ahikam, who defended Jeremiah's life when he was accused of blasphemy (26:24). God used Jeremiah's friends to save his life.

One does not have to be a famous prophet to be saved, however. Jeremiah 39 also documents the salvation of a slave:

> The word of the LORD came to Jeremiah while he was shut up in the court of the guard: "Go, and say to Ebed-melech the Ethiopian, 'Thus says the LORD of hosts, the God of Israel: Behold, I will fulfill my words against this city for harm and not for good, and they shall be accomplished before you on that day. But I will deliver you on that day, declares the LORD, and you shall not be given into the hand of the men of whom you are afraid. For I will surely save you, and you shall not fall by the sword, but you shall have your life as a prize of war, because you have put your trust in me, declares the LORD.'" (vv. 15–18)

These words explain what happened to Ebed-melech on the day of Jerusalem's judgment. God gave him a quintuple guarantee of salvation: "I will deliver you . . . you shall not be given into the hand of the men . . . I will surely save you . . . you shall not fall . . . you shall have your life as a prize of war." The Hebrew word translated "life" in this verse is actually the word for "booty," plunder taken in combat. Ebed-melech held on to his life like a battle prize.

Not even Ebed-melech's enemies were able to lay a finger on him. This perhaps refers to the officials he defied when he rescued Jeremiah from the mud (38:7–13). When Ebed-melech heard that Zedekiah had thrown Jeremiah into a cistern to die, he went to the king to plead for his life (38:8, 9). With the king's permission he pulled the prophet to safety. He was so thoughtful that he even took rags along to pad the ropes. Ebed-melech saved Jeremiah's life.

Later, when the slave's own life was in danger, God saved Ebed-melech. This is a hint from the Old Testament that God offers salvation in Jesus Christ to all the nations of the world. Ebed-melech was a Cushite from Ethiopia or the Nubian Empire. Thus he was one of the notable North Africans of the Bible. Like the Ethiopian eunuch whom Philip baptized (Acts 8:26–40), Ebed-melech shows that the gospel is for every tribe, people, and nation. It is for black, brown, red, and white.

The basis for Ebed-melech's salvation is important. He was not saved because God owed him a favor. He was not even saved because he rescued Jeremiah from the cistern. If ever a man could have been saved by works, it would have been Ebed-melech. His rescue operation demonstrated hatred of injustice and love for the ministry of God's Word. But when God promised to rescue him, he did not say one word about that courageous act.

Ebed-melech was not saved on the basis of any good work. He was saved by grace through faith: "I will surely save you . . . because you have put your trust in me" (39:18). "Ebed-Melech's trust in the Lord saved him from the fate of the rest of the city. God did not commend Ebed-Melech for his compassion or courage, but only for his trust in God."[7] This African slave was saved by grace, through faith—and this not from himself, it was the gift of God—not by works (cf. Ephesians 2:8, 9).

This is one place where the Old Testament teaches the doctrine of justification by faith alone, a doctrine more fully explained in the New Testament. Even someone who has performed as many good works as Mother Teresa of Calcutta (1910–1997), "The saint of the gutters," could not be declared righteous before God on the basis of personal merit. The believer does not stand before God on the basis of his or her own imperfect righteousness. Rather, the believer stands before God covered with the perfect righteousness of Jesus Christ, received by faith alone.

Snatched from the Flames

The story of the fall of Jerusalem gives a vivid picture of salvation from the judgment to come. Jeremiah and Ebed-melech were two brands plucked from the burning city.

In the same way, every sinner who comes to Christ in faith is like a branch snatched from the flames. This imagery is repeated throughout the Old Testament prophets. Amos said to Israel, "You were as a brand plucked out of the burning" (Amos 4:11). The angel of the Lord described Joshua the high priest as "a brand plucked from the fire" (Zechariah 3:2b). Every believer is a brand from the burning.

If every believer is a brand from the burning, then two things follow. First, every Christian can join Charles Wesley in praising God for a miraculous rescue:

Where shall my wondering soul begin?
How shall I all to heaven aspire?
A slave redeemed from death and sin,
A brand plucked from eternal fire,
How shall I equal triumphs raise,
Or sing my great Deliverer's praise?[8]

Second, saving other people from the flames is the responsibility of every Christian. There is too little urgency in the church for the salvation of the lost. What would the church be like if Christians understood that this post-Christian culture is about to be set aflame by the wrath of God? What would our witness be like if we saw the spiritual condition of unsaved family and friends as it actually is? And what if we accepted personal responsibility to help snatch them from the fire?

The book of Jude teaches Christians to think of themselves as spiritual firemen: "Have mercy on those who doubt; save others by snatching them out of the fire; to others show mercy with fear" (22, 23a). A whole course on Christian apologetics could be developed from these verses. But notice especially Jude's urgency: "Save others by snatching them out of the fire."

This is perhaps the best short description of evangelistic work in the Bible. It describes the work of missions, preaching, and personal evangelism: "Save others by snatching them out of the fire." Being snatched from the fire is exactly what happened to Jeremiah and Ebed-melech when Jerusalem fell. By God's grace, it is what will happen to every believer on the day of judgment.

The day of judgment will certainly come. On that dread day, every soul who has ever lived will be gathered before God. The same division will be made then as was made on the day Jerusalem fell. There will be only two kinds of people—the Jeremiahs and the Zedekiahs, the righteous and the unrighteous, the elect and the reprobate, the sheep and the goats, the redeemed and the damned.

On that day the enemies of God will be lost forever. They will be cast into the flames of Hell, to the praise of the glory of God's justice. But like brands from the burning, believers in the Lord Jesus Christ will be saved. They will escape final judgment and enter eternal life. Everyone who understands these things will be sure to come to Christ in faith and repentance and to help as many others as possible come to Christ with them.

The great Scotsman Thomas Boston once preached a long series of sermons on the final judgment. He closed with these words:

And now, if you would be saved from the wrath to come, and never go into this place of torment, take no rest in your natural state; believe the sinfulness and misery of it, and labour to get out of it quickly, fleeing unto Jesus Christ by faith. Sin in you is the seed of hell: and, if the guilt and reigning power of it be not removed in time, they will bring you to the second death in eternity. There is no other way to get them removed, but by receiving Christ, as he is offered in the gospel, for justification and sanctification: and he is now offered to you with all his salvation. . . . And the terrors of hell, as well as the joys of heaven, are set before you, to stir you up to a cordial receiving of him, with all his salvation; and to incline you unto the way of faith and holiness, in which alone you can escape the everlasting fire. May the Lord himself make them effectual to that end![9]

Anyone who heeds this warning will be saved, like a brand from the burning.

56

A Remnant Chosen by Grace

JEREMIAH 40:1—41:15

IF IT EXISTS AT ALL, what will the United States of America be like in the year 2050?

Some Christians prophesy a return to the glory days of "Christian America." They long for the rebuilding of the nation. They work to recapture the evangelical faith of our founding fathers. They hope to regain control of Congress and the media. They believe we are on the verge of a spiritual revival that will sweep the nation.

Is Nothing Sacred?

It is possible that the United States will still be at the center of world Christianity in the middle of the twenty-first century. Possible but unlikely. The effort to recover "Christian America" seems bound to fail. There is too much reliance on worldly methods to accomplish spiritual goals. There is too little faithful preaching of God's Word, which alone can prepare the way for genuine revival. Furthermore, it is doubtful whether "Christian America" ever existed. From the very beginning, Americans have been sinners as well as saints.[1]

There is another reason that efforts to rebuild "Christian America" are bound to fail: America is rapidly becoming a post-Christian culture. A television program in the fall of 1997 perfectly captured the spiritual climate of the nation. It was called *Nothing Sacred*, and it starred an irreverent and unorthodox priest. "I don't know if God exists or not," Father Ray told his congregation.

"Nothing Sacred" is a slogan for post-Christian times. The worship of God is not held as sacred. The ministry of God's Word is not sacred. Matrimony is not sacred. The family is not sacred. Is nothing sacred? Not even human life is sacred.

Barring an undeserved outpouring of the Holy Spirit, within a generation the influence of Christianity on American culture will be lost. The influence of the church on the city, education, politics, entertainment, and the media will dwindle until it virtually disappears. Therefore, what the church needs for the days to come is not a theology of growth, but a remnant theology.

God Will Preserve a Remnant

The events of Jeremiah 40, 41 provide a lesson in remnant theology. The main lesson is simply this: *God will preserve a remnant.* God's people may be besieged. They may be attacked. They may be oppressed. They may be scattered over the face of the earth. But they will never be lost, for God always preserves a remnant for himself.

A remnant is a leftover that is too useful to throw away, like an old piece of carpeting. My wife and I once lived in an apartment with drab, gray carpeting. (Come to think of it, we lived in such an apartment more than once, but once we actually did something about it.) We went to a carpet store and rummaged through the remnants until we found a piece of blue carpeting. We rolled it up and carried it home. It was not a fine Oriental carpet. It was not wall-to-wall carpeting. But it was decent enough to be functional. That is what God salvaged from the ruins of Jerusalem—a decent, useful remnant of his people.

The days following the fall of Jerusalem were terrible days. The houses, walls, and palaces of the city had been broken down and burned to the ground. Many leading citizens were deported. This was all because God was punishing the city for its sin: "The captain of the guard took Jeremiah and said to him, 'The LORD your God pronounced this disaster against this place. The LORD has brought it about, and has done as he said. Because you sinned against the LORD and did not obey his voice, this thing has come upon you'" (40:2, 3).

The commander sounded more like a prophet than a soldier. The people of Judah had been too blind to understand the ways of God, but "even a godless pagan could see what Yahweh was doing."[2] This Babylonian at least knew enough theology to figure out that God was punishing his people for their sins.

In the aftermath of judgment, things were so chaotic that Jeremiah temporarily got lost in the shuffle. King Nebuchadnezzar had given special orders that the prophet was not to be harmed (39:11, 12). Eventually Jeremiah was sent back home to his own people (39:13, 14), but not before being captured by some overzealous soldiers and marched to Ramah, the staging area or transit camp on the way to Babylon:

> The word that came to Jeremiah from the LORD after Nebuzaradan the captain of the guard had let him go from Ramah, when he took him bound in chains along with all the captives of Jerusalem and Judah who were being exiled to Babylon. The captain of the guard took Jeremiah and said to him . . . "I release you today from the chains on your hands. If it seems good to you to come with me to Babylon, come, and I will look after you well, but if it seems wrong to you to come with me to Babylon, do not come. See, the whole land is before you; go wherever you think it good and right to go. If you remain, then return to Gedaliah the son of Ahikam, son of Shaphan, whom the king of Babylon appointed governor of the cities of Judah, and dwell with him among the people. Or go wherever you think it right to go." (40:1, 2, 4, 5a)

Jeremiah 40 thus provides some details of Jeremiah's liberation that were omitted in chapter 39. While the relationship between the two accounts has puzzled some scholars, there is no contradiction. As Huey explains, "Jeremiah was released from the court of the guard on Nebuchadnezzar's orders and committed to the care of Gedaliah. In the confusion of captives being led away to Babylon, Jeremiah was not recognized and was arrested again and put in chains. He was recognized by officials in Ramah and released on Nebuzaradan's orders."[3]

Poor Jeremiah was in chains again, still suffering for the Lord. But he was freed by God's providence to remain among the remnant of God's people. "Then Jeremiah went to Gedaliah the son of Ahikam, at Mizpah, and lived with him among the people who were left in the land" (40:6). Generally speaking, the Jews who were hauled off to Babylon were the rich and the talented. The ones left behind were the poorest of the land, with a few notable exceptions:

> When all the captains of the forces in the open country and their men heard that the king of Babylon had appointed Gedaliah the son of Ahikam governor in the land and had committed to him men, women, and children, those of the poorest of the land who had not been taken into exile to Babylon, they went to Gedaliah at Mizpah—Ishmael the son of Nethaniah, Johanan the son of Kareah, Seraiah the son of Tanhumeth, the sons of Ephai the Netophathite, Jezaniah the son of the Maacathite, they and their men. (vv. 7, 8)

Although these names sound unfamiliar, they were (and are) well known to God. They were the survivors—the peasants, the refugees, and the leaders of the insurrection. They were God's remnant, chosen by grace.

Under the strong leadership of Gedaliah, the remnant started to grow:

> When all the Judeans who were in Moab and among the Ammonites and in Edom and in other lands heard that the king of Babylon had left a remnant in Judah and had appointed Gedaliah the son of Ahikam, son of Shaphan, as governor over them, then all the Judeans returned from all the places to which they had been driven and came to the land of Judah, to Gedaliah at Mizpah. (vv. 11, 12a)

Gedaliah had been appointed governor by the Babylonians. Soon he began to call the guerrilla leaders together and rally his troops.

The gathering of the remnant in Israel gives hope for post-Christian times. Like so many scraps of carpeting, the people of God have often been reduced to a remnant. In the days of Noah, only "a few, that is, eight persons" were saved in the ark when the earth was covered with water (1 Peter 3:20). In the days of Abraham, the destiny of God's people rested on a single man—Isaac, the son of promise. In the days of Jacob, God sent Joseph to Egypt "To preserve . . . a remnant on earth" (Genesis 45:7). In the days of the kings, only a remnant survived the fall of Jerusalem (2 Chronicles 36:20).

Concerning the exiles, Isaiah prophesied, "Though your people Israel be as the sand of the sea, only a remnant of them will return" (Isaiah 10:22). Micah promised that God would gather the remnant of Israel (Micah 2:12). The prophets were right. Only a remnant survived the exile. When they returned to Judah, they testified, "We are left a remnant that has escaped, as it is today" (Ezra 9:8–15). Even in the days of Jesus Christ, the disciples were no more than a "little flock" (Luke 12:32).

The people of God have never been wall-to-wall carpeting, but God has always preserved a remnant. This is remnant theology. It is hopeful theology. Although God's people are often in desperate straits, God has never gone without a people to love him and serve him.

And he never will. The eleventh chapter of Romans promises that God will always preserve a remnant. The Apostle Paul remembered the lament of the prophet Elijah, "how he appeal[ed] to God against Israel . . . 'Lord, they have killed your prophets, they have demolished your altars, and I alone am left, and they seek my life'" (vv. 2b, 3). Elijah felt sorry for himself. He thought the people of God had been reduced to a single individual. What he needed was a refresher course in remnant theology. Paul asked, "But what is

God's reply to [Elijah]? 'I have kept for myself seven thousand men who have not bowed the knee to Baal'" (v. 4). Elijah was not the only one. The remnant of God's people was 7,000 times larger than he realized.

Then Paul applied this lesson to the church: "So too at the present time there is a remnant, chosen by grace" (v. 5; cf. Acts 15:17). This promise is for the preservation of the righteous remnant, even in post-Christian times. The strength of the church is not in numbers. The strength of the church is not in growth strategies, management techniques, or survival skills. The strength of the church is God's gracious promise that he will preserve a people for himself.

God Will Provide for His Remnant

God not only preserves his people—he provides for them. The remnant of the Jews in Jerusalem was in a precarious position. Their very existence as a people was in jeopardy. But they had one thing going for them: God always provides for his remnant.

God began by making generous provision for his prophet Jeremiah. He made the Babylonians cover his expenses for room and board. When Nebuzaradan was finished meeting with Jeremiah, "The captain of the guard gave him an allowance of food and a present, and let him go" (40:5b). This was special treatment. One wonders what the Babylonians gave as parting gifts in those days or how much they gave for an allowance. But whatever Nebuzaradan gave Jeremiah, it was a reminder that God provides for his remnant people.

The story is told of a godly old woman who lived next door to an atheist. The two neighbors often argued about the existence of God and the power of prayer. One day the old woman ran out of food, so she knelt down and asked God to give her daily bread. The atheist overheard her prayer and seized the opportunity to disprove the existence of God. He ran to the market, bought a big sack of groceries, set it on the woman's porch, rang the bell, and hid in the bushes.

When the old woman opened the door and saw the groceries she said, "Praise God! My prayers are answered!"

But the atheist knew better. With a smirk he stepped out, held up his receipt from the market, and said, "God didn't buy those groceries—I did!"

"My dear young man," the old woman corrected him, "in that case, God not only provided the food, but he also had the devil pay the bill!"

In much the same way, God had the Babylonians pick up the tab for Jeremiah.

God's provision for the rest of his remnant was just as generous. The interim governor had full confidence that God would provide:

Gedaliah the son of Ahikam, son of Shaphan, swore to them and their men, saying, "Do not be afraid to serve the Chaldeans. Dwell in the land and serve the king of Babylon, and it shall be well with you. As for me, I will dwell at Mizpah, to represent you before the Chaldeans who will come to us. But as for you, gather wine and summer fruits and oil, and store them in your vessels, and dwell in your cities that you have taken." (vv. 9, 10)

This speech shows what a good leader Gedaliah was. His name means "The Lord is great!" (Incidentally, an inscription from this time period has been found at Lachish; it reads: "Belonging to Gedaliah, Over the House.")[4] The governor appealed for calm and pledged a return to prosperity.

At least one scholar calls Gedaliah's speech "propaganda,"[5] but these were not just idle campaign promises. When the remnant of the Jews gathered at Mizpah, "They gathered wine and summer fruits in great abundance" (v. 12b). They had lost everything they had. Their homes had gone up in smoke, and their fields had been trampled. Yet God gave them an abundant harvest from various trees and vines. (Grain is conspicuously absent from the harvest, no doubt because the siege had prevented planting that year.)

The lesson is that God always provides for his remnant. He gives his people what they need, even when it scarcely seems possible. In dangerous times, as in times of peace, God gives his people the blessings of the good life. If you belong to God, God will always take care of you. He will provide the work, clothing, home, and food you need to live. Many times a famine of adversity will be followed by a harvest of abundance.

The application, of course, is to trust God for everything you need:

God's providence gives us a security in this insecure, often violent world. The Lord sits enthroned over all the military, political, social and economic forces of our generation and his eternal predetermined purposes are ripening through it all. Nothing has got out of hand, nor will it. We can therefore live day by day knowing that the hands which hold our lives are the same hands which hold all things.[6]

God preserves and provides for his people, even when they are no more than a remnant.

God Will Keep His Promises to His Remnant

There is a third thing God will do for his remnant: He will keep his promises to them. Most of the book of Jeremiah consists of prophecies of judgment (not to mention fulfillments of judgment!). But Jeremiah also made many great and precious promises of blessing for God's people.

Some of Jeremiah's prophecies were for the remnant. In fact, Jeremiah mentions the remnant more often than any other book in the Bible. God promised, "I will gather the remnant of my flock out of all the countries where I have driven them, and I will bring them back to their fold, and they shall be fruitful and multiply" (23:3). That promise was fulfilled when God gathered his people from "Moab and among the Ammonites and in Edom and in other lands" (40:11).

God also said, "The people who survived the sword found grace in the wilderness" (31:2; cf. 2 Kings 19:31). That promise accurately describes the remnant that gathered around Gedaliah at Mizpah. Having survived the Babylonian sword, they received what God promised—favor in the desert, where they harvested an abundance of wine and summer fruit.

God had also promised an even richer harvest:

Sing aloud with gladness for Jacob,
    and raise shouts for the chief of the nations;
proclaim, give praise, and say,
    "O LORD, save your people,
    the remnant of Israel."
Behold, I will bring them from the north country
    and gather them from the farthest parts of the earth . . .
    and they shall be radiant over the goodness of the LORD,
over the grain, the wine, and the oil,
    and over the young of the flock and the herd." (31:7, 8, 12b)

These promises referred to the eventual return of the exiles from Babylon and the rebuilding of Jerusalem. But they began to be fulfilled immediately after the fall of Jerusalem. God preserved a remnant with Jeremiah, Gedaliah, and the tiny group of Jews under their care. Then God began to provide for the remnant. They rejoiced in a strong economy, the abundant fruits of the harvest (40:12).

God had also made a specific promise that the Jews would be saved if they surrendered to the Babylonians: "He who goes out and surrenders to the Chaldeans who are besieging you shall live and shall have his life as a prize of war" (21:9). God kept this promise when Gedaliah urged the people to submit to Babylonian rule, saying, "Do not be afraid to serve the Chaldeans. Dwell in the land and serve the king of Babylon, and it shall be well with you" (40:9). Things did go well. As long as God's people followed the interim governor, they were blessed. In all these ways, God fulfilled his promises to the remnant.

When things were at their bleakest, God began to bless. This shows that even in the most desperate times God keeps his promises to his remnant people.

There will be desperate times for the church. In some countries the church is in decline and Christians are outnumbered. In such places it is good to remember the remnant promise Jesus made to Peter: "I will build my church, and the gates of hell shall not prevail against it" (Matthew 16:18). God will keep that promise the way he keeps all his promises.

Put stock in the church. It is the only institution in the entire world that is guaranteed to survive. By the power of God the righteous remnant will survive all the onslaughts of Hell.

Et Tu, Ishmael?

As soon as God began to fulfill his remnant promises, the Jews at Mizpah faced a hellish onslaught of their own. After a bountiful harvest they were attacked and almost destroyed by Ishmael.

The trouble did not come without warning. Gedaliah received secret intelligence about a conspiracy. Some of his cabinet members warned him that he had an enemy in the camp. Ishmael's plot to assassinate the governor was so widely known that Gedaliah's friends assumed he knew about it already: "Now Johanan the son of Kareah and all the leaders of the forces in the open country came to Gedaliah at Mizpah and said to him, 'Do you know that Baalis the king of the Ammonites has sent Ishmael the son of Nethaniah to take your life?'" (40:13, 14a). (Archaeological note: Researchers have uncovered an ancient seal that reads, "Belonging to Baalis, King of Ammon").[7]

Rather foolishly, "Gedaliah the son of Ahikam would not believe them" (v. 14b), even when Johanan offered to eliminate his adversaries. "Then Johanan the son of Kareah spoke secretly to Gedaliah at Mizpah, 'Please let me go and strike down Ishmael the son of Nethaniah, and no one will know it. Why should he take your life, so that all the Judeans who are gathered about you would be scattered, and the remnant of Judah would perish?'" (v. 15). Johanan's explicit concern was for the remnant of God's people. "But Gedaliah the son of Ahikam said to Johanan the son of Kareah, 'You shall not do this thing, for you are speaking falsely of Ishmael'" (v. 16).

Sadly, what Johanan was saying about Ishmael proved to be more than a rumor, and Gedaliah's life was taken by a member of his own cabinet. The governor was forewarned but not forearmed:[8]

> In the seventh month, Ishmael the son of Nethaniah, son of Elishama, of the royal family, one of the chief officers of the king, came with ten men to Gedaliah the son of Ahikam, at Mizpah. As they ate bread together there at Mizpah, Ishmael the son of Nethaniah and the ten men with him rose up and struck down Gedaliah the son of Ahikam, son of Shaphan, with the

sword, and killed him, whom the king of Babylon had appointed governor in the land. (41:1, 2; cf. 2 Kings 25:25)

Gedaliah's death was a tragedy. For years afterward, the Jews held a fast to lament the day of his passing.[9] Like Julius Caesar ("*Et tu, Brute?*"), Gedaliah was betrayed by one of his own. His godly rule ended just months after it began because he listened too little and trusted too much. His unhappy fate paralleled that of Jerusalem: All of God's warnings were to no avail.

Gedaliah's death was also an act of terrorism. The murder took place during high-level talks, while the host and the guest "ate bread together" (41:1, 2), thus violating all conventions of hospitality. Like Judas Iscariot (Matthew 26:23), Ishmael betrayed his master while they were breaking bread.

The bloodshed did not stop with the governor. Ishmael became a serial killer. "Ishmael also struck down all the Judeans who were with Gedaliah at Mizpah, and the Chaldean soldiers who happened to be there" (41:3). Then, in an act of ruthless depravity, he deceived and slaughtered seventy holy men:

> On the day after the murder of Gedaliah, before anyone knew of it, eighty men arrived from Shechem and Shiloh and Samaria, with their beards shaved and their clothes torn, and their bodies gashed, bringing grain offerings and incense to present at the temple of the Lord. And Ishmael the son of Nethaniah came out from Mizpah to meet them, weeping as he came. As he met them, he said to them, "Come in to Gedaliah the son of Ahikam." When they came into the city, Ishmael the son of Nethaniah and the men with him slaughtered them and cast them into a cistern. But there were ten men among them who said to Ishmael, "Do not put us to death, for we have stores of wheat, barley, oil, and honey hidden in the fields." So he refrained and did not put them to death with their companions. Now the cistern into which Ishmael had thrown all the bodies of the men whom he had struck down along with Gedaliah was the large cistern that King Asa had made for defense against Baasha king of Israel; Ishmael the son of Nethaniah filled it with the slain. (vv. 4–9)

These eighty pilgrims were on their way to the temple, even though it was in ruins. They had traveled a great distance from the north. The condition of their hair and their clothes showed that they were in mourning, repenting for the sins of the nation. Ishmael met these holy men with crocodile tears and welcomed them in the name of Gedaliah. Since they had not heard the news of the governor's assassination, they did not know that they were in the wrong place at the wrong time. Ten of them managed to barter for their lives, but Ishmael slaughtered the rest and threw their bodies into a cistern built by King Asa (cf. 1 Kings 15:22).[10]

The massacre at Mizpah was a senseless act of violence against innocent victims, committed by a wicked, vicious man. Ishmael murdered God's governor, betrayed God's pilgrims, and piled the dead bodies in a hole in the ground.

Then he took God's people hostage (Jeremiah included, most likely) and prepared to hand them over to the Ammonites who, it turned out, were his sponsors:

> Then Ishmael took captive all the rest of the people who were in Mizpah, the king's daughters and all the people who were left at Mizpah, whom Nebuzaradan, the captain of the guard, had committed to Gedaliah the son of Ahikam. Ishmael the son of Nethaniah took them captive and set out to cross over to the Ammonites. (41:10)

For Ishmael, nothing was sacred. Hospitality was not sacred. Divinely appointed leadership was not sacred. The worship of God was not sacred. Even human life was not sacred.

A Remnant Belonging to Christ

Why did Ishmael commit these atrocities? The Bible gives at least a hint: He was "of the royal family" (41:1). In other words, Ishmael was of the house and line of David.

No doubt Ishmael was jealous. No doubt he considered Gedaliah a rival and considered that Judah's throne belonged to him by rights. Yet when Ishmael tried to grab power for himself, he became an antichrist. In other words, he set himself against the anointed one. He did not wait for God to put him on the throne as David had waited. He did not follow the way of the cross as Jesus did. Instead he tried to seize the kingdom of God by treachery and force.

Ishmael's example shows, by way of contrast, the humility of Jesus Christ. Jesus did not usurp God's throne. Instead he waited for God to exalt him to the highest place (Philippians 2:6–11). Nor did Jesus try to clobber people into his kingdom. Instead he came "humble, and mounted on a donkey" (Matthew 21:5), sweetly persuading us to come and have our sins forgiven.

Ishmael did just the opposite, which is why he should be considered a kind of antichrist. The Bible says there have been "many antichrists" (1 John 2:18). *Antichrist* is an appropriate title for Ishmael because he tried to destroy God's people. He killed their leader with an assassin's knife. Because of his violence, their numbers dwindled and they were enslaved by their enemies.

Similar things may happen to the American church in these post-Christian times. We may suffer the loss of courageous Christian leadership. Already there is a dearth of Bible-believing, Bible-teaching ministry. We may suffer the further loss of church members. Although a few denominations are active in evangelism and church planting, many are in sharp decline. We may undergo bondage to the spirits of the age—pleasure, prosperity, power.

All these things may happen to the church, but God's people will never be destroyed. A remnant chosen by grace will always endure. This was true in Jeremiah's day:

> But when Johanan the son of Kareah and all the leaders of the forces with him heard of all the evil that Ishmael the son of Nethaniah had done, they took all their men and went to fight against Ishmael the son of Nethaniah. They came upon him at the great pool that is in Gibeon. And when all the people who were with Ishmael saw Johanan the son of Kareah and all the leaders of the forces with him, they rejoiced. So all the people whom Ishmael had carried away captive from Mizpah turned around and came back, and went to Johanan the son of Kareah. But Ishmael the son of Nethaniah escaped from Johanan with eight men, and went to the Ammonites. (Jeremiah 41:11–15)

Johanan thus rescued the remnant of God's people, and they rallied to his cause. The place where it happened can still be seen at Gibeon, where there are ruins of a man-made pool eighty-two feet deep.[11] The pit is a monument to God's grace in preserving a people for himself.

This has been the story of God's people at all times and in all places. The first Christians were hunted by the emperors of Rome and scattered across the Middle East. The Christians of the Middle Ages were surrounded by barbarism. The Christians of the Reformation were branded as outlaws.

The struggles of the church continue to the present day. In the Middle East Christians are opposed by Islam. In China they are oppressed by Communism. In Europe they are worn down by atheism and secularism. Yet there still remains a remnant chosen by grace.

If you belong to the righteous remnant through faith in Jesus Christ you can say, with Christians down through the ages, "We are afflicted in every way, but not crushed; perplexed, but not driven to despair; persecuted, but not forsaken; struck down, but not destroyed" (2 Corinthians 4:8, 9). We are a remnant chosen by grace.

57

A Fatal Mistake

JEREMIAH 41:16—43:13

WHEN I WAS IN HIGH SCHOOL, I spent my autumn Friday nights in a crowded press box, announcing the football play-by-play for the Falcons of Wheaton North High School in Illinois. My loyal listeners on station WETN often heard shouting—not from me, usually, but from the coaches watching the game from the press box.

Football coaches can often sense disaster before it happens. Just as the quarterback starts to throw they start yelling, "No! Don't throw it!" It never did any good to yell, of course, but apparently it made the coaches feel better.

When the prophet Jeremiah traveled to Egypt, he was like a frustrated football coach. He kept telling his people, "No! Don't do it! Whatever you do, please don't go down to Egypt." But it did not do any good. Despite Jeremiah's many warnings and protests, the Jews went right on down to Egypt anyway.

Should We Stay or Should We Go?

Jeremiah's people started making their fatal mistake before they even realized what they were doing. They were refugees who had survived the fall of Jerusalem and witnessed the atrocities of war. They had watched their family and friends fall in battle, die of starvation, or march into exile. They had been held hostage by a crazed terrorist.

These hardships reduced God's people to a remnant of their former selves. They said, "We are left with but a few" (42:2b). The remnant was so small, in fact, that they feared for their lives:

> Then Johanan the son of Kareah and all the leaders of the forces with him took from Mizpah all the rest of the people whom he had recovered from

Ishmael the son of Nethaniah, after he had struck down Gedaliah the son of Ahikam—soldiers, women, children, and eunuchs, whom Johanan brought back from Gibeon. And they went and stayed at Geruth Chimham near Bethlehem, intending to go to Egypt because of the Chaldeans. For they were afraid of them, because Ishmael the son of Nethaniah had struck down Gedaliah the son of Ahikam, whom the king of Babylon had made governor over the land. (41:16–18)

The Jews had good reason to be afraid. There were certain to be reprisals when the Babylonians learned that the governor they appointed had been assassinated. So before the Babylonians could retaliate, the Jews decided to run back to Egypt, back to the house of bondage, back to the house of slavery. They wanted to return to the place of their exodus under Moses. It was almost as if they were trying to undo their salvation.

Going back to Egypt had "fatal mistake" written all over it. Jeremiah had often warned the Jews *not* to go to Egypt (2:18, 36; 24:8–10). Nevertheless, they were already halfway out the door. Maybe, they thought, it would be okay to go to Egypt just this once. So they traveled about five miles down the road. Then they started to have second thoughts. Should they stay or should they go?

Since the Jews were unsure what to do, they decided to consult Jeremiah.

Then all the commanders of the forces, and Johanan the son of Kareah and Jezaniah the son of Hoshaiah, and all the people from the least to the greatest, came near and said to Jeremiah the prophet, "Let our plea for mercy come before you, and pray to the Lord your God for us, for all this remnant—because we are left with but a few, as your eyes see us—that the Lord your God may show us the way we should go, and the thing that we should do." (42:1–3)

Asking God for directions is always the right thing to do. What does God want me to do with my life? What or where does God want me to study? What kind of work does God want me to do? Where should I live? Should I get married? Whom should I marry? Those are all important questions.

The trouble is, too many people do not start asking those questions until they are halfway down to Egypt. They only pretend to want to know God's will for their lives. What they really want is for God to put his rubber stamp on the plans they have already made. They say, "I've already made up my mind, but by the way, Lord, is this really what you want me to do?" They start to act before they begin to pray.

Another problem with the refugees was their inability to pray for themselves. They told Jeremiah, "Pray to the LORD your God for us" (v. 2). The prophet corrected them, of course. "Jeremiah the prophet said to them, 'I have heard you. Behold, I will pray to the LORD your God according to your request'" (v. 4a). The remnant would later speak of "The LORD our God" (v. 6).

Still, their use of the second person was revealing. The people felt like they had to get someone else to pray for them. They did not have a warm, personal relationship with God. They believed in his existence in a general sort of way, but they thought he was "somewhere out there." They were not close enough to God to engage in meaningful prayer.

Prayer is one of the best tests of your relationship with God. Do you pray? Do you know *how* to pray? If not, it may be because God is not *your* God.

In our natural, sinful condition we are God's enemies. The only way to become God's friend is to believe in Jesus Christ. God sent his only Son, Jesus Christ, to die on the cross for our sins so we could become friends of God. Once you believe that Jesus died for your sins, you enter an intimate friendship with God. Your heart opens up to God, and his heart opens up to you (Hebrews 10:19–22). You are able to communicate with him through prayer. But this only happens through faith in Jesus Christ, which is why Christians always pray "in Jesus' name."

To summarize, there were a couple of problems with the Jewish remnant's prayer: The prayer was late, and it was offered by a third party.

The remnant did know what to pray for, however. Their prayer itself was a good one. Anyone who wants to know the will of God should pray like this: "Show us the way we should go, and the thing that we should do" (42:3). That would be an excellent prayer to offer every day. In fact, Christians pray this way every time they use the words of the Lord's Prayer and say, "Your will be done" (Matthew 6:10). Praying for God's will to be done is another way of praying to go where God wants you to go and to do what God wants you to do.

The Jews not only prayed for God's will to be done—they promised to do it themselves. First, Jeremiah told them that he would give them the word of the Lord: "Behold, I will pray to the LORD your God according to your request, and whatever the LORD answers you I will tell you. I will keep nothing back from you" (42:4b). Then the Jews covenanted to obey God, no matter what:

> Then they said to Jeremiah, "May the LORD be a true and faithful witness against us if we do not act according to all the word with which the LORD your God sends you to us. Whether it is good or bad, we will obey the voice of the LORD our God to whom we are sending you, that it may be well with us when we obey the voice of the LORD our God." (42:5, 6)

This is the proper way to discover God's will for your life. Pray for guidance. Listen to God's Word, which today means reading the Bible rather than consulting a prophet. Then vow to do whatever the Lord says, no matter what.

Please Don't Go!

Once the remnant prayed for guidance, God gave it to them: "At the end of ten days the word of the LORD came to Jeremiah. Then he summoned Johanan the son of Kareah and all the commanders of the forces who were with him, and all the people from the least to the greatest" (42:7, 8). When they were all assembled, the prophet said, "Do not go to Egypt—do not collect $200." If they went to Egypt, the Babylonians would hunt them down and destroy them. But if they stayed in Judah they would live in peace.

It seemed like an easy decision. According to Jeremiah, the upside of staying in Judah was tremendous:

> [He] said to them, "Thus says the LORD, the God of Israel, to whom you sent me to present your plea for mercy before him: If you will remain in this land, then I will build you up and not pull you down; I will plant you, and not pluck you up; for I relent of the disaster that I did to you. Do not fear the king of Babylon, of whom you are afraid. Do not fear him, declares the LORD, for I am with you, to save you and to deliver you from his hand. I will grant you mercy, that he may have mercy on you and let you remain in your own land." (vv. 9–12)

These verses echo the call of Jeremiah, when God appointed him "over nations and over kingdoms" not only "To pluck up and to break down," but also "To build and to plant" (1:10). Though Jerusalem had been torn down, the Jews had nothing to be afraid of. God would plant his people back in their land. He would keep them safe. He would shower them with compassion. God would do all these things, provided they obeyed him.

Unfortunately, obeying God was not what the remnant had in mind. And God knew exactly what they were thinking: "We don't care how nice the benefit package sounds." "But if you say, 'We will not remain in this land,' disobeying the voice of the LORD your God and saying, 'No, we will go to the land of Egypt, where we shall not see war or hear the sound of the trumpet or be hungry for bread, and we will dwell there,' then hear the word of the LORD, O remnant of Judah" (42:13–15a). Humanly speaking, escape to Egypt was the best foreign policy. It was in a safe neighborhood a long, long way from Babylon, and the Egyptians had plenty of food and a stable economy; so going down to Egypt made a lot of sense.

There was only one problem with the flight to Egypt. It was against the will of God.

> Thus says the LORD of hosts, the God of Israel: If you set your faces to enter Egypt and go to live there, then the sword that you fear shall overtake you there in the land of Egypt, and the famine of which you are afraid shall follow close after you to Egypt, and there you shall die. All the men who set their faces to go to Egypt to live there shall die by the sword, by famine, and by pestilence. They shall have no remnant or survivor from the disaster that I will bring upon them. For thus says the LORD of hosts, the God of Israel: As my anger and my wrath were poured out on the inhabitants of Jerusalem, so my wrath will be poured out on you when you go to Egypt. You shall become an execration, a horror, a curse, and a taunt. You shall see this place no more. (vv. 15b–18)

Disaster would follow the remnant right down to Egypt. Everything that had happened in Jerusalem would happen on the Nile—sword, fear, famine, death, plague, disaster, wrath, cursing, horror, condemnation, and reproach.

Judgment was so certain that Jeremiah called going to Egypt a fatal mistake:

> The LORD has said to you, O remnant of Judah, "Do not go to Egypt." Know for a certainty that I have warned you this day that you have gone astray at the cost of your lives. For you sent me to the LORD your God, saying, 'Pray for us to the LORD our God, and whatever the LORD our God says declare to us and we will do it." And I have this day declared it to you, but you have not obeyed the voice of the LORD your God in anything that he sent me to tell you. Now therefore know for a certainty that you shall die by the sword, by famine, and by pestilence in the place where you desire to go to live. (vv. 19–22)

Understand the choice the remnant had to make. One option—staying in Judah—seemed dangerous. There were lots of enemies, but not very much food. The alternative—going down to Egypt—seemed really smart: no enemies and lots of food.

However, God knew things would turn out just the opposite of what people expected. The risky choice was really perfectly safe, while the easy way out was deadly. Therefore, to make the right decision, God's people had to put all their trust in God. Making the right choice meant living by faith.

We face the same kinds of spiritual decisions in our daily lives. Many things that seem risky are actually quite safe. It is safe to go into the jungle to do mission work. It is safe to make a lifetime vow of marital faithfulness. It is safe to raise a family. It is safe to give away your money to the poor. It is safe to do these things *provided* they are done in obedience to God. No matter how frightening it may seem at the time, it is always safest to obey God.

On the other hand, many things that seem safe turn out to be fatal mistakes. What is the harm in laughing at a vulgar joke with your coworkers? What is so dangerous about engaging in a little sexual activity before marriage? What does it matter if you steal some notepads from your corporation? Who cares if you cheat on your lab work?

Those things may sound relatively harmless, but they are no more safe than "safe sex." Disobeying God always has fatal side effects, spiritually speaking. Living for self always leads to death, not life.

Flight to Egypt

In the end, the remnant of the Jews decided to go their own way. They were like the friend (or former friend perhaps?) who asks for constructive criticism. "Don't just tell me what I'm doing right. I want to know what I can do to improve. Tell me what you really think." But as soon as you tell him what you really think, he gets so angry you wish you hadn't.

When Jeremiah said, "No! Stop! Don't do it!" the remnant was outraged. Davidson calls their response "blunt, angry and insolent."[1]

> When Jeremiah finished speaking to all the people all these words of the LORD their God, with which the LORD their God had sent him to them, Azariah the son of Hoshaiah and Johanan the son of Kareah and all the insolent men said to Jeremiah, "You are telling a lie. The LORD our God did not send you to say, 'Do not go to Egypt to live there,' but Baruch the son of Neriah has set you against us, to deliver us into the hand of the Chaldeans, that they may kill us or take us into exile in Babylon." (43:1–3)

The leaders of the remnant had already made up their minds. They refused to listen to Jeremiah, despite his flawless record as a prophet and despite their vow to do whatever God told them to do. Eugene Peterson puts it well: "Johanan and the people respected Jeremiah enough to ask for his prayers, but they didn't trust God enough to follow his counsel."[2] It never occurred to them that God's plans might be different from theirs. So when they asked for spiritual guidance in the first place, they were just fooling themselves. They said they wanted to follow God, but they didn't mean it. They were only willing to follow God if he was going their direction.

The trouble with a god who never disapproves of where you go or what you do is that he is no god at all. The real God is so wise and so holy that our plans often do not fit into his agenda. They are either foolish or downright sinful.

Do not be like the remnant, who assumed that God sits up in Heaven waiting to do what you want him to do. "All along (had they realized it) they had regarded God as a power to enlist, rather than as a lord to obey; and they still cannot believe that his will can be radically different from their own."[3] So off they went to Egypt, singing, "Have mine own way, Lord! Have mine own way! I am the potter; thou art the clay."

This is what John Calvin said should be learned from the remnant who neither trusted nor obeyed God: "We have then here set before us the hypocrisy of that people, so that we may learn that whenever we ask what pleases God, we should bring a pure and sincere heart, so that nothing may prevent or hinder us immediately to embrace whatever God may command us."[4]

The unrighteous remnant had two basic objections to Jeremiah's prophecy. They are the same two objections people use against God's Word to this very day.

First, they denied that it *was* the Word of God. They said to Jeremiah, "You are telling a lie. The LORD our God did not send you to say . . ." (43:2). In the same way, many people deny that the Bible is God's Word. They have their own ideas about what God is like, and they judge the Bible according to their own standards. They read what it teaches about God's wrath against sin, for example, and they say, "Oh no, our God would never say something like that. Our God is a God of love; he would never punish sin."

A second strategy for rejecting God's Word is to say it is only man's word. The remnant blamed Jeremiah's prophecy on his secretary: "Baruch the son of Neriah has set you against us" (v. 3). In the same way, many people say that the Bible is just like other ancient literature. It is an interesting collection of stories and opinions, but it is only a record of human thought. There is nothing divine or supernatural about it. So people turn to the New Testament teaching on the Incarnation or on sexuality or on the ordination of women and say, "That was only cultural. That was just Paul's opinion for Paul's times."

The truth is that the Bible is God's opinion for all time. "All Scripture is breathed out by God" (2 Timothy 3:16). It is the Word of God, written. The Holy Spirit used the experiences and talents of the Biblical authors to set down the very thoughts and commands of God on the pages of the Bible. "[Know] this first of all, that no prophecy of Scripture comes from someone's own interpretation. For no prophecy was ever produced by the will of man, but men spoke from God as they were carried along by the Holy Spirit" (2 Peter 1:20, 21).

Since the Bible is the written Word of God, it is only ignored at one's peril. The way to eternal life is found in the Bible and nowhere else. Where else will you learn that you are a guilty sinner who deserves eternal judgment? Where else will you read that Christ died on the cross for sinners? Where else will you discover that God raised Jesus from the dead to conquer sin and death? Where else will you be offered salvation from sin through faith in Jesus Christ? Nowhere else, which is why rejecting God's Word is a fatal mistake.

When the remnant of the Jews rejected God's Word by migrating to Egypt, they were writing their own death sentence.

> So Johanan the son of Kareah and all the commanders of the forces and all the people did not obey the voice of the LORD, to remain in the land of Judah. But Johanan the son of Kareah and all the commanders of the forces took all the remnant of Judah who had returned to live in the land of Judah from all the nations to which they had been driven—the men, the women, the children, the princesses, and every person whom Nebuzaradan the captain of the guard had left with Gedaliah the son of Ahikam, son of Shaphan; also Jeremiah the prophet and Baruch the son of Neriah. And they came into the land of Egypt, for they did not obey the voice of the LORD. And they arrived at Tahpanhes. (43:4–7)

Tahpanhes was on the frontiers of Egypt. When the remnant arrived in the Nile delta, Jeremiah gave them another gloomy prophecy: "Then the word of the LORD came to Jeremiah in Tahpanhes: 'Take in your hands large stones and hide them in the mortar in the pavement that is at the entrance to Pharaoh's palace in Tahpanhes, in the sight of the men of Judah'" (vv. 8, 9).

Jeremiah tore up the pavement in front of the royal house, a house that was uncovered by archaeologists a century ago.[5] The point of his object lesson was that the rulers of Babylon were going to come down to Egypt and set up camp on those very stones. "And say to them, 'Thus says the LORD of hosts, the God of Israel: Behold, I will send and take Nebuchadnezzar the king of Babylon, my servant, and I will set his throne above these stones that I have hidden, and he will spread his royal canopy over them'" (v. 10).

This is exactly what the Babylonian generals had done in Jerusalem: They sat in triumph over their enemies. "Though the Judean refugees have buried themselves in populous Egypt, they will be discovered and feel, as their compatriots had done, the weight of Babylonian might."[6]

Jeremiah went on to describe Egypt's defeat in graphic detail:

> He [Nebuchadnezzar] shall come and strike the land of Egypt, giving over to the pestilence those who are doomed to the pestilence, to captivity those

who are doomed to captivity, and to the sword those who are doomed to the sword. I shall kindle a fire in the temples of the gods of Egypt, and he shall burn them and carry them away captive. And he shall clean the land of Egypt as a shepherd cleans his cloak of vermin, and he shall go away from there in peace. He shall break the obelisks of Heliopolis, which is in the land of Egypt, and the temples of the gods of Egypt he shall burn with fire. (vv. 11–13)

The image of the shepherd is especially vivid. Literally the text reads: "As a shepherd picks his clothes clean of lice, so the king of Babylon will pick the land of Egypt clean, and then leave victorious" (v. 12b, *Good News Bible*).

That is precisely what happened, of course. The fragment of an ancient text describes how in "The 37th year (586/7 BC), Nebuchadnezzar, king of Bab[ylon] mar[ched against] Egypt to deliver a battle."[7] When he arrived, he "deloused" Egypt. As Derek Kidner states, "Egypt's impressive temples, gods and obelisks . . . would prove merely combustible, portable or breakable."[8] Portable indeed, for the idols and obelisks of the Egyptian sun god now decorate the museums and piazzas of Europe.

The defeat of Egypt was a sad ending to a sad story. For us, it is a cautionary tale about willful disobedience to the revealed will of God. The remnant of the Jews knew God's will for their lives, but they rejected it because they thought they knew better. A Biblical proverb aptly describes their fatal mistake: "There is a way that seems right to a man, but its end is the way to death" (Proverbs 14:12).

Loyal to the End

There is only one detail in this tragic report that seems to give any hope. The Bible lists some of the men and women who traveled down to Egypt. Among them were "Jeremiah the prophet and Baruch the son of Neriah" (43:6).

This is a remarkable statement of loyalty to God's people. Jeremiah did not have to go to Egypt.[9] In fact, he had several opportunities to go elsewhere. Just months before, the Babylonians had offered him a golden parachute—an all-expense-paid trip to Babylon. Nebuzaradan had said, "If it seems good to you to come with me to Babylon, come, and I will look after you well" (40:4). The prophet's enemies probably thought he would take the general up on his offer, for they had often accused him of being a traitor and a Babylonian sympathizer (37:13; 38:4).

But the great prophet was no Benedict Jeremiah. He was so devoted to God's people that he rejected the pension he richly deserved. He preferred to join the remnant of God's people rather than to walk on the plush carpets of

Babylon. He stayed with God's people even when they were almost beneath his dignity; they were "not pilgrims, nor captives, but deserters."[10]

To live with such cowards may have been the most courageous thing Jeremiah ever did. It was proof of his love for God and God's people. It also gave a glimpse of the love of God's Son for his elect people. Jesus identified himself with our sin and entered into our death for our salvation.

Jeremiah's loyalty is a good example for everyone who belongs to the church. There are always people in the church who are hard to love. Maybe there is someone in your Bible study who irritates you. Perhaps someone in your ministry has a way of saying the wrong thing at the wrong time. It is even possible that someone in the church has mistreated you. But if you claim to know Christ, you must love the unlovely. This is because Jesus Christ gave his very life for tax collectors, prostitutes, and all kinds of sinners, yourself included.

Jeremiah's loyalty is also a particular challenge for everyone who is thinking about leaving a local church. "The church isn't meeting my needs anymore," people say. "I don't like the pastor. The music doesn't minister to me. There is nothing for the children. I don't care for the snacks. Everything seems so dead."

True, some congregations are weak and ineffective. Some are apostate, which means there are some occasions when changing churches is the right thing to do. But there is something to be said for being loyal to God's people, not because they are perfect, but because they are sinners saved by grace.

The German pastor and theologian Dietrich Bonhoeffer once made the kind of decision Jeremiah made. Almost from the beginning Bonhoeffer was an outspoken critic of the Nazis. Gradually the Gestapo took away his freedoms. He was forbidden to lecture at the university. The doors of his theological institute were closed.

Eventually, in 1939, Bonhoeffer was offered a teaching post in New York. It seemed like such a perfect opportunity to escape the troubles in Germany that he came to America. Less than a month after he arrived, however, he returned suddenly to Nazi Germany. Here is how Bonhoeffer explained his change of heart:

> I have had time to think and to pray about my situation, and that of my nation, and to have God's will for me clarified. I have come to the conclusion that I have made a mistake in coming to America. I shall have no right to participate in the reconstruction of the Christian life in Germany after the war if I did not share in the trials of this time with my people. Christians in Germany face the terrible alternative of willing the defeat of their nation

in order that civilization may survive, or willing the victory of their nation and thereby destroying civilization. I know which of these alternatives I must choose. But I cannot make that choice in security.[11]

A few years later Bonhoeffer was sent to the concentration camp at Buchenwald, where he was hanged for his involvement in a plot to overthrow Adolf Hitler.

Did Dietrich Bonhoeffer make a fatal mistake when he returned to the church in Germany? In the light of eternity, his decision to be faithful to God and to God's people will turn out to be one of the best decisions he ever made, for God rewards his faithful servants with eternal life. In Heaven many things that seemed risky at the time will turn out to be perfectly safe, whereas in Hell many things that seemed safe will prove to have been fatal. Obeying the revealed will of Christ is always the safest thing to do.

58

The King or the Queen?

JEREMIAH 44:1–30

THE FORTY-FOURTH CHAPTER of Jeremiah contains the prophet's last recorded words. Jeremiah 45 is a short prophecy given to Baruch two decades before (605 BC; see 45:1). Chapters 46—51 contain prophecies previously given against the nations. The oracles against Egypt were spoken in 605 BC (46:2), while the judgments against Babylon were announced around 594 BC (51:59). Chapter 52 is an appendix to the book that, as the Bible indicates (51:64b), was not written by Jeremiah himself. Thus chapter 44 contains the last re-corded words of Jeremiah.

This is a good place, therefore, to recount the many sufferings of the Weeping Prophet. He was ignored, rejected, scorned, and humiliated. He was beaten, imprisoned, and put in the stocks. He was falsely accused and con-demned as a traitor. Twice he was cast into a dungeon and left for dead.

Finally, Jeremiah's devotion to the people of God carried him into exile. He spent his last years in Egypt, the land of the Sphinx and the pyramids. He must have lived there for some time, for by the time he uttered his last words the Jews had scattered along the Nile: "The word that came to Jeremiah con-cerning all the Judeans who lived in the land of Egypt, at Migdol, at Tahpan-hes, at Memphis, and in the land of Pathros" (44:1).

F. B. Meyer suggests that Jeremiah's sojourn in Egypt "partook of the same infinite sadness as the forty years of his public ministry." He goes on to point out the similarity between the sufferings of Jeremiah and the sufferings of Jesus Christ:

> It would appear that, so far as his outward lot was concerned, the prophet Jeremiah spent a life of more unrelieved sadness than has perhaps fallen to the lot of any other, with the exception of the Divine Lord. This was so

apparent to the Jewish commentators on the prophecies of Isaiah that they applied to him the words of the fifty-third chapter, which tell the story of the Man of Sorrows who was acquainted with grief, and stood as a sheep dumb before her shearers. Of course, in the light of Calvary, we see the depths of substitutionary suffering in those inimitable words which no mortal could ever realize; but it is nevertheless significant that in any sense they were deemed applicable to Jeremiah.[1]

Jeremiah was not *the* Suffering Servant, but he was *a* suffering servant to the very end.

Some People Never Learn

Jeremiah 44 provides a fitting close to the prophet's ministry because it shows him doing what he did best—preaching the holy justice of God against sin.

The prophet began by reminding the Jewish expatriates of something they could never forget—the fall of their city. "Thus says the LORD of hosts, the God of Israel: You have seen all the disaster that I brought upon Jerusalem and upon all the cities of Judah. Behold, this day they are a desolation, and no one dwells in them" (v. 2).

Jeremiah's words must have brought back all the nightmares of Judah's defeat at the hands of the Babylonians:

> The memories were all too painful, the gaunt faces of little children struggling against famine, flaming torches catapulted over the walls striking their mark, burning their homes, the dreadful sight of the battering ram breaking through the walls they thought impenetrable, the twisted faces of barbaric captains storming the streets of their defeated city. The stench of burning flesh, the sound of helpless cries, the sight of such calamity they bore forever in their memories.[2]

The refugees could not forget those horrific experiences if they tried. What they had trouble remembering was why they happened. So Jeremiah reminded them that they were defeated, as God himself put it,

> because of the evil that they committed, provoking me to anger, in that they went to make offerings and serve other gods that they knew not, neither they, nor you, nor your fathers. Yet I persistently sent to you all my servants the prophets, saying, "Oh, do not do this abomination that I hate!" But they did not listen or incline their ear, to turn from their evil and make no offerings to other gods. Therefore my wrath and my anger were poured out and kindled in the cities of Judah and in the streets of Jerusalem, and they became a waste and a desolation, as at this day. (vv. 3–6)

These verses summarize the whole Old Testament. The Jews never learned from the mistakes of the past, so they were doomed to repeat them. They never learned their lesson.

One is reminded of Christ's lament: "O Jerusalem, Jerusalem, the city that kills the prophets and stones those who are sent to it! How often would I have gathered your children together as a hen gathers her brood under her wings, and you were not willing! See, your house is left to you desolate" (Matthew 23:37, 38). The Jews kept ignoring the prophets whom God kept sending (7:25, 26; 25:4; 26:5; 29:19; 35:15), until finally Judah and Jerusalem lay in ruins.

After that catastrophe one might assume that God's people had finally learned their lesson. But they were in danger of forgetting. They were going right back to their former sins. So God posed to them a series of questions:

> And now thus says the Lord God of hosts, the God of Israel: Why do you commit this great evil against yourselves, to cut off from you man and woman, infant and child, from the midst of Judah, leaving you no remnant? Why do you provoke me to anger with the works of your hands, making offerings to other gods in the land of Egypt where you have come to live, so that you may be cut off and become a curse and a taunt among all the nations of the earth? Have you forgotten the evil of your fathers, the evil of the kings of Judah, the evil of their wives, your own evil, and the evil of your wives, which they committed in the land of Judah and in the streets of Jerusalem? They have not humbled themselves even to this day, nor have they feared, nor walked in my law and my statutes that I set before you and before your fathers. (44:7–10)

The remnant of the Jews had "no remorse for sin and no reverence for Yahweh."[3] All their suffering was in vain because it did not teach them to obey.

Some people never learn. Yet before becoming overcritical of the Jews, it is worth remembering how often God has to teach us the same lesson, and how many times we fall back into the same old sins.

The Queen of Heaven

Jeremiah had preached this kind of sermon before. Idolatry was one of his favorite themes. Once he compared worshiping a false god to drinking water from another cistern (2:13). Another time he said idols were nothing more than scarecrows in the cucumber field (10:5). In chapter 44, however, several new themes emerge.

The first is that goddess worship is a very great sin. Oh, how the Jews who settled in Egypt loved to worship their goddess! "But we will . . . make offerings to the queen of heaven and pour out drink offerings to her, as we did, both we and our fathers, our kings and our officials, in the cities of Judah and in the streets of Jerusalem" (44:17). They would rather worship the Queen of Heaven than serve the King of the universe!

The Queen of Heaven was not an Egyptian; she was the fertility goddess of Canaan, Assyria, and Babylonia. How ironic it was for the Jews, having fled from the Babylonians, to worship a Babylonian goddess! Yet ancient papyri from the Jewish community at Elephantina (an island on the Nile) reveal that the Jews freely mixed elements of Israelite and Canaanite religion.[4]

The Queen of Heaven went by different names in different dialects— Anat, Astarte, Ashteroth, and Ishtar, which is the pagan origin of Easter. Her cult was worshiped with the burning of incense, the pouring of libations, and the sacrifice of animals. In the palace kitchen at Mari, archaeologists have uncovered some of the baking molds used to the shape this goddess into sweet little cakes.[5]

Goddess worship may sound old-fashioned to postmodern ears, but it is becoming increasingly fashionable. In every period of history, sin takes feminine as well as masculine forms. Who are the goddesses of the present age?

First, there is Mary, the mother of Jesus, venerated as the Madonna in the Roman Catholic Church. The pope calls her "The woman promised in Eden, the woman chosen from eternity to be the Mother of the Word, the Mother of divine Wisdom, the Mother of the Son of God. Hail, Mother of God!"[6] Roman Catholics pray, "We have no greater help, no greater hope than you, O Most Pure Virgin."[7] Or again, "Come to my aid, dearest Mother, for I recommend myself to thee. In thy hands I place my eternal salvation, and to thee I entrust my soul."[8]

Worshiping Mary is not a harmless addition to the Christian faith. It is rank pagan idolatry. It is as wicked as worshiping the Queen of Heaven. Indeed, "Queen of Heaven" is one of the titles Catholics sometimes give to Mary. There is a thirty-five-foot shrine to Mary near Logan Airport in Boston, Massachusetts. A large billboard advertises the statue as "Madonna Queen." To call Mary the Queen of Heaven is to defy Scripture and embrace idolatry.

Mary was a good and godly woman. The humility of her servant's heart is an example to every believer (Luke 1:38). In submission to the will of God, she became the mother of Jesus Christ. But she is not the "Mother of God." She is not the "Mediatrix" or "Co-Redemptrix" of our salvation. She is neither more nor less than a sinner saved by grace.

In the first chapter of Acts, we read that the apostles and many other Christians gathered in an upper room to praise God. "All these with one accord were devoting themselves to prayer, together with the women and Mary the mother of Jesus, and his brothers" (Acts 1:14). The first Christians were giving praise to God and to his Son Jesus Christ. They were not praising Mary, for that would have been goddess worship. Instead they were joined by Mary in praise to Christ for their salvation.

Another goddess of this age is *Sophia*, which is the Greek word for *wisdom*. Sophia is increasingly popular in radical feminist theology. In their quest to discover feminine motifs in the Bible, some liberal Protestants have noticed that Proverbs describes wisdom as a woman: "Wisdom cries aloud in the street, in the markets she raises her voice" (Proverbs 1:20). Instead of recognizing this as the literary device known as personification, they have claimed Wisdom as their goddess: "Mother Goddess is reawakening and we can begin to recover our primal birthright, the sheer intoxicating joy of being alive. We can open our eyes and see that there is nothing to be saved from . . . no God outside the world to be feared and obeyed."[9]

During the 1990s women from several mainline denominations sang Sophia's praises, even devising their own unholy sacraments. In one of their hymns they sang:

OUR MAKER SOPHIA,
we are women in your image. . . .
We celebrate the sensual life you give us . . .
we celebrate our bodiliness, our physicality,
the sensations of pleasure,
our oneness with earth and water.[10]

The logical consequence of radical feminist theology is the worship of a female god.

Wicca, the witch-goddess, is another goddess of this age. She is the goddess of satanic power, and her witchcraft is on the rise. Witches greet one another as "God and Goddess."[11] Covens gather on All Hallow's Eve to pray for the corruption of children and the destruction of the church. It is not uncommon for witches to show up in religious studies departments at major universities. Furthermore, in the last two decades some eighty thousand nuns have left the Roman Catholic Church. A recent book by Donna Steicher documents that many of them have turned to witchcraft and other forms of the occult.[12] They have gone from the convent to the coven, exchanging one goddess for another.

Other goddesses could be mentioned, including Self. One of the battle cries of radical feminism is "I found God in myself, and I loved her fiercely."[13] Then there is mighty Aphrodite, the goddess of sex. One theology professor describes sexual intercourse as "sexual godding." In the words of one of her students, "My most profound experience of Goddess is with my lover—while we are having sex. . . . I feel a deep sense of her love and presence with me."[14]

Perhaps none of these goddesses clamors for your worship. But what about that temptress Glamor? She is universally adored. Consider the billions of dollars spent to promote Glamor in the newspapers, magazines, billboards, and television commercials. A woman has to have the right shoes, clothes, makeup, perfume, jewels, and accessories. The reason shopping is America's number one hobby is because Glamor is Queen.

What does the Bible say about Glamor? It teaches women (and men, for that matter) to "adorn themselves in respectable apparel, with modesty and self-control, not with braided hair and gold or pearls or costly attire, but with what is proper for women who profess godliness—with good works" (1 Timothy 2:9, 10). Modern Christians hear these instructions and hope God doesn't really mean it. Modesty? Propriety? No gold? No designer labels? But notice how the command ends: This is for "women who profess godliness." It is all about worship. The danger in the latest hairstyle, the shiniest jewelry, and the fanciest dress is that you will start worshiping the goddess of Glamor, Fashion, or Beauty—someone or something besides God himself.

The point of giving these examples of goddess worship is that the warnings of Jeremiah 44 apply to the contemporary Christian. It is tempting to read about Old Testament idolatry and think, "Who would ever do that?" Well, take a closer look at Western culture, where paganism is smuggled in, sometimes even under the guise of Christianity.

Perhaps you should even take a look at yourself. Will you worship the King, or will you allow some Queen to dethrone him? God alone is King. God alone rules over Heaven and earth. God alone made beauty and wisdom. God alone made woman in his image, and he chose Mary to be his handmaid. Thus God alone deserves all worship and praise.

The Family Altar

Human beings are made to worship. If they do not worship the King of kings, they will worship some other god or goddess. This is true for families as well as individuals. For better or for worse, families worship together.

The devotion of the Jews for the Queen of Heaven was a family affair involving both husbands and their wives. The husbands knew what their wives were doing. Jeremiah described them as "all the men who knew that their wives had made offerings to other gods" (44:15a). The husbands knew, and their wives knew that they knew: "And the women said, 'When we made offerings to the queen of heaven and poured out drink offerings to her, was it without our husbands' approval that we made cakes for her bearing her image and poured out drink offerings to her?'" (v. 19).

Idolatry was killing the souls of these families. The husbands failed to show spiritual leadership within the home. They were not strong in service for their King. Meanwhile, their wives were leading their families into pagan worship. As a result, their children were learning to love the Queen rather than to serve the King.

The same thing had happened back in Jerusalem. Many years before, God had said to Jeremiah, "Do you not see what they are doing in the cities of Judah and in the streets of Jerusalem? The children gather wood, the fathers kindle fire, and the women knead dough, to make cakes for the queen of heaven" (7:17, 18a). Goddess worship had become a family tradition. "Remember those little cakes Mama used to make? I loved the way she used to pour the batter into the mold and bake them in the shape of the Queen of Heaven!"

Worship starts at the end of mother's apron strings. It starts with the values learned in the kitchen. It starts around the family dinner table, which the Puritans called "The family altar." This is why every family must meet together regularly for prayer and Bible study. Families should discuss the sermon and the Sunday school lesson on the way home from church. They should sing hymns and spiritual songs. They should memorize Bible passages and learn their catechism.

All family worship takes is a Bible and a commitment to the spiritual health of your family. What traditions are you establishing for your children? Will they remember the Bible verses they memorized over breakfast? Will they remember your joy on the morning of the Lord's Day? Will they remember, as I can remember, the passionate prayers of their grandparents around the dinner table? Will they remember the songs of salvation you used to sing at bedtime?

These are questions every father must answer, for family worship is the father's particular responsibility. The women in Egypt understood that principle. Their excuse for worshiping the Queen of Heaven was, "our husbands knew what we were doing." They were appealing to the Biblical teaching about vows. If a wife made a foolish vow, her husband had the spiritual authority to overturn it (Numbers 30:10–15). In Egypt the women made a vow to worship the Queen of Heaven (44:25). It was a sinful vow, but their husbands said nothing about it. Thus the guilt for the sin rested upon the husbands as well as on their wives.

On Self-Destruct Mode

Fathers are responsible for the spiritual health of their homes. They must be men of prayer, fasting, and repentance, for families are made to worship together. If they fail to worship the King, the consequences are devastating. Sin is always self-destructive.

The remnant of the Jews did not understand what they were doing to themselves. They were so blind that they thought goddess worship was good for them! As they reminisced about the good old days when they worshiped the Queen of Heaven in Jerusalem, they claimed that they never had any troubles: "For then we had plenty of food, and prospered, and saw no disaster. But since we left off making offerings to the queen of heaven and pouring out drink offerings to her, we have lacked everything and have been consumed by the sword and by famine" (vv. 17b, 18).

The dispute between the Queen of Heaven and the King of kings was an argument about what *worked*. The remnant claimed that things were fine until they stopped worshiping the Queen of Heaven. Goddess worship brought them health and wealth, they claimed. All their subsequent troubles were to be blamed on the reformation under Josiah, when goddess worship was outlawed. The fall of Jerusalem and the exile in Egypt did not take place until *after* they abandoned their Queen.

The real truth was exactly the opposite. Goddess worship is what destroyed them! The main reason they ended up in Egypt was because of their idolatry:

> Then Jeremiah said to all the people, men and women, all the people who had given him this answer: "As for the offerings that you offered in the cities of Judah and in the streets of Jerusalem, you and your fathers, your kings and your officials, and the people of the land, did not the LORD remember them? Did it not come into his mind? The LORD could no longer bear your evil deeds and the abominations that you committed. Therefore your land has become a desolation and a waste and a curse, without inhabitant, as it is this day. It is because you made offerings and because you sinned against the LORD and did not obey the voice of the LORD or walk in his law and in his statutes and in his testimonies that this disaster has happened to you, as at this day." (vv. 20–23)

"As at this day," Jeremiah said. But they didn't see it. The refugees were blind to sin and its consequences. They were so blind that they did not even recognize that they were living in sin and were being judged for their sins.

Every sin turns out to be suicidal. This is the great danger of doing what works instead of doing what is right. If you live for yourself, you will destroy yourself. It can feel good to be angry, but anger leads to bitterness. Greed works if you want to make money, but it is the enemy of contentment. Sexual sin destroys sexual intimacy. And so on. Sin destroys the soul. It destroys relationships with other people and fellowship with God. In the end, sin recoils to devour the sinner.

This was true back when the Jews worshiped the Queen of Heaven in Jerusalem: "And they pour out drink offerings to other gods, to provoke me to anger. Is it I whom they provoke? declares the LORD. Is it not themselves, to their own shame?" (7:18b, 19).

It turned out to be equally true in Egypt, where God promised that judgment would be severe:

> Therefore thus says the LORD of hosts, the God of Israel: Behold, I will set my face against you for harm, to cut off all Judah. I will take the remnant of Judah who have set their faces to come to the land of Egypt to live, and they shall all be consumed. In the land of Egypt they shall fall; by the sword and by famine they shall be consumed. From the least to the greatest, they shall die by the sword and by famine, and they shall become an oath, a horror, a curse, and a taunt. I will punish those who dwell in the land of Egypt, as I have punished Jerusalem, with the sword, with famine, and with pestilence. (44:11–13)

These wounds would all be self-inflicted. As Jeremiah had asked, "Why do you commit this great evil against *yourselves*?" (v. 7a). "You will destroy *yourselves* and make yourselves a curse" (v. 8a NIV).

The way the Jews defied Jeremiah's warning was very sad. Sin has such a powerful hold on the sinner that sinners sometimes choose to destroy themselves.

> Then all the men who knew that their wives had made offerings to other gods, and all the women who stood by, a great assembly, all the people who lived in Pathros in the land of Egypt, answered Jeremiah: "As for the word that you have spoken to us in the name of the LORD, we will not listen to you. But we will do everything that we have vowed, make offerings to the queen of heaven" (vv. 15–17a).

Their wives had made the same choice:

> Jeremiah said to all the people and all the women, "Hear the word of the LORD, all you of Judah who are in the land of Egypt. Thus says the LORD of hosts, the God of Israel: You and your wives have declared with your mouths, and have fulfilled it with your hands, saying, 'We will surely perform our vows that we have made, to make offerings to the queen of heaven and to pour out drink offerings to her.'" (vv. 24, 25a)

These were practically the only vows the Jews actually kept. As a result, the patience of God finally came to an end. "Have it your way," he said in essence. "Make your covenant with the Queen of Heaven. But know that you will be cursed for breaking my covenant":

> Then confirm your vows and perform your vows! Therefore hear the word of the LORD, all you of Judah who dwell in the land of Egypt: Behold, I have sworn by my great name, says the LORD, that my name shall no more be invoked by the mouth of any man of Judah in all the land of Egypt, saying, 'As the Lord GOD lives.' Behold, I am watching over them for disaster and not for good. All the men of Judah who are in the land of Egypt shall be consumed by the sword and by famine, until there is an end of them. (vv. 25b–27)

The exiles could not swear, "As the Lord GOD lives" because they denied his very existence. God's threat to watch over them for harm was especially ominous. Back in chapter 29 God had said that he had good plans for the exiles in Babylon, plans for their "welfare" and not for "evil" (29:11). But his plans for the refugees in Egypt were not good.

This is the great difference between those who trust in God and those who do not. If you come to God through Jesus Christ, the King of the universe is watching out for you. But if you insist on worshiping the Queen of Heaven, you will come to harm.

This is a strong warning to anyone living in unrepentant sin. Sin is self-destructive, which is why sinners must repent and believe the gospel before it is too late. Eventually God allows sinners to have their own way. C. S. Lewis writes, "There are only two kinds of people in the end: those who say to God, 'Thy will be done,' and those to whom God says, in the end, 'Thy will be done.' All that are in Hell, choose it."[15]

The refugees in Egypt made a hell of their own choosing. And Jeremiah gave them a sign to confirm their choice:

> This shall be the sign to you, declares the LORD, that I will punish you in this place, in order that you may know that my words will surely stand against you for harm: Thus says the LORD, Behold, I will give Pharaoh Hophra king of Egypt into the hand of his enemies and into the hand of those who seek his life, as I gave Zedekiah king of Judah into the hand of Nebuchadnezzar king of Babylon, who was his enemy and sought his life. (44:29, 30)

That is exactly what happened. The Jews put all their trust in Hophra. After all, he was the Pharaoh who sent help to King Zedekiah (cf. 37:5). Once Hophra even claimed, "Not even a god can move me from my throne."[16] Yet

Herodotus describes how Ahmosis II rebelled, removed Hophra from the throne, and finally executed him in 566 BC.[17] Trusting in Hophra, like trusting in the Queen of Heaven, proved to be a poor choice.

The Remnant of the Remnant

Was there any hope for these sinners?

God was within his rights to utterly destroy them. He said, "None of the remnant of Judah who have come to live in the land of Egypt shall escape or survive or return to the land of Judah, to which they desire to return to dwell there. For they shall not return, except some fugitives" (v. 14). "Except some fugitives"—that is the key phrase. God *always* saves a remnant, or at least a remnant of the remnant, chosen by grace.

The remnant of the remnant was saved so everyone would know that God is King. "And those who escape the sword shall return from the land of Egypt to the land of Judah, few in number; and all the remnant of Judah, who came to the land of Egypt to live, shall know whose word will stand, mine or theirs" (v. 28). It was God's word against their word, the King against the Queen. In the end, the remnant of the remnant proved God's kingly justice against sin and his royal grace for sinners.

The remnant of the remnant was so small, it is hard to say if this chapter has a happy ending. Humanly speaking, Jeremiah's life did *not* have a happy ending. His ministry ended as it began, with words of judgment. Like nearly all the rest of his prophecies, his final words of judgment were largely ignored. In fact, rabbinic tradition holds that Jeremiah was stoned by the Jews in Egypt. Perhaps Hebrews 11:37 has Jeremiah in mind when it speaks of the stoning of the prophets.

Was Jeremiah a failure? If success in ministry is measured by what works, then Jeremiah was a failure, for he failed to turn back the tide of idolatry in his generation. However, if success is measured by faithfulness to God's call, Jeremiah was a supreme success. He was faithful to God's Word to the very end of his sufferings.

There is another sense in which Jeremiah's life and ministry was a success, for everyone who knows Jesus Christ is the happy ending to Jeremiah's ministry!

The apostle Peter explained how the prophets of the Old Testament longed for the coming of Jesus Christ:

> Concerning this salvation, the prophets who prophesied about the grace
> that was to be yours searched and inquired carefully, inquiring what person

or time the Spirit of Christ in them was indicating when he predicted the sufferings of Christ and the subsequent glories. It was revealed to them that they were serving not themselves but you, in the things that have now been announced to you through those who preached the good news to you by the Holy Spirit sent from heaven. (1 Peter 1:10–12)

In this book we have come to know Jeremiah in a deeply personal way. At times his sufferings have almost become our sufferings. Our affection for him becomes all the deeper when we realize that he suffered all these things *for us*. By the Spirit of God, Jeremiah understood that his mockings, beatings, tortures, and almost-executions were for the sake of God's people in centuries to come.

What message could possibly be so important that a man would suffer forty, fifty, or even sixty years to deliver it? What message would inspire a man to do all this, not for himself, but for the sake of people he would never meet? Only the message of salvation in Jesus Christ, that the Son of God would suffer and die to give his people eternal life.

Jeremiah's saving message cost him much suffering throughout his life. Its cost was all the sufferings of all the prophets and apostles. Most costly of all, it was paid for with the very lifeblood of Christ on the cross. Since that message comes at such great cost, should you not receive it, believe it, and proclaim it with your whole heart?

59

Attempt Small
Things for God

JEREMIAH 45:1–5

JEREMIAH 45 IS NOT ABOUT JEREMIAH. It is about his secretary Baruch, described by Sigmund Mowinckel as "The literary and spiritual heir to the preaching of Jeremiah and the one who has taken care of the spiritual remains of the prophet, the founder and carrier-on of the tradition about him, 'the author' of the book of Jeremiah."[1]

Baruch happens to be the only man from the Old Testament who has been fingerprinted. In 1975 a group of archaeologists purchased some clay document markers from an Arab antiquities dealer. The archaeologists did not decipher the markers—which were the bookmarks of the ancient world—until 1986. When they did, they discovered that one of them bears the seal of Baruch son of Neriah.[2] Since then another document marker has been discovered that bears not only Baruch's seal, but also a thumbprint, very probably the thumbprint of the scribe himself.[3] Baruch was a man of flesh, blood, and fingerprint.

Since Baruch was a man, he had all the weaknesses and failings common to humanity, including a sinful heart. There are times when it seems hard to relate to Jeremiah. He performed such brave deeds and spoke such bold words that he towers above the ordinary believer. But Baruch was more like us. His sins and his sorrows seem more familiar, more down-to-earth. What can we learn from his experience?

Baruch's Complaint

Jeremiah 45 is a flashback, or perhaps an appendix, to chapter 36. In that chapter Jeremiah dictated all his prophecies to Baruch, who wrote them down on a scroll. Then Jeremiah sent his scribe to read the prophecies during the fast at the temple. Subsequently the scroll was taken to King Jehoiakim. In an act of outright rebellion, the king slashed the very words of God into pieces and fed them into the winter fire.

Sometime during that infamous episode, Jeremiah gave Baruch a message from the Lord. "The word that Jeremiah the prophet spoke to Baruch the son of Neriah, when he wrote these words in a book at the dictation of Jeremiah, in the fourth year of Jehoiakim the son of Josiah, king of Judah" (45:1). The Scripture does not indicate at what moment this prophecy came, but it sounds as if Baruch had just put the finishing touches on Jeremiah's scroll.

God spoke to Baruch because he had been complaining: "Thus says the LORD, the God of Israel, to you, O Baruch: You said, 'Woe is me! For the LORD has added sorrow to my pain. I am weary with my groaning, and I find no rest'" (vv. 2, 3). One after another, these words convey great weariness of body and soul: "woe, sorrow, pain, weary, groaning, no rest." Baruch was discouraged, disheartened, and disillusioned.

It is not hard to guess why Baruch may have been depressed. The Bible says the word of the Lord came to him *after* he had written the scroll. He may have despaired because he knew no one would listen to Jeremiah. Or perhaps it was because the words of judgment were so severe. According to Jeremiah's prophecy, the reformation would fail, the city would fall, and the culture would be destroyed. His own people would fall victim to sword, famine, and plague.

Then there were the threats on Jeremiah's life, which might well extend to Baruch when he read Jeremiah's prophecy at the temple. The message was so dire, people might kill the messenger. So Baruch may have been afraid, both for his own life and for his dear friend Jeremiah. He was counting the heavy cost of suffering for God's Word.

It is also possible that Baruch started to complain later, when he learned that the king had burned his manuscript. It is very discouraging to have one's work go to waste. Once there was a man who lost the only copy of the typescript of his dissertation. Twice! He was so discouraged that he gave up and never finished his doctorate. Who can blame him? Anyone who has lost a day or two of work through computer failure knows that it can seem like a national crisis.

Baruch lost much more than a day or two of work, however. It must have taken weeks or even months to make a perfect copy of Jeremiah's prophecies. This was in the days before dictaphones or word processors. When Jehoiakim burned Baruch's manuscript, many weeks of hard labor for the Word of God went up in smoke. This could explain why the scribe said, *"Oy li"*—"Woe is me!"

Perhaps God's Word came to Baruch while he was making a second copy of Jeremiah's scroll. He complained that he was "weary." Day after day he had been getting out the scroll, painstakingly writing the letters, scratching out his mistakes with a knife. Baruch would have agreed with the philosopher who wrote Ecclesiastes: "Of making many books there is no end, and much study is a weariness of the flesh" (Ecclesiastes 12:12b). Hard work tires the body.

A weary body makes for a weary soul. But Baruch was more than tired—he was discouraged. He complained about his *"pain,"* which may refer to some physical problem, such as back pain. He spoke of his *"sorrow,"* which seems to refer to some grief, perhaps even the loss of a loved one. He mentioned his *"groaning,"* which hints at some secret burden carried in the heart.

The words of Baruch's lament thus describe all the difficulties of life in this fallen world. In one way or another, they touch every trouble of the human heart. When God's people come to worship on the Lord's Day, many of them are worn-out. They are tired from their professional work, their schoolwork, or their housework. Day by day, week by week, month by month, year by year their jobs, their families, and their ministries gradually wear them down.

Others have pain, especially physical pain. They have a life-threatening illness or suffer from a chronic ailment that will torment them until they die. For some, sorrow is added to pain. They remember the death of loved ones or lament the passing of happy days. Still others have groaning. They carry around secret wounds that are painful to the touch. "Woe to me!" we say because of all the weariness, pain, sorrow, and groaning of life.

It is good to know we do not suffer alone. The servants of God in the past had the same struggles we have. Yet they found God faithful in every situation. The Bible is not silent about the trials and sorrows of life. One of the reasons for its continual relevance is that it speaks to every troubled emotion of the soul. It assures us that sorrow and groaning are common to humanity.

The Bible also assures us that we have a Savior who understands the trials of life. Jesus Christ was "a man of sorrows" (Isaiah 53:3). He was worn out with groaning in the garden of Gethsemane. He went through the pain of dying for sins on the cross. Therefore, when we turn to God with our troubles, we are not turning to someone "who is unable to sympathize with our weaknesses" (Hebrews 4:15). On the contrary, Jesus has the most tender compassion for every one of his suffering children.

God's Answer

What counsel would you give to Baruch? Would you tell him to take a few days off? Would you lend him a sympathetic ear? Would you tell him to find an easier ministry? Would you tell him that God loves him and has a wonderful plan for his life? Would you remind him that "for those who love God all things work together for good" (Romans 8:28)?

On occasion, some of those things might be good to say to a discouraged believer. There is a time for resting, a time for listening, a time for changing jobs, and a time for trusting the sovereignty of God. But God had something else to say to Baruch. And very likely, he would say the same thing to anyone who says, "Woe is me!" He told Baruch, "And do you seek great things for yourself? Seek them not" (45:5a).

In other words, God was telling Baruch to stop being so selfish. God looked into his heart and saw how self-centered he was. Notice how often Baruch used the first person singular in his lament: "Woe is me! For the LORD has added sorrow to my pain. I am weary with my groaning, and I find no rest" (v. 3). He sounds even more self-centered in Hebrew, because nearly every word ends with a first person possessive pronoun: *my* woe, *my* pain, *my* being worn out, *my* groaning, *my* finding no rest. However much he may have hated his life, Baruch was still very deeply in love with himself!

Baruch's complaint yields two important insights about depression. The first is that every complaint is finally a complaint about God. Ultimately Baruch was blaming God for his troubles. It was "The LORD" who had added sorrow to his pain. Even when it has a physical component, despair is always a spiritual matter. Dissatisfaction with life is dissatisfaction with God. "It is all God's fault," people say. "God gave me this lousy job. God made me sick. God took away my loved ones." Whatever the trouble, God is to blame.

As depression turns against God, it turns inward upon the self. Baruch could not see beyond the boundaries of his own troubles. He spent all his time thinking about how tired he was, how much pain he was in, how many griefs he had to bear. But God cut right to the heart of Baruch's real problem: He was seeking something for *himself*.

The Bible does not mention what Baruch was seeking for himself. Maybe he wanted an easier life. Maybe he was tired of being an amanuensis and wanted a promotion—he wanted to be the prophet! After all, he was well educated. At one time his career prospects had been excellent, for he came from a prominent family. His grandfather Mahseiah had been the governor (32:12; cf. 2 Chronicles 34:8). His brother Seraiah was a high-ranking official (51:59). But now he was stuck taking dictation, doing Jeremiah's dirty work.

Whatever Baruch's ambition, he was being a very selfish man. So God told him to take his eyes off himself and look at what was happening to everyone else. If he thought he had problems, he should take a look at his neighbors. "Thus shall you say to him, Thus says the LORD: Behold, what I have built I am breaking down, and what I have planted I am plucking up—that is, the whole land. And do you seek great things for yourself? Seek them not, for behold, I am bringing disaster upon all flesh, declares the LORD" (45:4, 5).

God was speaking about a day of judgment. This may have referred to the momentous world event that took place later that year (605 BC)—the battle of Carchemish, in which the Egyptians defeated the Babylonians. Or it may refer to the final judgment. God said he would bring "disaster upon all flesh," meaning the whole creation.[4]

It was inappropriate for Baruch to be so selfish when the world was in such great danger. He was having his own private little pity party. Meanwhile, the rest of the world was going to Hell. God was going to judge them for their sins. If worldwide disaster is inevitable, why should someone like Baruch worry about his own petty concerns?

Baruch's rebuke is a reminder to be desperately concerned about the spiritual condition of family and friends. The eternal destiny of every soul hangs in the balance. Either you and your loved ones will spend eternity with God or you will be banished from his presence forever. Compared with that, the rest of life's troubles scarcely deserve mention.

Death to Self

Baruch's rebuke is also for everyone who desires to do something great. Deep down, every believer has a heartfelt passion to do something for God. The great missionary statesman William Carey (1761–1834) once preached a famous missionary sermon with the title, "Expect Great Things from God; Attempt Great Things for God."

What believer has not wanted to accept Carey's challenge and attempt something great for God? Generations after generations of believers have echoed the bold answer of Isaiah, who "heard the voice of the Lord saying, 'Whom shall I send, and who will go for us?' Then I said, 'Here I am! Send me'" (Isaiah 6:8). At some time or other, every Christian wants to stand with the prophet in the presence of God and say, "Here I am, Lord. Use me! Send me! I will go anywhere. I will do anything. I will suffer everything for the sake of the gospel of Jesus Christ."

Yet there can be something very self-centered about that prayer. "Here *I* am! Send *me*." Some Christians think the important thing is not that God's will gets done, but that *they* get to do it. They are happy for God to get the glory as long as they can share some of the limelight. How hard it is to attempt great things for God without attempting them also for self!

Baruch's example reminds us not to think of ourselves more highly than we ought. If God has given you a small place of ministry, then accept it. It is probably more than you can handle anyway. God will not ask you to do some greater thing until you have proven yourself faithful in a small thing.

Do not wait around for God to give you something great to do. Too many Christians put life on hold, waiting for some great task to come along. They are like Pip in Charles Dickens's novel *Great Expectations*. Pip was just a poor child, but he had a wealthy benefactor, so he grew up with "great expectations." He always knew great things were in store for him. So he left his family and went off to London to wait for those great things to come. But in the end his expectations failed. He did not get the money, the position, or anything else he expected.

If you are waiting to do some great thing, you may be wasting God's time. Most Christians will never do anything great. "And do you seek great things for yourself? Seek them not" (45:5a). Instead give your best for God in the small things. Be a good worker, lead one person to Christ, raise a godly family, support a missionary. The way to seek the glory of God is in the little things of the Christian life. Hudson Taylor (1832–1905) once said, "A little thing is just a little thing, but faithfulness in a little thing is a great thing." Not a great thing for *you*, understand, but a great thing for God. God is glorified greatly by the little things done for his glory. Attempt small things for God!

What does it take for a man like Baruch to stop seeking great things for himself? The answer is that he must die to himself. The self will not stop seeking greatness until it is put to death. But once the self is dead, the only thing left is to attempt small things (or great things) for the glory of God.

Reverend William Still served as minister of Gilcomston South Church for more than fifty years (1945–1997). The title of Mr. Still's autobiography summarizes his approach to ministry—*Dying to Live*. This is what he wrote about death to self:

> The deaths one dies before ministry can be of long duration—it can be hours and days before we minister, before the resurrection experience of anointed preaching. And then there is another death afterwards, sometimes worse than the death before. From the moment that you stand there dead in Christ and dead to everything you are and have and ever shall be and have,

every breath you breathe thereafter, every thought you think, every word you say and deed you do, must be done over the top of your own corpse or reaching over it in your preaching to others. Then it can only be Jesus that comes over and no one else. And I believe that every preacher must bear the mark of that death. Your life must be signed by the Cross, not just Christ's Cross (there is really no other) but your cross in his Cross, your particular and unique cross that no one ever died—the cross that no one ever could die but you and you alone: your death in Christ's death.[5]

I sometimes think of those words as I approach the pulpit to preach. I confess I have yet to see my self lying like a corpse upon the platform. That is the way the sinful self is; it is unwilling to lie down and die. It wants to come right up and minister in its own strength. It will take advantage of every opportunity to seek great things for itself.

That is why the self must die. That is why *your* self must die. And the place that selves go to die is the cross of Jesus Christ: "We know that our old self was crucified with him in order that the body of sin might be brought to nothing, so that we would no longer be enslaved to sin. For one who has died has been set free from sin" (Romans 6:6, 7). The self received its deathblow on the cross. Jesus was crucified for the selfishness of all our sins. Now the self is dying a long, slow death.

As your self lies dying, the thing to do is to bury it. "Consider yourselves dead to sin," the apostle went on to say, "and alive to God in Christ Jesus" (Romans 6:11). A part of you goes on living, of course, but it is only the part in which God himself lives. Now what your self says is, "I have been crucified with Christ. It is no longer I who live, but Christ who lives in me" (Galatians 2:20a).

This kind of death to self is a great help in suffering such as Baruch endured. As Bonhoeffer wrote, "When a person has completely given up the idea of making something of himself . . . then one throws oneself entirely into the arms of God, then one no longer takes seriously his own suffering."[6]

Blessed Assurance

God's counsel for Baruch may not sound very soothing. Just about the last thing someone wants to hear when he is depressed is to stop being so selfish. But God had Baruch's best interests at heart. He loved him and cared for him. So after he rebuked him, he promised him salvation, saying, "For behold, I am bringing disaster upon all flesh, declares the LORD. But I will give you your life as a prize of war in all places to which you may go" (45:5b). In this way, "Baruch is at once reassured and reprimanded."[7]

Baruch had been many places during his lifetime. He was with Jeremiah in prison when the prophet bought a field from his cousin Hanamel. He was the one who signed and sealed the deed and put the real estate documents in a clay jar for safekeeping (32:11–16). Baruch was also by Jeremiah's side when he dictated all the words of his prophecies (36:4).

Baruch went lots of other places after God gave him this message as well. He risked his life to read Jeremiah's scroll to all the Jews at the temple (36:8–10). After he gave the scroll to the royal cabinet, he went into hiding so the king could not arrest him (36:19, 26). Many years later Baruch went down to Egypt with the unrighteous remnant of God's people (43:6). There he was in danger again, as Public Enemy Number Two. The remnant blamed him for Jeremiah's prophecies, saying, "Baruch the son of Neriah has set you against us, to deliver us into the hand of the Chaldeans, that they may kill us or take us into exile in Babylon" (43:3).

Although Baruch found himself in many dangerous situations, he always survived. Wherever he went, God saved his life, just as he had promised. Baruch was not to seek great things for himself, but God did a great thing for Baruch. He saved him. As Jesus promised: "Whoever would save his life will lose it, but whoever loses his life for my sake and the gospel's will save it" (Mark 8:35).

The term used in chapter 45 for escaping with one's life is one Jeremiah had used before. God promised Ebed-melech, the African slave who rescued Jeremiah from the cistern, "I will surely save you, and you shall not fall by the sword, but you shall have your life as a prize of war" (39:18a). God promised that Baruch and Ebed-melech would escape with their lives as the spoils of battle.

Baruch clung to that promise the rest of his life, which is probably why the promise has been preserved in the Bible. Some scholars complain that this little chapter is out of place. It belongs back in chapter 36, they say. However, it is obvious that when Baruch arranged Jeremiah's scroll he put this prophecy right where it belonged. He treasured the promise God gave him. It reminded him of the way God answered him in his despair. So he put it here at the end of his life to show that God was faithful to his promise.

Everyone who believes in Jesus Christ has the same assurance Baruch had. God has promised to do a great thing for us. He has given us the guarantee of eternal life: "And this is the testimony, that God gave us eternal life, and this life is in his Son. Whoever has the Son has life; whoever does not have the Son of God does not have life. I write these things to you who believe in the name of the Son of God that you may know that you have eternal life" (1 John

5:11–13). This is where we find our true significance—not in doing something for ourselves, or even for God, but in what God has done for us.

Once we understand that we are nothing more than sinners saved by grace, we no longer seek great things for ourselves. We are content to glorify God in the little things of life. This attitude is beautifully expressed in a childlike hymn written by Anna Waring (1850):

> Father, I know that all my life is portioned out for me;
> the changes that are sure to come, I do not fear to see:
> I ask thee for a present mind, intent on pleasing thee.
>
> I would not have the restless will that hurries to and fro,
> seeking for some great thing to do, or secret thing to know;
> I would be treated as a child, and guided where I go.
>
> I ask thee for the daily strength, to none that ask denied,
> a mind to blend with outward life, while keeping at thy side,
> content to fill a little space, if thou be glorified.

60

God of All Nations

JEREMIAH 46:1—47:7

THE EMPEROR DIOCLETIAN (AD 245–313) was a great enemy of God. He once had a medal made that proclaimed, "The name of Christianity being extinguished." Then, as he expanded the Roman Empire into Spain, he erected a monument to himself bearing the following inscription:

> Diocletian Jovian Maximian Herculeus Caesares Augusti
> for having everywhere abolished the superstition of Christ
> for having extended the worship of the gods.[1]

In the same way, many nations before and since have set themselves up "against the LORD and against his Anointed" (Psalm 2:2b). Jeremiah 46—51 contains an international roll call of God's ancient enemies. The list runs from Egypt, which enslaved God's people for four hundred years, to Babylon, which held them captive for seventy.

These chapters are sometimes called "The Oracles Against the Nations." They are war oracles "summoning the people to battle, pronouncing defeat for the enemy, and often including a taunt against the enemy."[2]

"The Oracles Against the Nations" begin in a rather matter-of-fact way: "The word of the LORD that came to Jeremiah the prophet concerning the nations" (46:1). The chapters that follow contain prophecies about the fates of Egypt, Philistia, Moab, Ammon, Edom, Damascus, Kedar, Hazor, Elam, and Babylon. Ten nations are mentioned in all, covering nearly a million square miles of the globe. God takes the powers and superpowers of the ancient world and casually orders them around. Who does God think he is?

The Ruler of All Nations

God knows who he is. He is not a regional supervisor. He is not a tribal deity. He is the God of all nations. His sovereignty is not limited to a single culture, nation, or ethnic group. He has the whole world in his hands.

God staked his claim as ruler of all nations on the very first page of Jeremiah. When he called Jeremiah to the ministry he appointed him as "a prophet to the nations" (1:5b). With his "Oracles to the Nations," Jeremiah carried out the last part of his job description.[3] He took his message of judgment and grace and went international with it.

Jeremiah was a prophet to all nations because he served the God of all nations. The way God rules the nations is by his Word. The Old Testament was not written only to and for the Jews. The Holy Spirit took great pains to communicate God's Word to the nations.

The closing chapters of Jeremiah are not, Eugene Peterson says, "second-level works tossed off in a slovenly manner because they are for despised foreigners."[4] On the contrary, they contain some of the finest poetry in the Bible. They display such intimate knowledge of the ancient peoples that scholars sometimes struggle to explain what they mean. The "Oracles Against the Nations" contain references only someone from Moab, Edom, or Kedar could understand.

Consider God's comprehensive knowledge of ancient Egypt. He had heard Egypt's boast:

> Who is this, rising like the Nile,
>   like rivers whose waters surge?
> Egypt rises like the Nile,
>   like rivers whose waters surge.
> He said, "I will rise, I will cover the earth,
>   I will destroy cities and their inhabitants." (46:7, 8)

Every year the Nile flooded its banks and surged over the Nile delta. The Pharaohs boasted that they would rise and cover the earth in the same way.

God knew the geography of Egypt and the other kingdoms of North Africa:

> Declare in Egypt, and proclaim in Migdol;
>   proclaim in Memphis and Tahpanhes. (v. 14a)

> Let the warriors go out:
>   men of Cush and Put who handle the shield,
>   men of Lud, skilled in handling the bow. (v. 9b)

In those days, the kingdoms of Cush (Ethiopia), Put (Somalia), and Lud (Libya) contributed soldiers to the Egyptian alliance.

God was also aware of Egypt's military capabilities. His prophet Jeremiah used the proper terms for both of the kinds of shields the Egyptians used ("Prepare buckler and shield, and advance for battle!"; v. 3). He knew that Greek soldiers, who were first hired by Psammeticus I (c. 664–610 BC), formed the backbone of the Egyptian army. They were the "hired soldiers in her midst" (v. 21a).[5] In short, God knew everything there was to know about Egypt.

God's knowledge of Philistia was equally extensive. He knew the geography of the coastal plain as well as the Nile delta. He knew that the Phoenician cities of Tyre and Sidon turned to Gaza and Ashkelon for help (47:4a). He called the Philistines "The remnant of the coastland of Caphtor" (47:b; cf. Amos 9:7), which was the ancient name for Crete. God knew who they were, where they lived, and where they had come from, for Caphtor was the Mediterranean island to which the Philistines traced their heritage.

Jeremiah's point was that God is the ruler of all nations. Most of the gods of the ancient world were regional deities. They ruled one people in one place at one time. They were like mediocre sports teams: They usually won at home, but they always struggled on the road. However, the one true God rules the nations home and away.

The Apostle Paul once tried to explain this to the philosophers in Athens: "He [God] made from one man every nation of mankind to live on all the face of the earth, having determined allotted periods and the boundaries of their dwelling place" (Acts 17:26). God was omniscient about the ancient cultures of Egypt and Philistia. In the same way, he knows everything happening in the world at this instant.

Moreover, God is omnipotent in his government of world affairs. He is the God of history. He is working to bring his plan to completion in every kingdom, tribe, and nation. World events are the canvas where he paints his mighty acts.

One reason Christians should take an interest in international affairs is that their God rules over all nations:

> Biblical religion is aggressively internationalist. People who participate in the community of faith find themselves in a company of men and women who have a passion for crossing boundaries—linguistic, racial, geographic, cultural—in order to demonstrate that there is no spot on earth and no person on earth that is not included in the divine plan.[6]

If one wants to know what God is doing in the world, it is not enough to read the local paper. Since God is the ruler of all nations, every Christian should be a world Christian.

The Judge of All Nations

God is Judge of all nations as well as Ruler of all nations. He rules the nations in order to bring them to account for their sins. Thus Jeremiah's "Oracles Against the Nations" were primarily oracles of judgment.

Chapter 46 is the record of God's judgment against Egypt. Jeremiah's poetry came from the battlefront, where officers would give sharp orders as troops mustered for combat. Imagine the scene:

> Prepare buckler and shield,
>   and advance for battle!
> Harness the horses;
>   mount, O horsemen!
> Take your stations with your helmets,
>   polish your spears,
>   put on your armor! (vv. 3, 4)

The battle would be joined, but it would be over shortly after it began. The confidence of the soldiers would quickly turn to dismay. They would beat a hasty retreat, turning their heels in "Total, scrambling, unavailing flight."[7]

> Why have I seen it?
> They are dismayed
>   and have turned backward.
> Their warriors are beaten down
>   and have fled in haste;
> they look not back—
>   terror on every side!
>   declares the LORD. (v. 5)

Like the army Pharaoh lost in the Red Sea, the Egyptians would be swallowed in the watery depths, this time in the river that flowed through Babylon.

> The swift cannot flee away,
>   nor the warrior escape;
> in the north by the river Euphrates
>   they have stumbled and fallen. (v. 6)

The Egyptians would try to regroup, of course. Their general would call for his cavalry and infantry to mount another offensive:

Advance, O horses,
and rage, O chariots!
Let the warriors go out. (v. 9a)

But the counterattack would fail, and the soldiers would lie dying on the field, calling for the medics.

Go up to Gilead, and take balm,
O virgin daughter of Egypt!
In vain you have used many medicines;
there is no healing for you.
The nations have heard of your shame,
and the earth is full of your cry;
for warrior has stumbled against warrior;
they have both fallen together. (vv. 11, 12)

The irony is that during these days the Egyptians were world leaders in medicine. On the day of judgment, however, they would find themselves without medicine and without remedy, their wounds incurable.

The preceding account formed Jeremiah's message "concerning the army of Pharaoh Neco, king of Egypt, which was by the river Euphrates at Carchemish and which Nebuchadnezzar king of Babylon defeated in the fourth year of Jehoiakim the son of Josiah, king of Judah" (v. 2). The prophet vividly foretold what the battle of Carchemish would be like for Egypt. That battle, which took place in 605 BC, marked a major turning point in world history. The Babylonian victory shifted the balance of power from the Nile to the Euphrates.

Just four years later (601 BC), the Babylonians marched on Egypt. As the Scripture says, this is "The word that the LORD spoke to Jeremiah the prophet about the coming of Nebuchadnezzar king of Babylon to strike the land of Egypt" (v. 13). According to the *Babylonian Chronicle*, there were heavy losses on both sides.[8]

Again speaking prophetically, Jeremiah described the battle in vivid terms. It would begin with a battle cry sounded along the route the Babylonians would follow:

Declare in Egypt, and proclaim in Migdol;
proclaim in Memphis and Tahpanhes;
say, "Stand ready and be prepared,
for the sword shall devour around you." (v. 14; cf. 44:1)

But things would go badly for the Egyptians, almost like a slapstick comedy.

> Why are your mighty ones face down?
>> They do not stand
>> because the LORD thrust them down.
> He made many stumble, and they fell. (vv. 15, 16a)

The Babylonians would tower over the Egyptians like a high mountain on a flat plain.

> As I live, declares the King,
>> whose name is the LORD of hosts,
> like Tabor among the mountains
>> and like Carmel by the sea, shall one come. (v. 18)

Like the Jews, many of the Egyptians would be carried into exile:

> Prepare yourselves baggage for exile,
>> O inhabitants of Egypt!
> For Memphis shall become a waste,
>> a ruin, without inhabitant. (v. 19)

In the end, even the battle-hardened mercenaries would pack their bags and go home:

> . . . and they said one to another,
> "Arise, and let us go back to our own people
>> and to the land of our birth,
>> because of the sword of the oppressor." (v. 16b)

> Even her hired soldiers in her midst
>> are like fattened calves;
> yes, they have turned and fled together;
>> they did not stand,
> for the day of their calamity has come upon them,
>> the time of their punishment. (v. 21)

These deserters would taunt their former employer with a political insult. "Call the name of Pharaoh, king of Egypt, 'Noisy one who lets the hour go by'" (v. 17). In other words, "Pharaoh is a bigmouth; he has squandered his chance!"

Finally, the prophet used animal imagery to describe the Egyptian debacle:

> She makes a sound like a serpent gliding away;
>   for her enemies march in force
> and come against her with axes
>   like those who fell trees.
> They shall cut down her forest,
>   declares the LORD,
>   though it is impenetrable,
> because they are more numerous than locusts;
>   they are without number.
> The daughter of Egypt shall be put to shame;
>   she shall be delivered into the hand of a people from the north.
>   (vv. 22–24)

The locust is a conventional Biblical image for judgment (see Joel 2:1–11; Revelation 9:3–11). "[It] is both a pesky insect and an invading, irresistible army, too numerous to count, irresistible, destructive, intimidating, making one utterly helpless."[9] Here the locust also serves as a reminder of the plagues on Egypt during the days of Moses (Exodus 10:1–20).

The picture of the snake is especially clever. The snake was an emblem of Egyptian supremacy. It was part of Pharaoh's royal insignia. There is a snake, for example, coiled on top of the death mask of King Tutankhamen. But Jeremiah prophesied that when the day of judgment came, the Egyptians would have to slither away.

Jeremiah not only taunted the Egyptians, but he also insulted their gods: "A beautiful heifer is Egypt, but a biting fly from the north has come upon her" (v. 20). Describing Egypt as "a beautiful heifer" was a way of poking fun at Apis, the bull-god of the Egyptians. As far as Jeremiah was concerned, Apis was nothing more than a fattened calf (v. 21), and everyone knows what happens to them (except perhaps the calves themselves)!

God's victory over the Egyptians was also a defeat of their so-called gods: "The LORD of hosts, the God of Israel, said: 'Behold, I am bringing punishment upon Amon of Thebes, and Pharaoh and Egypt and her gods and her kings, upon Pharaoh and those who trust in him. I will deliver them into the hand of those who seek their life, into the hand of Nebuchadnezzar king of Babylon and his officers'" (vv. 25, 26a). The one true God has no rivals. This shows the folly of trusting the gods and generals of Egypt, as the Jews were tempted to do. There is only one God and Judge of all nations.

The Judge of All Nations, Continued

Jeremiah's prophecy against the Philistines was shorter, but no less severe. Most likely it was first given in 609 BC, when, according to Herodotus,

Pharaoh Neco attacked the city-states of Philistia.[10] "The word of the LORD that came to Jeremiah the prophet concerning the Philistines, before Pharaoh struck down Gaza" (47:1).

Soon an enemy would come from the north, and the Philistines would be swept away by the Babylonian tide:

Thus says the LORD:
Behold, waters are rising out of the north,
    and shall become an overflowing torrent;
they shall overflow the land and all that fills it,
    the city and those who dwell in it. (v. 2a)

The invasion would bring fear and despair. Even the sound of the approaching enemy would make the Philistine warriors too demoralized to defend their families:

Men shall cry out,
    and every inhabitant of the land shall wail.
At the noise of the stamping of the hoofs of his stallions,
    at the rushing of his chariots, at the rumbling of their wheels,
the fathers look not back to their children,
    so feeble are their hands. (vv. 2b, 3)

When the day of judgment comes, defeat will be total:

. . . the day . . . is coming to destroy
    all the Philistines,
to cut off from Tyre and Sidon
    every helper that remains.
For the LORD is destroying the Philistines,
    the remnant of the coastland of Caphtor. (v. 4)

It will be a day of lamentation as well as a day of judgment. Jeremiah described the rituals the Philistines would go through to mourn their losses:

Baldness has come upon Gaza;
    Ashkelon has perished.
O remnant of their valley,
    how long will you gash yourselves? (v. 5)

The lines of Jeremiah's poetry have become the facts of history. After the Battle of Carchemish, Nebuchadrezzar briefly turned his attention to the Philistines in 604 BC. As the *Chronicles of the Chaldean Kings* recount, Nebuchadrezzar "marched to the city of Ashkelon and captured it. . . . He captured its king and plundered it. . . . He turned the city into a mound and heaps of ruins."[11]

> A Babylonian prism, now in Istanbul, mentions the presence—presumably with little choice in the matter—of the kings of Tyre and Sidon (cf. v. 4), of Gaza (5) and of Ashdod, at the court of Nebuchadrezzar; while a prison list now in Berlin records the rations for the king of Ashkelon (5), among other noted prisoners (including Jehoiachin of Judah).[12]

These are the facts. What they mean is that God is the Judge of all nations. The battles of the ancient Near East were not merely political or historical events—they were the work of God in the world. "The LORD of hosts, the God of Israel, said: 'Behold, I am bringing punishment upon . . . Egypt'" (46:25).

These were holy wars in which God himself waged war on his enemies. Jeremiah repeatedly mentioned God's active role in the military campaigns against Egypt and Philistia:

> That day is the day of the Lord GOD of hosts,
>   a day of vengeance,
>   to avenge himself on his foes.
> The sword shall devour and be sated
>   and drink its fill of their blood.
> For the Lord GOD of hosts holds a sacrifice
>   in the north country by the river Euphrates. (46:10; cf. vv. 15, 18)

Significantly, Jeremiah called God by his warrior name: "The Lord GOD of hosts." This title indicates that God is the captain of his angelic army.

The Philistines would have to fight against the same awesome opponent who defeated Egypt:

> For the LORD is destroying the Philistines,
>   the remnant of the coastland of Caphtor. (47:4b)

> Ah, sword of the LORD!
>   How long till you are quiet?
> Put yourself into your scabbard;
>   rest and be still!
> How can it be quiet
>   when the LORD has given it a charge?
> Against Ashkelon and against the seashore
>   he has appointed it. (vv. 6, 7)

These nations were to be punished for taking their stand against God. The Judge of all nations would personally bring them to justice.

The God of all nations renders the same justice in the present age. David's promises about the Messiah's rule are still being fulfilled:

> For kingship belongs to the LORD,
>   and he rules over the nations. (Psalm 22:28)

> The LORD is at your right hand;
>   he will shatter kings on the day of his wrath.
> He will execute judgment among the nations,
>   filling them with corpses;
> he will shatter chiefs
>   over the wide earth. (Psalm 110:5, 6)

It is not easy to discern the purposes of God in the events of history. Nevertheless, God is at work. He was at work in the rise of the United States of America. He was at work in the fall of the Communist empire in Eastern Europe. He is still at work in the Far East, Africa, South America, and every part of the globe.

The judgments of God will continue until the end of history, when Jesus Christ will come again to judge the world. "When the Son of Man comes in his glory, and all the angels with him, then he will sit on his glorious throne. Before him will be gathered all the nations, and he will separate people one from another as a shepherd separates the sheep from the goats" (Matthew 25:31, 32). Jesus Christ is the Judge of all nations. He will bring kingdoms to justice as well as individuals.

This is good news! The book of Jeremiah ends with long chapters of judgment against the nations. Some scholars say these chapters are depressing, or even offensive. Walter Brueggemann, for example, complains that Jeremiah's prophecy about the Philistines is "so severe and so raw, and indeed shameless, unbothered about the theological authorization of brutality."[13]

True, there are times when God's judgment is severe. But the real question is this: Is it just for God to vanquish his enemies or not? Is it just for God to judge the Egyptians for enslaving his people (Exodus 1—14) and for slaying his king (Josiah, in 2 Kings 23:29, 30) or not? Is it just for God to avenge the Philistines for trying to kill his anointed one (David, in 1 Samuel 17) or not? If these things are just, then Jeremiah's oracles are exhilarating! They bring praise and glory to God's justice.

However squeamish contemporary scholars may feel about it, it is right and good for God to defeat all his enemies. In our family devotions we once read about the terrible deaths of Ahab and Jezebel. We were reading a solid Calvinist story Bible at the time, so no detail was spared. We read how Ahab was struck by a random arrow and bled to death in his chariot, where the dogs later licked his blood (1 Kings 22:34–38). We read how Jezebel was thrown down from a parapet for the wild dogs to devour her flesh (2 Kings 9:30–37). When we finished the story a little cheer went up from our dinner table as my four-year-old son said, "Yay!"

Frankly, I was shocked. Ahab and Jezebel met such bloody ends, it hardly seemed right to celebrate. But the more I thought about it, the more I realized that God's victory *is* something to cheer about. Ahab and Jezebel were the sworn enemies of God. They slaughtered God's prophets and led his people into idolatry. Therefore, it was perfectly holy and absolutely just for God to destroy them.

The Savior of All Nations

Divine judgment is good news for God and his people. It is wonderful to know that in the end God will defeat all his enemies. Neither a king nor a kingdom will remain on earth in defiance of God.

Through it all, God's people will remain safe. Lest they forget, Jeremiah spoke these words of reassurance:

> But fear not, O Jacob my servant,
>   nor be dismayed, O Israel,
> for behold, I will save you from far away,
>   and your offspring from the land of their captivity.
> Jacob shall return and have quiet and ease,
>   and none shall make him afraid.
> Fear not, O Jacob my servant,
>   declares the LORD,
>   for I am with you.
> I will make a full end of all the nations
>   to which I have driven you,
>   but of you I will not make a full end.
> I will discipline you in just measure,
>   and I will by no means leave you unpunished.
>   (46:27, 28; cf. 30:10–11)

This prophecy repeats the most frequent command in the Bible: "Fear not." Jeremiah's prophecies against Egypt and Philistia were not meant to frighten, but to encourage. The very acts that destroyed God's enemies would save his friends, for destruction and salvation are two sides of one coin. God will save his people and be with them.

God's impending victory over the nations ought to make Christians missionary-minded. As John Piper explains, "The Old Testament missionary hope is expressed repeatedly as exhortations, promises, prayers and plans for God's glory to be declared among the peoples and his salvation to be known among the nations."[14]

The Lord Jesus Christ has given a Great Commission to "go . . . and make disciples of all nations, baptizing them in the name of the Father and of the Son and of the Holy Spirit" (Matthew 28:19). Christians go to all nations because God rules all nations. There is no place in the world where Christ does not rule. His Spirit goes wherever his people go. So Christians venture boldly into the darkest parts of the globe with the message of salvation in Jesus Christ.

The message of salvation is for all nations, even Egypt and Philistia. Jeremiah tucked this promise in at the end of his oracle of judgment against Egypt: "Afterward Egypt shall be inhabited as in the days of old, declares the LORD" (46:26b).

Judgment never has the last word. "Mercy triumphs over judgment" (James 2:13b). God's ultimate purpose is to bring all nations to salvation in Christ. The Ruler and Judge of all nations is also the Savior of all nations.

Promises about Egypt's salvation are scattered throughout the Old Testament (Isaiah 19:19–25; Ezekiel 29:13–16). One of the most significant comes in Psalm 87, which has been made familiar by the first line of John Newton's (1725–1807) hymn, "Glorious Things of Thee Are Spoken, Zion, City of Our God."

What are these glorious things? They involve the salvation of the very nations that received Jeremiah's oracles of judgment

> Among those who know me I mention Rahab and Babylon;
>> behold, Philistia and Tyre, with Cush—
>> "This one was born there," they say.
> And of Zion it shall be said,
>> "This one and that one were born in her";
>> for the Most High himself will establish her.
> The LORD records as he registers the peoples,
>> "This one was born there." (Psalm 87:4–6)

"Rahab" is a Biblical code word for Egypt. Thus God promised to bring both Egypt and Philistia into his everlasting city.

There is a place for Egypt and Philistia in the plan of God, not just for judgment but also for salvation. This is why Jeremiah took pains to speak to these nations in terms they could understand. God has inscribed the names of Egyptians and Philistines in his Book of Life!

The promise of salvation for these nations has already begun to be fulfilled. Many Egyptians, and I suppose also many Philistines, have repented of their sins and have come to faith in Jesus Christ. May God save many more of them in days to come.

The hope of salvation is not just for Egypt and Philistia, however, but for all the nations of the world. "The God who chose Israel out of the nations and gave it a distinctive history remained also and always the God of the nations too. . . . He is concerned with the life of the nations for He is their God."[15]

Sometimes people wonder what in the world God is doing. What the God of all nations is doing is ruling and judging the nations in order to save them. William Carey, the great evangelist to the Indian people, once declared that it is God's intention "To prevail finally over all the power of the Devil, and to destroy all his works, and set up His own kingdom and interest among men, and extend it as universally as Satan had extended his. It was for this purpose that the Messiah came and died."[16] This is "The preaching of Jesus Christ . . . kept secret for long ages but has now been disclosed and . . . been made known to all nations . . . to bring about the obedience of faith" (Romans 16:25, 26).

61

The Pride of Life

JEREMIAH 48:1–47

WHEN JEREMIAH WAS JUST A LAD growing up in Anathoth, the land of Moab formed the eastern border of his world. As he looked out across the Dead Sea he could see a high plateau along the horizon. The Moabites lived there, the long-lost cousins of the Jews who traced their heritage back to Abraham's nephew Lot (Genesis 19:36, 37).

The Fall of Moab

Chapter 48 is the record of Jeremiah's prophecy to Moab. "Concerning Moab. Thus says the LORD of hosts, the God of Israel" (48:1a). By now we know what to expect from such a prophecy. The nation will be "specifically named, attentively described, seriously addressed."[1] The news will not be good. Jeremiah's prophecy about Moab—like his prophecies about Egypt and Philistia—will be a prophecy of judgment.

And so it was. Town by town, Moab was to be destroyed:

> Woe to Nebo, for it is laid waste!
>   Kiriathaim is put to shame, it is taken;
> the fortress is put to shame and broken down;
>   the renown of Moab is no more.
> In Heshbon they planned disaster against her:
>   "Come, let us cut her off from being a nation!"
> You also, O Madmen, shall be brought to silence;
>   the sword shall pursue you.
> A voice! A cry from Horonaim,
>   "Desolation and great destruction!" (vv. 1b–3)

From the outcry at Heshbon even to Elealeh, as far as Jahaz they utter their voice, from Zoar to Horonaim and Eglath-shelishiyah. For the waters of Nimrim also have become desolate. (v. 34)

Jeremiah lifted his eyes up to the eastern skyline and announced:

Judgment has come upon the tableland, upon Holon, and Jahzah, and Mephaath, and Dibon, and Nebo, and Beth-diblathaim, and Kiriathaim, and Beth-gamul, and Beth-meon, and Kerioth, and Bozrah, and all the cities of the land of Moab, far and near. The horn of Moab is cut off, and his arm is broken, declares the LORD. (vv. 21–25)

Once again, these oracles of judgment display Jeremiah's extensive knowledge of the geography of the Middle East. Twenty-five Moabite locations get mentioned in all.[2] The municipalities of Moab were well known to Jeremiah, and to God. To summarize:

The destroyer shall come upon every city,
    and no city shall escape;
the valley shall perish,
    and the plain shall be destroyed,
    as the LORD has spoken.
Give wings to Moab,
    for she would fly away;
her cities shall become a desolation,
    with no inhabitant in them. (vv. 8, 9)

Verse 9a in the NIV reads, "Put salt on Moab." Sowing salt was a symbol of curse in the ancient world. It showed that a town or city had been left completely desolate by a conquering army.

Jeremiah urged Moab's executioners to do their work with all possible haste: "Cursed is he who does the work of the LORD with slackness, and cursed is he who keeps back his sword from bloodshed" (v. 10). Since the Moabites were cursed, there would be no escape from divine judgment.

He who flees from the terror
    shall fall into the pit,
and he who climbs out of the pit
    shall be caught in the snare.
For I will bring these things upon Moab,
    the year of their punishment,
    declares the LORD.
In the shadow of Heshbon
    fugitives stop without strength,

for fire came out from Heshbon,
    flame from the house of Sihon;
it has destroyed the forehead of Moab,
    the crown of the sons of tumult. (v. 44, 45; cf. Isaiah 24:17, 18)

The Moabites would receive the same punishment the Israelites received:

Woe to you, O Moab!
    The people of Chemosh are undone,
for your sons have been taken captive,
    and your daughters into captivity. (v. 46)

The Moabites learned the same lesson the Egyptians and the Philistines learned. God is the Ruler and Judge of all nations. His kingship observes no political boundaries.

How do you say, "We are heroes
    and mighty men of war"?
The destroyer of Moab and his cities has come up,
    and the choicest of his young men have gone down to slaughter,
    declares the King, whose name is the LORD of hosts. (vv. 14, 15)

God is king of Moab as well as king of Israel. He is the King of all kings. There is no ethnocentrism to his sovereignty.

Remarkably, Jeremiah's prophecy was made while Moab still had a strong economy. Nevertheless, the prophet foresaw the sudden and total defeat of the Moabites. "Flee! Save yourselves! You will be like a juniper in the desert!" (v. 6). "The calamity of Moab is near at hand, and his affliction hastens swiftly" (v. 16). "For thus says the LORD: 'Behold, one shall fly swiftly like an eagle and spread his wings against Moab'" (v. 40; cf. Ezekiel 17:3, 4).

The eagle swooped as promised. Josephus reported how Nebuchadrezzar came from Babylon in 582 BC to destroy the Moabites.[3] Moab was scattered as promised, too. Jeremiah ordered:

Leave the cities, and dwell in the rock,
    O inhabitants of Moab!
Be like the dove that nests
    in the sides of the mouth of a gorge. (v. 28)

The findings of modern archaeology have confirmed Jeremiah's prophecies:

It was in its state of highest prosperity that the prophets foretold that the cities of Moab should become desolate, without any to dwell in them; and accordingly we find, that although the sites, ruins and names of many ancient cities of Moab can be traced, not one of them exists at the present day as tenanted by man. . . . Cyril Graham, who explored this region, found cities with buildings in a good state of preservation, yet everywhere uninhabited. "In the whole of these vast plains, north and south, east and west, desolation reigns supreme." The long-predicted doom of Moab is now fulfilled, and the forty-eighth chapter of Jeremiah is verified on the spot by the traveler.[4]

The tragedy of the Moabites shows that God's Word is true. Jeremiah was not simply a shrewd observer of the international scene. He was more than a good guesser. He was the mouthpiece of God. When everything he prophesied came true, it was a remarkable confirmation of God's Word.

It is sobering to realize that all these judgments have come to pass. The punishment of the Moabites is a warning to anyone who doubts the reality of God's wrath. The Bible says that "it is appointed for man to die once, and after that comes judgment" (Hebrews 9:27). The truth of that statement cannot be confirmed personally until after death. But since God says it, believe it! If the rest of the prophecies of divine judgment have been fulfilled, why would the threat of eternal judgment be any different?

God hates sin and must punish it. That is why sinners must take their sins to the cross where Christ was crucified. The wages of sin must be exacted in full. Sinners must either pay for their own sins, as the Moabites did, or have their sins paid for them on the cross. Becoming a Christian means giving your sins to Jesus Christ, trusting that they were paid for when he died on the cross. Otherwise, you will have to pay for them yourself at the final judgment.

The Sins of Moab

It was, of course, the sins of the Moabites that led to their destruction. The towns of Moab brought their judgment on themselves. Jeremiah mentioned at least five of their specific sins.

The first was rebellion. The Moabites were destroyed because they lived their whole lives in defiance of God:

Moab shall be destroyed and be no longer a people,
    because he magnified himself against the LORD.
Terror, pit, and snare
    are before you, O inhabitant of Moab!
    declares the LORD. (48:42, 43)

The Moabites had a long history of shaking their fists at God. Originally they were conceived through incest. One of the daughters of Lot had sexual relations with her father and gave birth to Moab, which means "from father" (Genesis 19:36, 37). Ever afterwards, the Moabites were sworn enemies of God's people. Balak king of Moab tried to persuade Balaam to pronounce a curse against Israel (Numbers 22—24). In the days of the judges, Moab was defeated by Ehud, the left-handed judge (Judges 3:12–30). In the days of the kings, David subdued the Moabites and made them pay tribute (2 Samuel 8:1, 2). Many years later the Moabites rebelled against Israel again, but God delivered them into the hands of Jehoshaphat (2 Kings 3; 2 Chronicles 20).

In Jeremiah's day, the Moabites defied God not by attacking God's people, but by making fun of them:

> Was not Israel a derision to you? Was he found among thieves, that whenever you spoke of him you wagged your head? (v. 27)

God allowed Moab to taunt his people for a time, but they would not be mocked forever.

In the end the Moabites themselves would be held in derision.

> Make him drunk, because he magnified himself against the LORD, so that Moab shall wallow in his vomit, and he too shall be held in derision. (v. 26)

> How it is broken! How they wail! How Moab has turned his back in shame! So Moab has become a derision and a horror to all that are around him. (v. 39)

This humiliating and degrading picture of drunkenness is an echo of 25:15–29, where God promised to pass the cup of his wrath around to the nations like a beer bottle at a frat party.

The drunken stupor of Moab is a warning to anyone who mocks God. God suffers himself to be ridiculed by his creatures. He allows comedians to make fun of him at the movies or on late-night television. He permits students to smirk at Christians for their moral scruples. He lets atheists take the Christian symbol of the fish, give it legs, and turn it into a symbol for Charles Darwin. God even suffered his own Son to be mocked on his way to the cross. But God will not be mocked forever. There was nothing humorous about Moab wallowing in her own vomit. Nor will there be anything funny about meeting God at his throne for judgment.

A second sin of the Moabites was idolatry, the worship of false gods:

> And I will bring to an end in Moab, declares the LORD, him who offers sacrifice in the high place and makes offerings to his god. (v. 35)

The Moabites had a long history of such idolatry. They were known to worship Chemosh, the god of the stars, and Chemosh worship was a bloody business. When Mesha king of Moab saw that he was about to be defeated by Jehoshaphat king of Judah, he sacrificed his firstborn son to Chemosh on the walls of Kir Hareseth (2 Kings 3:26, 27).

Despite his thirst for blood, Chemosh had often been a temptation to Israel. In the days of Balaam, Moabite women seduced the Israelites to worship their gods (Numbers 25). King Solomon later married Moabite women and set up an altar to Chemosh (1 Kings 11:1–13). Indeed, the Bible says that one reason Israel finally was divided into two kingdoms was because God's people worshiped "Chemosh the god of Moab," among other pagan deities (1 Kings 11:33).

God punished the Moabites to show his power over Chemosh. He sent Chemosh "into exile with his priests and his officials" (48:7b). The Moabite god thus became a trophy of war. The people of Moab became "ashamed of Chemosh, as the house of Israel was ashamed of Bethel, their confidence" (v. 13). This shows what happens to those who trust in Chemosh, or in any other god besides the true God. Such gods can save neither themselves nor others. Therefore, Judah's attempt to forge a confederacy with the Moabites was doomed to fail (594 BC; cf. 27:3).

Third, the Moabites were self-righteous. This is the basic instinct of fallen humanity. By nature, sinners have an unshakable confidence in their own goodness. The Moabites were no exception, and that was their downfall: "For, because you trusted in your works . . . you also shall be taken" (v. 7a).

No sinner has ever been saved by his or her own works. This is what sent Martin Luther into such great despair. As a young man, Luther had every reason to trust in his deeds:

> I was a good monk and kept my order so strictly that I could claim that if ever a monk were able to reach heaven by monkish discipline I should have found my way there. All my fellows in the house, who knew me, would bear me out in this. For if it had continued much longer I would, what with vigils, prayers, readings and other such works, have done myself to death.[5]

Luther knew he had to be perfectly righteous to stand before God. But he knew he was completely unrighteous. He spent as many as six hours at a time confessing his sins. But still there was no rest for his sinful soul.

Luther was in dark despair until he discovered that the gospel reveals a righteousness *from* God, a righteousness that is by faith alone from first to last (Romans 1:17a). The sinner does not give righteousness to God; God gives righteousness to the sinner. The best righteousness the sinner can bring to God is self-righteousness, which is no righteousness at all. "But now a righteousness from God . . . has been made known. . . . This righteousness from God comes through faith in Jesus Christ to all who believe" (Romans 3:21, 22 NIV). God's judgment against Moab shows the futility of trusting in one's own deeds, and therefore the necessity of receiving the righteousness of Jesus Christ by faith.

A fourth sin of the Moabites was greed: "You trusted in your works and your treasures" (48:7a). When Jeremiah gave this prophecy, the Moabites were riding an economic boom. They did not count their wealth in stocks and bonds in those days; they counted it in wine. Moab was the Napa Valley of the ancient Near East. Jeremiah thus referred to "The fruitful land of Moab" and "The wine . . . from the winepresses" (v. 33a).

Moab was also the sheepfold of the ancient Near East. To give an idea how many sheep the Moabites had, in the days of King Mesha they supplied Israel with one hundred thousand lambs and one hundred thousand fleeces in annual tribute (2 Kings 3:4).

The sins of the Moabites are starting to sound familiar—rebellion, idolatry, self-righteousness, greed. These are the same sins that characterize Western civilization in the early part of the twenty-first century.

There was one more sin of which the Moabites were guilty. It is the biggest sin of all, and also the sin Christians commit most easily. The main sin of Moab was pride.

> We have heard of the pride of Moab—
>   he is very proud—
> of his loftiness, his pride, and his arrogance,
>   and the haughtiness of his heart.
> I know his insolence, declares the LORD;
>   his boasts are false,
>   his deeds are false. (vv. 29, 30)

The *New English Bible* offers a more poetic translation:

> We have heard of Moab's pride, and proud indeed he is,
> Proud, presumptuous, overbearing, insolent.
> I know his arrogance, says the Lord;
> His boasting is false, false are his deeds. (v. 29 NEB)

This must have been a popular saying in those days, since Isaiah also quoted it (Isaiah 16:6). Presumably the Moabites were as proud in Jeremiah's day as they had been in Isaiah's. Jeremiah also referred to them as "sons of tumult" (48:45) or "noisy boasters" (NIV). However, even though the Moabites were full of idle boasts, their fleeting fame would soon come to an end. God was going to humble them.

> Come down from your glory,
>   and sit on the parched ground,
>   O inhabitant of Dibon!
> For the destroyer of Moab has come up against you;
>   he has destroyed your strongholds. (v. 18)

Perhaps the best word to describe the pride of the Moabites is "complacency," which the *Oxford English Dictionary* defines as "smug self-satisfaction." Jeremiah depicted Moab's complacency like this:

> Moab has been at ease from his youth
>   and has settled on his dregs;
> he has not been emptied from vessel to vessel,
>   nor has he gone into exile;
> so his taste remains in him,
>   and his scent is not changed. (v. 11)

Jeremiah imagined a jar of wine left long past the point of being mellow. Amazingly, the text of this verse has been preserved on an ancient wine seal found in the Middle East.[6] One expert explains that "newly fermented wine should be racked within one or two weeks after the completion of fermentation because off-odors may form as a result of the autolyzation of the yeasts in the lees."[7] Vintage wine is best, but not when it is "soured by standing on accumulated sediment."[8]

In the same way, the Moabites were sitting back and living the easy life. Given their thriving wine culture, the image was especially appropriate. They were affluent and indolent. Somebody needed to do something to shake them up. Otherwise, Moab would become clay in the hands of an angry potter.

> Therefore, behold, the days are coming, declares the LORD, when I shall send to him pourers who will pour him, and empty his vessels and break his jars in pieces. (v. 12)

If only the vintner had poured the Moabites from one bottle into another before it was too late!

Many Christians need to be decanted in the same way! Few institutions are more complacent, more smugly self-satisfied, than the traditional church. Complacent Christians are believers who have not entertained one new thought or made one new step of faith in months, if not years. They are at the same point in their Christian life now that they were at last year, and the year before that. Their behavior is no more godly. Their prayers are no more intimate. Their evangelism is no more persuasive. According to Jeremiah's image, they still taste the way they used to taste and smell the way they used to smell. Someone or something needs to stir them up before the wine of the Spirit grows sour in the dregs of a stagnant spirituality.

This theme is emphasized in an old missionary biography called *Hudson Taylor in the Early Years*. One of the book's chapters takes its title from Jeremiah 48:11: "Emptied from Vessel to Vessel."[9] It describes how unsettled Taylor was in the first few months of his second year in China. He moved from place to place. Nevertheless, because he was too unsettled to grow complacent, he was fruitful in his Christian work.

Like Hudson Taylor and like the Moabites, many Christians need to be stirred up. Unless something fresh is happening in your spiritual life, soon you will smell and taste like a sour Christian.

A Lament for Moab

Once divine judgment came to wine country, it would be too late for Moab to be stirred up and therefore refreshed.

> Gladness and joy have been taken away
> > from the fruitful land of Moab;
> I have made the wine cease from the winepresses;
> > no one treads them with shouts of joy;
> > the shouting is not the shout of joy. (v. 33; cf. Isaiah 16:10)

Like all the judgment passages of Jeremiah, chapter 48 is a warning about the wages of sin. But it is also an invitation to weep for the lost. Jeremiah's oracle against Moab was not angry but mournful. It was not a diatribe but a lament.

Jeremiah described the way the Moabites themselves would mourn over their destruction:

> A voice! A cry from Horonaim,
> > "Desolation and great destruction!"
> Moab is destroyed;
> > her little ones have made a cry.

For at the ascent of Luhith
   they go up weeping;
for at the descent of Horonaim
   they have heard the distressed cry of destruction." (vv. 3–5)

. . . the cities shall be taken
   and the strongholds seized.
The heart of the warriors of Moab shall be in that day
   like the heart of a woman in her birth pains. (v. 41)

When judgment came, Moab would be helpless. Once she had been vanquished, her inhabitants would begin the rituals of public mourning:

> For every head is shaved and every beard cut off. On all the hands are gashes, and around the waist is sackcloth. On all the housetops of Moab and in the squares there is nothing but lamentation, for I have broken Moab like a vessel for which no one cares. (vv. 37, 38; cf. Isaiah 15:2, 3)

The sound of children sobbing would reach from the mountains down to the plains, where Moab's neighbors would overhear it and join the lament:

Grieve for him, all you who are around him,
   and all who know his name;
say, "How the mighty scepter is broken,
   the glorious staff." (v. 17)

Stand by the way and watch,
   O inhabitant of Aroer!
Ask him who flees and her who escapes;
   say, "What has happened?"
Moab is put to shame, for it is broken;
   wail and cry!
Tell it beside the Arnon,
   that Moab is laid waste. (vv. 19, 20)

God's unsparing judgment would be Moab's unrelenting grief.

As he imagined this scene, the prophet himself was moved by Moab's plight. The Weeping Prophet, who had already wept for his own sins and the sins of his people, began to weep for the sins of his long-lost cousins:

Therefore I wail for Moab;
   I cry out for all Moab;
   for the men of Kir-hareseth I mourn.
More than for Jazer I weep for you,
   O vine of Sibmah!

Your branches passed over the sea,
   reached to the Sea of Jazer;
on your summer fruits and your grapes
   the destroyer has fallen. (vv. 31, 32; cf. Isaiah 16:7–9)

Jeremiah had deep sympathy—even empathy—for the sufferings of Moab.

It was remarkable enough for a Jew to weep for Moab. What is more remarkable still is that God himself joined the lament! These were God's words as well as Jeremiah's:

Therefore my heart moans for Moab like a flute, and my heart moans like a flute for the men of Kir-hareseth. Therefore the riches they gained have perished . . . for I have broken Moab like a vessel for which no one cares. (vv. 36, 38b; cf. Isaiah 16:11)

God is the one who broke Moab, yet he also played the piper at her funeral. What can it mean that Almighty God sheds tears over the destruction of his enemies? This is a mystery known only to God. But it is a reminder of the tears our Savior shed for the lost in his own city: "O Jerusalem, Jerusalem, the city that kills the prophets and stones those who are sent to it! How often would I have gathered your children together as a hen gathers her brood under her wings, and you were not willing! See, your house is left to you desolate" (Matthew 23:37, 38).

Christians who have the heart of Christ share his pity for the lost. They are deeply affected by the realities of impending judgment. They are mournfully aware of the desperate spiritual condition of unbelievers. They are firmly convinced of the necessity of turning to Jesus Christ for salvation. For Christians who pattern their lives after the life of Christ, evangelism is an act of the heart as well as the will.

One Monday morning I came into the sanctuary of Tenth Presbyterian Church to pray. (I write this even though it is likely to give you the wrong impression about my spirituality. The truth is that my heart is colder than most, as my wife can testify.) The previous day I had watched a man bring a young boy to church. He seemed ill at ease and went out the side door as soon as he had taken his son to Sunday school. It seemed like he was a good man who wanted to raise his son the right way. But it also seemed like he did not know Jesus Christ in a personal way.

I was so moved by the lostness of his condition that I agonized in prayer for his family that Monday morning. I prayed that the boy's Sunday school teachers would welcome him with the love of God. I prayed with many tears that someone would tell him the gospel. I begged God that he would send his Holy Spirit with power so that the boy and his family would come to saving faith in Jesus Christ.

The Bible does not teach that the power of prayer depends on our tears. In truth, the efficacy of prayer rarely depends on the emotional state of the one who prays. God glorifies himself by answering many halfhearted and lackluster prayers, I have found. So weeping may not be a good way to guarantee an answer to prayer. But because tears come from the heart, they do say something about the affections of the one who prays. Anyone who has God's heart for the lost will grieve over their spiritual condition.

This was true in the ministry of David Brainerd (1718–1747). Brainerd was one of the first missionaries to Native Americans. God blessed his preaching with many conversions before his death at the tender age of twenty-nine. This is what Brainerd wrote in his diary on April 19, 1742, when he was just twenty-three years old:

> God enabled me so to agonize in prayer that I was quite wet with sweat, though in the shade and the wind was cool. My soul was drawn out very much for the world. I gasped for the multitude of souls. I think I had more enlargement for sinners than for the children of God. I felt as if I could spend my life in cries for them both.[10]

A church will not see the lost coming to Christ by dozens and hundreds until Christians learn so to "agonize in prayer . . . for the multitude of souls."

The Restoration of Moab

God must have heard Jeremiah's lament, for the last words of his prophecy offered some hope for the lost tribe of Moab: "'Yet I will restore the fortunes of Moab in the latter days, declares the Lord.' Thus far is the judgment on Moab" (48:47). Earlier God had promised that the fortunes of Judah would be restored (33:11), but he also held out the same promise to Moab.

It is hard to know how God has fulfilled or will fulfill this promise. There is not a single word in the whole Bible concerning the salvation of a Moabite. There is, of course, a story about the salvation of a Moabitess. Although Ruth was from Moab, she clung to the God of Israel. When her mother-in-law Naomi was ready to return to Israel, Ruth said, "Where you go I will go, and where you lodge I will lodge. Your people shall be my people, and your God my God. Where you die I will die, and there will I be buried. May the Lord do so to me and more also if anything but death parts me from you" (Ruth 1:16, 17). Ruth was saved by her faith. God gave her a rich harvest of barley, redeemed her from poverty, and provided her with a husband. He even made her the grandmother of King David. Therefore, Jesus Christ, the son of David, had a Moabitess in his family tree.

But what of the Moabites today? A few survived the onslaught of Babylon, but by the Byzantine period they had been lost in the sands of the Middle East.[11] If their bloodline survives today, it runs through the veins of the Arabs of Jordan and other kingdoms of the Middle East.

If Jeremiah's promise can still be claimed, therefore, it can only be claimed on behalf of the Muslims of the Middle East. In the past, Arab Muslims have been overlooked by the church. In his book on Muslim evangelism, Bruce McDowell argues:

> The church is growing so slowly among Muslims not so much because Muslims are "hard" to convert, but because they have been largely ignored by the church. There are comparatively few people ministering to Muslims. Only about 2 percent of the Protestant missionary force is ministering to the over one billion Muslims, who make up almost 20 percent of the world's population.[12]

Nevertheless, the Muslims of the Middle East have not been overlooked by God. He pities their lost condition. He longs to see them come to faith in his Son. Every Christian should share God's love and pity for lost Muslims, praying and working for their salvation.

62

Most High over All the Earth

JEREMIAH 49:1–39

THE OLD TESTAMENT PEOPLE OF GOD lived in a bad neighborhood. The last chapters of Jeremiah serve as a reminder that the Jews were surrounded by fierce enemies. They constantly had trouble with gang violence and guerrilla warfare.

Five of Israel's enemies are mentioned in Jeremiah 49: to the west, the Ammonites (vv. 1–6); to the south, the Edomites (vv. 7–22); to the north, the Arameans (Damascus) (vv. 23–27); to the far west, the Elamites (vv. 34–39); and scattered here and there, the tribesmen of Kedar (vv. 28–33). These are the peoples who have tormented the Jews throughout history, down to this very day—the Jordanians, the Syrians, the Iranians, and the Palestinian Arabs.

These nations were not simply enemies of God's people—they were enemies of God himself. That is why Asaph once prayed that God would utterly destroy them:

> For they conspire with one accord;
>   against you they make a covenant—
> the tents of Edom and the Ishmaelites,
>   Moab and the Hagrites,
> Gebal and Ammon and Amalek. . . .
> Let them be put to shame and dismayed forever;
>   let them perish in disgrace,
> that they may know that you alone,
>   whose name is the LORD,
>   are the Most High over all the earth. (Psalm 83:5–7a, 17, 18)

Destined for Destruction

Eventually Asaph's prayers were answered. Jeremiah 49 shows what happened to God's enemies. The substance of Jeremiah's message was repeated hundreds of years later by the Apostle Paul: "For many . . . walk as enemies of the cross of Christ. Their end is destruction" (Philippians 3:18, 19a).

First, God promised to destroy the Ammonites. The Ammonites are now the Jordanians, whose capital city is called Amman. They were born in incest, for Ben-Ammi was the son of Lot's younger daughter after she slept with her father (Genesis 19:36–38).

Like the Moabites, therefore, the Ammonites were the long-lost cousins of the Jews. And like the Moabites, they had a family feud with the Jews. The feud was renewed in Jeremiah's day when Baalis, king of the Ammonites, plotted the assassination of Gedaliah, the governor of Jerusalem (40:14). But the feud had gone on for centuries. The Ammonites fought against both Saul and David; both times they were defeated (1 Samuel 11:1–11; 2 Samuel 10).

In the eighth century BC, Ammon occupied part of the land God had given to Israel. While Israel was busy fending off the Assyrian king Tiglath-pileser (734 BC), the greedy Ammonites moved in to annex the territory of Gad for themselves (Judges 11:4–33). Jeremiah said:

> Concerning the Ammonites.
>> Thus says the LORD:
>
>> "Has Israel no sons?
>>> Has he no heir?
>> Why then has Milcom [or Molech] dispossessed Gad,
>>> and his people settled in its cities?" (49:1)

The mention of Molech is a reminder that the Ammonites worshiped Molech, perhaps the most vile pagan deity of the ancient Near East. Molech worship required child sacrifice. It was a sign of Israel's utter depravity that Jeremiah had to preach against the Molech worshipers in Jerusalem (32:35: "They built the high places of Baal in the Valley of the Son of Hinnom, to offer up their sons and daughters to Molech, though I did not command them, nor did it enter into my mind, that they should do this abomination, to cause Judah to sin").

The Ammonites tried to destroy Israel militarily and spiritually, but soon they would be destroyed themselves. Even their gods would be taken into exile.

Therefore, behold, the days are coming,
   declares the LORD,
when I will cause the battle cry to be heard
   against Rabbah of the Ammonites;
it shall become a desolate mound,
   and its villages shall be burned with fire;
then Israel shall dispossess those who dispossessed him,
   says the LORD.

"Wail, O Heshbon, for Ai is laid waste!
   Cry out, O daughters of Rabbah!
Put on sackcloth,
   lament, and run to and fro among the hedges!
For Milcom [or Molech] shall go into exile,
   with his priests and his officials. . . .
Behold, I will bring terror upon you,
   declares the Lord GOD of hosts,
   from all who are around you,
and you shall be driven out, every man straight before him,
   with none to gather the fugitives." (49:2, 3, 5)

This prophecy was fulfilled. Some time after the Ammonites joined an international coalition to fight against Babylon (27:3), Nebuchadnezzar led his armies to conquer Ammon (582 BC).

Second, God promised to destroy the Edomites. The Edomites were also cousins of the Jews, for they traced their ancestry back to Esau, the brother of Jacob (Genesis 36:1). The sibling rivalry between those twins persisted through the centuries (Amos 1:11). The Edomites refused to let Moses and the children of Israel pass through their territory (Numbers 20:14–21). They tried to conquer Israel in the days of the judges (Judges 11). "And David made a name for himself when he returned from striking down 18,000 Edomites in the Valley of Salt" (2 Samuel 8:13). The Edomites, in turn, tried to get their revenge during the days of King Solomon (1 Kings 11:14–22). When Jerusalem fell to Babylon, all Edom rejoiced (Psalm 137:7).

Jeremiah prophesied that after centuries of mutual hostility, the destiny of Edom would be destruction:

Flee, turn back, dwell in the depths,
   O inhabitants of Dedan!
For I will bring the calamity of Esau upon him,
   the time when I punish him. (49:8)

For thus says the LORD: "If those who did not deserve to drink the cup must drink it, will you go unpunished? You shall not go unpunished, but you must drink. For I have sworn by myself, declares the LORD, that Bozrah shall become a horror, a taunt, a waste, and a curse, and all her cities shall be perpetual wastes." (vv. 12, 13; cf. 25:15–29)

I have heard a message from the LORD,
    and an envoy has been sent among the nations:
"Gather yourselves together and come against her,
    and rise up for battle!" (v. 14; cf. Obadiah 1)

Edom shall become a horror. Everyone who passes by it will be horrified and will hiss because of all its disasters. As when Sodom and Gomorrah and their neighboring cities were overthrown, says the LORD, no man shall dwell there, no man shall sojourn in her. (vv. 17, 18; cf. Isaiah 34:5–15)

It is not certain when Edom was destroyed. Most likely the Babylonians did it, since the Edomites were part of an anti-Babylonian federation (27:3) and since Babylon was often compared to an eagle (48:40). This fact fits in well with the end of Jeremiah's prophecy:

Behold, one shall mount up and fly swiftly like an eagle and spread his wings against Bozrah, and the heart of the warriors of Edom shall be in that day like the heart of a woman in her birth pains. (49:22)

Destined for Destruction, Continued

Third, God promised to destroy Damascus, the capital city of the Syrians. The Arameans, as they were known in those days, were fierce enemies of the Jews. Gangs of Arameans often ventured into Israel, especially during the days of Elijah and Elisha (1 Kings 20, 22; 2 Kings 5).

Like the Ammonites and the Edomites, the Arameans were destined for destruction:

Concerning Damascus:

"Hamath and Arpad are confounded,
    for they have heard bad news;
they melt in fear,
    they are troubled like the sea that cannot be quiet.
Damascus has become feeble, she turned to flee,
    and panic seized her;
anguish and sorrows have taken hold of her,
    as of a woman in labor.
How is the famous city not forsaken,
    the city of my joy?
Therefore her young men shall fall in her squares,
    and all her soldiers shall be destroyed in that day,

declares the LORD of hosts.
And I will kindle a fire in the wall of Damascus,
   and it shall devour the strongholds of Ben-hadad." (49:23–27)

This prophecy is hard to date, although it is known that Damascus became a vassal of Babylon in 605 BC.

Fourth, Jeremiah uttered a prophecy "concerning Kedar and the kingdoms of Hazor that Nebuchadnezzar king of Babylon struck down" (v. 28a). This prophecy referred to the Bedouin of the Middle East, wandering shepherds who lived in desert tents (Isaiah 60:7).

Since they were nomads, the Bedouin often escaped military conflict. But not this time. Their destiny was destruction:

Thus says the LORD:
"Rise up, advance against Kedar!
   Destroy the people of the east!
Their tents and their flocks shall be taken,
   their curtains and all their goods;
their camels shall be led away from them." (49:28b, 29a)

"Their camels shall become plunder,
   their herds of livestock a spoil.
I will scatter to every wind
   those who cut the corners of their hair,
and I will bring their calamity
   from every side of them,
   declares the LORD.
Hazor shall become a haunt of jackals,
   an everlasting waste;
no man shall dwell there;
   no man shall sojourn in her." (vv. 32, 33)

Even in the desert, their enemies would find them and surround them.

   . . . and men shall cry to them: 'Terror on every side!'
Flee, wander far away, dwell in the depths,
O inhabitants of Hazor!
   declares the LORD.
For Nebuchadnezzar king of Babylon
   has made a plan against you
   and formed a purpose against you. (vv. 29b, 30)

According to the *Babylonian Chronicle*, Kedar and Hazor were attacked and defeated in the year 599 BC in retaliation for trying to cut off Babylonian supply lines.[1]

Fifth and finally, this is "The word of the Lord that came to Jeremiah the prophet concerning Elam, in the beginning of the reign of Zedekiah king of Judah" (v. 34). The Elamites were the Persians who lived far to the east, in what is now southern Iran.

Like the other nations, the Elamites were destined for destruction:

> And I will bring upon Elam the four winds from the four quarters of heaven. And I will scatter them to all those winds, and there shall be no nation to which those driven out of Elam shall not come. I will terrify Elam before their enemies and before those who seek their life. I will bring disaster upon them, my fierce anger, declares the Lord. I will send the sword after them, until I have consumed them, and I will set my throne in Elam and destroy their king and officials, declares the Lord. (vv. 36–38)

The Elamites lived far from Israel, but they did not live outside the sovereignty of God. Perhaps their judgment came in 596 BC, the year in which the *Babylonian Chronicle* mentions a clash between Babylon and Elam.[2]

A pattern is beginning to emerge. God promised to defeat every last one of his enemies. Jeremiah collected years of prophecies at the end of his book to show, in the words of Asaph, that God is "The Most High over all the earth."

This is a comfort whenever world events are troubled. God's justice will prevail. One day nations that invade their neighbors, rule by terror, pervert justice, traffic in drugs, hire assassins, promote abortion, destroy what God has created, or stockpile chemical and biological weapons will be brought to account for their sins. (This includes, of course, our own nation.) The destiny of God's enemies is always destruction.

Who Is the Chosen One?

It is perfectly just for God to destroy his enemies. When God punishes sin, he is not revealing a flaw in his moral character. Quite the opposite. A king who allows himself to be mocked loses all respect. A ruler who refuses to stand up to his rivals loses his kingdom.

This is what destroyed King Arthur in the stories about the Knights of the Round Table. Sir Lancelot defied King Arthur by sleeping with Queen Guinevere. Camelot was destroyed because the king failed to respond to this challenge to his authority.

A true king defends himself. He has the courage and the strength to defeat his enemies. He does not allow evil men to take his land, enslave his people, or insult his royal dignity.

The God of Heaven and earth is a true king, able and willing to subjugate his enemies. All through Jeremiah's oracles of international judgment we have heard the voice of God: "I will cause the battle cry to be heard" (49:2). "I have stripped Esau bare" (v. 10). "I will kindle a fire in the wall of Damascus" (v. 27). "I will scatter to the winds those who are in distant places" (v. 32 NIV). "I will set my throne in Elam" (v. 38). By defeating his enemies, God defends his own royal authority.

There is a striking picture of God's kingship in the prophecy against Edom. Jeremiah explained God's royal sovereignty in terms the Edomites could understand. The forests of Edom were inhabited by wild animals in those days, so he drew a comparison with the king of the beasts:

> Behold, like a lion coming up from the jungle of the Jordan against a perennial pasture, I will suddenly make him [Edom] run away from her. And I will appoint over her whomever I choose. For who is like me? Who will summon me? What shepherd can stand before me? Therefore hear the plan that the LORD has made against Edom and the purposes that he has formed against the inhabitants of Teman: Even the little ones of the flock shall be dragged away. Surely their fold shall be appalled at their fate. At the sound of their fall the earth shall tremble; the sound of their cry shall be heard at the Red Sea. (vv. 19–21; cf. 50:44, 45)

God's statement demands an answer: "I will appoint over her whomever I choose" (v. 19). Who is the chosen one? Who is the lion? Who is the king? Who will defeat God's enemies?

In one of the most stunning prophecies from the Old Testament, the prophet Isaiah asked the same question:

> Who is this who comes from Edom,
>   in crimsoned garments from Bozrah,
> he who is splendid in his apparel,
>   marching in the greatness of his strength? (Isaiah 63:1a)

Like Jeremiah, Isaiah pronounced a curse against Bozrah, the city of the Edomites. He saw a warrior advancing with robes spattered red. And he posed the same question as Jeremiah: Who is this?

Unlike Jeremiah, the prophet Isaiah was given an answer. The warrior said, "It is I, speaking in righteousness, mighty to save" (Isaiah 63:1b). In other words, Isaiah saw the Lord God himself striding from Bozrah! God himself defeated the Edomites. He appointed himself as the one chosen to conquer his enemies. In this way, the prophets pointed forward to the coming of God's

Son Jesus Christ to defeat God's enemies and to rule as the Most High over all the earth.

The defeat of the Edomites is a picture of final judgment, when every last one of God's enemies will be utterly and eternally defeated. It is a vision of the victory of Jesus Christ. For God has placed his Son at his right hand and has promised to make all his enemies a footstool for his feet (Hebrews 1:13). Christ must win the victory over sin, death, Satan, and every prince and potentate who opposes him.

Friend or Foe?

The victory of Christ is good news. It means that someday Asaph's prayer will be answered, and God will be known as the Most High over all the earth. But this is only good news for God's friends, not for his enemies. For them it is the worst possible news. If Christ will defeat all his enemies, then it is desperately important to become one of his friends. Are you a friend of God, or are you still one of his foes?

To answer this question, it helps to know what makes someone a friend of God. These nations were God's enemies because they did not put their trust in him. They trusted other things instead, each nation depending on someone or something besides the true and living God.

The Ammonites trusted in their wealth.

> Why do you boast of your valleys,
>   O faithless daughter,
> who trusted in her treasures, saying,
>   "Who will come against me?" (49:4)

They did not think anyone could touch them because they lived in lush valleys.

The Edomites trusted their wisdom. They were very clever. As Jeremiah's insults reveal, they had a reputation for practical intelligence.

> Concerning Edom.
>   Thus says the LORD of hosts:
>
> "Is wisdom no more in Teman?
>   Has counsel perished from the prudent?
>   Has their wisdom vanished?" (v. 7)

The Edomites also trusted their defenses. They could retreat to Petra, an impregnable hiding place that could be entered only by a passage the width of a single soldier. Or they could flee to the imposing fortress of Bozrah. Jeremiah called the Edomites the ones "who live in the clefts of the rock, who hold the height of the hill" (v. 16b).

The Syrians trusted their fame. Jeremiah called Damascus "The famous city" (v. 25).

The Bedouin trusted themselves:

> Rise up, advance against a nation at ease,
>   that dwells securely,
>   declares the LORD,
> that has no gates or bars,
>   that dwells alone." (v. 31)

The nomads were carefree. They relied on their privacy and independence to save them.

Finally, the Elamites trusted their weapons. They were well known for their skill at archery (Isaiah 22:6). Jeremiah thus called the bow of Elam "The mainstay of their might" (49:35b).

Jeremiah 49 is history, but it is not a history lesson. The nations of Jeremiah's day trusted their wealth, their wisdom, and their weapons. People trust the same kinds of things today to make it through life—money, intelligence, popularity, independence, power. They count on their savings to provide for their needs. They think they are smart enough to beat the system. They base their happiness on the approval of others. They want to make it on their own. They try to manipulate things for their own advantage.

The same attitudes even prevail among Christians in these post-Christian times. Like the Ammonites, we stuff ourselves with rich food. Like the Edomites, we build our homes higher and higher up the hill. Like the Bedouin, we demand our space. And all the while we assume that divine judgment will never strike us.

Jeremiah 49 shows what happens to people who trust in anyone or anything besides the one true God. Wealth did not save the Ammonites. They were not able to buy their way out of judgment. Wisdom did not save the Edomites, nor did their military might:

> For behold, I will make you small among the nations,
>   despised among mankind.
> The horror you inspire has deceived you,
>   and the pride of your heart,
> you who live in the clefts of the rock,
>   who hold the height of the hill.
> Though you make your nest as high as the eagle's,
>   I will bring you down from there,
>   declares the LORD. (vv. 15, 16; cf. Obadiah 2–4)

Fame did not save the Arameans because God is no respecter of persons. Independence did not save the Bedouin; God found them in the wilderness and destroyed them just the same. Weapons did not save the Elamites. "Thus says the LORD of hosts: 'Behold, I will break the bow of Elam, the mainstay of their might'" (v. 35).

God's judgment of these nations proved the truth of something Jeremiah said much earlier: "Let not the wise man boast in his wisdom, let not the mighty man boast in his might, let not the rich man boast in his riches" (9:23a). Jeremiah went on to say: "Behold, the days are coming, declares the LORD, when I will punish all those who are circumcised merely in the flesh—Egypt, Judah, Edom, the sons of Ammon, Moab, and all who dwell in the desert who cut the corners of their hair" (9:25, 26a). God judged these nations to show that intelligence, power, and money cannot save.

The destiny of everyone who trusts in these things is destruction. Huey summarizes Jeremiah's message like this:

> Ammon depended on Molech and its riches (49:3–4). Edom depended on wisdom and its inaccessible location (49:7,16). Damascus depended on its fame (49:25). Kedar depended on its remoteness (49:31) and Elam on its bow (49:35–38), but all of them failed. The fate of those nations is a solemn reminder that dependence on human resources rather than on God will always fail.[3]

Do not let human resources lull you into a false sense of security. Investments cannot save you; they simply place you at the mercy of volatile international markets. Your intelligence cannot save you; test scores will not be checked at the gates of Heaven. Fame is fleeting. Independence leads to loneliness. Your strength will fail as you grow old.

The *Heidelberg Catechism* asks, "What is your only comfort, in life and in death?" (Q. 1). The answer is a reminder that salvation is found in Jesus Christ, and nowhere else: "That I belong—body and soul, in life and in death—not to myself but to my faithful Savior, Jesus Christ, who at the cost of his own blood has fully paid for all my sins and has completely freed me from the dominion of the devil."

Grace for the Needy

Jeremiah 49 is mainly about justice for God's enemies. However, like everywhere else in Jeremiah's book of prophecy, it also contains words of grace for God's friends.

God gave a hint of his grace to Edom. At first he promised that Edom would be completely destroyed, saying, "His children are destroyed, and his brothers, and his neighbors; and he is no more" (49:10b). However, God proceeded to say: "Leave your fatherless children; I will keep them alive; and let your widows trust in me" (v. 11).

This is a reminder that God gives grace to the humble, especially to needy children and lonely women. This theme is repeated throughout Scripture. God commanded his people to leave some grapes and grain in the fields for the widows and orphans to glean (Leviticus 19:10; Deuteronomy 24:21). And God promised to follow the same practice in his judgment against Edom:

> If grape gatherers came to you,
>   would they not leave gleanings?
> If thieves came by night,
>   would they not destroy only enough for themselves?
> But I have stripped Esau bare;
>   I have uncovered his hiding places,
>   and he is not able to conceal himself.
> His children are destroyed, and his brothers,
>   and his neighbors; and he is no more.
> Leave your fatherless children; I will keep them alive;
>   and let your widows trust in me. (49:9–11; cf. Obadiah 5–6)

God "upholds the widow and the fatherless" (Psalm 146:9). He takes special care of orphans and widows because they are so often sinned against. Even when they live with God's enemies, widows and orphans may be counted among God's friends. This is God's grace for the needy. His promise of protection can be claimed by widows, orphans, foster children, single moms, and anyone else who is vulnerable.

Grace for the Enemy

God's grace is not only for individuals, however, it is also for entire nations. Two of these oracles of judgment—and only two—end with a promise of grace. "But afterward I will restore the fortunes of the Ammonites, declares the LORD" (49:6). "But in the latter days I will restore the fortunes of Elam, declares the LORD" (v. 39). Jeremiah had already made similar promises to Egypt (46:26) and to Moab (48:47), as well as to Judah (30:18).

What does it mean for God to restore the fortunes of a nation? It may mean that God will bless a nation socially, politically, and economically. Although God judged the ancient peoples of Jordan and Iran, they were not permanently destroyed.[4] After 539 BC, Elam became the center of the Persian Empire. Its capital city of Susa was rebuilt by Darius in 494 BC.[5] The Ammonites were still around until the second century, when they were defeated by the Macca-beans. God restored the fortunes of the nations he promised to restore. Even to this day, they are populated and prosperous, at least to some degree.

But Jeremiah's promise of good fortune contained a hint of more lasting blessing. The Elamites were lost in the days of Jeremiah, scattered to the four winds. But they are found in the pages of the New Testament. Do you know where?

In the second chapter of Acts, Luke described how the Holy Spirit came upon the church with great power on the Day of Pentecost:

> And they were all filled with the Holy Spirit and began to speak in other tongues as the Spirit gave them utterance. Now there were dwelling in Jeru-salem Jews, devout men from every nation under heaven. And at this sound the multitude came together, and they were bewildered, because each one was hearing them speak in his own language. And they were amazed and astonished, saying, "Are not all these who are speaking Galileans? And how is it that we hear, each of us in his own native language? Parthians and Medes and Elamites . . . we hear them telling in our own tongues the mighty works of God." (Acts 2:4–9a, 11b)

When the Holy Spirit came on the church with great power, the Elamites heard the wonders of God in their own language. Surely at least a few of those Persians were among the three thousand who came to faith in Jesus Christ that day and were baptized by the apostles.

Jeremiah's promise was partly fulfilled at Pentecost, therefore, when God began to restore the fortunes of the Persians. But God has not stopped restor-ing the Persians. The gospel of Jesus Christ continues to spread among the people of Iran to this very day. There are more Iranian Christians alive today than at any other moment in history.[6] And since more than a million Iranians have come to the United States, Americans now have a wonderful opportunity to help fulfill the promise God made to Iran through the prophet Jeremiah. God has a plan to save the people of Iran by his grace.

The Mystery of Grace

The salvation of the Iranian people reveals something mysterious about grace. Why does God give his grace to some and not to others? All the nations men-tioned in Jeremiah 49 were enemies of God. They all deserved to be destroyed, but God saved some of them anyway. Why some and not others?

As Derek Kidner reflected on this mystery, he was reminded of the two thieves who were crucified on Calvary, one on either side of Christ. They were both sinners. They both hurled insults at Jesus (Matthew 27:44). They were both enemies of the cross of Christ. They were both destined for destruction.

Yet one of the robbers received the grace of God. As he hung on the cross he was convicted of his sin. We are punished justly, he said, "for we are receiving the due reward of our deeds." He confessed that Jesus Christ is the sinless one: "This man has done nothing wrong" (Luke 23:41). And then he asked for the free gift of eternal life: "Jesus, remember me when you come into your kingdom" (Luke 23:42). And Jesus gave the man the grace for which he prayed.

Here is the mystery: Why did Jesus save one thief and not the other? Kidner quotes an old saying: "One was saved, that none might despair; yet only one, that none might presume."[7] God's promise of grace for Elam teaches us not to despair. There is grace enough for God's enemies. At the same time, God's judgment against Edom, Damascus, Kedar, and Hazor is a warning not to presume upon God's grace. There is no hope for anyone who trusts anything except the mercy that God has shown in Jesus Christ.

63

"Full Atonement! Can It Be?"

JEREMIAH 50:1–46

THE ENGLISH POET Percy Bysshe Shelley (1792–1822) wrote a sonnet about a statue lying broken in the sand:

> I met a traveller from an antique land
> Who said: Two vast and trunkless legs of stone
> Stand in the desert. Near them on the sand
> Half sunk, a shatter'd visage lies, whose frown
> And wrinkled lip and sneer of cold command
> Tell that its sculptor well those passions read
> Which yet survive, stamp'd on these lifeless things,
> The hand that mock'd them and the heart that fed.

Although the statue lay in pieces, its inscription remained:

> And on the pedestal these words appear:
> 'My name is Ozymandias, king of kings:
> Look on my works, ye Mighty, and despair!'
> Nothing beside remains. Round the decay
> Of that colossal wreck, boundless and bare,
> The lone and level sands stretch far away.[1]

Shelley's sonnet witnesses the fall of an empire. It mocks the pride of Ozymandias, who styled himself the king of kings. His name no longer strikes fear into anyone's heart, for his kingdom lies half buried in the desert.

The Fall of Babylon

Jeremiah promised the same thing to Nebuchadnezzar, Evil-Merodach, Nabonidus, and all the rest of the cruel kings of Babylon. The mighty Babylonian empire would be toppled and buried in the sand.

This is the climax of Jeremiah's book. For decades he had prophesied that the Babylonians would defeat Judah, Egypt, Philistia, Moab, Ammon, Edom, Damascus, Kedar, and Elam. One by one Babylon conquered the kingdoms of the Middle East to become the greatest empire in the world (612–539 BC).

Throughout his ministry Jeremiah insisted that resistance was futile. Indeed, some have said that "The argument of the book of Jeremiah is that Babylon is implementing the judgment of God against Jerusalem."[2] Therefore, the Babylonians were to be feared, and even prayed for (29:7)!

Yet the Babylonians were not a law unto themselves. They were not God's friends, only his helpers. Therefore, like every other superpower, they had to answer to God for their sins:

> For this is the vengeance of the LORD:
>   take vengeance on her;
>   do to her as she has done. (50:15b)

Jeremiah 50 is the Biblical version of "what goes around comes around." Having judged all the other nations of the world, including Israel, God finally turned his attention to the great enemy—Babylon.

Jeremiah foretold the fall of Babylon in graphic detail. He began with a shout of triumph:

> The word that the LORD spoke concerning Babylon, concerning the land of the Chaldeans, by Jeremiah the prophet:
>
> "Declare among the nations and proclaim,
>   set up a banner and proclaim,
>   conceal it not, and say:
> 'Babylon is taken,
>   Bel is put to shame,
>   Merodach is dismayed.
> Her images are put to shame,
>   her idols are dismayed.'" (vv. 1, 2)

God would triumph over Babylon and her gods.

Once Jeremiah had issued his news flash, God told how he would triumph:

> For behold, I am stirring up and bringing against Babylon a gathering of great nations, from the north country. And they shall array themselves against her. From there she shall be taken. (v. 9a; cf. 6:22–24)
>
> Behold, a people comes from the north;
>   a mighty nation and many kings

are stirring from the farthest parts of the earth.
They lay hold of bow and spear;
    they are cruel and have no mercy.
The sound of them is like the roaring of the sea;
    they ride on horses,
arrayed as a man for battle
    against you, O daughter of Babylon!

The king of Babylon heard the report of them,
    and his hands fell helpless;
anguish seized him,
    pain as of a woman in labor. (vv. 41–43)

The nations that attacked Babylon would take their marching orders from Almighty God:

Set yourselves in array against Babylon all around,
    all you who bend the bow;
shoot at her, spare no arrows,
    for she has sinned against the LORD.
Raise a shout against her all around;
    she has surrendered;
her bulwarks have fallen;
    her walls are thrown down. . . .
Cut off from Babylon the sower,
    and the one who handles the sickle in time of harvest;
because of the sword of the oppressor,
    every one shall turn to his own people,
    and every one shall flee to his own land. (vv. 14, 15a, 16)

The battle would be over seemingly before it began. The enemies would shout; Babylon would surrender.

Many of the details in Jeremiah's blow-by-blow description of the battle were heavy with sarcasm. He prophesied:

Go up against the land of Merathaim,
    and against the inhabitants of Pekod.
Kill, and devote them to destruction,
    declares the LORD. (v. 21a)

Merathaim and Pekod were real locations in Babylon. Ironically, those place names sounded like the Hebrew words for "double rebellion" and "punishment."

There was more sarcasm to come:

> . . . do all that I have commanded you.
> The noise of battle is in the land,
>   and great destruction!
> How the hammer of the whole earth
>   is cut down and broken!
> How Babylon has become
>   a horror among the nations! (vv. 21b–23)

Babylon was used to doing the hammering, but the hammer itself would be pounded into submission. Babylon was also used to doing the trapping. But God said:

> I set a snare for you and you were taken, O Babylon,
>   and you did not know it;
> you were found and caught,
>   because you opposed the LORD. (v. 24)

Here is another irony—Babylon, which once had laid siege to Jerusalem, would be surrounded itself:

> Summon archers against Babylon, all those who bend the bow. Encamp around her; let no one escape. (v. 29a)

When the archers drew their bows, their arrows would find their marks:

> Their arrows are like a skilled warrior who does not return empty-handed. Chaldea shall be plundered; all who plunder her shall be sated, declares the LORD. (vv. 9b, 10)

Jeremiah prophesied that Babylon's defeat would be total. Her economy would be ruined.

> Come against her from every quarter;
>   open her granaries;
> pile her up like heaps of grain, and devote her to destruction;
>   let nothing be left of her. (v. 26)

Her brave young soldiers would fall in battle:

> Kill all her bulls;
>   let them go down to the slaughter.
> Woe to them, for their day has come,
>   the time of their punishment. . . .

> Therefore her young men shall fall in her squares, and all her soldiers shall be destroyed on that day, declares the LORD. (vv. 27, 30; cf. 49:26)

As the assault continued, everyone and everything in Babylon would come under attack.

> A sword against the Chaldeans, declares the LORD,
>   and against the inhabitants of Babylon,
>   and against her officials and her wise men!
> A sword against the diviners,
>   that they may become fools!
> A sword against her warriors,
>   that they may be destroyed!
> A sword against her horses and against her chariots,
>   and against all the foreign troops in her midst,
>   that they may become women!
> A sword against all her treasures,
>   that they may be plundered! (vv. 35–37)

The staccato rhythm of this poetry captures "The repetitious, irresistible hammering of destructive force. The utterance uses no verbs. The action is too abrupt; the assault is too quick."[3]

The story of the fall of Babylon in 539 BC is a remarkable one. The attack, which came from the northern side of the city, was made by a coalition of armies led by Cyrus the Persian. According to one account:

> Cyrus made his successful assault on a night when the whole city, relying on the strength of the walls, had given themselves up to the riot and debauchery of a grand public festival, and the king and his nobles were revelling at a splendid entertainment. Cyrus had previously caused a canal, which ran west of the city, and carried off the superfluous water of the Euphrates into the lake of Nitocris, to be cleared out, in order to turn the river into it; which, by this means, was rendered so shallow, that his soldiers were able to penetrate along its bed into the city.[4]

The Wasteland

The attack of Cyrus was only the first blow Babylon was to suffer. By the time God was finished, nothing but wasteland would remain.

> For out of the north a nation has come up against her, which shall make her land a desolation, and none shall dwell in it; both man and beast shall flee away."(v. 3)

For Babylon to come under northern attack was an amazing reversal. As Brueggemann puts it, the prophecy "which has so consistently summoned the 'foe from the north' (i.e., Babylon) now turns against the 'foe from the north,' and thereby transforms the role and position of Babylon. That great empire now is not the means of attack, but the object of Yahweh's attack."[5]

Babylon's boast would be turned into shame, her valleys into wilderness:

Though you rejoice, though you exult,
    O plunderers of my heritage,
though you frolic like a heifer in the pasture,
    and neigh like stallions,
your mother shall be utterly shamed,
    and she who bore you shall be disgraced.
Behold, she shall be the last of the nations,
    a wilderness, a dry land, and a desert.
Because of the wrath of the LORD she shall not be inhabited
    but shall be an utter desolation;
everyone who passes by Babylon shall be appalled,
    and hiss because of all her wounds. (vv. 11–13)

A drought against her waters,
    that they may be dried up!
For it is a land of images,
    and they are mad over idols. (v. 38)

Therefore wild beasts shall dwell with hyenas in Babylon, and ostriches shall dwell in her. She shall never again have people, nor be inhabited for all generations. As when God overthrew Sodom and Gomorrah and their neighboring cities, declares the LORD, so no man shall dwell there, and no son of man shall sojourn in her. (vv. 39, 40; cf. Genesis 19:24, 25; Isaiah 13:19–22)

According to this picture of utter desolation, the Babylonians would disappear; only the scavengers would remain.

Babylon thus met the same fate as Ozymandias. First the empire was toppled, and then it was half-buried in the desert. Now travelers who walk in that ancient land find nothing but ruins in the sand. This is what happened to that great city:

From [the fall of Babylon in 538 BC] its importance declined, for Cyrus made Susa the capital of his kingdom. It revolted against Darius Hystaspis, who again subdued it, broke down all its gates, and reduced its walls to the height of fifty cubits. According to Strabo, Xerxes destroyed the tower of Belus. Under the Persians, and under Alexander's successors, Babylon continued to decline, especially after Seleucus Nicator had founded Seleucia, and made it his residence. A great portion of the inhabitants of Babylon removed thither; and in Strabo's time, that is, under Augustus, Babylon had become so desolate, that it might be called a vast desert. . . . From this time onward, Babylon ceases almost to be mentioned; even its ruins have not been discovered until within the last two centuries. . . . The aspect of the whole region is dreary and forlorn. It is infested by noxious animals, and perhaps in no place under heaven is the contrast between ancient magnificence and present desolation greater than here.[6]

These are all matters of historical fact, but they must be understood theologically. The exiles knew who had defeated Babylon and why. When Babylon first fell, they carried the news back to Jerusalem.

> A voice! They flee and escape from the land of Babylon, to declare in Zion the vengeance of the LORD our God, vengeance for his temple. (v. 28)

God brings down the proud. He humiliates the arrogant. He destroys the violent. Although Babylon ruled over the ancient world, God had the last word, as he always does:

> Behold, I am against you, O proud one,
>   declares the Lord GOD of hosts,
> for your day has come,
>   the time when I will punish you.
> The proud one shall stumble and fall,
>   with none to raise him up,
> and I will kindle a fire in his cities,
>   and it will devour all that is around him. (vv. 31, 32)

A Strong Redeemer

The fall of Babylon is a story of defeat, one of the greatest defeats in the history of the world. But it is also a story of victory for the people of God. The destruction of Babylon meant salvation for God's people.

This chapter mentions five blessings of salvation, all of which point toward salvation in Jesus Christ. First, *redemption*. The fall of Babylon is one of the two great acts of redemption in the Old Testament. The first was the exodus, when God brought his people out of the land of Egypt, out of the house of bondage. The second was the return from exile, when God brought his people out of the city of Babylon and led them back home.

The Jews were in bondage in Babylon. Like Pharaoh, Nebuchadnezzar would not let God's people go:

> Thus says the LORD of hosts: The people of Israel are oppressed, and the people of Judah with them. All who took them captive have held them fast; they refuse to let them go. (v. 33; cf. Psalm 137)

The Jews languished in captivity, but God did not allow them to be tormented forever. He delivered them from bondage. After seventy years they received the instructions they had been longing to hear:

> Flee from the midst of Babylon, and go out of the land of the Chaldeans, and be as male goats before the flock. (v. 8)

They were to leave Babylon like rams charging out of a sheepfold.

God destroyed Babylon so he could save his people. Jeremiah specifically described this deliverance as redemption: "Their Redeemer is strong; the LORD of hosts is his name" (v. 34a).

Redeemer—or, to use the proper term for it, *kinsman-redeemer*—is one of God's best names. A kinsman-redeemer had the responsibility to rescue the members of his family from slavery and to avenge their enemies. Boaz served as a kinsman-redeemer when he rescued his cousin Ruth from poverty and slavery (Ruth 4:1–12; cf. Job 19:25). God described himself as a redeemer when he brought his people out of Egypt (Exodus 6:6; 15:13).

God also redeemed his people by saving them from Babylon. He was a strong redeemer:

> Behold, like a lion coming up from the thicket of the Jordan against a perennial pasture, I will suddenly make them run away from her, and I will appoint over her whomever I choose. For who is like me? Who will summon me? What shepherd can stand before me? Therefore hear the plan that the LORD has made against Babylon, and the purposes that he has formed against the land of the Chaldeans: Surely the little ones of their flock shall be dragged away; surely their fold shall be appalled at their fate. At the sound of the capture of Babylon the earth shall tremble, and her cry shall be heard among the nations. (vv. 44–46; cf. 49:19–21)

Like a mighty warrior, God worked salvation with his own hands:

> The LORD has opened his armory
>   and brought out the weapons of his wrath,
> for the Lord GOD of hosts has a work to do
>   in the land of the Chaldeans. (v. 25)

Jeremiah used a slightly different image when he described God as a lawyer who would defend his people:

> He will surely plead their cause, that he may give rest to the earth, but unrest to the inhabitants of Babylon." (v. 34b; cf. Isaiah 43:1, 14)

This was quite a reversal. At the beginning of Jeremiah's book, God brought charges against his people (2:9). By the end of the book, he has become their legal defender or advocate. He has gone from prosecuting attorney to defense attorney in order to redeem his people from slavery.

The name *redeemer* must have been precious to every exile who went back home to rebuild Jerusalem. But it is even more precious to every Christian. The Westminster *Shorter Catechism* asks, "Who is the Redeemer of God's elect?" (Q. 21). Then it gives this wonderful answer: "The only Redeemer of God's elect is the Lord Jesus Christ. . . ." Christ redeemed his people when he paid for their sins on the cross. He released us from the bondage of our guilt. He bought us back from sin, back from death, back from the devil. Christ accomplished this redemption with his own blood.

The Jews were redeemed from their captivity at the Babylonians' expense.

> Repay her according to her deeds; do to her according to all that she has done. For she has proudly defied the LORD, the Holy One of Israel. (v. 29b)

But we have been redeemed from our captivity to sin at God's expense. "You were ransomed from the futile ways inherited from your forefathers, not with perishable things such as silver or gold, but with the precious blood of Christ, like that of a lamb without blemish or spot" (1 Peter 1:18, 19).

Tears of Repentance

A second blessing of salvation is *repentance*. When God redeemed the Jews, they did not just go back to their city—they went back to their God:

> In those days and in that time, declares the LORD, the people of Israel and the people of Judah shall come together, weeping as they come, and they shall seek the LORD their God. (50:4; cf. 3:18; 29:13)

This prophecy was partly about reconciliation. Two alienated peoples would become one united people for God. But the prophecy was also about repentance, for seeking God with tears always means sorrow for sin.

The return from exile was well lubricated with tears. The Jews who went back to Jerusalem were keenly aware of their sin. When the priests read Scripture to them, they "wept as they heard the words of the Law" (Nehemiah 8:9). Later, when Ezra heard that the people were marrying pagans, he tore his tunic, pulled his hair, and fell to the ground in true repentance (Ezra 9:3–15). "While Ezra prayed and made confession, weeping and casting himself down before the house of God, a very great assembly of men, women, and children gathered to him out of Israel, for the people wept bitterly" (Ezra 10:1).

Turning back to God means turning away from sin, and turning away from sin means being sorry for sin. A sinner who grasps the holiness of God and receives the mercy of God must weep over his sins. It is a grievous thing to sin against a holy and merciful God.

True repentance is always tinged with sorrow. True penitents weep over their sins. The tax collector wept when he prayed at the temple. He "would not even lift up his eyes to heaven, but beat his breast, saying, 'God, be merciful to me, a sinner!'" (Luke 18:13). Peter wept when he denied Christ. After the rooster crowed the third time, "he went out and wept bitterly" (Matthew 26:75). God does not base his forgiveness on our tears of repentance. But since we are such great sinners, we must sometimes be touched by the anguish of our sin.

The proper way to confess sin is with sorrow. The Westminster *Shorter Catechism* asks (Q. 87), "What is repentance unto life?" The answer is: "Repentance unto life is a saving grace, whereby a sinner, out of a true sense of his sin, and apprehension of the mercy of God in Christ, doth, with grief and hatred of his sin, turn from it unto God, with full purpose of, and endeavour after, new obedience." The mention of grief is a reminder that repentance is often accompanied by tears.

This ought to be the experience of every Christian. Tearful repentance is one of the blessings of salvation. Once you grasp the perfect holiness of God and the boundless mercy of Christ, even the least sin becomes grievous. Turn away from sin and come back to God as the exiles did—with tears.

The Everlasting Covenant

A third blessing of salvation is *covenant*. Indeed, all God's promises and all the blessings of salvation are bound together in the covenant of grace.

Jeremiah promised that the exiles would set their faces toward the city of God. Once they arrived, they would never leave. They would add obedience to repentance.

> They shall ask the way to Zion, with faces turned toward it, saying, "Come, let us join ourselves to the LORD in an everlasting covenant that will never be forgotten." (50:5)

The Jews bound themselves to God in covenant. This is also what it means to be a Christian. A Christian is someone who is bound to God by covenant. A Christian becomes a member of the church, God's covenant community. A Christian is baptized in God's Triune Name and thus receives God's covenant sign. A Christian takes Communion, sitting down to God's covenant meal. And a Christian is identified as a Christian by living the covenant life.

These are all ways of keeping covenant with God. When Jeremiah mentioned the everlasting covenant, however, he was not talking about our covenant with God. He was talking about God's covenant with us.

Jeremiah was the prophet of the new covenant. He showed God's people how they had broken the old covenant, announcing its terms and its curses (11:1–13). He explained that God's people were banished from their city because they had "forsaken the covenant of the LORD their God and worshiped other gods and served them" (22:9). He lamented these unhappy events as the breakup of a marriage covenant: "My covenant . . . they broke, though I was their husband, declares the LORD" (31:32).

However, Jeremiah also announced the coming of a new covenant written on the mind and in the heart (31:31–34). The new covenant would establish a bond of friendship, so that God's people would belong to God and God would belong to his people. The new covenant, we learn in Jeremiah 50, would also be unforgettable. God has promised "an everlasting covenant that will never be forgotten" (v. 5b; cf. 32:40).

The problem with the old covenant was forgetfulness. God's people forgot God and their covenant with him. But the new covenant will last forever. It cannot be forgotten because it comes to us in Jesus Christ. According to Calvin, "This prophecy cannot be otherwise explained than of Christ's spiritual kingdom."[7] Jeremiah gave a clue that he was speaking about the coming Christ when he said, "In those days and in that time" (v. 4a).

The reason the new covenant cannot be forgotten is because God's own Son will always remember it. If the new covenant depended on us, it could not last forever. We are too forgetful. The new covenant does not depend on us, however, but on the person and work of Jesus Christ. We enter the covenant in and through him. Jesus Christ keeps covenant for his people. Therefore, the new covenant is everlasting.

Charles Haddon Spurgeon imagined God the Son making covenant promises to God the Father in eternity past, using words like these:

My Father, on my part I covenant that in the fullness of time I will become man. I will take upon myself the form and nature of the fallen race. I will live in their wretched world, and for my people I will keep the law

perfectly. I will work out a spotless righteousness, which shall be acceptable to the demands of thy just and holy law. In due time I will bear the sins
of all my people. Thou shalt exact their debts on me; the chastisement of
their peace I will endure, and by my stripes they shall be healed. My Father,
I covenant and promise that I will be obedient unto death, even the death
of the cross. I will magnify thy law, and make it honorable. I will suffer all
they ought to have suffered. I will endure the curse of thy law, and all the
vials of thy wrath shall be emptied and spent upon my head. I will then rise
again; I will ascend into heaven; I will intercede for them at thy right hand;
and I will make myself responsible for every one of them, that not one of
those whom thou hast given me shall ever be lost, but I will bring all my
sheep of whom, by my blood, thou hast constituted me the shepherd—I
will bring every one safe to thee at last.[8]

Whether he used these words or not, Jesus Christ kept every one of those
promises. He became a man. He obeyed the Law. He bore the curse for our
sins. He died on the cross. He was raised from the dead. He ascended into
Heaven. He prays for his people. He keeps us to the very end. All these truths
are summarized in the Biblical blessing:

> Now may the God of peace who brought again from the dead our Lord
> Jesus, the great shepherd of the sheep, by the blood of the eternal covenant,
> equip you with everything good that you may do his will, working in us
> that which is pleasing in his sight, through Jesus Christ, to whom be glory
> forever and ever. Amen. (Hebrews 13:20, 21)

The Good Shepherd

The mention of our great Shepherd brings us to a fourth blessing of salvation—*a good shepherd*.

Jeremiah had seen plenty of bad shepherds in his time. He often charged
other spiritual leaders with pastoral malpractice: "The shepherds are stupid,"
he complained, "and do not inquire of the LORD; therefore they have not prospered, and all their flock is scattered" (10:21). "Woe to the shepherds who
destroy and scatter the sheep of my pasture!" (23:1).

Bad shepherds are bad for their sheep. God's people wandered and became the lost sheep of the Old Testament:

> My people have been lost sheep. Their shepherds have led them astray,
> turning them away on the mountains. From mountain to hill they have
> gone. They have forgotten their fold. All who found them have devoured
> them, and their enemies have said, "We are not guilty, for they have sinned
> against the LORD, their habitation of righteousness, the LORD, the hope of
> their fathers." (50:6, 7)

Israel is a hunted sheep driven away by lions. First the king of Assyria devoured him, and now at last Nebuchadnezzar king of Babylon has gnawed his bones."(v. 17)

The Assyrians made mutton chops out of Israel when they conquered the northern tribes in 722 BC (2 Kings 17:1–6). A century and a half later the Babylonians came to gnaw on whatever bones were left.

What God's people needed was a good shepherd. They needed a shepherd to find them, rescue them, and bring them back to the fold.

> Therefore, thus says the LORD of hosts, the God of Israel: Behold, I am bringing punishment on the king of Babylon and his land, as I punished the king of Assyria. I will restore Israel to his pasture, and he shall feed on Carmel and in Bashan, and his desire shall be satisfied on the hills of Ephraim and in Gilead. (vv. 18, 19)

In these verses Jeremiah was looking back to the defeat of Assyria around 610 BC.

These verses also look forward, however, to everything the Bible says about Jesus Christ, the Good Shepherd. When the sheep are scattered, Jesus is the Good Shepherd who has compassion on them because they are "harassed and helpless, like sheep without a shepherd" (Matthew 9:36). When the sheep are lost, Jesus is the Good Shepherd who leaves the ninety-nine in the open country to "go after the one that is lost, until he finds it" (Luke 15:4). When the sheep are in danger, Jesus is the Good Shepherd who "lays down his life for the sheep" (John 10:11).

When the sheep are hungry, Jesus is the Good Shepherd who supplies whatever they need. Jeremiah promised that Israel's "desire" would be "satisfied" (50:19). Literally, he said that Israel's *soul* would be satisfied, which echoes the well-known psalm:

> The LORD is my shepherd; I shall not want.
> > He makes me lie down in green pastures.
> He leads me beside still waters.
> > He restores my soul. (Psalm 23:1–3a)

One wonders if Jeremiah realized just how good the Good Shepherd would be. Jesus is *so* good! No other shepherd has ever loved his sheep so deeply, searched for them so diligently, or provided for them so generously. No other shepherd has ever paid so great a price to save his sheep.

Do you know this Good Shepherd? Jesus says, "I am the good shepherd. I know my own and my own know me" (John 10:14). If you do not know Jesus Christ as your shepherd, he calls you to follow him. If you do know the Good Shepherd, then trust him now. He has already gone to the trouble to find you and save you at the cost of his own life. You can trust him to take care of everything else you need. Jesus is the Good Shepherd who cares tenderly for the bodies and souls of all his sheep.

Full Atonement

Jeremiah made one more salvation promise. It may have been the most remarkable promise of all, the promise of *atonement*:

> In those days and in that time, declares the LORD, iniquity shall be sought in Israel, and there shall be none, and sin in Judah, and none shall be found, for I will pardon those whom I leave as a remnant. (50:20; cf. 31:34; Micah 7:18)

One of the best places to look for Israel's guilt is the book of Jeremiah. How could anyone miss it? Jeremiah took great pains to document all of Israel's sins, in all their sordid detail—homicide, infanticide, adultery, idolatry, lying, cheating, stealing, and all the rest of them.

Yet Jeremiah imagined someone—maybe God himself?—going on a quest to find Israel's sin. But the quest was futile. The search was in vain. After a long hard search, there was no sin to be found. The guilt of God's people seemingly had vanished.

This is what Jesus Christ was doing when he died on the cross. The promise of the gospel is that Jesus Christ atoned for all the sins of every believer on the cross. If you know Christ, then Christ died for all your sins. This could be called the doctrine of the unlimited atonement.

Christ died for all the sins you committed before you became a Christian. No doubt some of them were heinous. Abortion? Adultery? Armed robbery? No matter how reprehensible, every last one of your former sins is forgiven. Furthermore, Christ died for all the sins you have committed *since* you became a Christian, including the sins you have yet to commit. Christ died for them all.

Christ died for all the sins you know about, plus all the ones you don't. He died for secret sins as well as open sins, small sins as well as big sins. On the cross Jesus Christ atoned for every sin committed by every believer who will ever live.

Philip P. Bliss (1838–1876) wrote a wonderful hymn about the atoning work of Christ on the cross. It is usually referred to by its first line: "Man of

Sorrows! What a Name." But the middle verse of that hymn praises Christ for the wonder of his unlimited atonement:

Guilty, vile, and helpless, we;
Spotless Lamb of God was he;
Full atonement! can it be?
Hallelujah! what a Savior.

64

"Fallen! Fallen Is Babylon the Great!"

JEREMIAH 51:1–64

JEREMIAH'S ORACLE OF JUDGMENT against Babylon seems to have been the heaviest prophecy in the Old Testament. Jeremiah chapters 50, 51 were so heavy that they sank to the bottom of the Euphrates River.

Babylon Is Sunk

It happened like this: Against Jeremiah's better judgment (27:1–22), King Zedekiah tried to rebel against Babylon in 594 BC. When the Babylonians got wind of the rebellion, they ordered Zedekiah back to Babylon to declare his allegiance to Nebuchadnezzar. He took his quartermaster, Seraiah, with him.

When Jeremiah heard about Seraiah's mission, he gave him the latest edition of his prophecy about Babylon:

> The word that Jeremiah the prophet commanded Seraiah the son of Neriah, son of Mahseiah, when he went with Zedekiah king of Judah to Babylon, in the fourth year of his reign. Seraiah was the quartermaster. Jeremiah wrote in a book all the disaster that should come upon Babylon, all these words that are written concerning Babylon. And Jeremiah said to Seraiah: "When you come to Babylon, see that you read all these words." (51:59–61)

Like his brother Baruch (32:12; 36:1–10), Seraiah served as Jeremiah's spokesperson. (Also like Baruch, his name has been found on an ancient seal).[1] Seraiah read what is now known as Jeremiah 50, 51—110 verses about the fall of the Babylonian empire.

When the quartermaster finished, he undoubtedly followed the rest of the prophet's instructions:

> And say, "O LORD, you have said concerning this place that you will cut it off, so that nothing shall dwell in it, neither man nor beast, and it shall be desolate forever." When you finish reading this book, tie a stone to it and cast it into the midst of the Euphrates, and say, "Thus shall Babylon sink, to rise no more, because of the disaster that I am bringing upon her, and they shall become exhausted." (51:62–64a)

This was another object lesson from a prophet who specialized in audio-visuals. Jeremiah buried a linen belt and dug it up to show that God would save the remnant of his people (13:1–11). He bought a clay jar from the potter and smashed it outside the city walls to show that God would destroy Jerusalem (19:1–15). He bought a field in enemy-occupied territory to show that God would bring his people back home (32:1–44). This time the message was obvious: Babylon was sunk! Unlike the linen belt, the scroll was beyond recovery. Thus Jeremiah 51 ends on a note of finality: "Thus far are the words of Jeremiah" (v. 64b).

The Bible does not say who heard Seraiah's recitation. Perhaps it was intended for the Babylonians, in which case Seraiah probably ended up a dead man. More likely he gathered the Jewish exiles to hear Jeremiah's prophecy. "By the waters of Babylon"—where they often sat down to weep for Zion (Psalm 137)—the captives heard God promise utterly to destroy their enemies. Then they stood peering into the black water, waiting to see if Jeremiah's prophecy would float back up to the surface.

The scroll never resurfaced. Like the Babylonian empire, it stayed submerged. Fortunately, however, Seraiah had made a copy, thereby preserving the prophecy for the pages of the Old Testament.

The Fall of Babylon

Together Jeremiah 50, 51 form one long prophecy, with chapter 51 repeating many themes from chapter 50.

As before, Jeremiah prophesied that Babylon would be attacked by a federation of armies, which would receive their marching orders from God himself.

> Thus says the LORD:
>
> "Behold, I will stir up the spirit of a destroyer
>   against Babylon,
>   against the inhabitants of Leb-kamai,

and I will send to Babylon winnowers,
    and they shall winnow her,
and they shall empty her land,
    when they come against her from every side
    on the day of trouble." (51:1, 2)

> Sharpen the arrows!
> Take up the shields!

The LORD has stirred up the spirit of the kings of the Medes, because his purpose concerning Babylon is to destroy it, for that is the vengeance of the LORD, the vengeance for his temple. (v. 11)

Set up a standard on the earth;
    blow the trumpet among the nations;
prepare the nations for war against her;
    summon against her the kingdoms,
    Ararat, Minni, and Ashkenaz;
appoint a marshal against her;
    bring up horses like bristling locusts.
Prepare the nations for war against her,
    the kings of the Medes, with their governors and deputies,
    and every land under their dominion." (vv. 27, 28)

Jeremiah mentioned the invaders by name. Babylon would be attacked by the Medes and the Ashkenazi, the peoples of Armenia and Kurdistan who were conquered by Cyrus and his Persian army in 550 BC. Their attack would be carefully coordinated:

Set up a standard against the walls of Babylon;
    make the watch strong;
set up watchmen;
    prepare the ambushes;
for the LORD has both planned and done
    what he spoke concerning the inhabitants of Babylon.
O you who dwell by many waters,
    rich in treasures,
your end has come;
    the thread of your life is cut. (vv. 12, 13)

Not only would the attack be well coordinated, but it would also be over-whelming:

The LORD of hosts has sworn by himself:
Surely I will fill you with men, as many as locusts,
    and they shall raise the shout of victory over you. (v. 14)

For thus says the Lord of hosts, the God of Israel:
The daughter of Babylon is like a threshing floor
    at the time when it is trodden;
yet a little while
    and the time of her harvest will come. (v. 33)

In other words, first Babylon would get pounded, then stripped bare.

Again in chapter 51 Jeremiah gives detailed descriptions of the battle. The attack will come so quickly that the Babylonians won't even have time to prepare for battle:

Let not the archer bend his bow,
    and let him not stand up in his armor.
Spare not her young men;
    devote to destruction all her army.
They shall fall down slain in the land of the Chaldeans,
    and wounded in her streets. (vv. 3, 4)

The land trembles and writhes in pain,
    for the Lord's purposes against Babylon stand,
to make the land of Babylon a desolation,
    without inhabitant.
The warriors of Babylon have ceased fighting;
    they remain in their strongholds;
their strength has failed;
    they have become women;
her dwellings are on fire;
    her bars are broken. (vv. 29, 30)

With a grand sense of drama, the prophet imagined the scene in the king's war cabinet rooms:

One runner runs to meet another,
    and one messenger to meet another,
to tell the king of Babylon
    that his city is taken on every side;
the fords have been seized,
    the marshes are burned with fire,
    and the soldiers are in panic. (vv. 31, 32)

Given our knowledge of ancient Babylon, it is not hard to fill in the details, as J. A. Thompson has done:

In the conduct of warfare in the ancient world specially trained runners brought news from the scene of the battle to the king. Babylon's runners were renowned, and it was these men who came running from every direction to announce to the king that the city had fallen. The first news seems to refer to the collapse of the defenses outside the city. These were vast. In addition to the two massive walls surrounding the heart of Babylon, an inner one some 21 feet thick and an outer one over 12 feet thick, there were great walls thrown up at intervals beyond the city together with a chain of fortresses north and south of the city. The Euphrates River gave protection, and a variety of waterways and large depressions flooded with water all combined to create the impression of an impregnable city. But the fords across the rivers and waterways were seized and the reedy swamps were set on fire. The burning of the swamp reeds would deprive refugees of a place to hide and would flush out any who might have escaped there already. Such news threw the warriors into a panic.[2]

The Aftermath

The news of Babylon's fall would create noise and confusion, not only in the king's chambers, but throughout the city:

A voice! A cry from Babylon!
    The noise of great destruction from the land of the Chaldeans!
For the LORD is laying Babylon waste
    and stilling her mighty voice.
Their waves roar like many waters;
    the noise of their voice is raised." (vv. 54, 55)

The city's defeat would come as a total surprise:

They shall roar together like lions;
    they shall growl like lions' cubs.
While they are inflamed I will prepare them a feast
    and make them drunk, that they may become merry,
then sleep a perpetual sleep
    and not wake, declares the LORD.
I will bring them down like lambs to the slaughter,
    like rams and male goats." (vv. 38–40)

I will make drunk her officials and her wise men,
    her governors, her commanders, and her warriors;
they shall sleep a perpetual sleep and not wake,
    declares the King, whose name is the LORD of hosts. (v. 57)

These prophecies were fulfilled in the life and death of King Belshazzar, who "made a great feast for a thousand of his lords and drank wine in front of the thousand. . . . They drank wine and praised the gods of gold and silver, bronze, iron, wood, and stone" (Daniel 5:1, 4). But while they were getting intoxicated, God sent a hand to write words of judgment on the wall of the banqueting hall (Daniel 5:5, 6). That very night (after he read the handwriting on the wall!), Belshazzar was slain, and the Medes took over his kingdom (Daniel 5:30, 31).

As a result, Babylon eventually became a wasteland, just as Jeremiah prophesied. Babylon would become like an extinct volcano:

> Behold, I am against you, O destroying mountain,
>> declares the LORD,
> which destroys the whole earth;
> I will stretch out my hand against you,
>> and roll you down from the crags,
>> and make you a burnt mountain.
> No stone shall be taken from you for a corner
>> and no stone for a foundation,
> but you shall be a perpetual waste,
>> declares the LORD. (vv. 25, 26)

To put it another way, Babylon would become like a desert waste.

> I will dry up her sea
>> and make her fountain dry,
> and Babylon shall become a heap of ruins,
>> the haunt of jackals,
> a horror and a hissing,
>> without inhabitant. (vv. 36b, 37)

> How Babylon is taken,
>> the praise of the whole earth seized!
> How Babylon has become
>> a horror among the nations!
> The sea has come up on Babylon;
>> she is covered with its tumultuous waves.
> Her cities have become a horror,
>> a land of drought and a desert,
> a land in which no one dwells,
>> and through which no son of man passes.
> And I will punish Bel in Babylon,
>> and take out of his mouth what he has swallowed.
> The nations shall no longer flow to him;
>> the wall of Babylon has fallen." (vv. 41–44)

The city's moats would dry up (including the renowned reservoir of Queen Nitocris), and the ziggurats would fall down all over Babylon, that most cos-

mopolitan of cities. Jeremiah's prophecy about the city walls demands special
notice.

> Thus says the LORD of hosts:
> The broad wall of Babylon
>   shall be leveled to the ground,
> and her high gates
>   shall be burned with fire.
> The peoples labor for nothing,
>   and the nations weary themselves only for fire. (v. 58)

According to Herodotus, the outer walls of Babylon were 300 feet high
and seventy-five feet wide, wide enough to drive several chariots abreast.[3]
Yet they would all fall down, furnishing more fuel for the flames of divine
judgment.

Another similarity between chapters 50 and 51 is the command to escape
from Babylon. The exiles were to flee, every man for himself:

> Flee from the midst of Babylon;
>   let every one save his life!
> Be not cut off in her punishment,
>   for this is the time of the LORD's vengeance,
>   the repayment he is rendering her." (v. 6)

> Go out of the midst of her, my people!
>   Let every one save his life
>   from the fierce anger of the LORD!
> Let not your heart faint, and be not fearful
>   at the report heard in the land,
> when a report comes in one year
>   and afterward a report in another year,
> and violence is in the land,
>   and ruler is against ruler. (vv. 45, 46)

> You who have escaped from the sword,
>   go, do not stand still!
> Remember the LORD from far away,
>   and let Jerusalem come into your mind. (v. 50)

Eventually the exiles would have to run for it. Until that time they were
to live in hope. Even when unsettling rumors circulated through the ghetto,
God's people were not to lose heart. The day of their salvation certainly would
come. The word God sent to the prophet Jeremiah was not a rumor, it was
news—news that has since become history.

The fall of Babylon would be so calamitous that Jeremiah was (almost) moved to pity:

Suddenly Babylon has fallen and been broken;
    wail for her!
Take balm for her pain;
    perhaps she may be healed. (v. 8; cf. 8:22)

In the end, however, he was forced to admit that the Babylonians were beyond redemption. The people of God had no choice but to flee:

We would have healed Babylon,
    but she was not healed.
Forsake her, and let us go
    each to his own country,
for her judgment has reached up to heaven
    and has been lifted up even to the skies. (v. 9)

Though Babylon should mount up to heaven,
    and though she should fortify her strong height,
yet destroyers would come from me against her,
    declares the LORD." (v. 53)

Babylon would meet the same fate as Babel, for "man's attempt to build himself up to the skies ends only in building up his judgment."[4]

Lessons Learned from Defeat

Jeremiah 50, 51 seems repetitive (not to say redundant), especially since the prophecy against Babylon is longer than the rest of Jeremiah's international oracles combined. There are two good reasons for this. One is because Jeremiah wanted to show how finally, definitely, utterly, and completely God would destroy Babylon.

The other reason was so that people would believe his prophecy. Calvin pointed out that unless Jeremiah prophesied at length, no one would believe him. Babylon was then at the height of her glory, with her fabulous Hanging Gardens, her mighty Ishtar Gate, and all the rest of her wonders. Jeremiah thus predicted "The ruin of Babylon, not in simple words, for nothing seemed then more unreasonable than to announce the things which God at length proved by the effect. As Babylon was then the metropolis of the East, no one could have thought that it would ever be possessed by a foreign power."[5]

Whether people believed Jeremiah or not, his prophecies came true. Babylon plunged like a rock to the bottom of the Euphrates.

The history of Babylon's fall teaches many valuable lessons. It teaches that God is *just*. "I will repay Babylon and all the inhabitants of Chaldea before your very eyes for all the evil that they have done in Zion, declares the LORD" (v. 24). Or again:

Babylon must fall for the slain of Israel,
    just as for Babylon have fallen the slain of all the earth. (v. 49)

. . . for a destroyer has come upon her,
    upon Babylon;
her warriors are taken;
    their bows are broken in pieces,
for the LORD is a God of recompense;
    he will surely repay. (v. 56)

Because God is just, he must repay evil for evil.

The fall of Babylon also teaches that God is *all-powerful*. Jeremiah paused in the middle of his prophecy to remember that the God of the nations is also the God of creation:

It is he who made the earth by his power,
    who established the world by his wisdom,
and by his understanding stretched out the heavens.
When he utters his voice there is a tumult of waters in the heavens,
    and he makes the mist rise from the ends of the earth.
He makes lightning for the rain,
    and he brings forth the wind from his storehouses. (vv. 15, 16)

The downfall of great cities is just one small part of God's rule over all things in Heaven and earth. He is all-powerful.

The fall of Babylon also teaches that God *answers prayer*. God's people prayed for the defeat of their enemies, especially Babylon. They cried:

"Nebuchadnezzar the king of Babylon has devoured me;
    he has crushed me;
he has made me an empty vessel;
    he has swallowed me like a monster;
he has filled his stomach with my delicacies;
    he has rinsed me out [NIV: has spewed me out].
The violence done to me and to my kinsmen be upon Babylon,"
    let the inhabitant of Zion say.
"My blood be upon the inhabitants of Chaldea,"
    let Jerusalem say. (vv. 34, 35; cf. Psalm 137:8, 9)

Nebuchadnezzar was a gluttonous dragon who gorged himself on God's people and then spat them out again. It was right for them to pray for the destruction of such a grotesque, bulimic monster.

It was also right to pray against the Babylonians for desecrating God's temple:

> We are put to shame, for we have heard reproach;
>> dishonor has covered our face,
> for foreigners have come
>> into the holy places of the LORD's house. (v. 51; cf. Psalm 74:1–23)

If it was right for God's people to utter such prayers, it was right for God to answer them. "Therefore thus says the Lord: 'Behold, I will plead your cause and take vengeance for you'" (v. 36a; cf. 50:34).

God is a defender, an advocate, and an avenger. It is his responsibility to defeat the enemies of his people. This is a reminder to pray for the kingly work of Jesus Christ as he conquers all his and our enemies.

American Babylon

Jeremiah 51 is not simply a history lesson from the past; it is also a warning for the present. Babylon is not just a historic city. It stands for everything hateful and odious to God.

Babylon is every culture that is proud, arrogant, wasteful, violent, and destructive. It represents every city that sets itself against the kingdom of God. Robert Linthicum thus calls it "a city which has no redeeming value, a city given over to the wholehearted worship and pursuit of evil."[6] Or, as urban missiologist Ray Bakke observes, "Throughout the Bible, Babylon is a symbol of the city which is anti-God. Literally the name means 'gate to God.' The Babylonian disease leads a city to build towers that breach heaven's gates. 'Move over, God, we're coming up,' might be their motto."[7]

Augustine wrote about Babylon in his great book *The City of God*. He viewed the history of the world as a conflict between two great cities—the City of Man and the City of God. As Augustine studied the Bible, he discovered that Babylon represented the City of Man standing against the City of God. Then, as he examined his own culture, he realized that Rome had become the capital City of Man.

If Augustine were alive today, he would add another metropolis to his list—Washington, DC, or perhaps New York City. For the sins of Babylon have become the most prevalent sins of American culture. Jeremiah 51 is a warning to the Babylon of post-Christian America.

What were the chief sins of Babylon? First, the worship of other gods:

> Every man is stupid and without knowledge;
>   every goldsmith is put to shame by his idols,
> for his images are false,
>   and there is no breath in them.
> They are worthless, a work of delusion;
>   at the time of their punishment they shall perish.
>   (vv. 17, 18; cf. 10:12–16)

The problem with idols, Jeremiah recognized, is that they are idle. They cannot do anything. They do not make any sense. They do not know anything. They cannot breathe. They have no value because they cannot save their worshipers from judgment.

The most popular idol in Babylon was Mammon. The idolmakers were chiefly goldsmiths, and Babylon herself was called "a golden cup" (v. 7). The Babylonians were "rich in treasures" (v. 13) because they plundered gold and jewels from all their enemies and carried them back to their fabulous palaces. Robert Linthicum issues this stinging indictment:

> In essence, all the rest of the world has become the third world to Babylon; Babylon was enriched but the price was the destitution of the other countries and peoples of the world. . . . Babylon's greed and lust for wealth and economic security raped the rest of the world, leaving it helpless and destitute, unable to cope either nationally or individually with the exigencies of life. The radical impoverishment of the world, both of its peoples and its natural resources, meant nothing to Babylon, as long as she could have her little niceties and obscene luxuries.[8]

"Economic security," "little niceties" and "obscene luxuries" are apt terms to describe the American Babylon, especially around Christmas. The day after Thanksgiving the cash registers start to ring, and they do not stop ringing until after New Year's Day. To sort through the mail-order catalogs, to hum the television jingles, and to press one's nose against the shop windows is to live among the Babylonians.

The trouble with gold—or any other idol—is that it is senseless, breathless, and worthless. It is nothing at all like the true God:

> Not like these is he who is the portion of Jacob,
>   for he is the one who formed all things,
> and Israel is the tribe of his inheritance;
>   the LORD of hosts is his name. (v. 19; cf. 10:16)

God is no idol. He is not a man-made object at all, for he himself is the Maker of all things.

God promised to reign supreme over all other gods, including the gods of the Babylonians. He said, "I will punish Bel in Babylon" (v. 44a).

> Therefore, behold, the days are coming
>> when I will punish the images of Babylon;
> her whole land shall be put to shame,
>> and all her slain shall fall in the midst of her. (v. 47)

> Therefore, behold, the days are coming, declares the LORD,
>> when I will execute judgment upon her images,
> and through all her land
>> the wounded shall groan. (v. 52)

Bel was the god of the Babylonians, but in the end God would ring Babylon's Bel.

The other great sin of Babylon was violence. The Babylonians were a fierce and warlike people. This is how Jeremiah described them:

> Babylon was a golden cup in the LORD's hand,
>> making all the earth drunken;
> the nations drank of her wine;
>> therefore the nations went mad. (v. 7; cf. 25:15–29)

When God addressed them, he said:

> You are my hammer and weapon of war:
> with you I break nations in pieces;
>> with you I destroy kingdoms;
> with you I break in pieces the horse and his rider;
>> with you I break in pieces the chariot and the charioteer;
> with you I break in pieces man and woman;
>> with you I break in pieces the old man and the youth;
> with you I break in pieces the young man and the young woman;
>> with you I break in pieces the shepherd and his flock;
> with you I break in pieces the farmer and his team;
>> with you I break in pieces governors and commanders.
>> (vv. 20–23; cf. 50:23)

The latter verses may be addressed to Cyrus, but they are better understood as words to Babylon. God used Babylon to carry out his judgments. Yet the Babylonians were responsible for the evil they committed, and they were finally cursed for their bloodthirsty ways.

Like Babylon, America has become an increasingly violent nation. Serial killers are considered a suitable subject for movies. The most popular video games for children feature horrific dismemberment. Not surprisingly, television viewers are routinely titillated with the latest details of gruesome homicides or school bombings on the evening news.

America is also like Babylon because it has the most powerful army in the world. In November 1997 the *Philadelphia Inquirer* ran a series of articles called "Blackhawk Down." The articles described a clash between US soldiers and Somalian civilians in the city of Mogadishu. Somalian warlords were waging civil war, and American soldiers were trying to keep the peace. But in the fog of war, they found themselves targeted for death and trying desperately to defend themselves.

One Somali described what it was like to see an American helicopter swerve over his house and fire its machine guns down the street. He could see no evidence that the helicopter was controlled by a human being. The creature who sat in the cockpit was entirely mechanized. He wore a helmet, goggles, gloves, and body armor. The Somali was gripped with an overwhelming sense of fear and despair at the approach of this inhuman beast raining death from the sky. People felt much the same way about the Babylonians. News of their approach sent entire cities into a panic.

This is not a wholesale indictment of the United States Armed Forces. It is, however, a recognition that America has become the modern Babylon. It is the mightiest, wealthiest nation in the history of the world. Yet power and prosperity pose grave spiritual dangers. They lead to arrogance and violence, greed and immorality. America is not a safe neighborhood. Like Babylon, our culture stands for much that is hateful and odious to God.

"Alas! Alas! You Great City"

There is hope for the future, however. Eventually Satan's lease on the City of Man will expire, and Babylon will be destroyed.

Jeremiah's prophecy contained a hint of something much bigger than the fall of historical Babylon. He promised that on the day of judgment,

> Then the heavens and the earth,
>   and all that is in them,
> shall sing for joy over Babylon,
>   for the destroyers shall come against them out of the north,
>   declares the LORD. (v. 48)

Jeremiah's prophecy was about universal, cosmic events that would affect everything in creation. He was speaking, therefore, about the eventual triumph of the City of God, the ultimate victory of Jesus Christ over everything that stands in opposition to him.

Jeremiah's prophecy was not just about Babylon past; it is also about Babylon future. It looks forward to the day of final judgment. As F. B. Meyer explained:

> One is disposed to enlarge the scope of the prophecy and to believe that every form of anti-Christian power, whether systems of false philosophy, structures of ancient superstition, or gigantic wrongs like the drink traffic and the opium trade, shall wither and die before the all-conquering might of Emmanuel, who was manifested to destroy the works of the devil. He must reign until all enemies are put beneath his feet. Let us strengthen our confidence in the certain prevalence of good over evil, of the Church over the world, and of Christ over Satan, as we consider the precise fulfillment of Jeremiah's predictions concerning the fall of Babylon.[9]

Jeremiah 50, 51 shows that Christ must win in the end.

What Jeremiah promised is repeated in another great prophecy about the defeat of Babylon. The prophecy comes near the end of the book of Revelation, where "Babylon" again has a double meaning: It stands both for Rome and for every institution that is hateful and odious to God.

The similarities between Jeremiah and Revelation are numerous. One might almost say that Revelation 17—19 is based on Jeremiah 50, 51. Like Jeremiah, John saw "a golden cup" in Babylon's hand (Revelation 17:4). He exposed her idolatry, especially her love for "luxurious living" (18:3; cf. 18:7, 11–19). He accused her of violence against the people of God (17:6; 18:7, 20). He warned God's people to flee from her on the day of judgment (18:4, 5).

Like Jeremiah, John exulted in the fall and desolation of Babylon:

Fallen, fallen is Babylon the great!
    She has become a dwelling place for demons,
a haunt for every unclean spirit,
    a haunt for every unclean bird. (18:2)

Pay her back as she herself has paid back others,
    and repay her double for her deeds;
    mix a double portion for her in the cup she mixed.
As she glorified herself and lived in luxury,
    so give her a like measure of torment and mourning.
      (18:6, 7a; cf. Jeremiah 25:15–29)

> Alas! Alas! You great city,
>   you mighty city, Babylon!
> For in a single hour your judgment has come. (18:10b)

Most striking of all, John's vision included a stone cast into the watery depths:

> Then a mighty angel took up a stone like a great millstone and threw it into the sea, saying,
>
>> So will Babylon the great city be thrown down with violence,
>>   and will be found no more. (18:21)

John's vision was as heavy as Jeremiah's prophecy. When Jeremiah caused a stone to be thrown into the Euphrates, he was prophesying about the end of history, when the City of Satan will sink to the bottom of the sea. Jeremiah was among the first to celebrate the victory of Jesus Christ over sin, death, the devil, and all the enemies of God.

Not Forsaken, but Vindicated: Hallelujah!

It is awesome to consider the end of history, the final judgment, and the ultimate defeat of all God's enemies. By awesome I mean frightening, something that inspires fear. What will happen to you on the day of judgment? Where will you stand?

In the middle of his prophecies of destruction, Jeremiah tried to reassure God's people. First he promised that God would keep track of them:

> For Israel and Judah have not been forsaken
>   by their God, the Lord of hosts,
> but the land of the Chaldeans is full of guilt
>   against the Holy One of Israel. (51:5)

Literally Jeremiah said that Israel and Judah would not be widowed. God would remember the vows he made when he entered into a marriage covenant with his people (cf. 2:2). Despite their sin, God would not reject them. He would remain faithful to the very end.

The other promise Jeremiah made was that God's people would live to tell about God's mighty judgments. They would not perish when Babylon fell. They would escape to give this testimony of praise:

> The Lord has brought about our vindication;
>   come, let us declare in Zion
>   the work of the Lord our God. (v. 10)

The promise of vindication meant that sin would be dealt with—not ignored, but paid for. Ultimately God's people were vindicated on the cross when Jesus Christ died for their sins.

This is such good news, Jeremiah promised, that it would be announced all over Zion. Even after Babylon was destroyed, Zion would remain standing. God's people would return to God's city to celebrate God's victory, for the destruction of God's enemies means the salvation of God's people.

The fall of Babylon is good news; indeed, it is the very best news of all! The same will be true at the end of history, when God's people will celebrate their vindication and God's victory for all eternity. In his vision of Heaven, the apostle John heard them:

> After this I heard what seemed to be the loud voice of a great multitude in heaven, crying out,
>
> > "Hallelujah!
> > Salvation and glory and power belong to our God,
> >   for his judgments are true and just;
> > for he has judged the great prostitute [Babylon]
> >   who corrupted the earth with her immorality,
> >   and has avenged on her the blood of his servants."
>
> Once more they cried out,
>
> > "Hallelujah!
> > The smoke from her goes up forever and ever." . . .
>
> Then I heard what seemed to be the voice of a great multitude, like the roar of many waters and like the sound of mighty peals of thunder, crying out,
>
> > "Hallelujah!
> > For the Lord our God
> >   the Almighty reigns." (Revelation 19:1–3, 6)

It is good to remember that the great "Hallelujah" passages from Revelation—including the "Hallelujah Chorus" from Handel's *Messiah*—celebrate the fulfillment of Jeremiah's prophecies about the fall of Babylon. The City of God will triumph over the City of Man and over the City of Satan. Hallelujah and hallelujah! Amen and amen.

65

"How Lonely Sits the City"

JEREMIAH 52:1-34

HOW IS THIS FOR A HAPPY ENDING?

> How lonely sits the city
> that was full of people! . . .
> She weeps bitterly in the night,
> with tears on her cheeks. . . .
> Judah has gone into exile because of affliction
> and hard servitude. . . .
> The enemy has stretched out his hands
> over all her precious things;
> for she has seen the nations
> enter her sanctuary. . . .
> For these things I weep;
> my eyes flow with tears;
> for a comforter is far from me,
> one to revive my spirit.
> (Lamentations 1:1a, 2a, 3a, 10a, 16a; cf. Psalm 74:4–7)

These are the words of a forlorn poet. They come from the book of Lamentations, in which the prophet Jeremiah mourned for the city he loved and lost.

The same events are described rather differently in the book of Jeremiah. That book does not end with the strophes of a poet or the expectations of a prophet, but with the facts of a historian.

Jeremiah's own words ended with the close of chapter 51, as the Bible indicates (51:64b; cf. 1:1). This editorial remark is one of the reasons this commentary has accepted the book of Jeremiah as the prophet's own work. Some scholars have tried to interpret Jeremiah as a hodgepodge of writings from different sources. Yet the Biblical writers were extremely careful to say who wrote what. Even a prophecy as short as Obadiah—which contains only twenty-one verses—has been preserved with the prophet's own copyright.

The same care has been taken to preserve Jeremiah's authorship. The final editor (Baruch?) closed the book on Jeremiah with the story of the fall of Jerusalem, largely borrowed from 2 Kings 24:18—25:30.[1] He wanted to make sure nobody mistook these words—inspired though they were—for Jeremiah's words. So he clearly stated where the poetry ended and the history began.

A Concluding Historical Postscript

The scribe who wrote the epilogue to Jeremiah had a historian's eye for detail. He did not shed any tears for Jerusalem. He simply reported how the city was captured. He did not tell how he felt—he just told what happened. His report was that when Jerusalem fell in the year 586 BC, it was dethroned (52:1–11), demolished (vv. 12–16), desecrated (vv. 17–23), and depopulated (vv. 24–30).[2]

Jerusalem's troubles began with an act of royal rebellion. "Zedekiah was twenty-one years old when he became king, and he reigned eleven years in Jerusalem. His mother's name was Hamutal the daughter of Jeremiah of Libnah. And he did what was evil in the sight of the LORD, according to all that Jehoiakim had done. . . . And Zedekiah rebelled against the king of Babylon" (vv. 1, 2, 3b). Jeremiah repeatedly begged Zedekiah to surrender to the Babylonian yoke, but the king was too fearful to obey God's will (38:17–19).

So the Babylonian army marched on the city to teach Zedekiah a military and spiritual lesson: "And in the ninth year of his reign, in the tenth month, on the tenth day of the month, Nebuchadnezzar king of Babylon came with all his army against Jerusalem, and laid siege to it. And they built siegeworks all around it" (52:4).

This is how war was waged in ancient days. Attackers would surround the city. Then they would build a ramp of earth and stones up to the city wall.

> The ramp would be reinforced with wooden planks (Jer. 6:6), so it could support the siege machines, such as the battering rams, that were used for breaching the defenders' walls or sapping under the walls to gain entrance. The wooden beam of the battering ram, equipped with a metal point, was suspended from the war machine by thick ropes. The body of the battering ram, mobilized by four to six wheels, was enclosed to protect its operators from the defenders' missiles.[3]

The invaders kept pounding on the city gate until it collapsed. In this case the attack lasted for more than a year—"The city was besieged till the eleventh year of King Zedekiah" (52:5).

One can scarcely imagine how desperate things became inside the city toward the very end. Jeremiah described it like this:

> The tongue of the nursing infant sticks
>   to the roof of its mouth for thirst;
> the children beg for food,
>   but no one gives to them. (Lamentations 4:4)

> We must pay for the water we drink;
>   the wood we get must be bought. (Lamentations 5:4)

> We get our bread at the peril of our lives,
>   because of the sword in the wilderness.
> Our skin is hot as an oven
>   with the burning heat of famine. (Lamentations 5:9, 10)

Thus spoke the poet, but the historian was more matter-of-fact: "On the ninth day of the fourth month the famine was so severe in the city that there was no food for the people of the land" (52:6).

Just as the food ran out, the Babylonians breached the walls of the city. "Then a breach was made in the city, and all the men of war fled and went out from the city by night by the way of a gate between the two walls, by the king's garden, and the Chaldeans were around the city" (v. 7a; cf. 39:1–4). With the fate of the city hanging in the balance, the army of Judah lost its nerve and ran for the wilderness.

They managed to slip through enemy lines, but there was no escape, especially for the king:

> And they went in the direction of the Arabah. But the army of the Chaldeans pursued the king and overtook Zedekiah in the plains of Jericho, and all his army was scattered from him. Then they captured the king and brought him up to the king of Babylon at Riblah in the land of Hamath, and he passed sentence on him. The king of Babylon slaughtered the sons of Zedekiah before his eyes, and also slaughtered all the officials of Judah at Riblah. He put out the eyes of Zedekiah, and bound him in chains, and the king of Babylon took him to Babylon, and put him in prison till the day of his death. (vv. 7b–11)

The last thing Zedekiah ever saw was the execution of his sons. If only he had trusted the Lord rather than his own wits!

So much for the king; he was dethroned. What happened to his kingdom? It was demolished:

> In the fifth month, on the tenth day of the month—that was the nineteenth year of King Nebuchadnezzar, king of Babylon—Nebuzaradan the captain of the bodyguard, who served the king of Babylon, entered Jerusalem. And he burned the house of the LORD, and the king's house and all the houses of Jerusalem; every great house he burned down. And all the army of the Chaldeans, who were with the captain of the guard, broke down all the walls around Jerusalem. (vv. 12–14; cf. 39:8)

The excavations along the Kidron Valley confirm that the Babylonians systematically tore down the walls of Jerusalem.[4] This was in fulfillment of Jeremiah's calling "To pluck up and to break down" nations and kingdoms (1:10).

The conquerors also torched Jerusalem's civic buildings. The fire spread, and the whole city burned. Even the beautiful cedars that Solomon brought from Lebanon to build his palace became fuel for the fire. This, too, is in the archaeological record, for Babylonian arrowheads have been found among the ashes of Jeremiah's Jerusalem.[5]

Next the invaders committed the ultimate sacrilege. They desecrated the temple, laying unholy hands on the sacred articles in God's house.

> And the pillars of bronze that were in the house of the LORD, and the stands and the bronze sea that were in the house of the LORD, the Chaldeans broke in pieces, and carried all the bronze to Babylon. And they took away the pots and the shovels and the snuffers and the basins and the dishes for incense and all the vessels of bronze used in the temple service; also the small bowls and the fire pans and the basins and the pots and the lampstands and the dishes for incense and the bowls for drink offerings. What was of gold the captain of the guard took away as gold, and what was of silver, as silver. As for the two pillars, the one sea, the twelve bronze bulls that were under the sea, and the stands, which Solomon the king had made for the house of the LORD, the bronze of all these things was beyond weight. As for the pillars, the height of the one pillar was eighteen cubits, its circumference was twelve cubits, and its thickness was four fingers, and it was hollow. On it was a capital of bronze. The height of the one capital was five cubits. A network and pomegranates, all of bronze, were around the capital. And the second pillar had the same, with pomegranates. There were ninety-six pomegranates on the sides; all the pomegranates were a hundred upon the network all around. (52:17–23; cf. 1 Kings 7:15–37; 2 Kings 25:13–17)

All these things were used in the worship of God for lighting candles, tending the altar, and making various sacrifices.[6] The inventory is precise down to the last pomegranate because it was written by a historian who loved to get his facts straight.

The Babylonians had looted the temple once before—in 597 BC—but then there had been too much to carry. This time, in addition to gold and silver, they recovered more bronze than they could even weigh. The bronze sea alone must have weighed tons. It held 10,000 gallons of water and stood eight feet tall by fifteen feet wide—all solid bronze.[7] No doubt the temple furnishings were a valuable addition to the Babylonian treasury.

The Babylonians, however, were interested in more than sprinkling bowls and bronze pillars. After they dethroned, demolished, and desecrated Jerusalem, they proceeded to depopulate it. They took revenge on the members of the royal cabinet:

> And the captain of the guard took Seraiah the chief priest, and Zephaniah the second priest and the three keepers of the threshold; and from the city he took an officer who had been in command of the men of war, and seven men of the king's council, who were found in the city; and the secretary of the commander of the army, who mustered the people of the land; and sixty men of the people of the land, who were found in the midst of the city. And Nebuzaradan the captain of the guard took them and brought them to the king of Babylon at Riblah. And the king of Babylon struck them down and put them to death at Riblah in the land of Hamath. (vv. 24–27a)

The Babylonians also wanted cheap labor. So the sacking of Jerusalem marked the beginning of the Babylonian Captivity—seventy years of exile for God's people.

> And Nebuzaradan the captain of the guard carried away captive some of the poorest of the people and the rest of the people who were left in the city and the deserters who had deserted to the king of Babylon, together with the rest of the artisans. But Nebuzaradan the captain of the guard left some of the poorest of the land to be vinedressers and plowmen. . . . So Judah was taken into exile out of its land. (vv. 15, 16, 27b; cf. 39:9, 10)

Since he was writing a history, the writer made a careful count of all the Jews who were deported:

> This is the number of the people whom Nebuchadnezzar carried away captive: in the seventh year, 3,023 Judeans; in the eighteenth year of Nebuchadnezzar he carried away captive from Jerusalem 832 persons; in the twenty-third year of Nebuchadnezzar, Nebuzaradan the captain of the guard carried away captive of the Judeans 745 persons; all the persons were 4,600. (vv. 28–30)

Since these totals are smaller than the numbers given in 2 Kings, they probably include only the male adults. In all, a remnant of perhaps twenty thousand Jews were taken into captivity (cf. 2 Kings 24:14, 16).

"Because of the Anger of the Lord"

Those are the facts, but what do they mean? What spiritual lessons can be drawn from the fall of Jerusalem?

The most obvious lesson is that God "will by no means clear the guilty" (Exodus 34:7). He is a righteous judge who brings people to account for their misdeeds.

The key to interpreting Jeremiah 52 (not to mention the rest of the book's calamities) comes near the beginning: "For because of the anger of the LORD it came to the point in Jerusalem and Judah that he cast them out from his presence" (52:3a). There is no reason to wonder why Jerusalem was destroyed. The city lay deserted because of the Lord's anger, and the cause of the Lord's anger was sin, as the Scripture clearly shows.

After all the sins of Judah—idolatry and adultery, ingratitude and injustice—there was only one suitable way for Jeremiah's book to end. Siege, famine, invasion, fire, looting, and captivity were no more than the citizens of Jerusalem deserved for rebelling against Almighty God.

It is significant that God spoke of casting his people from his presence (v. 3). To stand in the presence of God is the greatest blessing any human being can ever know. It is the hope of every believer:

One thing have I asked of the LORD,
 that will I seek after:
that I may dwell in the house of the Lord
 all the days of my life,
to gaze upon the beauty of the LORD
 and to inquire in his temple. (Psalm 27:4)

To stand in the divine presence is a blessing reserved for those who love God.

The presence of God is no place for sinners. The unholy cannot survive the presence of the Holy One. This was David's fear when he sinned against the Lord. "Cast me not away from your presence," he prayed (Psalm 51:11a). Yet this is exactly what happened to God's people: They were banished from God's sight because of their sins. The fall of Jerusalem and the exile in Babylon were expressions of God's holiness.

The God who does not leave the guilty unpunished is not only holy, he is also just. Many times his prophet warned what would happen if his people did not repent of their sins. Jeremiah said enemies would come from the north (6:22, 23; 10:22; 13:20). He prophesied that they would surround Jerusalem (4:16, 17; 6:3–6). He foresaw that the city and the country would lie in ruins (4:20, 27; 9:11; 12:10–12; 19:10–13). He foretold of famine and death in the streets (9:20–22; 14:1–6, 18). He warned Zedekiah that unless he repented he would be handed over to Nebuchadnezzar (34:1–3; 37:17; 38:17, 18). He prophesied that Jerusalem would be burned to the ground (37:10; 38:18, 23), even describing how the palace cedars would be cast into the flames (22:7). He warned that the Babylonians would loot the temple (27:19–22). Finally, Jeremiah told how God's people would be carried into exile (10:17, 18; 13:17; 16:13; 25:11).

Nearly every verse in Jeremiah 52 is a fulfilled prophecy. In fact, reading the chapter is a good way to review the entire book of Jeremiah. The facts speak for themselves: Jeremiah spoke the true words of God. This chapter not only vindicates Jeremiah, it vindicates the holiness and justice of God. It proves that God says what he means and does what he says.

As the citizens of Jerusalem gazed upon the smoldering remains of their city, they should have recalled all Jeremiah's prophecies. They should have recognized that they had brought destruction upon themselves:

> Your ways and your deeds
>   have brought this upon you.
> This is your doom, and it is bitter;
>   it has reached your very heart. (4:18)

> I will punish you according to the fruit of your deeds. (21:14)

The fall of Jerusalem teaches that God is a righteous judge who does not leave the guilty unpunished. Matthew Henry thus ends his commentary on the book by saying:

> No word of God shall fall to the ground, but the event will fully answer the prediction; and the unbelief of man shall not make God's threatenings, any more than his promises, of no effect. The justice and truth of God are here written in bloody characters, for the conviction or the confusion of all those that make a jest of his threatenings. Let them *not be deceived, God is not mocked.*[8]

The Bible contains many warnings about the judgment still to come. It says that the wages of sin is death (Romans 6:23). It promises that a day of judgment is coming, when Jesus Christ will return in power and might. It announces that "it is appointed for man to die once, and after that comes judgment" (Hebrews 9:27). It warns us that all the enemies of God will be banished from his sight forever (Matthew 25:41, 46).

What God says, he will do. As the Apostle Paul told the Thessalonians, "You yourselves are fully aware that the day of the Lord will come like a thief in the night. While people are saying, 'There is peace and security,' then sudden destruction will come upon them as labor pains come upon a pregnant woman, and they will not escape" (1 Thessalonians 5:2, 3).

These and many similar warnings about judgment ought to give us sober thoughts about the life to come. The fear of divine judgment compels us to preach the message of salvation in Jesus Christ. It should compel everyone who hears the message to receive it. If final judgment is a myth, then Christ's death on the cross is an irrelevance. But if final judgment is a certainty, then the work of Christ is a necessity for everyone who wishes to stand in God's presence. There is no other way to be saved, no other way to remain in God's presence, except through the work of Christ on the cross.

As quoted a bit earlier, "It is appointed for man to die once, and after that comes judgment" (Hebrews 9:27). That Scripture goes on to say that if we wish to be saved on the day of judgment, we must put our trust in Jesus Christ. "So Christ, having been offered once to bear the sins of many, will appear a second time, not to deal with sin but to save those who are eagerly waiting for him" (Hebrews 9:28).

Moving Day

The fall of Jerusalem also pleads with us to remain faithful to the Lord. Jerusalem had every spiritual advantage. It was built to be God's chosen city. It was governed by God's chosen king. It was populated with God's chosen people. Best of all, it was the location for God's chosen temple. Yet all of this was lost to the Babylonians because God's people did not remain faithful to him.

Jeremiah had warned that this could happen. Many years before, God had sent him on a field trip to Shiloh. For several hundred years Shiloh was the place where God made his dwelling on earth. The tabernacle was set up there, with the ark of the Lord inside.

By Jeremiah's day, however, Shiloh had become a ruin because the people had been unfaithful. The Lord said, "Go now to my place that was in Shiloh, where I made my name dwell at first, and see what I did to it because of the evil of my people Israel . . . therefore I will do to the house that is called by my name, and in which you trust, and to the place that I gave to you and to your fathers, as I did to Shiloh" (7:12, 14). By the end of Jeremiah's ministry, Jerusalem had become another one of God's former addresses. Like Shiloh, the temple, which bore God's name, was pillaged by pagans.

The fall of Jerusalem thus pleads with us to remain faithful to the Lord. No tabernacle, no temple, no church holds a permanent lease on God's Spirit. The evangelical church in America has nearly every spiritual advantage the temple in Jerusalem had. Since it is a Christian church, the evangelical church bears the name of Christ. It enjoys the presence of the Holy Spirit in worship. Like Jerusalem, the evangelical church has received a spiritual inheritance from its fathers in the faith.

Yet the day may come when God forecloses on his spiritual loan to the evangelical church. Imagine what moving day would be like—hymnals stacked and boxed for recycling, pews unbolted from the floor and loaded onto a truck, the rest of the ecclesiastical artifacts sold at auction, perhaps destined to become decorations at a theme restaurant.

Or even worse, the church would continue to bear the name of Christ without being filled by his Spirit. Only a small remnant would believe the Bible to be the Word of God written, or defend the sovereignty of God, or maintain the doctrine of justification by grace alone through faith alone.

It is easy to say, "Never, Lord! Not in my church!" But it could happen. The evangelical church could become another spiritual wasteland, the way Jerusalem became another Shiloh. If it could happen to God's own temple, it could happen anywhere.

If these things did happen, we would mourn the passing of evangelicalism the way Jeremiah mourned for Jerusalem, saying, "How deserted lies the church!" But our sorrow would have to include confession of our own sins. For as we lamented the passing of the church, we would be forced to admit that we were part of the problem. The church declined because we declined. We were content with what we had already achieved in the Christian life. We confronted the sins of others without ever confessing our own sins. We knew how to talk about Christ, but we never loved the Lord.

The truth is that the evangelical church is as desperately needy for God's grace as it was the very day it was founded. And we ourselves are as desperately needy for God's grace as we were the moment we first came to Christ. The fall of Jerusalem pleads with us to throw ourselves again and again on the mercy of Christ and to remain faithful to the Lord.

A Hopeful Ending

Is there any hope? Can anything be done to save the people of God?

There is hope. Jeremiah 52 is about the future of God's people as well as their past. As John Bright argues, "In its present context the chapter seems to say: the divine word both has been fulfilled—and will be fulfilled."[9]

For the Jews, there was some hope in the list of items taken from the temple. At first it seemed as if the gods of Babylon had triumphed over the God of Israel. But the historian made careful remembrance of the items that belonged in God's house. He did so because Jeremiah had promised that the temple furnishings would be returned to Jerusalem (27:21, 22).

The inventory was for future reference. When the exile was over and God's people returned to Jerusalem, they knew exactly what to take back with them. Ezra records:

> Cyrus the king also brought out the vessels of the house of the LORD that Nebuchadnezzar had carried away from Jerusalem and placed in the house of his gods. Cyrus king of Persia brought these out in the charge of Mithredath the treasurer, who counted them out to Sheshbazzar the prince of Judah. And this was the number of them: 30 basins of gold, 1,000 basins of silver, 29 censers, 30 bowls of gold, 410 bowls of silver, and 1,000 other vessels; all the vessels of gold and of silver were 5,400. All these did Sheshbazzar bring up, when the exiles were brought up from Babylonia to Jerusalem. (Ezra 1:7–11; cf. 5:14, 15)

Later Ezra weighed out the gold, silver, and other articles that the Babylonians offered the Jews to furnish the temple (8:24–30). Temple worship was restored in Jerusalem, just the way the last chapter in Jeremiah promised.

Then there is another and greater hope—the hope of a king to rule God's city. An ancient Jewish prayer expresses the longing for God to bless his city again: "To Jerusalem thy city return with compassion, O Lord, and dwell therein as thou hast promised. Rebuild thou thy city speedily in our days, O God, a structure everlasting. And the throne of David thy servant speedily establish there. Blessed art thou, O Lord, the builder of Jerusalem. Amen."[10] The only hope for the city that lay deserted was that God would rebuild it and send his servant to rule on David's throne.

The hope of a king clearly is held out in the closing verses of the book of Jeremiah. It would be too much to expect Jeremiah to have a happy ending, but it does have a hopeful ending. The historian who wrote the epilogue included this postscript:

> And in the thirty-seventh year of the exile of Jehoiachin king of Judah, in the twelfth month, on the twenty-fifth day of the month, Evil-merodach king of Babylon, in the year that he began to reign, graciously freed

Jehoiachin king of Judah and brought him out of prison. And he spoke kindly to him and gave him a seat above the seats of the kings who were with him in Babylon. So Jehoiachin put off his prison garments. And every day of his life he dined regularly at the king's table, and for his allowance, a regular allowance was given him by the king, according to his daily needs, until the day of his death, as long as he lived. (vv. 31–34)

This ending is hopeful because it shows that King Jehoiachin was still alive and well, even after nearly four decades in prison. Thirty-seven years after arriving in Babylon, he traded his prison clothes for royal robes. Literally, the king of Babylon "spoke good things with him." He was given a seat at the king's table. In fact, Jehoiachin's name appears on tablets discovered near the Ishtar Gate in Babylon. These documents, which list the names of foreigners who were entitled to eat the king's food, refer to Jehoiachin as "king of the Jews."[11]

This is important because Jehoiachin was David's rightful heir. In his Messianic prophecies, Jeremiah promised that God would put a son of David back on the throne (23:5, 6; 30:8, 9, 21; 33:14–17). The ending of Jeremiah's book showed that the line of David was not extinguished. There was still hope that God would send a king to save his people.

Some scholars doubt whether Jeremiah has a hopeful ending after all. One reason for this is their denial that the Messiah could come from Jehoiachin's line. Their argument is based on the prophecy at the end of Jeremiah 22:

Is this man Coniah [or, Jehoiachin] a despised, broken pot,
    a vessel no one cares for?
Why are he and his children hurled and cast
    into a land that they do not know?
O land, land, land,
    hear the word of the LORD!
Thus says the LORD:
"Write this man down as childless,
    a man who shall not succeed in his days,
for none of his offspring shall succeed
    in sitting on the throne of David
    and ruling again in Judah." (vv. 28–30)

These verses form a Messianic puzzle. If Jehoiachin was considered "childless," how could he have "children"? And if none of his "offspring" would sit on David's throne, why is it that Jesus of Nazareth was a direct descendant of Jehoiachin?

There are two ways of resolving this apparent contradiction. One is to say that the curse on Jehoiachin was temporary. Jeremiah Jehoiachin would not prosper "in his days" (v. 30). This may have left open the possibility that his descendants would rule at some point in the future.

A better answer is that verse 30 was not spoken about Jehoiachin at all, but about Zedekiah. This is the solution offered by J. Carl Laney, who argues that in Jeremiah 22 the experiences of three former kings are used as a warning to Zedekiah. On this reading, the chapter begins and ends with words addressed specifically to King Zedekiah. Laney's explanation is worth quoting in full:

> In the first part of the chapter, God speaks to Zedekiah and warns him concerning the consequences of continued injustice and oppression (vv. 1–9). In the rest of the chapter, Zedekiah is reminded of God's judgment on his predecessors. This is intended to serve as an incentive to obedience and loyalty to Yahweh. Shallum (Jehoahaz) reigned only three months before being carried away to Egypt (vv. 10–12). Jehoiakim died and received a donkey's burial (vv. 13–23). Coniah (Jehoiachin) reigned only three months and then was taken captive to Babylon (vv. 24–28).
>
> The prophecy concludes with application to Zedekiah (vv. 21–22). He is the man who would die childless and have no descendant on the throne of David. This is precisely what happened. With the capture of Jerusalem, Zedekiah's children were slain and the king was blinded and exiled to Babylon (2 Kings 25:6–7). None of Zedekiah's descendants sat on the throne of David.
>
> We conclude that there is no curse on Coniah. The rhetorical question raised in verse 28, "Is this man Coniah a despised, shattered jar?" expects the answer, "no." Although exiled from the land due to disobedience to the covenant, Coniah was preserved in Babylon. He was later released from prison, given a living allowance, and set on a throne in Babylon (2 Kings 25:27–30).[12]

Laney's solution is a good one. It places God's curse where it belongs— on Zedekiah rather than on Jehoiachin.

If there is no curse on Jehoiachin, then the ending of Jeremiah holds the promise of a sequel. It is the final chapter of one story, but only the beginning of the next.

The rest of the story can be found in the New Testament Gospels:

> And after the deportation to Babylon: Jechoniah [that is, Jehoiachin] was the father of Shealtiel, and Shealtiel the father of Zerubbabel, and Zerubbabel the father of Abiud, and Abiud the father of Eliakim, and Eliakim the father of Azor, and Azor the father of Zadok, and Zadok the father of Achim, and Achim the father of Eliud, and Eliud the father of Eleazar, and Eleazar the father of Matthan, and Matthan the father of Jacob, and Jacob

the father of Joseph the husband of Mary, of whom Jesus was born, who is called Christ. (Matthew 1:12–16)

This is the happy ending Jeremiah always hoped for, but never got to write. It is a happy ending for everyone who believes, because this Jesus, who is called Christ, came to save us from our sins.

LAMENTATIONS

66

Five Laments: An Epilogue

LAMENTATIONS 1—5

SHE SITS AMONG THE RUINS, slumped slightly to one side. Her elbow rests on the arm of her throne. Her gaze is turned downward in a resolute frown. Her aspect reveals that she has endured great suffering, a grief too deep for words, perhaps even for tears. Though the crown on her head gives her a regal air, she is despondent.

The queen who answers to this description was carved into stone by William Wetmore Story (1819–1895). Story's sculpture establishes an imposing presence in the galleries of Philadelphia's Pennsylvania Academy of the Fine Arts. The inscription at the base of the woman's throne identifies her as "Jerusalem in Her Desolation."

The queenly city William Story carved into stone is Jerusalem personified, the Jerusalem that barely survived the tragic events described at the end of the book of Jeremiah. She had already experienced all the indignities and indecencies of the Babylonian assault. After a long siege, the city finally fell to Nebuchadnezzar in 587 BC, and her citizens were deported to Babylon. Story's sculpture depicts the aftermath—a city still numb with grief. The crumbled bits of mortar around her suggest a city in ruins. Yet the most significant detail is the tiny serpent slithering near the queen's feet. The serpent stands for sin, showing that Jerusalem's desolation was the result of her disobedience.

Not surprisingly, Story based his work on Lamentations, a forgotten book written in the days following Jerusalem's fall to Babylon. Lamentations is closely related to the events described in the book of Jeremiah. It is not so much a sequel to Jeremiah, however, as it is a response. The book's melancholy, almost plaintive tone is apparent from its very first verse, which laments the triple disaster of childlessness, widowhood, and slavery:

How lonely sits the city
that was full of people!
How like a widow has she become,
she who was great among the nations!
She who was a princess among the provinces
has become a slave. (1:1)

Suffering, A to Z

Strictly speaking, the book of Lamentations is anonymous. The work does not name its author. Nevertheless, Lamentations has long been attributed to the prophet who also wrote Jeremiah, and there are several good reasons for thinking that this tradition may be correct.

Lamentations was written by an eyewitness of the siege and fall of Jerusalem. Its descriptions of those terrible events are fresh and vivid. They bear all the marks of firsthand experience. In all likelihood, Lamentations was written in or near the ruined city itself—if not by Jeremiah himself, then at least by one of his contemporaries.

Two clues about the book's authorship come from other Biblical documents. One comes from the introduction to Lamentations in the Septuagint, the earliest Greek translation of the Hebrew Old Testament. The Septuagint provides this heading for the book: "And it came to pass, after Israel was taken captive and Jerusalem laid waste, that Jeremiah sat weeping and lamented with this lamentation over Jerusalem and said. . . ." The other clue comes from the end of the Chronicles: "Jeremiah also uttered a lament for Josiah; and all the singing men and singing women have spoken of Josiah in their laments to this day. They made these a rule in Israel; behold, they are written in the Laments" (2 Chronicles 35:25). It is probable—if not actually certain—that "The Laments" mentioned in this verse are the very laments that form the book of Lamentations.

Some scholars maintain that there are many similarities between Jeremiah and Lamentations, especially in the vocabulary and tone of the two books. It is perhaps worth noting that a lament is literally a *jeremiad*, a memorial dirge for a ruined society. The prophet Jeremiah had begun to take up a lament long before the Babylonian attack (e.g., Jeremiah 14:17). It would be only natural for the Weeping Prophet to continue shedding tears after his beloved city finally fell.

For all its pathos, Lamentations is not an emotional outburst. The book is actually a collection of elegies, formal poems written for a funeral. The poems were written with deliberate artistry. While some aspects of Hebrew poetry remain a mystery to scholars, it seems that Lamentations has a rhythm all its own. The poetic phrasing used throughout the book is distinctive. Some think the Jews used this special cadence for funerals and other occasions of sorrow.

Each of the five chapters in Lamentations is a complete poem in itself. The book thus consists of five separate laments for a fallen city and a fallen people. What is important to know is that each lament was composed in the form of an alphabetic acrostic. In other words, each chapter (with one exception, as we shall discover) is divided into twenty-two separate sections, one for every letter in the Hebrew alphabet. Each verse, or set of verses, begins with a successive letter of the alphabet. Lamentations thus describes the sufferings of God's people from A to Z, from *aleph* to *taw*.

The elaborate artistry of these five laments communicates something important about their purpose. The lamentations are not simply cries from the heart, although they certainly are that. They are rather an attempt to reflect on the meaning of human suffering. The book of Lamentations is a *theodicy*, an attempt to explain the ways of God to humanity. The writer wants to do something more than vent his feelings. He also seeks to gain perspective on suffering, and to share that perspective with his fellow sufferers. The book of Jeremiah ended with a factual account of the last, desperate days of the Jerusalem Jeremiah knew and loved. The book of Lamentations is an attempt to interpret the meaning of that catastrophe.

Since this catastrophe was shared by an entire society, the identity of the person who wrote the five laments is relatively unimportant. Lamentations is not about the sufferings of an individual. The five poems that make up the book are communal rather than personal laments. This is what distinguishes Lamentations from another Biblical theodicy, the book of Job. Whereas Job deals with the problem of personal suffering, Lamentations deals with the problem of national suffering. There is a further difference as well: Job's sufferings were undeserved, whereas Jerusalem deserved her desolation.

The communal focus of Lamentations makes its message continually relevant for the church and the world. The book of Job helps people make sense of personal losses and tragedies. The book of Lamentations helps people make sense of national disasters like famine, warfare, and genocide. For example, Lamentations is where the Jews turned for help and comfort when their temple was destroyed by the Romans in AD 70. It is also where the American-Jewish composer Leonard Bernstein (1918–1990) turned for the text of the last movement of his first symphony, "Jeremiah," which was composed and performed during the Holocaust of the 1940s. In a world of overwhelming human suffering, Lamentations gives voice to the deepest agonies of grief, with the hope that some comfort may come from crying out to God for mercy.

First Lament: Suffering for Sin

The first lament opens with Jerusalem's response to her sad predicament: "She weeps bitterly in the night, with tears on her cheeks" (1:2a). There was much to be lamented:

> From on high he sent fire;
>   into my bones he made it descend;
> he spread a net for my feet;
>   he turned me back;
> he has left me stunned,
>   faint all the day long.
>
> My transgressions were bound into a yoke;
>   by his hand they were fastened together;
> they were set upon my neck;
>   he caused my strength to fail;
> the Lord gave me into the hands
>   of those whom I cannot withstand.
>
> The LORD rejected
>   all my mighty men in my midst;
> he summoned an assembly against me
>   to crush my young men;
> the Lord has trodden as in a winepress
>   the virgin daughter of Judah. (vv. 13–15)

Jerusalem was devastated. In the words of one commentator, she "mourned by this time less for what she had suffered than for what she had become."[1]

Jerusalem had been betrayed by her allies, especially Egypt:

> Among all her lovers
>   she has none to comfort her;
> all her friends have dealt treacherously with her;
>   they have become her enemies. . . .
>
> When her people fell into the hand of the foe,
>   and there was none to help her,
> her foes gloated over her;
>   they mocked at her downfall. . . .
>
> I called to my lovers,
>   but they deceived me;
> my priests and elders
>   perished in the city,

> while they sought food
>   to revive their strength. (vv. 2b, 7b, 19; cf. Jeremiah 37:7)

Many of her inhabitants had been sent into exile in Babylon:

> Judah has gone into exile because of affliction
>   and hard servitude;
> she dwells now among the nations,
>   but finds no resting place;
> her pursuers have all overtaken her
>   in the midst of her distress. . . .
>
> Her foes have become the head;
>   her enemies prosper . . .
> her children have gone away,
>   captives before the foe. . . .
>
> . . . hear, all you peoples,
>   and see my suffering;
> my young women and my young men
>   have gone into captivity." (vv. 3, 5a, 5c, 18b)

The holy city, the seat of David, had suffered countless losses. Pilgrims no longer thronged to "The festival" (v. 4a). Merchants no longer walked through her gates (v. 4b). The "majesty" had departed from her temple (v. 6a). Her princes were "like deer that find no pasture; they fled without strength before the pursuer" (v. 6b). Her palaces were looted and her Holy of Holies was defiled:

> Jerusalem remembers
>   in the days of her affliction and wandering
> all the precious things
>   that were hers from days of old. . . .
>
> The enemy has stretched out his hands
>   over all her precious things;
> for she has seen the nations
>   enter her sanctuary,
> those whom you forbade
>   to enter your congregation. (vv. 7a, 10)

In the streets, desperate people negotiated for their very lives.

> All her people groan
>   as they search for bread;

they trade their treasures for food
  to revive their strength. (v. 11a; cf. v. 19b)

After suffering all these calamities, the survivors were reduced to bitter and unrelieved anguish:

The roads to Zion mourn,
  for none come to the festival;
all her gates are desolate;
  her priests groan;
her virgins have been afflicted,
  and she herself suffers bitterly. . . .

For these things I weep;
  my eyes flow with tears;
for a comforter is far from me,
  one to revive my spirit;
my children are desolate,
  for the enemy has prevailed. (vv. 4, 16)

The reason for Jerusalem's defeat, and thus for her sorrow, was not hard to find. The prophet Jeremiah had been warning about it for decades. He had seen it all coming—the failed alliances (Jeremiah 2:18, 36, 37; 37:7), the deadly siege (4:16, 17; 6:3–6), the desperate famine (5:17; 8:13; 9:15; 12:10–13; 14:1–6), the fallen temple (7:12–15; 27:16–22), and the forgotten festivals (7:34; 16:1–9; 25:10), followed by a long exile (9:16; 10:18; 13:18, 19; 25:8–11). All this was the result of Judah's sin: "The Lord has afflicted her for the multitude of her transgressions" (Lamentations 1:5b). The word Jeremiah uses for "Transgressions" here suggests outright rebellion. To emphasize the point, he compares Jerusalem "To a debased, slatternly harlot, shamelessly exposing her nakedness and indifferent to the marks of menstrual blood."[2]

Jerusalem sinned grievously;
  therefore she became filthy;
all who honored her despise her,
  for they have seen her nakedness;
she herself groans
  and turns her face away.

Her uncleanness was in her skirts;
  she took no thought of her future;
therefore her fall is terrible;
  she has no comforter. (vv. 8, 9a)

What Jerusalem experienced was just punishment for her sins. When, if ever, would she repent?

Finally the city speaks. Interspersed with the poetic description of her woes are several comments addressed directly to God, not by the prophet Jeremiah, but by the city of Jerusalem. "O Lord, behold my affliction, for the enemy has triumphed!" (v. 9c). "Look, O Lord, and see, for I am despised" (v. 11b). What follows is Jerusalem's complaint about the mistreatment she has received at the hands of her enemies, with an appeal for God to judge them:

> They heard my groaning,
>   yet there is no one to comfort me.
> All my enemies have heard of my trouble;
>   they are glad that you have done it.
> You have brought the day you announced;
>   now let them be as I am.
>
> Let all their evildoing come before you,
>   and deal with them
> as you have dealt with me
>   because of all my transgressions;
> for my groans are many,
>   and my heart is faint. (vv. 21, 22)

Even while the city cries for vengeance, however, she confesses her many sins:

> The Lord is in the right,
>   for I have rebelled against his word. . . .
>
> Look, O Lord, for I am in distress;
>   my stomach churns;
> my heart is wrung within me,
>   because I have been very rebellious.
> In the street the sword bereaves;
> ·   in the house it is like death. (vv. 18a, 20)

The English poet John Donne (1572–1631) summed up Jerusalem's contrition in a rhyming couplet: "But yet the Lord is just, and righteous still, I have rebelled against his holy will."[3]

The book of Lamentations is one long illustration of the eternal principle that "whatever one sows, that will he also reap" (Galatians 6:7b). As Jerusalem discovered, most of sin's wounds are self-inflicted. Rudyard Kipling (1865–1936) made this point in a poem called "Natural Theology." The poem was Kipling's way of wrestling with the question, why does God let bad things happen to good people? In the poem, suffering souls wrestle with the meaning of their afflictions. Each of them asks, "Why have the gods afflicted me?" This was Kipling's answer:

> This was none of the good Lord's pleasure;
> For the Spirit He sets in Man is free;
> But what comes after is measure for measure
> And not a God that afflicteth thee.
> As was the sowing so the reaping
> Is now, and evermore shall be.
> Thou art delivered to thine own keeping.
> Only thyself hath afflicted thee.[4]

There is a major problem with Kipling's theology. Suffering *is* the Lord's pleasure, the result of his providence as well as his justice. Jerusalem suffered what God *decreed* that she should suffer:

> Zion stretches out her hands,
>   but there is none to comfort her;
> the LORD has commanded against Jacob
>   that his neighbors should be his foes;
> Jerusalem has become
>   a filthy thing among them. (Lamentations 1:17)

Yet the point Kipling was trying to make is valid: Measure for measure, the wounds of sin are self-inflicted. In the end, Jerusalem got exactly what she deserved, and she had only herself to blame.

Happily, the message of the Bible is that God has provided a way to escape his wrath. There is a hint of this in Judah's first lament, which includes a verse Christians have long considered descriptive or even prophetic of the sufferings of Christ:

> Is it nothing to you, all you who pass by?
>   Look and see
> if there is any sorrow like my sorrow,
>   which was brought upon me,
> which the LORD inflicted
>   on the day of his fierce anger. (v. 12)

In a work entitled "Crucifixion," the musician John Stainer (1840–1901) put the words of this cry into the mouth of Christ on the cross: "Is it nothing to you, all ye that pass by?"

This verse is considered a foreshadowing of the cross for three reasons.

First, the crucifixion was the most severe of all sufferings, involving both the spiritual pain of the Son's separation from the Father and the physical pain of his long, slow asphyxiation. Was any suffering like his suffering? Furthermore, what Christ endured on the cross was the wrath of God. God brought suffering on the crucified Christ in "The day of his fierce anger." Finally, no one recognized what was being accomplished on the cross—namely, the redemption of lost sinners. The people who passed by considered Christ nothing, pausing only long enough to give him their mockery and abuse.

Like Jerusalem before him, Jesus was not simply despised and rejected—he was also ignored. *The Interpreter's Bible* draws this comparison:

> Years ago there was painted a picture that haunts the memory of those who have seen it. It is a scene in some public place. Christ is at the center, not on a cross, but tied by his hands with a rope to a kind of altar, head bowed, a crown of thorns on it, his body bent low in suffering. Near by is the inscription *Deo Ignoto*—"To the Unknown God." Past him is flowing, on one side and the other, a crowd of people representative of our modern life, men and women in rich dress and poor people in ragged attire; clergymen engaged in heated theological discussion; men reading newspapers, a priest intoning a prayer, a mother and her child—all sorts of people. Only one of them looks at the suffering figure of the Savior, and she but for one shocked glance. Is it nothing to you, all ye that pass by? What a picture of our modern life in its neglect of the Christ![5]

Postmodern life is even more neglectful, of course, scarcely considering the claims of Christ at all. Yet even to those who ignore it, the cross still poses this question: "Is it nothing to you, all you who pass by?"

Those who stop long enough for an answer discover that the cross means everything in the world. It means forgiveness of sin, peace with God, and everlasting life. Thus the Christian lingers at the cross, and sings:

> O glorious King, we bless thee, no longer pass thee by;
> O Jesus, we confess thee, the Son enthroned on high.
> Lord, grant to us remission; life through thy death restore;
> Yea, grant us the fruition of life forevermore.[6]

Second Lament: The Days That Are No More

Jeremiah's second lament recounts many of the same calamities as the first. There is something healthy about this. Healing comes through memory, not forgetfulness, and a vital part of the grieving process is honestly confronting what has been lost. The second lament thus deals with a particular kind of sorrow, the sorrow that comes from remembering the days that are no more.

As he lamented the irrecoverable past, the prophet would have recognized the truth in this line from Alfred, Lord Tennyson (1809–1892): "A sorrow's crown of sorrow is remembering happier things."[7]

Jerusalem seemed to have lost everything. She had lost her glorious temple, and with it a place to meet with God and make sacrifice for sin:

> How the LORD in his anger
>   has set the daughter of Zion under a cloud!
> He has cast down from heaven to earth
>   the splendor of Israel;
> he has not remembered his footstool
>   in the day of his anger. . . .
>
> He has laid waste his booth like a garden,
>   laid in ruins his meeting place;
> the LORD has made Zion forget
>   festival and Sabbath,
> and in his fierce indignation has spurned king and priest.
>
> The LORD has scorned his altar,
>   disowned his sanctuary. (2:1, 6, 7a)

Jerusalem had lost her homes and her ramparts, her palaces and her gates, all pillaged and burned to the ground:

> The LORD has swallowed up without mercy
>   all the habitations of Jacob;
> in his wrath he has broken down
>   the strongholds of the daughter of Judah;
> he has brought down to the ground in dishonor
>   the kingdom and its rulers.
>
> He has cut down in fierce anger
>   all the might of Israel;
> he has withdrawn from them his right hand
>   in the face of the enemy;
> he has burned like a flaming fire in Jacob,
>   consuming all around. . . .
>
> He has swallowed up all its palaces;
>   he has laid in ruins its strongholds,
> and he has multiplied in the daughter of Judah
>   mourning and lamentation. . . .
>
> He has delivered into the hand of the enemy
>   the walls of her palaces;

they raised a clamor in the house of the Lord
    as on the day of festival.

The LORD determined to lay in ruins
    the wall of the daughter of Zion;
he stretched out the measuring line;
    he did not restrain his hand from destroying;
he caused rampart and wall to lament;
    they languished together.

Her gates have sunk into the ground;
    he has ruined and broken her bars. (vv. 2, 3, 5b, 7b–9a)

The city had lost her leaders, both political and spiritual:

Her king and princes are among the nations;
    the law is no more,
and her prophets find
    no vision from the LORD. (v. 9b)

As far as the prophets were concerned, perhaps it was just as well, for they had
ceased to speak for God:

Your prophets have seen for you
    false and deceptive visions;
they have not exposed your iniquity
    to restore your fortunes,
but have seen for you oracles
    that are false and misleading.
        (v. 14; cf. Jeremiah 23:16–22; 27:10, 15)

But the loss of King Jehoiachin was catastrophic, for it seemed to mark
the end of the house of David, and the end of God's promise.

Jerusalem lost her dignity. She was scorned by the nations:

All who pass along the way
    clap their hands at you;
they hiss and wag their heads
    at the daughter of Jerusalem:
"Is this the city that was called
    the perfection of beauty,
    the joy of all the earth?"

All your enemies
    rail against you;

> they hiss, they gnash their teeth,
>   they cry: "We have swallowed her!
> Ah, this is the day we longed for;
>   now we have it; we see it!" (vv. 15, 16)

Worst of all was the effect that the invasion had on the people of the city, especially the women and children. What had happened to them was so shocking that none of the survivors could think of anything to say. All they could do was assume a posture of lamentation:

> The elders of the daughter of Zion
>   sit on the ground in silence;
> they have thrown dust on their heads
>   and put on sackcloth;
> the young women of Jerusalem
>   have bowed their heads to the ground. (v. 10)

The writer, too, was devastated by what he had seen, and joined the mourners:

> My eyes are spent with weeping;
>   my stomach churns;
> my bile is poured out to the ground
>   because of the destruction of the daughter of my people.
>   (v. 11a; cf. Jeremiah 14:17)

What the people of Jerusalem had witnessed was an appalling loss of life, a famine in the city that led to starvation:

> Infants and babies faint
>   in the streets of the city.
>
> They cry to their mothers,
>   "Where is bread and wine?"
> as they faint like a wounded man
>   in the streets of the city,
> as their life is poured out
>   on their mothers' bosom. (vv. 11b, 12)

During the last days of the siege the poet had seen it for himself—children dying "on their mothers' bosom."

What was amazing about these losses was that they were all the Lord's doing. To be sure, they were the result of Judah's sin. But the reality still had to be faced: God had turned against his own people. He had not simply allowed his own city to be defeated—he had helped destroy it. God had used the Babylonians to do the destroying, of course, but he was still the ultimate cause of Jerusalem's affliction. God had hurled down the temple and torn down the battlements. God had burned the city and left its people to die in the streets:

> He has bent his bow like an enemy,
>   with his right hand set like a foe;
> and he has killed all who were delightful in our eyes
>   in the tent of the daughter of Zion;
> he has poured out his fury like fire.
>
> The LORD has become like an enemy;
>   he has swallowed up Israel. (vv. 4, 5a)

In a strange twist on the Old Testament motif of the divine warrior, God was not fighting *for* his people, but *against* them.

If the people had only listened to Jeremiah, they would not have been surprised to find God as their enemy. The prophet had long predicted that Judah would be judged for her sins. When judgment finally came, he said:

> The LORD has done what he purposed;
>   he has carried out his word,
>   which he commanded long ago;
> he has thrown down without pity;
>   he has made the enemy rejoice over you
>   and exalted the might of your foes. (v. 17)

The sufferings of Jerusalem were part of God's decree—not only the eternal decree of his divine will, but also the decree he issued through his prophet Jeremiah.

Since it was in keeping with his decree, the fall of Jerusalem revealed many of the perfections of God. It was an act of divine justice, intended to repay a wayward people for their rebellion. Yet it was also an act of divine love, intended to chasten God's people and thus to turn them away from their sins. Through the sufferings of defeat and exile, God's people finally learned not to place their confidence in kings or temples, but only in God himself.

Extreme hardship often plays a similar role in the life of the Christian. Suffering is one of the benefits of belonging to God by adoption in Jesus Christ. Indeed, it is one of the surest proofs of sonship: "For the Lord disciplines the one he loves, and chastises every son whom he receives" (Hebrews 12:6). Being chastened by suffering draws the believer into closer fellowship with God the Father.

Even when suffering is intended for good, however, it can be hard to accept. The pitiable fall of Jerusalem left the prophet Jeremiah with far more questions than answers.

> What can I say for you, to what compare you,
>   O daughter of Jerusalem?
> What can I liken to you, that I may comfort you,
>   O virgin daughter of Zion?
> For your ruin is vast as the sea;
>   who can heal you? (2:13)

The last of Jeremiah's questions—"Who can heal you?"—echoed a medical complaint he had made long before: "Is there no balm in Gilead?" (Jeremiah 8:22).

There was only one who could possibly answer the prophet's cry for healing, and that was God himself. Even Jeremiah was unsure how the city might be healed. The one thing—the only thing—he could do was pray, begging for God's grace in the midst of God's justice.

First the prophet invited others to join him:

> Their heart cried to the LORD.
>   O wall of the daughter of Zion,
> let tears stream down like a torrent
>   day and night!
> Give yourself no rest,
>   your eyes no respite!
>
> Arise, cry out in the night,
>   at the beginning of the night watches!
> Pour out your heart like water
>   before the presence of the LORD!
> Lift your hands to him
>   for the lives of your children,
> who faint for hunger
>   at the head of every street.
>   (Lamentations 2:18, 19; cf. Jeremiah 9:17–20)

Then Jeremiah turned his suffering into intercession, which is the general movement of the book of Lamentations. One commentator calls the prayer at the end of the second lament "a desperate recounting of utmost woe."[8] It is the prayer of someone suffering a crisis of faith because he has witnessed unspeakable horrors, of someone who has no answers, only questions:

Look, O Lord, and see!
　　With whom have you dealt thus?
Should women eat the fruit of their womb,
　　the children of their tender care?
Should priest and prophet be killed
　　in the sanctuary of the Lord?

In the dust of the streets
　　lie the young and the old;
my young women and my young men
　　have fallen by the sword;
you have killed them in the day of your anger,
　　slaughtering without pity.

You summoned as if to a festival day
　　my terrors on every side,
and on the day of the anger of the Lord
　　no one escaped or survived;
those whom I held and raised
　　my enemy destroyed." (vv. 20–22)

The second lament thus ends with cannibalism and sacrilege, with unburied corpses mounded in the streets—the fearful results of divine wrath. Jeremiah hardly knows how to pray about such things, but at least he can bring them to the Lord's remembrance.

Third Lament: Mercy for the One Who Suffers

Lamentations 3 is longer than Jeremiah's other laments. Like the others, it is an alphabetic acrostic with twenty-two sections, one for each of the twenty-two letters of the Hebrew alphabet. Unlike the others, however, it is a triple acrostic, with three verses for every letter. In the Hebrew Bible, the first three verses all start with *aleph*, the second three verses with *beth*, and so forth. Thus the third lament contains sixty-six verses rather than the twenty-two we have come to expect.

This difference in form is matched by a difference in content, a difference that is apparent from the outset:

I am the man who has seen affliction
　　under the rod of his wrath;
he has driven and brought me
　　into darkness without any light;
surely against me he turns his hand
　　again and again the whole day long. (3:1–3)

The third lament begins with the pronoun "I." It is personal rather than communal. While some think it is intended to come from the mouth of Jerusalem, it is better understood as coming from the mouth of Jeremiah. Lamentations 3 is the prophet's personal response to the sufferings of his people.

Jeremiah's personal lament is a reminder that suffering is always personal. When nations go through times of tragedy and tribulation, the greatest suffering always takes place at the individual level.

Many details in the third lament match the circumstances of Jeremiah's life, providing further evidence that Lamentations was written by the prophet himself. By this moment, late in his career, Jeremiah could rightly say, "He has made my flesh and my skin waste away" (v. 4a). Since he was imprisoned in the king's cistern during part of the siege (see Jeremiah 37:16; 38:1–6), it would also be appropriate for him to say,

> He has besieged and enveloped me
> with bitterness and tribulation;
> he has made me dwell in darkness
> like the dead of long ago.
>
> He has walled me about so that I cannot escape;
> he has made my chains heavy . . .
> he has blocked my ways with blocks of stones;
> he has made my paths crooked. (Lamentations 3:5–7, 9)

Further reminders of Jeremiah's imprisonment come much later in the lament:

> I have been hunted like a bird
> by those who were my enemies without cause;
> they flung me alive into the pit
> and cast stones on me;
> water closed over my head;
> I said, "I am lost." (vv. 52–54)

These verses, especially, sound more like the trials of Jeremiah than the tribulations of Jerusalem.

There are many other points of comparison as well. There were times when Jeremiah was forbidden to intercede for his people (7:16; 11:14; 14:11). So who better to say, "Though I call and cry for help, he shuts out my prayer" (Lamentations 3:8)? And who better than Jeremiah, the pariah, to utter these words: "I have become the laughingstock of all peoples, the object of their taunts all day long" (v. 14; cf. Jeremiah 16:1–9)? Or who better to write, "My soul is bereft of peace; I have forgotten what happiness is" (v. 17) than the man who so often warned against the dangers of prophesying peace when there is no peace (Jeremiah 6:14; 8:11)?

God practically turned into the prophet's personal enemy. God was the predator; Jeremiah was the prey.

> He is a bear lying in wait for me,
>   a lion in hiding;
> he turned aside my steps and tore me to pieces;
>   he has made me desolate. (Lamentations 3:10, 11)

To change the image, God was the archer, and Jeremiah was the target.

> He bent his bow and set me
>   as a target for his arrow.
> He drove into my kidneys
>   the arrows of his quiver. (vv. 12, 13)

God was the hunter who pursued his prophet with deadly skill.

There were times when all these sufferings tempted Jeremiah to become bitter. He had tasted the wormwood and the gall.

> He has filled me with bitterness;
>   he has sated me with wormwood.
> He has made my teeth grind on gravel,
>   and made me cower in ashes. (vv. 15, 16)

Everything he had ever dreamed for had vanished, and he could only lament his loss. "So I say, 'My endurance has perished; so has my hope from the LORD'" (v. 18).

This last exclamation seems to have brought a change to Jeremiah's melancholy mood, which shows the importance of holding on to God in the midst of suffering. For the mere mention of the divine name ("LORD") had a dramatic effect on the prophet's outlook. He could never forget the bitter trials he had faced. Yet before the Weeping Prophet fell into utter despair, he remembered God and his perfections.

> Remember my affliction and my wanderings,
>   the wormwood and the gall!
> My soul continually remembers it
>   and is bowed down within me.
> But this I call to mind,
>   and therefore I have hope:

The steadfast love of the LORD never ceases;
his mercies never come to an end;
they are new every morning;
great is your faithfulness.
"The LORD is my portion," says my soul,
"Therefore I will hope in him." (vv. 19–24)

These verses are reminiscent of the "Confessions" in the book of Jeremiah (e.g., 20:7–18). They are familiar to many Christians because they form the basis for the well-known hymn by Thomas O. Chisholm (1866–1960):

Great is Thy faithfulness, O God my Father!
There is no shadow of turning with Thee;
Thou changest not; Thy compassions, they fail not:
As Thou hast been Thou forever wilt be.

Great is Thy faithfulness! Great is Thy faithfulness!
Morning by morning new mercies I see;
All I have needed Thy hand hath provided—
Great is Thy faithfulness, Lord, unto me.

The story of how Chisholm came to write his great hymn reveals a profound truth about God's faithfulness. Some great hymns are written in response to a dramatic spiritual experience. That is not the case with "Great Is Thy Faithfulness," however. It was not the product of a single experience but of a lifetime of God's faithful care. Not long before his death, Chisholm wrote:

My income has never been large at any time due to impaired health in the earlier years which has followed me on until now. But I must not fail to record here the unfailing faithfulness of a covenant keeping God and that He has given me many wonderful displays of His providing care which have filled me with astonishing gratefulness.[9]

When the text for Chisholm's hymn is placed in its proper Biblical context, the wonder of God's providing care becomes all the more apparent. What Jeremiah wrote were the words of a survivor, of a man who had suffered great evil without abandoning his confidence in God's faithfulness.

Indeed, it was because Jeremiah suffered so greatly that he was able to appreciate the little mercies of daily life. His experience reveals the truth in these stanzas from Robert Browning Hamilton:

I walked a mile with Pleasure;
She chattered all the way,

But left me none the wiser
For all she had to say.

I walked a mile with Sorrow;
And ne'er a word said she;
But, oh, the things I learned from her
When sorrow walked with me.[10]

Jeremiah's sorrows had produced character. Among the many things he learned from his sufferings were important truths about the nature of God. He had learned to praise God for his love, his compassion, and his covenant faithfulness. It is perhaps significant that the word "mercies" (v. 22) is plural. With each new day, the Weeping Prophet had fresh experiences of divine compassion. Even to wake up in the morning was to be reminded of God's constant care.

The God who had covenanted to care for Jeremiah was not a distant deity, a mere abstraction of the human mind. The prophet addressed him personally and directly: "Great is *your* faithfulness" (v. 23). In the process of remembering God's attributes, Jeremiah was drawn back into living fellowship and intimate communion with his faithful God. He did not merely list God's attributes—he praised God for them, so that his theology became his doxology.

Jeremiah was able to learn from his sufferings because he endured them patiently. His testimony is a reminder of the blessings that come through waiting on God:

The LORD is good to those who wait for him,
    to the soul who seeks him.
It is good that one should wait quietly
    for the salvation of the LORD. (vv. 25, 26)

Christians who suffer do more than suffer. They also wait. This is not the passive waiting of stoic endurance. It is rather an active resting in the goodness of God, with the hopeful expectation that someday one's trials will come to an end. There are times when the only thing a sufferer can do is wait for God. But waiting is good because God is worth waiting for. His salvation will come in due course, provided one surrenders to his will and to his timing.

These verses, in which Jeremiah praises God for his faithful mercies and surrenders to his timetable for salvation, form the climax of the book of Lamentations. According to the canons of Hebrew poetry, the most important truths are contained in a work's center. In these verses, which form the heart of

Jeremiah's third lament, the prophet reaches a place of comfort and hope that marks a turning point in his spiritual experience.

In the verses that follow, Jeremiah offers his brief theodicy, a "vindication of divine righteousness in the light of the covenant relationship."[11] His time of waiting brought new insight into the causes and meaning of suffering:

> It is good for a man that he bear
> > the yoke in his youth.
>
> Let him sit alone in silence
> > when it is laid on him;
> let him put his mouth in the dust—
> > there may yet be hope;
> let him give his cheek to the one who strikes,
> > and let him be filled with insults.
>
> For the LORD will not
> > cast off forever,
> but, though he cause grief, he will have compassion
> > according to the abundance of his steadfast love;
> for he does not afflict from his heart
> > or grieve the children of men. (vv. 27–33)

Here Jeremiah speaks of God's unfailing love, a love that makes him reluctant to see his people suffer and that guarantees they will not suffer forever. Yet suffer they must, for God is just:

> To crush underfoot
> > all the prisoners of the earth,
> to deny a man justice
> > in the presence of the Most High,
> to subvert a man in his lawsuit,
> > the LORD does not approve. (vv. 34–36)

Whatever Jerusalem has suffered is not unfair, for God is a God of justice. There is no use, therefore, in complaining to God. Nor is there any use arguing with him about the judgments he, in his providence, has ordained.

> Who has spoken and it came to pass,
> > unless the LORD has commanded it?
> Is it not from the mouth of the Most High
> > that good and bad come?
> Why should a living man complain,
> > a man, about the punishment of his sins? (vv. 37–39)

When suffering is deserved, it ought to produce confession rather than complaint. The sin that caused the suffering in the first place must be repented of and renounced. Thus Jeremiah calls God's people to careful self-examination, followed by heartfelt corporate confession of national sin:

> Let us test and examine our ways,
>   and return to the LORD!
> Let us lift up our hearts and hands
>   to God in heaven:
> "We have transgressed and rebelled,
>   and you have not forgiven.
>
> You have wrapped yourself with anger and pursued us,
>   killing without pity;
> you have wrapped yourself with a cloud
>   so that no prayer can pass through.
> You have made us scum and garbage
>   among the peoples.
>
> All our enemies
>   open their mouths against us;
> panic and pitfall have come upon us,
>   devastation and destruction." (vv. 40–47)

The tone of these verses is not accusatory. Rather, these verses acknowledge that everything Judah has suffered is a direct result of her rebellion.

Jeremiah knew, of course, that mere words are not enough. One of the surest signs of genuine repentance is sorrow for sin. He himself was a man of sorrows, acquainted with grief by the sins of his people:

> My eyes flow with rivers of tears
>   because of the destruction of the daughter of my people.
> My eyes will flow without ceasing,
>   without respite,
> until the LORD from heaven
>   looks down and sees;
> my eyes cause me grief
>   at the fate of all the daughters of my city. (vv. 48–51)

Jeremiah's weeping over sin was to serve as a model for Judah's penitence.

Despite his many sorrows, there was an element of joy in Jeremiah's confession. The prophet was confident that his prayers would be answered and that Judah's sins would be forgiven:

> I called on your name, O Lord,
>   from the depths of the pit;
> you heard my plea, "Do not close
>   your ear to my cry for help!"
> You came near when I called on you;
>   you said, "Do not fear!" (vv. 55–57)

After this reassurance of God's presence, the third lament ends with a cry for vengeance. Perhaps it is Jerusalem's cry for justice against her enemies. Or perhaps it is Jeremiah's cry to be defended from those who plotted against him (see Jeremiah 26:1–15; 38:1–6). The fact that the prayer is offered "from the depths of the pit" (Lamentations 3:55) makes the latter suggestion especially plausible. Either way the plea is the same—that the God who grants mercy to the one who suffers would also carry out his curse against the one who oppresses.

> You have taken up my cause, O Lord;
>   you have redeemed my life.
> You have seen the wrong done to me, O Lord;
>   judge my cause.
> You have seen all their vengeance,
>   all their plots against me.
>
> You have heard their taunts, O Lord,
>   all their plots against me.
> The lips and thoughts of my assailants
>   are against me all the day long.
> Behold their sitting and their rising;
>   I am the object of their taunts.
>
> You will repay them, O Lord,
>   according to the work of their hands.
> You will give them dullness of heart;
>   your curse will be on them.
> You will pursue them in anger and destroy them
>   from under your heavens, O Lord. (vv. 58–66)

This cry for vengeance is another echo from the book of Jeremiah, where the prophet frequently asked God to destroy his enemies (see Jeremiah 11:20; 12:3; 15:15; 17:18; 18:21–23). Having received God's mercy, he committed his cause to God's infinite justice.

Fourth Lament: A Failure of Leadership

The third lament ends with a cry for vengeance; the fourth returns to the situation in Jerusalem. It opens by drawing a memorable comparison:

How the gold has grown dim,
    how the pure gold is changed!
The holy stones lie scattered
    at the head of every street. (4:1)

Although gold does not tarnish, it does lose its shine when it is covered with dust, which is precisely what happened to the golden articles from Jerusalem's temple. They were trampled in the city's dusty streets, for her glory had departed.

Far more precious than gold were the young men of Jerusalem. Yet they, too, were trampled underfoot, like fragments of broken pottery.

The precious sons of Zion,
    worth their weight in fine gold,
how they are regarded as earthen pots,
    the work of a potter's hands! (v. 2)

The connection with Jeremiah's ministry is unmistakable. Many years before, the prophet had gone to the potter's house, purchased a clay jar, and dashed it into a thousand pieces (Jeremiah 19). That was meant to be a sign of impending judgment. And that situation happened exactly the way Jeremiah said it would: God's people were treated like so many shards of broken pottery.

Most of the other events described in the fourth lament have been mentioned earlier in this study. Lamentations 4 contains yet another, even more horrific description of famine in the streets of Jerusalem:

Even jackals offer the breast;
    they nurse their young,
but the daughter of my people has become cruel,
    like the ostriches in the wilderness.

The tongue of the nursing infant sticks
    to the roof of its mouth for thirst;
the children beg for food,
    but no one gives to them.

Those who once feasted on delicacies
    perish in the streets;
those who were brought up in purple
    embrace ash heaps.

For the chastisement of the daughter of my people has been greater
    than the punishment of Sodom,
which was overthrown in a moment,
    and no hands were wrung for her.

Her princes were purer than snow,
  whiter than milk;
their bodies were more ruddy than coral,
  the beauty of their form was like sapphire.

Now their face is blacker than soot;
  they are not recognized in the streets;
their skin has shriveled on their bones;
  it has become as dry as wood.

Happier were the victims of the sword
  than the victims of hunger,
who wasted away, pierced
  by lack of the fruits of the field.

The hands of compassionate women
  have boiled their own children;
they became their food
  during the destruction of the daughter of my people.
    (vv. 3–10; cf. Jeremiah 14:1–6; 19:9; 52:6)

Hunger gnawed away at the bones of Jerusalem's citizens. The living envied the dead as they scavenged for food in the city garbage dump. They became walking skeletons. Indeed, they could hardly be recognized, for their skin was blackened from malnutrition and exposure. Even maternal instinct wasted away, for children not only died in their mothers' arms—they died at their mothers' hands.

Once again the prophet makes it clear that this was all the Lord's doing. God himself had set the city ablaze:

The LORD gave full vent to his wrath;
  he poured out his hot anger,
and he kindled a fire in Zion
  that consumed its foundations. (v. 11)

Jerusalem was suffering at the hands of God's justice. But what had aroused his anger? More than anything else, what had invited divine judgment was the negligence of the city's spiritual leaders:

The kings of the earth did not believe,
  nor any of the inhabitants of the world,
that foe or enemy could enter
  the gates of Jerusalem.

> This was for the sins of her prophets
>   and the iniquities of her priests,
> who shed in the midst of her
>   the blood of the righteous. (vv. 12, 13)

The prophets had sinned, leaving the people to starve for God's Word as well as for food. The temple priests had shed innocent blood. Thus they had to bear the humiliation of God's wrath:

> They wandered, blind, through the streets;
>   they were so defiled with blood
> that no one was able to touch
>   their garments.
>
> "Away! Unclean!" people cried at them.
>   "Away! Away! Do not touch!"
> So they became fugitives and wanderers;
>   people said among the nations,
>   "They shall stay with us no longer."
>
> The LORD himself has scattered them;
>   he will regard them no more;
> no honor was shown to the priests,
>   no favor to the elders. (vv. 14–16)

The king, too, had failed to provide godly leadership. He had established unholy alliances with godless nations like Egypt, and the help he was promised never came:

> Our eyes failed, ever watching
>   vainly for help;
> in our watching we watched
>   for a nation which could not save.
>
> They dogged our steps
>   so that we could not walk in our streets;
> our end drew near; our days were numbered,
>   for our end had come.
>
> Our pursuers were swifter
>   than the eagles in the heavens;
> they chased us on the mountains;
>   they lay in wait for us in the wilderness.
>   (vv. 17–19; cf. Lamentations 1:3, 19; Jeremiah 27:1–7)

In the end, the king himself was betrayed into the hands of his enemies:

> The breath of our nostrils, the LORD's anointed,
>   was captured in their pits,
> of whom we said, "Under his shadow
>   we shall live among the nations." (v. 20)

The people of God thus learned the futility of merely political solutions to spiritual problems.

What is striking about this section of Lamentations is the failure of all three branches of Israel's leadership. Going back at least to the days of Eusebius of Caesarea (c. 260–c. 340), careful students of the Bible have identified three offices in Old Testament Israel—prophet, priest, and king. God gave his people prophets, priests, and kings to lead them both spiritually and politically. Often when one leader failed, another leader was able to get the nation back on course. When King David sinned, for example, the prophet Nathan rebuked him and led him to repentance (2 Samuel 12). Or, to give another example, King Joash repaired the temple when the priests allowed it to deteriorate (2 Kings 12).

One of the reasons Jerusalem fell to the Babylonians was because the prophets, priests, and kings had all forsaken divine guidance. The kings had become cowards and apostates. The prophets—save Jeremiah—no longer spoke for God. And the priests were abusing their sacred office. What Jeremiah lamented, therefore, was an appalling lack of spiritual leadership.

Ultimately, what Jeremiah was looking for was the kind of leadership that can only be found in Jesus Christ. Jesus Christ is the true prophet, the holy priest, and the servant king. Thus viewing the Old Testament in terms of these three offices is a good way to understand his work. The Westminster *Shorter Catechism* provides a helpful description of the prophetic, priestly, and kingly ministries of Christ:

> Q. 23. What offices doth Christ execute as our Redeemer?
> A. 23. Christ, as our Redeemer, executeth the offices of a prophet, of a priest, and of a king, both in his estate of humiliation and exaltation.
>
> Q. 24. How doth Christ execute the office of a prophet?
> A. 24. Christ executeth the office of a prophet, in revealing to us, by his word and Spirit, the will of God for our salvation.
>
> Q. 25. How doth Christ execute the office of a priest?
> A. 25. Christ executeth the office of a priest, in his once offering up of himself a sacrifice to satisfy divine justice, and reconcile us to God; and in making continual intercession for us.

Q. 26. How doth Christ execute the office of a king?
A. 26. Christ executeth the office of a king, in subduing us to himself, in ruling and defending us, and in restraining and conquering all his and our enemies.

At their best, the prophets, priests, and kings of the Old Testament fore-shadowed Christ's coming. At their worst, they showed why his coming was so necessary. As we have seen, Lamentations does not have all the answers to the problem of suffering. One thing it does do, however, is raise some of the kinds of questions God has answered in Jesus Christ. In this case, Lamenta-tions helps to show why Jesus is the true prophet, the holy priest, and the servant king God's people have always needed. Unlike Judah's lying prophets, he always gives God's true Word. Unlike her unholy priests, he has offered perfect atonement for sin, once and for all. And unlike her selfish kings, he bravely defends his people from all their enemies.

Somewhat surprisingly, the fourth lament ends on a hopeful note. Not-withstanding Judah's desperate lack of effective leadership, one of her oldest enemies would be defeated:

Rejoice and be glad, O daughter of Edom,
    you who dwell in the land of Uz;
but to you also the cup shall pass;
    you shall become drunk and strip yourself bare. (4:21)

Because of their treachery against Judah, the Edomites would be forced to drink the wine of God's fury (cf. Jeremiah 25:15–29; 49:7–22).

Mixed in with this cry for vengeance is a promise that Judah's exile will end:

The punishment of your iniquity, O daughter of Zion, is accomplished;
    he will keep you in exile no longer;
but your iniquity, O daughter of Edom, he will punish;
    he will uncover your sins. (Lamentations 4:22)

One day the punishment will be over, and the exile will come to an end. Thus there is hope for Zion, the city of God, which is not so much a place as it is a people—the populace of God's eternal kingdom.

This promise was fulfilled in Israel's history, but only partially. After sev-enty years of exile, God's people were released from captivity and returned to Jerusalem. But God's people still wait for their God to establish his eternal city. While we live in the ruined city of humanity, we wait for the new Jerusalem, the glorious haven described in Bernard of Cluny's famous twelfth-century hymn:

Jerusalem the golden, with milk and honey blest,
Beneath your contemplation sink heart and voice oppressed.
I know not, O I know not, what joys await us there;
What radiancy of glory, what bliss beyond compare.

O sweet and blessed country, the home of God's elect!
O sweet and blessed country that eager hearts expect!
Jesus, in mercy bring us to that dear land of rest;
Who are, with God the Father and Spirit, ever blest.

Fifth Lament: A Prayer for Renewal

The fifth and final poem in Lamentations is not so much a lament as a prayer. It is a prayer of last desperation, for times when everything else has failed to bring suffering to an end.

Perhaps this sense of desperation explains why Lamentations 5 is not an acrostic. The poem is divided into twenty-two verses, but they do not begin with successive letters of the Hebrew alphabet. This has led some scholars to think that the fifth lament is only a rough draft the writer later intended to work into an acrostic. But an acrostic is such an obvious literary structure that it is hard to believe a lament could have slipped into the book without being reworked. More likely, the decision not to arrange the fifth lament in alphabetical order was deliberate, with the intention that the poem's disorderly structure would mirror the chaotic state of the city.

Jeremiah's final lament begins with an appeal for God to recall what his people have suffered:

> Remember, O LORD, what has befallen us;
> look, and see our disgrace! (5:1)

This appeal is followed by a somber recitation of Jerusalem's degradation—occupation, abandonment, bereavement, thirst, poverty, inflation, invasion, famine, dependency, slavery, exposure, rape, humiliation, and exhaustion:

> Our inheritance has been turned over to strangers,
>   our homes to foreigners.
> We have become orphans, fatherless;
>   our mothers are like widows.
> We must pay for the water we drink;
>   the wood we get must be bought.
> Our pursuers are at our necks;
>   we are weary; we are given no rest.
> We have given the hand to Egypt, and to Assyria,
>   to get bread enough.

Our fathers sinned, and are no more;
   and we bear their iniquities.
Slaves rule over us;
   there is none to deliver us from their hand.
We get our bread at the peril of our lives,
   because of the sword in the wilderness.
Our skin is hot as an oven
   with the burning heat of famine.
Women are raped in Zion,
   young women in the towns of Judah.
Princes are hung up by their hands;
   no respect is shown to the elders.
Young men are compelled to grind at the mill,
   and boys stagger under loads of wood. (vv. 2–13)

There is a reminder, too, of the emotional impact that all this suffering has had on the citizens of Jerusalem:

The old men have left the city gate,
   the young men their music.
The joy of our hearts has ceased;
   our dancing has been turned to mourning.
The crown has fallen from our head;
   woe to us, for we have sinned!
For this our heart has become sick,
   for these things our eyes have grown dim,
for Mount Zion which lies desolate;
   jackals prowl over it. (vv. 14–18; cf. Jeremiah 16:1–9)

Jeremiah describes a silent, lonely city. "Woe to us, for we have sinned!" he laments (v. 16b). To translate the verse more accurately, "If only we had never sinned!" His beloved Jerusalem has become a place without music, merriment, or mirth. The sacred temple mount has become a haunt for scavengers.

The fall of Jerusalem did not, however, mean the end of God's kingship. The dominance of Babylon never posed a threat to his sovereign rule. If anything, the destruction of Jerusalem and the deportation of her citizens demonstrated that God still ruled the nations, that he was continuing to work out his purpose in human history. In spite of the sufferings of his people, Jeremiah recognized that God was still in control. He testified, "But you, O Lord, reign forever; your throne endures to all generations" (v. 19).

Even though he knew he was a citizen of a greater and more enduring kingdom, the prophet still had a question. He wondered whether there was still a place in God's plan for the Jewish people. He asked:

Why do you forget us forever,
why do you forsake us for so many days?
Restore us to yourself, O LORD, that we may be restored!
Renew our days as of old—
unless you have utterly rejected us,
and you remain exceedingly angry with us. (vv. 20–22)

In the words of one commentator, "The Lord's stern discipline has awakened within Judah a sense of her own sinfulness, worthlessness, and helplessness. And finally, out of the depths of the bitterness occasioned by divine chastisement, she invokes God's grace and compassion."[12] Lamentations thus ends with a prayer for national restoration and spiritual renewal. Jeremiah understood that renewal is up to God, that it depends on his divine initiative. Regeneration always precedes repentance. Before God's people return, they must first be restored, which only God can do.

Jeremiah knew that God *could* restore Jerusalem, but he wondered if he *would*. His prayer seems doubtful as well as hopeful, raising the unwelcome prospect that Jerusalem is beyond redemption. Has God utterly rejected his people? Is he angry beyond measure? The possibility of being beyond redemption is so alarming that many Jews refuse to end their reading of Lamentations with the book's final verse. To this day, whenever the book is read, it is the custom in many synagogues to repeat verse 21 after verse 22.

That is not how Lamentations was written, however. The book ends the way God intended it to end, with the kind of unresolved anguish we have come to expect from the Weeping Prophet. Yet Lamentations was never intended to have the last word. The questions it raises were ones Jeremiah could not fully answer.

There are many times when Christians find themselves asking the same kinds of questions: Has God rejected me? Can I still be saved? Is there any hope? Will my sufferings ever come to an end? In this troubled world, similar questions often need to be asked about the sufferings of others: Why does God allow persecution and oppression? What purpose does he hope to accomplish through warfare and famine?

Unlike Jeremiah, we can do more than ask such questions. We can trust the answer God has provided through the atoning death of Jesus Christ, who makes this promise: "Blessed are those who mourn, for they shall be comforted" (Matthew 5:4).

Soli Deo Gloria!

Notes

Preface

1. Kathleen Norris, *The Cloister Walk* (New York: Riverhead, 1996), p. 34.
2. Francis Schaeffer, *Death in the City* (Downers Grove, IL: InterVarsity, 1969), p. 70.
3. Philip Graham Ryken, *Courage to Stand: Jeremiah's Battle Plan for Pagan Times* (Wheaton, IL: Crossway, 1998).

Chapter One: A Prophet to the Nations

1. Eugene H. Peterson, *Run with the Horses: The Quest for Life at Its Best* (Downers Grove, IL: InterVarsity, 1983), p. 38.
2. F. B. Meyer, *Jeremiah: Priest and Prophet*, rev. ed. (Fort Washington, PA: Christian Literature Crusade, 1993), p. 17.
3. J. R. R. Tolkien, *The Fellowship of the Ring* (Boston: Houghton Mifflin, 1965), p. 70.
4. R. E. O. White, *The Indomitable Prophet: A Biographical Commentary on Jeremiah* (Grand Rapids, MI: Eerdmans, 1992), pp. 4, 5.

Chapter Two: When the Almond Tree Blossoms

1. Douglas Rawlinson Jones, *Jeremiah,* New Century Bible Commentary (Grand Rapids, MI: Eerdmans, 1992), p. 73.
2. John Calvin, *A Commentary on Jeremiah*, 5 vols., vol. 1 (Edinburgh: Banner of Truth, 1989), p. 64.
3. Jones, *Jeremiah*, p. 79.
4. Moses Maimonides, chap. 37 in *A Guide of the Perplexed*, trans. M. Friedlander, (Mineola, NY: Dover, 1904).
5. Derek Kidner, *The Message of Jeremiah: Against Wind and Tide*, The Bible Speaks Today (Downers Grove, IL: InterVarsity, 1987), p. 28.
6. John Geree, quoted in J. I. Packer, *Among God's Giants* (Eastbourne, UK: Kingsway, 1991), frontispiece.
7. John Bunyan, *The Pilgrim's Progress* (New York: New American Library, 1964), pp. 93, 94.

Chapter Three: God Files for Divorce

1. Sheldon Vanauken, *A Severe Mercy* (London: Hodder and Stoughton, 1977; repr. 1989), p. 29.
2. Thomas Boston, "The Sin of People's Forsaking God and Betaking Themselves to the Creature in His Stead," *The Complete Works of the Late Rev. Thomas Boston*, ed. by Samuel M'Millan, 12 vols., vol. 10 (London, 1853; repr. Wheaton, IL: Richard Owen Roberts, 1980), pp. 145–77 (esp. p. 147).

3. Derek Kidner, *The Message of Jeremiah: Against Wind and Tide,* The Bible Speaks Today (Downers Grove, IL: InterVarsity, 1987), p. 33.

4. Andrew Comiskey, *Pursuing Sexual Wholeness: How Jesus Heals the Homosexual* (Lake Mary, FL: Creation House, 1989), p. 100.

5. R. K. Harrison, *Jeremiah and Lamentations,* Tyndale Old Testament Commentaries (Downers Grove, IL: InterVarsity, 1973), p. 60.

6. K. E. Bailey and W. L. Holladay, "The 'Young Camel' and 'Wild Ass' in Jeremiah 2:23–25," *Vetus Testamentum* 18 (1968), pp. 258, 259.

7. Ibid., p. 259.

8. Raymond Ortlund Jr., *A Passion for God* (Wheaton, IL: Crossway, 1994), p. 205.

9. Ibid., pp. 205, 206.

Chapter Four: The Way Back Home

1. Walker Percy, quoted in *First Things* (May 1993), p. 48.

2. Derek Kidner, *The Message of Jeremiah: Against Wind and Tide*, The Bible Speaks Today (Downers Grove, IL: InterVarsity, 1987), p. 35.

3. Eric Konigsberg, "The Vampires of Delancey Street," *Philadelphia* (March 1996), p. 68.

4. Max Lucado, cited in *Leadership* (Spring 1996), p. 71.

5. John Calvin, *A Commentary on Jeremiah*, 5 vols., vol. 1 (Edinburgh: Banner of Truth, 1989), p. 164.

6. John Shaw, *The Character of a Pastor According to God's Heart* (Ligonier, PA: Soli Deo Gloria, 1992), pp. 12, 13.

7. Cited in Kidner, *The Message of Jeremiah*, p. 37.

Chapter Five: True Repentance

1. Philip Yancey, *Disappointment with God: Three Questions No One Asks Aloud* (Grand Rapids, MI: Zondervan, 1988).

2. Ancient Irish poem, c. 8th century; trans. Mary E. Byrne, 1905; versified by Eleanor H. Hull, 1912.

3. R. K. Harrison, *Jeremiah and Lamentations,* Tyndale Old Testament Commentaries (Downers Grove, IL: InterVarsity, 1973), p. 67.

4. John Calvin, *A Commentary on Jeremiah,* 5 vols., vol. 1 (Edinburgh: Banner of Truth, 1989), p. 192.

5. Francis A. Schaeffer, *Death in the City* (Downers Grove, IL: InterVarsity, 1969), p. 17.

6. T. S. Eliot, "The Hollow Men" (1925), in *The Complete Poems and Plays, 1909–1950* (New York: Harcourt Brace, 1971), p. 59.

7. Merton P. Stromann, *Five Cries of Youth* (New York: Harper & Row, 1974); Merton P. Stromann, *Five Cries of Parents* (San Francisco: Harper & Row, 1985).

8. "Love Song for a Savior," Jars of Clay (Pogostick Music, BMI/Bridge Building Music, 1995).

Chapter Six: Lament for a City

1. R. K. Harrison, *Jeremiah and Lamentations,* Tyndale Old Testament Commentaries (Downers Grove, IL: InterVarsity, 1973), p. 70.

2. Sir George Adam Smith, April 26, 1891, *The Historical Geography of the Holy Land*, quoted in Peter C. Craigie, Page H. Kelley, and Joel F. Drinkard Jr., *Jeremiah 1—25*, Word Biblical Commentary, vol. 26 (Dallas: Word, 1991), p. 76.

3. See especially M. Fishbane, "Jeremiah *IV* 23–26 and Job *III* 3–13," *Vetus Testamentum* 21 (1971), pp. 151–67.

4. Robert Davidson suggests this image in his *Jeremiah*, Daily Study Bible, 2 vols., vol. 1 (Philadelphia: Westminster, 1983), p. 52.

5. Herodotus, *The Histories*, trans. A. de Sélincourt (New York: Penguin, 1972), I.104–106 (pp. 84, 85).

6. John Calvin, *A Commentary on Jeremiah*, 5 vols., vol. 1 (Edinburgh: Banner of Truth, 1989), p. 233.

7. F. B. Meyer, *Jeremiah: Priest and Prophet*, rev. ed. (Fort Washington, PA: Christian Literature Crusade, 1993), p. 36.

8. Ibid., p. 38.

Chapter Seven: A Good Man Is Hard to Find

1. R. K. Harrison, *Jeremiah and Lamentations*, Tyndale Old Testament Commentaries (Downers Grove, IL: InterVarsity, 1973), p. 74.

2. Os Guinness and John Seel, eds., *No God but God: Breaking with the Idols of Our Age* (Chicago: Moody, 1992).

3. *Time*, May 27, 1996, p. 17.

4. William Foxwell Albright, *The Archaeology of Palestine* (New York: Penguin, 1949), pp. 141, 142.

Chapter Eight: What Will You Do in the End?

1. John Guest, *Jeremiah, Lamentations,* The Communicator's Commentary, vol. 17 (Waco, TX: Word, 1988), pp. 67, 68.

2. George Whitefield, "The Method of Grace," in *The Rutherford Journal of Church & Ministry*, 2.2 (Winter 1995), pp. 8–11 (p. 8).

3. Ruth Gledhill, "Sacked priest compares his fate to Jeremiah's," *The Times* (8/1/94), p. 1.

Chapter Nine: At the Crossroads

1. Cited in James Montgomery Boice, *Two Cities, Two Loves: Christian Responsibility in a Crumbling Culture* (Downers Grove, IL: InterVarsity, 1996), p. 74.

2. Oscar Handlin, "The Unmarked Way," *The American Scholar* (Summer 1996), pp. 335–55 (p. 335).

3. Charles Hodge, quoted by A. A. Hodge, *The Life of Charles Hodge* (New York, 1880), p. 521.

4. Johanna McGeary, "The Right Way to Peace?" *Time*, June 10, 1996, p. 30.

5. See, for example, William L. Holladay, *A Commentary on the Book of the Prophet Jeremiah, Chapters 1–25* (Philadelphia: Fortress, 1986), p. 223.

6. John Guest, *Jeremiah, Lamentations,* The Communicator's Commentary, vol. 17 (Waco, TX: Word, 1988), p. 69.

7. Derek Kidner, *The Message of Jeremiah: Against Wind and Tide*, The Bible Speaks Today (Downers Grove, IL: InterVarsity, 1987), p. 47.

Chapter Ten: What the Church Needs Now Is Reformation!

1. Pope Leo X, *Exsurge Domine* (1520), quoted in Roland H. Bainton, *Here I Stand: A Life of Martin Luther* (New York: Abingdon, 1950), p. 147.

2. John Calvin, *A Commentary on Jeremiah*, 5 vols., vol. 4 (Edinburgh: Banner of Truth, 1989), p. 366.

3. Robert Davidson, *Jeremiah, Daily Study Bible*, 2 vols., vol. 1 (Philadelphia: Westminster, 1983), p. 73.

Chapter Eleven: The Family That Worships Together

1. Frederika Bremer, quoted in Avi Kempinski, "Sweden in South Philly: The American Swedish Historical Museum," *Scandinavian Review* (Autumn 1995), pp. 85–89 (p. 87).

2. Peter C. Craigie, Page H. Kelley, and Joel F. Drinkard Jr., *Jeremiah 1—25*, Word Biblical Commentary, vol. 26 (Dallas: Word, 1991), p. 124.

3. Derek Kidner, *The Message of Jeremiah: Against Wind and Tide*, The Bible Speaks Today (Downers Grove, IL: InterVarsity, 1987), p. 50.

4. Os Guinness and John Seel, eds., *No God but God: Breaking with the Idols of Our Age* (Chicago: Moody, 1992), p. 18.

5. *Christianity Today* (April 8, 1996), p. 94.

6. *Christianity Today* (June 20, 1994), p. 23.

7. Naomi Goldenberg, *Changing of the Gods: Feminism and the End of Traditional Religions* (Boston: Beacon, 1979), pp. 4, 25.

8. Oscar Handlin, "The Unmarked Way," *The American Scholar* (Summer 1996), p. 350.

9. *In The Confession of Faith* (Inverness: The Publications Committee of the Free Presbyterian Church of Scotland, 1970), p. 3.

10. Ibid., p. 6.

Chapter Twelve: The Valley of Slaughter

1. Philip J. King, *Jeremiah: An Archaeological Companion* (Louisville: Westminster/John Knox, 1993), p. 139.

2. L. E. Stager and S. R. Wolff, *Biblical Archaeology Review* (October 1, 1984), pp. 31–51. See also A. R. W. Green, *The Role of Human Sacrifice in the Ancient Near East* (Missoula, MT: Scholars, 1975).

3. John Calvin, *A Commentary on Jeremiah*, 5 vols., vol. 1 (Edinburgh: Banner of Truth, 1989), p. 412.

4. Steven Pinker, quoted in *LifeLines* (vol. 6, no. 6), p. 8.

5. R. K. Harrison, *Jeremiah and Lamentations*, Tyndale Old Testament Commentaries (Downers Grove, IL: InterVarsity, 1973), p. 88.

6. Derek Kidner, *The Message of Jeremiah: Against Wind and Tide*, The Bible Speaks Today (Downers Grove, IL: InterVarsity, 1987), p. 52.

7. Walter Brueggemann, *Jeremiah 1–25: To Pluck Up, To Tear Down*, International Theological Commentary (Grand Rapids, MI: Eerdmans, 1988), p. 81.

Chapter Thirteen: Wrongly Dividing the Word of Truth

1. William Bradshaw, quoted in I. D. E. Thomas, *A Puritan Golden Treasury* (Edinburgh: Banner of Truth, 1977), p. 238.

2. George Barna, *What Americans Believe* (Ventura, CA: Regal, 1991), p. 290.

3. Cited in John A. Broadus, *On the Preparation and Delivery of Sermons*, 4th ed. (San Francisco: Harper & Row, 1979), p. 184.

4. R. E. O. White, *The Indomitable Prophet: A Biographical Commentary on Jeremiah* (Grand Rapids, MI: Eerdmans, 1992), p. 77.

5. David F. Wells, *God in the Wasteland* (Grand Rapids, MI: Eerdmans, 1994), p. 88.

6. Ibid., p. 30.

7. *Philadelphia Inquirer* (June 19, 1996), A1, p. 16.

Chapter Fourteen: There Is a Balm in Gilead

1. C. S. Lewis, *A Grief Observed* (New York: Bantam, 1976), pp. 7, 8.

2. Francis A. Schaeffer, *Death in the City* (Downers Grove, IL: InterVarsity, 1969), p. 41.

3. Os Guinness and John Seel, eds., *No God but God: Breaking with the Idols of Our Age* (Chicago: Moody, 1992), p. 18.

4. Derek Kidner, *The Message of Jeremiah: Against Wind and Tide*, The Bible Speaks Today (Downers Grove, IL: InterVarsity, 1987), pp. 54, 55.

Chapter Fifteen: Something to Boast About

1. John Calvin, *A Commentary on Jeremiah*, 5 vols., vol. 1 (Edinburgh: Banner of Truth, 1989), p. 496.

2. Henry Wadsworth Longfellow, *The Reaper and the Flowers*, quoted in Robert Davidson, *Jeremiah*, Daily Study Bible, 2 vols., vol. 1 (Philadelphia: Westminster, 1983), p. 90.

3. Peter C. Craigie, Page H. Kelley, and Joel F. Drinkard Jr., *Jeremiah 1—25*, Word Biblical Commentary, vol. 26 (Dallas: Word, 1991), p. 148.

4. J. A. Thompson, *The Book of Jeremiah*, New International Commentary on the Old Testament (Grand Rapids, MI: Eerdmans, 1980), p. 316.

5. Francis A. Schaeffer, *Death in the City* (Downers Grove, IL: InterVarsity, 1969), p. 71.

6. Thomas Jefferson Hogg, *The Life of Percy Bysshe Shelley* (London, 1858).

7. Calvin, *Jeremiah*, vol. 1, p. 503.

Chapter Sixteen: The Scarecrow in the Melon Patch

1. Derek Kidner, *The Message of Jeremiah: Against Wind and Tide*, The Bible Speaks Today (Downers Grove, IL: InterVarsity, 1987), p. 56.

2. John Calvin, *Institutes of the Christian Religion*, trans. Ford Lewis Battles, ed. John T. McNeill, 2 vols., Library of Christian Classics (Philadelphia: Westminster, 1960), I.11.3.

3. David F. Wells, *God in the Wasteland* (Grand Rapids, MI: Eerdmans, 1994), p. 52.

4. Calvin, *Institutes*, I.11.8.

5. Richard Keyes, "The Idol Factory," in Os Guinness and John Seel, eds., *No God but God: Breaking with the Idols of Our Age* (Chicago: Moody, 1992), pp. 29–48 (p. 38).

6. Ibid., p. 33.

Chapter Seventeen: This Is (Not) Your Life

1. Derek Kidner, *The Message of Jeremiah: Against Wind and Tide*, The Bible Speaks Today (Downers Grove, IL: InterVarsity, 1987), p. 57.

2. Rodney Clapp, *Families at the Crossroads* (Downers Grove, IL: InterVarsity, 1993), p. 24.

3. R. E. O. White, *The Indomitable Prophet: A Biographical Commentary on Jeremiah* (Grand Rapids, MI: Eerdmans, 1992), p. 80.

4. Anthony Flew, *A Dictionary of Philosophy* (New York: St. Martin's, 1979), p. 111.

5. Matthew Henry, *Commentary on the Whole Bible* (New York: Revell, n.d.), 6 vols.

6. Ulrich Zwingli, quoted in W. P. Stephens, *Zwingli: An Introduction to His Thought* (Oxford: Oxford University Press, 1992), p. 48.

7. Ibid.

8. Ibid., p. 46.

Chapter Eighteen: Amen, Lord!

1. F. B. Meyer, *Jeremiah: Priest and Prophet*, rev. ed. (Fort Washington, PA: Christian Literature Crusade, 1993), p. 52.

Chapter Nineteen: How Can You Run with Horses?

1. Geerhardus Vos, "Jeremiah's Plaint and Its Answer," *The Princeton Theological Review*, vol. 26 (1928), pp. 481–95.

2. Derek Kidner, *The Message of Jeremiah: Against Wind and Tide*, The Bible Speaks Today (Downers Grove, IL: InterVarsity, 1987), p. 60.

Chapter Twenty: Paradise Regained

1. Robert Burns, "The Lament," *The Complete Illustrated Poems, Songs and Ballads of Robert Burns* (London: Lomond, 1990), pp. 145–48.

2. Elizabeth Achtemeier, "Preaching the Prophets with Honor," *Leadership* (Fall 1997), p. 58.

3. John Milton, *Paradise Regained*, Book 1, Lines 1–7.

4. Gustav Niebuhr, "Christian Split: Can Nonbelievers Be Saved?" *New York Times* (August 22, 1996), A1.

Chapter Twenty-One: *Corruptio Optimi Pessima*

1. Aristotle, *Nichomachean Ethics*, VIII.10.

2. R. E. O. White, *The Indomitable Prophet: A Biographical Commentary on Jeremiah* (Grand Rapids, MI: Eerdmans, 1992), p. 58.

3. John Calvin, *A Commentary on Jeremiah*, 5 vols., vol. 2 (Edinburgh: Banner of Truth, 1989), p. 170.

4. Edmund Spenser, *The Faerie Queene*, eds. Robert Kellogg and Oliver Steele (Indianapolis: Bobbs-Merrill, 1965), I.viii.46, 49.

Chapter Twenty-Two: For God's Sake, Do Something!

1. Alan Paton, *Cry, the Beloved Country* (New York: Macmillan, 1987), p. 229.

2. C. S. Lewis, *A Grief Observed* (New York: Bantam, 1976), p. 8.

3. D. P. Walker, *The Decline of Hell: Seventeenth-Century Discussions of Eternal Torment* (London: Routledge & Kegan Paul, 1994).

4. John Blanchard, *Whatever Happened to Hell?* (Durham: Evangelical Press, 1993; Wheaton, IL: Crossway, 1995).

5. John Calvin, *A Commentary on Jeremiah*, 5 vols., vol. 2 (Edinburgh: Banner of Truth, 1989), p. 243.

6. F. B. Meyer, *Elijah* (Fort Washington, PA: Christian Literature Crusade, 1992), p. 87.

Chapter Twenty-Three: When God Lets You Down

1. Robert Davidson, *Jeremiah*, Daily Study Bible, 2 vols., vol. 1 (Philadelphia: Westminster, 1983), p. 123.

Chapter Twenty-Four: Jeremiah, the Pariah

1. John Guest, *Jeremiah, Lamentations*, The Communicator's Commentary, vol. 17 (Waco, TX: Word, 1988), p. 131.

2. Robert Davidson, *Jeremiah*, Daily Study Bible, 2 vols., vol. 1 (Philadelphia: Westminster, 1983), p. 132.

3. Peter C. Craigie, Page H. Kelley, and Joel F. Drinkard Jr., *Jeremiah 1—25*, Word Biblical Commentary, vol. 26 (Dallas: Word, 1991), p. 216.

4. Walter Brueggemann, *Jeremiah 1—25: To Pluck Up, To Tear Down*, International Theological Commentary (Grand Rapids, MI: Eerdmans, 1988), p. 146.

5. Derek Kidner, *The Message of Jeremiah: Against Wind and Tide,* The Bible Speaks Today (Downers Grove, IL: InterVarsity, 1987), p. 70.

6. Philip J. King, *Jeremiah: An Archaeological Companion* (Louisville: Westminster/John Knox, 1993), p. 100.

7. R. K. Harrison, *Jeremiah and Lamentations*, Tyndale Old Testament Commentaries (Downers Grove, IL: InterVarsity, 1973), p. 105.

8. Robert Hotchkins, quoted in Leonard Sweet, *Faith Quakes* (Nashville: Abingdon, 1994), p. 46.

Chapter Twenty-Five: Like a Tree

1. Ralph Waldo Emerson, "Self-Reliance," in *Essays and English Traits*, The Harvard Classics, vol. 5 (New York: Collier, 1909), pp. 63–88.

2. R. K. Harrison, *Jeremiah and Lamentations*, Tyndale Old Testament Commentaries (Downers Grove, IL: InterVarsity, 1973), p. 106.

3. Derek Kidner, *The Message of Jeremiah: Against Wind and Tide*, The Bible Speaks Today (Downers Grove, IL: InterVarsity, 1987), p. 72.

4. Thomas Boston, *Human Nature in Its Fourfold State* (Edinburgh: Banner of Truth, 1989), p. 299.

5. Edgar Allan Poe, *A Collection of Stories* (New York: Tom Doherty, 1988), pp. 156–61.

6. Jean Bethke Elshtain, "The Newtape File II," *First Things* (April 1993), p. 12.

7. C. S. Lewis, *The Screwtape Letters* (New York: Macmillan, 1971), p. 5.

8. Walter Brueggemann, *Jeremiah 1—25: To Pluck Up, To Tear Down*, International Theological Commentary (Grand Rapids, MI: Eerdmans, 1988), p. 153.

Chapter Twenty-Six: Keep the Lord's Day Holy

1. John Calvin, *A Commentary on Jeremiah*, 5 vols., vol. 2 (Edinburgh: Banner of Truth, 1989), p. 379.

2. Volkman Fritz, *The City in Ancient Israel* (Sheffield, UK: Sheffield Academic Press, 1995), pp. 178, 179.

3. Ibid., p. 179.

4. Robert Davidson, *Jeremiah*, Daily Study Bible, 2 vols., vol. 1 (Philadelphia: Westminster, 1983), pp. 146, 147.

5. James Montgomery Boice, *The Gospel of John: An Expositional Commentary*, 2 vols., vol. 2 (Grand Rapids, MI: Zondervan, 1976), pp. 43–46.

6. Donald Grey Barnhouse, "The Christian and the Sabbath," *Commentary on Romans 14:5, 6* (Philadelphia: Bible Study Hour, 1958), p. 11.

7. F. F. Bruce, *The Epistle to the Hebrews*, rev. ed., New International Commentary on the New Testament (Grand Rapids, MI: Eerdmans, 1990), p. 110.

Chapter Twenty-Seven: In the Potter's Hands

1. William Shakespeare, *The Tragedy of Hamlet, Prince of Denmark*, ed. William W. Main (New York: Odyssey, 1963), V.1.

2. John Calvin, *A Commentary on Jeremiah*, 5 vols., vol. 2 (Edinburgh: Banner of Truth, 1989), p. 393.

3. J. A. Thompson, *The Book of Jeremiah*, New International Commentary on the Old Testament (Grand Rapids, MI: Eerdmans, 1980), p. 433.

4. Edmund Calamy, "England's Looking-Glasse," in William S. Barker, *Puritan Profiles* (Fearn, Ross-shire, UK: Mentor, 1996), p. 210.

5. Eugene H. Peterson, *Run with the Horses: The Quest for Life at Its Best* (Downers Grove, IL: InterVarsity, 1983), p. 77.

6. F. B. Meyer, *Jeremiah: Priest and Prophet*, rev. ed. (Fort Washington, PA: Christian Literature Crusade, 1993), p. 80.

7. Samuel Macauley Jackson, *Huldreich Zwingli, the Reformer of German Switzerland* (New York: n.p., 1901), p. 148.

Chapter Twenty-Eight: Vessels of Wrath

1. Philip J. King, *Jeremiah: An Archaeological Companion* (Louisville: Westminster/John Knox, 1993), p. 165.

2. Jonathan Edwards, "The Justice of God in the Damnation of Sinners," *The Works of Jonathan Edwards*, vol. 1 (Edinburgh and Carlisle, PA: Banner of Truth, 1976), pp. 668–79.

3. Ibid., p. 678. These arguments are well summarized in James Montgomery Boice, *Romans*, vol. 3 (Grand Rapids, MI: Baker, 1993), pp. 1103–106.

4. Oliver Bowles, *De Evangelico Pastore Tractatus*, vol. II (London, n.p., 1648), p. 77: "*ad aedificationem, non ad destructionem.*"

5. John Bunyan, *The Pilgrim's Progress* (New York: New American Library, 1964), pp. 17–19.

Chapter Twenty-Nine: Dark Night of the Soul

1. Kathleen Norris, *The Cloister Walk* (New York: Riverhead, 1996), p. 31.

2. Ibid., pp. 31–35.

3. Vance Havner, "Resigned or Re-Signed," *Pulpit Helps* (August 1998), p. 12.

4. John Calvin, *A Commentary on Jeremiah*, 5 vols., vol. 3 (Edinburgh: Banner of Truth, 1989), p. 38.

5. Dietrich Bonhoeffer, *Letters and Papers from Prison*, in Robert Davidson, Jeremiah, Daily Study Bible, 2 vols., vol. 1 (Philadelphia: Westminster, 1983), p. 165.

6. Compare Jeremiah 20:16 with Genesis 19:24–28.

7. R. E. O. White, *The Indomitable Prophet: A Biographical Commentary on Jeremiah* (Grand Rapids, MI: Eerdmans, 1992), p. 162.

8. Calvin, *Jeremiah*, vol. 3, p. 44.

9. Derek Kidner, *The Message of Jeremiah: Against Wind and Tide*, The Bible Speaks Today (Downers Grove, IL: InterVarsity, 1987), p. 81.

10. J. G. McConville, *Judgment and Promise: An Interpretation of the Book of Jeremiah* (Leicester, UK: Apollos, 1993), pp. 73, 74.

Chapter Thirty: No King but Christ

1. Josephus, "The Antiquities of the Jews," in *The Works of Josephus*, trans. William Whiston (Peabody, MA: Hendrickson, 1987), X.vi.3 (p. 272).

2. See D. J. Wiseman, *Illustrations from Biblical Archaeology* (Downers Grove, IL: InterVarsity, 1958), p. 73.

3. Derek Kidner, *The Message of Jeremiah: Against Wind and Tide*, The Bible Speaks Today (Downers Grove, IL: InterVarsity, 1987), p. 87.

4. Peter Menzel, *Material World* (San Francisco: Sierra, 1994).

5. Kidner, *The Message of Jeremiah*, p. 87.

6. BBC World Service, February 15, 1983.

7. J. Gresham Machen, *Christianity and Liberalism* (Grand Rapids, MI: Eerdmans, 1946), p. 144.

8. *Christianity Today* (August 12, 1996), 20.

9. William Wells Brown, "Narrative of William W. Brown, a Fugitive Slave," in *The Norton Anthology of African American Literature*, eds. Henry Louis Gates Jr., Nellie Y. McKay, et al. (New York: Norton, 1997), pp. 245–76 (p. 248).

Chapter Thirty-One: Music for the Messiah

1. John Guest, *Jeremiah, Lamentations*, The Communicator's Commentary, vol. 17 (Waco, TX: Word, 1988), p. 170.

2. Barna Research Group, quoted in *The Church Around the World* (December 1996).

3. *The Church Around the World* (December 1996).

Chapter Thirty-Two: I Had a Dream!

1. "Lies," Violent Femmes 3, Gorno Music Publishing, 1988.

2. Derek Kidner, *The Message of Jeremiah: Against Wind and Tide*, The Bible Speaks Today (Downers Grove, IL: InterVarsity, 1987), p. 92.

3. Martin Luther, quoted in Karl Barth, *Church Dogmatics: The Doctrine of the Word of God*, trans. G. T. Thomson (Edinburgh: T & T Clark, 1936), 1/1:101.

4. Kidner, *The Message of Jeremiah*, p. 91.

5. H. Richard Niebuhr, *The Kingdom of God in America* (New York: Harper & Row, 1937), p. 193.

6. F. B. Huey Jr., *Jeremiah, Lamentations*, New American Commentary (Nashville: Broadman, 1993), p. 213.

7. D. A. Carson, *The Gagging of God: Christianity Confronts Pluralism* (Grand Rapids, MI: Zondervan, 1996), pp. 439, 440.

8. Francis A. Schaeffer, *Death in the City* (Downers Grove, IL: InterVarsity, 1969; reprinted in vol. 4, *The Complete Works of Francis A. Schaeffer*, Wheaton, IL: Crossway, 1982).

9. Dick Keyes, address at "The Word and the Image: Ethics in Media," Westminster Theological Seminary, Philadelphia (March 12, 1997).

Chapter Thirty-Three: Two Baskets of Figs

1. C. S. Lewis, *The Great Divorce* (New York: Macmillan, 1946), pp. 72, 73.

2. John Guest, *Jeremiah, Lamentations*, The Communicator's Commentary, vol. 17 (Waco, TX: Word, 1988), p. 176.

3. J. I. Packer, *Knowing God* (Downers Grove, IL: InterVarsity, 1973), p. 29.

4. Charles Haddon Spurgeon, "A New-Year's Benediction," in *War Cry* (January 1, 1994).

5. J. G. McConville, *Judgment and Promise: An Interpretation of the Book of Jeremiah* (Leicester, UK: Apollos, 1993), p. 85.

6. R. K. Harrison, *Jeremiah and Lamentations*, Tyndale Old Testament Commentaries (Downers Grove, IL: InterVarsity, 1973), p. 126.

Chapter Thirty-Four: "Take from My Hand This Cup"

1. George Herbert, "The Agony," *George Herbert and the Seventeenth-Century Religious Poets*, ed. Mario A. Di Cesare (New York: Norton, 1978), p. 14.

2. Mr. Merriton, in Thomas Case, ed., *The Morning Exercise Methodized* (London, n.p., 1660), p. 283.

Chapter Thirty-Five: Delivered from Death

1. This striking fact was noted by Mark A. Noll in "Diamond Devotional," *The Reformed Journal* (July 1989), pp. 6, 7.

2. John Sedgwick, quoted in I.D.E. Thomas, ed., *A Puritan Golden Treasury* (Edinburgh: Banner of Truth, 1977), p. 167.

3. Walter Brueggemann, *To Build, To Plant: A Commentary on Jeremiah 26—52*, International Theological Commentary (Grand Rapids, MI: Eerdmans, 1991), p. 5.

4. Robert Davidson, *Jeremiah*, Daily Study Bible, 2 vols., vol. 2 (Philadelphia: Westminster, 1983), p. 50.

Chapter Thirty-Six: Under the Yoke

1. Philip J. King, *Jeremiah: An Archaeological Companion* (Louisville: Westminster/John Knox, 1993), pp. 159–62.

2. D. J. Wiseman, *The Chronicles of Chaldaean Kings (625–556 b.c.) in the British Museum* (London: Trustees of the British Museum, 1956).

3. Gerald L. Keown, Pamela J. Scalise, Thomas G. Smothers, *Jeremiah 26—52*, Word Biblical Commentary, vol. 27 (Waco, TX: Word, 1995), p. 48.

4. Daniel Fleming, *Marks of a World Christian* (New York: Association Press, 1925).

5. David Bryant, *In the Gap: What It Means to Be a World Christian* (Ventura, CA: Regal, 1984), p. 93.

6. Ibid., p. 98.

7. Ibid., p. 206.

8. Patrick Johnstone, *Operation World: The Day-by-Day Guide to Praying for the World* (Wheaton, IL: ACMC, 1993).

9. James Montgomery Boice, *Daniel: An Expositional Commentary* (Grand Rapids, MI: Zondervan, 1989), pp. 56, 57.

Chapter Thirty-Seven: A Yoke of Iron

1. Francis A. Schaeffer, *Death in the City* (Downers Grove, IL: InterVarsity, 1969), pp. 60, 61.

2. John Calvin, *A Commentary on Jeremiah*, 5 vols., vol. 3 (Edinburgh: Banner of Truth, 1989), pp. 391, 392.

3. Elisabeth Elliot, *Through Gates of Splendor* (New York: Harper, 1957), pp. 235, 236.

4. Derek Kidner, *The Message of Jeremiah: Against Wind and Tide*, The Bible Speaks Today (Downers Grove, IL: InterVarsity, 1987), p. 99.

5. See D. A. Carson's article "On Banishing the Lake of Fire," in *The Gagging of God: Christianity Confronts Pluralism* (Grand Rapids, MI: Zondervan, 1996), pp. 515–36.

6. Lesslie Newbigin, "Confessing Christ in a Multi-Religion Society," *Scottish Bulletin of Evangelical Theology*, 12 (1994), pp. 130, 131.

Chapter Thirty-Eight: Seek the Welfare of the City

1. Robert C. Linthicum, *City of God, City of Satan: A Biblical Theology of the Urban Church* (Grand Rapids, MI: Zondervan, 1991), p. 145.

2. Thomas Jefferson, quoted in Harvie M. Conn, *The American City and the Evangelical Church* (Grand Rapids, MI: Baker, 1994), p. 31.

3. John Todd, *The Sabbath School Teacher*, quoted in ibid., p. 38.

4. Augustine, *The City of God*, ed. Philip Schaff, *Nicene and Post-Nicene Fathers, First Series*, vol. 2 (Peabody, MA: Hendrickson, 1994), XV.1.

5. James M. Boice, *Two Cities, Two Loves: Christian Responsibility in a Crumbling Culture* (Downers Grove, IL: InterVarsity, 1996), p. 35.

6. Pieter Bos, *City Cries*, quoted in Floyd McClung, *Seeing the City with the Eyes of God* (Tarrytown, NY: Revell, 1991), p. 72.

7. Roger S. Greenway and Timothy M. Monsma, *Cities: Mission's New Frontier* (Grand Rapids, MI: Baker, 1989), p. 44.

8. Ronald J. Sider, "The State of Evangelical Social Concern, 1978," *Evangelical Newsletter*, vol. 5, no. 13 (June 30, 1978).

9. John Perkins, *With Justice for All* (Ventura, CA: Regal, 1982), p. 65.

10. John Bright, *Jeremiah*, Anchor Bible (Garden City, NY: Doubleday, 1965), p. 206.

11. Jacques Ellul, *The Meaning of the City* (Grand Rapids, MI: Eerdmans, 1970), p. 181.

12. Clifford J. Green, ed., *Churches, Cities, and Human Community: Urban Ministry in the United States, 1945–1985* (Grand Rapids, MI: Eerdmans, 1996), p. viii.

13. Paul Volz, *Der Prophet Jeremia*, Kommentar Zum Alten Testament, vol. 10 (Leipzig: Deichert, 1928), p. 269.

14. See Linthicum, *City of God, City of Satan*, pp. 149–53.

Chapter Thirty-Nine: The Best-Laid Plans

1. R. K. Harrison, *Jeremiah and Lamentations*, Tyndale Old Testament Commentaries (Downers Grove, IL: InterVarsity, 1973), p. 126. For a helpful discussion of the seventy years, see the excursus in Gerald L. Keown, Pamela J. Scalise, Thomas G. Smothers, *Jeremiah 26—52*, Word Biblical Commentary, vol. 27 (Waco, TX: Word, 1995), pp. 73–75.

2. R. E. O. White, *The Indomitable Prophet: A Biographical Commentary on Jeremiah* (Grand Rapids, MI: Eerdmans, 1992), p. 108.

3. Edward Callan, introduction to Alan Paton, *Cry, the Beloved Country* (New York: Macmillan, 1987), p. xxvii.

4. Theodore Laetsch, *Bible Commentary*, *Jeremiah* (St. Louis: Concordia, 1965), pp. 234, 235.

5. See Robert Davidson, *Jeremiah*, Daily Study Bible, 2 vols., vol. 2 (Philadelphia: Westminster, 1983), pp. 64, 65.

6. Oswald Sanders, *Spiritual Leadership* (Chicago: Moody, 1967), p. 141.

Chapter Forty: "And Ransom Captive Israel"

1. Ernst Wilhelm Hengstenberg, *Christology of the Old Testament, and A Commentary on the Messianic Predictions*, 4 vols., vol. 2 (Grand Rapids, MI: Kregel, 1956), p. 424.

2. R. E. O. White, *The Indomitable Prophet: A Biographical Commentary on Jeremiah* (Grand Rapids, MI: Eerdmans, 1992), pp. 121, 122.

3. John Guest, *Jeremiah, Lamentations*, The Communicator's Commentary, vol. 17 (Waco, TX: Word, 1988), p. 217.

4. Walker Percy, *The Thanatos Syndrome* (New York: Farrar, Straus and Giroux, 1987), p. 123.

5. Derek Kidner, *The Message of Jeremiah: Against Wind and Tide*, The Bible Speaks Today (Downers Grove, IL: InterVarsity, 1987), p. 103.

6. J. A. Thompson, *The Book of Jeremiah*, New International Commentary on the Old Testament (Grand Rapids, MI: Eerdmans, 1980), p. 555.

7. Gerald van Groningen, *Messianic Revelation in the Old Testament* (Grand Rapids, MI: Baker, 1990), p. 712.

8. Walter Brueggemann, *To Build, To Plant: A Commentary on Jeremiah 26—52*, International Theological Commentary (Grand Rapids, MI: Eerdmans, 1991), p. 52.

9. *The Book of Common Prayer* (New York: Church Hymnal Corporation, 1945), p. 6.

10. For example, Brueggemann, *To Build, To Plant*, p. 51.

Chapter Forty-One: Messiah in the City

1. Elsie Houghton, *Christian Hymn-Writers* (Bryntirion, Bridgend, Mid Glamorgan, UK: Evangelical Press of Wales, 1982), p. 227.

2. F. B. Huey Jr., *Jeremiah, Lamentations*, New American Commentary (Nashville: Broadman, 1993), p. 266n.

3. Gerald L. Keown, Pamela J. Scalise, Thomas G. Smothers, *Jeremiah 26—52*, Word Biblical Commentary, vol. 27 (Waco, TX: Word, 1995), p. 105.

4. Ibid., pp. 109, 110.

5. E. Margaret Clarkson, "Our Cities Cry to You" (Wheaton, IL: Hope Music, 1987).

6. Derek Kidner, *The Message of Jeremiah: Against Wind and Tide*, The Bible Speaks Today (Downers Grove, IL: InterVarsity, 1987), p. 105.

7. Geerhardus Vos, "Jeremiah's Plaint and Its Answer," The Princeton Theological Review, vol. 26 (1928), p. 296.

8. Gerald van Groningen, *Messianic Revelation in the Old Testament* (Grand Rapids, MI: Baker, 1990), pp. 713, 714.

Chapter Forty-Two: Rachel, Dry Your Tears

1. Madeleine L'Engle, *The Glorious Impossible* (New York: Simon & Schuster, 1990).

2. Jonathan Kozol, *Rachel and Her Children: Homeless Families in America* (New York: Crown, 1988), p. 71.

3. John Calvin, *A Commentary on Jeremiah*, 5 vols., vol. 4 (Edinburgh: Banner of Truth, 1989), p. 91.

4. Derek Kidner, *The Message of Jeremiah: Against Wind and Tide*, The Bible Speaks Today (Downers Grove, IL: InterVarsity, 1987), p. 109.

5. Matthew Henry, *Commentary on the Whole Bible*, 6 vols., vol. 4 (New York: Fleming Revell, n.d.), n.p.

6. J. A. Thompson, *The Book of Jeremiah*, New International Commentary on the Old Testament (Grand Rapids, MI: Eerdmans, 1980), p. 571.

7. Ibid., p. 575.

8. See Robert Davidson, *Jeremiah*, Daily Study Bible, 2 vols., vol. 2 (Philadelphia: Westminster, 1983), p. 81.

9. Thompson, *The Book of Jeremiah*, pp. 575, 576 lists the main interpretive possibilities.

10. So says Davidson, *Jeremiah*, vol. 2, p. 84.

11. Matthew Henry, *Commentary on the Whole Bible*, 6 vols., vol. 4 (New York: Fleming Revell, n.d.), n.p.

12. Thompson, *The Book of Jeremiah*, p. 575.

Chapter Forty-Three: The New Covenant

1. O. Palmer Robertson, *The Christ of the Covenants* (Phillipsburg, NJ: Presbyterian and Reformed, 1980), p. 4.

2. John Murray, *The Covenant of Grace* (Phillipsburg, NJ: Presbyterian and Reformed, 1953), p. 31.

3. Robert Davidson, *Jeremiah*, Daily Study Bible, 2 vols., vol. 2 (Philadelphia: Westminster, 1983), p. 88.

4. Herman Witsius, *The Economy of the Covenants Between God and Man*, 2 vols. (London, 1773; repr. Escondido, CA; Den Dulk Christian Foundation, 1990), I.1.9.

5. Gerhard Von Rad, *Old Testament Theology*, trans. D.M.G. Stalker, 2 vols., vol. 2 (New York: Harper & Row, 1960), p. 213.

6. J. A. Thompson, *The Book of Jeremiah*, New International Commentary on the Old Testament (Grand Rapids, MI: Eerdmans, 1980), p. 580.

7. Robertson, *The Christ of the Covenants*, p. 281.

8. F. B. Huey Jr., *Jeremiah, Lamentations*, New American Commentary (Nashville: Broadman, 1993), p. 279.

9. R. K. Harrison, *Jeremiah and Lamentations*, Tyndale Old Testament Commentaries (Downers Grove, IL: InterVarsity, 1973), p. 140.

10. John Calvin, *A Commentary on Jeremiah*, 5 vols., vol. 4 (Edinburgh: Banner of Truth, 1989), p. 130.

11. Ibid., p. 126.

12. Robertson, *The Christ of the Covenants*, p. 190.

13. Thomas à Kempis, quoted in *Urban Mission* (June 1997), p. 30.

14. Jonathan Edwards, *The Works of Jonathan Edwards*, 2 vols., vol. 2 (Edinburgh: Banner of Truth, 1974), p. 765.

15. Murray, *The Covenant of Grace*, p. 31.

16. Thompson, *The Book of Jeremiah*, p. 581.

17. Oliver O'Donovan, *The Desire of the Nations: Rediscovering the Roots of Political Theology* (Cambridge, MA: Cambridge University Press, 1996), p. 285.

18. Thomas Boston, *The Complete Works of the Late Rev. Thomas Boston, Ettrick*, ed. Samuel M'Millan, 12 vols., vol. 8 (London, 1853; repr. Wheaton, IL: Richard Owen Roberts, 1980), p. 430.

Chapter Forty-Four: Buyer's Market

1. William L. Ventolo Jr. and Martha R. Williams, *Fundamentals of Real Estate Appraisal*, 6th ed. (Chicago: Dearborn Financial, 1994), p. 59.

2. Walter Brueggemann, *To Build, To Plant: A Commentary on Jeremiah 26—52*, International Theological Commentary (Grand Rapids, MI: Eerdmans, 1991), p. 79.

3. John Calvin, *A Commentary on Jeremiah*, 5 vols., vol. 4 (Edinburgh: Banner of Truth, 1989), p. 160.

4. Titus Livius Pataviensis, *From the Founding of the City*, trans. Aubrey de Sélincourt (Baltimore: Penguin, 1965), XXVI.11 (p. 368).

5. Derek Kidner, *The Message of Jeremiah: Against Wind and Tide*, The Bible Speaks Today (Downers Grove, IL: InterVarsity, 1987), p. 112.

6. Calvin, *A Commentary on Jeremiah*, vol. 4, p. 168.

7. Kidner, *The Message of Jeremiah*, p. 113.

8. In Phillip E. Johnson, *Reason in the Balance: The Case Against Naturalism in Science, Law and Education* (Downers Grove, IL: InterVarsity, 1995), pp. 12, 13.

9. Ibid., pp. 7, 8.

10. John Calvin, *Institutes of the Christian Religion*, ed. John T. McNeill, trans. Ford Lewis Battles, 2 vols., Library of Christian Classics, Vols. 20, 21 (Philadelphia: Westminster, 1960).

11. John Guest, *Jeremiah, Lamentations*, The Communicator's Commentary, vol. 17 (Waco, TX: Word, 1988), p. 234.

Chapter Forty-Five: Is Anything Too Hard for God?

1. Herman Bavinck, *The Doctrine of God*, trans. William Hendriksen (Edinburgh: Banner of Truth, 1977), p. 242.

2. Herbert Schlossberg, *Idols for Destruction* (Wheaton, IL: Crossway, 1990), p. 255.

3. J. G. McConville, *Judgment and Promise: An Interpretation of the Book of Jeremiah* (Leicester, UK: Apollos, 1993), p. 100.

4. Walter Brueggemann, *To Build, To Plant: A Commentary on Jeremiah 26—52*, International Theological Commentary (Grand Rapids, MI: Eerdmans, 1991), p. 87.

5. Gerald L. Keown, Pamela J. Scalise, Thomas G. Smothers, *Jeremiah 26—52*, Word Biblical Commentary, vol. 27 (Waco, TX: Word, 1995), p. 160.

6. John Calvin, *A Commentary on Jeremiah*, 5 vols., vol. 4 (Edinburgh: Banner of Truth, 1989), p. 217.

Chapter Forty-Six: "Pardon for Sin and a Peace That Endureth"

1. J. A. Thompson, *The Book of Jeremiah*, New International Commentary on the Old Testament (Grand Rapids, MI: Eerdmans, 1980), p. 598n.

2. F. B. Huey Jr., *Jeremiah, Lamentations*, New American Commentary (Nashville: Broadman, 1993), p. 298.

3. Gerald L. Keown, Pamela J. Scalise, Thomas G. Smothers, *Jeremiah 26—52*, Word Biblical Commentary, vol. 27 (Waco, TX: Word, 1995), p. 170.

4. William Still, *Toward Spiritual Maturity* (Glasgow: Nicholas Gray, 1986), p. 13.

5. John Calvin, *The Epistles of Paul the Apostle to the Romans and to the Thessalonians*, trans. Ross Mackenzie, eds. David W. Torrance and Thomas F. Torrance, Calvin's Commentaries (Edinburgh: Saint Andrew, 1961), pp. 111, 112.

6. Thomas Boston, *Human Nature in Its Fourfold State* (Edinburgh: Banner of Truth, 1989), p. 144.

7. Robert Davidson, *Jeremiah*, Daily Study Bible, 2 vols., vol. 2 (Philadelphia: Westminster, 1983), p. 100.

Chapter Forty-Seven: While Shepherds Watched Their Flocks

1. Leon Morris, *The Gospel According to St. Luke: An Introduction and Commentary*, Tyndale New Testament Commentaries (Grand Rapids, MI: Eerdmans, 1974), p. 84.

2. Walter L. Liefeld, *Luke*, The Expositor's Bible Commentary (Grand Rapids, MI: Zondervan, 1984), p. 844.

3. Matthew Henry, *Commentary on the Whole Bible*, 5 vols., vol. 4 (New York: Fleming Revell, n.d.), n.p.

4. Ibid.

Chapter Forty-Eight: God Never Fails

1. C. S. Lewis, *Till We Have Faces* (London: Harcourt Brace, 1956), pp. 184ff.

2. Melvin Calvin, *Chemical Evolution* (Oxford: Clarendon, 1969), p. 258.

3. Nancy R. Pearcey and Charles B. Thaxton, *The Soul of Science: Christian Faith and Natural Philosophy* (Wheaton, IL: Crossway, 1994), p. 28.

4. James Gleick, *Chaos: Making a New Science* (New York: Penguin, 1987), p. 5.

Chapter Forty-Nine: The Emancipation Revocation

1. J. A. Thompson, *The Book of Jeremiah*, New International Commentary on the Old Testament (Grand Rapids, MI: Eerdmans, 1980), p. 608.

2. R. E. O. White, *The Indomitable Prophet: A Biographical Commentary on Jeremiah* (Grand Rapids, MI: Eerdmans, 1992), pp. 112, 113 is among those who point out that "Piety and penitence apart, the king's action had prudential advantages. Freed slaves need not be fed, and they could join laborers and soldiers defending the city."

3. Frederick Douglass, quoted in James M. McPherson, *Battle Cry of Freedom* (New York: Ballantine, 1988), p. 558.

4. Booker T. Washington, *Up From Slavery*, in Henry Louis Gates Jr. and Nellie Y. McKay, eds., *The Norton Anthology of African American Literature* (New York: Norton, 1997), pp. 497, 498.

5. White, *The Indomitable Prophet*, p. 113.

6. Flavius Josephus, *Antiquities of the Jews*, 3 vols., vol. 3 (Grand Rapids, MI: Baker, 1984), p. 72.

7. John Calvin, *A Commentary on Jeremiah*, 5 vols., vol. 4 (Edinburgh: Banner of Truth, 1989), p. 286.

8. Walter Brueggemann, *To Build, To Plant: A Commentary on Jeremiah 26—52*, International Theological Commentary (Grand Rapids, MI: Eerdmans, 1991), p. 110.

9. J. Gresham Machen, *Christianity and Liberalism* (Grand Rapids, MI: Eerdmans, 1946), p. 144.

10. Charles Wesley, "Blow Ye the Trumpet, Blow!" (1750).

Chapter Fifty: Promise Keepers

1. R. E. O. White, *The Indomitable Prophet: A Biographical Commentary on Jeremiah* (Grand Rapids, MI: Eerdmans, 1992), p. 91.

2. F. B. Meyer, *Jeremiah: Priest and Prophet*, rev. ed. (Fort Washington, PA: Christian Literature Crusade, 1993), p. 121.

3. A. A. Hodge, *The Confession of Faith* (Edinburgh: Banner of Truth, 1869; repr. 1983), p. 288.

4. Ibid., p. 287.

5. Booker T. Washington, *Up From Slavery*, in Henry Louis Gates Jr. and Nellie Y. McKay, eds., *The Norton Anthology of African American Literature* (New York: Norton, 1997), pp. 495, 496.

6. Robert Davidson, *Jeremiah*, Daily Study Bible, 2 vols., vol. 2 (Philadelphia: Westminster, 1983), pp. 111, 112.

7. Derek Kidner, *The Message of Jeremiah: Against Wind and Tide*, The Bible Speaks Today (Downers Grove, IL: InterVarsity, 1987), p. 119.

Chapter Fifty-One: Book Burning

1. Thomas Watson, *A Body of Divinity*, rev. ed. (London: n.p., 1692; repr. Edinburgh: Banner of Truth, 1965), p. 27.

2. John Guest, *Jeremiah, Lamentations*, The Communicator's Commentary, vol. 17 (Waco, TX: Word, 1988), p. 253.

3. Derek Kidner, *The Message of Jeremiah: Against Wind and Tide*, The Bible Speaks Today (Downers Grove, IL: InterVarsity, 1987), p. 119.

4. *God's Word Today*, P.O. Box 2000, Philadelphia, PA 19103.

5. Small Groups Ministries International, 8776 Driftwood Drive, Riverside, CA 92503.

6. Gemariah is one of the Biblical figures whose existence can be confirmed from extra-Biblical sources. A clay document marker (*bulla*) found near Jerusalem in 1983 reads: "belonging to Gemariah, son of Shaphan the scribe." See Y. Shiloh, "A Group of Hebrew Bullae from the City of David," *Israel Exploration Journal* 36 (1986), pp. 16–38.

7. D. Ussishkin, "King Solomon's Palaces," *Biblical Archaeology* 36 (1973), cited in Philip J. King, *Jeremiah: An Archaeological Companion* (Louisville: Westminster/John Knox, 1993), p. 109.

8. J. I. Packer, sermon on Jeremiah 36, preached at Westminster Theological Seminary, Philadelphia (c. 1990).

9. J. I. Packer, *Truth and Power: The Place of Scripture in the Christian Life* (Wheaton, IL: Harold Shaw, 1996), n.p.

10. *Hall's Chronicle: Containing the History of England* (London, n.p., 1809), pp. 762, 763, quoted in David Daniell, *William Tyndale: A Biography* (New Haven, CT: Yale University Press, 1994), pp. 196, 197.

Chapter Fifty-Two: Benedict Jeremiah?

1. Robert Davidson, *Jeremiah*, Daily Study Bible, 2 vols., vol. 2 (Philadelphia: Westminster, 1983), pp. 8, 9.

2. J. G. McConville, *Judgment and Promise: An Interpretation of the Book of Jeremiah* (Leicester, UK: Apollos, 1993), p. 114.

3. F. B. Meyer, *Jeremiah: Priest and Prophet*, rev. ed. (Fort Washington, PA: Christian Literature Crusade, 1993), p. 160.

4. J. A. Thompson, *The Book of Jeremiah*, New International Commentary on the Old Testament (Grand Rapids, MI: Eerdmans, 1980), p. 632.

5. Ibid., pp. 633, 634.

6. Davidson, *Jeremiah*, vol. 2, p. 122.

7. Francis A. Schaeffer, *Death in the City* (Downers Grove, IL: InterVarsity, 1969), p. 66.

8. Ibid., pp. 66, 67.

9. Ibid., p. 67.

10. Ibid.

11. John Calvin, *A Commentary on Jeremiah*, 5 vols., vol. 4 (Edinburgh: Banner of Truth, 1989), p. 383.

Chapter Fifty-Three: In and Out of the Cistern

1. F. B. Meyer, *Jeremiah: Priest and Prophet*, rev. ed. (Fort Washington, PA: Christian Literature Crusade, 1993), p. 7.

2. John Calvin, *A Commentary on Jeremiah*, 5 vols., vol. 4 (Edinburgh: Banner of Truth, 1989), p. 384.

3. Cited in *Christian American* (March/April 1996).

4. John Guest, *Jeremiah, Lamentations*, The Communicator's Commentary, vol. 17 (Waco, TX: Word, 1988), p. 268.

5. Calvin, *A Commentary on Jeremiah*, vol. 4, p. 393.

6. John Milton, *Paradise Lost* (New York: Holt, Rinehart, and Winston, 1951), Book 5, lines 897–903.

7. John Dominic Crossan takes this view in *The Historical Jesus: The Life of a Mediterranean Jewish Peasant* (San Francisco: Harper San Francisco, 1991). For a rebuttal, see Ben Witherington III, *The Jesus Quest: The Third Search for the Jew of Nazareth* (Downers Grove, IL: InterVarsity, 1995), pp. 58–92.

Chapter Fifty-Four: A Private Audience

1. Douglas Rawlinson Jones, *Jeremiah*, New Century Bible Commentary (Grand Rapids, MI: Eerdmans, 1992), p. 455.

2. Dietrich Bonhoeffer, quoted in *Christianity Today* (August 12, 1996), p. 22.

3. Eugene H. Peterson, *Run with the Horses: The Quest for Life at Its Best* (Downers Grove, IL: InterVarsity, 1983), pp. 163, 164.

4. R. E. O. White, *The Indomitable Prophet: A Biographical Commentary on Jeremiah* (Grand Rapids, MI: Eerdmans, 1992), p. 115.

5. R. K. Harrison, *Jeremiah and Lamentations*, Tyndale Old Testament Commentaries (Downers Grove, IL: InterVarsity, 1973), p. 156.

6. Derek Kidner, *The Message of Jeremiah: Against Wind and Tide*, The Bible Speaks Today (Downers Grove, IL: InterVarsity, 1987), p. 125.

7. B. Duhm, quoted in J. P. Hyatt, "Introduction and Exegesis, Jeremiah," *The Interpreter's Bible*, vol. 5 (Nashville: Abingdon, 1956), pp. 773ff.

8. John Guest, *Jeremiah, Lamentations*, The Communicator's Commentary, vol. 17 (Waco, TX: Word, 1988), p. 272.

9. Robert Davidson, *Jeremiah*, Daily Study Bible, 2 vols., vol. 2 (Philadelphia: Westminster, 1983), p. 127.

Chapter Fifty-Five: Brands from the Burning

1. Flavius Josephus, as paraphrased in John Guest, *Jeremiah, Lamentations*, The Communicator's Commentary, vol. 17 (Waco, TX: Word, 1988), p. 277. See also Flavius Josephus, "The Antiquities of the Jews," in *The Works of Josephus*, trans. William Whiston (Peabody, MA: Hendrickson, 1987), X.8.1–5.

2. J. A. Thompson, *The Book of Jeremiah*, New International Commentary on the Old Testament (Grand Rapids, MI: Eerdmans, 1980), p. 647.

3. John Calvin, *A Commentary on Jeremiah*, 5 vols., vol. 4 (Edinburgh: Banner of Truth, 1989), p. 421.

4. John Blanchard, *Whatever Happened to Hell?* (Durham, UK: Evangelical Press, 1993; repr. Wheaton, IL: Crossway, 1995). See also the chapter "On Banishing the Lake of Fire" in D. A. Carson, *The Gagging of God: Christianity Confronts Pluralism* (Grand Rapids, MI: Zondervan, 1996), pp. 515–36.

5. Walter Brueggemann, *To Build, To Plant: A Commentary on Jeremiah 26—52*, International Theological Commentary (Grand Rapids, MI: Eerdmans, 1991), p. 156.

6. William Shakespeare, *The Tragedy of King Lear*, eds. Tucker Brooke and William Lyon Phelps (New Haven, CT: Yale University Press, 1947), III.7.

7. F. B. Huey Jr., *Jeremiah, Lamentations*, New American Commentary (Nashville: Broadman, 1993), p. 346.

8. Charles Wesley, "The Wesleys' Conversion Hymn," quoted in J. I. Packer, *Knowing God* (Downers Grove, IL: InterVarsity, 1973), p. 189.

9. Thomas Boston, *Human Nature in Its Fourfold State* (Edinburgh: Banner of Truth, 1964), pp. 505, 506.

Chapter Fifty-Six: A Remnant Chosen by Grace

1. See Mark A. Noll, Nathan O. Hatch, and George M. Marsden, *The Search for Christian America* (Wheaton, IL: Crossway, 1983).

2. Gerald L. Keown, Pamela J. Scalise, Thomas G. Smothers, *Jeremiah 26—52*, Word Biblical Commentary, vol. 27 (Waco, TX: Word, 1995), p. 237.

3. F. B. Huey Jr., *Jeremiah, Lamentations*, New American Commentary (Nashville: Broadman, 1993), pp. 340, 341.

4. J. A. Thompson, *The Book of Jeremiah*, New International Commentary on the Old Testament (Grand Rapids, MI: Eerdmans, 1980), p. 653.

5. See Keown, Scalise, and Smothers, *Jeremiah 26—52*, p. 237.

6. Bruce Milne, *Know the Truth* (Leicester, UK: InterVarsity, 1982), p. 88.

7. Robert Deutsch, "Seal of Ba'alis Surfaces," *Biblical Archaeological Review*, vol. 25, no. 2 (March/April 1999), pp. 46–49.

8. John Guest, *Jeremiah, Lamentations*, The Communicator's Commentary, vol. 17 (Waco, TX: Word, 1988), p. 288.

9. Huey, *Jeremiah, Lamentations*, p. 353. See also Zechariah 7:5; 8:19.

10. The cistern has been excavated by C. C. McCown, *Tell en Nasbeh I, Archaeological and Historical Results* (Berkeley: University of California Press, 1947).

11. J. B. Pritchard, "The Water System at Gibeon," *Biblical Archaeology*, vol. 19, no. 4 (1956), pp. 66–75.

Chapter Fifty-Seven: A Fatal Mistake

1. Robert Davidson, *Jeremiah*, Daily Study Bible, 2 vols., vol. 2 (Philadelphia: Westminster, 1983), p. 146.

2. Eugene H. Peterson, *Run with the Horses: The Quest for Life at Its Best* (Downers Grove, IL: InterVarsity, 1983), p. 201.

3. Derek Kidner, *The Message of Jeremiah: Against Wind and Tide*, The Bible Speaks Today (Downers Grove, IL: InterVarsity, 1987), p. 131.

4. John Calvin, *A Commentary on Jeremiah*, 5 vols., vol. 4 (Edinburgh: Banner of Truth, 1989), p. 480.

5. See W. M. F. Petrie, *Tanis II* (1888), pp. 47ff.

6. R. K. Harrison, *Jeremiah and Lamentations*, Tyndale Old Testament Commentaries (Downers Grove, IL: InterVarsity, 1973), p. 165.

7. James B. Pritchard, ed., *Ancient Near Eastern Texts* (Princeton, NJ: Princeton University Press, 1955), p. 308.

8. Kidner, *The Message of Jeremiah*, p. 132.

9. There is nothing in the text to suggest that Jeremiah and Baruch were taken to Egypt against their will, as some scholars suggest. Such coercion is implausible. Why would the remnant court disaster by bringing along the prophet who opposed them?

10. Kidner, *The Message of Jeremiah*, p. 132.

11. Dietrich Bonhoeffer, quoted in *Glimpses* (Worcester, PA: Christian History Institute), no. 63.

Chapter Fifty-Eight: The King or the Queen?

1. F. B. Meyer, *Jeremiah: Priest and Prophet*, rev. ed. (Fort Washington, PA: Christian Literature Crusade, 1993), pp. 189, 190.

2. John Guest, *Jeremiah, Lamentations*, The Communicator's Commentary, vol. 17 (Waco, TX: Word, 1988), pp. 305, 306.

3. J. A. Thompson, *The Book of Jeremiah*, New International Commentary on the Old Testament (Grand Rapids, MI: Eerdmans, 1980), p. 673.

4. Derek Kidner, *The Message of Jeremiah: Against Wind and Tide*, The Bible Speaks Today (Downers Grove, IL: InterVarsity, 1987), p. 134.

5. Philip J. King, *Jeremiah: An Archaeological Companion* (Louisville: Westminster/John Knox, 1993), p. 105; see also Gerald L. Keown, Pamela J. Scalise, Thomas G. Smothers, *Jeremiah 26—52*, Word Biblical Commentary, vol. 27 (Waco, TX: Word, 1995), pp. 266–68.

6. Pope John Paul II, quoted in Paul G. Schrotenboer, *Roman Catholicism: A Contemporary Evangelical Perspective* (Grand Rapids, MI: Baker, 1988), p. 40.

7. *Novena Prayers in Honor of Our Mother of Perpetual Help* (Uniontown, PA: Sisters of St. Basil, 1968), p. 16.

8. Ibid., p. 19.

9. Miriam Starhawk, *Yoga Journal* (May–June 1986), p. 59, cited in Ruth Tucker, *Another Gospel: Alternative Religions and the New Age Movement* (Grand Rapids, MI: Zondervan, 1989), p. 340.

10. Re-Imagining Conference, Minneapolis, 1993; reported in *Good News: A Forum for Scriptural Christianity within the United Methodist Church* (January 1994), p. 13.

11. Naomi R. Goldberg, *Changing of the Gods: Feminism and the End of Traditional Religions* (Boston: Beacon, 1989), p. 89.

12. Donna Steichen, *Ungodly Rage* (San Francisco: Ignatius, 1993).

13. Carol Christ, "Why Women Need the Goddess: Phenomenological, Psychological and Political Reflections," in *Womanspirit Rising: A Feminist Reader in Religion*, eds. Carol Christ and Judith Plaskow (San Francisco: Harper & Row, 1979), p. 277.

14. Carter Heyward, *Touching Our Strength: The Erotic as Power and the Love of God* (San Francisco: HarperCollins, 1989), p. 88, quoted in David F. Wells, *God in the Wasteland* (Grand Rapids, MI: Eerdmans, 1994), p. 52.

15. C. S. Lewis, *The Great Divorce* (New York: Macmillan, 1946), pp. 72, 73.

16. F. B. Huey Jr., *Jeremiah, Lamentations*, New American Commentary (Nashville: Broadman, 1993), p. 370.

17. Herodotus, cited in Thompson, *The Book of Jeremiah*, p. 682.

Chapter Fifty-Nine: Attempt Small Things for God

1. Sigmund Mowinckel, *Prophecy and Tradition* (Oslo: n.p., 1946), p. 61.

2. N. Avigad, *Hebrew Bullae from the Time of Jeremiah* (Jerusalem: Israel Exploration Society, 1986), no. 9.

3. Herschel Shanks, "Fingerprints of Jeremiah's Scribe," *Biblical Archaeology Review*, vol. 22, no. 2 (March/April 1996), pp. 36–38.

4. Walter Brueggemann, *To Build, To Plant: A Commentary on Jeremiah 26—52*, International Theological Commentary (Grand Rapids, MI: Eerdmans, 1991), p. 207.

5. William Still, *Dying to Live* (Fearn, Ross-shire, UK: Christian Focus, 1991), p. 136.

6. Dietrich Bonhoeffer, *"Widerstand und Ergebung*, quoted in F. B. Huey Jr., *Jeremiah, Lamentations*, New American Commentary (Nashville: Broadman, 1993), p. 372.

7. Gerald L. Keown, Pamela J. Scalise, Thomas G. Smothers, *Jeremiah 26—52*, Word Biblical Commentary, vol. 27 (Waco, TX: Word, 1995), p. 273.

Chapter Sixty: God of All Nations

1. Charles Haddon Spurgeon, *The Treasury of David: Psalms 1—26* (Grand Rapids, MI: Zondervan, 1968), p. 10.

2. Gerald L. Keown, Pamela J. Scalise, Thomas G. Smothers, *Jeremiah 26—52*, Word Biblical Commentary, vol. 27 (Waco, TX: Word, 1995), p. 275.

3. Note, however, that the Septuagint version of the Hebrew Bible places these oracles after 25:13.

4. Eugene H. Peterson, *Run with the Horses: The Quest for Life at Its Best* (Downers Grove, IL: InterVarsity, 1983), p. 185.

5. R. K. Harrison, *Jeremiah and Lamentations*, Tyndale Old Testament Commentaries (Downers Grove, IL: InterVarsity, 1973), p. 171.

6. Peterson, *Run with the Horses*, p. 182.

7. Derek Kidner, *The Message of Jeremiah: Against Wind and Tide*, The Bible Speaks Today (Downers Grove, IL: InterVarsity, 1987), p. 138.

8. Harrison, *Jeremiah and Lamentations*, p. 170.

9. Walter Brueggemann, *To Build, To Plant: A Commentary on Jeremiah 26—52*, International Theological Commentary (Grand Rapids, MI: Eerdmans, 1991), p. 224.

10. J. A. Thompson, *The Book of Jeremiah*, New International Commentary on the Old Testament (Grand Rapids, MI: Eerdmans, 1980), p. 696.

11. *Chronicles of the Chaldean Kings*, quoted in Douglas Rawlinson Jones, *Jeremiah*, New Century Bible Commentary (Grand Rapids, MI: Eerdmans, 1992), p. 491.

12. Kidner, *The Message of Jeremiah*, p. 141.

13. Brueggemann, *To Build, To Plant*, p. 235.

14. John Piper, *Let the Nations be Glad!: The Supremacy of God in Missions* (Grand Rapids, MI: Baker, 1993), p. 204.

15. D. T. Niles, *Upon the Earth* (New York: McGraw Hill, 1962), p. 250.

16. William Carey, *An Enquiry*, quoted in Ruth and Vishal Mangalwadi, *William Carey: A Tribute by an Indian Woman* (New Delhi: Nivedit Good, 1993), p. 73.

Chapter Sixty-One: The Pride of Life

1. Eugene H. Peterson, *Run with the Horses: The Quest for Life at Its Best* (Downers Grove, IL: InterVarsity, 1983), p. 188.

2. For more information about Moabite place names, see Gerald L. Keown, Pamela J. Scalise, Thomas G. Smothers, *Jeremiah 26—52*, Word Biblical Commentary, vol. 27 (Waco, TX: Word, 1995), pp. 310–19.

3. Flavius Josephus, "The Antiquities of the Jews," in *The Works of Josephus*, trans. William Whiston (Peabody, MA: Hendrickson, 1987), 10.9.7.

4. Samuel Fallows, *The Popular and Critical Bible Encyclopaedia and Scriptural Dictionary*, 3 vols., vol. 2 (Chicago: Howard-Severance, 1914), p. 1173.

5. Martin Luther, quoted in Bernard M. G. Reardon, *Religious Thought in the Reformation* (London: Longman, 1981), p. 51.

6. W. A. Irwin, "An Ancient Biblical Text," *American Journal of Semitic Languages and Literature* (1931), p. 184.

7. Keown, Scalise, and Smothers, *Jeremiah 26—52*, p. 315.

8. R. E. O. White, *The Indomitable Prophet: A Biographical Commentary on Jeremiah* (Grand Rapids, MI: Eerdmans, 1992), p. 84.

9. Howard Taylor, *Hudson Taylor in the Early Years* (CIM, 1911).

10. David Brainerd, quoted by Roger Carswell, "Doing the Work of an Evangelist," Sandy Cove Bible Conference (August, 15, 1996).

11. R. K. Harrison, *Jeremiah and Lamentations*, Tyndale Old Testament Commentaries (Downers Grove, IL: InterVarsity, 1973), p. 178.

12. Bruce A. McDowell, *Muslims and Christians at the Table: Promoting Biblical Understanding Among North American Muslims* (Phillipsburg, NJ: Presbyterian & Reformed, 1999), p. 26.

Chapter Sixty-Two: Most High over All the Earth

1. R. K. Harrison, *Jeremiah and Lamentations*, Tyndale Old Testament Commentaries (Downers Grove, IL: InterVarsity, 1973), p. 182.

2. F. B. Huey Jr., *Jeremiah, Lamentations*, New American Commentary (Nashville: Broadman, 1993), p. 406.

3. Ibid., p. 407.

4. See W. Rudolph, *Jeremiah*, Handbuch zum Alten Testament, pp. 249, 255.

5. Douglas Rawlinson Jones, *Jeremiah*, New Century Bible Commentary (Grand Rapids, MI: Eerdmans, 1992), p. 520.

6. Don M. McCurry, ed., *Sharing the Gospel with Iranians* (Altadena, CA: Samuel Zwemer Institute, 1982), p. 47.

7. Derek Kidner, *The Message of Jeremiah: Against Wind and Tide*, The Bible Speaks Today (Downers Grove, IL: InterVarsity, 1987), p. 143.

Chapter Sixty-Three: "Full Atonement! Can It Be?"

1. Percy Bysshe Shelley, "Ozymandias," in *The Norton Anthology of English Literature*, rev. ed., ed. M. H. Abrams (New York: Norton, 1968), p. 1579.

2. Walter Brueggemann, *To Build, To Plant: A Commentary on Jeremiah 26—52*, International Theological Commentary (Grand Rapids, MI: Eerdmans, 1991), p. 257.

3. Walter Brueggemann, "Texts That Linger, Words That Explode," *Theology Today*, vol. 54, no. 2 (July 1997), pp. 180–99 (p. 195).

4. *International Bible Dictionary* (Plainfield, NJ: Logos, 1977), pp. 49, 50

5. Brueggemann, *To Build, To Plant*, p. 257.

6. *International Bible Dictionary*, p. 50.

7. John Calvin, *A Commentary on Jeremiah*, 5 vols., vol. 5 (Edinburgh: Banner of Truth, 1989), p. 131.

8. Charles Haddon Spurgeon, "The Blood of the Everlasting Covenant," in *The New Park Street Pulpit*, vol. 5 (Pasadena, TX: Pilgrim, 1975), pp. 419, 420.

Chapter Sixty-Four: "Fallen! Fallen Is Babylon the Great!"

1. F. B. Huey Jr., *Jeremiah, Lamentations*, New American Commentary (Nashville: Broadman, 1993), p. 430.

2. J. A. Thompson, *The Book of Jeremiah*, New International Commentary on the Old Testament (Grand Rapids, MI: Eerdmans, 1980), p. 760.

3. R. E. O. White, *The Indomitable Prophet: A Biographical Commentary on Jeremiah* (Grand Rapids, MI: Eerdmans, 1992), p. 146.

4. Derek Kidner, *The Message of Jeremiah: Against Wind and Tide*, The Bible Speaks Today (Downers Grove, IL: InterVarsity, 1987), p. 151.

5. John Calvin, *A Commentary on Jeremiah*, 5 vols., vol. 5 (Edinburgh: Banner of Truth, 1989), p. 122.

6. Robert C. Linthicum, *City of God, City of Satan: A Biblical Theology of the Urban Church* (Grand Rapids, MI: Zondervan, 1991), p. 279.

7. Ray Bakke, *A Theology as Big as the City* (Downers Grove, IL: InterVarsity, 1997), p. 184.

8. Linthicum, *City of God, City of Satan*, pp. 282, 283.

9. F. B. Meyer, *Jeremiah: Priest and Prophet*, rev. ed. (Fort Washington, PA: Christian Literature Crusade, 1993), p. 152.

Chapter Sixty-Five: "How Lonely Sits the City"

1. The two passages are nearly identical, except that Jeremiah 52 includes the number of deportees (vv. 28–30) and omits the assassination of Gedaliah (2 Kings 25:22–26).

2. Derek Kidner, *The Message of Jeremiah: Against Wind and Tide*, The Bible Speaks Today (Downers Grove, IL: InterVarsity, 1987), p. 159.

3. Philip J. King, *Jeremiah: An Archaeological Companion* (Louisville: Westminster/John Knox, 1993), pp. 77, 78.

4. See, for example, Kathleen Kenyon, *Digging Up Jerusalem* (New York: Praeger, 1974).

5. King, *Jeremiah: An Archaeological Companion*, p. 72.

6. The temple furnishings are described in G. E. Wright, *Biblical Archaeology*, rev. ed. (Philadelphia: Westminster, 1962), pp. 137–46.

7. King, *Jeremiah: An Archaeological Companion*, p. 117.

8. Matthew Henry, *Commentary on the Whole Bible*, 6 vols., vol. 4 (New York: Fleming Revell, n.d.), n.p.

9. John Bright, *A History of Israel* (London: SCM, 1980), p. 370.

10. Robert C. Linthicum, *City of God, City of Satan: A Biblical Theology of the Urban Church* (Grand Rapids, MI: Zondervan, 1991), p. 278.

11. See William Foxwell Albright, "King Jehoiachin in Exile," *Biblical Archaeology*, vol. 5 (1942), pp. 39–55.

12. J. Carl Laney, *Answers to Tough Questions from Every Book of the Bible* (Grand Rapids, MI: Kregel, 1997), p. 133.

Chapter Sixty-Six: Five Laments: An Epilogue

1. H. L. Ellison, "Lamentations," in *The Expositor's Bible*, ed. Frank E. Gaebelein, 12 vols., vol. 6 (Grand Rapids, MI: Zondervan, 1986), p. 702.

2. Ibid., p. 705.

3. John Donne, "The Lamentations of Jeremy, for the most part according to Tremelius," in *Chapters into Verse: Poetry in English Inspired by the Bible*, eds. Robert Atwan and Laurance Wieder, 2 vols., vol. 1 (Oxford: Oxford University Press, 1993), pp. 418–20 (lines 69, 70).

4. Rudyard Kipling, "Natural Theology," in *The Years Between* (Garden City, NY: Doubleday, 1919).

5. "Lamentations," in *The Interpreter's Bible*, 12 vols. vol. 6 (New York: Abingdon, 1956), p. 12.

6. Arthur T. Russell, "O Jesus, We Adore Thee" (1851).

7. Alfred Lord Tennyson, "Locksley Hall," in *Tennyson's Poetry*, ed. Robert W. Hill Jr. (New York: Norton, 1971), pp. 94–100 (line 76).

8. Ellison, "Lamentations," p. 715.

9. Thomas Chisholm, quoted in Kenneth W. Osbeck, *Amazing Grace: 366 Inspiring Hymn Stories for Daily Devotions* (Grand Rapids, MI: Kregel, 1990), p. 348.

10. Robert Browning Hamilton, quoted in Harry Emerson Fosdick, *Successful Christian Living: Sermons on Christianity Today* (New York: Harper, 1937), p. 229.

11. R. K. Harrison, *Jeremiah and Lamentations*, Tyndale Old Testament Commentaries (Downers Grove, IL: InterVarsity, 1973), p. 1201.

12. J. G. S. S. Thomson, "Lamentations," in *The Biblical Expositor*, ed. Carl F. H. Henry, 3 vols., vol. 2 (Grand Rapids, MI: Baker, 1985), p. 223.

Scripture Index

General Index

Index of Sermon
Illustrations

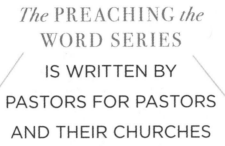